Mastering Microsoft 365 Security Technologies

Design and implement Microsoft security, compliance, and identity

Pramiti Bhatnagar

bpb

www.bpbonline.com

First Edition 2025

Copyright © BPB Publications, India

ISBN: 978-93-65892-871

To View Complete
BPB Publications Catalogue
Scan the QR Code:

Dedicated to

*My little twins **Aadi** and **Shiv***

and

My parents

About the Author

Pramiti Bhatnagar is a seasoned professional with over twenty years of deep technical experience in Microsoft technologies, including Microsoft Entra, Microsoft Purview, Microsoft Defender, Microsoft 365 Windows, and Microsoft Endpoint Manager. Pramiti holds an honours degree in applied psychology from the University of Delhi and has numerous technical certifications, such as Certified Information Privacy Manager, Microsoft Certified: Cybersecurity Architect Expert, and Project Management Professional (PMP).

Currently, Pramiti serves as a Principal Product Manager for Microsoft Entra, primarily focusing on Copilot for Security and Entra External Identities. Pramiti has also held various roles at Microsoft, including Global Black Belt, Cloud Solution Architect, and Partner Technology Strategist.

About the Reviewers

❖ **Mahesh Kohli** is a product manager at Microsoft, holding CISM certification and Microsoft Certified Trainer credentials, with over 18 years of experience in the IT industry. He is currently focused on enhancing Microsoft Defender solutions, managing roadmaps, overseeing customer expectations, conducting market research, and providing strategic advice to security leadership to help customers strengthen their overall security posture.

Additionally, Mahesh specializes in delivering security-focused training sessions and webinars for both internal and external stakeholders. Before transitioning to a product management role, he served as a Premier Field Engineer, managing security and compliance solutions. In this role, he acted as a trusted advisor, conducting security assessments, health assessments, and workshops, while assisting customers with implementing security controls based on best practices. Outside of his professional role, Mahesh is an avid reader with a passion for classic novels, non-fiction and IT-related books.

❖ **Taresh Mehra** is a data protection and cyber security QA Engineer with over 18 years of experience in Edison, New Jersey. He specializes in backup and storage solutions, ransomware mitigation, and data indexing, ensuring data integrity in modern IT environments. His expertise spans AI/ML applications in data security, REST API testing, and cloud technologies.

Taresh has also shaped industry standards through his leadership in the Cloud Security Alliance and extensive contributions as a cyber security publication reviewer. His work advancing the field through IEEE conference papers and technical evaluations at major hackathons earned him the prestigious 2024 SILVER GLOBEE® AWARD for Cyber Security Professional of the Year. As both an IEEE Senior Member and RSA Fellow, he continues to influence the direction of enterprise security, helping define best practices and innovation benchmarks across the industry.

Acknowledgement

I would like to express my sincere gratitude to all those who contributed to the completion of this book.

First and foremost, I want to extend my heartfelt thanks to my family who have offered their unwavering support during the development of this book.

I also want to thank my colleagues, managers and mentors at Microsoft who have provided me with numerous opportunities to learn and grow and become capable of writing a book.

I am immensely grateful to BPB Publications for offering me the opportunity to share my knowledge. Their guidance and expertise in bringing this book to fruition has been incredible. Their support and assistance were invaluable in navigating the complexities of the publishing process.

I would also like to acknowledge the reviewers, technical experts, and editors who provided valuable feedback and contributed to the refinement of this book. Their insights and suggestions have significantly enhanced the quality of the book.

Finally, I want to express my gratitude to the readers who have shown interest in this book. Your support and encouragement have been deeply appreciated.

Thank you to everyone who has played a part in making this book a reality.

Preface

Security is top of mind for most organizations today. With the increasing number of cyber-attacks and shortage of skilled professionals, organizations are struggling to protect themselves from bad actors. At the same time, data is exploding making it even tougher for organizations to keep themselves and their data safe. M365 Security technologies provide end-to-end solutions for protecting and organisation's data, identities and applications.

This book covers end-to-end Microsoft security solutions. Section 1 of this book focuses on Microsoft's identity and access management solution Microsoft Entra. The five chapters in this section introduce Microsoft Entra and then guide the reader through implementation of Microsoft Entra and managing, protecting and governing identities using Microsoft Entra ID Governance, Microsoft Entra Privileged Identity Management. It also introduces the reader to Microsoft Entra Secure Services Edge, Microsoft's Zero Trust network access solution.

Section 2 focuses on protecting the organization against threats. It introduces Microsoft Defender XDR as Microsoft's extended detection and response solution. The chapters in this section shed light on how Microsoft Defender solutions can help protect devices, identities, M365 and non-M365 applications from external threats.

Section 3 shifts the focus on protecting data. This section explains how organizations can protect structured and unstructured data in Microsoft 365 and multi-cloud environments using Microsoft Purview Information Protection, prevent accidental or intentional data exfiltration using Microsoft Purview Data Loss Prevention, identify insider risks and manage regulatory compliance and privacy.

This book is designed to help experienced and novice security professionals become experts in administering and implementing Microsoft security solutions. Through practical examples, comprehensive explanations, hand-on labs, and a structured approach, this book aims to equip readers with a solid understanding of Microsoft security solutions. Whether you are a novice or an experienced learner, this book will serve as a valuable resource as you work towards advancing your cybersecurity career.

Chapter 1: Introduction to Microsoft Entra- This chapter introduces the Microsoft Entra product family. Microsoft Entra is a family of products that help organisations create and manage users and govern user access to applications and services. This chapter introduces the components of the Microsoft Entra and how they can help organisations address their identity and access management requirements. It touches on the licensing options for each capability. This chapter explains how to create users using Microsoft Entra, the external collaboration capabilities using Microsoft Entra External ID. It also introduces new capabilities like Microsoft Entra Permissions Management, Microsoft Entra Verified ID and Global Secure Access.

Chapter 2: Implementing Identity- Many organizations worldwide use on-premises Active Directory for managing their identities. When they decide to move to the cloud, they would want to provide their end users with seamless access to both cloud and on-premises applications and resources. This chapter describes how these organizations can sync their on-premises Active Directory identities to Microsoft Entra ID securely so that users can use the same credentials to access both on-premises and cloud resources. It goes on to explain the password synchronization methods like password hash sync and pass-through authentication. It explains the password protection capabilities available in Microsoft Entra ID and how these can be extended to on-premises Active Directory. It also talks about setting up single sign-on for applications and end user self-service in Microsoft Entra ID.

Chapter 3: Identity Management- One of the main tasks of an identity and access management administrator is to make sure that the right system resources are accessible to the right users. This can be a challenging task since there are thousands of user identities in any organisation. This chapter introduces the group management features in Microsoft Entra ID to handle these identities and protect your organisation's resources effectively. It also covers the key concept of role based access control, which aids in understanding the other Microsoft capabilities explained in this book.

Chapter 4: Identity Protection- Identity is the key to access. Hence, a secure cloud deployment relies on a secure identity. Identity attacks have increased dramatically in recent years. Organisations need to enforce rigorous identity protection strategies while also offering a smooth work experience to their end users. This chapter describes the different identity protection features in Microsoft Entra ID like multifactor authentication, passwordless sign-in, unphishable credentials like passkeys. It also explains how Microsoft Entra ID Protection feature like risk-based conditional access policies can help prevent identity-based attacks.

Chapter 5: Identity Governance- Each identity goes through a lifecycle that needs to be managed from when a user joins the organisation to when they leave. The user access must be kept up to date across the joiner-mover-leaver scenario and this must be done efficiently. This chapter shows how to use entitlement management to give the users the right access that they need to do their job. Access reviews can be used to check the user's access to data and applications regularly, making sure that they do not have more access than necessary to fulfil their job roles. Lastly, it explores how Privilege Identity Management can be used to give just in-time access to the users that have the most sensitive access.

Chapter 6: Microsoft Defender XDR- Organizations these days are exposed to a myriad of threats ranging from viruses, malware, phishing attacks, ransomware and more. They need to have effective threat protection strategies which include a combination of proactive prevention, real-time detection and rapid response. They need to deploy security solutions like firewalls, antivirus software, intrusion detection and protection systems to protect their networks, devices and data from potential harm. Microsoft Defender XDR is a suite of solutions that helps with detection, prevention, investigation and response of threats across endpoints, identities, email and applications. It provides integrated protection against sophisticated cyber-attacks.

Chapter 7: Protecting Identities- Many organizations still have big on-premises Active Directory infrastructures that can be compromised by attackers. Organizations must have tools to identify attacks against these identities and protect them from being stolen or abused. This chapter explores how Microsoft Defender for Identity helps organizations avoid breaches by spotting threats, investigating and responding to incidents. Microsoft Defender for Identity is a cloud-based solution that helps your SecOps teams provide a modern identity and threat detection solution across hybrid environments. It helps stop breaches, identify threats, examine dubious activities and react to attacks.

Chapter 8: Protecting Endpoints- In today's hybrid working environment, users are using a multitude of devices from a multitude of locations. Gone are the days when users used to work only from their offices safe behind the corporate firewall. This exposes user endpoints to threats like never before. The attackers are also becoming very sophisticated. Organizations need modern and intelligent tools to protect their users' devices from bad actors. Microsoft Defender from Endpoint is an enterprise endpoint security platform designed to help enterprise networks prevent, detect, investigate, and respond to advanced threats. Coupled with Microsoft Defender Vulnerability Management, it offers proactive protection and visibility into the vulnerabilities in the environment and provides recommendations to strengthen the security posture. Organizations today also use operational technology and Internet of Things devices. It is important for an organization to gain visibility into these devices and the threats surrounding them. Microsoft Defender for IoT provides device discovery and threat protection services for OT and IoT networks across cloud, on-premises and air-gapped infrastructure.

Chapter 9: Protecting M365 Apps- Many organisations are now shifting to cloud-based services. Microsoft is the world's top collaboration SaaS provider. Most organisations store a lot of data in the M365 cloud, Exchange Online, SharePoint Online, OneDrive for Business and Teams. Attackers try to compromise these applications using different methods like phishing and spoofing. This chapter explains Exchange Online Protection and Microsoft Defender for Office 365 and their roles in defending, detecting, investigating and responding to attacks aimed at your M365 environment.

Chapter 10: Protecting Non-Microsoft Cloud Apps- Today, end users have access to a wide variety of SaaS applications that help them work more efficiently. However, this poses a major challenge for Security Administrators as they might not have visibility of which applications are in use, their security posture and how they are being used. These applications introduce new threat vectors for an organization in terms of cyber-attacks and more avenues for data exfiltration. This chapter explores Microsoft Defender for Cloud Apps and how it can help identify the use of Shadow IT, approve and disapprove applications and ultimately track the usage of those applications to protect your organisation's data and assets.

Chapter 11: Security Management Using Microsoft Sentinel- This chapter introduces the concepts of **Security Incident and Event Monitoring (SIEM)** and **Security Orchestration Automation and Response (SOAR)**. It then goes on to introduce Microsoft Sentinel as Microsoft's cloud-native SIEM and SOAR solution. It explains how Microsoft Sentinel helps SOC analysts manage hundreds of alerts daily, preventing critical security incidents. The chapter covers the setup of Microsoft Sentinel, connecting data sources, handling incidents, creating playbooks, and automating responses. It also highlights the integration with Microsoft solutions and non-Microsoft clouds, the use of Threat Intelligence, and the creation of visual reports.

Chapter 12: Protect and Govern Sensitive Data- Data is the most valuable resource that an organisation has. In today's world data is everywhere and organisations need tools to find the sensitive data, safeguard it from unauthorized access and manage it through its lifecycle. This chapter explores Microsoft Purview Information Protection and how it can be used to find and protect sensitive content; Microsoft Purview Data Loss Protection to prevent sensitive information from being shared with unauthorized parties. It also explains how Microsoft Purview Data Lifecycle Management and Records Management can be used to govern the life cycle of the data from the time it was created till when it is securely disposed of.

Chapter 13: Managing Insider Risks- Data does not move itself, people move data. To understand the user intent behind moving the data, we need to know not only how, but also why the data moved. This chapter explains Microsoft Purview Insider Risk Management and Microsoft Purview Communication Compliance solutions to set up policies that can track user behaviour over time and prevent insiders from leaking sensitive content. It also covers Adaptive Protection and how to gather forensic evidence for investigations.

Chapter 14: Managing eDiscovery Cases- When something goes wrong, an organization might need to show proof to regulators, legal authorities or their own investigators. This chapter introduces Microsoft Purview eDiscovery as the tool investigate such incidents by creating cases, assigning custodians and conducting searches across the organization to find the data that is most important for the investigation. It can examine and filter the data in-place to save time and money when doing an eDiscovery investigation.

It is also important for organizations to be aware of user and admin activity happening in their environment. Microsoft Purview Audit serves as a comprehensive record of system activities, user actions, and changes to data. This chapter explains it can aid in investigating and resolving incidents of unauthorized access, data breaches, or other security violations.

Chapter 15: Managing Regulatory Compliance- Most organizations are subject to more than one industry or government regulation that they must adhere to. Remaining compliant with these regulations is an arduous task. Organizations invest a lot of time and money to achieve this. Microsoft Purview Compliance Manager is a simple SaaS based solution that helps organizations remain compliant with the regulations by providing easy to use templates and step-by-step guidance to meet the regulation requirements.

Chapter 16: Managing Privacy- Many organizations have a lot of PII stored in unstructured data in different locations. This PII can be mishandled and lead to serious consequences like loss of customer trust and reputation. Microsoft Priva helps a privacy officer to find out where PII is stored, how it moves within the organization and how old it is. It also empowers the user to make smart data handling decisions by providing timely trainings. Microsoft Priva Subject Rights Request is the tool that helps organizations to quickly answer Data Subject Requests. This chapter also introduces Preview capabilities of Consent management, Tracker scanning and Privacy assessments.

Chapter 17: Best Practices- The concluding chapter of this book takes the reader through identity, security and compliance best practices that further enhance the understanding of the concepts. This also enables administrators to take best decisions based on their organization business use cases and requirements.

Code Bundle and Coloured Images

Please follow the link to download the
Code Bundle and the *Coloured Images* of the book:

https://rebrand.ly/am8kms4

The code bundle for the book is also hosted on GitHub at
https://github.com/bpbpublications/Mastering-Microsoft-365-Security-Technologies.
In case there's an update to the code, it will be updated on the existing GitHub repository.

We have code bundles from our rich catalogue of books and videos available at
https://github.com/bpbpublications. Check them out!

Errata

We take immense pride in our work at BPB Publications and follow best practices to ensure the accuracy of our content to provide with an indulging reading experience to our subscribers. Our readers are our mirrors, and we use their inputs to reflect and improve upon human errors, if any, that may have occurred during the publishing processes involved. To let us maintain the quality and help us reach out to any readers who might be having difficulties due to any unforeseen errors, please write to us at :

errata@bpbonline.com

Your support, suggestions and feedbacks are highly appreciated by the BPB Publications' Family.

Did you know that BPB offers eBook versions of every book published, with PDF and ePub files available? You can upgrade to the eBook version at www.bpbonline. com and as a print book customer, you are entitled to a discount on the eBook copy. Get in touch with us at :

business@bpbonline.com for more details.

At **www.bpbonline.com**, you can also read a collection of free technical articles, sign up for a range of free newsletters, and receive exclusive discounts and offers on BPB books and eBooks.

Piracy

If you come across any illegal copies of our works in any form on the internet, we would be grateful if you would provide us with the location address or website name. Please contact us at **business@bpbonline.com** with a link to the material.

If you are interested in becoming an author

If there is a topic that you have expertise in, and you are interested in either writing or contributing to a book, please visit **www.bpbonline.com**. We have worked with thousands of developers and tech professionals, just like you, to help them share their insights with the global tech community. You can make a general application, apply for a specific hot topic that we are recruiting an author for, or submit your own idea.

Reviews

Please leave a review. Once you have read and used this book, why not leave a review on the site that you purchased it from? Potential readers can then see and use your unbiased opinion to make purchase decisions. We at BPB can understand what you think about our products, and our authors can see your feedback on their book. Thank you!

For more information about BPB, please visit **www.bpbonline.com**.

Join our book's Discord space

Join the book's Discord Workspace for Latest updates, Offers, Tech happenings around the world, New Release and Sessions with the Authors:

https://discord.bpbonline.com

Table of Contents

CHAPTER 1
Introduction to Microsoft Entra

Introduction

This chapter introduces you to Microsoft Entra. Microsoft Entra is a family of products that help organisations create, manage, and govern user access to enterprise applications and services. In this chapter, we will learn the components of the Microsoft Entra and how they can help organisations address their identity and access management requirements. We will also explore the licensing options for each capability. This chapter will demonstrate how to create users using Microsoft Entra, the external collaboration capabilities using Microsoft Entra External ID. It will also introduce new capabilities like Microsoft Entra Permissions Management, Microsoft Entra Verified ID and Global Secure Access.

Structure

The chapter covers the following topics:

- Microsoft Entra ID
- Microsoft Entra ID Governance
- Microsoft Entra External ID
- Microsoft Entra Permissions Management
- Microsoft Entra Workload ID

- Microsoft Entra Verified ID
- Global Secure Access

Objectives

By the end of this chapters, readers will be able to explain the different components of the Microsoft Entra product family. You will be able to understand the different licensing options available to organisations when they buy Microsoft Entra ID and the identity governance capabilities in Microsoft Entra ID. This chapter also explains how Microsoft Entra enables secure collaboration with external vendors, partners and customers using Microsoft Entra External ID. Finally, you will understand the new capabilities Microsoft Entra Permissions Management, Microsoft Entra Workload ID, Microsoft Entra Verified ID and Global Secure Access.

The future chapters in this book build on the concepts covered in this chapter.

Microsoft Entra ID

Microsoft Entra ID, previously known as Azure Active Directory, is Microsoft's cloud-based service for identity and access management. This allows users in the organisation to access internal and external resources like Microsoft 365, Azure and many other third-party cloud applications.

Microsoft Entra ID serves many purposes for users in an organisation depending on their role:

- **IT admins**: They can use Microsoft Entra ID to create and manage user accounts and control access to applications and other resources.
- **Application developers**: They can use Microsoft Entra ID to authenticate users and provide **single sign-on** (**SSO**) for their applications. This allows users to access applications with their Entra ID login information.
- **Microsoft 365, Office 365, Azure or Dynamics CRM online users**: Microsoft Entra ID enables users to authenticate and gain access to resources required to do their job.

Licensing

Microsoft Online business services such as Microsoft 365 or Microsoft Azure rely on Microsoft Entra ID to enable sign-in for users and help secure their identities. If your organisation uses any of these services, you already have the free version of Microsoft Entra ID.

To access other advanced user management and identity governance features, you can purchase Entra ID P1 or Entra ID P2.

Following is a short description of these license types:

- **Microsoft Entra ID free**: It is included in Microsoft cloud subscriptions such as Microsoft 365 and Azure. It offers basic user and group administration, on-premises directory sync, SSO and basic reporting features.

- **Microsoft Entra ID P1**: This plan offers all the features of the free plan, plus it allows hybrid users to access applications both on-premises and in the cloud. It also gives advanced administration options like dynamic groups, self-service group management and self-service password reset for on-premises users. It can be purchased as a separate product. It is included in Microsoft 365 E3 and Microsoft 365 Business Premium.

- **Microsoft Entra ID P2**: P2 offers all the capabilities of free and P1 and adds identity protection features such as risk-based Conditional Access and Privileged Identity Management that give access to administrators only when needed. It can be purchased on its own or comes with Microsoft 365 E5.

Creating new Entra ID tenant

All administrative tasks related to Microsoft Entra ID are done using the Microsoft Entra admin centre. You will begin by creating a new tenant for your organisation.

Prerequisites

To get started with Microsoft Entra ID you need to create an Entra ID tenant. For this, you need the following:

- An Azure subscription.
- An account with the Tenant Creator role assigned.

Note: If you do not have an Azure subscription create a free account by going to https://azure.microsoft.com/en-us/free/.

Steps

Following are the steps to create a new Microsoft Entra ID tenant:

1. Login to the Azure portal at **https://portal.azure.com** with an account that has the Tenant Creator role assigned.
2. Select **Microsoft Entra ID**.
3. Navigate to **Overview | Manage tenants** and then click **Create**.
4. On the **Basics** page, select **Microsoft Entra ID** and click **Next: Configuration** as shown in the following figure:

Home > Contoso | Overview > Manage tenants >

Create a tenant ···
Microsoft Entra ID

*Basics   *Configuration   Review + create

Microsoft Entra ID and Azure AD B2C enable users to access applications published by your organization, and share same administration experiences. Learn more

Tenant type

Select a tenant type *
- ● Microsoft Entra ID
- ○ Azure AD B2C

Help me choose...

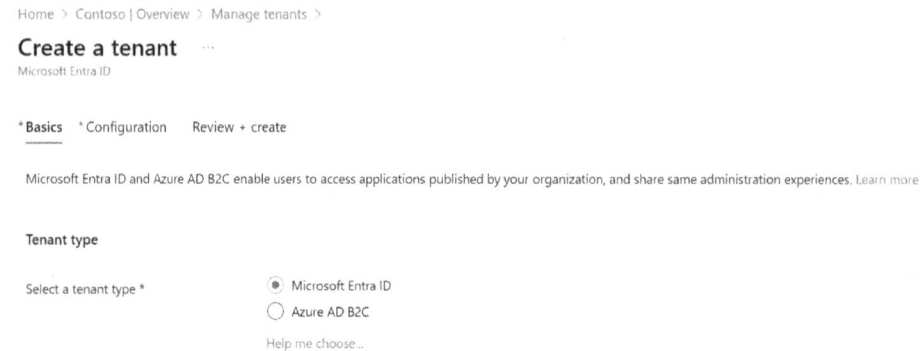

Figure 1.1: Creating a new tenant

5. On the **Configuration,** page enter the **Organisation name, Initial domain name** and **Location** and click **Next: Review + create**.

   Refer to the following figure:

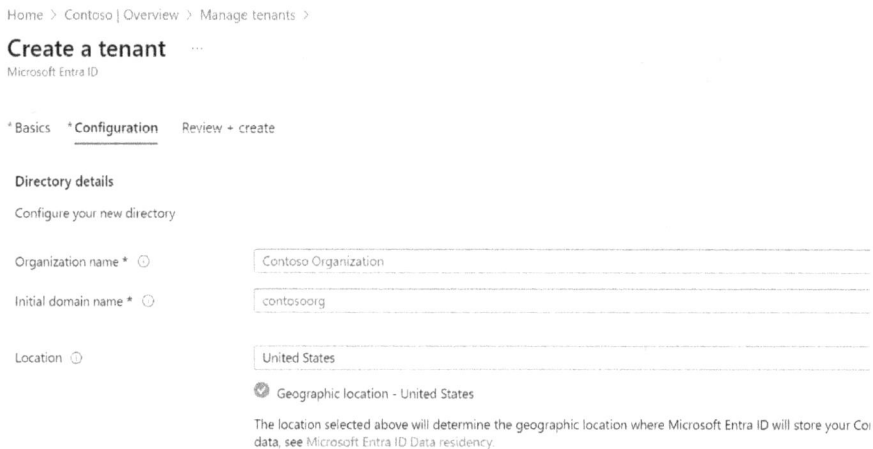

Home > Contoso | Overview > Manage tenants >

Create a tenant ···
Microsoft Entra ID

*Basics   *Configuration   Review + create

Directory details
Configure your new directory

Organization name * ⓘ | Contoso Organization

Initial domain name * ⓘ | contosoorg

Location ⓘ | United States

✅ Geographic location - United States

The location selected above will determine the geographic location where Microsoft Entra ID will store your Co
data, see Microsoft Entra ID Data residency.

Figure 1.2: Enter organisation details

The new tenant will be created with the domain **domainname.onmicrosoft.com**.

When you create a new Microsoft Entra tenant, you become the Global Administrator of the tenant. You are also listed as the technical contact for the tenant.

Adding custom domain name in Entra ID

Microsoft Entra tenants are created with an initial domain like **youorganisationname. onmicrosoft.com**. The user IDs are hence in the format **user1@youorganisationname. onmicrosoft.com**. This cannot be changed or deleted but an additional domain name can be added to the tenant. This creates an additional domain name that is, familiar to the users, such as **user1@youorganisationname.com**.

Following are the steps to add a custom domain name:

1. Login to **https://entra.microsoft.com** with an ID that has the Domain Name Administrator role assigned.

2. Browse to **Identity | Settings | Domain names | Add custom domain.**

3. Click on **Add custom domain**. Enter your organisation's domain and click **Add domain**.

   Refer to the following figure:

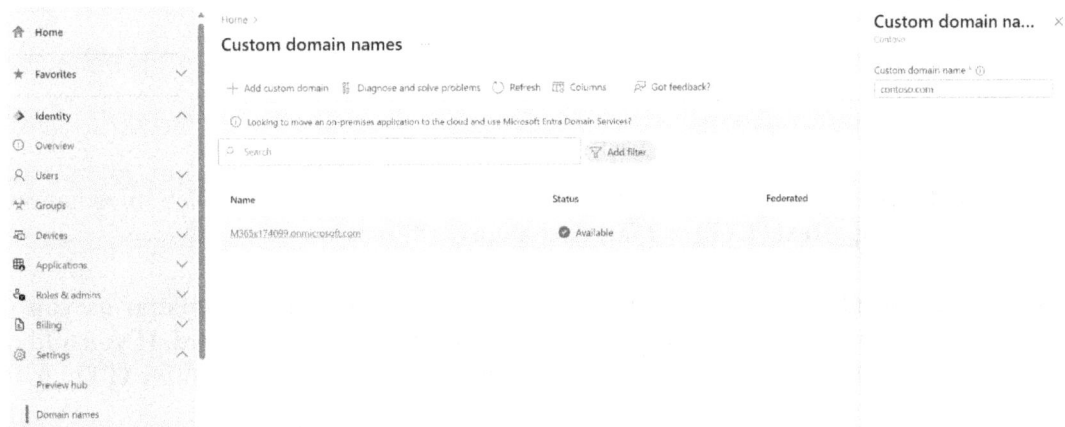

Figure 1.3: Adding a custom domain name

Note: The custom domain name must include `.com`, `.net` or any other top-level extension for this to work. The organization should already have a top-level domain registered with a domain registrar.

4. The unverified domain is added, showing the DNS information as in the screen below. This will be required to validate your ownership of the domain. Save this information.

   Refer to the following figure:

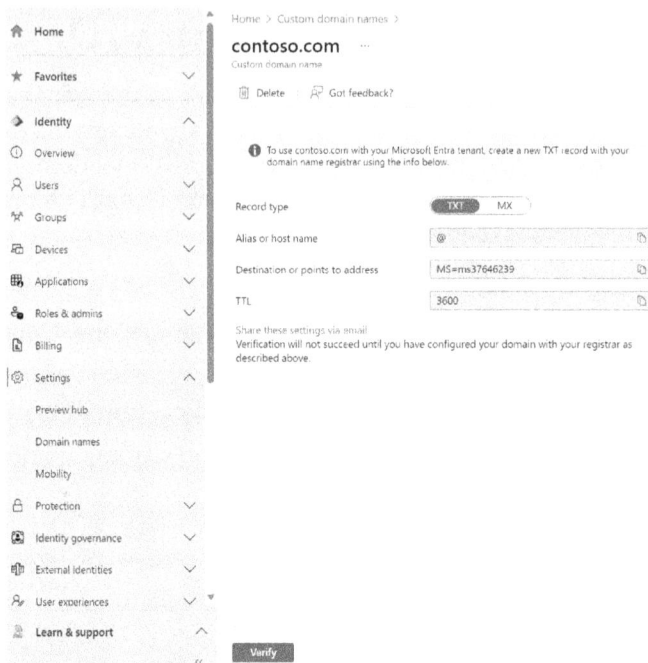

Figure 1.4: Unverified domain added

5. Next, update your record with your domain registrar with this DNS information by creating a **Text (TXT)** or **Mail Exchange (MX)** record.

Note: You can add as many custom domains with your domain registrar as you like, but keep in mind that each domain gets its own TXT or MX record. If you add incorrect or duplicate information you will have to wait for the time to live (TTL) to expire before you can try again.

6. After adding the DNS information with the domain registrar, ensure that the domain is valid in Microsoft Entra as shown in *Figure 1.4,* click the **Verify** button to verify the domain name.

Common verification issues

If you cannot verify a custom domain name, try the following suggestions:

- Try again after an hour
- Ensure there are no errors in the domain information
- Make sure the domain is not in use in another directory
- Ensure there are no unmanaged Power BI tenants

Microsoft Entra ID Governance

Microsoft Entra ID Governance is an identity governance solution that enables organisations to improve productivity, strengthen security and meet regulatory and compliance requirements. It helps ensure that the right people have the right access to the right resources. It helps organisations mitigate access and identity risks by protecting monitoring and auditing access to critical assets.

Microsoft Entra ID helps organisations to perform the following:

- Understand how the users are using the access assigned to them
- Ensure there are controls in place to manage access
- Audit that the controls are working effectively

With Microsoft Entra ID Governance, organisations can govern the identity and access lifecycle of user and privileged accounts.

Governing user accounts

Identity lifecycle refers to the stages a user identity goes through from the time it is created when a user joins the organisation, to the time it is deleted when they leave the organisation. It is also referred to as the **joiner-mover-leaver** scenario.

Refer to the following figure:

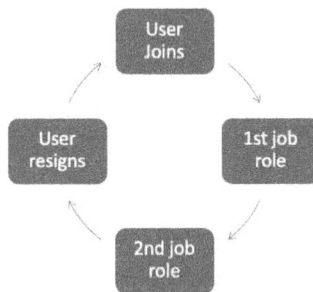

Figure 1.5: The identity lifecycle

When a user joins an organization their user ID is created in the organisation's HR system. In most organizations, it takes a few days for the user to become productive due to the time-consuming processes of identity provisioning. Organizations need to automate this process so that the new joiners can be productive on the first day.

Microsoft Entra ID Governance can help organisations accelerate identity provisioning by performing the following:

- Automating retrieving new user account from HR systems like Workday and SuccessFactors and provisioning the identities in Active Directory and Microsoft Entra ID.

- Maintaining the user access over time as they move from one role to another and when they leave the organisation.

- Automatically granting access to resources that they need for their role thereby eliminating the need for the users to request for access for each resource.

- Automatically provisioning and maintaining user accounts in other applications such as legacy on-premises applications and third-party **software as a service (SaaS)** applications.

The two key capabilities that help govern user access are **entitlement management** and **access reviews**. We will explore these capabilities in detail in *Chapter 5, Identity Governance*.

Governing privileged accounts

Privileged accounts are accounts that have administrative access, like Global Administrators, User Administrators, etc. Governing privileged accounts is a key aspect of modern identity management given the risks associated with the misuse of these accounts.

Microsoft Entra ID **Privileged Identity Management** (**PIM**) provides controls tailored to secure access rights for resources across Microsoft Entra, Azure, Microsoft 365 and other applications. Capabilities such as **just-in-time** (**JIT**) access, multi-factor authentication and Conditional Access provide a comprehensive set of controls to help secure your organisation's resources. There are rich auditing and alerting capabilities which help alert administrators about unexpected role elevation or unexpected admin activities.

Licensing

Microsoft Entra ID Governance licenses offer more identity governance features for Microsoft Entra ID P1 and P2 customers, besides the licensing options already mentioned. They are available as two products: Microsoft Entra ID Governance and Microsoft Entra ID Governance Step up for Microsoft Entra ID P2.

These two products have the basic identity governance features that are part of Microsoft Entra ID P2 as well. Additionally, they have more advanced identity governance features. These features are the same in both products. The only difference is that they require different prerequisites.

To purchase **Entra ID Governance** license, the tenant needs an active subscription of **AAD Premium** or **AAD Premium P2**. This requirement is met if you have Microsoft Entra ID P1, Microsoft 365 E3/E5, EMS E3/E5 or Microsoft 365 F1/F3.

To purchase **Microsoft Entra ID Governance step up for Microsoft Entra ID P2**, the tenant needs **AAD Premium P2**. This requirement is met if you have Microsoft Entra ID P2, Microsoft 365 E5, EMS E5, M365 E5/F5 Security or M365 F5 Security and Compliance.

Microsoft Entra External ID

Microsoft Entra External ID lets you work securely with users who are not part of your organisation, such as partners, contractors, suppliers, vendors and distributors. With Microsoft Entra External ID, external users can use their existing identities to sign in. They can have a corporate identity or a non-corporate identity like *Google*, *Yahoo* or *Facebook*. Their identity provider takes care of their user identity. You are only required to control that identity's access to your applications.

External identities have the following capabilities:

- **B2B collaboration**: Securely collaborate with business partners, vendors or contractors by letting them use their credentials to access resources and applications in your organisation's tenant. They are typically represented in your organisation's tenant as Guest accounts.

- **B2B direct connect**: Using this feature, you can establish a two-way trust with another organisation for seamless collaboration. This supports *Teams* shared channels which lets external users access your resources from their instances of Teams. B2B direct connect users are not represented as guests in your directory.

- **Azure AD B2C**: This feature enables you to publish modern SaaS applications or custom-developed applications to customers and consumers. It uses Azure AD B2C for identity and access management. Azure AD B2C does not support the publishing of Microsoft apps to external users.

- **Microsoft Entra multi-tenant organisation**: Using this feature, you can collaborate with multiple tenants from a single Microsoft Entra organisation via cross-tenant collaboration.

These concepts will be covered in detail in *Chapter 2, Implementing Identity.*

Pricing

Microsoft Entra ID charges you based on **Monthly Active Users** (**MAU**) which is the number of unique authentication activities in a month. To use MAU billing, you need to connect your Microsoft Entra tenant to an Azure subscription. If you have already done that, your tenant will automatically use the MAU model for billing. If you have not connected your Microsoft Entra tenant to an Azure subscription, you need to do that to enable MAU billing.

Following are the steps to connect your Microsoft Entra tenant to an Azure subscription:

1. Sign in to **https://entra.microsoft.com** using an account that has at least the Contributor role.

2. In the Microsoft Entra admin centre toolbar, click on the **Settings** icon in the portal toolbar. Then, on the **Portal settings | Directories + subscriptions** page, find your directory under the **Directory name** list, as follows:

Portal settings | Directories + subscriptions

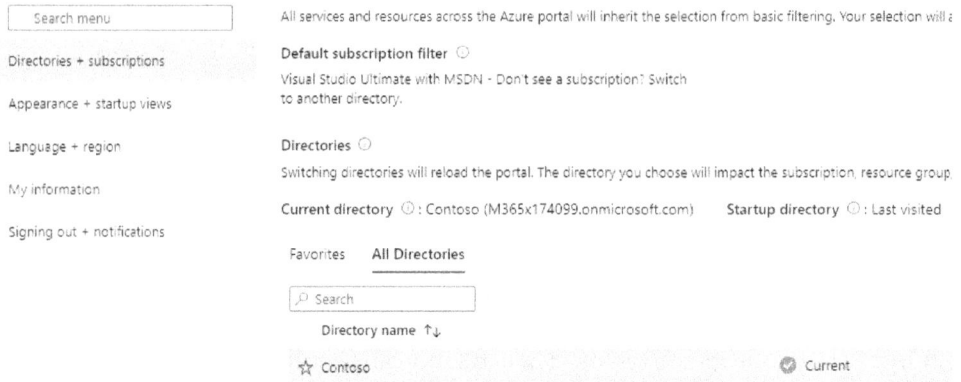

All services and resources across the Azure portal will inherit the selection from basic filtering. Your selection will a

Search menu

Directories + subscriptions

Appearance + startup views

Language + region

My information

Signing out + notifications

Default subscription filter ⓘ

Visual Studio Ultimate with MSDN - Don't see a subscription? Switch to another directory.

Directories ⓘ

Switching directories will reload the portal. The directory you choose will impact the subscription, resource group.

Current directory ⓘ : Contoso (M365x174099.onmicrosoft.com)   Startup directory ⓘ : Last visited

Favorites   **All Directories**

🔎 Search

Directory name ↑↓

☆ Contoso   ✓ Current

Figure 1.6: Directories and subscriptions

3. Navigate to **Identities** | **External Identities** | **Overview**.

4. Under **Subscriptions**, click on **Linked subscriptions**.

5. In the tenant list, select the checkbox next to the tenant you want to link and click on **Link subscription**.

    Refer to the following figure:

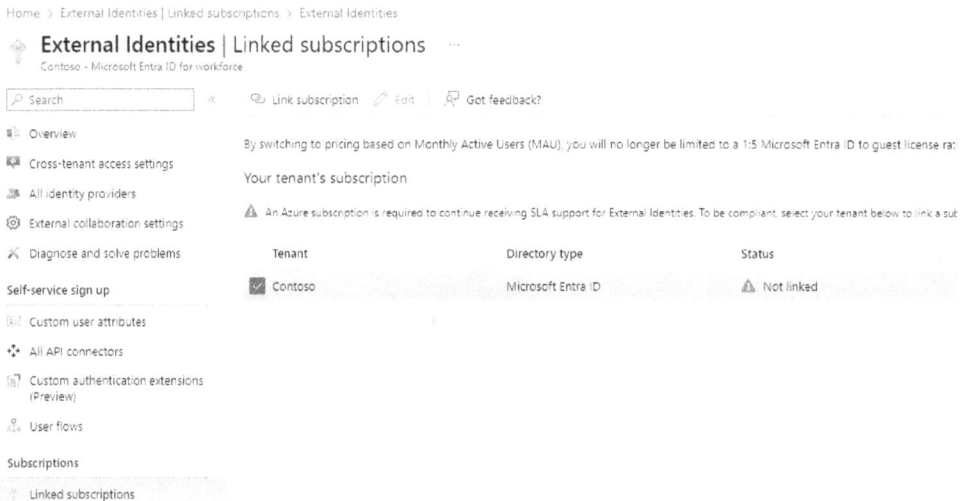

Home > External Identities | Linked subscriptions > External Identities

External Identities | Linked subscriptions ···
Contoso - Microsoft Entra ID for workforce

🔎 Search   «   ↺ Link subscription   ✎ Edit | ⮐ Got feedback?

▪ Overview

▧ Cross-tenant access settings

▨ All identity providers

⚙ External collaboration settings

✕ Diagnose and solve problems

Self-service sign up

▦ Custom user attributes

✦ All API connectors

▥ Custom authentication extensions (Preview)

▨ User flows

Subscriptions

▸ Linked subscriptions

By switching to pricing based on Monthly Active Users (MAU), you will no longer be limited to a 1:5 Microsoft Entra ID to guest license rat

Your tenant's subscription

⚠ An Azure subscription is required to continue receiving SLA support for External Identities. To be compliant, select your tenant below to link a sub

Tenant	Directory type	Status
☑ Contoso	Microsoft Entra ID	⚠ Not linked

Figure 1.7: Link subscription

6. In the **Link a subscription** fly-out pane, select a **Subscription** and **Resource group** and click **Apply**.

    Refer to the following figure as an example:

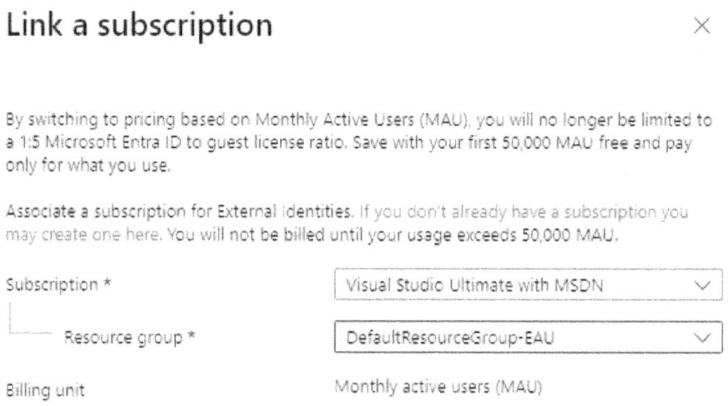

Link a subscription   ✕

By switching to pricing based on Monthly Active Users (MAU), you will no longer be limited to a 1:5 Microsoft Entra ID to guest license ratio. Save with your first 50,000 MAU free and pay only for what you use.

Associate a subscription for External Identities. If you don't already have a subscription you may create one here. You will not be billed until your usage exceeds 50,000 MAU.

Subscription *	Visual Studio Ultimate with MSDN ⌄
⌐ Resource group *	DefaultResourceGroup-EAU ⌄
Billing unit	Monthly active users (MAU)

Figure 1.8: Link subscription

Microsoft Entra Permissions Management

Microsoft Entra Permissions Management is a **Cloud Infrastructure Entitlement Management** (**CIEM**) solution that provides visibility to permissions assigned to all identities across multi-cloud infrastructure in **Microsoft Azure**, **Amazon Web Services** (**AWS**) and **Google Cloud Platform** (**GCP**). Permission management detects, remediates and continuously monitors excessive and unused permissions.

Following are the capabilities provided by Microsoft Entra Permissions Management:

- **Discover**: Assess the gap between permission granted and permissions used. This helps understand if excessive permissions have been granted.
- **Remediate**: Right-size permissions based on usage, grant more appropriate permissions and allow for just-in-time access to resources.
- **Monitor**: Detect anomalous activities with machine learning-powered alerts and generate rich forensic reports.

Prerequisites

Before you begin, you will need access to the following tools:

- A local BASH shell with Azure CLI or Azure Cloud Shell using BASH environment.
- AWS, Azure and GCP consoles
- A user with the Global Administrator role

Set-up Permissions Management

Follow are the steps to onboard Permissions Management for the first time:

1. Login to the Entra admin centre at **https://entra.microsoft.com** with an account that has at least the Billing Administrator role assigned.

2. Navigate to Permissions Management on the left pane and in the right pane select Launch Portal.

Note: If you do not have a Permissions Management license, you can sign up for a free 45-day trial. Go to https://entra.microsoft.com, in the left pane select Permissions Management and then in the right pane click on Try for free.

Onboard your multi-cloud environment

There are multiple steps involved in onboarding your cloud environments to Microsoft Entra Permissions Management. This section discusses these steps.

Set the controller

The controller lets you choose the level of access you want to give to users in Permissions Management. Based on this decision, you will either enable or disable the controller, as follows:

- **Enabling** the controller during onboarding grants write access to the Permissions Management admin. Using this access the Permissions Management admin can right-size and remediate permissions via the Permissions Management portal.
- **Disabling** the controller or never enabling it grants the Permissions Management admin read-only access to your environment.

Note: If you do not enable controller during the onboarding process, you will have the option to enable it later.

Configure data collection

There are three data collection modes in Permissions Management, as follows:

- **Automatic (recommended)**: Permissions Management automatically detects and onboards all current and newly created subscriptions.
- **Manual**: Enter each subscription one by one for Permissions Management to find, add and track. You can choose up to 100 subscriptions for each collector.
- **Select**: This option automatically identifies all current subscriptions that the CIEM application can access.

Note: For Automatic or Select modes, the controller must be enabled.

Follow are the steps to enable Permissions Management to collect data from the cloud resources.

1. In the Entra Permissions Management portal, click on the Settings option on the top right corner.

2. On the Data Collectors tab, select AWS, Azure or GCP.

3. Click Create Configuration.

From here you can follow the specific steps to configure data collection for AWS, GCP or Azure. Refer to the Microsoft Online documentation for the detailed steps.

Once the data collectors are configured, the status column shows the progress of data collection, as follows:

- **Pending**: Data collection has not started detecting or onboarding.
- **Discovering**: Authorization systems are being detected.
- **In Progress**: Authorization systems have been detected, and onboarding has started.
- **Onboarded**: Data collection is complete, and all detected systems are onboarded.

To view the data, select the Authorisation Systems tab. The Status column displays Collecting data. The data collection process can take some time depending on the size of the authorisation system and the amount of data available for collection.

> Note: Effective 1st April 2025, Microsoft Entra Permissions Management is no longer available for purchase for new customers. Effective 1st October 2025, Microsoft Entra Permissions Management will be retired, and Microsoft will discontinue support for this product.

Microsoft Entra Workload ID

A workload identity is a way of giving an application, script or container an identity that can use Microsoft Entra ID to connect to other services or resources. For instance, a workload identity could be given to GitHub Actions, so it can access an Azure subscription.

Applications, service principals and managed identities are the types of workload identities in Microsoft Entra.

An **application** is a type or model that is determined by its application object. The application object is a universal identifier that can be used among all tenants.

A **service principal** is a representation of an application object in a tenant, which is specific to that tenant. An application object acts as a template for creating a service principal in each tenant where the application is used. It specifies the app's capabilities in the tenant, the resources that can interact with the app and the users that can access it.

A **managed identity** is a kind of service principle that developers use to handle credentials. This means the developers do not have to create and manage credentials in the application they are building.

Key scenarios

Following are some of the ways in which you can use workload identities in Microsoft Entra:

- Service principals can be granted access to resources depending on certain conditions.
- You can utilise risk-based Conditional Access policies and Continuous Access Evaluation.
- You can manage custom security attributes for an app.
- Microsoft Entra Identity Protection can help to detect risky identities like leaked credentials.
- Use Microsoft Entra to access protected resources without having to deal with secrets for workloads that run on Azure.
- You can perform access reviews for service principles.

Microsoft Entra Verified ID

In today's digital world, we use identities to manage every aspect of our personal and professional lives whether it is booking tickets, ordering food or shopping most of our identities are controlled by third parties. We are constantly granting apps access to our personal information and data. It will be impossible for us to keep track of which party has access to which pieces of information.

Microsoft is collaborating with customers, partners and the community on the new version of **Decentralised Identities** (**DIDs**). DIDs are identifiers that users create, own, and are globally unique, with special features. Microsoft's verifiable credential solution uses DIDs to sign securely as evidence that a third party (verifier) is confirming that the information shown is a verifiable credential.

Understanding verifiable credentials

IDs are a part of our everyday lives. Some kind of IDs are driver's license, passports, certificates from universities. We can secure this important identity information when we work over the unprotected internet by verifying credentials in data objects that contain claims by the issuer confirming information about a subject. These claims have a schema and include DID of the issuer and subject. The issuer's DID make a digital signature as evidence that they agree with the information.

Verifiable credentials in action

John is a user who logs in to his company's network with his user id and password to access resources. His company is using a verifiable credential solution that lets employees easily prove that they work there. *John* wants to get a loan from a bank that has lower rates for his company's employees. He requests a proof of employment from his company. His company gives him a signed verifiable credential that he can store in a digital wallet. He can show this credential to the bank and get a lower rate of interest. The wallet application records this transaction and *John* can see when and where he used his proof of employment.

Global Secure Access

Global Secure Access is Microsoft's **Security Services Edge** (**SSE**) solution.

Microsoft Entra Internet Access and Microsoft Entra Private Access comprise Microsoft's SSE solution. Global Secure Access is the unified term used for both these technologies. It is built upon principles of Zero Trust.

Following figure depicts how identities, endpoints and networks use Global Secure Access to access resources in the public cloud and in the on-premises data centre:

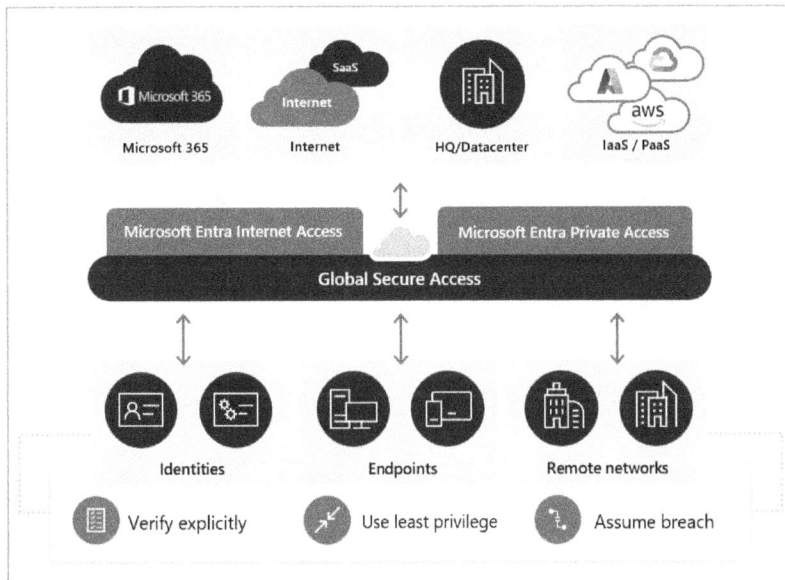

Figure 1.9: Global Secure Access

Microsoft Entra Internet Access

Microsoft Entra Internet Access securely connects to Microsoft 365, SaaS and public internet apps and safeguards users, devices and data. It offers an identity-centric **Secure Web Gateway** (**SWG**) solution for SaaS applications and other internet traffic. It enhances Conditional Access policies with network conditions to defend against harmful internet traffic. For M365 applications, it provides security and visibility as well as quicker and smoother access.

Microsoft Entra Private Access

Microsoft Entra Private Access is a SWG that focuses on identity and gives users secure access to private and corporate resources no matter where they work from. It extends the features of Microsoft Entra application proxy. Remote users can access private apps on any device in different cloud environments, private networks and data centres without a VPN. This service provides adaptive access per app based on Conditional Access policies which are more secure than a VPN.

Internet Access and Private Access along with Microsoft Defender for Cloud Apps make up the Microsoft SSE solution.

Conclusion

Microsoft Entra is a suite of products that protects the communication between people, apps, resources, and devices with capabilities for multi-cloud identity and network access. It consists of the following products:

- **Identity and access management**
  - o Microsoft Entra ID (formerly Azure Active Directory)
  - o Microsoft Entra ID Governance
  - o Microsoft Entra External ID
- **New identity categories**
  - o Microsoft Entra Verified ID
  - o Microsoft Entra Permissions Management
  - o Microsoft Entra Workload ID
- **Network access**
  - o Microsoft Entra Internet Access
  - o Microsoft Entra Private Access

Multiple choice questions

1. **Which of the following offer identity management as a service?**
   a. Microsoft Entra ID
   b. Microsoft Entra Private Access
   c. Microsoft Entra External ID
   d. Active Directory

2. **Which of the following services is used to govern privileged accounts?**

    a. Microsoft Entra Verified ID

    b. Microsoft Entra Permissions Management

    c. Microsoft Entra Identity Governance

    d. Global Secure Access

3. **Which license is required to use Entitlement Management?**

    a. Microsoft Entra ID P1

    b. Microsoft Entra ID P2

    c. Microsoft Entra ID Governance

    d. It is based on Monthly Active Users

Answer key

1. a

2. c

3. c

Join our book's Discord space

Join the book's Discord Workspace for Latest updates, Offers, Tech happenings around the world, New Release and Sessions with the Authors:

https://discord.bpbonline.com

CHAPTER 2
Implementing Identity

Introduction

Many organizations worldwide use on-premises **Active Directory** (**AD**) for managing their identities. When they decide to move to the cloud, they would want to provide their end users seamless access to both cloud and on-premises applications and resources. This chapter describes how these organizations can sync their on-premises AD identities to Microsoft Entra ID securely so that users can use the same credentials to access both on-premises and cloud resources. It goes on to explain the password synchronization methods like password hash sync and Pass-through authentication. It explains the password protection capabilities available in Microsoft Entra ID and how these can be extended to on-premises Active Directory. It also talks about setting up single sign-on for applications and end user self-service in Microsoft Entra ID.

Structure

This chapter covers the following topics:

- Determine identity model
- Cloud-only identity
- Hybrid identity
- Authentication methods

- Password protection
- Single sign-on
- End user self-service

Objectives

By the end of this chapter, you will be able to understand the scenarios where cloud and hybrid identity could be implemented. You should be able to create and manage user accounts in the Microsoft Entra ID tenant, implement hybrid identity using Microsoft Entra Cloud Sync and Microsoft Entra Cloud Connect, and explain the difference between the two. You will be able to explain the difference between password hash synchronization and pass-through authentication and identify the right authentication method for a given scenario. Lastly, you should be able to implement different end user self-service capabilities, single sign-on, and explain the password protection capabilities available in Microsoft Entra ID.

Determine identity model

A good identity infrastructure is essential for an enterprise, as it enables better security and user productivity. When you design an identity infrastructure for your organization, you must consider various factors.

Some of these are as follows:

- The current identity model used by the organization
- The future desired state
- The organization's security strategy
- The regulatory landscape the organization is subject to

The first decision would be to decide between cloud-only identity and hybrid identity. This will be based on your organization's identity requirements, if you have an on-premises AD infrastructure, how much you rely on it, and the need to keep it.

The following table explains the two identity models:

Attribute	Cloud-only identity	Hybrid identity
Definition	User accounts exist only in Microsoft Entra tenant.	User accounts exist in on-premises AD and are synchronized to the Microsoft Entra ID tenant.
Management	Entra ID portal or PowerShell.	User accounts are primarily managed in the on-premises AD and changes are synchronized to the cloud.

Attribute	Cloud-only identity	Hybrid identity
Authentication	The Microsoft Entra ID tenant performs authentication for the identities.	Authentication can be handled either by on-premises AD or the Microsoft Entra ID tenant depending on how the synchronization is set up.
Best for	Organizations that do not need an on-premises AD infrastructure.	Organizations that have investments and dependency on their on-premises AD.
Advantage	Simple, easy to setup and use.	Users can use the same credentials while accessing legacy and cloud-based applications.
Limitation	Organizations cannot enforce their own password policy.	Complex to set up and maintain

Table 2.1: Cloud identity models

Cloud-only identity

If you choose to use the cloud-only identity, you must sign up for a Microsoft Entra ID tenant. The steps to do so have been explained in *Chapter 1, Introduction to Microsoft Entra*. Once you have created the Entra ID tenant, you are ready to manage users and groups.

Creating and managing user accounts

For organizations that use cloud-only identity, user accounts are created and managed in Microsoft Entra ID. Organizations can create user accounts one-by-one or in bulk. The following sections explain each of these methods.

One-by-one

With this method, administrators would use the Microsoft Entra ID portal to create the user accounts.

The following are the steps for the same:

1. Login to **https://entra.microsoft.com** with an account that has at least the User Administrator role assigned.
2. In the left pane, expand **Identity | Users | All users**.
3. In the right pane, click on **All users | New user | Create new user**, as shown in *Figure 2.1*:

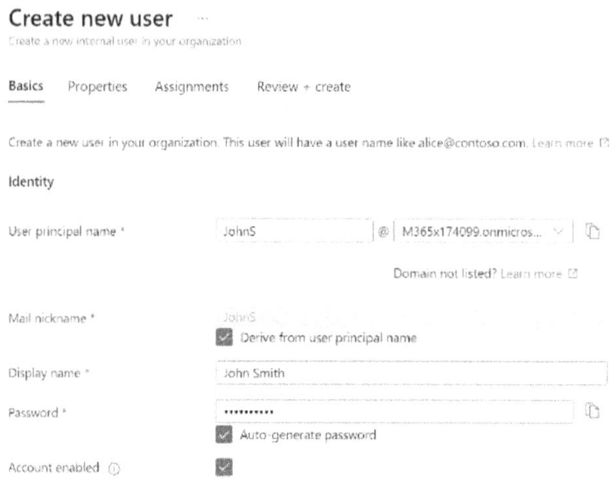

Figure 2.1: Create a new user account

4. Fill in the **Display name** and **User principal name**. The user principal name must be unique in the directory. Ensure that the boxes **Derive from user principal name**, **Auto-generate password**, and **Account enabled** are checked. Click on **Next: Properties** button, as shown in the following figure:

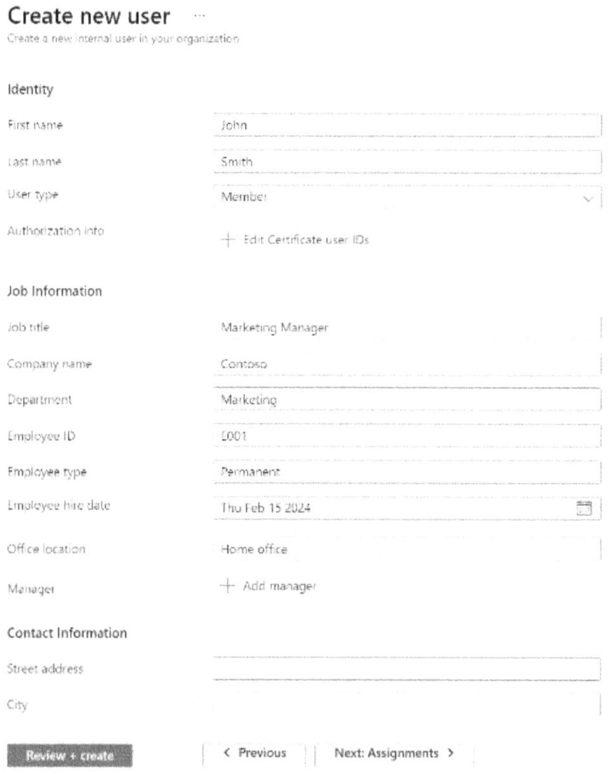

Figure 2.2: User properties

5. On the **Properties** page, enter the user details as appropriate and click on **Next: Assignments**.

6. On the **Assignments** page, you can assign the user to appropriate Administrative Units, Groups, and Roles. These concepts will be discussed in the next chapter. For now, accept the defaults and click **Next: Review + create**.

7. On the **Review + create** page, click **Create**.

Bulk import

This method allows you to use a **.csv** file to add a group of users to Microsoft Entra ID.

Following are the steps to bulk create users in Microsoft Entra ID:

1. Login to **https://entra.microsoft.com** with an account that has at least the User Administrator role assigned.

2. In the left pane, expand **Identity | Users | All users**.

3. In the right pane, click on **Bulk operation | Bulk create**. In the fly-out pane, click on **Download** to download a sample **.csv** file, as shown in the following figure:

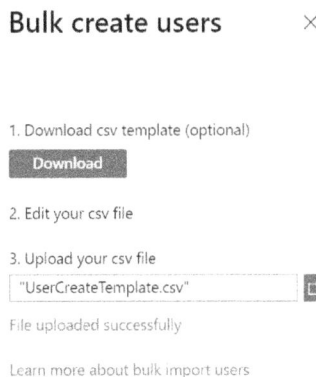

Bulk create users   ✕

1. Download csv template (optional)

Download

2. Edit your csv file

3. Upload your csv file

"UserCreateTemplate.csv"

File uploaded successfully

Learn more about bulk import users

Figure 2.3: Bulk create users

4. Complete the **.csv** file with the details of the users to be created. Upload the updated **.csv** file in the portal and click on **Submit**. While entering the user details in the **.csv** ensure that the fields marked as Required are filled in. Also, ensure that the user principal name is unique in the directory. If there are any data validation issues, the bulk import will fail. Correct the errors in the **.csv** and retry.

5. To view the status of each user account, click on **Bulk operation results** in the left pane. The right pane displays the results of each bulk upload operation.

    Refer to the following figure:

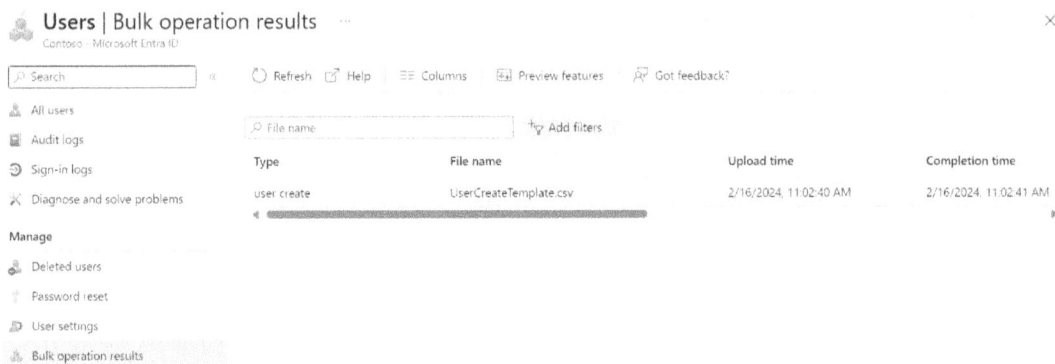

Figure 2.4: Bulk operation results

Windows PowerShell

PowerShell is a cross-platform task automation solution consisting of a command line shell, a scripting language and a configuration management framework. It can run on Windows, macOS and Linux.

You can create user accounts in bulk using a PowerShell script. The first step is to connect to your Microsoft 365 tenant using Windows PowerShell. You should have the Microsoft Graph PowerShell SDK installed on your computer.

Pre-requisites: The Microsoft Graph PowerShell SDK requires that you have the components following installed on your computer:

- Windows PowerShell 5.1 or later
- .NET Framework 4.7.2 or later

The following steps explain how to connect to your M365 tenant using PowerShell and create users:

1. Open a PowerShell command prompt window by right-clicking and selecting Run as Administrator. Run the following command to change the Windows PowerShell Execution Policy to **RemoteSigned**:

   ```
   Set-ExecutionPolicy RemoteSigned -Force
   ```

2. Install the v1 module of the SDK using the following command:

   ```
   Install-Module Microsoft.Graph -Force
   ```

3. To connect to your Microsoft 365 tenant, use the following command:

   ```
   Connect-MgGraph -Scopes "User.ReadWrite.All"
   ```

   This command will open a window prompting you to sign in with your credentials. Once done you will see a success message. You only need to sign in once per session.

4. To create a single user account, use the following command:

```
New-MsolUser -DisplayName <display name> -FirstName <first
name> -LastName <last name> -UserPrincipalName <sign-in name>
-UsageLocation <ISO 3166-1 alpha-2 country code> -LicenseAssignment
<licensing plan name> [-Password <Password>]
```

5. To create user accounts in bulk, first create the **.csv** file we discussed in the previous section and then use the following syntax to import it into the Entra ID tenant:

```
Import-Csv -Path <Input CSV File Path and Name> | foreach
{New-MsolUser -DisplayName $_.DisplayName -FirstName $_.FirstName
-LastName $_.LastName -UserPrincipalName $_.UserPrincipalName -Us-
ageLocation $_.UsageLocation -LicenseAssignment $_.AccountSkuId
[-Password $_.Password]} | Export-Csv -Path <Output CSV File Path
and Name>
```

Hybrid identity

In a hybrid identity model user accounts are created in on-premises AD and are synchronized to Microsoft Entra ID. Most user account changes flow from on-premises to Entra ID. When hybrid identity is implemented the on-premises AD remains authoritative for account information. This means that you will be performing administrative tasks on-premises and changes will be synchronized to Entra ID.

Synchronizing on-premises AD with Microsoft Entra ID can be a complex process, and there are several common pitfalls to be aware of, as follows:

1. **Duplicate user accounts**: If user attributes like UPN, email, or proxy address are not properly matched, duplicate user accounts can be created in Entra ID.

2. **ImmutableID issues**: The **ImmutableID** attribute is crucial for linking on-premises AD objects with Entra ID objects. Incorrect or missing **ImmutableID** values can cause synchronization problems.

3. **Synchronization delays**: Synchronization can sometimes be delayed due to network issues, large data volumes, or misconfigurations. This can result in outdated information and access issues.

Sometimes, manual intervention is needed to resolve synchronization issues, such as moving problematic user objects to a non-synchronized **organizational unit** (**OU**) and manually triggering a sync cycle.

There are two ways to synchronize on-premises AD to Entra ID.

Microsoft Entra Cloud Sync

Microsoft Entra Cloud Sync is a new service from Microsoft that synchronizes on-premises AD and Microsoft Entra ID using Microsoft online services. A light-weight agent acts as a bridge between Microsoft Entra ID and AD and stores the configuration in Microsoft Entra ID. The agent provides cloud sync and on-premises app provisioning capabilities.

It uses **System for Cross-domain Identity Management 2.0 (SCIM)**, which is a common user schema that helps users move between apps. SCIM is becoming a standard for provisioning and works with federation standards like **Security Assertion Markup Language (SAML)** and OpenID Connect to give administrators a complete solution for access management.

It provides the following benefits:

- Synchronize multiple disconnected AD forests to a single Microsoft Entra tenant.
- Simple installation using a lightweight provisioning agent.
- Supports groups with up to 50,000 members. If you have groups which have more than 50,000 members you will have to use Microsoft Connect Sync.
- Multiple provisioning agents can be used to address high availability scenarios.

Deployment scenarios

Microsoft Entra Cloud Sync supports the following deployment scenarios:

- Integrate a single AD forest with a single Microsoft Entra tenant.
- Integrate multiple AD forests with a single Microsoft Entra tenant.
- There is already an existing forest with Microsoft Entra Connect, and a new forest is synchronized using Microsoft Entra Cloud sync.
- Synchronize disconnected AD forests to a single Microsoft Entra tenant.

In addition to the above scenarios, Microsoft Entra Cloud Sync also supports the following scenarios.

- **HR-driven provisioning**: It involves creating user accounts in Microsoft Entra ID directly from a supported HR system. When a new employee joins a company, they are entered into the HR system. When this happens, their identity is automatically created in the Microsoft Entra ID tenant. It also supports employee attribute changes, such as when employees move across teams, and their attributes, such as manager name, department, etc., are updated. When employees leave the organization and their account in the HR system is terminated the same is updated in Microsoft Entra ID as well.
- **App provisioning**: This refers to automatically creating user identities in the cloud applications that the users need access to. It also includes maintenance and removal of user identities. Common scenarios include provisioning a Microsoft

Entra ID into cloud-based applications like Dropbox, Salesforce, ServiceNow and more.

This chapter will only focus on synchronizing objects from on-premises AD to Entra ID.

Key components

There are two key components of Microsoft Entra Cloud Sync, as follows:

- **A provisioning agent**: Built on the same server-side technology as application proxy and pass-through authentication, the provisioning agent requires only outbound connections to the Microsoft Cloud. The agent is auto updated.

- **A provisioning service**: This is the service responsible for updating changes to the Microsoft Entra ID tenant every two minutes.

Installing Microsoft Entra Cloud Sync

The following sections explain the pre-requisites and the steps to install and configure Microsoft Entra Cloud Sync in your environment.

Pre-requisites: Before you install the Microsoft Cloud Sync agent, ensure that the following requirements are met:

- A Domain Administrator or Enterprise Administrator account.

- A Microsoft Entra tenant with a custom domain name verified.

- A Hybrid Identity Administrator account created as a user in Microsoft Entra ID.

- An on-premises server or virtual machine running Windows 2016 or later with 4GB RAM and .NET 4.7.1+ runtime. TLS 1.2 should be enabled. NTLM should not be enabled.

- The agent should be able to make outbound requests to Microsoft Entra ID over ports 80, 443, and 8080.

- The PowerShell execution policy on the server should be set to Undefined or RemoteSigned.

- Group Managed Service Accounts are managed domain accounts that provide automatic password management, simplified service principal name management, ability to delegate management and extend the functionality to multiple servers. Administrative credentials are required to create this account and they appear as **domain\provAgentgMSA$**. Creating and configuring Group Managed Service Accounts is beyond the scope of this book. Refer to the Microsoft online documentation for the detailed steps.

Installation steps: The following steps must be completed on the server selected to run the Cloud Sync agent.

1. Go **to https://portal.azure.com,** and select **Microsoft Entra ID.**

2. In the left pane, click on **Microsoft Entra Connect**.

3. On the **Microsoft Entra Connect** page, in the left pane, click on **Cloud sync**.

4. On the **Cloud sync** page, on the left pane, click on **Agents**.

5. In the right pane, click on **Download on-premises agent**. In the fly out pane, click on **Accept terms and Download**.

6. Once the package has downloaded double click on `AADConnectProvisioningAgentSetup.exe` to start the installation.

7. On the splash screen, accept the license terms and conditions, and click on **Install**.

8. Once the installation is complete, the configuration wizard will start. Click **Next** to start the configuration.

9. On the **Select Extension** page, select **HR-driven provisioning (Workday and SuccessFactors)/Azure AD Connect Cloud Sync** and click **Next**, as shown in the following figure:

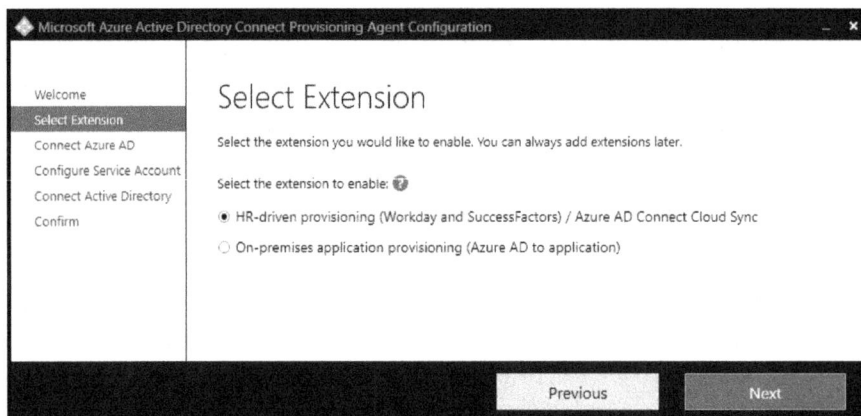

Figure 2.5: Select the provisioning option

10. On the page, click on **Authenticate** and sign in with your Microsoft Entra Global Administrator or Hybrid Identity Administrator credentials.

11. On the **Configure Service Account** page, choose the option **Create gMSA** and enter your AD Domain Administrator credentials to create the `provAgentgMSA$`. This will be created in the same domain where your sync server has joined. You can also choose to **Use custom gMSA** to specify a gMSA that you may have manually created for this purpose. It is however, recommended to let the tool create the gMSA for you. Once done, click on **Next**. Refer to *Figure 2.6:*

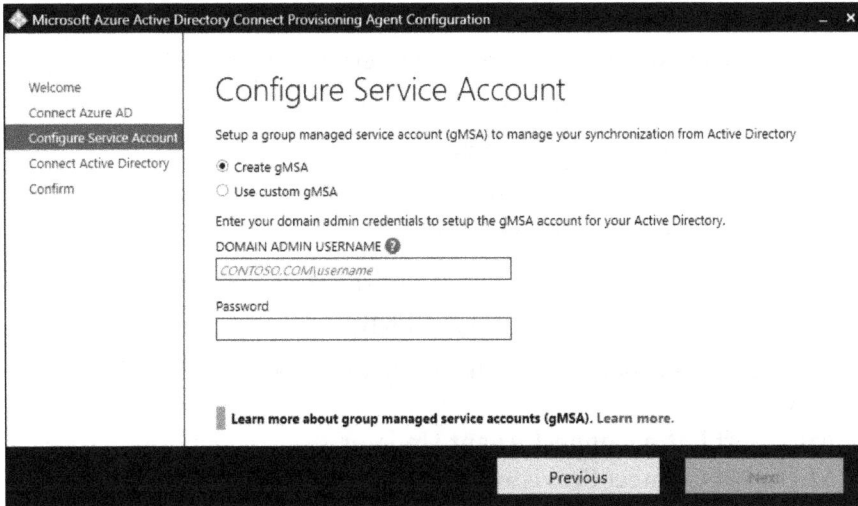

Figure 2.6: *Create a new gMSA*

12. On the **Connect Active Directory** page, if your domain is listed under **CONFIGURED DOMAINS** proceed to the next step. If not, enter your AD domain name, and click on **Add Directory**. Enter your Domain Administrator credentials, click on **OK,** and then click on **Next**.

    Refer to *Figure 2.7*:

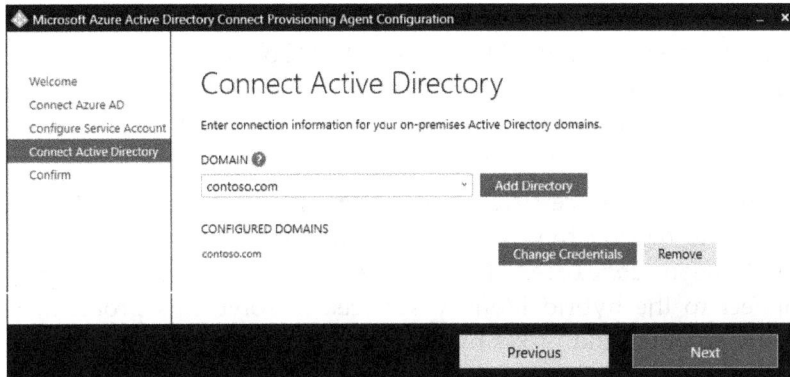

Figure 2.7: *Connect Active Directory*

13. On the **Configuration complete** page, click **Confirm** to register and restart the agent.

14. Once complete, you will see a message `Your agent configuration was successfully verified`. Click on **Exit** to close the configuration wizard.

Verify the installation: You would need to verify that the cloud sync agent is successfully installed and working. This must be done both in the Microsoft Entra ID tenant and the local server.

To verify the installation in Microsoft Entra ID tenant, following are the steps:

1. Sign into **https://portal.azure.com,** and select **Microsoft Entra ID**.

2. In the left pane, click on **Microsoft Entra Connect**.

3. In the left pane, click on **Cloud sync**.

4. On the **Cloud Sync** page, you will see the agents installed. Confirm that the agent is displayed, and the status is **Healthy**.

Following are the steps on the local server to confirm:

1. Sign into the server with a **Local Administrator** account.

2. Open the **Services** snap-in and ensure that the status of the following services is **Running**.
   a. **Microsoft Entra Connect Agent Updater**
   b. **Microsoft Connect Provisioning Agent**

Common installation problems

Several problems could arise while installing the agent. Some of them are explained, as follows:

- **Agent failed to start**: You might get an error `Service 'Microsoft Entra Provisioning Agent' failed to start. Verify that you have sufficient privileges to start the system services`.

  This problem is caused by a group policy preventing permissions to be applied to the local NT service account (NT Service\AADConnectProvisioningAgent) created by the installer. To solve this problem, go to the **Microsoft Entra Provisioning Agent** service in the **Services** console and on the **Log On** tab change the account to a domain admin and restart the service.

- **Agent times out or certificate is not valid**: You might get an error while attempting to register the service `Time out has expired and the operation has not been completed`. This problem is caused when the agent is not able to connect to the hybrid identity service. To solve this problem, you need to configure an outbound proxy by adding your proxy server name and port to the file `C:\Program Files\Microsoft Azure AD Connect Provisioning Agent\ AADConnectProvisioningAgent.exe.config`.

- **Agent registration fails**: If the agent registration fails due to a security error, it could be because it is not able to run PowerShell scripts due to local PowerShell execution policies. Ensure that the machine and user PowerShell execution policy on the server are set to Undefined or RemoteSigned.

Microsoft Entra Connect

Earlier called Azure AD connect, this is an on-premises application that is designed to synchronize identities from on-premises AD to Microsoft Entra ID. This involves installing an on-premises infrastructure, that includes a SQL Server. If you are just starting with your cloud synchronization journey, consider using Microsoft Entra Cloud Sync. However, there might be several scenarios where you would still need to use Microsoft Entra Connect, as follows:

- You do not want to synchronize your user account passwords to the cloud.
- You want to connect to LDAP directories.
- You want to allow advanced customization for attribute flows.
- You need support for merging user attributes from multiple domains.
- You need support for unlimited objects per AD domain.
- You have large groups with up to 250,000 members.

You have a large-scale deployment that will benefit from the performance and stability provided by a backend SQL Server.

Microsoft Entra ID Connect offers the following features:

- **Password hash synchronization**: A sign-in method that synchronizes a hash of the users' on-premises AD password with Microsoft Entra ID. This will be discussed in detail in the next section.
- **Pass-through authentication**: A sign-in method that allows the users to use the same password for both on-premises and cloud applications without synchronizing the passwords to the cloud. It also does not require installing extensive infrastructure. This will be discussed in detail in the next section.
- **Federation integration**: Microsoft Entra Connect can be used to create a hybrid environment using an on-premises AD Federation Services infrastructure. This will be discussed in detail in the next section.
- **Synchronization**: Microsoft Entra Connect Synchronization services (Microsoft Entra Cloud Sync) is the main component of Microsoft Entra Connect. It is a service that synchronizes identity data between on-premises AD and cloud. This sync service consists of two components, the on-premises Microsoft Entra Connect Sync and the service side component called **Microsoft Entra Connect Sync service**. This service was earlier called **DirSync** and then Azure AD Sync.
- **Health monitoring**: It provides robust monitoring in a central location within the Microsoft Entra admin center.

Installation requirements

Before you proceed with the installation of Microsoft Entra Connect, ensure that the requirements are met.

The following are the pre-requisites for the installation:

- A cloud-only identity with the **Hybrid Identity Administrator** permissions.
- A Microsoft Entra ID tenant with a verified domain name.

- Prepare your on-premises data using the IdFix tool to identify errors like duplicates or formatting issues before synchronizing to the cloud.
- An on-premises AD environment with schema version and forest functional level at Windows Server 2003 or later.
- PowerShell execution policy set to RemoteSigned.
- Connectivity to a DNS server to enable name resolution for both internet and intranet.
- Network connectivity to all configured domains and to the root domain of all configured forests.
- Open Microsoft Entra Connect ports if you are using firewalls on your intranet. For a complete list of ports, refer to **https://learn.microsoft.com/en-us/entra/identity/hybrid/connect/reference-connect-ports**.
- Allow the Office 365 URLs in your firewall to ensure connectivity to Microsoft Online Services. For a complete list of URLs refer to Microsoft online documentation.

Note: The IdFix tool is used to perform remediation of identity objects and their attributes in an on-premises AD environment in preparation for migration to Microsoft Entra ID. It can be downloaded from GitHub. https://github.com/Microsoft/idfix.

The following are some important considerations:

- Read-only domain controllers are not supported.
- Using on-premises forests or domains that contain dot (.) NetBIOS names is not supported.
- Enabling AD recycle bin is recommended.
- Microsoft Entra Connect cannot be installed on Small Business Server or Windows Server Essentials before 2019.
- The server should have full GUI support. Windows Server Core is not supported.

Connect server requirements

The server on which the Microsoft Entra Connect Sync will be installed should meet the following requirements:

- A domain-joined Windows Server 2016 or later.
- .NET Framework version 4.6.2 or later.
- Microsoft PowerShell 5.0 or later.
- TLS 1.2 enabled.

The memory, CPU, and hard disk requirements differ according to the number of objects to be synchronized from the on-premises AD.

Refer to the following table for the exact requirements:

Number of objects in AD	CPU	Memory	Hard drive size
Fewer than 10,000	1.6 GHz	6 GB	70 GB
10,000 – 50,000	1.6 GHz	6 GB	70 GB
50,000 – 100,000	1.6 GHz	16 GB	100 GB
100,000 – 300,000	1.6 GHz	32 GB	300 GB
300,000 - 600,000	1.6 GHz	32 GB	450 GB
More than 600,000	1.6 GHz	32 GB	500 GB

Table 2.2: Minimum hardware requirements for Entra Connect

SQL server requirements

Microsoft Entra Connect uses a SQL database to store identity data. By default, a SQL Server 2019 Express LocalDB is installed. This enables you to manage 100,000 objects. If your AD contains more than 100,000 objects, you need to install the full version of SQL. For performance reasons it is recommended to install the SQL server on the same server as the Microsoft Entra Connect tool.

Installation types

Microsoft Entra Connect offers two installation choices. Refer to the following table to decide which one is appropriate for your environment:

Express	Custom
You have a single AD forest on-premises.	You have or want to synchronize more than one AD forests.
You have an Enterprise Administrator account.	You do not have access to an Enterprise Administrator account.
You have less than 100,000 objects in on-premises AD.	You have more than 100,000 objects in on-premises AD.
You plan to use password hash sync for authentication.	You plan to use federation or pass-through authentication.
You want to synchronize all objects in the domain or OU.	You want to synchronize a subset of the objects.

Table 2.3: Express vs. custom settings

Installation steps

The steps to install Microsoft Entra Connect differ depending on the options you choose. Before you begin the installation, login as Local Administrator on the server you want to install Microsoft Entra Connect. Download the tool from **https://www.microsoft.com/en-us/download/details.aspx?id=47594** and execute the `AzureADConnect.msi` to launch the installation wizard.

From here, the steps will differ depending on the authentication method you choose. Those steps will be discussed in detail when we discuss the authentication methods in the next section.

Object filtering

By default, Microsoft Entra Connect synchronizes all objects from the on-premises Active Directory to Microsoft Entra ID, which is the recommended configuration. In some scenarios, you might want to control which objects are synchronized to Microsoft Entra ID. The following are some possible scenarios:

- You are running pilot and want to test with a subset of users first.

- You have non-personal accounts, like service accounts, that you do not want synchronized to Microsoft Entra ID.

- You do not delete on-premises accounts, but you want only active accounts in Microsoft Entra ID.

In these scenarios, you can use object filtering to synchronize only a subset of the accounts. There are four filtering options available:

- **Group-based filtering**: Filtering based on a single group is only possible during the initial installation of Microsoft Entra Connect, under the Custom installation in the installation wizard. This option is used when running a pilot deployment. Once the pilot is complete, you can use one of the other filtering methods. Once group-based filtering is disabled, it cannot be re-enabled.

- **Domain-based filtering**: This option enables you to choose which domains you want to synchronize to Microsoft Entra ID. You can do this at the first install of the Microsoft Entra Connect tool by using the Custom settings and selecting the domains to synchronize on the Domain and OU filtering page. This can also be done at a later stage by re-running the Microsoft Entra Connect installation wizard.

- **OU-based filtering**: This option enables you to select specific OUs to synchronize to Microsoft Entra ID. You can do this at the first install of the Microsoft Entra Connect tool by using the Custom settings and selecting the OUs to synchronize on the Domain and OU filtering page. This can also be done at a later stage by re-running the Microsoft Entra Connect installation wizard.

- **Attribute-based filtering**: This is the most flexible method of object filtering as you can control nearly every aspect of the objects synchronized. This uses the user account attributes to determine which user account should be synchronized to Microsoft Entra ID.

Microsoft Entra Connect Health

Installed along with Microsoft Entra Connect, the Microsoft Entra Connect Health provides monitoring for your on-premises identity infrastructure. Login to the Microsoft Entra Connect Health portal via **https://aka.ms/aadconnecthealth** to view alerts, performance metrics, and usage analytics.

Authentication methods

There are various methods of enabling authentication when on-premises identities are synchronized to Microsoft Entra ID. Choosing the right authentication type is the first concern for organizations wanting to move to the cloud.

This is a very important decision because of the following reasons:

- It is the first decision an organization will make when they plan to move to the cloud.
- Authentication controls access to all cloud data and resources.
- It is the foundation of all other advanced security measures that will be implemented in the future.
- It is nearly impossible to change.

Microsoft Entra Connect offers three authentication choices, that is, password hash sync, Pass-through authentication, and Federated authentication. We will learn more about these in the following sections.

Password hash sync

Password hash sync is the simplest method to enable authentication for on-premises AD objects in the cloud. In this method, password hashes are synchronized to Microsoft Entra ID. The users can use the same usernames and passwords for all on-premises and cloud applications.

It offers the following key advantages:

- Requires the least amount of administrative effort in terms of deployment, infrastructure, and maintenance.
- Advanced identity protection features like leaked credential reports are available only with this method.
- Provides business continuity. If your on-premises AD infrastructure is not available, the users will still be able to authenticate.
- Password hash sync can be used as a fallback mechanism for the other two authentication methods. If you have certain business requirements that are not met by password hash sync, you can use one of the other two methods and use

password hash sync as a fallback method to continue providing authentication services to your end users in case your on-premises infrastructure is unavailable.

The following figure illustrates a hybrid identity architecture with password hash sync:

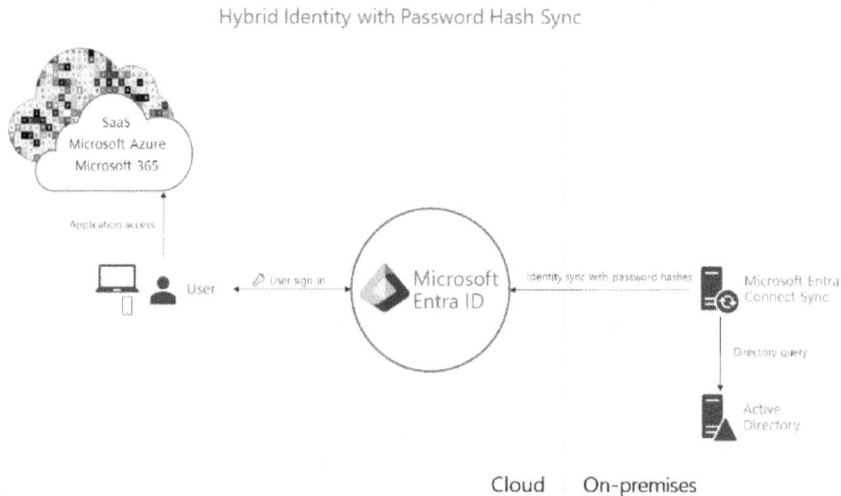

Figure 2.8: Password hash sync

The on-premises AD stores user passwords as a MD4 hash value of the original password. This is the result of a hashing algorithm, which is a one-way mathematical function. There is no way that a hashed value can be reversed to the obtain the original password.

Microsoft Entra Connect sync extracts the password hash from AD and applies additional security to the hashed password before synchronizing it with Microsoft Entra ID. The passwords are synchronized every two minutes, and this interval cannot be modified.

On the first run, all passwords of in-scope users are synchronized to Microsoft Entra ID. You can use staged rollout to test user groups with capabilities like **multi-factor authentication** (**MFA**), Conditional Access, Identity Protection, and Identity Governance.

This section explains in detail how the password hash sync agent securely synchronizes passwords from on-premises AD to Microsoft Entra ID.

Following are the steps for the same:

1. The password hash synchronization agent on the Microsoft Entra Connect server requests stored passwords from a Domain Controller every two minutes. The MS-DRSR protocol is used. It is the standard protocol used to replicate data between DCs. The service account should have the Replicate Directory Changes and Replicate Directory Changes All AD permissions. These permissions are granted when the agent is installed.

2. The Domain Controller encrypts the MD4 password hash with a MD5 hash key and a **salt**. It then sends the result over **Remote Procedure Call** (**RPC**) to the

password hash synchronization agent. The DC also sends the salt to the password hash synchronization agent using the MS-DRSR protocol so that the agent can decrypt the package.

> **Note:** A salt is random data added as additional input to the password to make it more secure. MD4 and MD5 are cryptographic hash functions used in hashing algorithms.

3. The password hash synchronization agent uses **MD5CryptoServiceProvider** and the salt to generate a key to decrypt the received package back to its MD4 value. It never has the password in clear text. MD5 is only used to achieve replication protocol compatibility with the DC.

4. The 16-byte binary password hash is then converted to a 32-byte hexadecimal string, and then back to binary using UTF-16 encoding. This expands the original hash to 64 bytes.

5. A 10-byte length per user salt is then added to the 64-byte binary for added security.

6. The MD4 hash and the per user salt is then combined, and sent into the PBKDF2 function. This is then hashed 1000 times using the HMAC-SHA256 algorithm.

> **Note:** Password-based Key Derivation Function 2 (PBKDF2) is a key derivative function used to reduce vulnerability to brute force attacks. Hash-based message authentication code (HMBAC) is a specific message authentication code used to verify data integrity and authenticity. SHA256 is a cryptographic function that is used in the calculation of an HMBAC.

7. The resulting 32-byte hash is then combined with the per user salt and the SHA256 iterations. It is then sent to Microsoft Entra ID over TLS.

8. When a user enters their password, it is run through the same process, MD4+salt+PBKDF2+HMAC-SHA256. If the resulting hash matches the hash stored in Microsoft Entra ID, the password is verified, and the user is granted access.

Important considerations

The following are some important considerations for password hash synchronization:

- The plain-text passwords are never exposed to password hash synchronization agent or to Microsoft Entra ID.
- The passwords are never stored in SQL. They are only processed in memory and then sent to Microsoft Entra ID.
- Users are authenticated against the passwords stored in Microsoft Entra and not on the on-premises AD.

- Since the MD4 hash is not transmitted to Microsoft Entra ID, if the Microsoft Entra ID password is stolen, it cannot be deciphered back to the original password stored in on-premises AD. This protects the passwords from pass-the-hash attack.

- For synchronized users, the on-premises AD password complexity policies override the password complexity policies in Microsoft Entra ID. Users created directly in the cloud still get the Microsoft Entra ID password complexity policy.

- For synchronized users, the password in Microsoft Entra ID is set to Never Expire. The account expiry attribute is not synchronized to Microsoft Entra ID from on-premises AD. It is possible for users to login to cloud services even if their on-premises password has expired. It is recommended using a PowerShell script, using the **Set-ADUser** cmdlet, that disables a user's Entra ID account once their on-premises AD account expires.

- Organizations usually provide a temporary password to new users and turn on the flag **User must change password at next logon**. To turn on temporary password support in Microsoft Entra ID for synchronized users, you should run the following command on your Entra Connect server:

```
Set-ADSyncAADCompanyFeature -ForcePasswordChangeOnLogOn $true
```

This feature should only be used if you have Self Service Password Reset and Password Writeback enabled in your tenant.

Selective password hash synchronization

Once you enable password hash synchronization, all users' passwords will be synchronized to Microsoft Entra ID. If you would like to synchronize a subset of the users, you can use selective password hash synchronization.

Include versus exclude

The first decision you would need to make is the number of users whose passwords you would like to synchronize to Microsoft Entra ID. To reduce administrative effort, you will follow different steps if the included users are more than the excluded users, and vice versa.

Both the scenarios use the **adminDescription** attribute. Rules are applied based on the value of this attribute and that is what makes selective password hash synchronization work. If the number of excluded users is less than the included users, the value of the **adminDescription** attribute should be **PHSFiltered**. If the number of excluded users is more than the included users, the value should be **PHSIncluded**.

The Microsoft Entra Connect synchronization scheduler must be disabled before implementing selective password hash synchronization.

Follow these steps:

1. Open Windows PowerShell and enter the following command to disable the scheduler:

   ```
   Set-ADSyncScheduler -SyncCycleEnabled $false
   ```

2. Confirm that the scheduler is disabled with the following command:

   ```
   Get-ADSyncScheduler
   ```

Now, you are ready to configure selective password hash synchronization.

Following are the steps, if excluded users are less than included users:

1. Open the Synchronization Rules Editor from the application menu on the computer where you have Microsoft Entra Connect sync installed. Select On in the Password Sync dropdown box and Standard in the Rule Type dropdown box.

2. In the box beneath, select the default synchronization rule for which you want to configure selective password hash synchronization and click on Edit. A box will appear asking you to disable the rule create an editable copy. Click Yes.

3. Give the rule a meaningful name like **In from AD—User AccountEnabled—Excluded Users**. Change the precedence value to a number below 100. Uncheck the boxes next to Enable Password Sync and Disabled. Click **Next**.

4. On the Scoping filter page, click on Add clause. In the attribute column, select **adminDescription** from the dropdown list. Select EQUAL from the operator dropdown list. In the value field, enter **PHSFiltered**.

5. Leave the rest of the settings as default. Click Save. A box will pop-up notifying that a full synchronization will run during the next synchronization cycle. Click OK.

6. Once again select the default rule and click on Edit. In the box prompting to disable the rule and create an editable copy, click Yes.

7. Give the rule a meaningful name like **In from AD—User AccountEnabled—Included Users**. Change the precedence value to a number lower than the previous rule. Check the box next to Enable Password Sync and uncheck the box next to Disabled. Click Next.

8. On the Scoping filter page, click on Add clause. In the attribute column, select **adminDescription** from the dropdown list. Select NOTEQUAL from the operator dropdown list. In the value field enter **PHSFiltered**.

9. Leave the rest of the settings as default. Click Save. A box will pop-up notifying that a full synchronization will run during the next synchronization cycle. Click OK.

10. Back in the main screen, remove all filters and you should be able to see the rules you just created.

If the number of excluded users is more than the number of included users, the following are the steps.

1. Open the Synchronisation Rules Editor. Select On in the Password Sync dropdown box and Standard in the Rule Type dropdown box.

2. In the box below, select the default synchronisation rule for which you want to configure selective password hash synchronisation and click on Edit. A box will appear asking you to disable the rule create an editable copy. Click Yes.

3. Give the rule a meaningful name like **In from AD—User AccountEnabled— Excluded Users**. Change the precedence value to a number below 100. Uncheck the boxes next to Enable Password Sync and Disabled. Click Next.

4. On the Scoping filter page, click on Add clause. In the attribute column, select `adminDescription` from the dropdown list. Select NOTEQUAL from the operator dropdown list. In the value field enter `PHSIncluded`.

5. Leave the rest of the settings as default. Click Save. A box will pop-up notifying that a full synchronisation will run during the next synchronisation cycle. Click OK.

6. Once again select the default rule and click on Edit. In the box prompting to disable the rule and create an editable copy, click Yes.

7. Give the rule a meaningful name like **In from AD—User AccountEnabled— Included Users**. Change the precedence value to a number lower than the previous rule. Check the box next to Enable Password Sync and uncheck the box next to Disabled. Click Next.

8. On the Scoping filter page, click on Add clause. In the attribute column, select `adminDescription` from the dropdown list. Select EQUAL from the operator dropdown list. In the value field enter `PHSIncluded`.

9. Leave the rest of the settings as default. Click Save. A box will pop-up notifying that a full synchronisation will run during the next synchronisation cycle. Click OK.

10. Back in the main screen, remove all filters and you should be able to see the rules you just created.

Once all the configuration is completed, you need to edit the value of the attribute `adminDescription` and re-enable the synchronization scheduler.

Following are the steps to edit the `adminDescription` attribute for all users in AD:

1. On your on-premises Domain Controller, open AD Users and Computer snap-in.

2. Navigate to OU and select the user whose attribute you want to update.

3. Double click on the user object and click on the Attribute Editor tab. Select the `adminDescription` attribute and enter the appropriate value as per the table above depending on if you want to include or exclude the user in selective password hash synchronization.

You can also do this using the following PowerShell commands:

```
set-adusermyuser-replace@{adminDescription="PHSFiltered"}
```

You can also use the following:

```
set-adusermyuser-replace@{adminDescription="PHSIncluded"}
```

Following are the steps to re-enable the synchronization scheduler:

1. Open Windows PowerShell and enter the following command to disable the scheduler:

   ```
   Set-ADSyncScheduler -SyncCycleEnabled $True
   ```

2. Confirm that the scheduler is enabled, as follows:

   ```
   Get-ADSyncScheduler
   ```

Setup password hash synchronization

Password hash synchronization is automatically enabled when you install Microsoft Entra Connect using the **Express** settings by following these steps:

1. Sign in as **Local Administrator** on the server where you want to install Microsoft Entra Connect. This will serve as the sync server.
2. Download the Microsoft Entra Connect from the Microsoft download center. Double click **AzureADConnect.msi** to start the installation.
3. Accept the licensing terms and click **Continue**.
4. On the **Express settings** page click on the button **Use express settings**.
5. On the **Connect to Azure AD** page, enter the username and password of an account that has the Hybrid Identity Administrator role assigned.
6. On the **Connect to AD DS** page, enter the username and password of the Enterprise Administrator account.
7. On the **Ready to configure page,** click **Install**. You can check the box **Start the synchronization process when configuration completes** if you want to start synchronization immediately, you can clear this box if you want to add filtering. You also have the option to enable hybrid deployment of Exchange. You can use this option if you plan to have mailboxes both in Exchange Online and on-premises Exchange Servers.
8. Click **Exit** once the installation completes.

Pass-through authentication

This is an alternative to the password hash sync method offering the same benefits of users being able to use the same username and password for both on-premises and cloud services. However, some organizations that want to enforce their own AD security and password policies can choose pass-through authentication. In this method, passwords remain stored on the on-premises AD. When the user tries to access an application, Microsoft Entra ID sends the authentication request to the on-premises AD and if the password matches the user is allowed access. Pass-through authentication offers the following benefits:

- Users can use the same username and password to access both on-premises and cloud applications.
- It is easy to deploy and administer. A simple lightweight agent is deployed.
- On-premises passwords are never stored in the cloud in any form.
- The agent makes only outbound connections from your network.
- Administrators can enforce on-premises password policies.

Following figure illustrates a hybrid identity architecture with Pass-through authentication:

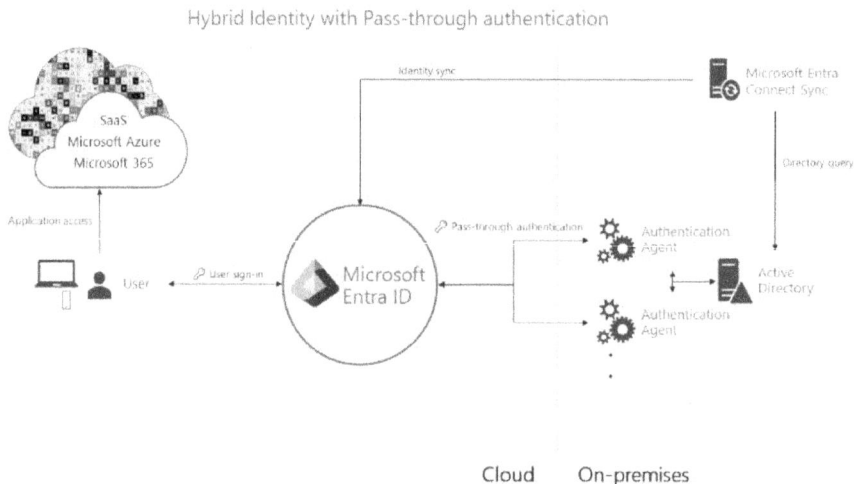

Figure 2.9: Pass-through authentication

Configuration pre-requisites

Before configuring Pass-through authentication, ensure that the following requirements are met:

- A cloud-only account with the Hybrid Identity Administrator permissions.
- One or more custom domain names added to the Microsoft Entra tenant.
- A server running Windows Server 2016 or later to with Microsoft Entra Connect installed.
- If you have a firewall between the servers and your Entra ID tenant, the following configuration is required:
  - o Authentication agents should be able to make outbound requests over ports 80, 443 and 8080.

o Add the following URLs to the Allow list ***.msapproxy.net** and ***.servicebus.windows.net**.

o The authentication agent should be able to access **login.windows.net** and **login.microsoftonline.com**.

o Unblock the following URLs to validate certificates: **crl3.digicert.com:80**, **crl4.digicert.com:80**, **ocsp.digicert.com:80**, **www.d-trust.net:80**, **root-c3-ca2-2009.ocsp.d-trust.net:80**, **crl.microsoft.com:80**, **oneocsp.microsoft.com:80**, and **ocsp.msocsp.com:80**.

o Allow the URL **autologon.microsoftazuread-sso.com** if you have an outgoing HTTP proxy.

o Inline inspection and termination on outbound TLS communications should be avoided between the Azure Passthrough Agent and the Azure Endpoint.

Enable Pass-through authentication

Pass-through authentication is enabled through Microsoft Entra Connect Custom settings. On the User sign-in page, select Pass-through authentication as the Sign On method. The pass-through agent is installed on the same server as Microsoft Entra Connect, and the feature is enabled on the tenant.

Test Pass-through authentication

Following are the steps to confirm that the configuration is completed successfully:

1. Sign in to **https://entra.microsoft.com** as Hybrid Identity Administrator and select Microsoft Entra ID.

2. Click on Microsoft Entra Connect.

3. Confirm that Pass-through authentication is Enabled.

4. Click on Pass-through authentication. The page should list the servers where the Authentication Agent is installed.

Federated authentication

Federation relies on an external trusted system to authenticate users. The on-premises AD can be federated with Microsoft Entra ID. This method ensures that all authentication occurs on the on-premises AD servers.

Microsoft Entra ID connect supports federation with **Active Directory Federation Service (AD FS)** and PingFederate. This book only covers Active Directory Federation Service. For details on configuring federation with PingFederate, refer to Microsoft online documentation.

Federation typically requires significant investment in on-premises infrastructure. Most organizations that choose this option already have an on-premises federated environment. It is arduous to maintain and will require significant hardware investment to provide load-balancing and business continuity. However, there are some business scenarios that are only available with federation. You might choose federation if you have the following:

- Use a third-party multifactor provider requiring federation.
- Use third-party authentication services.

  Use a sign-in that requires sAMAccountName instead of **User Principal Name (UPN)**. For example, **CONTOSO\Johnd** instead of **johnd@contoso.com**.

Federated authentication is illustrated in *Figure 2.10*:

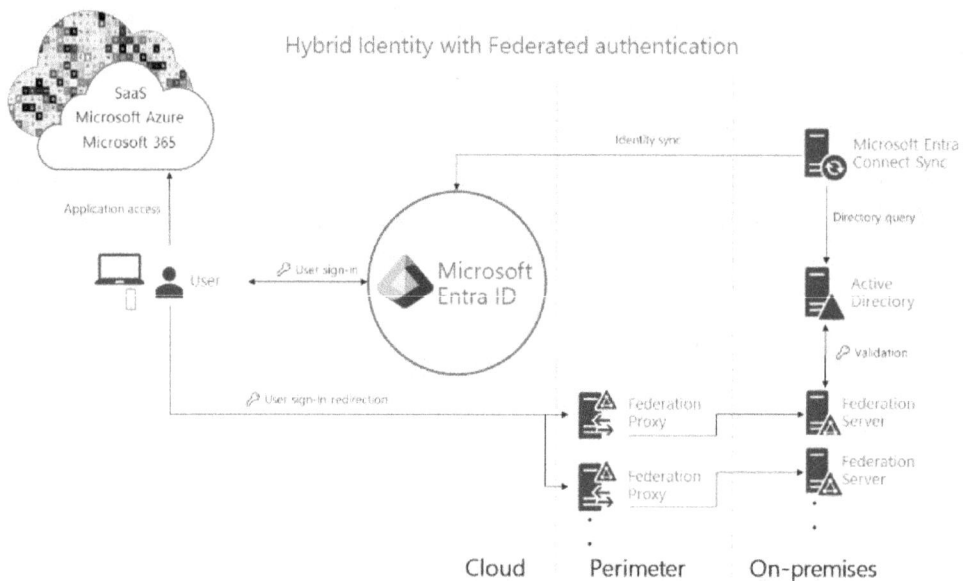

Figure 2.10: *Federated authentication*

Requirements

To configure federation between Microsoft Entra ID and AD FS you should have an on-premises AD FS environment. This typically consists of one or more AD FS servers and one or more AD FS proxy servers in the perimeter network. You need proxy servers so that you do not have to expose your AD FS servers to the internet. You can configure federation with only one AD FS and one proxy server; however, it is recommended to have two of each for business continuity and redundancy.

Following are the minimum requirements to configure an AD FS environment:

- Windows Server 2012 R2 or later for AD FS servers with remote management enabled.

- Windows Server 2012 R2 or later for Web Application Proxy with remote management enabled.
- TLS/SSL certificate for the federation service name.
- Set up DNS record for AS FS name.

Note: Installation of AD FS farm is beyond the scope of this book. Please refer to Microsoft documentation for detailed steps.

Enable Federation in Microsoft Entra Connect

Federation is enabled using the Microsoft Entra Connect installation wizard.

Following are the steps:

1. During the installation, choose Custom settings. On the User sign-in page, select Federation with AD FS.
2. On the Connect to Microsoft Entra ID page, enter a Hybrid Identity Administrator account. Do not use an account that is in a domain to you plan to enable for federation. You can use an account in the default **onmicrosoft.com** domain. This account is used to create a service account in Microsoft Entra ID and is not required after installation finishes.
3. On the AD FS Farm page, you can choose to use an existing farm or configure a new farm. If you choose and exiting farm, you will see a page to configure the trust relationship between AS FS and Microsoft Entra ID. If you decide to configure a new farm, specify the server where AD FS will be installed.
4. Next, specify the Web Application Proxy servers.
5. Next, enter the credentials to enable Web Application Proxy servers can connect to the AS FS servers. These should be a local administrator account on the AD FS server.
6. Next, specify the service account used by the AD FS service.
7. Lastly, select the Microsoft Entra ID tenant to be federated.

Choosing right method

Following is a handy decision tree that you can use to determine which authentication method is best suited for your business needs:

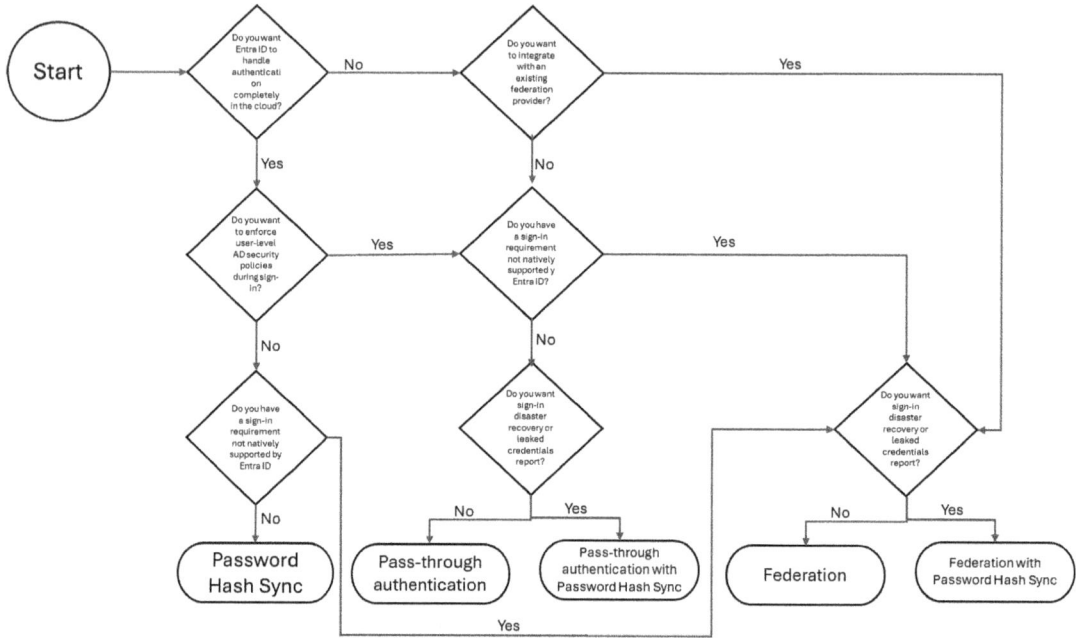

Figure 2.11: Authentication decision tree

Following is a comparison table:

Consideration	Password hash sync	Pass-through authentication	Federation
Where does authentication occur?	In Microsoft Entra ID	Microsoft Entra ID authenticates the user after verifying the password with the on-premises AD.	On-premises AD.
What are the on-premises infrastructure requirements?	None	A lightweight agent is installed on a virtual or physical server. Additional servers are required if more than one agent needs to be deployed.	Two or more ADFS servers. Two or more WAP servers installed in DMZ.
What are the networking requirements?	None	Outbound internet access from the servers that run the authentication agents.	Inbound internet access to the WAP servers. Inbound access from the WAP servers to the ADFS servers. Network Load Balancing

Consideration	Password hash sync	Pass-through authentication	Federation
Is a TLS/SSL certificate required?	No	No	Yes
Is health monitoring available?	Not required	Status of agents is available in the Microsoft Entra ID Admin center.	Microsoft Entra Connect Health can be used to provide health status.
Which advanced scenarios are supported?	Smart password lockout. Leaked credential report.	Smart password lockout.	Multisite low-latency authentication system. ADFS extranet lockout. Integration with third-party IdPs.

Table 2.3: Comparing authentication methods

Password protection

Passwords are increasingly becoming the single point of failure in identity attacks. Organizations enforce strong password policies, which lead to users following bad password practices. While you can provide guidance on the use of strong passwords, weak passwords are still used. Microsoft Entra ID offers password protection features that can prevent users from using weak passwords and their variants.

Global banned password list

Microsoft Entra constantly receives and analyses telemetry for commonly used weak, insecure, and compromised passwords. If any weak passwords are found, they are added to the global banned password list. This list is automatically applied to all users in a Microsoft Entra ID tenant. This list is solely maintained by *Microsoft*. The entries in this list are not based on any external source but a result of analysis of the telemetry received by Microsoft. When a user resets their password, the password is checked against the global banned password list to ensure that the new password is not on the list.

Custom banned password list

Microsoft Entra ID offers the ability for organizations to create and maintain a list of banned passwords. This is applied to user accounts in addition to the global banned password list. Some organizations might have a list of passwords that they do not want used. For example, they might want to prevent users from using the organization's name or its variants in their passwords. An administrator can add up to 1000 passwords in the custom banned password list. When a user attempts to change their password, it is evaluated against both the global banned password list and the custom banned password list.

Password spray attacks

Password spray attack is a form of brute force attack in which an attacker uses commonly used passwords on many accounts in an attempt to find the password. They do not attempt an account more than a few times as this can lead to detection. Most of the password spray attacks use a small number of passwords against each account. Microsoft Entra ID blocks commonly known weak passwords, thereby protecting the accounts against password spray attacks.

Supporting on-premises

The above capabilities are only helpful if you have your passwords synchronized to Microsoft Entra ID using password hash synchronization. In scenarios where customers are storing passwords on their on-premises AD you can deploy agents on on-premises to extend the password protection capabilities to on-premises AD. This agent needs to be installed on all domain controllers in the on-premises AD forest. It is responsible for forwarding the password policy download requests from the domain controllers to Microsoft Entra ID and send the responses from Microsoft Entra ID to the domain controller.

Single sign-on

Microsoft Entra ID supports **single sign-on** (**SSO**) with many third-party cloud applications. Once this is enabled, the users can sign in to these applications using their Microsoft Entra ID account. There are three methods of enabling SSO for an application:

- **SSO with SAML**: SAML is an XML-based open standard for exchanging authentication and authorization information between an application and an identity provider. It tells the external application that a user is who they say they are. Microsoft Entra ID has thousands of pre-integrated applications that use SSO.

- **Linked SSO**: This option provides SSO to an application that is already using SSO in another service. It does not provide SSO using Microsoft Entra ID. It directs a user to another location when they select the application in their MyApps portal. It is most used when links are used for a custom web application that uses federation.

- **OpenID Connect (OIDC)**: Based on the OAuth2 protocol, it uses a standard method from OIDC to provide identity services. It is typically used when user consent is required to sign in to a web application.

- **Password-based authentication**: In this method Microsoft Entra collects, encrypts and stores the user's application password in its directory and supplies the credentials when the user needs to sign in. It is used when an application does not support SAML and authenticates with a username and password instead of authentication tokens.

To enable SSO for enterprise applications, following are the steps:

1. Login to **https://entra.microsoft.com.**
2. In the left pane, expand **Identity** I **Applications** I **Enterprise Applications**.
3. Click on **All applications**.
4. In the right pane, select the application for which you want to enable SSO.
5. On the application overview page, click on **single sign-on**.
6. In the right pane, select the SSO method and follow the on-screen instructions.

Note: The final steps will be different for each application type and the SSO method it supports.

End user self-service

Microsoft Entra ID offers several end user self-service capabilities to ease the administrative overhead, empower the workforce and reduce helpdesk calls. This section explores some of these self-service options. These options are available from the MyApplications portal.

Self-service password reset

If a user account is locked or if they forget their password, they can unlock it or reset their own passwords without requiring calling the helpdesk. This feature has added security as the users reset their own passwords and the helpdesk does not have to verify the identity of the user calling for password reset.

While setting up end user self-service password reset, administrators can configure the authentication options a user can use to verify their identity online if they need to reset their password or unlock their account. These methods are as follows:

- **Mobile application notification**: Users will receive a notification on the Microsoft Authenticator app on their mobile phones.
- **Mobile application code**: Users will receive a code on the Microsoft Authenticator app on their mobile and they will have to enter the same code on the self-service portal.
- **Email**: Users can configure an alternative email address to use during the verification process.
- **Mobile phone**: Users will receive a call or text on their configured mobile phone.
- **Office phone**: Users will receive a call on their configured office phone.

- **Security questions**: User can configure security questions and answers. They will be asked to answer one or more of the security questions during the verification process.

Following are the steps to configure end user self-service password reset:

1. Login into **https://entra.microsoft.com** with an account that has at least Authentication Policy Administrator role.

2. In the left pane, click on **Identity** | **Protection** | **Password reset**.

3. Click on **Properties,** and in the right pane, select if you want to enable password reset for All users or selected users. If you choose selected users, you will be prompted to select the group for which you want to enable SSPR. Once done, click **Save**.

Refer to *Figure 2.12:*

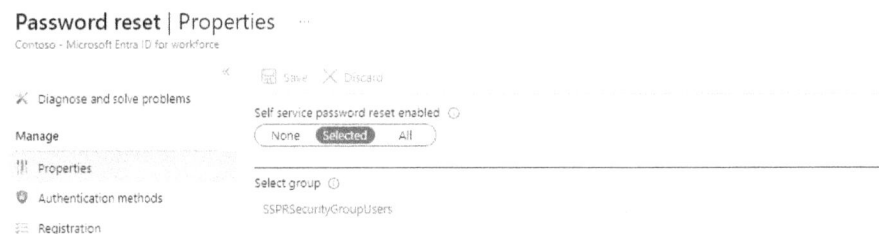

Password reset | Properties
Contoso - Microsoft Entra ID for workforce

⤬ Diagnose and solve problems

Manage

⌘ Properties
🛡 Authentication methods
☰ Registration

🔲 Save ✕ Discard

Self service password reset enabled ⓘ
(None **Selected** All)

Select group ⓘ
SSPRSecurityGroupUsers

Figure 2.12: *Configure SSPR group*

4. Click on **Authentication methods**. In the right pane, select the number of methods users are required to fulfill to reset their passwords. Under the **Methods available to users,** select the methods you want to make available to users to use during their password reset process. Click **Save**.

Refer to *Figure 2.13:*

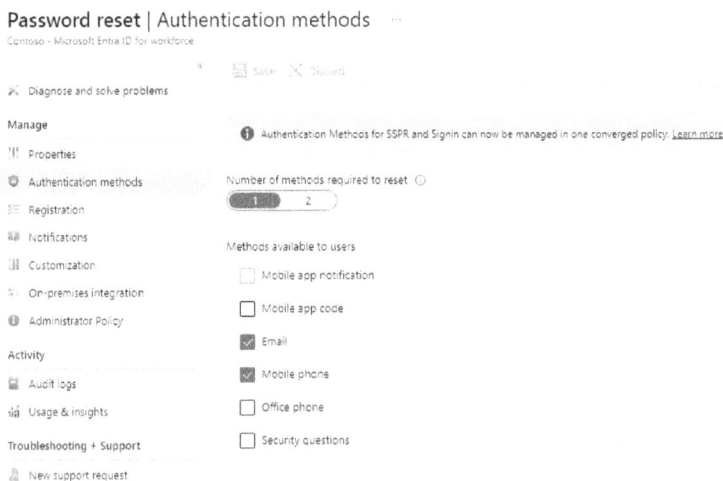

Password reset | Authentication methods
Contoso - Microsoft Entra ID for workforce

⤬ Diagnose and solve problems

Manage
⌘ Properties
🛡 Authentication methods
☰ Registration
📱 Notifications
� JII Customization
🔗 On-premises integration
ⓘ Administrator Policy

Activity
📊 Audit logs
📈 Usage & insights

Troubleshooting + Support
📄 New support request

🔲 Save ✕ Discard

ⓘ Authentication Methods for SSPR and Signin can now be managed in one converged policy. Learn more

Number of methods required to reset ⓘ
(**1** 2)

Methods available to users
☐ Mobile app notification
☐ Mobile app code
☑ Email
☑ Mobile phone
☐ Office phone
☐ Security questions

Figure 2.13: *SSPR methods*

Note: These settings only affect user accounts. Administrative user accounts are always enabled for self-service password reset and are required to use two authentication methods to reset their passwords.

Tip: If an end user must reset their password, they should go to https://aka.ms/ sspr. The first time they will be promoted to set up the authentication methods you configured above.

Self-service group management

Using Microsoft Entra ID, you can enable users to create and manage their own Microsoft 365 or Security groups. This offloads a considerable amount of work from IT to the end users. The group owners are responsible for maintaining group membership.

To set up self-service group management, follow these steps:

1. Login to **https://entra.microsoft.com** using an account which has at least the Group Administrator role assigned.

2. In the left pane, click on **Identity** | **Groups** | **Group settings**.

3. In the **General** page, make the following settings:

   a. **Owners can manage group membership requests in the Access Panel: Yes**

   b. **Restrict user ability to access group features in the Access Panel: No**

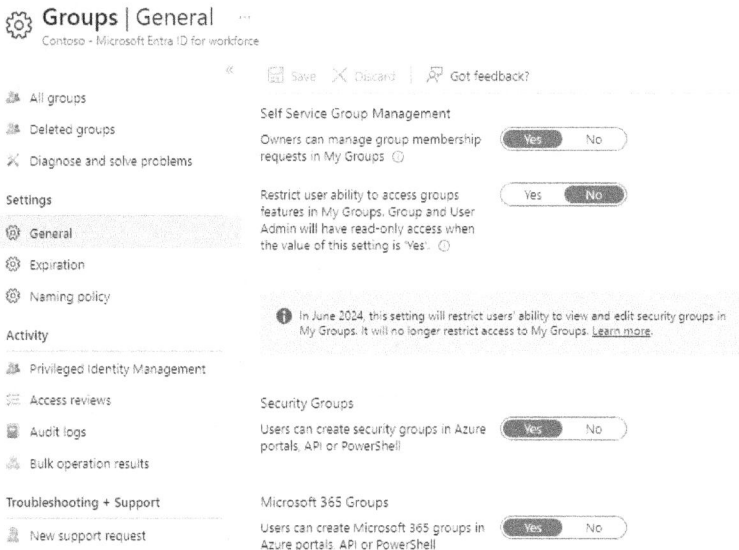

Figure 2.14: Self-service group management settings

4. Click **Save**.

Tip: End users can create and manage groups from the Groups Access Panel in MyApps portal. Go to https://myapplications.microsoft.com, select My Groups from the drop-down list.

Self-service application assignment

Microsoft Entra allows users to discover applications from the MyApps portal. With this feature, admins can:

- Add users to preconfigured groups that have access to applications.
- Allow up to 10 business users to approve or deny application requests.
- Allow business users to set application passwords that users can use to sign into applications.
- Automatically assign applications to business users based on their role.

Note: SSO for the application should be enabled before self-service can be configured. These steps are explained in the previous section.

Follow the steps to enable self-service application assignment:

1. Login to **https://entra.microsoft.com** with an account that has the Cloud Application Administrator role assigned.
2. Navigate to **Identity | Application | Enterprise Applications | All applications**.
3. In the list of applications, find the application that you want to enable self-service for. Click on the application name. In the page that opens, click on **Self-service**.
4. In the right pane, switch the toggle next to **Allow users to request access to this application?** to **Yes**.
5. Click on **Select group**, next to **To which group should assigned users be added?**, select a group, and click **Select**. When a user request is approved, they are added to this group.
6. If business approval is required before user access is approved, select **Yes** next to **Require approval before granting access to this application?**
7. Click on **Select approvers**, next to **Who is allowed to approve access to this application?** and select the user(s) who can approve access. Groups are not supported. Up to 10 users can be selected as approvers. If multiple approvers are selected, any one user can approve the request.
8. Choose the role to which these users should be assigned by clicking on **Select a role** next to **To which role should users be assigned in this application?** This option is to assign users to a role within the application.
9. Click on **Save**.

In addition to the self-service options discussed above, the MyApplications portal offers other self-service options as well, such as:

- **My Sign-ins**: Users can access their own sign-in activity and report any malicious sign-ins to their organization.

- **MyAccess**: Employees and guests can request access to different application packages, which enable them to get access to applications and services. This will be discussed in detail in *Chapter 5, Identity Governance*.

- **Devices**: Users can view and manage the list of devices connected to their Microsoft Entra ID account.

- **Security info**: Users can update their verification methods.

Conclusion

In this chapter, we learnt the capabilities of Microsoft Entra ID for administrators, end users, and applications.

Microsoft Entra ID offers two methods of configuring and managing identity: cloud only identity and hybrid identity. There are three methods of configuring hybrid identity. They are Microsoft Entra Cloud Sync, Microsoft Entra Connect and Federation using AD FS. The method you choose depends on your organization's current and future identity requirements. The hybrid identity method offers two options to synchronize user accounts to Microsoft Entra ID: Password hash sync and Pass-through authentication. Microsoft Entra ID also offers password protection capabilities for both cloud and on-premises deployments.

Microsoft Entra ID enables end users to manage aspects of their identities themselves. They can use self-service password reset to unlock their accounts or change their passwords. They can use self-service group management to create and manage M365 and Security groups. They can also request access to applications, view their sign-in history, and connected devices using the MyApplications portal.

Lastly, we learned the various ways in which SSO can be configured for applications.

In the next chapter, you will learn about the identity management features of Microsoft Entra ID.

Multiple choice questions

1. **Your organization has been using on-premises Active Directory for the last 15 years. You decide to move to the cloud and choose Microsoft Entra ID as your identity provider. The organization wants to provide single sign-on for all applications. The on-premises Active Directory should remain authoritative for user authentication. You need to implement a solution with the least amount of**

administrative effort and infrastructure requirements. **Which identity model is best suited?**

   a. Cloud-only identity

   b. Hybrid identity with password hash synchronization

   c. Hybrid identity with pass-through authentication

   d. Hybrid identity with federation

2. **Which of the following is possible only if Microsoft Entra Connect Sync is used?**

   a. Connecting multiple on-premises AD forests to Microsoft Entra ID

   b. Support for federation

   c. Support for groups with up to 250,000 members

   d. Support for Seamless SSO

3. **As an IT administrator you want to reduce the number of helpdesk calls by providing users self-service capabilities. What are some of the user self-service capabilities available with Microsoft Entra ID? Select all that apply.**

   a. Users can be enabled to reset their own passwords

   b. Managers can be enabled to reset passwords for their team

   c. Users can be enabled to create and manage groups

   d. Managers can be enabled to create user accounts for their team

4. **Under which scenario would you use federation?**

   a. You use third party MFA

   b. You want to leverage the leaked credential report

   c. You want to minimize the on-premises infrastructure

   d. You want to allow users to sign in with DOMINAN\username.

Answer key

  1. c

  2. c

  3. a, c

  4. d

CHAPTER 3
Identity Management

Introduction

One of the main tasks of an identity and access management administrator is to make sure that the right system resources are accessible to the right users. This can be a challenging task since there are thousands of user identities in any organization. This chapter shows you how you can use the group management features in Microsoft Entra ID to handle these identities and protect your organization's resources effectively. It also covers the key concept of role-based access control, which will help you understand the other Microsoft capabilities explained in this book. It also teaches how you can logically segment your Microsoft 365 tenant administration by using admin units. It ends by introducing you to protected actions and how they further strengthen security.

Structure

This chapter covers the following topics:

- User and group management
- Microsoft Entra roles
- Administrative units
- Protected actions

Objectives

By the end of this chapter, readers will be able to create and delete user accounts, assign roles and licenses to users and groups. You will also be able to understand the different types of groups in Microsoft Entra ID, create groups, add members and understand group-based licensing. This chapter will also explain **role-based access control (RBAC)** in Microsoft Entra ID. You will also learn how you can create and manage admin units to decentralize management of the M365 tenant and use protected actions to protect high-impact permissions.

User and group management

In the previous chapters, you learned how to set up an Entra ID tenant, determine the correct identity model for your organization and choose the right authentication method.

Let us begin by understanding the types of user accounts in Microsoft Entra ID. Before creating a user account, it is important to determine the user's relationship with the organization. Based on that you can decide whether the user should be created as an internal user or external user.

Following are the types of user accounts available in Microsoft Entra ID:

- **Internal member**: These are the organization's full-time employees.
- **Internal guest**: These users have accounts in the Microsoft Entra ID tenant but have guest privileges. They might have been created before B2B collaboration was introduced.
- **External member**: These users authenticate using an external account but have member level privileges. These are common in multitenant organizations like conglomerates, divesture and merger and acquisition scenarios.
- **External guest**: These are external users who sign-in using external accounts and have guest level privileges.

Inviting guest user

The steps to create a new user account were explained in *Chapter 1, Introduction to Microsoft Entra.*

Following are the steps to explain how you can invite a guest in the Microsoft Entra ID tenant:

1. Sign in to **https://entra.microsoft.com** with an account that has the Guest Inviter role assigned.
2. In the left pane, navigate to **Identity | Users | All users**.
3. In the right pane, click on **New user | Invite external user** as shown in the following figure:

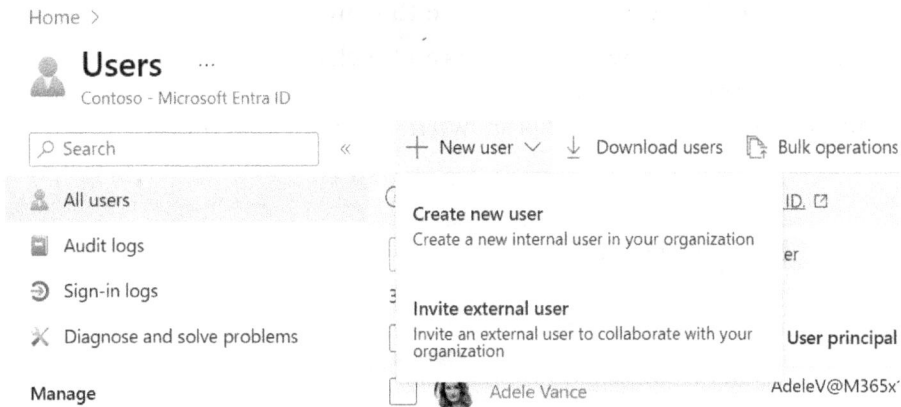

Figure 3.1: *Creating an external user*

4. On the next page, enter the email address of the external user where the invite will be sent as shown in *Figure 3.2*. Optionally, enter a **Display name**. Make sure the box next to **Send invite message** is checked. Optionally, type a message to the external user and enter any **Cc recipient** you want them to be notified for the invite. This could be the internal sponsor for the external user. Click on **Next: Properties** as shown in the following figure:

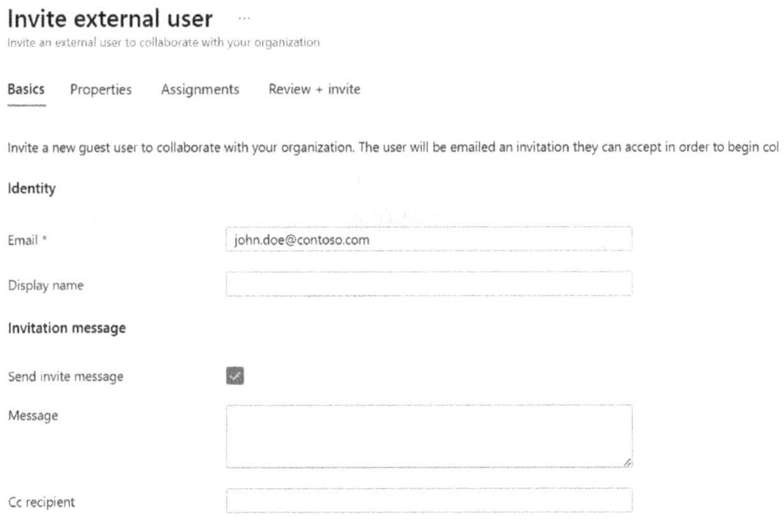

Figure 3.2: *Invite external user*

5. On the **Properties** page, add details about the external user as appropriate and click **Next: Assignments**.

6. On the **Assignments** page, you can add the guest user to roles and groups as required. The guest user will be assigned those roles and groups once they activate

their account. Once done click on **Next: Review + invite**.

7. On the last page, review your settings and click on **Invite**. Once done, the external user will receive an email on the email address you configured to join your organization. A sample email is shown in the following figure:

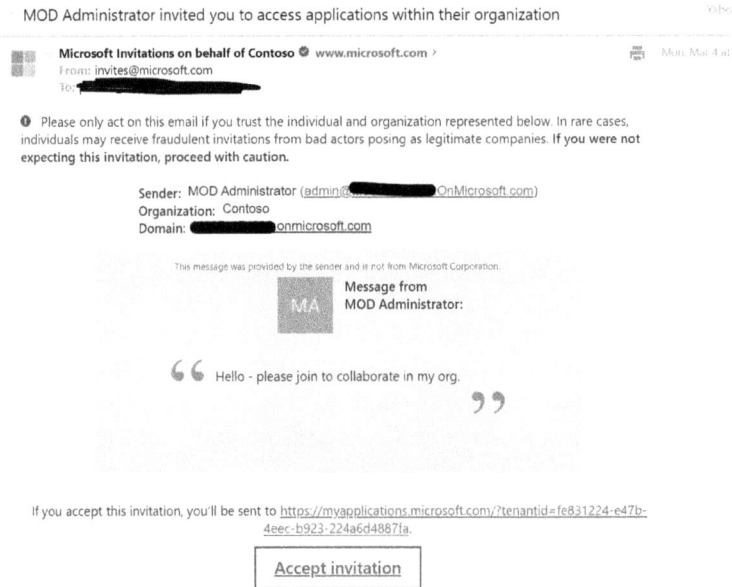

Figure 3.3: Guest user invite sample mail

8. You can check the status of the invitation in the guest user properties. In the Microsoft Entra ID portal, click on the guest user account and check the status under **B2B invitation**. You can also resend the invitation from here, as shown in the following figure:

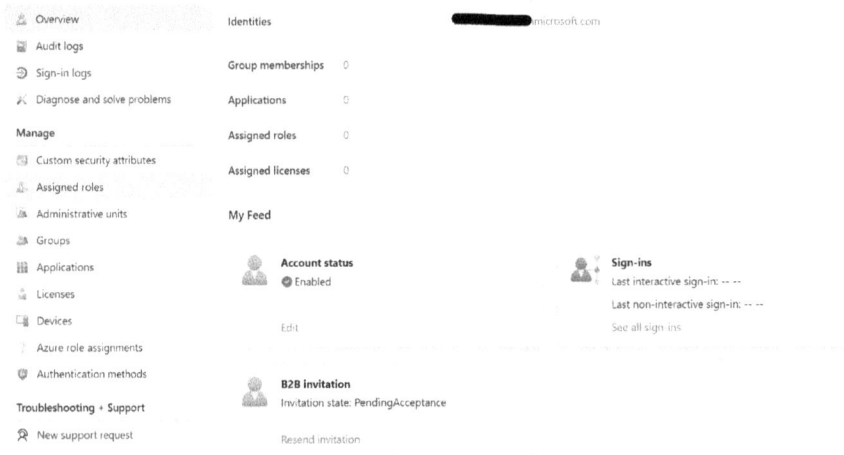

Figure 3.4: Check guest invite status

Deleting user account

Before you delete a user account, following factors should be considered:

- The administrator account used to delete a user account should be a Global Administrator, Privileged Authentication Administrator or User Administrator.
- Global Administrator and Privileged Authentication Administrator can delete all user accounts including other administrators.
- User Administrator can delete Helpdesk Administrator, other User Administrators and non-admin accounts.

Following are the steps to delete a user account:

1. Sign into **https://entra.microsoft.com** and navigate to **Identity | Users | All users**.
2. In the right pane, click on the user account that you would like to delete and click on **Delete**.

The deleted user account is moved to the Deleted users page for 30 days after which it is permanently deleted.

Creating new group

With Microsoft Entra ID, you can use groups to make management of user accounts easier. Using groups enables administrators to grant permissions and assign licenses to groups rather than individual users. You can also manage access to applications using groups. There are two types of groups available in Microsoft Entra ID, as follows:

- **Security**: These groups are used to manage user access to shared resources.
- **Microsoft 365**: These groups offer collaboration capabilities across shared mailboxes, SharePoint sites and more.

Group membership can be managed in three ways, as follows:

- **Assigned**: Administrators can add each individual user to groups.
- **Dynamic user**: Using this method, administrators can use rules to dynamically assign users to groups. For example, you could create a group for all users in the Legal department. This is based on the users' Microsoft Entra ID attributes. Once created, all users whose Department field in Microsoft Entra ID is Legal will be dynamically added to this group. As and when the user's Entra ID attributes are updated the group membership is dynamically updated.
- **Dynamic device**: Using this group type you can dynamically add or remove devices to a group based on their attributes.

Following are the steps to create a new group:

1. Login to **https://entra.microsoft.com** with an account that has at least the User Administrator role assigned.

2. Navigate to **Identity** | **Groups** | **All groups**.

3. In the right pane, click on **New group**.

4. Select the appropriate **Group type** as `Security` or `Microsoft 365` as shown in *Figure 3.5*.

5. Enter the name of the group and an optional description.

6. If you want Microsoft Entra roles to be assigned to this group switch the toggle under **Microsoft Entra roles can be assigned to the group** to **Yes**. Role-assignable groups are explained in the next section.

7. Select the appropriate group membership types as `Assigned`, `Dynamic User` or `Dynamic Device`.

8. You can choose **Owners** and add **Members** to the group at the time of creation or it can be done later.

9. Click on **Create** to create the group, as shown in the following figure:

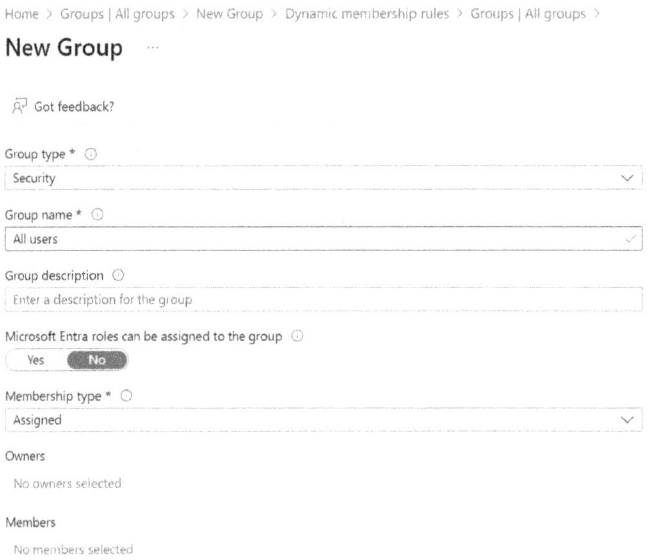

Home > Groups | All groups > New Group > Dynamic membership rules > Groups | All groups >

New Group ⋯

⟳ Got feedback?

Group type * ⓘ
| Security | ⌄ |

Group name * ⓘ
| All users | ✓ |

Group description ⓘ
| Enter a description for the group |

Microsoft Entra roles can be assigned to the group ⓘ
(Yes **No**)

Membership type * ⓘ
| Assigned | ⌄ |

Owners
No owners selected

Members
No members selected

Figure 3.5: Creating a new group

Role-assignable groups

Using Microsoft Entra ID P1, you can create groups to which roles can be assigned. These are called **role-assignable groups**. This simplifies management of the role, ensures consistent access and makes auditing straightforward. Groups can be assigned built-in roles or custom roles.

Consider a scenario where there are several people who manage the IT helpdesk, and a part of their role is to reset end user passwords. Instead of assigning the Helpdesk

Administrator role to each individual, a role-assignable group can be created, and the Helpdesk Administrator role can be assigned to this group. This way if people change roles and are removed from the group they lose the Helpdesk Administrator role. Also, when new people join the IT Helpdesk they can be added to this group, and they will automatically get the role. This helps ensure that individuals do not have more privileges than they require to do their job. It also frees up the Global Administrator or the Privileged Role Administrator from assigning and removing roles as people move between jobs as the group administration can be delegated.

There are certain considerations to be kept in mind while creating role-assignable groups, as follows:

- The role-assignable property can be set only for new groups. Existing groups cannot be changed to role-assignable groups.
- Once a role-assignable group is created, this property cannot be changed.
- A maximum of 500 role-assignable groups can be created a Microsoft Entra tenant.
- Roles cannot be assigned groups that are created in on-premises AD.

Protecting role-assignable groups

If a role is assigned to a group, the administrator who manages the membership of that group can also manage the membership of the role. For example, if there is a group called User Administrators and it has the Helpdesk Administrator role assigned, any administrator who can modify the membership of the group can add themselves to the group and become a Helpdesk Administrator and be able to reset user passwords. This way, administrators could elevate their permissions in ways that are not intended.

Role-assignable groups can help prevent these scenarios and potential breaches as they have the following restrictions:

- Only Global Administrators and Privileged Role Administrators can create role-assignable groups.
- The membership type of a role-assignable group must be Assigned. It cannot be Dynamic.
- By default, only Global Administrators or Privileged Role Administrators can manage membership of a role-assignable group. You can, however, delegate the management to other users by adding group owners.
- Another group cannot be nested within a role-assignable group.

PIM and role-assignable groups

If you do not want members to have standing access to the role, you can use Microsoft Entra **Privileged Identity Management** (**PIM**) to make the group eligible for the role. This way the group members can get elevated permissions for a certain amount of time. PIM is explained in *Chapter 5, Identity Governance*.

Adding members to group

If you did not add members to the group at the time of creation or if additional members need to be added at a later stage, following steps add members to a group that has membership type defined as **Assigned**:

1. Login to **https://entra.microsoft.com** with an account that has at least the User Administrator role assigned.

2. Navigate to **Identity | Groups | All groups**.

3. In the right pane, click on the group to which you want to add members.

4. Click on **Members**.

5. In the right pane, click on **Add members**. In the window that pops up select the user accounts you want to add to this group and click **Select**.

To add members to a group that has group membership defined as **Dynamic User** or **Dynamic Device**, a query needs to be defined while creating the group. Follow the steps to create a new group and select the appropriate **Membership type**. Under **Dynamic user members** or **Dynamic device members** click on **Add dynamic query**. In the next screen, you can define the query.

The following figure shows how you can dynamically add users in the **Marketing department** to a group:

Home > Groups | All groups > New Group > Dynamic membership rules > Groups | All groups > New Group >

Dynamic membership rules   …   ✕

🖫 Save   ✕ Discard   ⌨ Got feedback?

Configure Rules   Validate Rules (Preview)

You can use the rule builder or rule syntax text box to create or edit a dynamic membership rule. ⊙ Learn more

And/Or	Property	Operator	Value	
	department	Equals	Marketing	🗑
And	Choose a Property	Choose an Operator	Add a value	🗑

+ Add expression + Get custom extension properties ⊙

Rule syntax   ✎ Edit

(user.department -eq "Marketing")

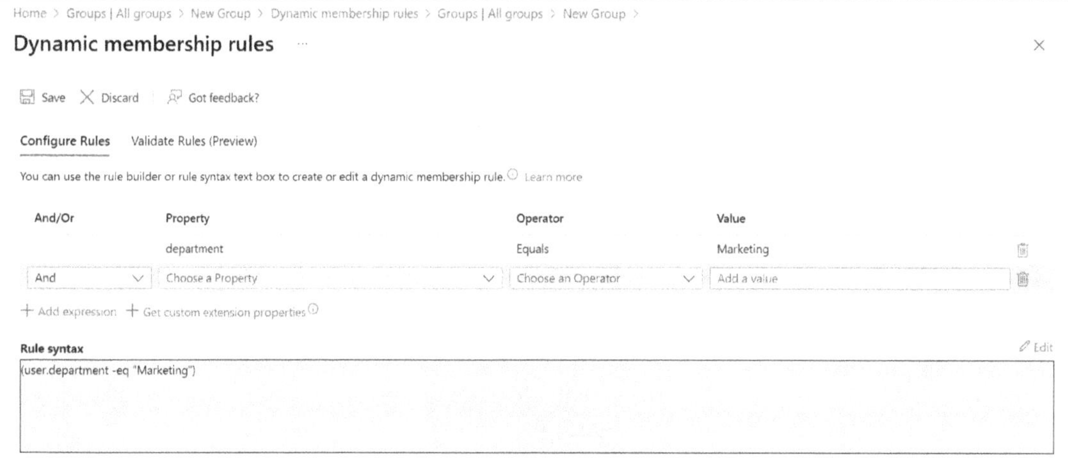

Figure 3.6: Adding users in the Marketing department to a group

The following figure shows how you can add all devices with a specific device model to a group:

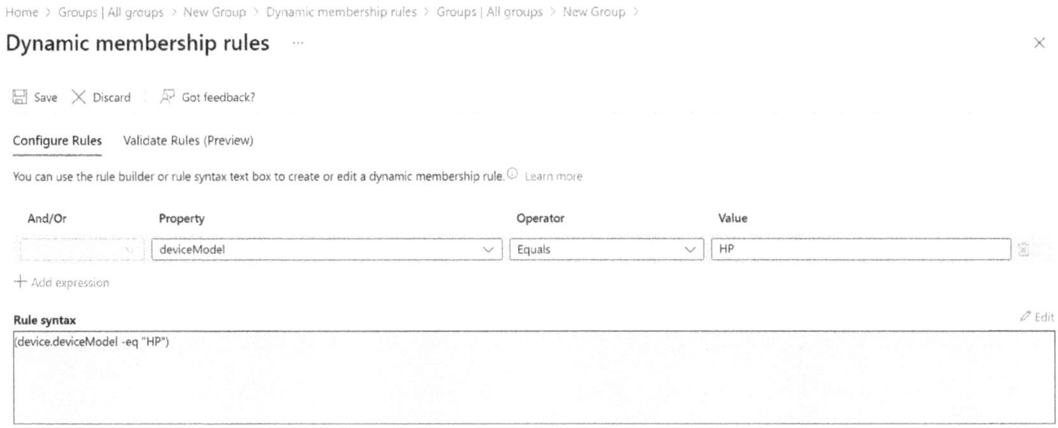

Figure 3.7: *Dynamically adding devices to a group*

Nested group

Security groups can be added to other security groups. These are called **nested groups**. You need the Groups Administrator or User Administrator role to do so. This helps in better management of access permissions and assigning resources to groups. For example: you could have a group called All Employees with nested groups such as All Employees: Americas, All Employees: EMEA and All Employees: Asia. This way you can assign resources applicable to all employees at the parent group level and apply region specific resources to nested groups.

Nested groups do not support the following scenarios:

- Groups cannot be added to groups that are synced from on-premises AD.
- Security groups cannot be nested within Microsoft 365 groups.
- Microsoft 365 groups cannot be nested within Security groups or other Microsoft 365 groups.
- Licenses cannot be applied to nested security groups.
- Exchange Distribution groups cannot be nested within security groups.
- Security groups cannot be added as members in mail-enabled security groups.
- Groups cannot be added as members to role-assignable groups.

Group-based licensing

In Microsoft Entra, licenses can be assigned to groups. This is easier than assigning licenses to individual users as Microsoft Entra takes care of assigning licenses to each individual user who is a member of the group. As new members join the group, they are automatically assigned licenses and when members leave, their licenses are removed.

Every user who is a member of the license assigned group should have one of the following licenses assigned:

- Microsoft Entra ID P1
- Microsoft 365 Business Premium or Office 365 Enterprise E3

The following are some main features of group-based licensing:

- Licenses can be assigned to any security group whether the group is created in Microsoft Entra ID or synchronized from on-premises AD.
- When a license is assigned to a group, the administrator can disable one or more service plans in the product.
- All Microsoft cloud services that support user-level licensing can be assigned to groups.
- Microsoft Entra automatically adds and removes licenses from users who are added or removed from the group.
- A user can be a member of multiple groups that have licenses assigned and have licenses assigned outside the group membership. If a user is assigned the same license via multiple groups, or directly, the license is consumed only once.

Assigning licenses to user or group

Most services in Microsoft 365 are subscription-based licenses and for users to be able to access these services, appropriate licenses should be applied to their user accounts.

The following are the steps to assign licenses to a user or group:

1. Sign in to **https://entra.microsoft.com** with an account that has the License Administrator role assigned.
2. Navigate to **Identity | Billing | Licenses**.
3. Click on **All products**. This page shows the total number of licenses available in the tenant. It also shows how many licenses are assigned and how many are available for use as shown in *Figure 3.8*:

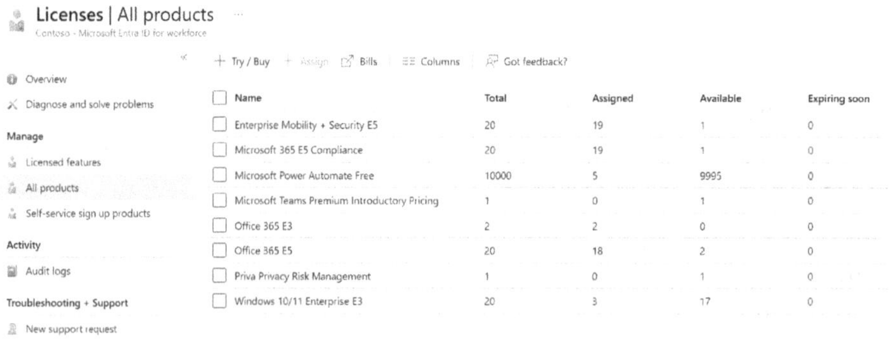

Figure 3.8: All products

4. Select the licenses you want to assign.

5. On the next page, click on **Assign**.

6. On the next page, click on **Add users or groups**.

7. In the search box, select the user account or group to which you want to assign the license and click **Select**, as shown in the following figure:

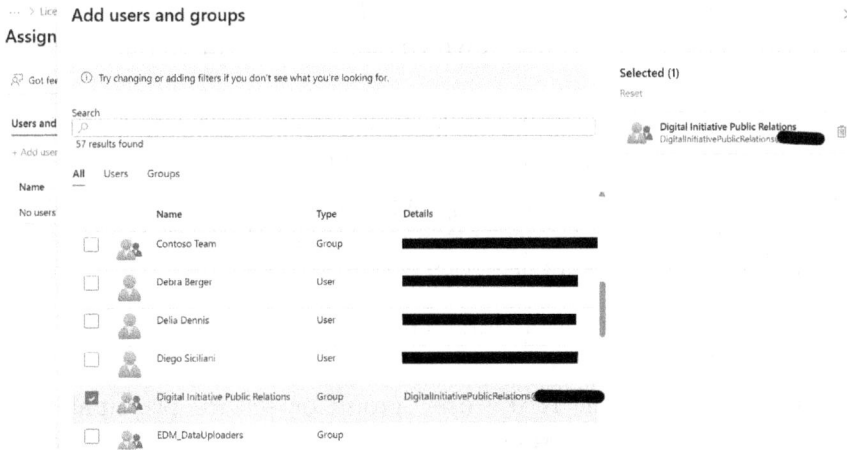

Figure 3.9: Assign licenses to users or groups

8. Click on **Next: Review + assign** and ensure that all required licenses are **On**. If you want to disable any service for a group switch the toggle next to that service to **Off**. Click on **Review + assign** to assign the licenses, as shown in *Figure 3.10*:

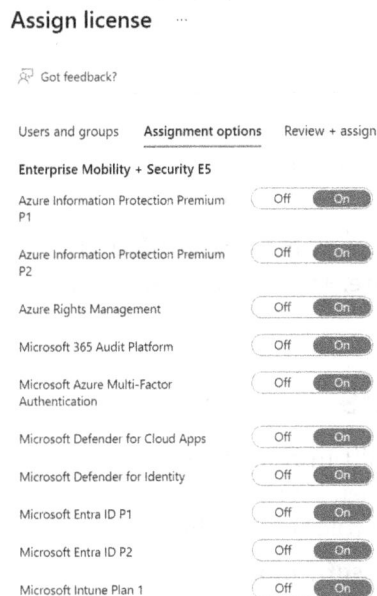

Figure 3.10: Assignment options

Microsoft Entra roles

A Microsoft Entra role is a set of rules that assigns specific permissions to administrators based on the principle of least privilege access. These roles allow fine-grained control over permissions assigned to administrators, ensuring that they have the appropriate permissions to do their job. Not more, not less. These roles assign permissions on resources such as users, devices, groups and applications. Microsoft Entra ID has several built-in roles and organizations can create their own custom roles based on their requirements, as follows:

- **Built-in roles** are available out of the box and have a defined set of permissions assigned. These cannot be changed or modified.

- **Custom roles** support specific organization needs to be more granular in the permissions they assign to their administrators. A Microsoft Entra ID P1 license is required for each user that has a custom role assigned.

A role can be assigned to a user by creating a role assignment. A role assignment consists of three elements, as follows:

- **Security principal**: This is the user, group or service principal that gets the permissions defined in the role.

- **Role definition**: A role is also called a role definition and is a collection of permissions. These define the actions such as create, edit, delete and update that can be performed on Microsoft Entra ID resources.

- **Scope**: These are the resources to which the role definitions assign the permissions. When a role is assigned, scope can be defined as the entire tenant, administrative unit or a particular resource.

A role can be assigned, as follows:

- To a **user**. This is the most common method of assigning roles.

- To a **group**. With Microsoft Entra ID P1, you can create role-assignable groups and assign roles to groups.

- Using **PIM**. Just-in-time access can be provided to these roles. Microsoft Entra ID P2 is required for this feature. This will be discussed in detail in *Chapter 5, Identity Governance*.

View role definitions

Microsoft Entra ID has over 60 built-in roles that can be assigned to administrators. In addition, organizations can create their own custom roles specific to their needs. Following are the steps to view all the built-in roles in the Microsoft Entra admin center:

1. Login to **https://entra.microsoft.com.**

2. In the left pane navigate to **Identity** I **Roles and administrators** I **Roles and administrators**.

3. *Figure 3.11* shows the built-in roles. If you create a custom role, it will also appear in the same screen, as follows:

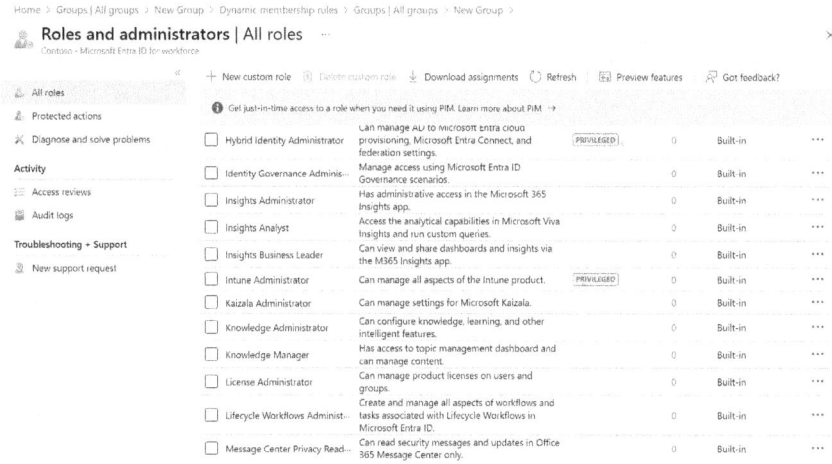

Figure 3.11: *Microsoft Entra built-in roles*

4. Click on any role to explore further and then click on **Description**. In the right pane you will be able to see the role description and the exact permissions that make up this role.

Figure 3.12 shows the description page of the **Compliance Administrator** role:

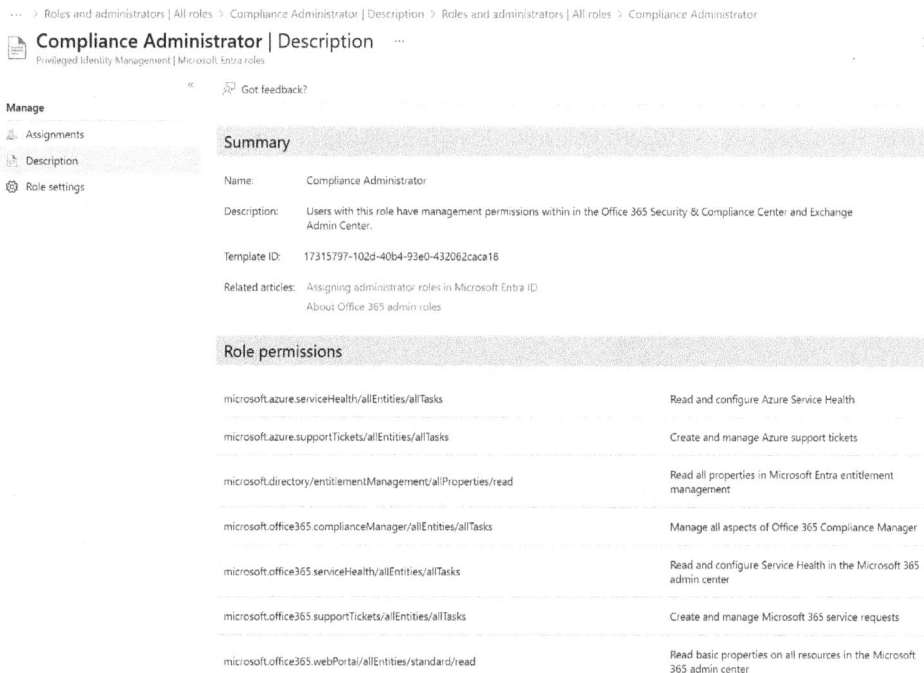

Figure 3.12: *Compliance Administrator role description*

You can also view role definitions programmatically by using PowerShell or the Microsoft Graph API. Refer to the Microsoft online documentation for the detailed steps.

View role assignments

In Microsoft Entra, roles can be assigned at an organizational level or at an application level. Roles assigned at the organization level are added to and can be seen in the list of application-level roles assignments, but roles assigned at application level are not added to and cannot be seen in the list of organization level role assignments.

To view the roles assigned to yourself, go to the **Roles and administrators** page. In the right pane, your roles appear at the top as shown in the following figure:

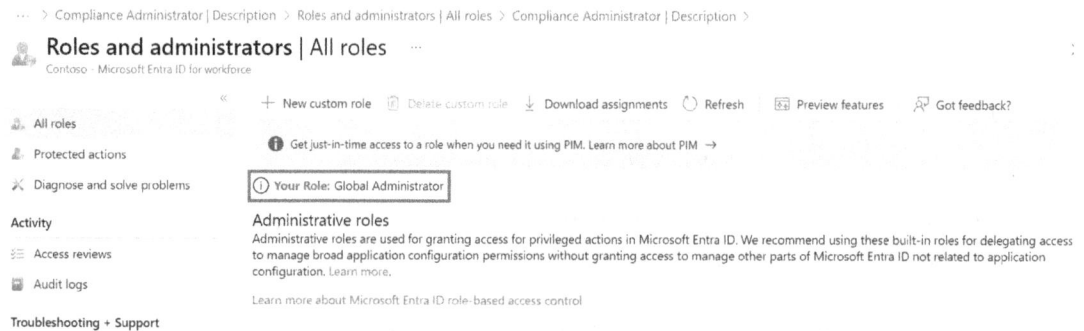

Figure 3.13: Viewing your own role

From this page you can also download the role assignments by clicking on **Download assignments**. This will download all role assignments in the form of a **.csv** file. An example of the **.csv** file is shown in the following figure:

A	B	C	D	E	F	G	H	I	J	K	L
roleAssignmentId	roleDefinitionId	roleDisplayName	isBuiltIn	principalId	userPrincipalName	displayName	objectType	userType	directoryScopeId	directoryScopeName	directoryScopeType
cqeYdnt4yEqQH2D	7698a772-787b-4	Cloud Device Administrator	TRUE	c2cb7576-2ff1-	NestorW@M365x1	Nestor Wilke	user	Member	/bea37a3e-228a-4	'-deleted-	'-
l1cxFy0QtECT4EM	17315797-102d-4	Compliance Administrator	TRUE	77f6dcfc-992a-	AllanD@M365x174	Allan Deyoung	user	Member	/	Contoso	Directory
4-PYiFWPHkqVOp	88d8e3e3-8f55-4	Directory Readers	TRUE	549d730b-0a57	00000014-0000-00	Microsoft.Azure.SyncFabric	servicePrincipal		/	Contoso	Directory
4-PYiFWPHkqVOp	88d8e3e3-8f55-4	Directory Readers	TRUE	9513749d-8d64	0000001a-0000-00	MicrosoftAzureActiveAuthn	servicePrincipal		/	Contoso	Directory
lAPpYvVpN0KRkAEl	62e90394-69f5-4	Global Administrator	TRUE	9bfe558a-9e69-	admin@M365x174	MOD Administrator	user	Member	/	Contoso	Directory
lAPpYvVpN0KRkAEl	62e90394-69f5-4	Global Administrator	TRUE	77f6dcfc-992a-	AllanD@M365x174	Allan Deyoung	user	Member	/	Contoso	Directory
5wuT_mJe20eRr5j	fe930be7-5e62-4	User Administrator	TRUE	77f6dcfc-992a-	AllanD@M365x174	Allan Deyoung	user	Member	/administrativeUn	Legal Users	administrativeUnit
5wuT_mJe20eRr5j	fe930be7-5e62-4	User Administrator	TRUE	425bf4bc-bf2f-4	RaulR@M365x1740	Raul Razo	user	Member	/administrativeUn	Marketing users	administrativeUnit

Figure 3.14: Role assignments downloaded as .csv file

Viewing assignments for a role

You can view role assignments in the Microsoft Entra admin center, using PowerShell and Graph API. This section describes using Microsoft Entra admin center. For using PowerShell and Graph API refer to Microsoft online documentation as shown in the following steps:

1. Login to **https://entra.microsoft.com**.
2. In the left pane navigate to **Identity | Roles and administrators | Roles and administrators**.

3. Click on a role to open its properties. The right pane lists all the users who have this role assigned. The below picture shows **Active assignments** for the **Compliance Administrator** role. The are also options for **Eligible assignments** and **Expired assignments**. This will be discussed in detail under PIM in *Chapter 5, Identity Governance*.

   Refer to the following figure:

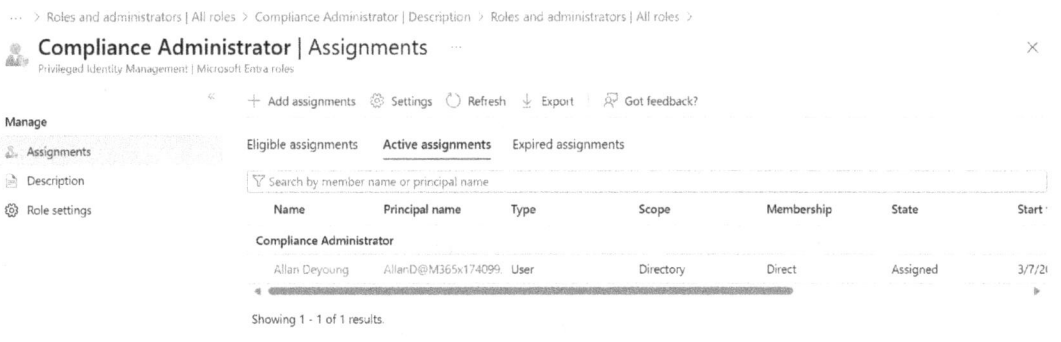

Figure 3.15: Active role assignments for Compliance Administrator role

You can also download the role assignments in the form on a .csv file by clicking on the **Export** button. A sample **.csv** file for the **Compliance Administrator** role is shown in the following figure:

	A	B	C	D	E	F	G	H
1	Assignment State	User Group Name	Role Name	Email	PrincipalName	Member Type	Assignment Start Time (UTC)	Assignment End Time (UTC)
2	Active	Allan Deyoung	Compliance Administrator	AllanD@M	AllanD@M365x	Direct	2024-03-07 03:09:22Z	Permanent
3								

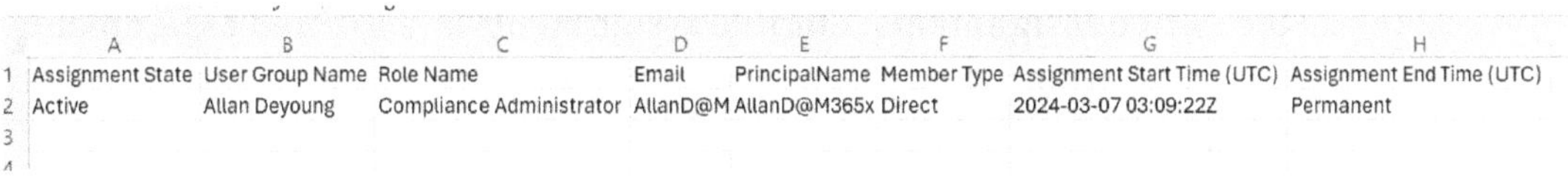

Figure 3.16: .csv file for Compliance Administrator role assignments

Viewing role assignments for an application

In Microsoft Entra applications can also have roles assigned. You can view the roles assigned to an application in the Microsoft Entra admin portal, as shown in the following steps:

1. Login to **https://entra.microsoft.com**.
2. In the left pane, navigate to **Identity | App registrations**.
3. In the right pane, select the app and on the next page click on **Roles and administrators**. The right pane shows the Microsoft Entra roles assigned to the selected application as shown in the following figure:

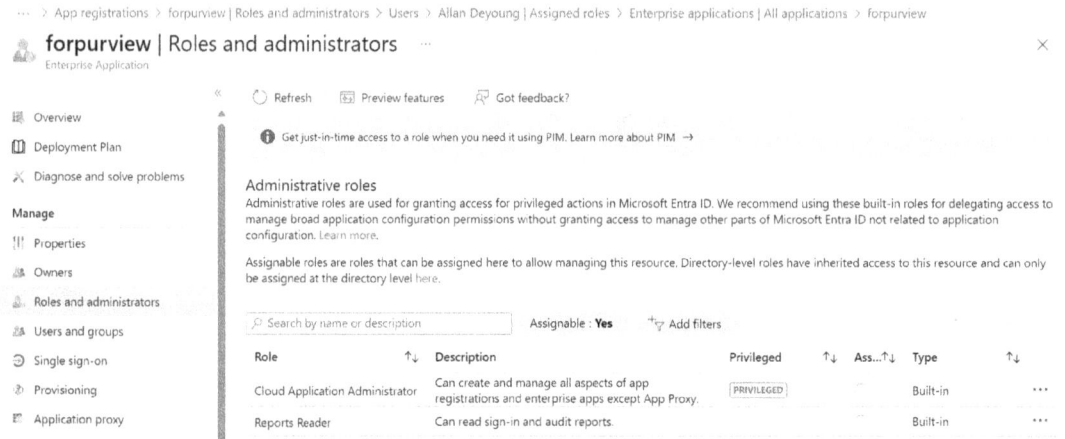

Figure 3.17: Viewing roles assigned to an application

Viewing role assignments for a user

Following are the steps to view the Microsoft Entra roles assigned to a user:

1. Login to **https://entra.microsoft.com.**
2. In the left pane, navigate to **Identity** | **Users** | **All users**.
3. Select the user and in the next screen, click on **Assigned roles**. The right pane will show all the **Active assignments**, **Eligible assignments** and **Expired assignments**. The below picture shows the **Active assignments** for a user called *Allan Deyoung* as shown in the following figure:

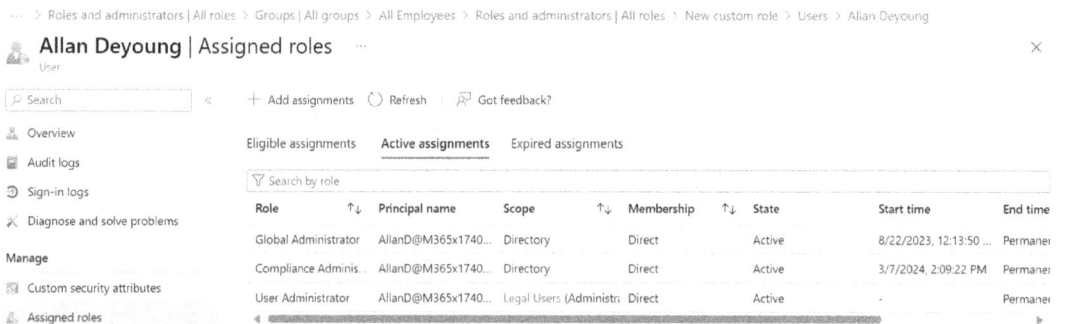

Figure 3.18: Active assignments for Allan Deyoung

Viewing role assignments for a group

Following are the steps to view the Microsoft Entra roles assigned to a group:

1. Login to **https://entra.microsoft.com.**
2. In the left pane navigate to **Identity** | **Groups** | **All groups**.

3. Select the group and in the next screen click on **Roles and administrators**. The pane will show all the roles assigned to the group.

Creating custom roles

As already mentioned, Microsoft Entra has more than 60 built-in roles already available for use. However, sometimes these do not suffice, and organizations want to create further granular roles to suit their administrative needs. Microsoft Entra provides organizations the option to create custom roles to meet their specific needs.

To create a custom role the following pre-requisites must be met:

- Microsoft Entra ID P1 or P2 license

- An account with **Privileged Role Administrator** or **Global Administrator** role assigned.

Following are the steps to create a role in the Microsoft Entra admin center.

1. Login to **https://entra.microsoft.com.**

2. In the left pane, navigate to **Identity** | **Roles and administrators** | **Roles and administrators.**

3. In the right pane, click on **New custom role**.

4. On the **Basics** page enter a name and description for the new role and select if you want start from scratch or clone from another custom role. Click on **Next**, as shown in the following figure:

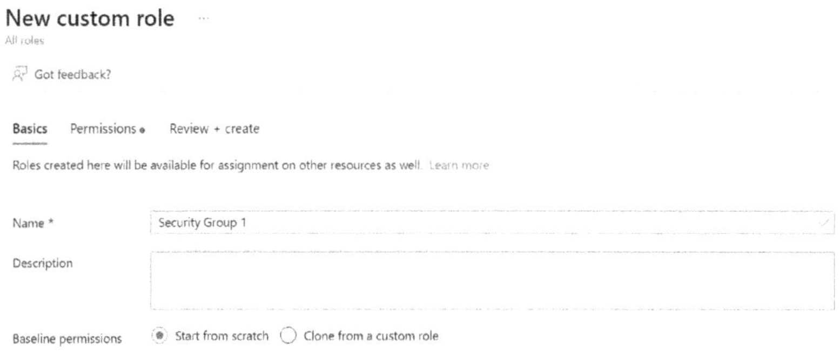

Figure 3.19: Create a custom role

5. The **Permissions** page lists all available permissions in Microsoft Entra. Choose the permissions you want to assign to this custom role and click **Next**, as shown in the following figure:

New custom role ...
All roles

⟩

🔊 Got feedback?

Basics   **Permissions**   Review + create

Add permissions for this custom role. Currently, permissions for Application registrations and Enterprise applications are supported in custom roles. Learn more

🔍 Search by permission name or description

	Permission	↑↓	Description	↑↓	Privileged	↑↓
☐	microsoft.directory/applicationPolicies/allProperties/read		Read all properties (including privileged properties) on application policies			
☐	microsoft.directory/applicationPolicies/allProperties/update		Update all properties (including privileged properties) on application policies			
☐	microsoft.directory/applicationPolicies/basic/update		Update standard properties of application policies			
☑	microsoft.directory/applicationPolicies/create		Create application policies			
☑	microsoft.directory/applicationPolicies/createAsOwner		Create application policies, and creator is added as the first owner			
☑	microsoft.directory/applicationPolicies/delete		Delete application policies			

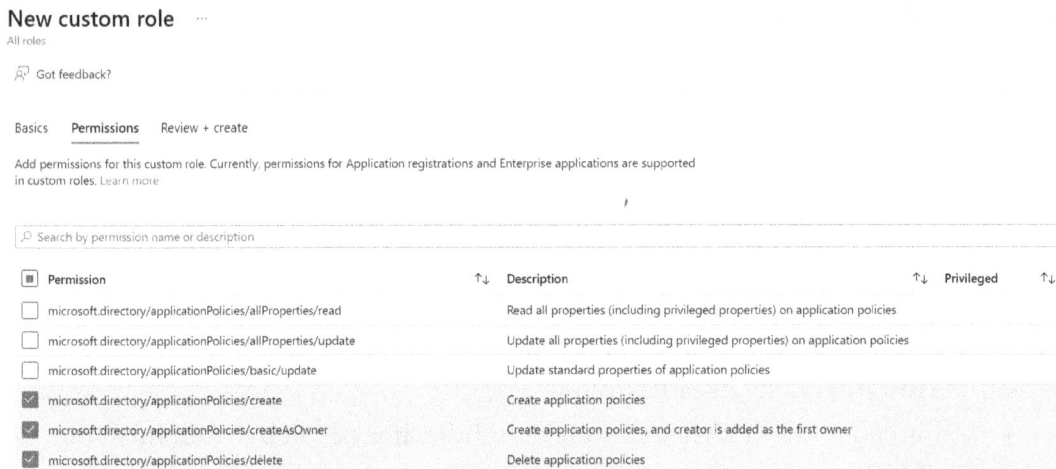

Figure 3.20: Choose permissions for the custom role

6. In the last screen, review your information and click on **Create**.

Assigning roles to users and groups

Now that you have learnt about built-in roles and how to create custom roles, let us see how these roles can be assigned to users and groups to grant them permissions on Microsoft Entra resources.

Assigning roles to users

You must assign roles to users to enable them to perform tasks in Microsoft Entra. To be able to assign roles you should have the **Privileged Role Administrator** or **Global Administrator** role assigned.

Following are the steps to assign roles in the Microsoft Entra admin center:

1. Login to **https://entra.microsoft.com**.
2. In the left pane, navigate to **Identity | Roles and administrators | Roles and administrators**.
3. From the right pane, select the role to which you want to assign users. Click on **Add assignments**.
4. Click on **No member selected** and, in the fly, out pane pick one or more users to whom you want to assign this role and click on **Select** as shown in the following figure:

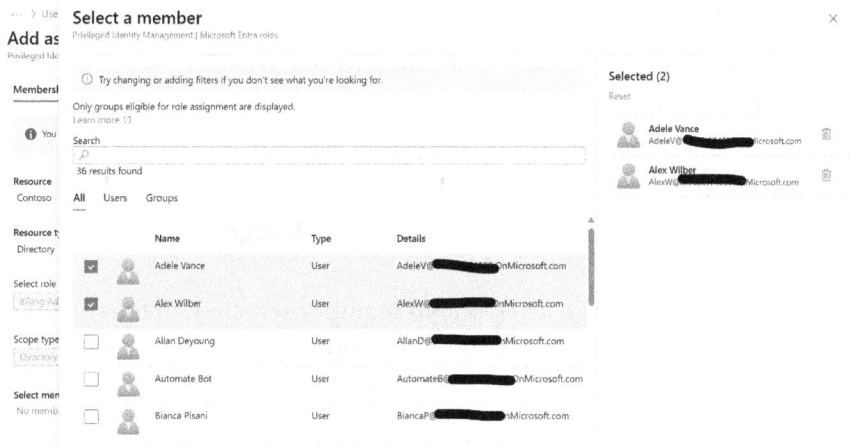

Figure 3.21: Select users to add to role

5. In the **Add assignments** page, click on **Next**.

6. In the **Settings** page select the **Assignment type** as **Active**. Enter a justification and ensure that the **Permanently eligible** box is checked and click on **Assign**. Refer to *Figure 3.22*. The other options will be discussed when PIM will be discussed in *Chapter 5, Identity Governance*.

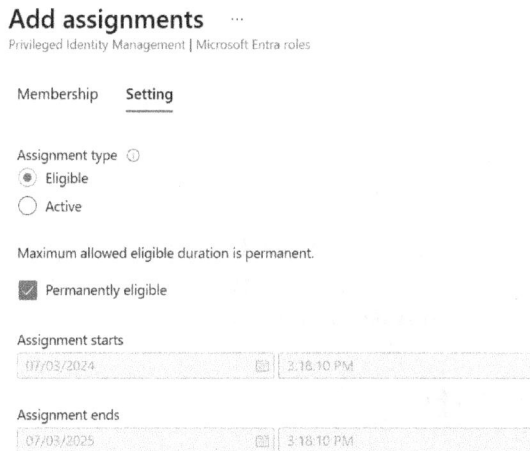

Figure 3.22: Permanently assign a user to a role

Assigning roles to groups

To make role management easier, Microsoft Entra offers the option to assign roles to groups instead of individual users. To assign roles to groups you should have the following:

- Microsoft Entra ID P1 license.

- An account with the **Privileged Role Administrator** role assigned.

- A role-assignable group created. This is explained earlier in this chapter.

Following are the steps to assign a role to a group in Microsoft Entra admin portal:

1. Login to **https://entra.microsoft.com.**

2. In the left pane, navigate to **Identity | Roles and administrators | Roles and administrators**.

3. From the list of roles select the role. In the **Assignments** page, click on **Add assignments**.

4. On the **Membership** page, click on **No member selected**. In the fly out pane. click on **Groups** and select the role assignable group that you want to assign the role to. Click **Select** as shown in the following figure:

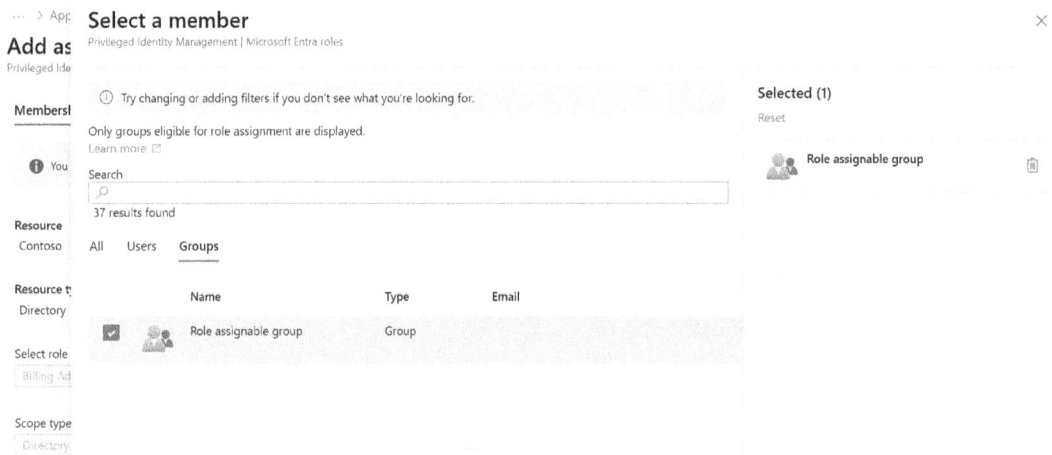

Figure 3.23: Select a group to add to a role

5. Back on the **Membership** page, click on **Next**. On the settings page, select the **Assignment type** as **Active**. Ensure that the **Permanently assigned** box is checked, enter a justification, and click on **Assign**. Refer to *Figure 3.22*.

Administrative units

Administrative units allow you to segment your organization into smaller blocks based on location, department, business unit etc. That can allow specific administrators to manage only members of that unit. For example, you could have separate admin units for Americas, EMEA and Asia. You can then assign separate admins to control access, manage users and set policies for those specific geographies.

It is important to note that a single object can be included in multiple administrative units depending on its scope. In the above example, if the organization has further administrative units for departments like Marketing, Finance, HR, a marketing user in EMEA could be member of two administrative units, that is, EMEA and Marketing.

To create admin units, you need the following:

- Microsoft Entra P1 license for each administrative unit administrator.
- An account that has the Privileged Role Administrator role assigned.

Restricted management administrative units

In some scenarios, organizations might want to protect specific objects from modification by anyone other than a specific set of administrators. For example, you might want to protect the C-level executives and their devices from modification by the first level helpdesk. You could assign them to a restricted management administrative unit and assign a separate administrator to that admin unit.

Users, devices and security groups can be added to a restricted management administrative unit. Only administrators that are assigned as administrators at the restricted management administrative unit scope level can perform all action related to users, devices and security groups in that admin unit. Other administrators, including Global Administrator cannot perform all actions.

Table 3.1 summarizes the allowed and unallowed actions:

Action	Blocked	Allowed
Read standard user properties like name, photo		Y
Modify properties of the user, device or group	Y	
Delete the user, device or group	Y	
Reset the password for a user	Y	
Modify group members or owners	Y	
Add users, groups or devices in other groups		Y
Modify email and mailbox settings for users in Exchange		Y
Apply Intune policies to a device		Y
Add or remove a group as a site owner in SharePoint		Y

Table 3.1: Actions for the restricted management admin unit scope

Table 3.2 summarizes which administrators can modify the Microsoft Entra properties of objects (users, devices and security groups) in a restricted management admin unit:

User role	Blocked	Allowed
Global administrator	Y	
Tenant-scoped administrator	Y	
Administrators assigned to the restricted management admin unit		Y

User role	Blocked	Allowed
Administrators assigned to another restricted management admin unit of which the object is a member		Y
Administrators assigned to another regular admin unit of which the object is a member	Y	
Administrators assigned at the scope of a resource	Y	
Owners of groups and devices added to restricted management admin units	Y	

Table 3.2: Blocked and allowed actions by administrative scope

At the time of this writing, restrictive management administrative units were in Public Preview and had the following limitations:

- Restricted management administrative units can be configured only at the time of creation. This setting cannot be changed later.
- Groups in restricted management administrative units cannot be managed using Microsoft Entra ID Governance capabilities.
- Membership of a role-assignable group cannot be modified once it is added to a restricted management administrative unit.
- Group owners cannot modify the membership of a group that is included in a restricted management administrative unit. Only Global Administrator and Privileged Role Administrator can modify membership.
- Some actions cannot be performed on objects that are in a restricted management administrative group. For example, if a Global Administrator account is in a restricted management administrative unit, another administrator cannot reset their password. They will have to be removed from the admin unit to do this.
- Distribution groups, mail-enabled groups and Microsoft 365 groups cannot be members of the restricted management administrative units.

Creating administrative unit

Following are the steps for creating an administrative unit:

1. Login to **https://entra.microsoft.com**.
2. Navigate to **Identity | Roles and administrators | Admin Units**.
3. In the right pane, click on **Add**.
4. Enter a name for the admin unit and optionally enter a description.
5. If you do not want the tenant-level admins to be able to modify the members switch the **Restricted management administrative unit** toggle to **Yes**. Click on **Next: Assign roles** as shown in the following figure:

Figure 3.24: *Creating an administrative unit*

6. On the **Assign roles** page, select a role to assign to this administrative unit. This is optional. Click on **Next: Review + create**.

Adding members to administrative unit

Following are the steps to add members in an administrative unit:

1. Login to **https://microsoft.entra.com** with an account that has at least the **Privileged Role Administrator** or the **Global Administrator** role assigned.

2. Navigate to **Identity** | **Roles and administrators** | **Admin units**. In the right pane, select the newly created admin unit.

3. Click on **Users** and in the right pane, click on **Add member** to pick the members from the list. You can also add users in bulk by clicking on **Bulk operations** | **Bulk add members**. You will be prompted to upload a `.csv` file as shown in the following figure:

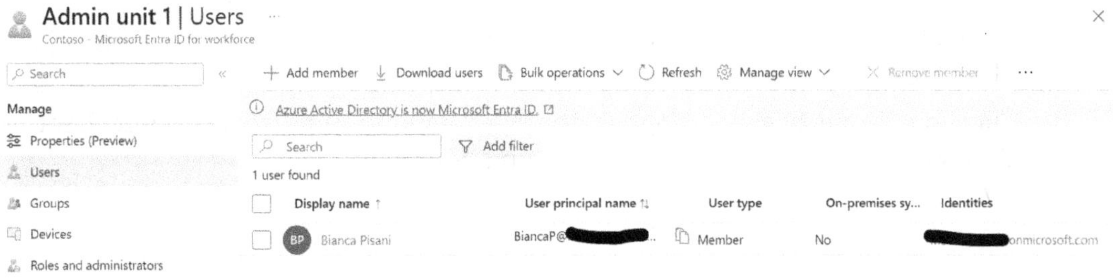

Figure 3.25: *Adding users to an administrative group*

4. To add groups, click on **Groups** and in the right pane, click on **Add** and pick the group from the list. You can also create a new group from within the admin unit by clicking on **New group**. This will take you to the page to create a new group as shown in the following figure:

Admin unit 1 | Groups ⋯
Contoso - Microsoft Entra ID for workforce

	Name	Object Id	Group Type	Membership Type	Email	Source
	Ask HR	00d43026-5e61-449d...	Microsoft 365	Assigned	askhr@▮▮▮	Cloud

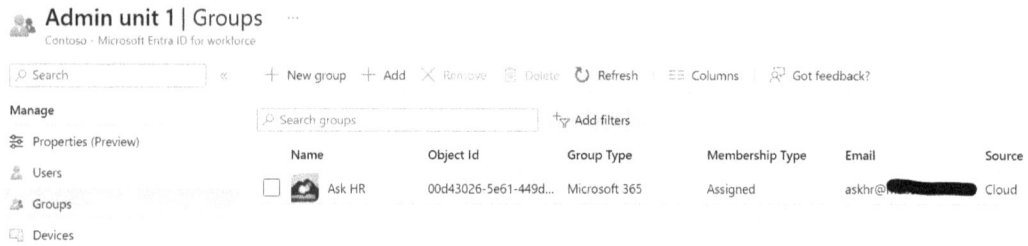

Figure 3.26: Adding groups to administrative units

> **Note: To create a new group from within the administrative unit you should have the Global Administrator role assigned.**

5. To add devices, click on **Devices** and in the right pane, click on **Add device**. Pick the devices from the list.

Dynamically add members to administrative unit

Adding individual members to administrative units can be quite cumbersome. When users move between departments or locations the administrative unit membership will have to be manually updated. This can be quite a big administrative overhead. To make this simpler and automated you can dynamically add members to an administrative unit using object attributes. At the time of this writing, this feature was in Public Preview.

> **Note: To dynamically assign members to an administrative unit Microsoft Entra ID P1 license is required for each admin unit administrator and member.**

Following are the steps to dynamically add members to an admin unit:

1. Login to **https://entra.microsoft.com** with an account that has at least the **Privileged Role Administrator** or the **Global Administrator** role assigned.

2. Navigate to **Identity** | **Roles and administrators** | **Admin units**. In the right pane select the newly created admin unit.

3. Click on **Properties** and change the **Membership type** to **Dynamic User** or **Dynamic Device** a shown in the following figure:

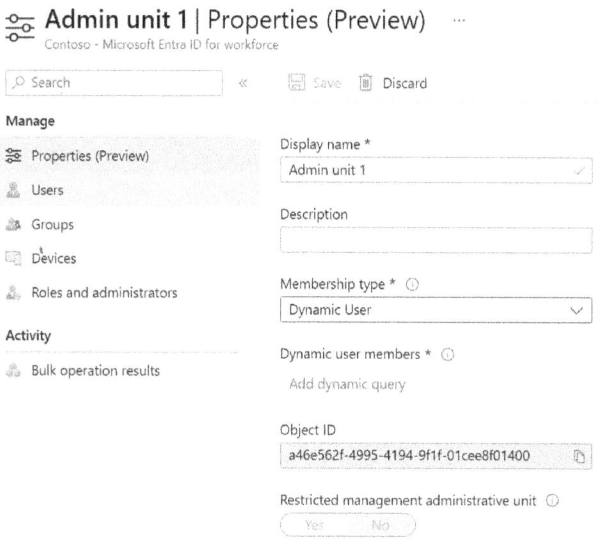

Figure 3.27: *Change admin unit membership to Dynamic User*

4. Click on **Add dynamic query**. In the next screen, select the **Property**, **Operator** and type in the **Value**. You can build complex queries to meet your requirements. Once done, click on **Save**, as shown in the following figure:

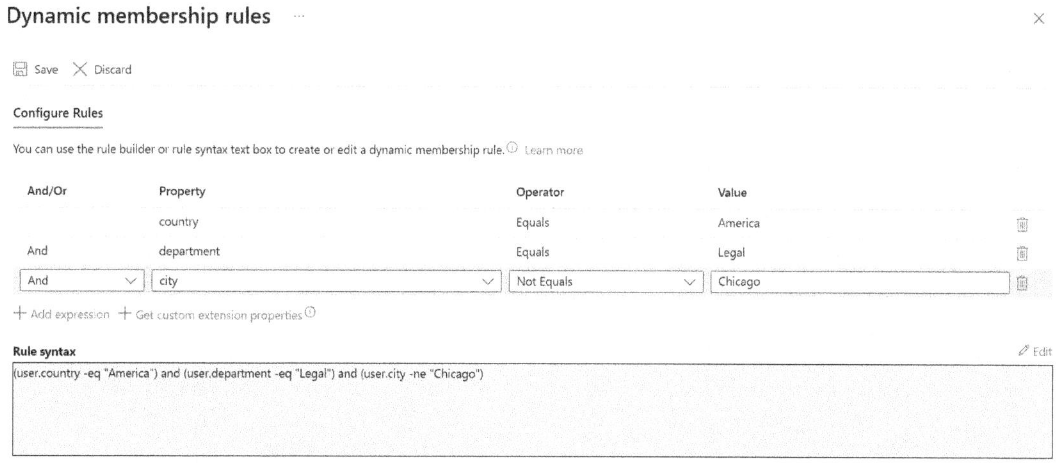

Figure 3.28: *Dynamic membership rules in admin units*

Assigning administrative roles to administrative unit

Once you have created an administrative unit and added members to it, either manually or dynamically, the next step would be to determine which users, groups or service principals can perform administrative actions on members of that administrative unit. This is done by assigning roles to that administrative unit scope. Members of that role will then have permissions only on the object within the administrative unit scope and not on other objects in the tenant. For example, if the Helpdesk Administrator role is assigned to admin unit 1, members of the Helpdesk Administrator role group will be able to reset passwords for only users in admin unit 1 and not for other users in the tenant.

Following are the only Microsoft Entra roles can be assigned to an administrative unit scope:

- Authentication Administrator
- Cloud Device Administrator
- Groups Administrator
- Helpdesk Administrator
- License Administrator
- Password Administrator
- Printer Administrator
- SharePoint Administrator
- Teams Administrator
- Teams Devices Administrator
- User Administrator

In addition, custom roles can also be assigned to an administrative scope if the custom role has permissions relevant to users, groups or devices.

Following permissions are restricted if the target of the operation is another administrator:

- Read or modify user authentication methods or reset passwords.
- Modify user properties like phone numbers, alternate email addresses or OAuth secret keys.
- Delete or restore user accounts.

Following security principals can be assigned a role at the administrative unit scope:

- Users
- Role-assignable groups
- Service principals

Service principals and guest user accounts do not receive the directory read permissions by default so they cannot be assigned to an administrative unit scope unless they are also assigned permissions to read the objects that are members of the administrative unit.

Following are the steps to assign a role to an administrative unit:

1. Login to **https://entra.microsoft.com** with an account that has at the Privileged Role Administrator role assigned.

2. Navigate to **Identity | Roles and administrators | Admin units**.

3. In the right pane, click the admin unit that was just created, and click on **Roles and administrators**.

4. In the right pane, select the role that you would like to assign to this administrative unit as shown in the following figure:

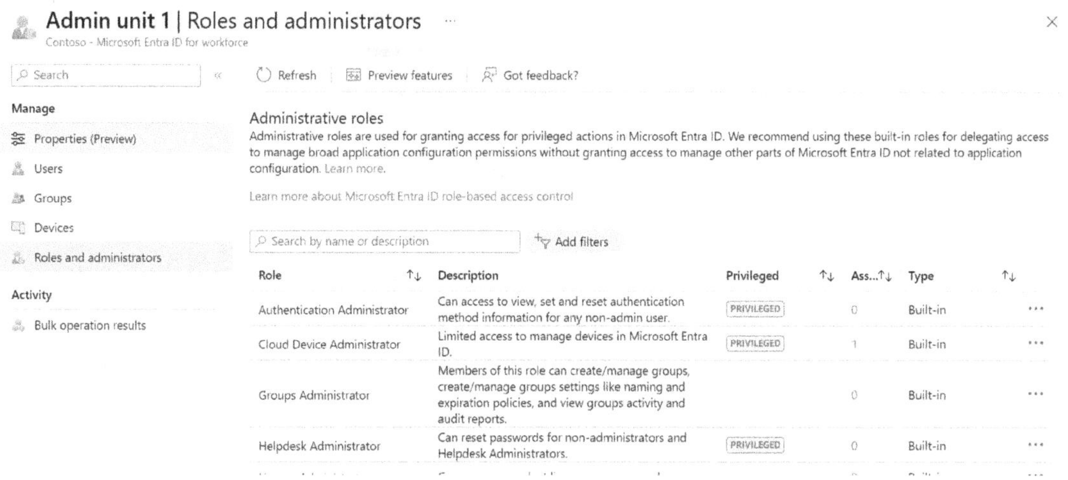

Figure 3.29: *Adding roles to an administrative unit*

5. Click on **Add assignments**, as shown in the following figure:

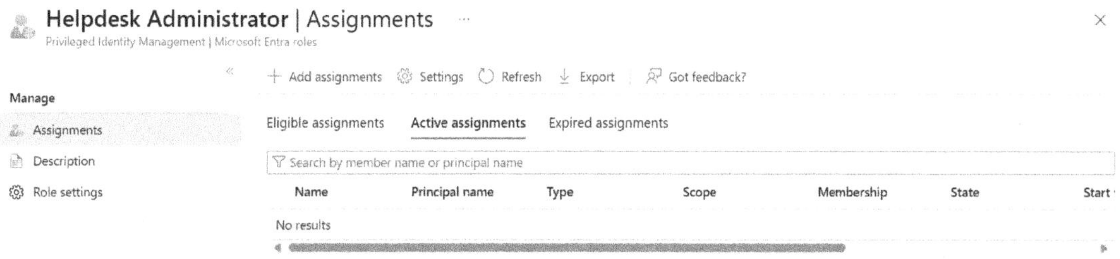

Figure 3.30: *Adding role assignment*

6. Under membership, click on **No member selected** and from the list pick the user, group or service principal and click on **Select**, as shown in the following figure:

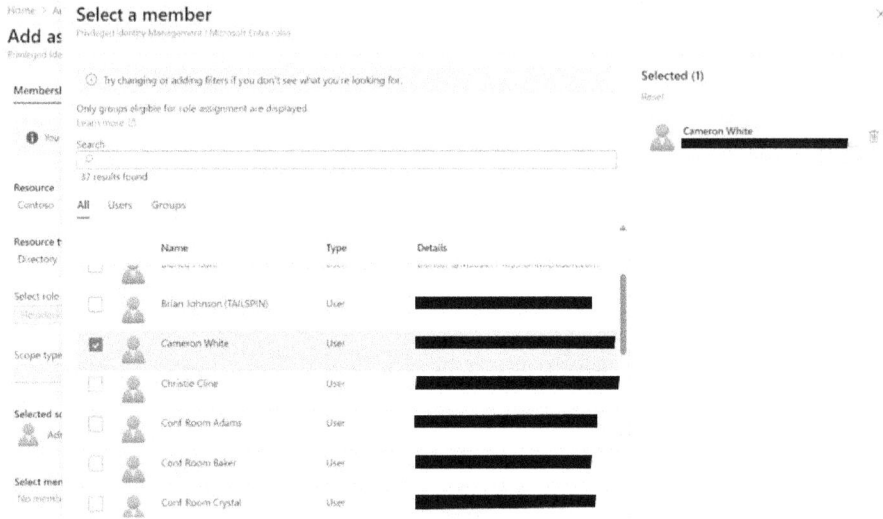

Figure 3.31: Select the security principal

7. Click **Next**. On the **Settings** page, make the appropriate selections and click on **Assign**, as shown in the following figure:

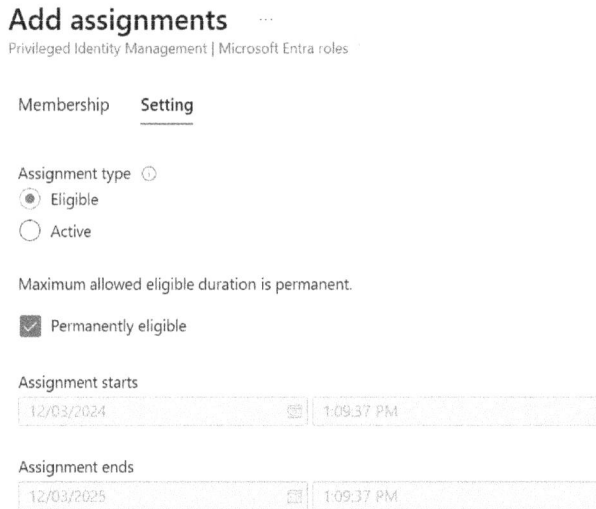

Figure 3.32: Select assignment type

Protected actions

Protected actions are Microsoft Entra ID permissions that are protected by Conditional Access policies. They are used when organizations want to add an additional layer of security. They can be applied to actions that require strong protection regardless of the role carrying out that action.

Conditional Access policies can be applied to a small subset of permissions in Microsoft Entra ID.

Following are the areas where protected actions can be applied:

- Conditional Access policy management
- Cross-tenant access settings management
- Custom rules that define network locations
- Protected action management

The Conditional Access policy applied to the permission triggers when the user attempts to carry out the action and not during the user sign-in.

Protected actions can be used along with PIM role activation to further strengthen security. PIM role activation can also be protected using Conditional Access policies. In this case, Conditional Access policy is applied when the user attempts to activate the privileged role while protected actions protect the high-impact permissions regardless of the user role.

Note: Conditional Access policies and PIM will be discussed in the subsequent chapters.

Prerequisites

Before configuring protected actions, ensure that your Microsoft Entra tenant meets the following requirements:

- Microsoft Entra P1 license
- Conditional Access Administrator or Security Administrator role.

Configuring protected actions

Following are the steps to use protected actions. These steps should be followed in sequence for proper configuration:

1. Login to **https://entra.microsoft.com**.
2. Navigate to **Identity** | **Protection** | **Conditional Access**.
3. Click on **Authentication contexts,** and in the right pane click on **New authentication context**. In the fly out pane, give the authentication context a name and click **Save** as shown in the following figure:

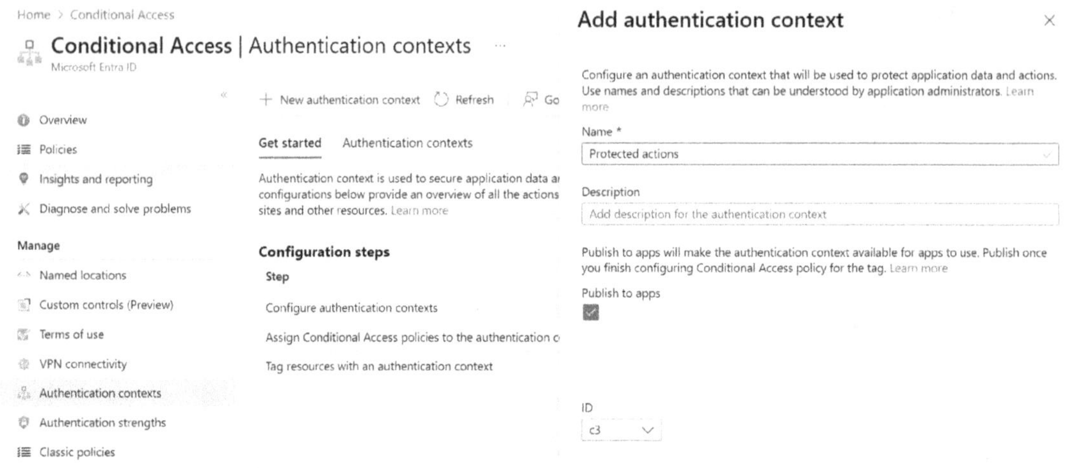

Figure 3.33: New authentication context

4. Navigate to **Identity** | **Roles and administrators** | **Roles and administrators**.

5. Click on **Protected actions** and in the right pane click on **Add protected actions**.

6. In the Conditional Access authentication context, select the authentication context created in *Step 3*. Click on **Select permissions,** and from the fly out pane select the permissions that you want to protect, and click on **Add** and then, click on **Save** as shown in the following figure:

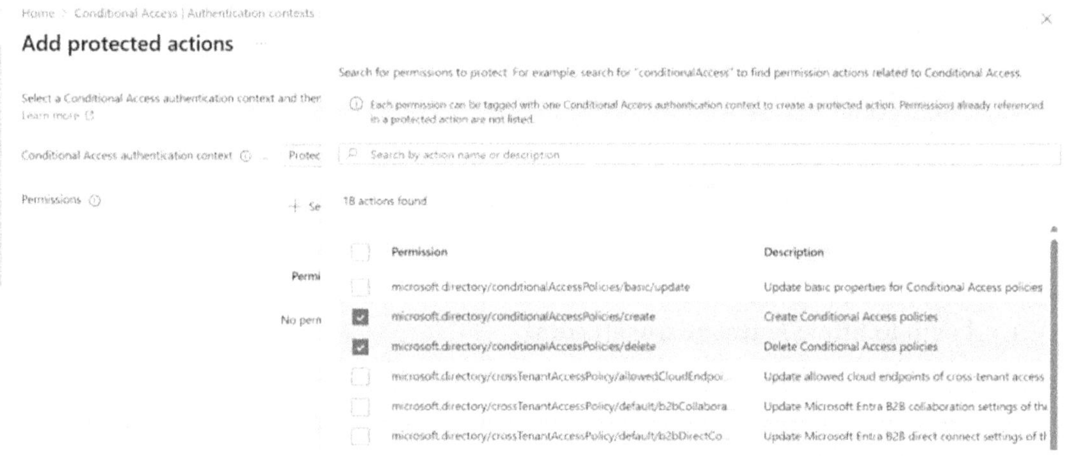

Figure 3.34: Add protected actions to authentication context

7. Once this is done, you can create a Conditional Access policy using this authentication context. Steps to create a Conditional Access policy will be discussed in detail in the next chapter.

Conclusion

In this chapter, you learned user and group management capabilities in Microsoft Entra ID. You learned how to invite guest users to your tenant and how to create different types of groups. You also learned several features like assigning roles and licensing to groups that make user management simpler. The chapter explained RBAC in Microsoft Entra ID. You learned about the different role groups available in Microsoft Entra ID and how they grant permissions to users over Microsoft Entra resources. There are several out of the box roles available and custom roles can be created to serve the organization specific needs.

Some organizations also need to decentralize management of user accounts and groups based on region, department or other attributes. Microsoft Entra administrative units are a way of creating logical boundaries within your tenant and then assigning administrative permissions to users to be manage these administrative units. You learnt how to create administrative units and add members to them dynamically as well as manually.

At the end, the chapter explained the concept of protected actions. Protected actions are permissions that can be subject to conditional access policies so that users will have to satisfy certain conditions before they can execute the action. Protected actions can be used along with PIM to further strengthen security.

In the next chapter, you will learn how you can manage and govern identities using the features of Microsoft Entra Identity Governance.

Multiple choice questions

1. **What are the different types of groups available in Microsoft Entra ID? Select all that apply.**
   a. Security groups
   b. Mail-enabled security groups
   c. Microsoft 365 groups
   d. Distribution groups

2. **How can a user be assigned licenses in Microsoft Entra ID? Select all that apply.**
   a. At the user level
   b. At the organization level
   c. At the administrative unit level
   d. At group level

3. **Can a Microsoft Entra role be assigned to a group?**

   a. Yes

   b. No

4. **You are the IT administrator in a large multinational corporation. You want to decentralize the management of users and groups by geography. Which Microsoft Entra feature can you use?**

   a. Dynamic security groups

   b. Administrative units

   c. Role-based access control

   d. Custom roles

Answer key

1. a, c
2. a, d
3. a
4. b

Join our book's Discord space

Join the book's Discord Workspace for Latest updates, Offers, Tech happenings around the world, New Release and Sessions with the Authors:

https://discord.bpbonline.com

CHAPTER 4
Identity Protection

Introduction

It is now recognized that identity is the new front door. Identity is the key to access. Users use their identities to access all applications, services and data to perform their job responsibilities. It is, therefore, evident that protecting identities is key to protecting the organization's crown jewels. Identity attacks have increased dramatically in recent years. Organizations need to enforce rigorous identity protection policies while also offering a smooth work experience to their end users. This chapter will explore the different identity protection capabilities in Microsoft Entra ID.

Structure

The chapter covers the following topics:

- Understanding authentication methods
- Understanding Conditional Access
- Configuring combined registration
- Multi-factor authentication
- Passwordless sign-in
- Microsoft Entra ID Protection

Objectives

By the end of this chapter, you will be able to understand the identity protection capabilities in Microsoft Entra ID. These include enabling multi-factor authentication, designing and implementing Conditional Access policies including risk-based policies. You will also learn how to identify risky users and risky sign-ins and how to implement controls to protect your organization against them. This chapter will also cover the various authentication methods like multi-factor authentication and passwordless authentication. This chapter will prepare you to design and implement an identity protection strategy for your organization.

Understanding authentication methods

Username and password are the typical way of logging into any app or service. Users have been using this method for years and are very familiar with it. However, as more and more services go online, users now must create and remember multiple usernames and passwords. This results in poor password habits like using the same password for many systems or using passwords that are not secure or predictable. Users also give their passwords to their friends and co-workers.

Meanwhile, attackers are becoming more advanced and are finding new ways to hack user passwords. There is a huge rise in password spray and brute force attacks. Besides teaching users how to create strong passwords, organizations need to enforce stricter measures to secure their user identities. Passwords are not enough to safeguard user identities. They need to be supported with extra authentication methods or, even better, be replaced. This section will cover the different authentication methods that Microsoft Entra ID offers to help defend user accounts from identity-based attacks.

Figure 4.1 summarizes the authentication methods available with Microsoft Entra ID. They broadly fall under two categories, that is, multi-factor authentication and passwordless:

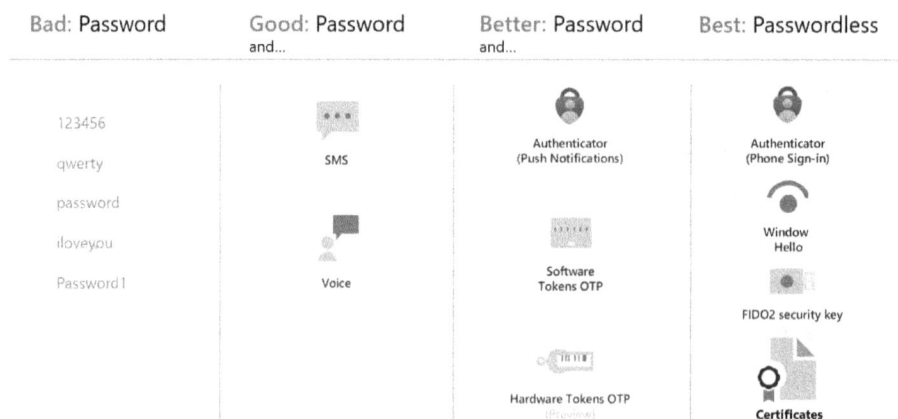

Figure 4.1: Authentication methods

Some of these authentication methods are used as a primary factor when a user signs in while others can only be used as a secondary factor with MFA and **self-service password reset (SSPR)**. It is now possible for end users to register their security information for both MFA and SSPR in a single step. This is called **combined registration** and is explained in the next section.

Table 4.1 summarizes how each authentication method works:

Authentication method	Primary	Secondary
Windows Hello for Business	Yes	MFA
Microsoft Authenticator (Push)	No	MFA and SSPR
Microsoft Authenticator (Passwordless)	Yes	No
FIDO2 security key	Yes	MFA
Certificate-based authentication	Yes	MFA
OATH hardware tokens	No	MFA and SSPR
OATH software tokens	No	MFA and SSPR
Temporary Access Pass (TAP)	Yes	MFA
SMS	Yes	MFA and SSPR
Voice call	No	MFA and SSPR
Password	Yes	No

Table 4.1: Authentication methods usability

While configuring the authentication methods, Windows Hello for Business does not serve as a step-up MFA credential on its own but can provide MFA for credentials being used in FIDO2 keys. Passwordless sign-in can only be used for secondary authentication if certificate-based authentication is enabled.

Enabling authentication methods

Before users can start using these authentication methods, administrator have to enable them in Microsoft Entra ID portal. The following are the steps:

1. Login to **https://entra.microsoft.com** with an account that has the Authentication Policy Administrator role assigned.

2. Navigate to **Protection | Authentication methods | Policies**.

3. In the right pane, you will see a list of all authentication methods available. Click on each to explore the options and to turn them on or off as follows:

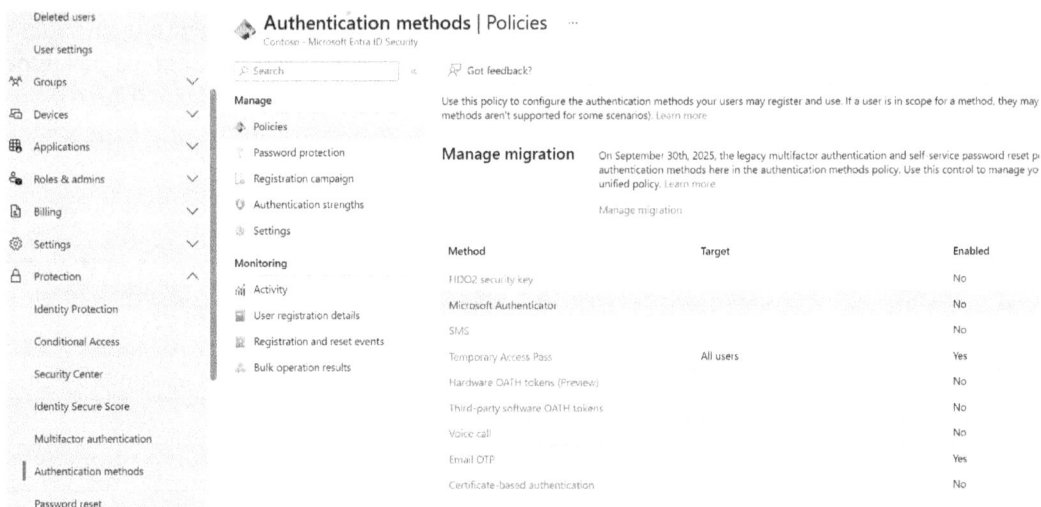

Figure 4.2: *Available authentication methods*

Understanding Conditional Access

At the core of Entra ID protection is Conditional Access. As the security perimeter now extends beyond the traditional boundaries, organizations need to use new identity-driven measures to secure corporate resources. Conditional Access is Microsoft's Zero Trust policy engine. It takes signals from various sources and then enforces policy decisions. In simplest terms, Conditional Access policies can be defined as if-then statements. For example, if a user wants to access their email, they must complete an MFA challenge. Using Conditional Access administrators can help users be productive anywhere and anytime, while protecting the organization's resources. Conditional Access policies are enforced after the user has been authenticated.

The minimum license required to use Conditional Access is **Microsoft Entra ID P1**.

Figure 4.3 is a graphical representation of how Conditional Access works:

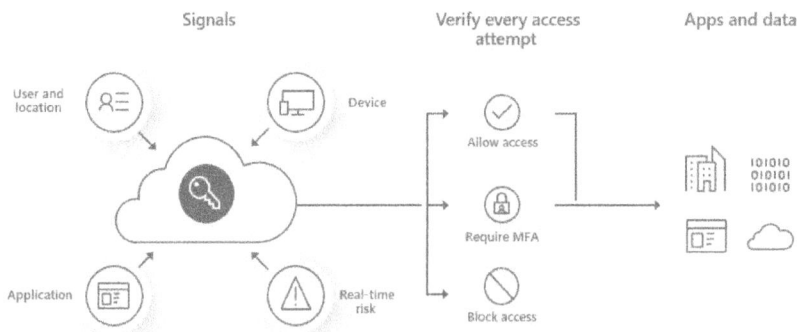

Figure 4.3: *Conditional Access overview*

Using Conditional Access policies an administrator can define conditions under which a user is granted or denied access to corporate resources based on their sign-in conditions. For example, if a user is accessing a corporate resource from a company managed laptop from a trusted network location, they can be allowed access to the corporate resource. If they are accessing a corporate resource from a company managed laptop but from an untrusted network location, they may be prompted for MFA before access is granted. However, if they are accessing corporate resources from an airport kiosk, they can be completely denied access to the corporate resources.

Using Conditional Access policies, you can define granular control over access of corporate resources based on user risk.

Following are the common signals that Conditional Access policy decisions are based on:

- **User or group**: Policies can be applied to individual users or based on group membership.
- **User location**: Policies can be applied based on the user's network location. Organizations can define a list of trusted locations like their corporate or VPN IP address ranges to be excluded from policy.
- **Device**: Various device states like operating system version, patch level, compliance level can be taken into consideration while applying a policy.
- **Application**: Conditional Access policies can be triggered depending on the application or the corporate resource the user is attempting to access.

Based on the above signals, one of the following decisions can be taken:

- Block access
- Grant access
- Grant access subject to user satisfying conditions like MFA, ensuring device compliance, forcing password change and so on.

An administrator can create Conditional Access policies from the Microsoft Entra administrator portal.

Following are the steps:

1. Login to **https://entra.microsoft.com** with an account that has the Conditional Access Administrator role assigned.
2. Navigate to **Protection | Conditional Access**.
3. In the right-pane, click on **Create new policy** to configure your policy.

There are several controls available in Conditional Access. Discussing each control is beyond the scope of this book. It is recommended reading Microsoft's online documentation.

Figure 4.4 shows the Conditional Access policy configuration page:

New ...
Conditional Access policy

Control access based on Conditional Access
policy to bring signals together, to make
decisions, and enforce organizational policies.
Learn more ☐

Name *

Example: 'Device compliance app policy'

Assignments

Users ⓘ

0 users and groups selected

Target resources ⓘ

No target resources selected

Conditions ⓘ

0 conditions selected

Access controls

Grant ⓘ

0 controls selected

Session ⓘ

0 controls selected

Enable policy

(Report-only) On   Off

Create

Figure 4.4: *Configure Conditional Access policy*

Configuring combined registration

If both MFA and SSPR are enabled in your tenant, users can now register their security information for both in a single step. This is called **combined registration.** Before combined registration was available, users had to register their security information twice, once for MFA and once for SSPR. This was confusing as they were completing similar steps. Combined registration now makes it easy for users by eliminating the need to register twice.

Combined registration can be configured in two modes, as follows:

- **Interrupt mode**: In this mode, the user is interrupted during sign-in, and a wizard is presented where they must refresh or register their security information for MFA and SSPR.
- **Managed mode**: In this mode, the user can go to **https://aka.ms/mysecurityinfo** and register for SSPR and MFA.

Note: If users had registered for MFA before combined registration was enabled, they will have to complete the MFA challenge to complete combined registration.

Combined registration can be enabled using Conditional Access policies.

Following are the steps:

1. Login to **https://entra.microsoft.com** using an account that has the Conditional Access Administrator role assigned.

2. Navigate to **Protection | Conditional Access**.

3. In the right pane, click on **New Policy**. Type a meaningful name for your policy.

4. Under **Users** select the users and groups you want to enable for combined registration.

5. Under **Target resources** select **User actions** and check the box **Register security information**, as shown in the following figure:

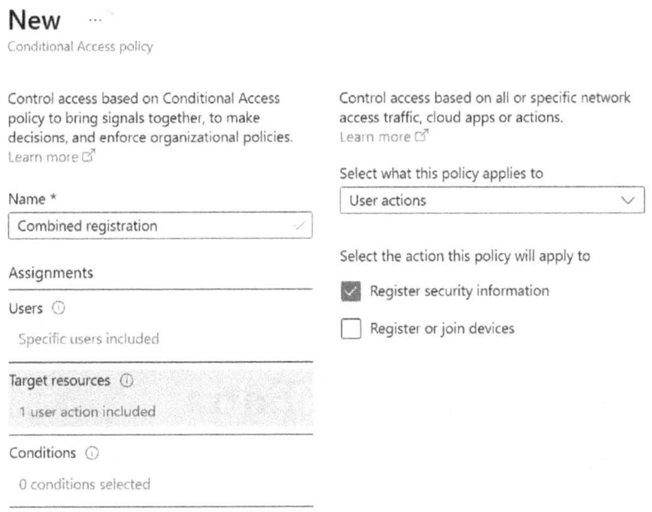

New ⋯
Conditional Access policy

Control access based on Conditional Access policy to bring signals together, to make decisions, and enforce organizational policies. Learn more ☐

Name *
┌──────────────────────────────────┐
│ Combined registration   ⌄ │
└──────────────────────────────────┘

Assignments

Users ⓘ

Specific users included

Target resources ⓘ

1 user action included

Conditions ⓘ

0 conditions selected

Control access based on all or specific network access traffic, cloud apps or actions. Learn more ☐

Select what this policy applies to
┌──────────────────────────────────┐
│ User actions   ⌄ │
└──────────────────────────────────┘

Select the action this policy will apply to

☑ Register security information

☐ Register or join devices

Figure 4.5: Conditional Access policy for combined registration

6. Under **Conditions,** choose the conditions under which the user should be prompted for combined registration. It could be if they are signing in from an untrusted location, unmanaged device or accessing from an unallowed app.

7. Under **Grant**, select **Block access**.

8. Ensure that the **Enable policy** toggle is set at **On** and click on **Create**.

Now, that we have discussed the basic concepts of identity protection, let us discuss the specifics and understand the different authentication methods, their use and configuration.

Multi-factor authentication

MFA is a process in which a user is prompted for a second authentication method once their username and password are validated. This increases security as the second authentication method is not something that is easy for an attacker to duplicate or obtain. MFA is a combination of the following:

- Something that you know, like your username or password
- Something that you have, like a phone or hardware key
- Something that you are, biometrics like fingerprint or face

Microsoft Entra ID MFA works by prompting a user to provide two or more of the authentication methods before granting them access. For example, once you enter your username and password you could be prompted to provide **one-time password (OTP)** sent to your mobile device.

Prerequisites

Before you start deploying MFA it is important to consider your current setup, as follows:

- If you are deploying MFA in a cloud only environment there are no prerequisites, and you can skip to the deployment steps.
- If you have a hybrid identity environment, make sure that you have Microsoft Entra Connect deployed and identities synchronized to Microsoft Entra ID.
- If you have on-premises legacy applications that can be accessed from the cloud, ensure that you have Microsoft Entra application proxy deployed.

Enabling MFA in Microsoft Entra

There are two ways to enable MFA in Microsoft Entra as discussed in this section.

Security defaults

The simplest way to enable MFA in the organization is to enable security defaults. These are a set of security features which are turned on in a single mouse click making it easier for administrators to protect their organization from identity-based attacks. These settings are preconfigured by *Microsoft* and are available for all tenants. They are enabled by default for all M365 tenants created after October 22, 2019.

The basic security features turned on by security defaults are as follows:

- **Require all users to register for MFA**: After enabling security defaults all existing tokens should be revoked. This will force all users to register for MFA. This can be done using the Revoke-AzureADUserAllRefreshToken PowerShell cmdlet. The users will now have 14 days to register for MFA using the Microsoft Authenticator app. After 14 days users will not be able to sign-in unless MFA registration is completed. The 14 day period for a user begins when they login interactively for the first time after security defaults is enabled.

- **Turn on MFA for all administrators**: The administrator roles will be prompted for MFA each time they login after security defaults are enabled, as follows:

  o   Global Administrator

  o   Application Administrator

  o   Authentication Administrator

  o   Authentication Policy Administrator

  o   Billing Administrator

  o   Cloud Application Administrator

  o   Conditional Access Administrator

  o   Exchange Administrator

  o   Helpdesk Administrator

  o   Identity Governance Administrator

  o   Password Administrator

  o   Privileged Authentication Administrator

  o   Privileged Role Administrator

  o   Security Administrator

  o   SharePoint Administrator

  o   User Administrator

- **Turn on MFA for all users when necessary**: Microsoft decides when a user should be prompted for MFA depending on factors such as location, device, role and task. This is to prevent users from being prompted for MFA each time, thus leading to MFA fatigue.

- **Block legacy authentication protocols**: After enabling security defaults all authentication requests made by older protocols like IMAP, SMTP or POP3 will be blocked.

- **Require MFA for signing on to Azure services**: After turning on security defaults any user or administrator logging on to Microsoft Entra admin center, Azure PowerShell and Azure CLI will be prompted for MFA each time.

Following are the security defaults that are ideal and useful for organizations:

- Do not have premium licenses to turn on Conditional Access policies.

- Do not use any clients with legacy authentication protocols.

- Want to improve their security posture but are not sure where to start.

Following are the steps to turn on security defaults in your tenant:

1. Login to **https://entra.microsoft.com** with an account that has at least the Security Administrator role assigned.

2. Navigate to **Identity** | **Overview** | **Properties**.

3. Select **Manage security defaults**. In the fly out pane, select **Enabled** from the drop-down list and click on **Save**.

Note: **Security defaults are not available if you have Conditional Access policies configured in your tenant.**

MFA registration policy

To effectively roll out MFA to end users, you can use the MFA registration policy which will force users to register for MFA regardless of the app they are signing into.

Following are the steps to configure an MFA registration policy:

1. Login to **https://entra.microsoft.com** with an account that has the Security Administrator role assigned.

2. Navigate to **Protection** | **Identity Protection** | **Multi-factor authentication registration policy**.

3. In the right-pane, click on to include users and group in the policy, as follows:

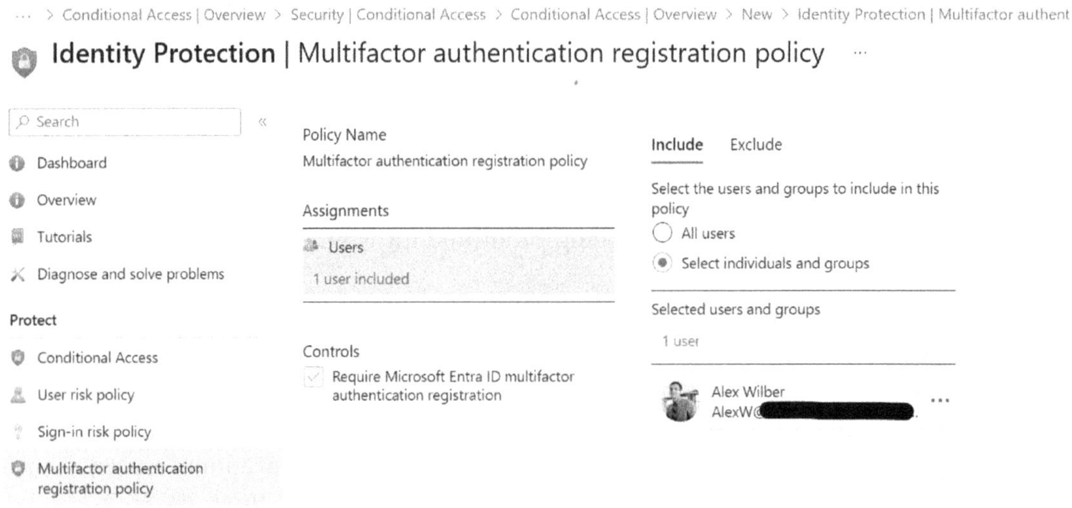

··· > Conditional Access | Overview > Security | Conditional Access > Conditional Access | Overview > New > Identity Protection | Multifactor authent

Identity Protection | Multifactor authentication registration policy ···

🔍 Search ≪	**Policy Name**	**Include** Exclude
ⓘ Dashboard	Multifactor authentication registration policy	
ⓘ Overview		Select the users and groups to include in this policy
▦ Tutorials	**Assignments**	◯ All users
✕ Diagnose and solve problems	🔱 Users	⦿ Select individuals and groups
	1 user included	
Protect		Selected users and groups
🛡 Conditional Access	**Controls**	1 user
🧍 User risk policy	☑ Require Microsoft Entra ID multifactor authentication registration	Alex Wilber
⚡ Sign-in risk policy		AlexW@▬▬▬▬▬. ···
🛡 Multifactor authentication registration policy		

Figure 4.6: Selecting users for MFA registration

4. Ensure that the **Policy enforcement** toggle is set to **Enabled,** and click on **Save,** as follows:

Policy enforcement

Enabled Disabled

Save

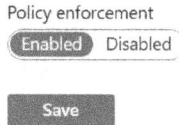

Figure 4.7: *Policy enforcement toggle*

Microsoft Entra ID will now prompt the user to register for MFA the next time they sign-in interactively. The users can skip the registration process for 14 days after which they will not be allowed to sign in unless they register.

You can also use Conditional Access policies to roll out MFA. However, the MFA registration policy is the most efficient way for MFA to roll out as it is not dependent on the user trying to access a specific application. Once you have turned on the MFA registration policy you can use additional Conditional Access policies to prompt users to complete MFA challenge based on certain conditions.

Now that we know how to configure MFA let us discuss the various authentication methods available to users to complete an MFA challenge.

Microsoft Authenticator app

The authenticator app can be used as an MFA option to approve or deny sign in requests when in **Push** mode. Users can view the prompt on their authenticator app and click on **Approve** if it is a legitimate request, else click on **Deny**.

It can also be used as a software token to generate OATH verification codes. The users can then enter the verification code at the sign-in stage.

Figure 4.8 shows an example of the Microsoft Authenticator app generating OATH verification codes:

Figure 4.8: *Microsoft Authenticator app showing OATH codes for various applications*

Note: OATH codes are not supported for certificate-based authentication. Users can have a maximum of five OATH tokens or authenticator applications configured for use at any time.

Before users can use the Microsoft Authenticator app as an MFA method, administrator must enable it in authentication methods. Refer to the section on *Enabling authentication methods.* Ensure that the **Push** mode is selected, as shown in the following figure:

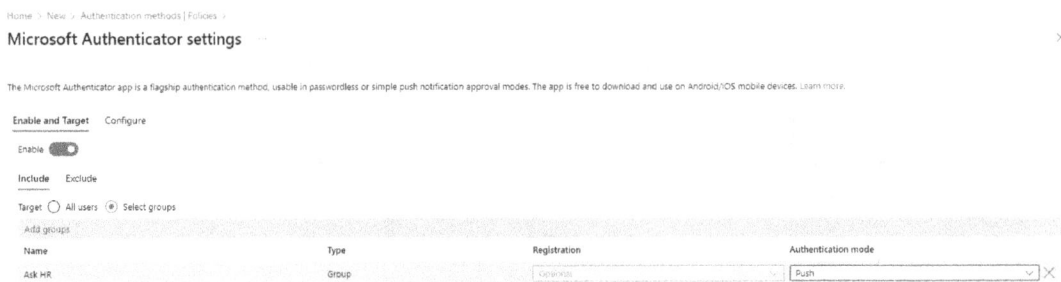

Figure 4.9: Enable Microsoft Authenticator app in Push mode

To register the Microsoft Authenticator app as an MFA method, users use the MySecurityInfo page. Following are the steps

1. Login to **https://aka.ms/mysecurityinfo** with your Entra ID credentials.

2. Make sure you are on the **Security Info** page.

3. Click on **Add sign-in method**. In the drop down, select **Authenticator app** and click on **Add**, as follows:

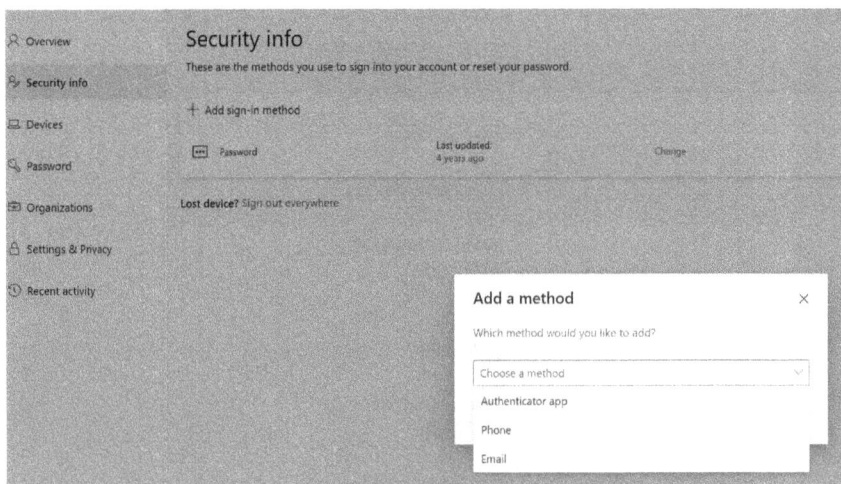

Figure 4.10: User registering to use the Microsoft Authenticator app

4. You will be promoted to install the app. Install the app from your iOS or Android store and click on **Next**.

Figure 4.11: *Install the Authenticator app*

5. On the **Set up your account** screen, click **Next,** as shown in the following figure:

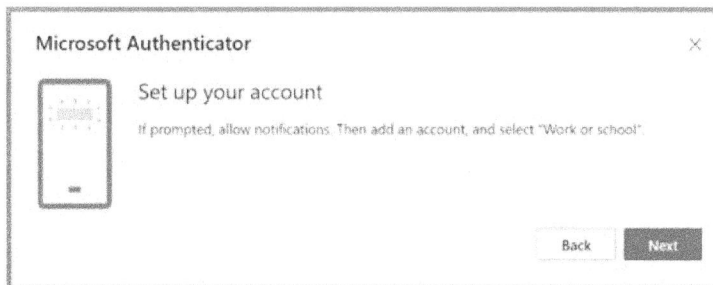

Figure 4.12: *Set up your account*

6. Next, you will be prompted to scan the QR code to use the app. This will connect the app with your account. On your smartphone, open the authenticator app and click on the + sign on the top right. Select **Work or school account** and select **Scan QR code**. This will open the camera, which you can use to scan the QR code displayed on the screen. This will add the account to your authenticator app. On the screen below, click **Next,** as shown in the following figure:

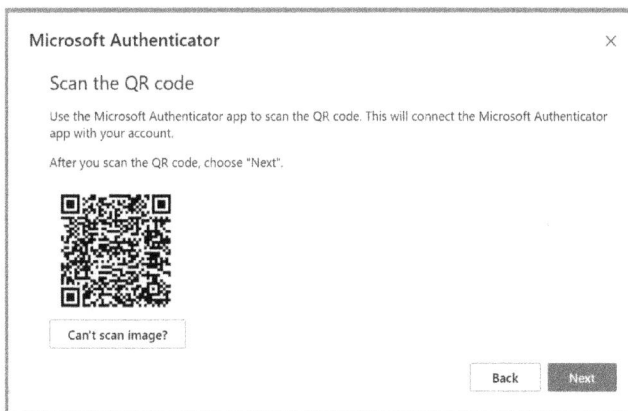

Figure 4.13: *Scan QR Code*

7. You might be prompted to confirm by entering a code on a prompt in the app. Enter the code to confirm.

Figure 4.14 shows the MySecurityInfo page, displaying a code that the user must input into the Microsoft Authenticator app on their mobile phone to complete the process:

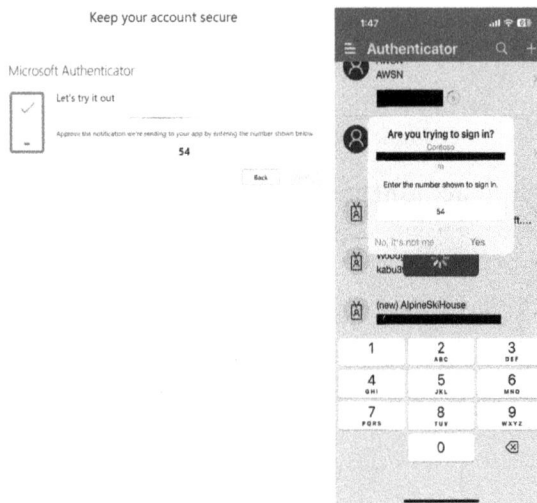

Figure 4.14: *Validate authenticator*

8. You will be prompted with a screen saying **Notification approved**. Click on **Next**. Microsoft Authenticator will now be displayed on the MySecurityInformation page as an authentication method, as shown in the following figure:

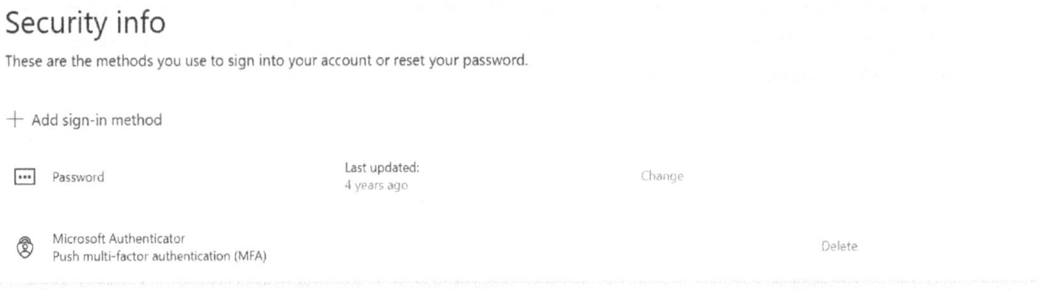

Figure 4.15: *Authentication methods listed on MySecurityInfo page*

OATH software token

OATH software tokens are applications such as the Microsoft Authenticator app that generate a secret key or seed that is entered into the app and used to generate OTP. When in Push mode, the authenticator app automatically generates codes and is therefore not dependent on internet connectivity. To enable users to use OATH software token as an

MFA authentication option administrator will need to enable it in the Microsoft Entra ID portal as described in the first section of this chapter.

OATH hardware token

OATH Hardware tokens are small devices that display a 6-digit number that refreshes every 30 or 60 seconds. With Microsoft Entra ID you can use OATH-TOTP SHA-1 tokens. There are several vendors that sell these types of hardware tokens.

Figure 4.16 shows one such hardware token:

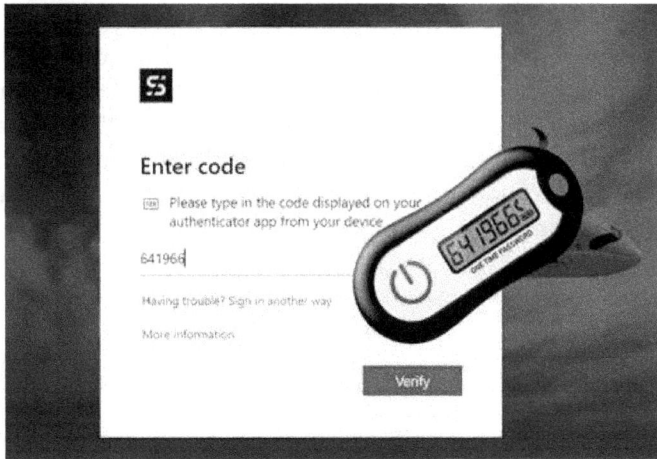

Figure 4.16: OATH hardware token

OATH hardware tokens usually come with a secret key or seed that is pre-programmed into the token. These keys must be entered into Microsoft Entra ID. Secret keys are limited to 128 characters, can only contain *a-z* characters in upper or lower case and digits 2-7. They must be encoded in *Base32*.

To enable users to use OATH hardware tokens administrator will need to configure them in the Microsoft Entra ID tenant.

Following are the steps:

1. Acquire the hardware tokens from a supported vendor.
2. Login to **https://entra.microsoft.com** with an account that has the Authentication Policy Administrator role assigned.
3. Navigate to **Protection | Authentication methods | Policies**.
4. In the right pane, click on **Hardware OATH tokens**. In the next screen, switch the toggle next to **Enable** and then to **On**. You can choose to enable this for all users in the tenant or selected groups. Once done, click on **Save** as shown in the following figure:

Hardware OATH tokens (Preview) settings   ···   ✕

Hardware OATH tokens are physical devices that use the OATH TOTP standard and a secret key to generate 6-digit codes used to authenticate. This policy control specifically manages the ability to register and use Hardware OATH tokens. Learn more.

Enable and Target

Enable ⬤◯

Include   Exclude

Target ⦿ All users ◯ Select groups

Name	Type	Registration
All users	Group	Optional ⌄

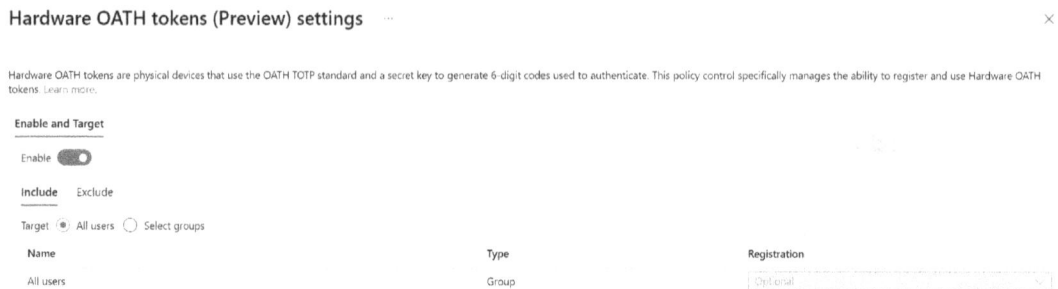

Figure 4.17: Enable OATH hardware token

5. Now, the tokens must be uploaded into the portal. To do this, the details of the hardware tokens will have to be entered in a **.csv** file. You can download the format of the **.csv** file by going to **Protection** | **Multi-factor authentication** | **OATH tokens**. In the right pane click on **Download**. Complete the **.csv** files with the details of the hardware tokens and upload it by clicking on the **Upload** button, as shown in the following figure:

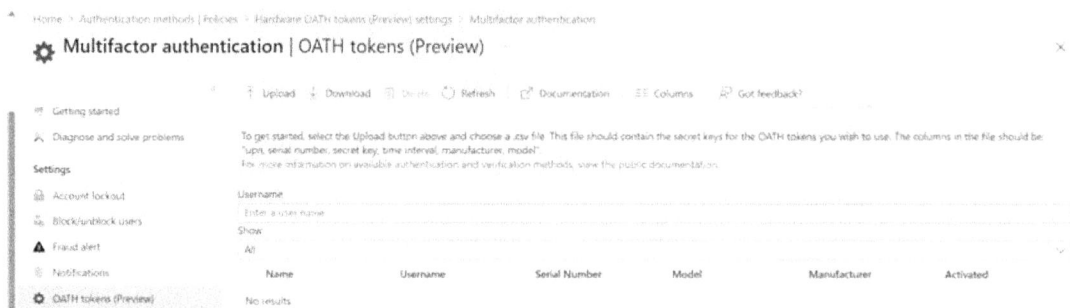

Home > Authentication methods | Policies > Hardware OATH tokens (Preview) settings > Multifactor authentication

⚙ Multifactor authentication | OATH tokens (Preview)   ✕

⬆ Upload ⬇ Download 🗑 Delete ↻ Refresh   📄 Documentation   ≡≡ Columns   🖉 Got feedback?

■ Getting started

Diagnose and solve problems   To get started, select the Upload button above and choose a .csv file. This file should contain the secret keys for the OATH tokens you wish to use. The columns in the file should be:
                                  "upn, serial number, secret key, time interval, manufacturer, model".
Settings   For more information on available authentication and verification methods, view the public documentation.

🔒 Account lockout   Username
🔓 Block/unblock users   Enter a user name
⚠ Fraud alert   Show
🔔 Notifications   All
⚙ OATH tokens (Preview)

Name	Username	Serial Number	Model	Manufacturer	Activated
No results					

Figure 4.18: Upload OATH hardware tokens

The **.csv** file can take a few minutes to process depending on its size. You can check the status by clicking on the **Refresh** button. If there are errors, download the file, fix the errors and upload again. Once all errors are fixed, the tokens will be available in the Entra ID portal. You can then activate each token by clicking on **Activate** next to each token and entering the OTP displayed on the token. A maximum of 200 OATH tokens can be activated every five minutes.

Users can manage and add OATH tokens by registering them on the **MySecurityInfo** page by going to **https://aka.ms/mysecurityinfo.** Once registered, when the user is prompted for MFA during sign in, they can check the digits displayed on the hardware token and enter the same digits in the MFA prompt on their screen. If the number matches, the user is allowed access.

OATH tokens are very useful in highly regulated industries like banking or defense where users may not be allowed to carry their mobile phones, thus being unable to use the Microsoft Authenticator app.

Note: At the time of this writing, OATH hardware tokens were in public preview.

Phone options

In addition to the above options, traditional MFA methods like SMS and Voice call are also available as authentication options with Microsoft Entra ID. Microsoft, however, recommends moving away from these methods and move to the modern authentication methods described above.

Passwordless sign-in

Passwordless is considered the most secure sign-in method as it eliminates the need for a user to enter their password during sign-in. Users can bootstrap passwordless methods using an existing MFA option or using a TAP. Let us explore the passwordless authentication options offered by Microsoft Entra ID.

Passkey authentication

Passkeys, developed by the **Fast Identity Online** (**FIDO**) Alliance, offer an innovative approach to secure authentication. They eliminate the need for traditional passwords by leveraging FIDO2 standards. These keys depend on public key cryptography to authenticate identities, offering a higher level of security by minimizing vulnerabilities such as phishing, password-related breaches, and weak passwords. By replacing passwords with cryptographic credentials, passkeys simplify the sign-in process while enhancing protection against cyber threats.

Passkeys are supported on modern systems like Windows 10 (version 1903 or higher) and are integrated into tools like the Microsoft Authenticator, empowering organizations to adopt robust, password-free security solutions.

The FIDO2 specification requires each security key vendor to provide an **Authenticator Attestation GUID** (**AAGUID**), which is a 128-bit identifier indicating the key type. Passkey providers on desktops and mobiles are also expected to provide an AAGUID during registration.

This section will explain how you can enable your users to use passkeys in the Microsoft Authenticator app.

Before enabling passkeys, ensure that the following requirements have been met:

- Microsoft Entra multifactor authentication should be enabled in the organization.
- Users should have the Microsoft Authenticator app installed on their devices.
- Users' devices should support passkey authentication. The following devices are supported:

      o   Entra ID joined devices should be running Windows 10 version 1903 or higher.

      o   Hybrid joined devices should be running Windows 10 version 2004 or higher.

Enable passkeys

Following are the steps to enable passkey as an authentication method:

1. Login to **https://entra.microsoft.com** with an account that has the **Authentication Policy Administrator** role assigned.

2. Navigate to **Protection | Authentication methods | Policies**.

3. Click on **Passkey (FIFO2)** and click on **Enable**. Select the user to include or exclude from the policy, as shown in the following figure:

Figure 4.19: Enable passkeys

4. Click on **Configure,** and make the settings, as shown in *Figure 4.20*:

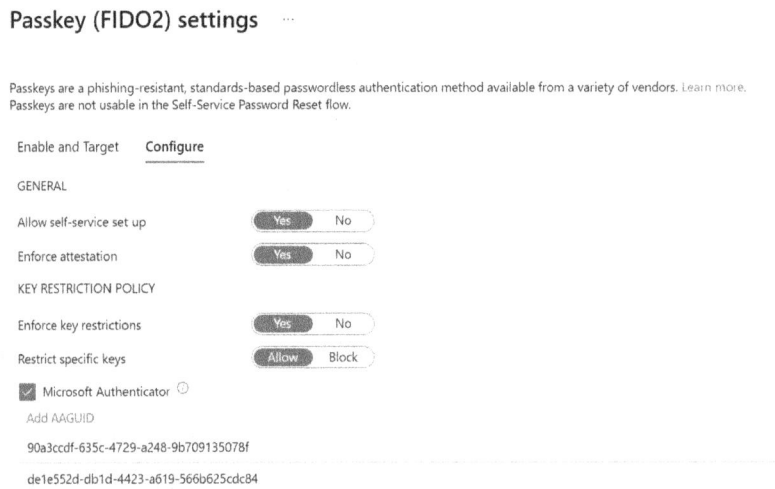

Figure 4.20: Passkey configuration

- Set **Allow self-service set up** to **Yes** to enable users to register for a passkey using their *My security info* page.

- Set **Enforce attestation** to **Yes** to ensure that the FIDO2 security keys are from a genuine and legitimate vendor
- Set **Enforce key restrictions** to **Yes** if you want to allow or disallow certain key models or passkey providers, identified by their AAGUID. When this setting is set to **Yes**, you can select Microsoft Authenticator to automatically add the Authenticator app AAGUIDs in the key restriction list.

5. Once done, click **Save**.

6. You can now create a Conditional Access policy to require users to register and use passkeys.

Registering passkey

Users can manually register for passkey using the following steps:

1. As an end user, go to **https://mysignins.microsoft.com**
2. In the left pane, click on **Security info**.
3. In the right pane, click on **Add sign-in method** and then, click on **Passkey**.
4. Before adding a passkey, you will have to complete MFA. If you do not have MFA method registered, you will have to do so before being able to add a passkey.
5. A dialog box will open asking where you would like to store your passkey, as shown in the following figure:

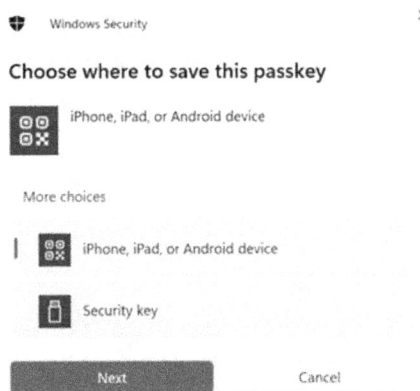

Figure 4.21: *Save passkey*

6. Choose **iPhone, iPad or Android device** and follow the guidance on the screen to save your passkey to your Microsoft Authenticator app.

Sign-in with passkey

Once a user has stored a passkey on their authenticator app, they can use it to sign-in passwordlessly using the following steps:

1. Go to **https://portal.office.com** and enter your username, and click on **Next**.
2. Click on **Sign-in options** and select **Face, fingerprint, PIN or security key**. Click **Next.**
3. Choose **iPhone, iPad or Android device** and click **Next**.
4. A QR code will be displayed. Scan the QR code using your device camera. Tab **Sign-in with a passkey** on your device. The device will connect to your computer using Bluetooth.
5. Click **Continue** on your device to sign-in using the passkey.

Temporary Access Pass

A TAP is a time-limited passcode that can be configured for single or multiple use. Using this, the users can register themselves for passwordless authentication from within the Microsoft Authenticator app without ever needing a password.

To provide a TAP to users, administrator must first configure a TAP authentication method policy.

Following are the steps:

1. Sign in to **https://entra.microsoft.com** with an account that has the Authentication Policy Administrator role assigned.
2. Navigate to **Protection** | **Authentication methods** | **Policies.**
3. In the right pane, click on **Temporary Access Pass**.
4. Click on **Enable** and then select the users to include or exclude from policy as shown in the following figure:

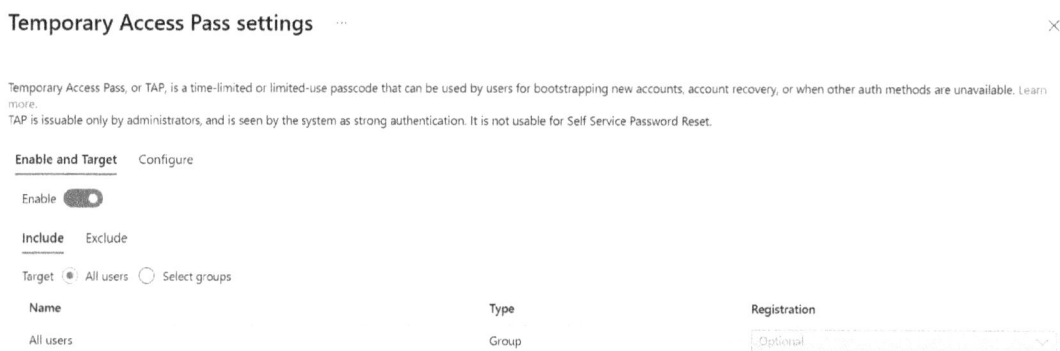

Temporary Access Pass settings   ···   ✕

Temporary Access Pass, or TAP, is a time-limited or limited-use passcode that can be used by users for bootstrapping new accounts, account recovery, or when other auth methods are unavailable. Learn more.
TAP is issuable only by administrators, and is seen by the system as strong authentication. It is not usable for Self Service Password Reset.

Enable and Target   Configure

Enable ◖O◗

Include   Exclude

Target ⦿ All users ◯ Select groups

Name	Type	Registration
All users	Group	Optional ⌄

Figure 4.22: Enable Temporary Access Pass

5. Click on **Configure** to edit the configuration of the TAP. Once done, click on **Update** as shown in the following figure:

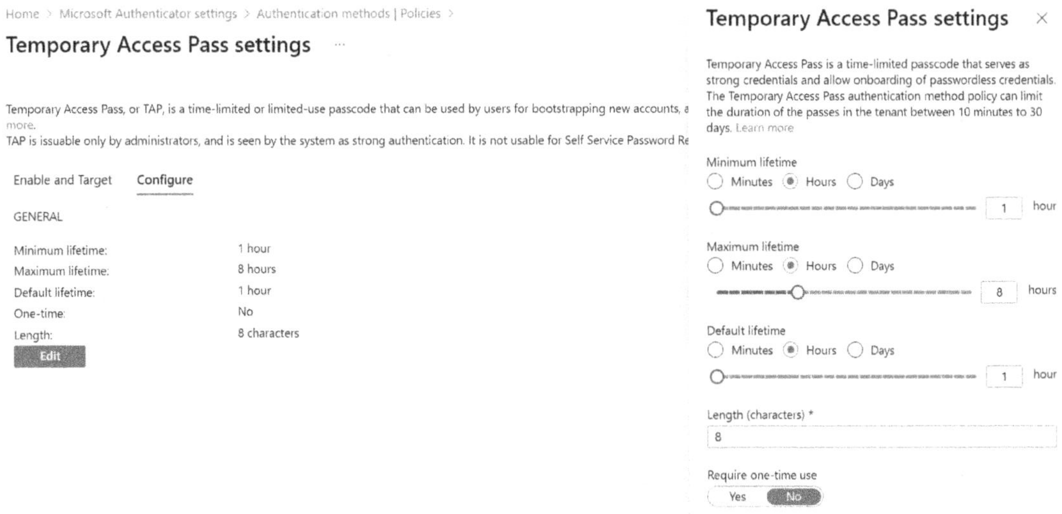

Home > Microsoft Authenticator settings > Authentication methods | Policies >

Temporary Access Pass settings ...

Temporary Access Pass, or TAP, is a time-limited or limited-use passcode that can be used by users for bootstrapping new accounts, a more.
TAP is issuable only by administrators, and is seen by the system as strong authentication. It is not usable for Self Service Password Re

Enable and Target   **Configure**

GENERAL

Minimum lifetime:	1 hour
Maximum lifetime:	8 hours
Default lifetime:	1 hour
One-time:	No
Length:	8 characters

Edit

Temporary Access Pass settings ✕

Temporary Access Pass is a time-limited passcode that serves as strong credentials and allow onboarding of passwordless credentials. The Temporary Access Pass authentication method policy can limit the duration of the passes in the tenant between 10 minutes to 30 days. Learn more

Minimum lifetime
○ Minutes ⦿ Hours ○ Days

○────────────────────────── [1] hour

Maximum lifetime
○ Minutes ⦿ Hours ○ Days

────────○────────────────── [8] hours

Default lifetime
○ Minutes ⦿ Hours ○ Days

○────────────────────────── [1] hour

Length (characters) *
[8]

Require one-time use
(Yes **No**)

Figure 4.23: Temporary Access Pass option configuration

6.   Click on **Save** to enable the TAP policy.

Creating Temporary Access Pass

You can now create a TAP for end users to enable them to set up passwordless authentication.

Table 4.2 summarizes the Microsoft Entra ID roles and the actions they can take on TAP:

Microsoft Entra ID role	Available actions
Global Administrator	Create, delete and view TAP for all users (except themselves).
Privileged Identity Administrator	Create, delete and view TAP for all users and admins (except themselves).
Authentication Administrator	Create delete and view TAP for all users (except themselves).
Global Reader	View TAP details for all users but cannot view the actual code.

Table 4.2: TAP actions available for Microsoft Entra ID roles

Following are the steps to generate TAP for a user:

1.   Login in to **https://entra.microsoft.com** with a role that has the Authentication Policy Administrator role assigned.

2.   Navigate to **Identity | Users | All users**.

3.   In the right pane select a user and click on **Authentication methods**.

4.   In the right pane click on **Add authentication method**.

5. In the fly out pane, select **Temporary Access Pass** from the drop-down menu. Define the activation time, duration and if it will be a one-time use or multiple. Once done click **Add**, as shown in the following figure:

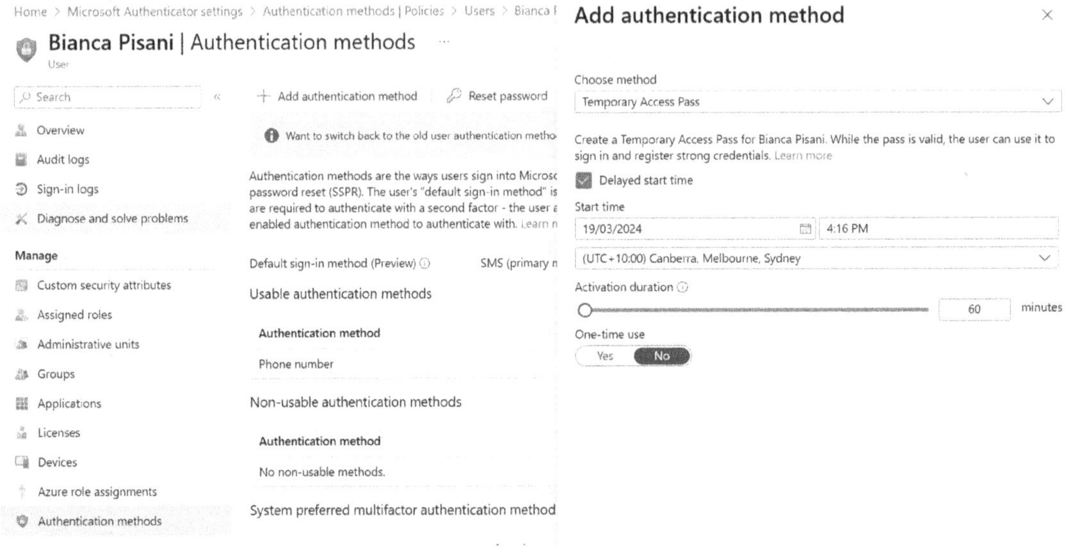

Figure 4.24: Generate TAP for a user

6. Once added, the details of TAP are displayed. Make a note of the passcode as this will have to be provided to the user. Click **OK**, as shown in the following figure:

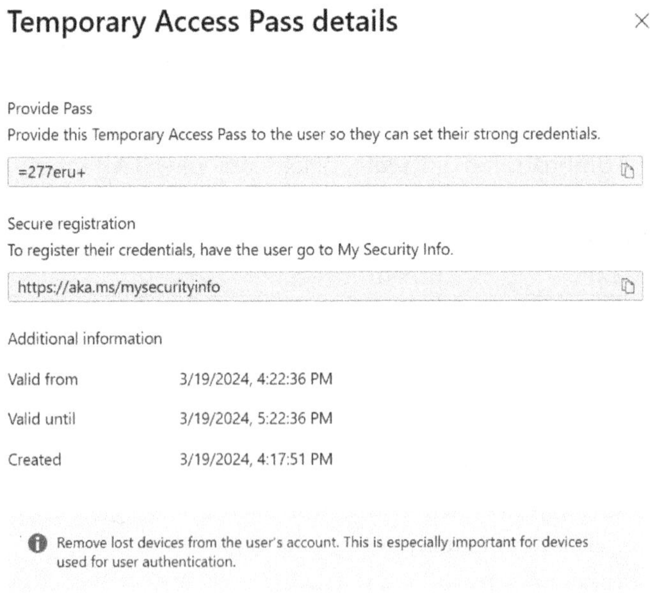

Figure 4.25: User TAP details

Using TAP

If a new user has joined your organization, you can get them started passwordlessly using a TAP. They can use the TAP to join their Windows 10 or 11 device to your Entra ID tenant without ever needing a password. During the domain-join process on a Windows 10 or 11 device, users can authentication using a TAP instead of a password. They can then register for Windows Hello for Business, which will be used for subsequent sign-ins.

As with all other authentication methods, users can manage their TAP by going to the **MySecurityInfo** page. If a user has a password it is listed as the default authentication method on this page. If the user does not have a password or any other registered authentication methods, they will see a banner at the top of the page asking them to add a new sign-in method. They can click on the banner and add their TAP. They can then continue to add additional sign-in methods.

Microsoft Authenticator app

The Microsoft Authenticator app can be used to enable passwordless authentication to Microsoft Entra ID accounts and other accounts like your personal *Hotmail* or *Outlook* accounts. It uses key-based authentication to enable user credentials that are tied to a device that uses a PIN or biometric. Using the Microsoft Authenticator app, a user can use their iOS or Android phone to sign in passwordlessly into any application that supports passwordless authentication.

When passwordless sign in is enabled, once the user enters their username, instead of entering a password they receive a prompt on their Microsoft Authenticator app.

The left part of *Figure 4.26* shows the user entering their username in Outlook and the right part of *Figure 4.26* shows the prompt they receive on their Microsoft Authenticator app on their mobile device:

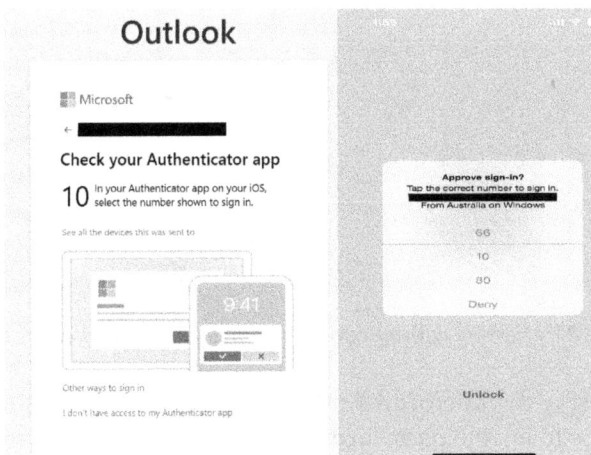

Figure 4.26: Outlook requesting passwordless sign in using authenticator app

Following steps describe the authentication flow during a passwordless sign-in:

1. The user enters their username.

2. Microsoft Entra recognizes that the user has strong credentials enabled and starts using the strong credential flow.

3. A push notification is sent to the Microsoft Authenticator app.

4. The user opens the app on receiving the push notification.

5. The Microsoft authenticator app calls Microsoft Entra ID and receives a proof-of-presence challenge and nonce.

6. The user completes the challenge by entering their biometric or PIN to unlock the private key.

7. The nonce is signed with the private key and sent back to Microsoft Entra ID.

8. Microsoft Entra ID performs the public/private key validation and returns a token.

Following prerequisites must be met before passwordless sign-in using the Microsoft Authenticator app is enabled:

- Ensure the users have the latest version of the Microsoft Authenticator app on their smartphones.

- For Android, the device on which the app is installed must be registered to an individual user.

- For iOS, the device must be registered with each tenant when the Microsoft Authenticator app is used to sign-in.

Before users can use the Microsoft Authenticator app as an MFA method, administrator must enable it in authentication methods. Refer to the section on *Enabling authentication methods*. Ensure that the **Passwordless** mode is selected, as shown in the following figure:

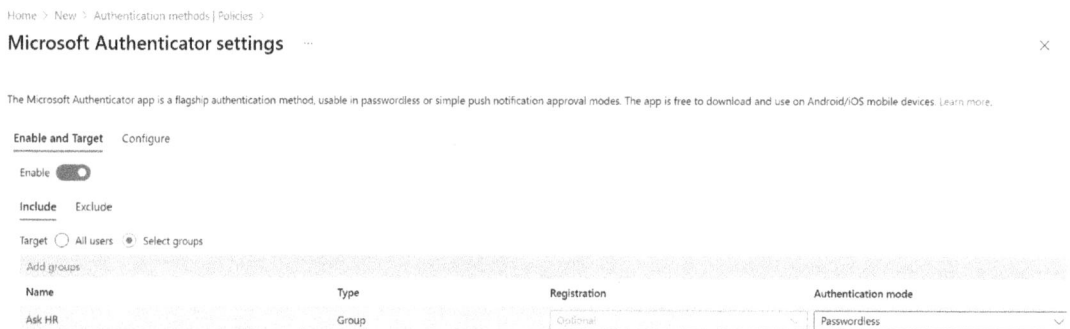

Figure 4.27: Microsoft authenticator app configured for passwordless sign-in

If users are already using the Microsoft Authenticator app for multi-factor authentication, following are the steps to enable passwordless sign-in:

1. On your Android or iOS device, open the Microsoft Authenticator app.

2. Select the account for which you would like to enable phone sign-in and tap on **Enable phone sign-in**. Follow the on-screen instructions to complete the configuration for passwordless sign-in.

First time users can register themselves for passwordless authentication from within the Microsoft Authenticator app without first needing to register the authenticator app. They will need to download the Microsoft Authenticator app on their smartphones and obtain a TAP from the administrator.

Following are the steps on their iOS or Android device:

1. On the device, open the Microsoft Authenticator app and tap on **Add account** and choose **Work or School account**.

2. Click on **Sign-in**. Enter the Microsoft Entra ID username.

3. User will be prompted to provide the TAP. Follow the on-screen instructions to complete the registration.

4. Once complete, follow the above steps to enable phone sign-in for the account.

Windows Hello for Business

Windows Hello for Business is a passwordless authentication method using which users can sign into Windows devices using biometrics such as facial recognition or fingerprint or a PIN, instead of a password. It is a phishing-resistant, two-factor authentication that has brute-force protection built-in. When used with FIDO/WebAuthN, Windows Hello for Business can also be used to sign into various websites thus eliminating the need to remember multiple passwords.

Windows Hello for Business offers the following benefits:

- It protects credential theft. An attacker must have both the device and the PIN to gain access.
- Since no passwords are used, it circumvents phishing and brute force attacks. It prevents server breaches and replay attacks as credentials are asymmetric and generated within the **Trusted Platform Module** (**TPM**).
- The PIN can only be used with the device it was configured with. So even if an attacker knows the PIN, they will still need the device to access the data. Moreover, Windows Hello for Business has brute force protection-built in.

Windows Hello for Business uses a two-factor authentication that combines device-specific credentials with a biometric. The credential is tied to Microsoft Entra ID. During provisioning, Windows Hello is set up on the device and the user is asked to provide a gesture that will be used to verify their identity and unlock the device. The biometric data is stored on the Windows device making it impossible to steal as it never leaves the device.

Windows Hello for Business supports facial recognition, fingerprint scanning and iris recognition. Major hardware vendors are now shipping hardware devices that are compatible with Windows Hello for Business.

Deploying Windows Hello for Business can be divided into the following phases:

- **Device registration phase**: All devices enabled for Windows Hello for Business must be registered with Microsoft Entra ID so that they receive an identity that is used to authenticate the device when a user signs-in. Microsoft Entra ID is the identity provider for cloud and hybrid deployments and the device registers with the Device Registration Service. For on-premises deployments the identity provider is AD FS and the device registers with the Enterprise Device Registration Service.

- **Provisioning phase**: Provisioning begins once the registration is successful, and the device receives a policy that enables Windows Hello. A **Cloud eXperience Host (CXH)** window is launched to guide the user through the provisioning experience.

  Following steps describe the flow during the provisioning phase:

  1. In the CXH window, the user is prompted to authenticate to Microsoft Entra ID with MFA.

  2. After MFA is successful, the user must provide a biometric gesture and a PIN.

  3. Once the PIN is created, a Windows Hello container is created.

  4. A public or private key pair is generated and bound to the TPM.

  5. The private key is stored locally and protected by the TPM and cannot be exported.

  6. The public key is registered with Microsoft Entra ID mapped with the user account. For cloud and hybrid deployments the Device Registration service writes the key to the user object in Microsoft Entra ID. For on-premises deployments AD FS writes the key to the user account in Active Directory.

- **Key synchronization**: In hybrid deployments once a user provisions Windows Hello for Business the key must be synchronized from Microsoft Entra ID to Active Directory. This is not applicable for cloud only deployments.

- **Certificate enrolment**: If Windows Hello is deployed using certificates, after the key is generated, the client generates a certificate request. The organization's **Public Key Infrastructure (PKI)** issues a certificate to the user which is stored on the user's Hello container and is used to authenticate the user to on-premises resources.

- **Authentication**: In this phase the user signs-in to the device using biometrics or PIN. Authentication occurs using the private portion of the credential which triggers Windows to use the private key to cryptographically sign the data before it is sent to the identity provider. Microsoft Entra ID authenticates the user by mapping the user account to the public key registered during the provisioning phase.

Windows Hello for Business deployment

There are a wide variety of ways in which Windows Hello for Business can be deployed in your environment. Multiple technologies come together to make Windows Hello for Business work. The final deployment model will depend on your current infrastructure and some aspects might already be determined.

Windows Hello for Business can be deployed in the following environments:

- Cloud-only
- Hybrid
- On-premises

This section will describe in detail the various deployment models and their requirements. This will enable you to decide which model is best suited to your environment.

Trust types

A deployment trust type determines how Windows Hello for Business clients authenticate to Active Directory. Windows Hello for Business authentication to Microsoft Entra ID always uses the key and not the certificate. Hence, trust type is not applicable for cloud-only deployments.

Table 4.3 shows the three trust types available:

Trust type	Description
Cloud Kerberos	Authentication to Active Directory occurs when users request a **Ticket Granting Ticket** (**TGT**) from the Microsoft Entra ID, using Microsoft Entra Kerberos. The on-premises domain controllers remain responsible for Kerberos service tickets and authorization.
Key	Authentication to Active Directory occurs using a device-bound hardware or software key that is created during the Windows Hello for Business provisioning experience. It requires that certificates be distributed to domain controllers.
Certificates	Certificates are issued to the users, and they authenticate using a device-bound hardware or software key created during the Windows Hello for Business provisioning experience.

Table 4.3: Trust types for Windows Hello for Business

Issuing certificates to Domain Controllers and users requires additional infrastructure, making Cloud Kerberos the recommended option to deploy Windows Hello for

Business. It offers several advantages and simpler deployment as compared to the Key trust and Certificate trust deployment types.

Following are some of the advantages:

- There is no need to deploy an additional PKI infrastructure.
- There is no need to synchronize public keys between Microsoft Entra ID and Active Directory.

Following table summarizes deployment models with their trust types and PKI requirements:

Deployment model	Trust type	PKI required
Cloud-only	N/A	No
Hybrid	Cloud Kerberos	No
Hybrid	Key	Yes
Hybrid	Certificate	Yes
On-premises	Key	Yes
On-premises	Key	Yes

Table 4.4: Deployment model summary for Windows Hello for Business

Operating system requirements

All supported Windows 10, 11 and Server versions can be used with Windows Hello for Business. However, cloud Kerberos trust requires some specific client and server versions. They are listed, as follows:

- Windows 10 21 H2 with KB5010415 or later
- Windows 11 21 H2 with KB5010414 or later
- Windows Server 2016 with KB3534307 or later
- Windows Server 2019 with KB4534231 or later

Authentication

Regardless of the deployment model, users can authenticate to Microsoft Entra ID using federated authentication or cloud authentication and the requirements vary based on trust type as summarized in the following table:

Deployment model	Trust type	Authentication to Microsoft Entra ID	Requirements
Cloud-only	n/a	Cloud authentication	n/a
Cloud-only	n/a	Federated authentication	Non-MS federation service
Hybrid	Cloud Kerberos	Cloud authentication	**Password hash sync (PHS)** or **pass-through authentication (PTA)**
Hybrid	Cloud Kerberos	Federated authentication	AD FS or non-MS federation service
Hybrid	Key	Cloud authentication	PHS or PTA
Hybrid	Key	Federated authentication	AD FS or non-MS federation service
Hybrid	Certificate	Federated authentication	PHS or PTA are not supported. AD must be federated with Microsoft Entra ID using AD FS.

Table 4.5: Authentication requirements for Windows Hello deployment models

Device registration

The devices enabled for Windows Hello for Business must be registered with the identity provider so that it can be authenticated when the user signs in. For on-premises deployment the AS FS server is responsible for device registration. For cloud-only and hybrid deployments Microsoft Entra ID is responsible for device registration.

Table 4.6 summarizes the device states and the device registration responsibility for each deployment model:

Deployment model	Device join state	Device registration responsibility
Cloud-only	Microsoft Entra joined Microsoft Entra registered	Microsoft Entra ID
Hybrid	Microsoft Entra joined Microsoft Entra hybrid joined Microsoft Entra registered	Microsoft Entra ID
On-premises	Active Directory Domain joined	AD FS

Table 4.6: Device state and registration responsibility for Windows Hello for Business

Multi-factor authentication

Windows Hello for Business aims at helping organizations move away from passwords by providing them a strong credential that enables MFA. It accepts a user's username and password as the first factor authentication, but the user must provide a second factor authentication before it can provision a strong credential. Depending on your deployment model the MFA options can differ.

For cloud-only and hybrid deployments, organizations can use Microsoft Entra ID MFA or a non-Microsoft MFA. For on-premises deployments, organizations must use an MFA that can integrate as an AD FS multifactor adapter.

Key registration

The Windows Hello for Business, provisioning experience creates an asymmetric key pair that is bound to the device as the user credentials. The private key is protected by the device's security modules. The credential is a user key. During provisioning the user's public key is registered with the identity provider. For cloud-only and hybrid deployments this identity provider is Microsoft Entra ID and for on-premises deployments it is AD FS.

Directory synchronization

As we know hybrid deployments use Microsoft Entra Connect Sync to synchronize identities from Active Directory to Microsoft Entra ID. In Windows Hello for Business scenarios, during the provisioning phase, the public portion of the user's credential is registered with Microsoft Entra ID which is then synchronized to Active Directory to provide SSO to on-premises resources.

In the case of Windows Hello for Business, on-premises deployments use directory synchronization to import users from Active Directory to the Azure MFA server which sends the MFA data to cloud services to perform verification.

Device configuration

Windows Hello for Business policy can be configured using Intune **configuration service providers** (**CSP**) or Active Directory **Group Policy Object** (**GPO**). If the devices are managed using Intune, it is ideal to deploy and manage Windows Hello for Business policy using CSP. For devices that are managed by on-premises Active Directory, GPO can be used to roll out Windows Hello for Business policy.

Licensing requirements

Windows Hello for Business does not require a premium license. However, some dependencies like Intune automatic enrolment and Conditional Access do. If you are using automatic enrolment in Intune or applying Conditional Access policies for Windows Hello for Business, make sure you have premium licenses. Users can also manually enroll their devices into Intune to eliminate the requirement of premium licenses.

Enrolling a certificate using the AD FS registration authority requires devices to authenticate to an AD FS server, which requires device write-back and a premium license is required.

> **Note: The detailed steps for configuring Windows Hello for Business in cloud-only, hybrid and on-premises deployments is beyond the scope of this book. Please refer to the Microsoft Online documentation.**

Microsoft Entra ID Protection

So far, we have learnt how to implement policies to protect user identities. In this section we will learn about a set of capabilities that help organizations detect, investigate and remediate identity-based risks. These risk signals can then be used by Conditional Access policies to make access decisions. They can also be sent to a **Security Information and Event Management** (**SIEM**) tool for further investigation and correlation.

The full set of Microsoft Entra ID Protection features is available with Microsoft Entra ID P2 licenses.

Understanding risk conditions

In Microsoft Entra ID Protection any suspicious action related to a user account is considered a risk. Risk can be categorized as **user risk** and **sign-in risk**. They can be calculated in real-time or offline. Real-time risks show up in reporting within five to ten minutes whereas, Offline risks might show up in 48 hours.

A user risk is detected at the user level and a sign-in risk is the possibility that the sign-in attempt is made by someone other than the owner of the account. Both these risks contribute to the overall risk score for the user.

Table 4.7 summarizes the risk types, license requirements and detection type:

Risk detection	Detection type	License requirement
Sign-in risk		
Atypical travel	Offline	Premium
Anomalous token	Real-time or Offline	Premium
Suspicious browser	Offline	Premium
Unfamiliar sign-in properties	Real-time	Premium
Malicious IP address	Offline	Premium
Suspicious inbox manipulation riles	Offline	Premium

Risk detection	Detection type	License requirement
Password spray	Offline	Premium
Impossible travel	Offline	Premium
New country	Offline	Premium
Activity from anonymous IP address	Offline	Premium
Suspicious inbox forwarding	Offline	Premium
Mass Access to Sensitive Files	Offline	Premium
Verified threat actor IP	Real-time	Premium
Additional risk detected	Real time or Offline	Nonpremium
Anonymous IP address	Real-time	Nonpremium
Admin confirmed user compromise	Offline	Nonpremium
Microsoft Entra threat intelligence	Real-time or Offline	Nonpremium
User risk		
Possible attempt to access **Primary Refresh Token** (**PRT**)	Offline	Premium
Anomalous user activity	Offline	Premium
User reported suspicious activity	Offline	Premium
Suspicious API traffic	Offline	Premium
Suspicious sending patterns	Offline	Premium
Additional risk detected	Real-time or Offline	Nonpremium
Leaked credentials	Offline	Nonpremium
Microsoft Entra threat intelligence	Offline	Nonpremium

Table 4.7: Risk types and detection

Note: For detailed definition of the above risks, refer to the Microsoft online documentation.

In addition to user and sign-in risk, Microsoft Entra ID Protection also helps in securing workload identities helping detect, investigate and remediate risks related to applications and service principals. A workload identity is an identity assigned to an application and allows it to access resources. Unlike a user account a workload identity cannot perform MFA and does not have a lifecycle. They also need a secure location to store their credentials or secrets. Due to this they are more vulnerable to attacks. Microsoft Entra ID Protection detects risks related to workload identities across sign-in behavior and offline indicators of compromise. These detections include Microsoft Entra Threat Intelligence, suspicious sign-ins, admin confirmed service principal compromise, leaked credentials, malicious application, suspicious application and anomalous service principal activity.

Microsoft Entra ID Protection assigns one of the three risk levels to each identified risk: low, medium and high. Microsoft calculates this risk based on its own threat intelligence and the threat signals it receives from the telemetry collected from the millions of systems running Microsoft commercial and consumer services worldwide. It does not provide specific details about how these risk levels are calculated. The customer organizations cannot define parameters for assigning specific risk levels. This is completely managed by Microsoft.

Risk-based access policies

Conditional Access policies can be applied to protect organizations when a sign-in or user risk is detected. These are called **risk based conditional access policies**. Administrators can create these policies to take specific actions based on the identified risk level. Once configured, during each sign-in Microsoft Entra ID Protection sends the detected risk level to Conditional Access and the policies apply if the conditions are satisfied.

Figure 4.28 shows where you can configure the user risk and sign-in risk while configuring a Conditional Access policy:

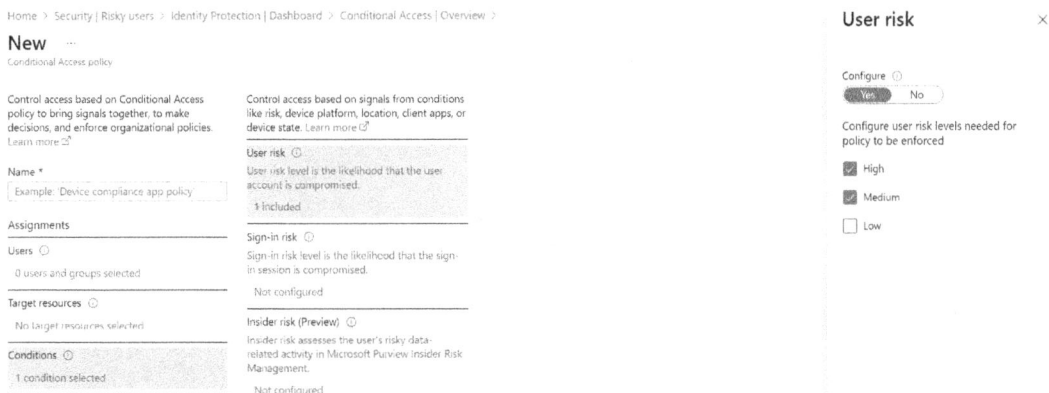

Figure 4.28: *Configuring risk-based conditional access policy*

Based on this the risk levels following actions can be taken by the Conditional Access policy for a sign-in risk detection:

- Block access
- Allow access
- Require MFA

For user risk detection, following actions can be taken:

- Block access
- Allow access but force a password change

If risk is detected users can perform required controls like MFA or secure password reset to remediate the risky event and close the event thereby, reducing noise for the administrator.

Investigate and remediate risks

Using Microsoft Entra ID Protection, administrators can access reporting that can be used to investigate user risk, sign-in risk, risky workload identities and risk detections. These reports are found on the Microsoft Entra admin center under **Protection** | **Identity Protection**.

Risky users

The risky users report lists all user accounts that are considered at risk of compromise. Administrators can investigate risky users and take appropriate action to remediate the user account to prevent unauthorized access to resources. A user account can be listed in the risky users report if they have performed one or more risky sign-ins or risks are detected in the user account as shown in *Table 4.7*.

To investigate a risk user, access the **Risky users** report by navigating to **Protection** | **Identity Protection** in your Microsoft Entra administrator portal.

Following figure shows the **Risky users** report:

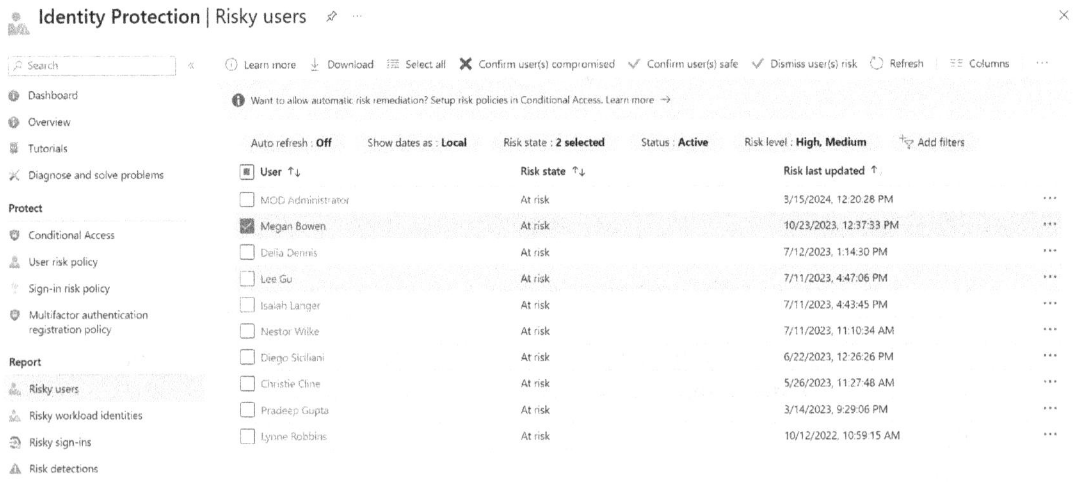

Figure 4.29: *Risky users report*

Click on any user account to view the details of the risk detection.

Figure 4.30 shows an example. Also, the various administrative actions are as shown in the figure:

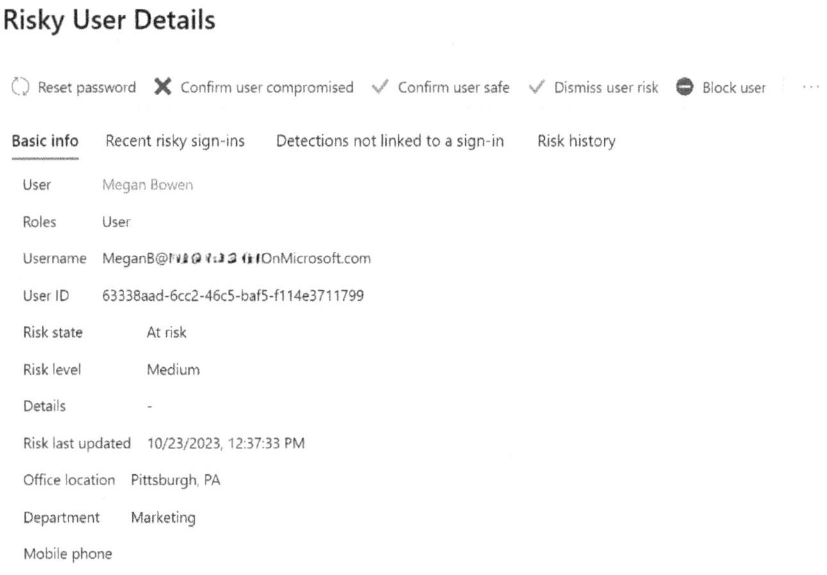

Risky User Details

◯ Reset password   ✕ Confirm user compromised   ✓ Confirm user safe   ✓ Dismiss user risk   ⊖ Block user   ⋯

Basic info   Recent risky sign-ins   Detections not linked to a sign-in   Risk history

User	Megan Bowen
Roles	User
Username	MeganB@M3 Q 7·3 3 (·10nMicrosoft.com
User ID	63338aad-6cc2-46c5-baf5-f114e3711799
Risk state	At risk
Risk level	Medium
Details	-
Risk last updated	10/23/2023, 12:37:33 PM
Office location	Pittsburgh, PA
Department	Marketing
Mobile phone	

Figure 4.30: Risky user details

Risky sign-ins

The risky sign-ins report shows the risk sign-in events for the last 30 days. With this report, administrators can find which sign-ins are classified at risk, if they are confirmed compromise, confirmed safe, remediated or dismissed. They can also find the device information, MFA details, if any Conditional Access policies were applied and much more. They can then decide to either confirm the sign-in as compromised or safe.

Following figure shows the **Risky sign-ins** report:

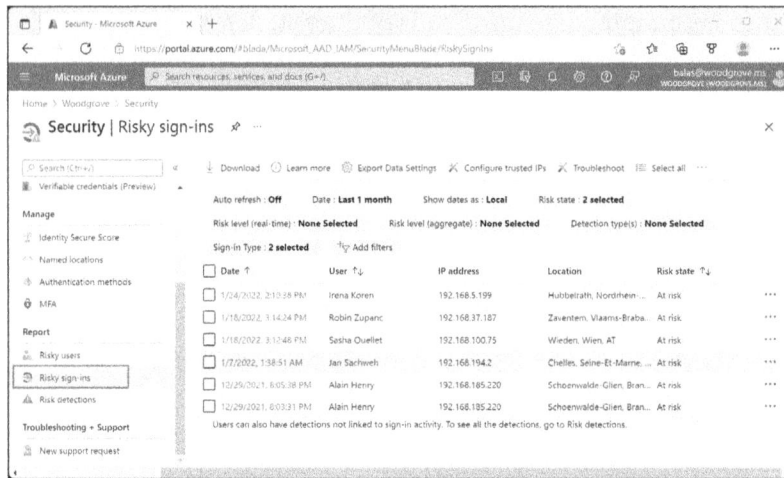

Figure 4.31: Risky sign-ins report

Risky workload identities

To find risky workload identities navigate to the risky workload identities section of the reports.

In the following figure, note the various options available to administrators to remediate identified risk:

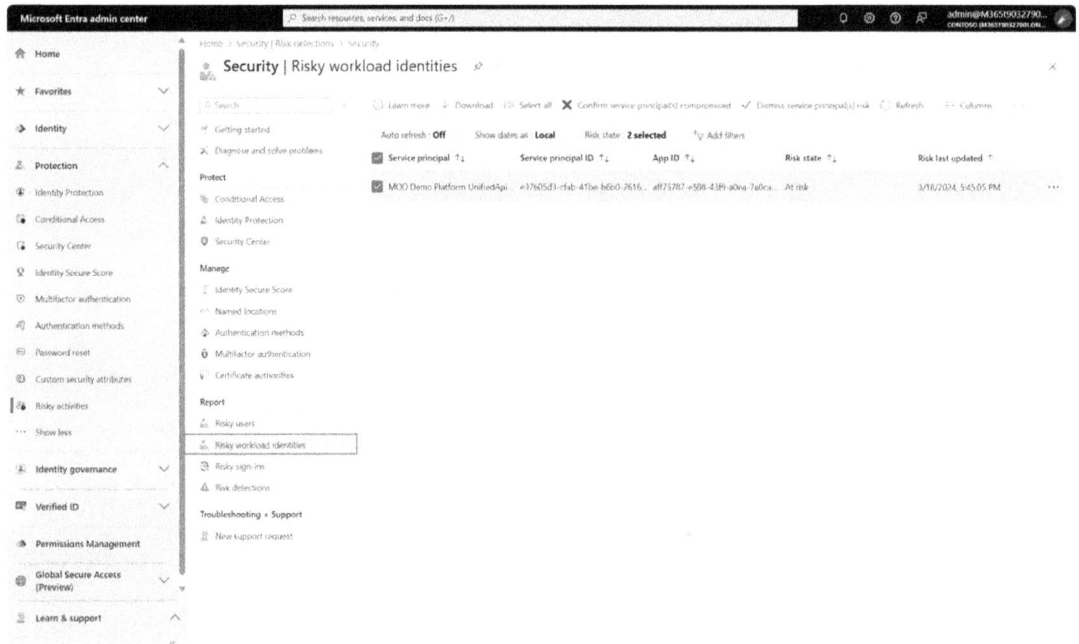

Figure 4.32: Risky workload identities report

Risk detections

The risk detections report shows detected risks from the last 90 days. With this report, administrators can find details about each risk detection, other risks triggered at the same time and sign-in location. This report gives administrators additional information using which they can take actions in the **Risky users** and **Risky sign-ins** reports. The **Risk detections** report is available in the Entra portal by navigating to **Protection** | **Identity protection** | **Risk detections.**

Refer to *Figure 4.33:*

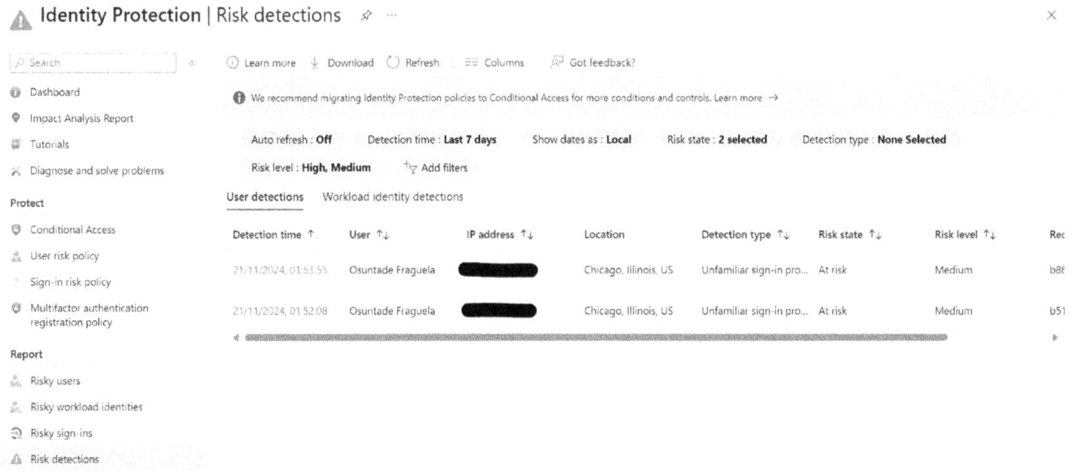

Figure 4.33: *Risk detections report*

Conclusion

This chapter went deep into understanding the identity protection concepts available in Microsoft Entra ID. You should now be able to explain the different authentication methods and when they can be used as primary or secondary authentication methods. This chapter introduced you to Conditional Access policies and explained how to configure them to provide granular control over your security posture.

We also discussed in detail multi-factor authentication and passwordless as the modern authentication methods and their advantages over traditional authentication methods of using just passwords. You also learnt the various methods of implementing MFA and passwordless.

Finally, this chapter concluded with discussing Microsoft Entra ID Protection and its risk-based capabilities to protect, detect, remediate identity-based risks.

In the next chapter, you will learn how identities can be governed using the Entra ID capabilities.

Multiple choice questions

1. In which ways can the Microsoft Authenticator app be used during authentication? Select all that apply.

   a. Multi-factor authentication

   b. OATH Soft token

   c. Passwordless

   d. All of the above

2. You are the security administrator for your organization that owns Microsoft Entra ID Free licenses. You have been tasked to turn on MFA for all users in your organization. What is the easiest way to do so? The solution should require least amount of administrative effort.

   a. Security defaults

   b. Conditional Access policies

   c. MFA registration policy

   d. Risk based policy

3. Which of the following authentication methods offer passwordless capabilities?

   a. Microsoft authenticator app in Push mode

   b. Windows Hello for Business

   c. OATH tokens

   d. Phone options

Answer key

1. d

2. a

3. b

Join our book's Discord space

Join the book's Discord Workspace for Latest updates, Offers, Tech happenings around the world, New Release and Sessions with the Authors:

https://discord.bpbonline.com

CHAPTER 5

Identity Governance

Introduction

Each identity goes through a lifecycle that needs to be managed from when a user joins the organization to when they leave. The user's access must be kept up to date during their time with the organization and this must be done efficiently. This chapter explains how to use entitlement management to ensure the users have the right access they need to do their job. It demonstrates how access reviews can be used to review the user's access to data and applications periodically, ensuring they do not have more access than necessary to fulfil their job roles. It also explores how PIM can be used to give just-in-time access to the most sensitive resources. Lastly, it introduces the new feature of lifecycle workflows that helps organizations manage users by automating the lifecycle processes of joiner, mover and leaver.

Structure

The chapter covers the following topics:

- Microsoft Entra ID Governance
- Entitlement management
- Access reviews

- Privileged Identity Management
- Lifecycle workflows

Objectives

By the end of this chapter, you will be able to use the features of Microsoft Entra ID Governance to create entitlement management packages to ensure that users have access to the resources they need as they begin their job responsibilities. You will also be able to configure access reviews to ensure that user access is maintained as they move across the organization. You will be able to use the features of PIM to protect the highly privileged accounts, group ownership and membership and critical Azure resources in the environment. You will also be able to use lifecycle workflows to create workflows to manage users across the joiner-mover-leaver scenario.

Microsoft Entra ID Governance

Microsoft Entra ID Governance is a set of solutions that help organizations improve user productivity, strengthen security and ensure regulatory compliance. It helps ensure that the right people have the right access to do their job. Microsoft Entra ID Governance helps in understanding the following:

- Which users have access to which resources?
- What are they doing with that access?
- Are controls in place to manage access?
- Can the controls be audited?

Using Microsoft Entra ID Governance, you can govern the identity and access lifecycle for your users and guests and protect privileged administrator accounts.

Identity and access lifecycle

Each identity goes through a lifecycle from when the user joins the organization and their identity is created (joiner), changes roles (mover) to when they resign, and their identity is removed from the system (leaver).

Organizations must ensure that the users' identities are provisioned and reprovisioned quickly so that they can become productive as soon as possible.

Using the entitlement management, access reviews and lifecycle workflows features of Microsoft Entra ID Governance organizations can manage provisioning of new users at scale ensuring that users have access to the resources they need to do their job, maintain user access as they move across roles and remove access once they leave the organization.

Privileged access lifecycle

Administrators and other privileged accounts can be misused if there is a rouge administrator or if there is an authorized user inadvertently making changes to IT systems. Therefore, it is important to monitor and govern the use of privileged accounts. Additionally, if a highly privileged account is compromised, the attacker can make changes to the IT systems that can severely hamper operations or bring them to a standstill. Organizations might also want to regulate access to Azure resources and membership and ownership of certain groups. Using Microsoft Entra ID PIM, organizations can provide JIT access to Microsoft Entra roles, Azure resources and M365 groups. This ensures that users do not have standing access to privileged role, Azure resources or groups.

Now, let us explore each of these features in detail.

Entitlement management

When users join an organization, they need access to several resources like SharePoint sites, Teams channels and applications. New employees may not know which resources they need access to. After joining, they might spend time understanding what access is required. Once they know, they might have to find people to approve their access. Precious time is lost as it takes time for the employee to start being productive. This problem is further complicated when collaborating with other organizations. There might not be a single individual who would know all the specific people in the external organization who need access to resources.

Entitlement management is a Microsoft Entra ID Governance feature that simplifies the identity and access lifecycle management for users and guests. It automates requesting and assigning access. It uses access packages which are based on catalogs to manage and maintain user access.

Access packages

An access package is a bundle of all the resources that employees might need to perform their job duties.

Following resources can be included in an access package:

- Microsoft Entra security groups
- M365 groups and teams
- Microsoft Entra enterprise applications
- SharePoint online sites
- Microsoft Entra roles

An administrator can create an access package containing the resources required for a job role. For example, an access package for a user in the marketing department could include membership of the marketing Teams channel, membership of marketing security groups, access to the marketing application and the marketing SharePoint site. Policies can then be defined based on which the assignment of the access package can be controlled.

A policy can define the following:

- The users or guests who can request access to this package.
- If the request is automatically approved or by designated approvers.
- If and when the access package assignment expires.

Catalog

A catalog is a container of resources and access packages. A catalog is created when all related resources need to be grouped together. For example, you might want to group all marketing resources into one catalog. This catalog might include M365 groups and teams related to marketing, marketing SharePoint sites and some marketing applications. This catalog can then be used to create access packages for marketing users. An access package might contain all or a subset of resources from the catalog.

By default, a Global Administrator and Identity Governance Administrator can manage all aspects of entitlement management like creating catalogs and access packages. However, they may not know to which business resources access has to be granted and for how long. This is further complicated as each business unit may have different requirements. An IT administrator can delegate the task of creating and assigning catalogs and access packages to administrators in the business units.

There are three ways of delegating access, as follows:

- The Identity Governance Administrator can create the catalog and then assign catalog owners to add resources and manage the catalog going forward.
- If resources do not have owners, administrators can create catalogs and add the resources. They can then assign catalog owners to manage the catalog going forward.
- If resources have owners, administrators can grant the catalog creator role to non-IT administrators who can then create their own catalogs.

Connected organizations

A connected organization is an external organization that your organization works with and needs to share resources like applications and SharePoint sites. Mostly, users in external organizations do not exist in your Microsoft Entra directory. You can use entitlement management to bring them into your directory as needed.

Connected organizations provide a way for users in these external organizations to request an access package and be able to access applications and SharePoint sites.

There are four ways to specify the users that form a connected organization, as follows:

- Users in another Microsoft Entra tenant.
- Users in a non-Microsoft directory that is configured for SAML/WS-Fed IdP federation.
- Users in a non-Microsoft directory whose email addresses have the same domain name. Ensure that email one-time passcode authentication is turned on for these users to be able to authenticate while requesting access and later while accessing resources.
- Users with a Microsoft account such as `hotmail.com`.

Add a connected organisation

Global Administrator or Identity Governance Administrator is the required role.

Following are the steps to add a connected organization:

1. Login to **https://entra.microsoft.com** and navigate to **Identity governance** | **Entitlement management** | **Connected organizations**.
2. Click on **Add connected organizations**.
3. On the **Basics** page, enter a **Name** and **Description**. The state will be automatically set as **Configured**. A connected organization can have one of the following two states:
   a. A **configured** connected organization is one that is fully connected and allows users to request access. It has been manually created and configured by the administrator.
   b. A **proposed** connected organization is an automatically created connected organization that the administrator has not added. This happens when an external user that is not a part of any connected organization is assigned to or requests an access package.
4. Click on next, **Directory + domain**, as shown in the following figure:

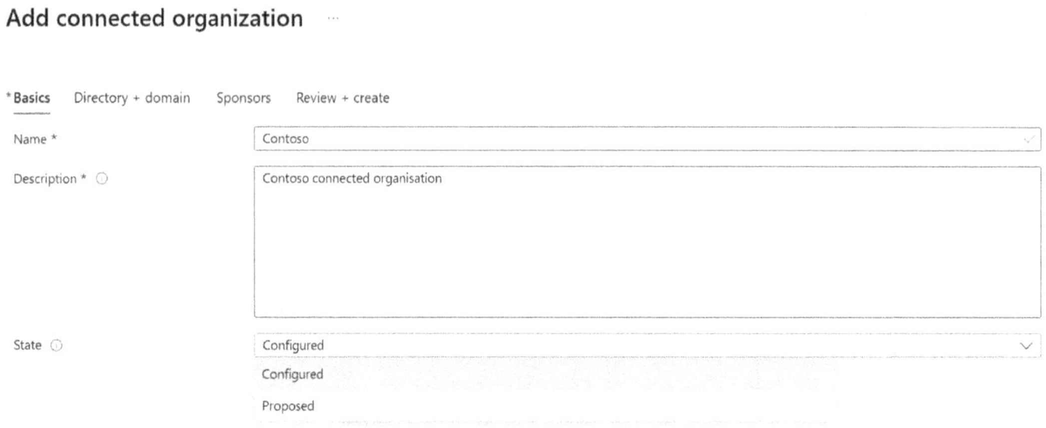

Add connected organization   ...

*Basics   Directory + domain   Sponsors   Review + create

Name *	Contoso
Description * ○	Contoso connected organisation
State ○	Configured
	Configured
	Proposed

Figure 5.1: Connected organization basics

5. Click on **Add directory + domain**. In the fly out pane, type the name of the external Microsoft Entra domain name. You can also add a non-Microsoft Entra domain name. Ensure that you type the entire domain name correctly.

    Following figure shows examples of a Microsoft Entra ID domain and non-Microsoft Entra domain name being added as connected organizations. Once done click on **Add** and then click on **Select**. Click on **Next: Sponsors**, as shown in the following figure:

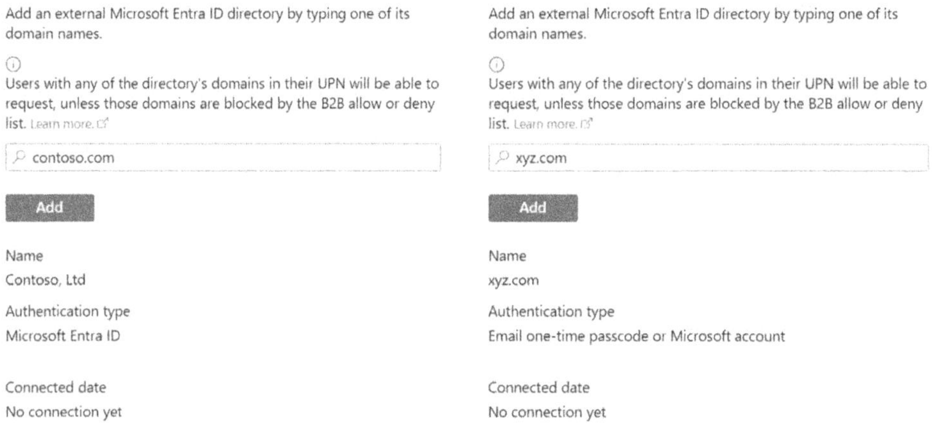

Add an external Microsoft Entra ID directory by typing one of its domain names.

ⓘ
Users with any of the directory's domains in their UPN will be able to request, unless those domains are blocked by the B2B allow or deny list. Learn more. ◻

    🔎 contoso.com

    Add

Name
Contoso, Ltd

Authentication type
Microsoft Entra ID

Connected date
No connection yet

Add an external Microsoft Entra ID directory by typing one of its domain names.

ⓘ
Users with any of the directory's domains in their UPN will be able to request, unless those domains are blocked by the B2B allow or deny list. Learn more. ◻

    🔎 xyz.com

    Add

Name
xyz.com

Authentication type
Email one-time passcode or Microsoft account

Connected date
No connection yet

Figure 5.2: Adding connected organization domain name

6. Sponsors are internal or external individuals who manage the relationship between the two organizations. Internal sponsors are users within your organization. External sponsors are external guests that already exist in your directory and are the points of contact for these connected organizations. Sponsors can be used as approvers when users in the connected organizations request an access package.

7. Click **Review + create** as shown in the following figure:

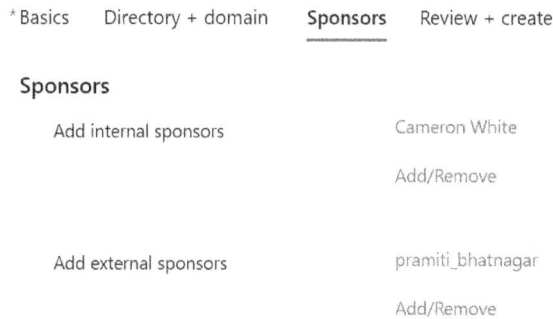

Basics   Directory + domain   **Sponsors**   Review + create

Sponsors

Add internal sponsors   Cameron White

                                         Add/Remove

Add external sponsors   pramiti_bhatnagar

                                         Add/Remove

Figure 5.3: Adding internal and external sponsors

8. On the **Review + create** page, click on **Create**.

Roles in entitlement management

Entitlement management has roles that allow non-IT administrators to manage catalogs and access packages.

These roles are summarized in the following table:

Role	Description
Catalog creator	Can create and manage catalogs. Typically assigned to non-IT administrators to create catalogs. The person who creates the catalog automatically becomes the first catalog owner and then can add more owners. They can only see and manage the catalogs they create.
Catalog owner	Can add, edit and manage access packages and other resources within a catalog. They must be listed as the owners of the resources before they can add the resource to a catalog.
Catalog reader	Can view existing access packages within a catalog.
Access package manager	Can edit and manage existing access packages within a catalog.
Access package assignment manager	Can edit and manage existing access packages' assignments.

Table 5.1: Entitlement management roles

Configure entitlement management

Now that we understand the components of entitlement management, we are ready to create and assign access packages. This section explains the steps for creating a catalog, assigning non-IT administrators and creating and assigning access packages. We will also discuss the end user experience of requesting access.

Delegate to catalog creator

Identity Governance Administrator or Global Administrator is the required role.

If you would like to delegate the creation of catalog to non-IT administrators, you will have to give them the catalog creator role.

Following are the steps to add catalog creators:

1. Login to **https://entra.microsoft.com** and navigate to **Identity Governance** | **Entitlement management** | **Settings**. At the top click on **Edit**.

2. Under **Delegate entitlement management**, click on **Add catalog creators** and select the users who you want to grant the catalog creator role to and click on **Select**, as shown in the following figure:

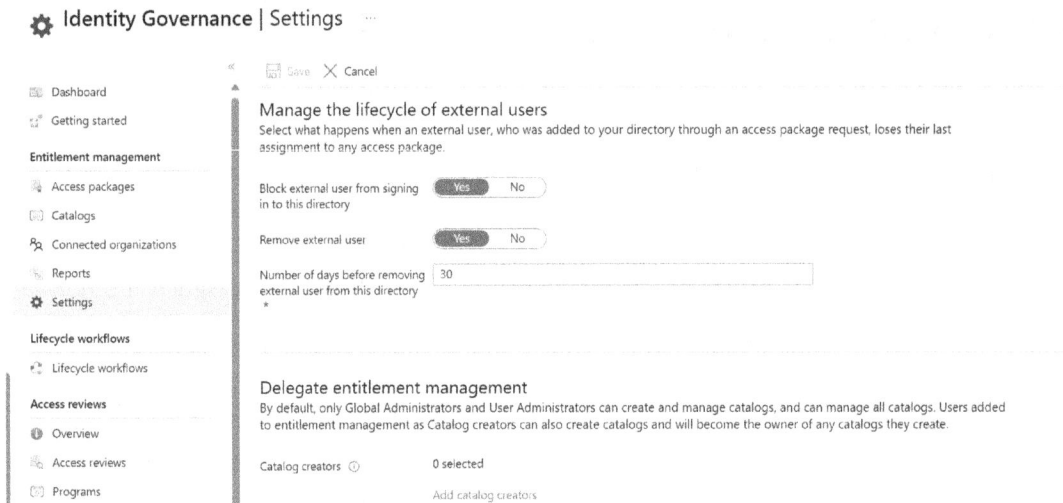

Figure 5.4: Delegate to catalog creator

3. Click **Save**.

Allow access to Microsoft Entra portal

Identity Governance Administrator or Global Administrator is the required role.

By default, delegated roles like catalog creators are not able to access the Microsoft Entra admin portal. To allow them to log in to the portal the following are the steps:

1. Login to **https://entra.microsoft.com** and navigate to **Identity** | **Users** | **User settings**.

2. Ensure the **Restrict access to Microsoft Entra admin center** toggle is set to **No**, as shown in the following figure:

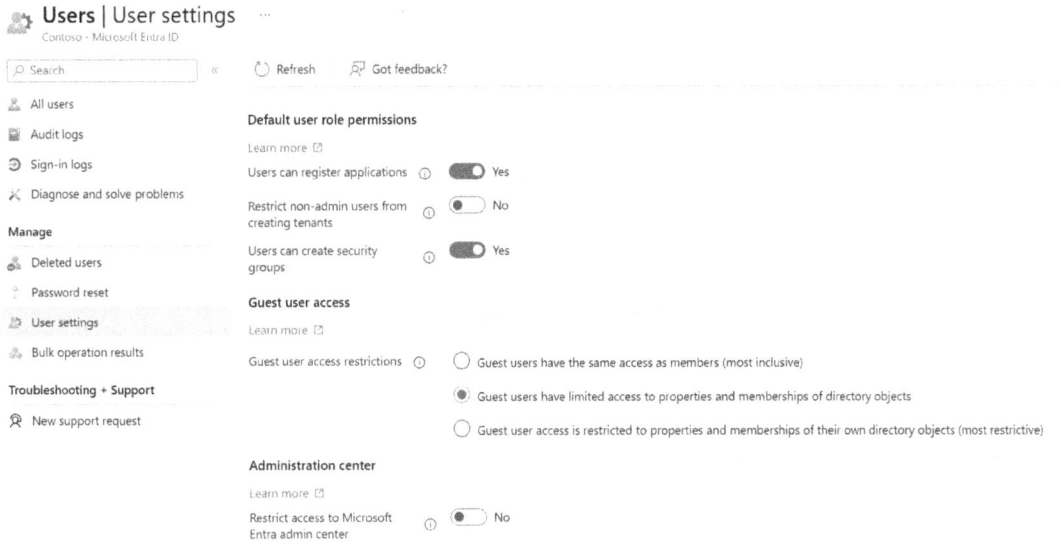

Figure 5.5: Allow access to Microsoft Entra portal

Creating catalog

Identity Governance Administrator or Global Administrator or Catalog creator is the required role.

Following are the steps to create a new catalog:

1. Login to **https://entra.microsoft.com** and navigate to **Identity Governance** | **Entitlement management** | **Catalogs**.

2. In the right pane, click on **New catalog**.

3. Give a **Name** and **Description** for the new catalog.

4. Make sure **Enabled** toggle is set to **Yes**.

5. If you want to make this catalog available for external users switch **Enabled for external users** to **Yes**, as shown in the following figure:

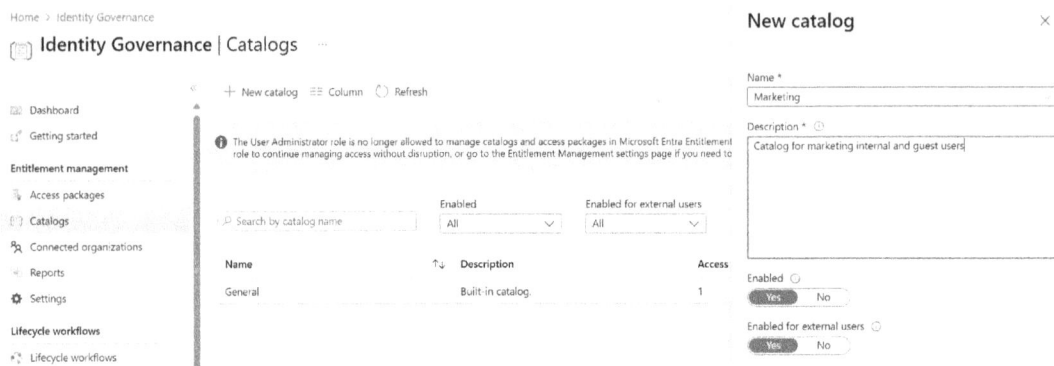

Figure 5.6: Catalog creation

6. Click **Create**.

Add additional roles

Identity Governance Administrator or Global Administrator or catalog owner is the required role. However, this step becomes optional.

The catalog creator who creates the catalog becomes the first catalog owner. They can add additional roles to the catalog to further delegate management of the catalog to others.

Following are the steps:

1. On the **Catalogs** page, click on **Roles and administrators**. You will see the page in *Figure 5.7*.

2. From this page, you can **Add catalog owner**, catalog readers, access package managers and access package assignment managers.

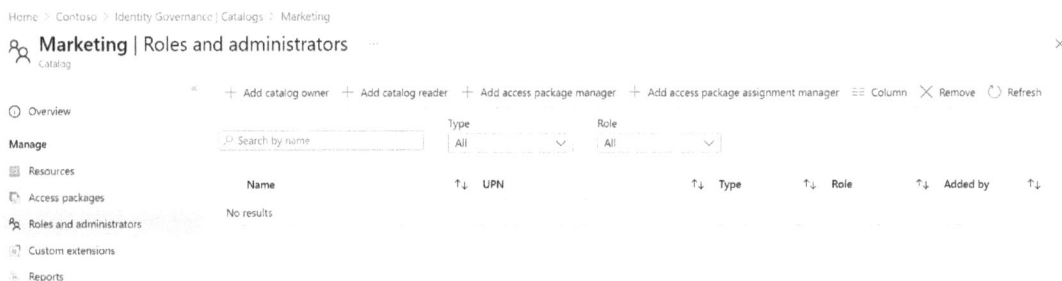

Figure 5.7: Add additional roles to catalog

Add resources to catalog

Identity Governance Administrator or Global Administrator or catalog owner is the required role.

Now that the catalog has been created, resources should be added to the catalog. These resources will be available to be added to the access package. M365 groups and teams, application, SharePoint online sites and Microsoft Entra roles are the resources that can be added to the catalog.

Following are the steps to add resources to the newly created catalog:

1. Click on the catalog that was just created and click on **Resources**. In the right pane click on **Add resources**. At the top, click on each of the buttons to add the relevant resources, as shown in the following figure:

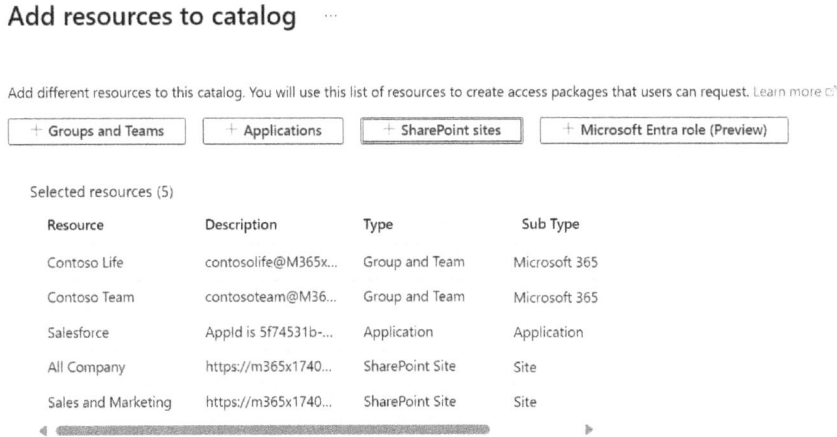

Add resources to catalog ...

Add different resources to this catalog. You will use this list of resources to create access packages that users can request. Learn more ☁

| + Groups and Teams | + Applications | + SharePoint sites | + Microsoft Entra role (Preview) |

Selected resources (5)

Resource	Description	Type	Sub Type
Contoso Life	contosolife@M365x...	Group and Team	Microsoft 365
Contoso Team	contosoteam@M36...	Group and Team	Microsoft 365
Salesforce	AppId is 5f74531b-...	Application	Application
All Company	https://m365x1740...	SharePoint Site	Site
Sales and Marketing	https://m365x1740...	SharePoint Site	Site

Figure 5.8: Add resources to the catalog

2. Once all resources have been added, click **Add**.

Add resource attributes in the catalog

Identity Governance Administrator or Global Administrator or catalog owner is the required role. However, this step is optional.

Resource attributes are the fields that requestors will be required to answer when they submit access requests. These answers will be shown to the approvers and stamped on the user object in Microsoft Entra ID. All attributes configured require an answer when the user requests an access package. If an answer is not provided the request cannot be submitted.

Following are the steps to require attributes for access requests:

1. Click on the ellipsis next to the newly added resource and select **Require attributes**, as shown in the following figure:

Figure 5.9: Adding attributes to resources

2. You can choose from **Built-in** or **Directory schema extension** attribute types. The built-in ones are the Microsoft Entra user profile attributes. Directory schema extension is a way to store more data in Microsoft Entra user objects. If you choose **Built-in** attribute, in the **Attribute type** dropdown list select the attribute from the dropdown. If you choose **Directory schema extension** attribute, you will have to type the name of the attribute.

> **Note: To add directory schema extensions to a user account in Microsoft Entra ID Microsoft Graph or PowerShell can be used. This will only be required if you require an attribute that is not already present in the Microsoft Entra ID user object or synchronized from on-premises Active Directory.**

3. In the **Default display string,** type the question you want the user to see.

4. Select the **Answer format**. You can choose from **Short text**, **Long text** or **Multiple choice**.

5. Under **Attribute value is editable** select **Yes** if you want the attribute value to be editable during assignment and self-service requests. If **No** is selected and the attribute value is empty the users can enter the value of the attribute. Once the value is saved, the attribute cannot be edited. If the attribute value is not empty, the user will not be able to update the attribute.

6. After making the changes, click **Save**, as shown in the following figure:

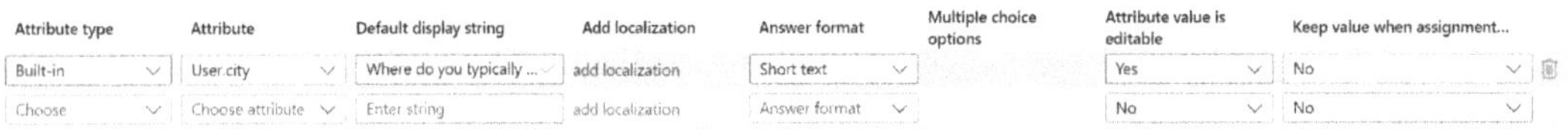

Figure 5.10: Editing attribute values

Create an access package

Identity Governance Administrator or Global Administrator or catalog owner or access package manager is the required role.

Following are the steps to create a new access package:

1. Login to **https://entra.microsoft.com** and navigate to **Identity Governance** | **Entitlement management** | **Access packages**.

2. In the right pane, click on **New access package**.

3. Enter the **Name** and **Description** of the access package and select the **Catalog** you want to base the access package on. Click on **Next: Resource roles**, as shown in the following figure:

| *Basics | Resource roles | *Requests | Requestor information | *Lifecycle | Custom extensions | Review + create |

Access package
Create a collection of resources that users can request access to.

Name *	Marketing access package
Description * ⓘ	Access package for marketing users
Catalog * ⓘ	Marketing

Learn more ⧉   Create new catalog

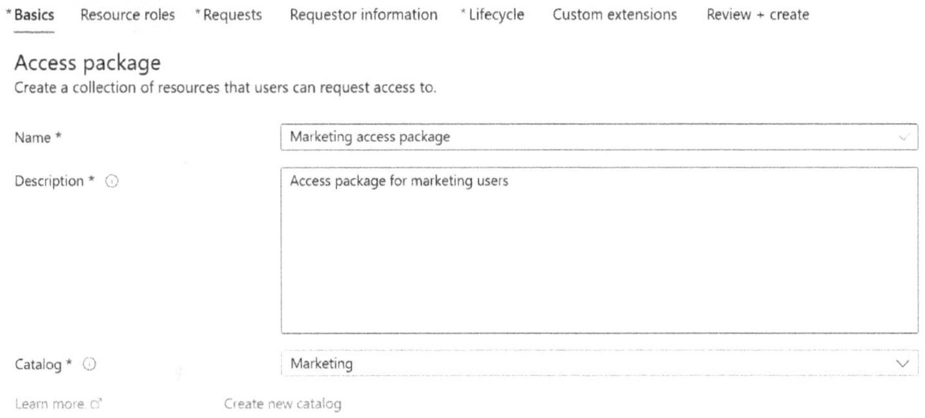

Figure 5.11: New access package

4. On the **Resource roles** page, click on each of the options to add the resources to the access package. *Figure 5.12* shows the groups and teams available to be added to the access package. Note that these are the same resources that were added to the catalog earlier. You can add all available resources or choose a few. Click on **Select** to add the resource to the access package, as shown in the following figure:

| *Basics | **Resource roles** | *Reques |

Add different resources to this access p ⧉

| + Groups and Teams | + |

Resource

ⓘ Try changing or adding filters if you don't see what you're looking for.

☐ See all Group and Team(s) not in the 'Marketing' catalog. You must have the correct permissions to add them in this access package.

Search
🔍 Search by name
2 results found

| All | Users | Groups | Devices | Enterprise applications | App registrations | Administrative units |

	Name	Type	Details
☐	Contoso Life	Group	contosolife@M365x174099.onmicrosoft.com
☐	Contoso Team	Group	contosoteam@M365x174099.onmicrosoft.com

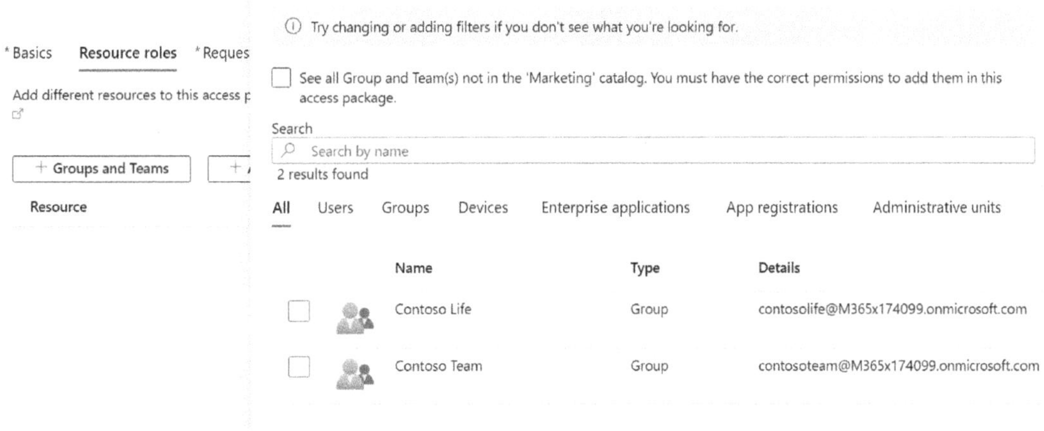

Figure 5.12: Add resources to access package

5. In the **Role** drop down menu, select the appropriate role you want to assign to the users on that resource. The roles differ by resource type. *Figure 5.13* shows an example of the available roles for a M365 group, Salesforce application and a SharePoint site. Once all roles have been selected, click **Next: Requests**, as shown in the following figure:

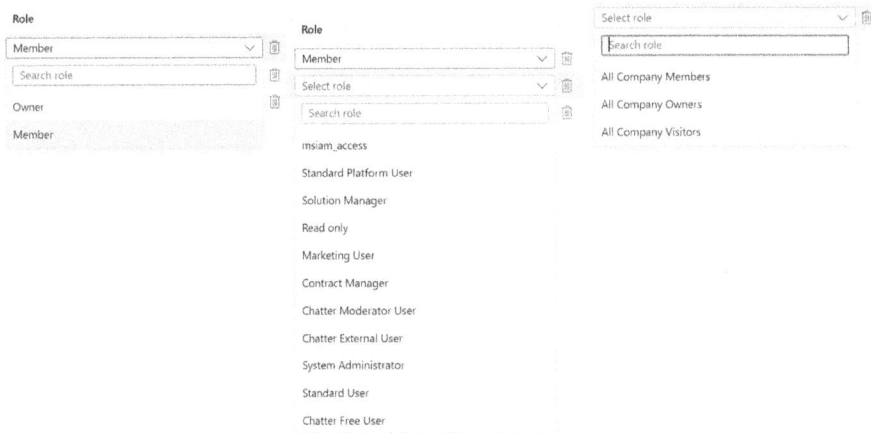

Figure 5.13: *Add roles to resources*

6. On the **Requests** page, you can select who can request this access package. Following are the available options:

  - **For users in your directory**: Review the options, as shown in the following figure:

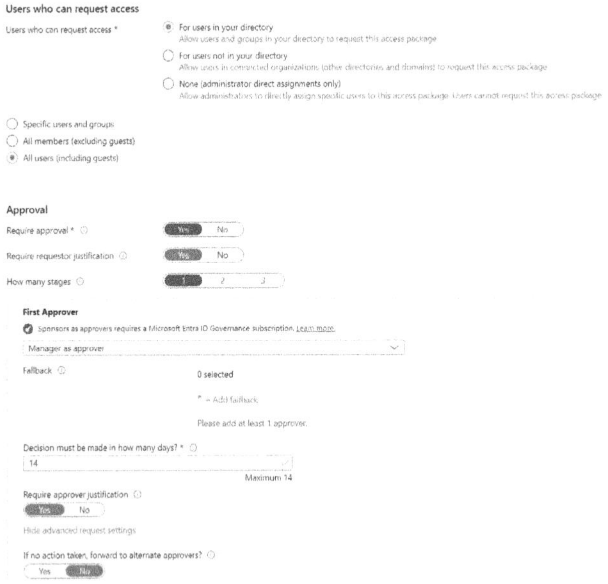

Figure 5.14: *Access package for users in your directory*

- **For users not in your directory**: This option allows users in connected organizations to request this access package. Connected organizations include only the organizations in configured state, as shown in the following figure:

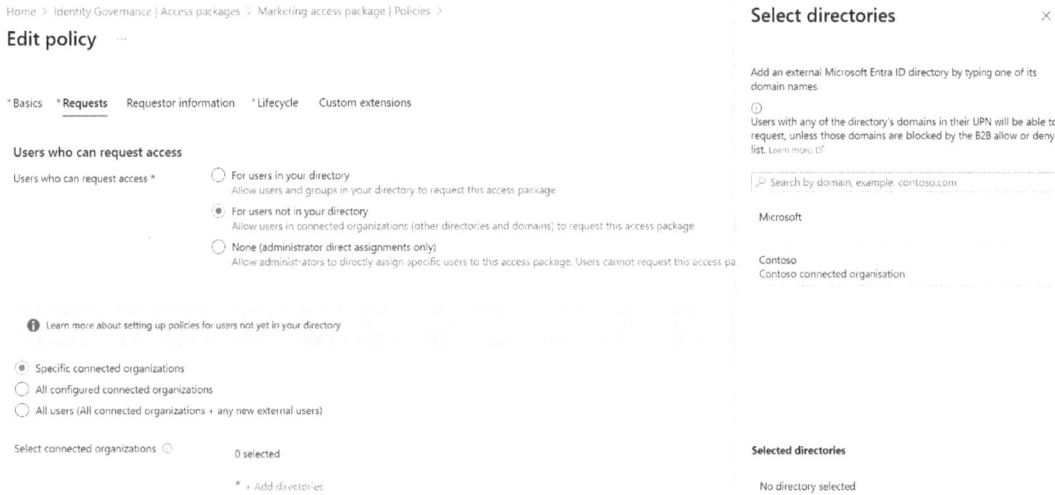

Home > Identity Governance | Access packages > Marketing access package | Policies >

Edit policy ...

*Basics   *Requests   Requestor information   *Lifecycle   Custom extensions

Users who can request access

Users who can request access *

- ○ For users in your directory
  Allow users and groups in your directory to request this access package
- ● For users not in your directory
  Allow users in connected organizations (other directories and domains) to request this access package
- ○ None (administrator direct assignments only)
  Allow administrators to directly assign specific users to this access package. Users cannot request this access pa

ⓘ Learn more about setting up policies for users not yet in your directory

- ● Specific connected organizations
- ○ All configured connected organizations
- ○ All users (All connected organizations + any new external users)

Select connected organizations ○   0 selected

* + Add directories

Select directories   ✕

Add an external Microsoft Entra ID directory by typing one of its domain names.

ⓘ
Users with any of the directory's domains in their UPN will be able to request, unless those domains are blocked by the B2B allow or deny list. Learn more ⧉'

🔍 Search by domain, example: contoso.com

Microsoft

Contoso
Contoso connected organisation

Selected directories

No directory selected

Figure 5.15: Access package for guests

- **None**: Selecting this option makes the access package unavailable for requests and only administrators can directly assign it to users.

7. Ensure that the toggle is **Yes** for **Enable new request**. If it is set to **No,** new requests to this access package cannot be made. Click, **Next: Requestor information**.

8. Use the **Requestor information** page to collect more information about the requestor. This page can be configured to ask the requestor questions which will be shown on the request form. Review the option and click on **Next: Lifecycle**, as shown in the following figure:

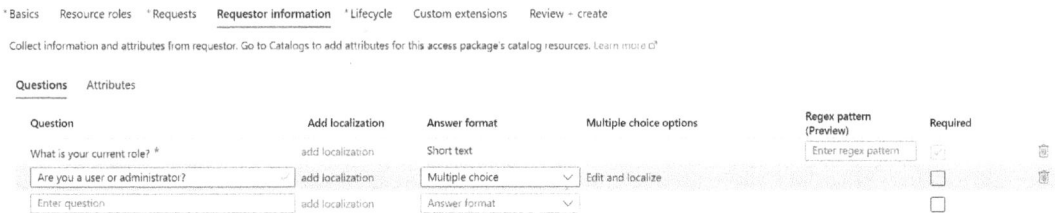

*Basics   Resource roles   *Requests   **Requestor information**   *Lifecycle   Custom extensions   Review + create

Collect information and attributes from requestor. Go to Catalogs to add attributes for this access package's catalog resources. Learn more ⧉'

Questions   Attributes

Question	Add localization	Answer format	Multiple choice options	Regex pattern (Preview)	Required	
What is your current role? *	add localization	Short text		Enter regex pattern	☑	🗑
Are you a user or administrator?	add localization	Multiple choice ∨	Edit and localize		☐	🗑
Enter question	add localization	Answer format ∨			☐	

Figure 5.16: Collecting requestor information

9. On the **Lifecycle** page, you can choose if and when the access package expires and if access reviews are required for this access package. Review the options and click **Next: Rules**, as shown in the following figure:

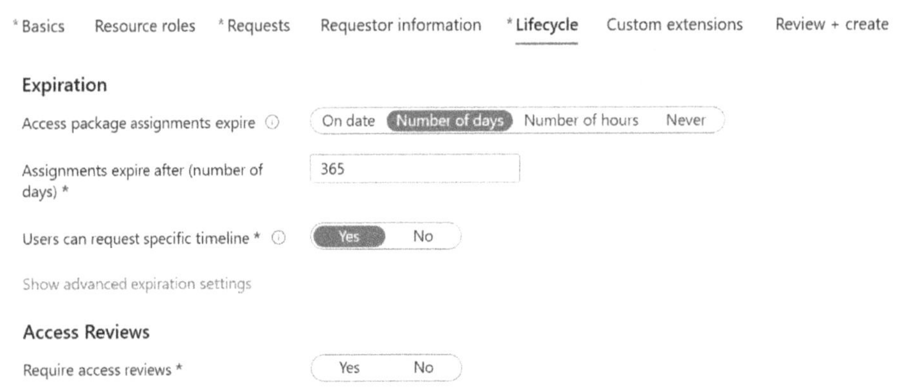

Figure 5.17: Access package lifecycle

10. Skip the **Custom extensions** step, and click on **Next: Review + create**. On the **Review + create** page, review the selected settings and click on **Create**.

11. Once the access package is created, the **My access portal link** will be displayed. This is the link the users will use to request this access package. Copy this link and provide it to the users, as shown in the following figure:

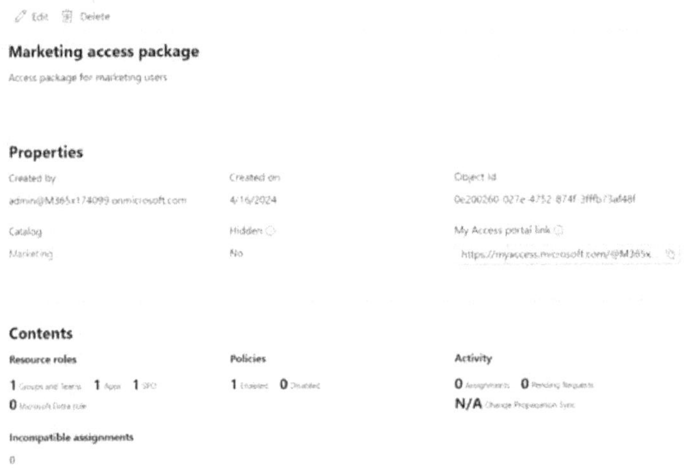

Figure 5.18: My access portal link

Request access

Internal user is the required role.

As an end user, following are the steps to request access to the Marketing access package:

1. Open a new browser window and go to the My Access portal link copied in the previous step. Enter your Microsoft Entra ID credentials.

2. You should see the **Marketing access package** pop up on the screen. You can view the details of the access package. Select the **Resources** tab to see the resources that access packages give access to. Click **Continue**, as shown in the following figure:

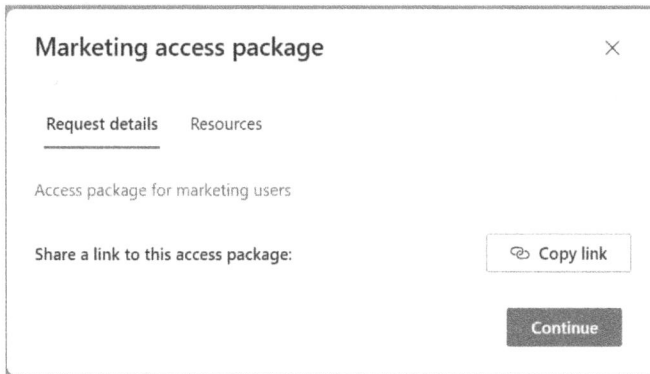

Figure 5.19: Access package on My Access page

3. You will now see the questions configured while creating the access package. Answer the questions and click on **Submit request**, as shown in the following figure:

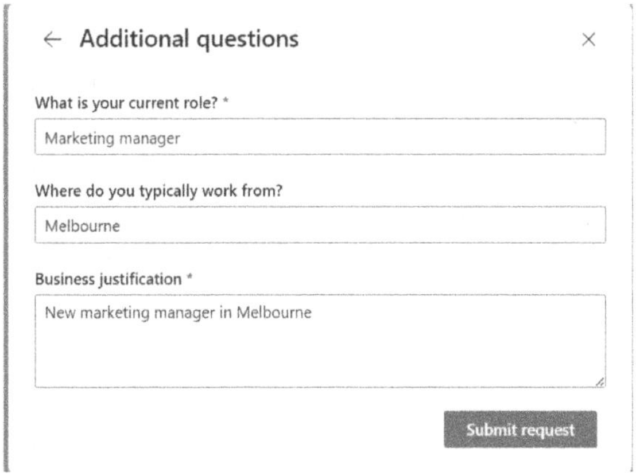

Figure 5.20: Additional questions while requesting access package

Approve access

Access package approver is the required role.

If the access package is subject to manual approvals, the access request will have to be approved before it is delivered to the end user. As the access package login to **https://myaccess.microsoft.com**. In the left pane, click on **Approvals**. The right pane will display all the pending access requests. Click on **Review** to review the inputs made by the user. Click on **Approve** or **Deny**. Enter a reason for your decision and click on **Submit**, as shown in the following figure:

Figure 5.21: Approve or deny access requests

Validate that worked

Identity Governance Administrator or Global Administrator or catalog owner or access package manager or access package assignment manager is the required role.

Following are the steps to ensure that the access package was delivered to the requestor:

1. Login to **https://entra.microsoft.com** and navigate to **Identity | Identity governance | Entitlement management**.

2. Click on **Access packages**. Select the appropriate access package and click on **Requests**.

3. In the right pane, ensure that the **Status** column displays **Delivered**, as shown in the following figure:

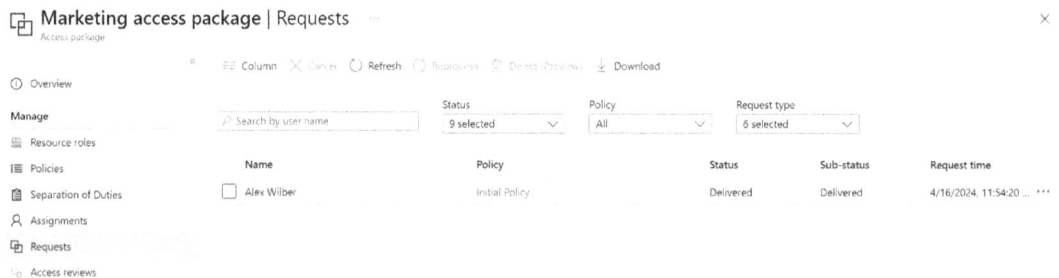

Figure 5.22: Access package delivered

Manually assigning an access package

Identity Governance Administrator or Global Administrator or catalog owner or access package manager or access package assignment manager is the required role.

If the access package has been created with the option **None (administrator direct assignment only)** administrators will have to manually assign the access package to users.

Following are the steps to manually assign an access package:

1. Login to **https://entra.microsoft.com** and navigate to **Identity | Identity governance | Entitlement management**.

2. Click on **Access packages** and select the access package to which you want to assign users.

3. Click on **Assignments**.

4. Click on **New assignment**. Fill in the required details and click on **Add,** as shown in the following figure:

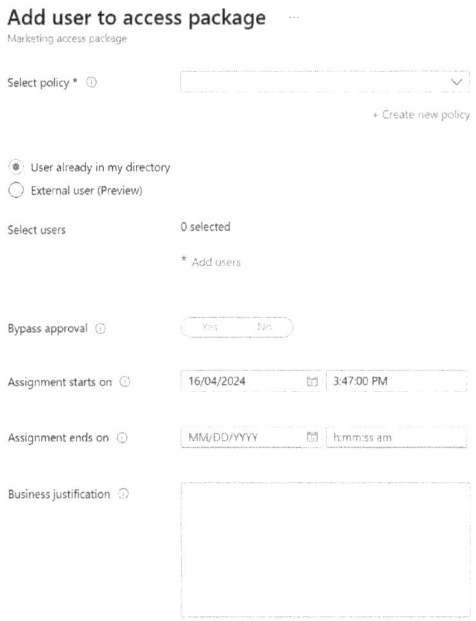

Figure 5.23: Manually add users to access package

Auto assigning users to an access package

Global Administrator or Identity Governance Administrator is the required role.

In some situations, you might want to automatically add users to access packages based on their Microsoft Entra ID attributes. For example, you might want to add all users in the marketing department to the Marketing access package.

Following are the steps to auto-assign an access package based on user attributes:

1. Login to **https://entra.microsoft.com** and navigate to **Identity | Identity governance | Entitlement management**.

2. Click on **Access packages** and select the access package to which you want to assign users.

3. Click on **Policies**.

4. Click on **Add auto assignment policy**.

5. In the **Configure Rules** page click on **Edit**. Select the user property from the **Property** drop down and select the appropriate **Operator**. In the **Value** box type in the value of the user property. See example below. Click **Save** to save the rule.

6. The boxes to **Automatically create assignments** and **Automatically remove assignments** are already checked. Doing this ensures that the users are automatically added and removed from the access package as their configured Microsoft Entra ID attributes change. For example, when a new user joins the Marketing department, they will be automatically added to this access package based on their Entra ID user attribute. Now, if the user moves from Marketing to Sales and their Entra ID user attribute is updated they will be automatically removed from this access package and lose access to all resources that this access package grants access to. You can also configure a grace period to retain user access to this access package for a pre-defined period once they go out of scope. Click on **Next**, as shown in the following figure:

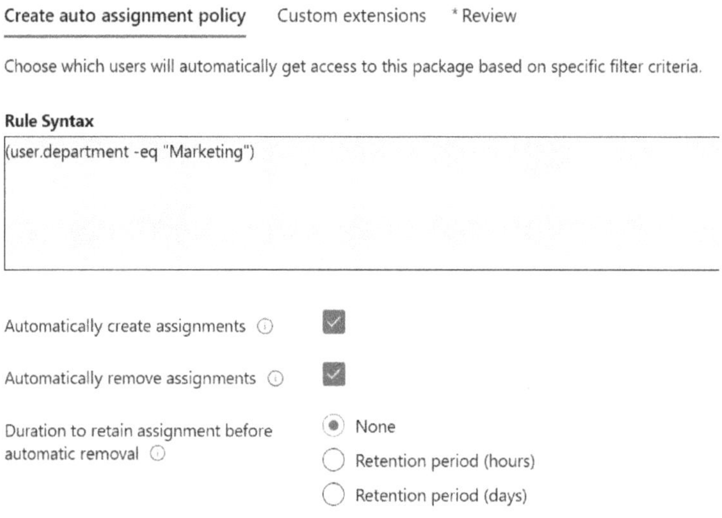

Create auto assignment policy   Custom extensions   * Review

Choose which users will automatically get access to this package based on specific filter criteria.

Rule Syntax

(user.department -eq "Marketing")

Automatically create assignments ⓘ   ☑

Automatically remove assignments ⓘ   ☑

Duration to retain assignment before automatic removal ⓘ
- ● None
- ○ Retention period (hours)
- ○ Retention period (days)

Figure 5.24: Create a dynamic rule

7. Skip the **Custom extensions** page, and click on **Next**.

8. On the **Review** page, type in **Name** and **Description** and click **Create**.

Licensing requirements

Entitlement management has the following licensing requirements.

- A Microsoft Entra ID Governance license.
- Each user that can request an access package must have a license assigned.
- Identity Governance Administrators do not need a license.
- A license is required for each auto-assignment policy.

Access reviews

Using Microsoft Entra ID users in the organization can collaborate with other internal users and with external guests. The self-service capabilities in Microsoft Entra ID makes it easy for internal users and external guests to request and receive access to resources. However, this poses a new challenge, users may have access to resources for longer than required or have more access than required to do their job. Checks and balances should be in place to ensure that users need continued access to the resources. Using access reviews organizations can review users access to Security and M365 groups, Applications, access packages, Microsoft Entra and Azure resource roles. Some scenarios where access reviews could be used are as follows:

- There are too many users in privileged roles.
- Automation is not possible. For example, HR data cannot be synchronized with Microsoft Entra ID.
- If you want to repurpose a group for a different use.
- When users have access to business-critical data or applications you might want to periodically review access to ensure their job role still requires them to access that data or application.

Following are some key features of access reviews:

- They can be ad-hoc or scheduled.
- They can be delegated to non-IT administrators or business owners.
- Users can self-attest their access or reviewers can be designated.
- Insights can be used to decide whether a user's access should be continued or discontinued.
- Outcomes such as continuing or removing access can be automated.
- They can be tracked for compliance or policy reasons.

Figure 5.25 shows the access review workflow:

Figure 5.25: Access review workflow

Multi-stage reviews

Access reviews support up to three review stages. This enables multiple approvers to review access to resources before a decision is made. This helps organizations meet certification and audit requirements, design more efficient reviews and reduce the number of decisions each reviewer is responsible for.

Multi-stage reviews help meet the following use cases:

- **Reach consensus across multiple reviewers**: This might be useful when access to highly critical resources is being reviewed or when there is a diverse set of reviewees, and it is hard for a single reviewer to make the decision.

- **Get input on unreviewed decisions**: If the first stage approvers are not able to decide, second stage and third stage reviewers can help.

- **Reduce burden on later-stage reviewers**: Reviews can be configured in such a way that if a deny decision is made at an earlier stage, those users are not reviewed at the later stages. This way the subsequent stage approvers see a filtered down list.

The options available while configuring multi-stage review are as follows:

- **Reviewers**: Group owners, selected users or groups, users themselves or managers of users can be configured as reviewers. For group owners and managers of reviewers, fallback reviewers can be configured. These will be used if primary reviewers do not exist.

- **Stage duration**: This specifies the number of days within which reviewers at each stage must respond to the review request.

- **Review results**: Reveal or hide the decision taken by earlier stage reviewers by selecting or unselecting **Show previous stage(s) decision to later stage reviewers** check box.

- **Review recurrence**: Specify if the access review is one time or recurring. The available options are **One time**, **Weekly**, **Monthly**, **Quarterly**, **Semi-annually**, **Annually**. If you choose a recurring review, you can specify start date and end options like **Never**, **End on specific date** or **End after number of occurrences**.

- **Reviewees for next stage**: Decide if you want to send all or only a subset of reviewees to the next stage. The available options are **All**, **Approved reviewees**, **denied reviewees**, **Not reviewed reviewees**, **Reviewees marked as Don't know**.

Refer to the following figure:

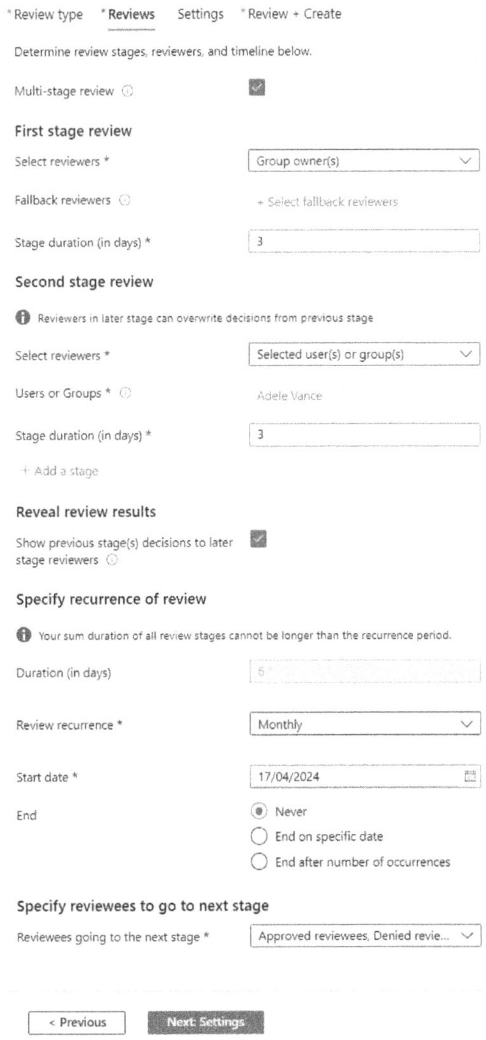

Figure 5.26: Configuring multi-stage review

Guest user reviews

Guest user reviews help organizations that use B2B collaboration. Guest access should be reviewed regularly to ensure that they still need access to the resources. When access reviews are configured with scope **Guest users only** an additional setting is available that allows is as follows:

- Removing guest user access from the resource.
- Blocking the guest user access for 30 days and then removing the user from the tenant.

Note: This option is not available if the review scope is All Microsoft 365 groups with guest users.

Refer to the following figure:

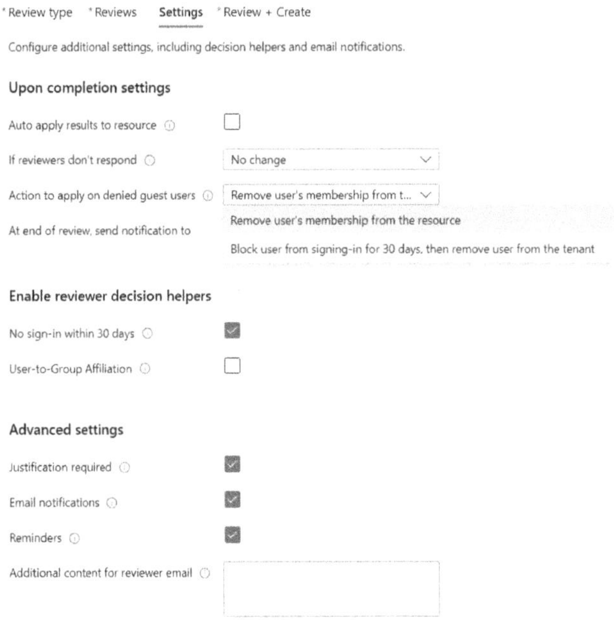

Figure 5.27: Review guest user access

Now, let us explore how access reviews are created and managed for each of the resources listed above.

Groups and applications

To be able to perform access reviews on applications they must be integrated with Microsoft Entra ID and be listed on the Microsoft Entra admin portal under **Identity** | **Applications** | **Enterprise applications**. To ensure that a listed application is ready for access review click on the application and switch to the **Properties** page for that application. The **Assignment required?** toggle must be set to **Yes**. If it is set to **No** users can access the application but access reviews cannot be performed, as shown in the following figure:

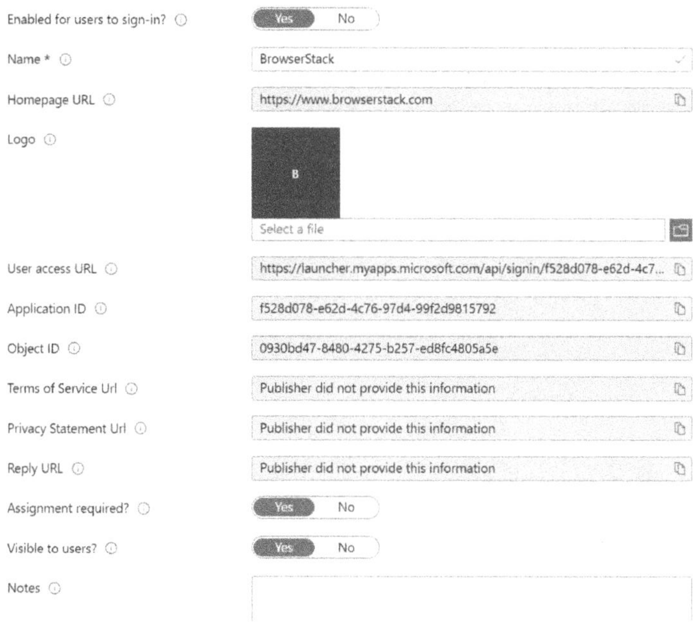

Figure 5.28: Prepare application for access review

Access reviews can be performed on groups created directly in Microsoft Entra ID. While access reviews can be scheduled and maintained for groups synchronized from AD, group membership cannot be changed as the source of authority for these groups is AD. To bypass this limitation, use **Group Writeback** or use a custom script to apply the results to AD. Dynamic groups and role-assignable groups cannot be included in access reviews.

Creating access review

Global administrator or Identity Governance administrator is the required role.

Following are the steps to create an access review for groups and applications:

1. Login to **https://entra.microsoft.com** and navigate to **Identity | Identity Governance | Access reviews**.

2. In the right pane, click on **New access review**.

3. In the **Select what to review**, select the appropriate option. If you choose the following:

   a. `Teams + Groups` you have the option to select.

      i. **All Microsoft 365 groups with guest users**. You can choose to exclude some groups from the scope of the access review. The **Scope** will be automatically selected as **Guest users only**. You have the option to perform the access review on only inactive guest users by checking the box **Inactive users**. You can specify the number of days of inactivity.

Refer to *Figure 5.29*:

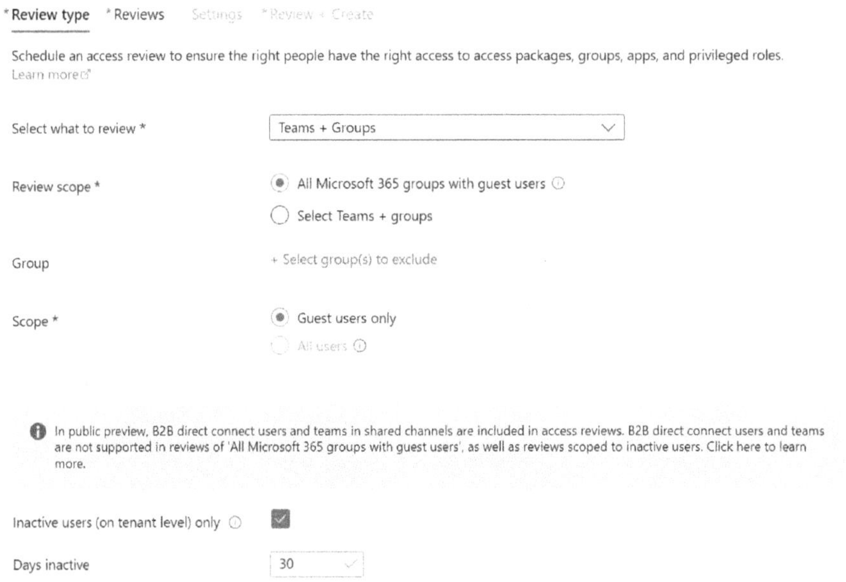

Figure 5.29: Access review for guest users

ii. **Select Teams + groups**. You can select the team and groups you want to perform the access review on. Review the options, as shown in the following figure:

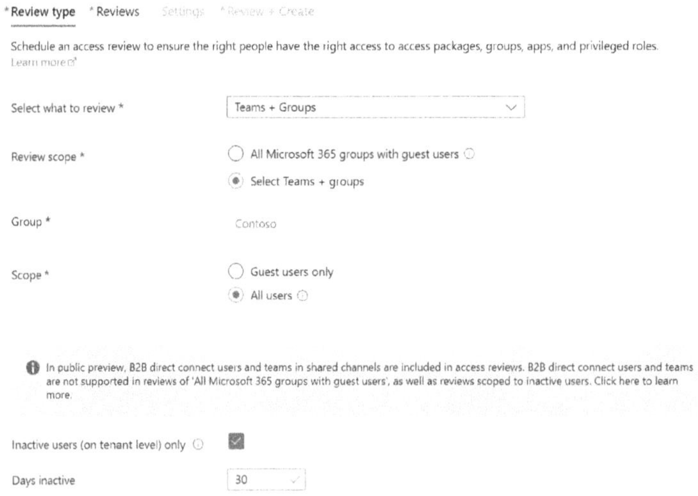

Figure 5.30: Access review for teams and groups

b. **Applications**. Choose the applications for access review and choose if you want to review access only for guest users or all users. Click on **Next: Reviews**, as shown in the following figure:

* **Review type**   * Reviews   Settings   * Review + Create

Schedule an access review to ensure the right people have the right access to access packages, groups, apps, and privileged roles.
Learn more⧉

Select what to review *	Applications ⌄
Application *	BrowserStack
Scope *	⦿ Guest users only ◯ All users ⓘ

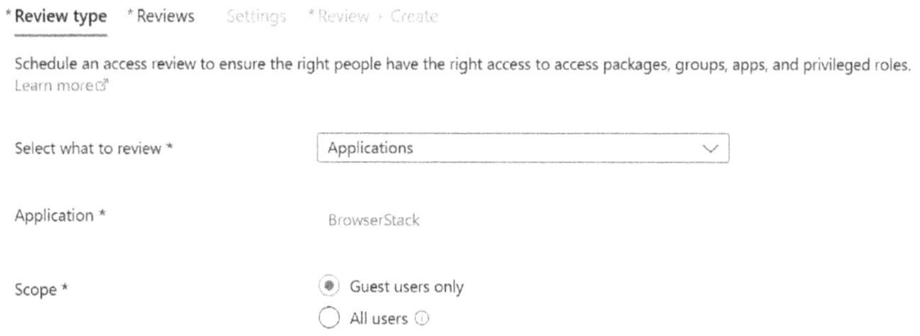

Figure 5.31: Access review for applications

4. On the **Reviews** page, choose if you want to configure a **multi-stage review**. The various options are explained in the section on multi-stage reviews. Refer to *Figure 5.26*. Click on **Next: Settings**.

5. On the **Settings** page select the appropriate options. The key ones are explained, as follows:

   a. **Auto apply results to resource** will automatically apply the decision of the access review to the resource. For example, if the user's access to is denied their access to the resource will be revoked once the review is completed.

   b. **If reviewers don't respond**, it specifies the action that will be taken if the reviewers do not respond. The available options are **No change**, **Remove access**, **Approve access**, **Take recommendations**.

   c. **Enable reviewer decision helpers** will give insights to reviewers, if there has been no sign-in in the last 30 days and highlight users who have low affiliation with other users within the group.

   d. If you chose the scope as **Guest users only**, two additional options are available. These are explained in the *Guest user reviews* section above.

6. Review the other settings on the page below and click on **Next: Review + Create**, as shown in the following figure:

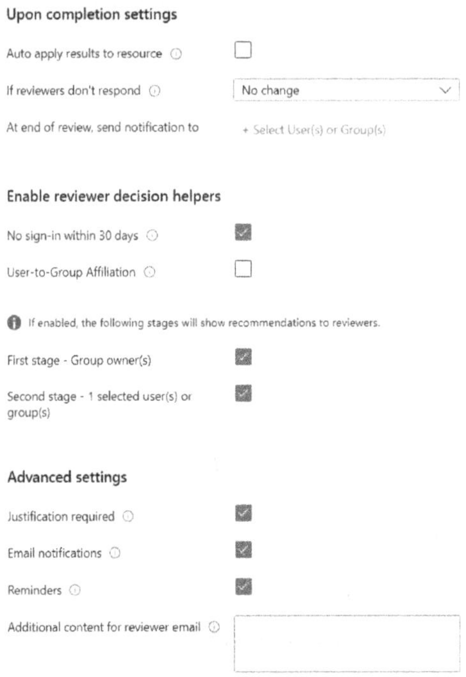

Upon completion settings

Auto apply results to resource ⓘ ☐

If reviewers don't respond ⓘ | No change ⌄ |

At end of review, send notification to + Select User(s) or Group(s)

Enable reviewer decision helpers

No sign-in within 30 days ⓘ ☑

User-to-Group Affiliation ⓘ ☐

ⓘ If enabled, the following stages will show recommendations to reviewers.

First stage - Group owner(s) ☑

Second stage - 1 selected user(s) or group(s) ☑

Advanced settings

Justification required ⓘ ☑

Email notifications ⓘ ☑

Reminders ⓘ ☑

Additional content for reviewer email ⓘ | |

Figure 5.32: Upon completion settings

7. On the **Review + Create** page, add a **Review name** and click on **Create**.

Review access

Access reviewer is the required role.

If email notifications have been configured, the access reviewer will receive an email asking them to start the review. They can click on **Start review** in the email or directly go to the My Access portal. From there, following are the steps:

1. Ensure that you are on the **Access reviews** page on **https://myaccess.microsoft. com**. The right pane will show the access reviews, as shown in the following figure:

Access reviews

1 review

Groups and Apps	Access packages

Name	Due	Resource	Progress
Review Contoso	Apr 20, 2024	Contoso	0 / 23

Figure 5.33: Access reviews on My Access portal

2. Click on the access review name to view a list of users. Click on **Details** to view the available options. You can see the recommendation is to deny user access as the user has not signed into the tenant in the last 30 days. Review the other available options. Click on **Submit** once done. You can select multiple users and click on **Approve, Deny** or **Don't know** to take bulk actions. You can also click on **Accept recommendations** to accept the recommendations provided by access review, as shown in the following figure:

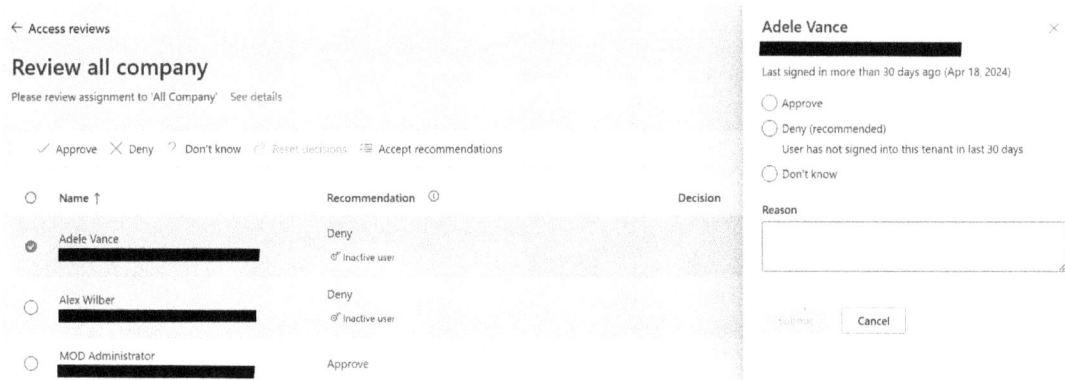

Figure 5.34: View user details

If you are the second or third stage reviewer, you will also see the decisions made by the earlier stage approvers, if the administrator has enabled that setting while creating the access review.

Access packages

You can create access reviews for an access package at the time of creation or by editing an existing access package assignment policy.

Creating access review

Global administrator or Identity Governance administrator or catalog owner or access package manager is the required role.

To create an access review for an access package at the time of creation, follow the steps in the section *Create an access review.* On the **Lifecycle** page, switch the **Require access reviews** toggle to **Yes**. Review the available options, as shown in the following figure:

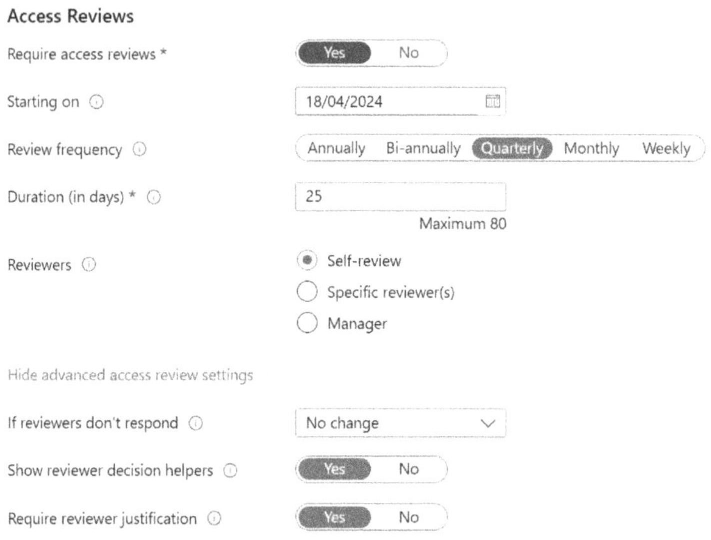

Access Reviews

Require access reviews *	**Yes** No
Starting on ⓘ	18/04/2024 📅
Review frequency ⓘ	Annually Bi-annually **Quarterly** Monthly Weekly
Duration (in days) * ⓘ	25
	Maximum 80
Reviewers ⓘ	● Self-review
	○ Specific reviewer(s)
	○ Manager

Hide advanced access review settings

If reviewers don't respond ⓘ	No change ⌄
Show reviewer decision helpers ⓘ	**Yes** No
Require reviewer justification ⓘ	**Yes** No

Figure 5.35: Access review for access package

To add an access review to an already created access package, following are the steps:

1. In the Microsoft Entra admin center, navigate to **Identity** | **Identity Governance** | **Entitlement management** | **Access package**. Select the access package from the right pane and select **Policies**.

2. From the list of policies, select the policy to which you want to add the access review. Click on the ellipses and select **Edit**.

3. In the policy, navigate to the **Lifecycle** page and add the access review.

Review access

Like reviewing access for groups and applications, access for access packages is also reviewed from the My Access portal. Once you login to the My Access portal as an access reviewer navigate to **Access reviews** and in the right pane click on **Access packages**. Refer to *Figure 5.33*. All access reviews for access packages where you are listed as reviewer will be displayed. Follow the steps described in the previous section to complete the access reviews.

Microsoft Entra roles and Azure resource roles

Following are the required roles:

*   **For Microsoft Entra roles**: Global Administrator or Privileged Role Administrator.

*   **For Azure resource roles**: Resource Owner or User Access Administrator.

Creating an access review

To configure access reviews for Microsoft Entra roles, following are the steps:

1. Login to **https://entra.microsoft.com** and navigate to **Identity Governance** | **Privileged Identity Management**. In the right pane, select either **Microsoft Entra roles** or **Azure resources** and then, click on **Access reviews**.

2. At the top, click **New**. Review the options on the below page and make the appropriate settings, as shown in the following figure:

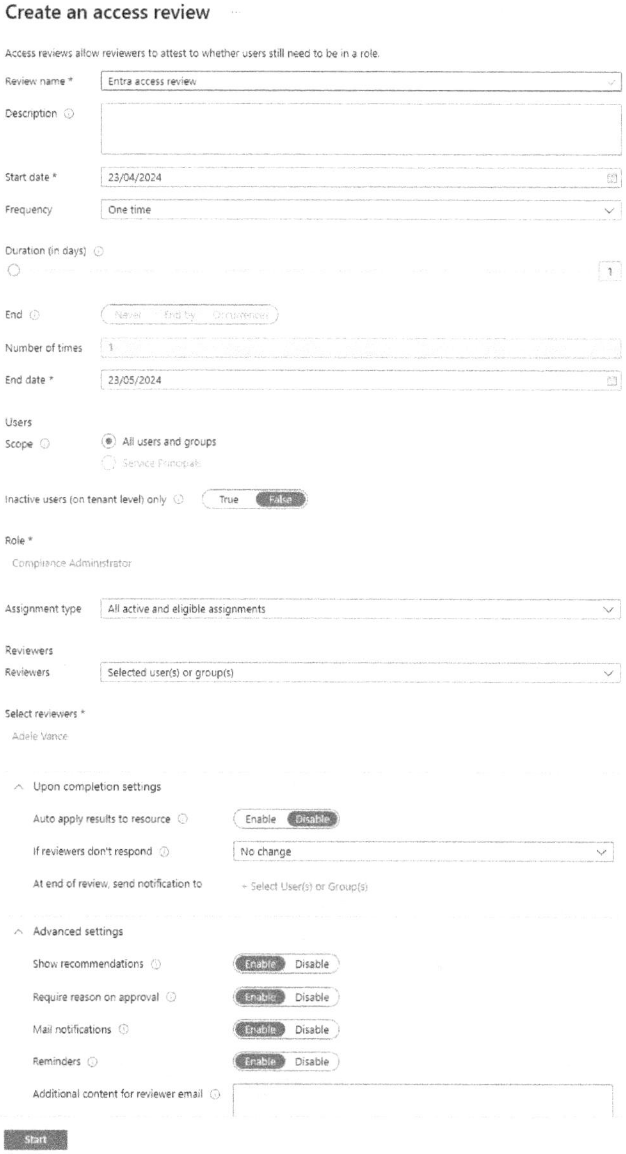

Figure 5.36: Access review for Entra roles

3. Click on **Start**.

Review access

If communications are configured, the reviewer might get an email that an access review has been initiated. To review access, the reviewer can either click on the link in the email or to the Microsoft Entra admin center directly.

Following are the steps:

1. Login to **https://entra.microsoft.com** and navigate to **Identity Governance | Privileged Identity Management | Review access**.

2. The right pane will show the available access reviews. Click on the name of the access review. The next page will show the user accounts whose access needs to be reviewed. Select the user to **Approve** or **Deny** access, as shown in the following figure:

Figure 5.37: Review access for Entra roles

License requirements

Access reviews have the following licensing requirements:

- Microsoft Entra ID Governance license.
- All users who are reviewing access or having their access reviewed must have a license.

Privileged Identity Management

Microsoft Entra PIM is a service that enables organizations to manage, control and monitor access to important resources like Microsoft Entra ID and Azure. PIM provides time-based and approval-based role activation that minimizes the risk of excessive, unnecessary or misused access permissions on resources.

Following are some key features of PIM:

- It provides just-in-time access to Microsoft Entra ID and Azure resources.
- It provides time-bound access to resources.
- It can require approval to activate privileged roles.
- It can enforce MFA to activate privileged roles.
- It can ask for justification to activate the privileged role.
- Access reviews can be conducted to ensure users still need the roles.

PIM can be used with the following:

- **Microsoft Entra roles**: It includes built-in and custom roles.
- **Azure resource roles**: These include built-in and custom roles that grant access to management groups, subscriptions, resources groups and resources in Azure.
- **Groups**: Using PIM just-in-time access can be set up to assign users as members or owners of a Microsoft Entra security group.

Using PIM, **Users** and **Groups** can be assigned to any of the above.

There are two types of assignments. *Table 5.2* summarizes the assignment options available in PIM:

Type	Description
Permanent eligible	The user account is always eligible to activate the role
Permanent active	The user account is a permanent member of the role
Time-bound eligible	The user account is eligible to activate the role for a specified time duration
Time-bound active	The user account is member of a role for a specified duration.

Table 5.2: Types of assignments in PIM

Note: It is recommended having zero permanently active members for roles other than two break-glass accounts that Global Administrators. A role cannot be assigned for a duration of less than five minutes and the assignment cannot be removed within five minutes of being assigned.

PIM for Microsoft Entra roles

Enabling PIM for Microsoft Entra roles has a few steps. Following are the steps:

Prepare the role for PIM

Global Administrator or Privileged Role Administrator is the required role.

In preparation to use PIM for Microsoft Entra roles, it is recommended that the roles be prepared for PIM. This is done by configuring role settings.

Following are the steps to configure role settings:

1. Login to **https://entra.microsoft.com** and navigate to **Identity Governance** | **Privileged Identity Management** | **Microsoft Entra roles** | **Roles**. The right pane will display all roles available in Microsoft Entra ID that can be configured with PIM.

2. Select a role and click on **Role settings**. Click on **Edit** to make the changes. Review the options, as shown in the following figure:

Note: For detailed explanation on each of the options refer to the Microsoft online documentation.

{⚙} **Exchange Administrator** | Role settings
Privileged Identity Management | Microsoft Entra roles

🖉 Edit

Manage

▫ Assignments

▫ Description

⚙ Role settings

Activation

Setting	State
Activation maximum duration (hours)	8 hour(s)
On activation, require	Azure MFA
Require justification on activation	Yes
Require ticket information on activation	No
Require approval to activate	No
Approvers	None

Assignment

Setting	State
Allow permanent eligible assignment	Yes
Expire eligible assignments after	-
Allow permanent active assignment	Yes
Expire active assignments after	-
Require Azure Multi-Factor Authentication on active assignment	No
Require justification on active assignment	Yes

Send notifications when members are assigned as eligible to this role:

Type	Default recipients	Additional recipients	Critical emails only
Role assignment alert	Admin	None	False
Notification to the assigned user (assignee)	Assignee	None	False
Request to approve a role assignment renewal/extension	Approver	None	False

Send notifications when members are assigned as active to this role:

Type	Default recipients	Additional recipients	Critical emails only
Role assignment alert	Admin	None	False
Notification to the assigned user (assignee)	Assignee	None	False
Request to approve a role assignment renewal/extension	Approver	None	False

Send notifications when eligible members activate this role:

Type	Default recipients	Additional recipients	Critical emails only
Role activation alert	Admin	None	False
Notification to activated user (requestor)	Requestor	None	False
Request to approve an activation	Approver	None	False

Figure 5.38: Role settings

Assigning role

Global Administrator or Privileged Role Administrator is the required role.

Following are the steps to assign a role:

1. In the Microsoft Entra admin center, navigate to the **Roles** page as described in previous step.

2. Select the role for which assignments need to be added and click on **Add assignments** at the top.

3. On the **Membership** page, click on **No member selected** to select members. In the fly out pane select the users you want to add to the role and click on **Select**. On the next screen, click on **Next**, as shown in the following figure:

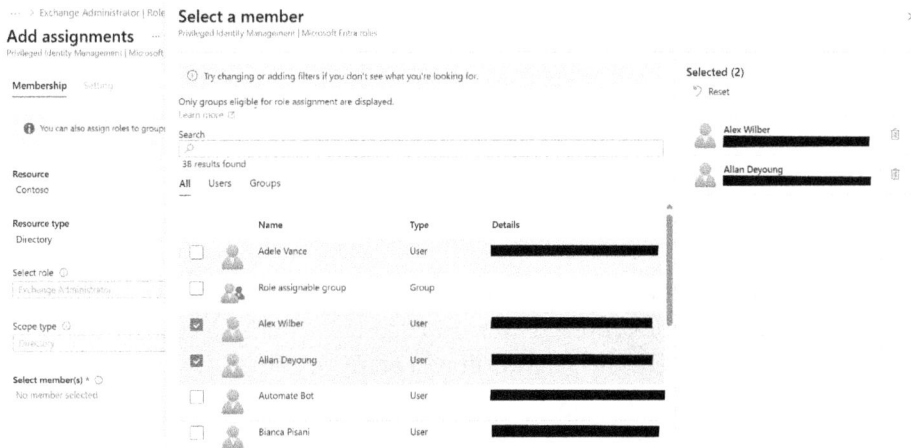

Figure 5.39: Add users to role

4. On the **Settings** page, select if the assignment type is **Eligible** or **Active**. Unchecking the **Permanently eligible** box will make the role time-bound, and a start and end date can be selected. Click on **Assign**, as shown in the following figure:

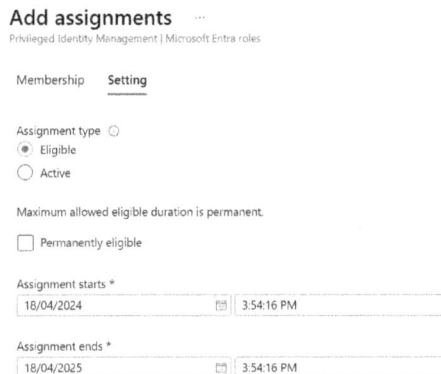

Figure 5.40: Role assignment settings

Activating role

An eligible user is the required role. If a user has been assigned an Active role assignment, they are added to the role group with no further action from their end. However, if they were made Eligible for the role, they will have to activate the role before they can perform privileged actions.

Following are the steps to activate a role:

1. In the Microsoft Entra admin center, navigate to **Identity Governance** | **Privileged Identity Management** | **My roles**. The right pane will list all the **Eligible assignments,** as shown in the following figure:

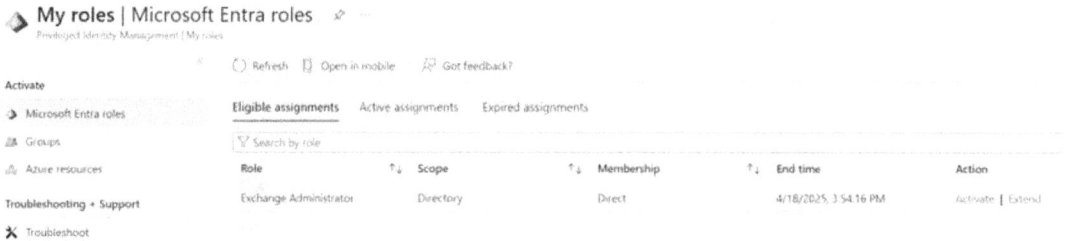

Figure 5.41: Eligible assignments

2. Click on **Activate**. In the fly out pane, enter an activation duration, provide a reason for activation and click on **Activate**. You can also choose a custom activation start time. If this is selected, the activation will start from that time.

   The role will be activated on 18th April 2024 at 4:30PM and will be active for two hours, as shown in the following figure:

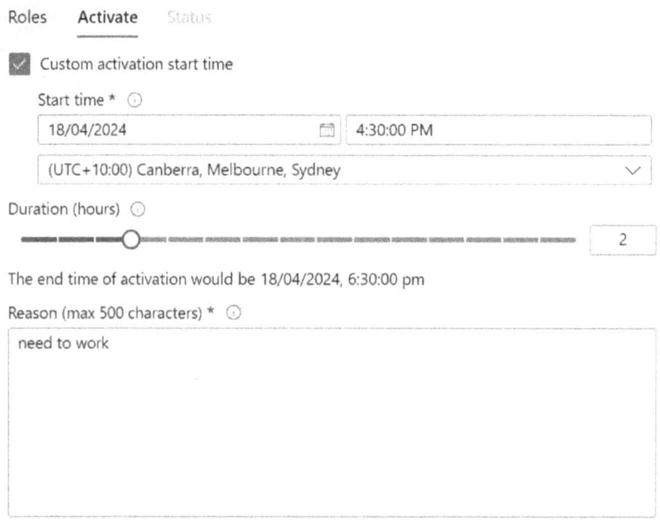

Figure 5.42: Activate the role

Note: When a role is activated, PIM creates active assignments (adds user to the role) within seconds. When the activation expires, either due to expiry of time or due to manual deactivation, PIM removes the active assignment (remove user from the role) within seconds.

Approve assignment

Designated approver is the required roles.

Following are the steps to approve an assignment:

1. If role settings required that the activation request be approved, it would be sent to an approver before activation. To approve PIM requests login to **https://entra.microsoft.com** and navigate to **Identity Governance | Privileged Identity Management | Approve requests**. Under **Request for role activations** review each request and click on **Approve** or **Deny**, as shown in the following figure:

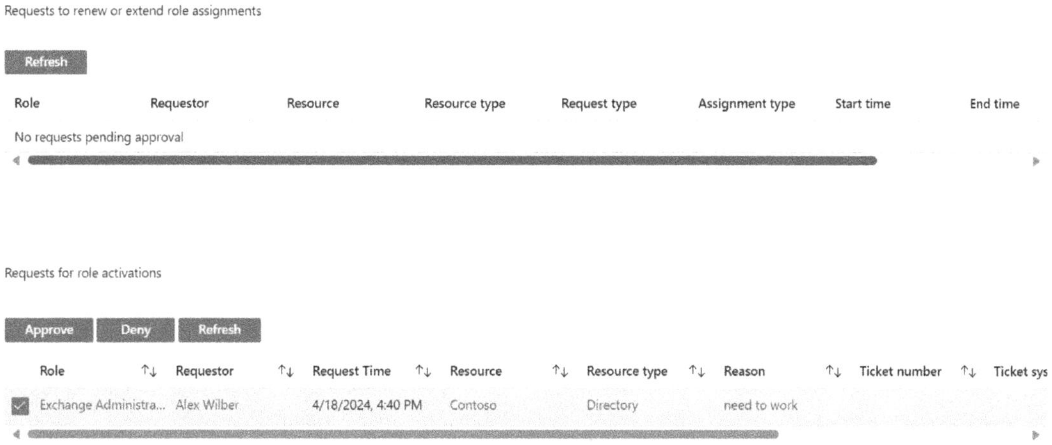

Requests to renew or extend role assignments

Refresh							
Role	Requestor	Resource	Resource type	Request type	Assignment type	Start time	End time
No requests pending approval							

Requests for role activations

Approve	Deny	Refresh								
Role	↑↓	Requestor	↑↓	Request Time	↑↓	Resource	↑↓	Resource type	↑↓	Reason	↑↓	Ticket number	↑↓	Ticket sys
✓ Exchange Administra...	Alex Wilber		4/18/2024, 4:40 PM	Contoso		Directory		need to work		

Figure 5.43: Approve requests

Extend assignment

Both active and eligible assignments become eligible for extension 14 days prior to expiry. In the above example, the assignment for the Exchange Administrator is set to expire on 18th April 2025. Refer to *Figure 5.41*. On 4th April 2025, this assignment will become eligible for extension and the **Extend** link will be activated. To request an assignment, the user can click on the **Extend** link and enter a justification for the extension request. The administrator will approve or reject the extension request from the **Approve requests** page of the portal as shown in *Figure 5.43*.

Administrators can also extend the request without the user having to request an extension. This can be done from the **Assignments** page of the selected role.

PIM for Azure resource roles

Using PIM, you can provide just-in-time access to Azure resources.

Select Azure resources

Administrators require the Microsoft.Authorization/roleAssignments/write permissions to the Azure resources. **User Access Administrator** and **Owner** roles have this permission is the required role.

Following are the steps to look for the Azure resources you want to manage using PIM:

1. Login to **https://entra.microsoft.com** and navigate to **Identity Governance | Privileged Identity Management | Azure resources**.

2. You can search at **Management groups** level, **Subscriptions level**, **Resource groups** level or **Resources** level. Make the appropriate selections and click on Manage resources. The resource group Purview is being chosen for management as shown in the following figure:

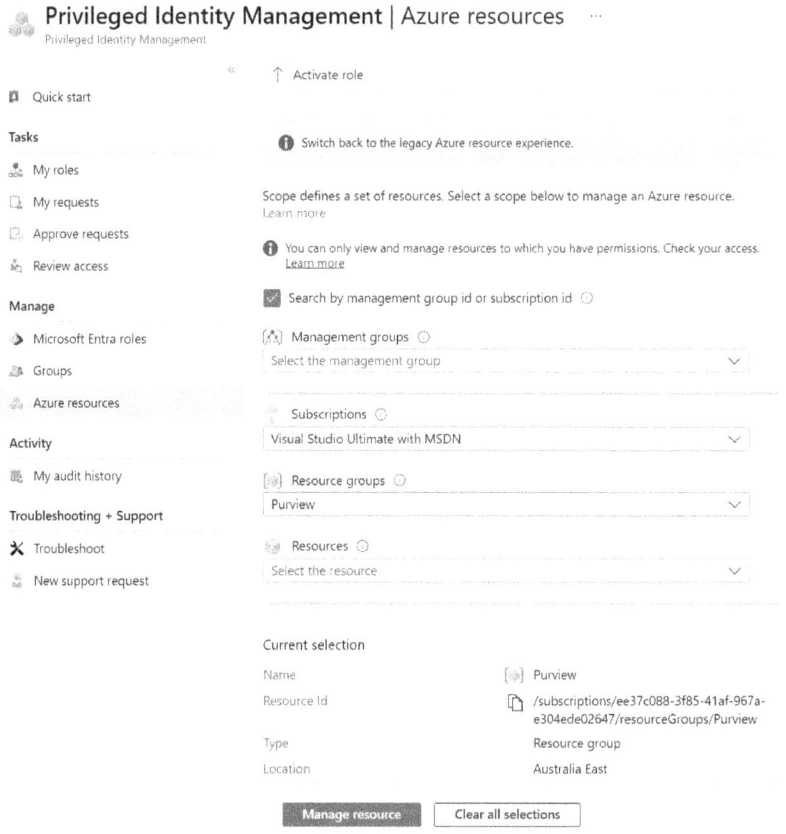

Figure 5.44: Discover Azure resources

3. The next screen will display a summary of PIM activity on the selected Azure resource. *Figure 5.45* shows a summary of PIM activity on the **Purview** Resource group:

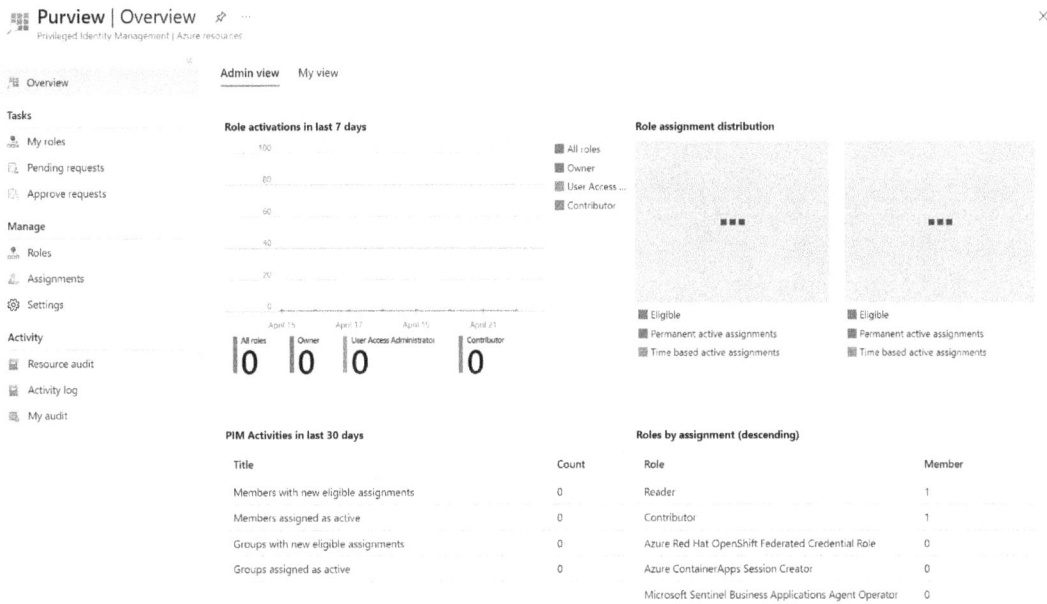

Figure 5.45: PIM activity

Preparing role for PIM

Similar to preparing a Microsoft Entra role for PIM, you can also prepare an Azure role for PIM.

Following are the steps:

1. As shown in *Figure 5.45*, click on **Settings**.
2. The screen will list all the available roles. Select the role you want to prepare and make the appropriate changes by clicking on **Edit**.

Assigning role

User Access Administrator or Owner or Global Administrator is the required role.

Following are the steps to assign a role:

1. As shown in *Figure 5.45*, click on **Roles** and at the top click on **Add assignments**.
2. On the **Membership** page select the role you want to assign to the selected resource and select the user who the role must be assigned to. Click **Select** and then click

Next as shown in the following figure:

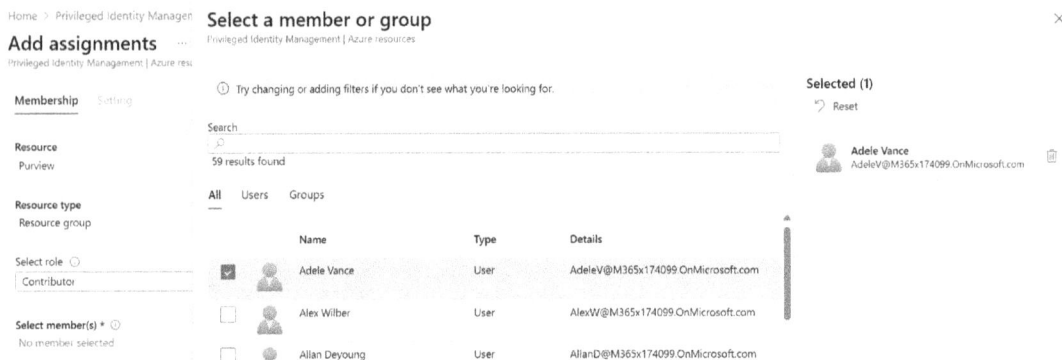

Figure 5.46: Assign a role

3. On the **Settings** page, select the appropriate **Assignment type** and select the start and end time and click on **Assign**, as shown in the following figure:

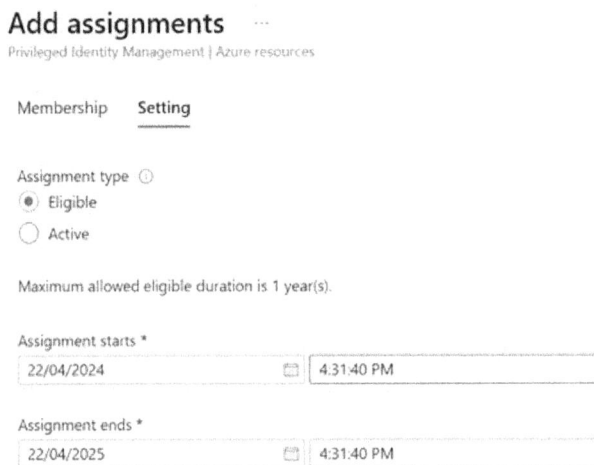

Figure 5.47: Assignment settings

The steps to activate, approve and extend Azure roles are similar to activating, approving and extending a PIM role. Refer to the previous section for the exact steps.

PIM for groups

Using PIM, you can provide just-in-time membership or ownership of a group. PIM supports Microsoft Entra Security groups or M365 groups. Using nested groups is not recommended.

Bring groups under PIM

Table 5.3 summarizes the role required to bring groups under PIM management:

Group type	Roles required
Role-assignable group	Global Administrator Privileged Role Administrator Group Owner
Non-role assignable groups	Global Administrator Directory Writer Groups Administrator Identity Governance Administrator User Administrator Group Owner

Table 5.3: Roles required for groups

Following are the steps to bring Groups under PIM management:

1. Login to **https://entra.microsoft.com** and navigate to **Identity Governance** | **Privileged Identity Management** | **Groups**.

2. At the top click, on **Discover resources** and select the groups that you would like to manage with PIM and click on **Manage groups**. You will be prompted to onboard selected groups. Click on **OK** as shown in the following figure:

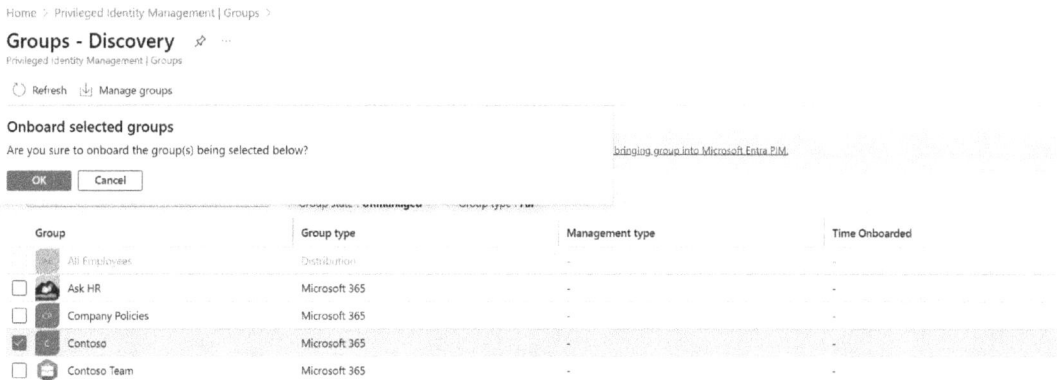

Figure 5.48: Manage groups

Note: Once a group is managed, it cannot be removed from PIM management.

Preparing group for PIM

Once a group is added under PIM scope, various settings can be configured as described in the following steps:

1. On the **Groups** page, you will now see the group listed.

2. Click on the group and then click on **Settings**. You will see options for **Owners** and **Members**. Click on any one of them to open its settings. Review the settings for the **Member** of a group in Figure 5.49. Click on **Edit** to make changes:

Role setting details - Member
Privileged Identity Management | Groups

✎ Edit

Activation

Setting	State
Activation maximum duration (hours)	8 hour(s)
On activation, require	None
Require justification on activation	Yes
Require ticket information on activation	No
Require approval to activate	No
Approvers	None

Assignment

Setting	State
Allow permanent eligible assignment	No
Expire eligible assignments after	1 year(s)
Allow permanent active assignment	No
Expire active assignments after	6 month(s)
Require Azure Multi-Factor Authentication on active assignment	No
Require justification on active assignment	Yes

Send notifications when members are assigned as eligible to this role:

Type	Default recipients	Additional recipients	Critical emails only
Role assignment alert	Admin	None	False
Notification to the assigned user (assignee)	Assignee	None	False
Request to approve a role assignment renewal/extension	Approver	None	False

Send notifications when members are assigned as active to this role:

Type	Default recipients	Additional recipients	Critical emails only
Role assignment alert	Admin	None	False
Notification to the assigned user (assignee)	Assignee	None	False
Request to approve a role assignment renewal/extension	Approver	None	False

Send notifications when eligible members activate this role:

Type	Default recipients	Additional recipients	Critical emails only
Role activation alert	Admin	None	False
Notification to activated user (requestor)	Requestor	None	False
Request to approve an activation	Approver	None	False

Figure 5.49: Owner settings for groups

Assigning role

Roles can now be assigned to the group by following these steps:

1. Click on the group name and click on **Roles**. This page will show the number of current **Members** and **Owners.**

2. Click on **Add assignments** and select the role from the dropdown list. **Member** and **Owner** are the choices available.

3. Click on **No member selected** to bring up a list of users. Select the user(s) you want to assign to the group and click on **Select**. Then click on **Save**.

The steps to activate, approve and extend Group assignments are similar to activating, approving and extending PIM role. Refer to the previous section for the exact steps.

Auditing

The **Resource audit** section of PIM shows all assignments and activations for Microsoft Entra roles, Azure resource roles and Groups for the past 30 days. To access the **Resource audit** section, navigate to **Privileged Identity Management** and select Microsoft Entra role, **Azure resources** or Groups. Then select **Resource audit**.

Following figure is an example of the **Resource audit** page for Microsoft Entra roles:

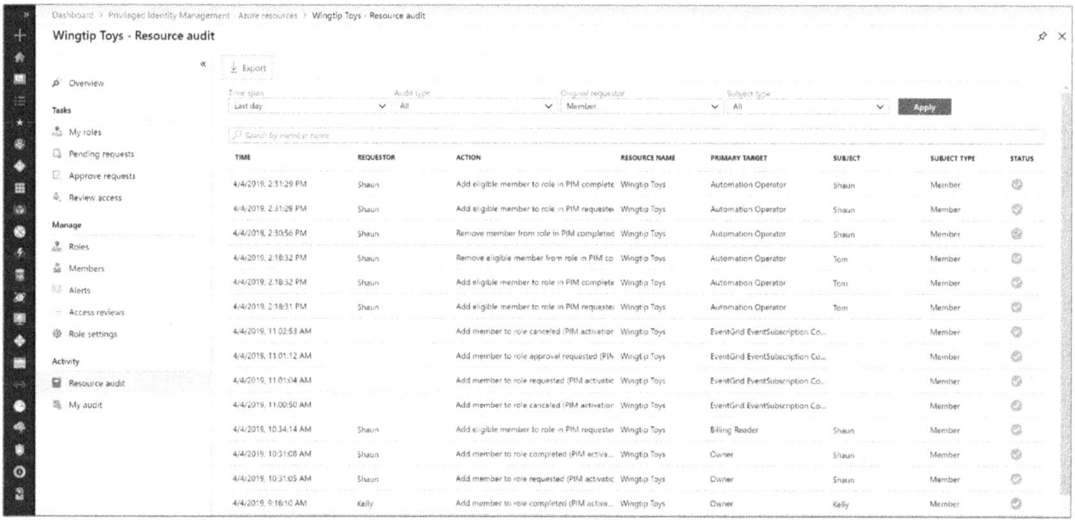

Figure 5.50: Resource audit

To view a list of all activities performed by the logged in user account, click on **My audit** on the screen above.

Licensing requirements

PIM has the following licensing requirements:

- Microsoft Entra ID Governance license.
- Users with eligible and/or time-bound assignments to Microsoft Entra ID or Azure roles must be assigned a license.

- Users with eligible and / or time-bound assignments as members of owners or PIM for Groups must be assigned a license.
- Users who can approve or reject activation requests must be assigned a license.

Lifecycle workflows

Lifecycle workflows is a new feature in Microsoft Entra ID Governance that enables organizations to manage users by automating the lifecycle processes of joiner, mover and leaver.

Lifecycle workflows are best suited for the following scenarios:

- Automatic user provisioning from HR tools.
- Automatic group membership.
- Automate user account management.

Components

Microsoft Entra provides predefined templates ready for use by the administrator. This helps with quicker deployment of workflows.

Following figure shows examples of these templates:

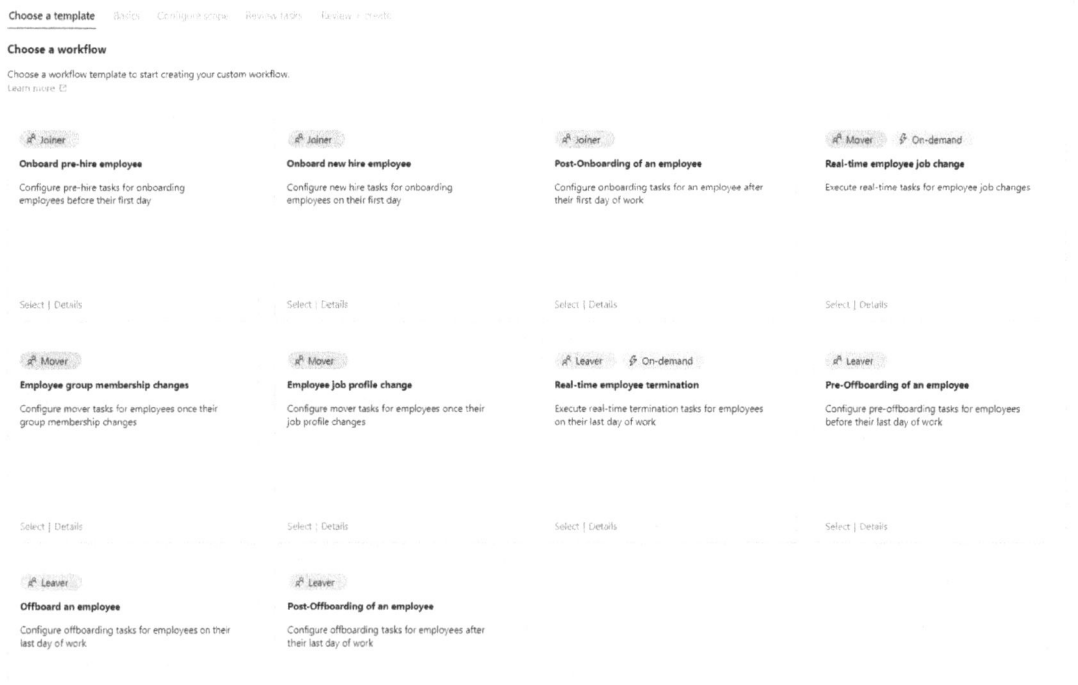

Figure 5.51: Lifecycle workflow templates

The **joiner** workflows are triggered based on the employee join date user attribute and the **leaver** workflows are triggered based on the employee leave date user attribute. The employee join date user attribute can be set in the user account in Microsoft Entra ID. To configure the employee, leave date attribute, Graph API needs to be used. Refer to Microsoft online documentation for the details. **https://learn.microsoft.com/en-us/graph/tutorial-lifecycle-workflows-set-employeeleavedatetime?tabs=http**.

> Note: These attributes can also be synchronized via HR inbound provisioning. If you are synchronizing users from AD, and want to use lifecycle workflows, you will have to use custom attributes as there is no employee hire date or employee leave date in on-premises AD.

Tasks

Each workflow comes with **built-in tasks** that help to automate common lifecycle management scenarios. These tasks can also be used to build custom workflows. These tasks can send welcome email to new hire, generate a TAP and email it to manager, add users to groups and teams and do much more. A complete list of built-in tasks can be seen in *Figure 5.54*. In addition to built-in tasks, **custom task extensions** can also be used for more complex scenarios.

Triggers

Triggers define when the workflow will run. The available trigger types are as follows:

- **Time based attribute**: If this is selected, the workflow will run when the selected date time attributes value is reached. For example, seven days before the date of employee hire.
- **Attribute changes**: If this is selected, the workflow will run when the selected user attribute changes. For example, when the user's department changes.
- **Group membership changes**: If this is selected, the workflow will run when the user is added or removed from selected groups.

Scope

Scope defines who the workflow will affect. Depending on the triggers selected, the scope options will change.

Creating lifecycle workflow

Global Administrator or Lifecycle Workflow Administrator is the required role.

Following are the steps to create a lifecycle workflow:

1. Login to **https://entra.microsoft.com** and navigate to **Identity Governance |
   Privileged Identity Management | Lifecycle workflows**. In the right pane, click
   on **Create workflow**.

2. You will see all the workflow templates as shown in *Figure 5.51*. Click on **Select** on
   the workflow that you want to create.

3. On the **Basics** tab, enter a name and description for the workflow. Select the **Trigger
   type** and configure the corresponding conditions. Click on **Next: Configure scope**
   as shown in the following figure:

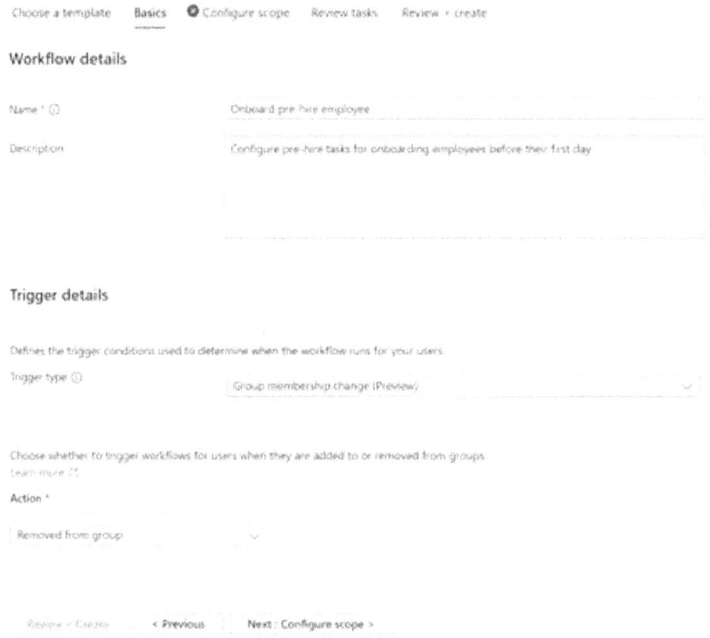

Figure 5.52: Workflow basics

4. On the **Configure scope** page, make the appropriate selections and click **Next:
   Review tasks** as shown in *Figure 5.53*:

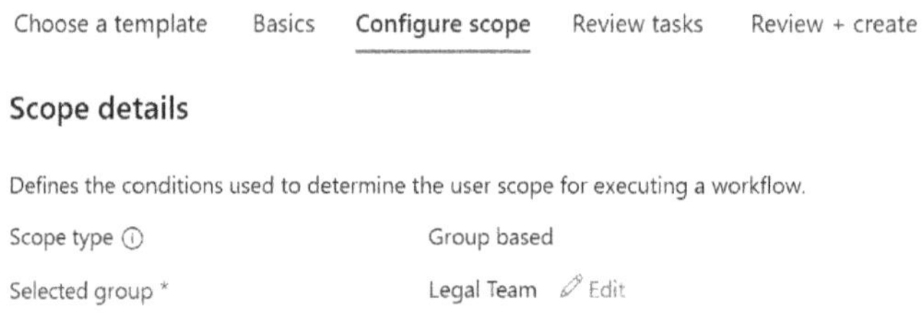

Figure 5.53: Configure scope

5. On the **Review tasks** page, tasks will be added as per the selected template. You
   can create more tasks by clicking on **Add tasks** for a complete list of tasks as shown
   in the following figure:

Select tasks ×

Onboard pre-hire em

Select the tasks you want to add to your workflow.

🗩 Got feedback?

	Name	Description	Category
	Add user to groups	Add user to selected groups	Joiner, Leaver, Mover
	Disable User Account	Disable user account in the directory	Joiner, Leaver
	Enable User Account	Enable user account in the directory	Joiner, Leaver
	Remove user from selected groups	Remove user from membership of selected Azure AD groups	Joiner, Leaver, Mover
	Generate TAP and Send Email	Generate Temporary Access Pass and send via email to user's manager	Joiner
	Send Welcome Email	Send welcome email to new hire	Joiner
	Add user to selected teams	Add user to Teams	Joiner, Leaver, Mover
	Remove user from selected Teams	Remove user from membership of selected Teams	Joiner, Leaver, Mover
	Run a Custom Task Extension	Run a Custom Task Extension to callout to an external system.	Joiner, Leaver, Mover
	Send onboarding reminder email	Send onboarding reminder email to user's manager	Joiner
	Request user access package assignment	Request user assignment to selected access package	Joiner, Mover
	Assign licenses to user (Preview)	Assign selected licenses to the user	Joiner, Mover

Create custom workflows by selecting a
Learn more ☑

Choose a template   Basics   Con

Workflow tasks

You can use the pre-defined tasks for thi
Learn more ☑

+ Add task   ⊘ Disable   ⌕ Enab

	Task order	Name
	1	⚙ Generate

Figure 5.54: *Add tasks*

6. Once done, click on **Next: Review + create**. Review the selected options and check the box **Enable schedule** if you would like to enable the workflow and click on **Create**. You can keep choose to keep the workflow disabled while you test it as shown in the following figure:

Choose a template   Basics   Configure scope   Review tasks   <u>Review + create</u>

Basics

Name	Onboard pre-hire employee
Description	Configure pre-hire tasks for onboarding employees before their first day
Category	Joiner
Trigger type	Group membership change (Preview)
Action	Removed from group

Configure

Scope type	Group based
Selected group	Legal Team

Review tasks

Generate TAP and Send Email	Enabled

Schedule workflow

Enable schedule   ☐

Figure 5.55: *Create workflow*

Testing workflow

Before you enable the workflow, you can test it by running it on demand. To run a workflow on demand, following are the steps:

1. Navigate to **Identity Governance** | **Privileged Identity Management** | **Lifecycle workflows** | **Workflows**.

2. Select the workflow and click on **Run** on demand, as shown in the following figure:

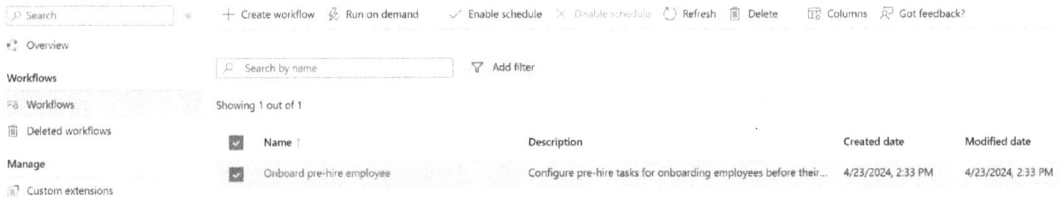

Figure 5.56: Test the workflow

3. You will be prompted to select users. Select a set of users to test this workflow on and click on **Run workflow**.

4. To view the status of the workflow, click on the workflow to open it and click on **Workflow history**. On this screen, you can see a summary of the workflow runs, the users processed by the workflow and the tasks run, as shown in the following figure:

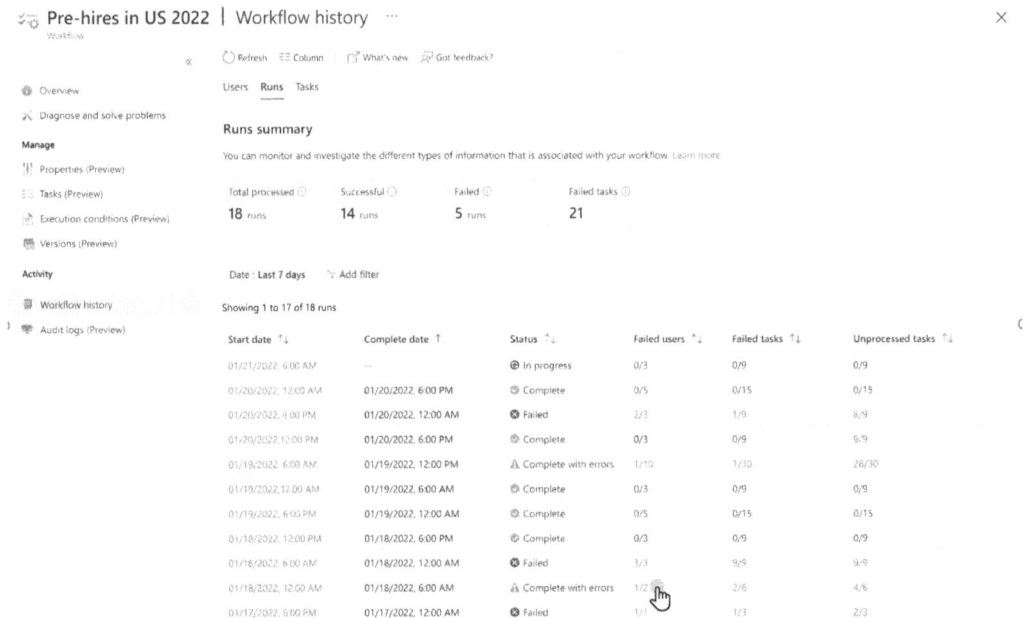

Figure 5.57: Workflow history

Licensing requirements

Lifecycle Workflow have the following licensing requirements:

- Microsoft Entra ID Governance license.
- Each Lifecycle Workflow Administrator requires a license.
- Each user who is in the scope of a workflow requires a license.

Conclusion

In this chapter, you learnt the Microsoft Entra ID Governance features in detail. This chapter described how you can use entitlement management to create access packages that users and guests can request to get started on their first day. You also learnt how to use access reviews to ensure that users and guests have continuous requirements for the access that they have. This chapter also went in depth explaining how PIM can be used to provide just-in-time access to groups, Microsoft Entra and Azure resource roles. Lastly, this chapter introduced the new feature of lifecycle workflows and how it can be used to automate tasks that need to be completed when a user joins the organization, moves roles and finally leaves the organization. You should now be able to use these Microsoft Entra ID Governance features to manage and identity lifecycle.

In the next chapter, we will discuss how to detect, protect and respond to threats using Microsoft Defender XDR.

Multiple choice questions

1. **You are an IT administrator and are tasked with ensuring that new joiners have access to all the resources they need to do their job. Which Microsoft Entra ID Governance feature will you use?**

   a. Lifecycle management

   b. Entitlement management

   c. Access reviews

   d. PIM

2. **Your organization wants to ensure that no administrator should have permanent membership to privileged roles. They should be able to elevate their access when they want to perform administrative tasks for a short duration. What should you configure?**

   a. Access package

   b. Lifecycle management

    c. PIM for Microsoft Entra roles

    d. PIM for groups

3. **You are the designated approver for access packages. As users request access packages you need to approve them so that the access packages can be delivered to them. Which portal should you use?**

    a. Microsoft Entra Administrator portal

    b. Intune portal

    c. Your mailbox

    d. My access portal

Answer key

  1. b.

  2. c.

  3. d.

Join our book's Discord space

Join the book's Discord Workspace for Latest updates, Offers, Tech happenings around the world, New Release and Sessions with the Authors:

https://discord.bpbonline.com

CHAPTER 6

Microsoft Defender XDR

Introduction

Organizations these days are exposed to a myriad of threats ranging from viruses, malware, phishing attacks, ransomware and more. They need to have effective threat protection strategies which include a combination of proactive prevention, real-time detection and rapid response. They need to deploy security solutions like firewalls, antivirus software, intrusion detection and protection systems to protect their networks, devices and data from potential harm. Microsoft Defender XDR is a suite of solutions that helps with detection, prevention, investigation and response of threats across endpoints, identities, email and applications. It provides integrated protection against sophisticated cyber-attacks.

Structure

The chapter covers the following topics:

- Microsoft Defender XDR
- Microsoft Secure Score

Objectives

In this chapter, you will learn about Microsoft Defender XDR and its features. You will see how Microsoft Defender XDR consolidates threat signals from other Microsoft solutions and provides a unified view to the security analyst. You will explore the incident investigation and response features including automated investigation and response. You will discover the new features like automatic attack disruption and deception capability. You will also learn how to use advanced hunting and threat analytics to proactively look for threats in your environment. You will find out how organizations can get help from Microsoft in their incident investigation and response efforts by using endpoint attack notifications and Microsoft Defender Experts. Finally, you will learn how you can use Microsoft Secure Score to evaluate and enhance your organization's security posture. The next chapters will elaborate on the topics covered in this chapter.

Microsoft Defender XDR

Microsoft Defender XDR is an **extended detection and response** (**XDR**) solution that aids in detection, prevention, investigation and response of threats across endpoints, email, identities and applications. It is a cloud-based pre-breach and post-breach enterprise suite of products. It receives and correlates signals from the following products to paint a single pane of glass for **security operations center** (**SOC**) teams:

- **Microsoft Defender for Endpoint** (**MDE**)
- **Microsoft Defender for Office 365** (**MDO**)
- **Microsoft Defender for Identity** (**MDI**)
- **Microsoft Defender for Cloud Apps** (**MDCA**)
- Microsoft Defender for Vulnerability Management
- **Microsoft Defender for Cloud** (**MDC**)
- Microsoft Entra ID Protection
- Microsoft Purview Data Loss Prevention
- App Governance
- Microsoft Purview Insider Risk Management

This helps them stitch together the threat signals and understand the full scope and impact of a threat.

Following are some of the key features of Microsoft Defender XDR:

- Provides a single pane of glass through the Microsoft Defender portal.
- Combines incident queues from the above products so that the SOC teams have a single screen to look when monitoring for security threats.
- Can take automatic remediation actions on threats.

- Uses AI to enable self-healing for compromised devices, identities and mailboxes.
- Enables threat hunting across the products.

The customer data collected by Microsoft Defender XDR is stored in Azure data centers in the *European Union, United Kingdom, United States, Australia, Switzerland* and *India*.

> **Note: Microsoft Defender XDR is aligned to the MITRE ATT&CK framework and shows how and where each attack has progressed across the kill chain. To understand the concepts in this section, it will be beneficial for the reader to understand the MITRE ATT&CK framework. Visit https://attack.mitre.org to learn more.**

Licensing requirements

To be able to access Microsoft Defender XDR features from the Microsoft Defender portal, organizations must own one of the following licenses:

- Microsoft 365 E5
- Microsoft 365 E3 + Microsoft 365 E5 Security
- Microsoft 365 E3 + EMS E5
- Windows 10 Enterprise E5
- Windows 11 Enterprise E5
- Office 365 E5
- Microsoft Defender for Identity
- Microsoft Defender for Endpoint
- Microsoft Defender for Cloud Apps
- Microsoft Defender for Office 365 (Plan 2)
- Microsoft 365 Business Premium
- Microsoft Defender for Business

Roles required

Each Microsoft Defender service, Microsoft Purview and Microsoft Entra have their own permission models. While Microsoft Defender XDR continues to honor the Microsoft Entra ID roles, it now offers a unified **role-based access control** (**RBAC**) model that provides a centralized permissions management solution for the following solutions:

- Microsoft Defender XDR
- Microsoft Defender for Endpoint
- Microsoft Defender for Office 365
- Microsoft Defender for Identity

- Microsoft Defender for Cloud
- Microsoft Defender Vulnerability Management
- Microsoft Secure Score

You must be a Global Administrator or Security Administrator in Microsoft Entra ID to be able to access the **Permissions and roles** page in the Microsoft Defender portal and manage roles in unified RBAC.

To be able to use the Microsoft Defender XDR unified RBAC model, relevant workloads must be activated in the Microsoft Defender portal. Login to **https://security.microsoft. com** and navigate to **Settings | Microsoft Defender XDR | Permissions and roles**. In the right pane, activate the required workloads, as shown in the following figure:

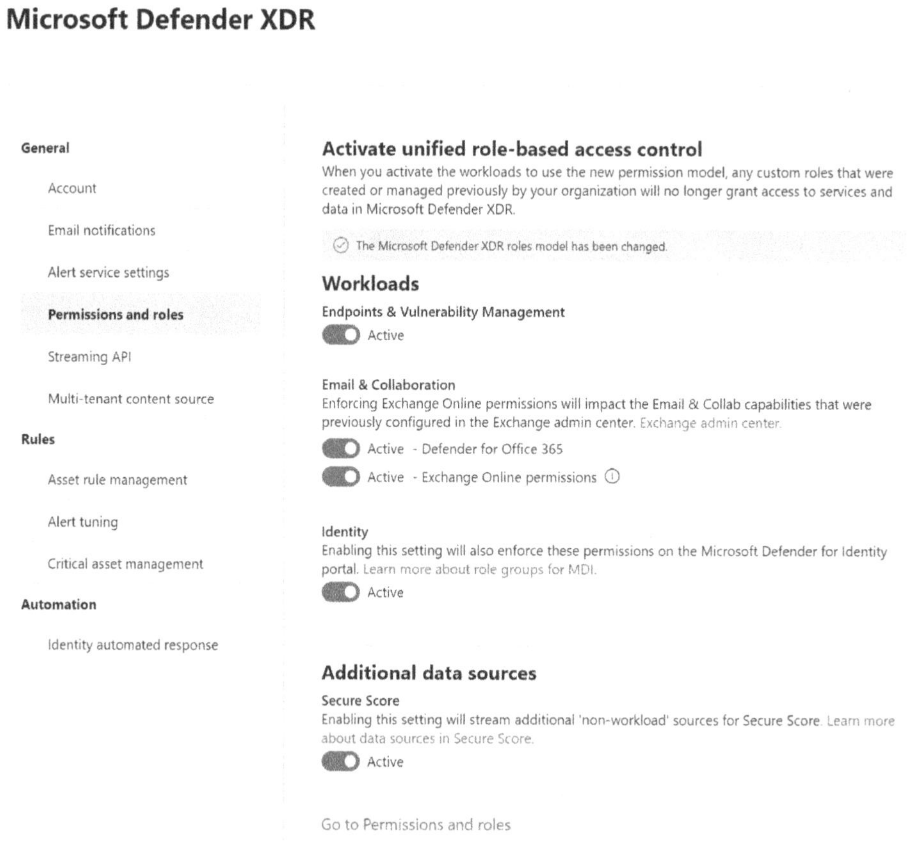

Microsoft Defender XDR

Activate unified role-based access control

When you activate the workloads to use the new permission model, any custom roles that were created or managed previously by your organization will no longer grant access to services and data in Microsoft Defender XDR.

⊘ The Microsoft Defender XDR roles model has been changed.

Workloads

Endpoints & Vulnerability Management
Active

Email & Collaboration
Enforcing Exchange Online permissions will impact the Email & Collab capabilities that were previously configured in the Exchange admin center. Exchange admin center.
Active - Defender for Office 365
Active - Exchange Online permissions ⓘ

Identity
Enabling this setting will also enforce these permissions on the Microsoft Defender for Identity portal. Learn more about role groups for MDI.
Active

Additional data sources

Secure Score
Enabling this setting will stream additional 'non-workload' sources for Secure Score. Learn more about data sources in Secure Score.
Active

Go to Permissions and roles

(left navigation pane)
General
Account
Email notifications
Alert service settings
Permissions and roles
Streaming API
Multi-tenant content source
Rules
Asset rule management
Alert tuning
Critical asset management
Automation
Identity automated response

Figure 6.1: Activate workloads for unified RBAC

Permissions for the activated workloads are now completely controlled by the Microsoft Defender XDR unified RBAC model.

Now you can create custom roles or import existing RBAC roles from the above listed solutions. This can be done in the Microsoft Defender portal by going to **Permissions** and selecting **Roles** under **Microsoft Defender XDR**.

Getting started

Before you can begin using it, you must turn on Microsoft Defender XDR in the Microsoft Defender portal. Ensure that you have the required licenses. You must be a Global Administrator or Security Administrator in Microsoft Entra ID. Login to the Microsoft Defender portal by going to **https://security.microsoft.com** and navigate to **System | Settings**. In the right pane, click on **Microsoft Defender XDR**. You will be shown a message while the system turns on XDR. It will take a few minutes and then, you will be shown a screen that shows the data center location where Microsoft Defender XDR will store the data. You will also be shown your **Tenant ID** and **Org ID** and an option to turn on **Preview Features**.

Refer to the following figure:

Microsoft Defender XDR

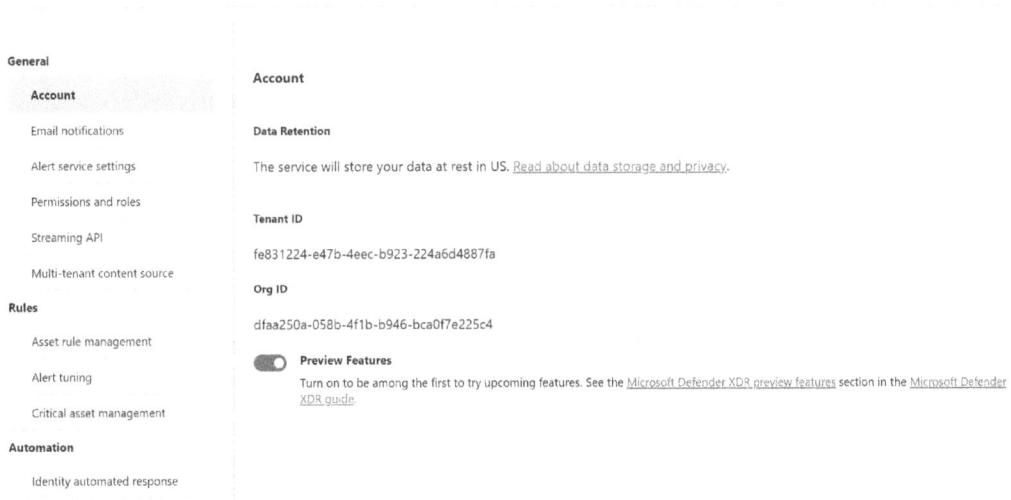

General

    Account

    Email notifications

    Alert service settings

    Permissions and roles

    Streaming API

    Multi-tenant content source

Rules

    Asset rule management

    Alert tuning

    Critical asset management

Automation

    Identity automated response

Account

Data Retention

The service will store your data at rest in US. Read about data storage and privacy.

Tenant ID

fe831224-e47b-4eec-b923-224a6d4887fa

Org ID

dfaa250a-058b-4f1b-b946-bca0f7e225c4

Preview Features

Turn on to be among the first to try upcoming features. See the Microsoft Defender XDR preview features section in the Microsoft Defender XDR guide.

Figure 6.2: Turn on Microsoft Defender XDR

Once the service is provisioned, it will add Incidents management, Alerts queue, action center for managing automated investigation and response, advanced hunting and threat analytics.

The Microsoft Defender XDR portal defaults to the UTC time zone. To change to your local time zone, go to **Settings | Microsoft Defender portal** and adjust the time zone.

Figure 6.3 shows the home page of the Microsoft Defender portal. Note the options available in the left navigation menu. Depending on the services deployed, you may see additional or fewer options.

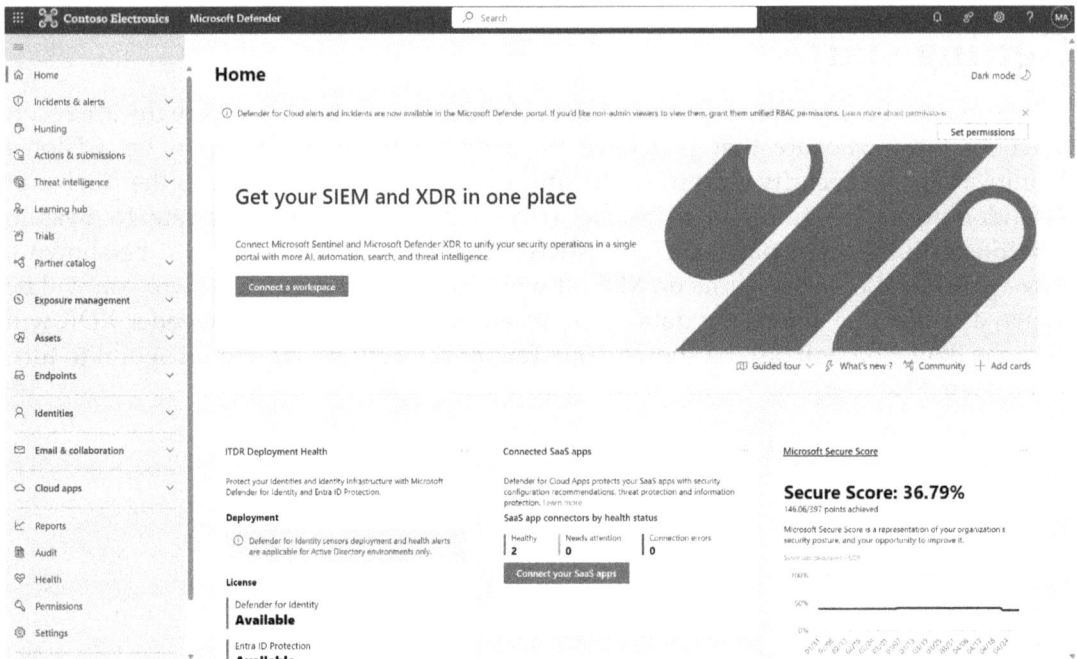

Figure 6.3: *Microsoft Defender portal home page*

Security Copilot in Defender

Security Copilot for security introduces AI to enable security teams to respond to attacks faster. Copilot for security is now embedded into the Microsoft Defender portal. It helps security teams be more efficient and tackle investigations quicker and with precision.

Following are the key features of Copilot for security:

- **Summarize incidents**: Analysts are faced with multiple incidents every day. Understanding and prioritizing these incidents can be very time-consuming. To quickly understand an incident, Copilot for security can summarize an incident in a natural language explaining what happened during the attack, which assets were involved and the timeline.

- **Take action on incidents**: Copilot for security offers guided responses specific to each incident using which security teams can quickly investigate and resolve incidents.

- **Analyze scripts**: These days most attackers rely on sophisticated malware that may be hidden in the form of scripts. Copilot can quickly analyze scripts and explain in natural language saving security teams hours.

- **Generate device summaries**: Copilot for security summarizes a device's information that includes its security posture, unusual behaviors, vulnerable software etc.

- **Analyze files**: Just life devices, Copilot for security can analyze suspicious files quickly.

- **Write incident reports**: Security teams spend a considerable amount of time writing incident summaries that include what actions were taken, what was the result, which team members were involved etc. Copilot can quickly consolidate these pieces of information and generate incident reports.

- **Writing hunting queries**: Microsoft Defender uses **Keyword Query Language (KQL)** to write advanced hunting queries. Security teams must learn KQL to be able to efficiently perform advanced hunting. Using the query assistant, security teams can now write their query in natural language and Copilot can convert it into KQL.

- **Monitor threat intelligence**: Copilot can monitor the threat intelligence feeds and quickly provide a summary of the latest threats that the organization may be exposed to.

Now that we understand Microsoft Defender XDR, let us discuss how to use it to investigate and respond to security incidents, automate threat investigation and response and hunt for threats with advanced hunting.

Incident investigation and response

Microsoft 365 services create **alerts** when they detect suspicious or malicious activity. Attackers seldom use a single attack vector. They employ various techniques against devices, emails and applications. This results in multiple alerts which are difficult to stitch together. Individual alerts provide valuable information about the activity, but they tell only a part of the story. Microsoft Defender XDR automatically aggregates related alerts and their associated information into **incidents** that tell the complete story of the attack. Grouping alerts into incidents provides a comprehensive view of where the attack started, what tactics were used, what is the scope of the attack and how much the attack has spread in your environment.

To view the incidents in the Microsoft Defender portal, go to **https://security.microsoft. com** and in the left pane, navigate to **Incidents & alerts | Incidents**. The incident page shows all incidents from the last six months as shown in the following figure:

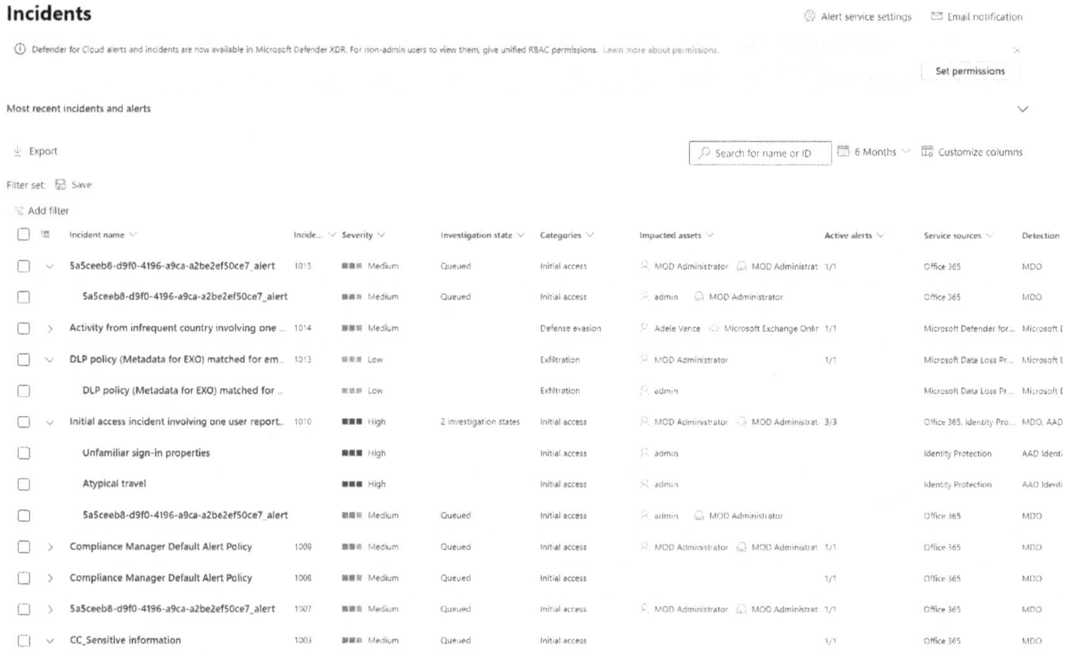

Figure 6.4: *Incident queue in Microsoft Defender*

From this screen, you can export the current list of incidents by clicking on the **Export** option. You can also add or remove columns using the **Customize columns** option.

Click on any incident to open the incident page which provides more information about the incident story including an incident graph which shows the assets involved in the incident. Following figure shows a data exfiltration incident:

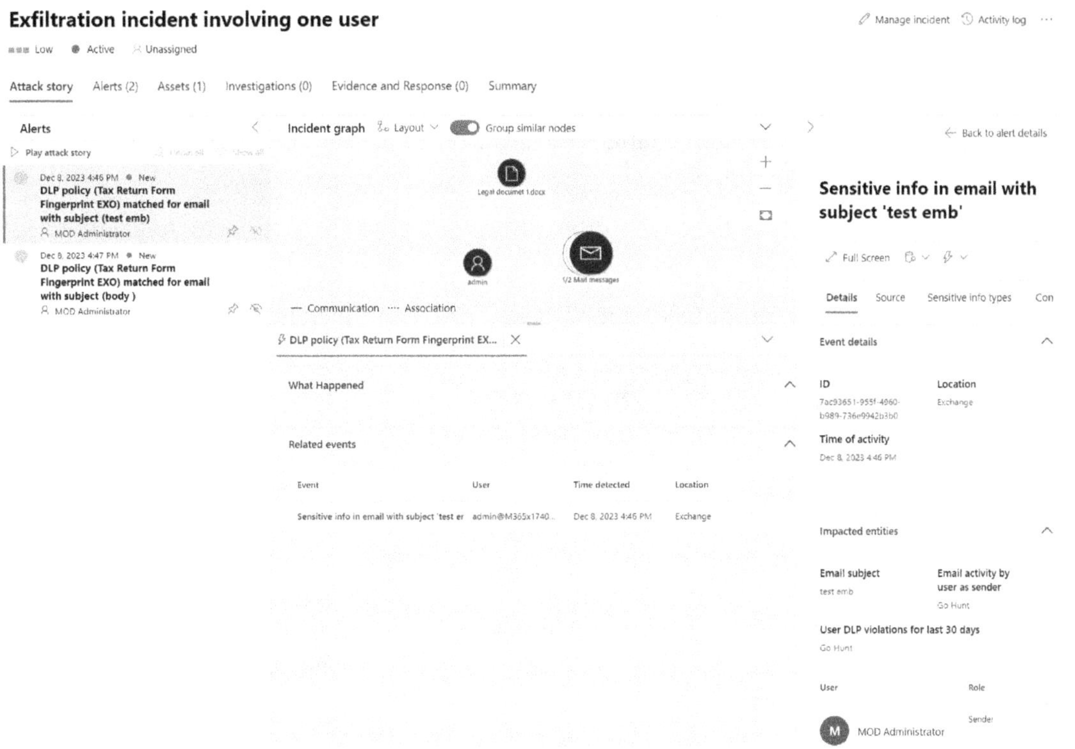

Exfiltration incident involving one user

✏ Manage incident ⏱ Activity log ⋯

▪▪▪ Low   ● Active   ◔ Unassigned

Attack story   Alerts (2)   Assets (1)   Investigations (0)   Evidence and Response (0)   Summary

Alerts   ‹   Incident graph   ⊿ Layout ∨   ⬤ Group similar nodes   ∨   ›   ← Back to alert details

▷ Play attack story

Dec 8, 2023 4:46 PM ● New
**DLP policy (Tax Return Form
Fingerprint EXO) matched for email
with subject (test emb)**
🔏 MOD Administrator

Dec 8, 2023 4:47 PM ● New
**DLP policy (Tax Return Form
Fingerprint EXO) matched for email
with subject (body)**
🔏 MOD Administrator

Legal document 1.docx

admin   1/2 Mail messages

— Communication ⋯⋯ Association

🔏 DLP policy (Tax Return Form Fingerprint EX...   ✕

What Happened   ⌃

Related events   ⌃

Event	User	Time detected	Location
Sensitive info in email with subject 'test e...	admin@M365x1740...	Dec 8, 2023 4:46 PM	Exchange

**Sensitive info in email with
subject 'test emb'**

✏ Full Screen   ⬚ ∨   ⬚ ∨

Details   Source   Sensitive info types   Con

Event details   ⌃

ID   Location
7ac93651-955f-4860-   Exchange
b989-736e9942b1b0

Time of activity
Dec 8, 2023 4:46 PM

Impacted entities   ⌃

Email subject   Email activity by
test emb   user as sender
                             Go Hunt

User DLP violations for last 30 days
Go Hunt

User   Role
                             Sender
Ⓜ MOD Administrator

Figure 6.5: Detailed incident page

The detailed incident page shown in *Figure 6.5* has the following tabs:

- **Attack story**: This tab includes the timeline of the attack, a graph showing all alerts and assets and any remediation actions taken. Clicking on each of the entities in the graphic will open the details page of the entity for further investigation and taking remediation action like isolating a device, deleting a file or suspending user in Entra ID.

- **Alerts**: This tab shows all the alerts that make up this incident. Details include the severity of the alerts, entities involved, source of the alert and the reason why the incidents were linked together.

- **Assets**: All assets like devices, users, mailboxes, apps that have been affected by the incident.

- **Investigations**: All the automated investigations that were triggered.

- **Evidence and response**: The suspicious entities in the alert that constitute evidence. These could be IP addresses, files, URLs and more.

- **Summary**: This page gives a snapshot of the top things to notice about the incident.

You can click on **Manage incident** on the top right to change the incident name, adjust the severity, assign the incident to someone and update the **Status** to **In progress** or **Resolved**.

Comments can also be added. You can also set the incident **Classification**. You can specify if the incident is a **True positive**, **False positive** or **Informational**.

The **Activity log** displays a list of all comments and actions related to the incident. All the user (comments) and system changes (audit) to the incident appear here. You can add comments from this page too.

Clicking on the ellipses next to the **Activity log** will give the option to **Ask Defender Experts**.

Now, let us look at some of the key capabilities of Microsoft Defender XDR.

Automated investigation and response

Security teams are bombarded with thousands of alerts every day. Given the volume of alerts it is challenging for humans to investigate and respond to all these alerts timely. As security alerts are triggered, security analysts start to prioritize and investigate the incidents. However, alerts continue to flow while previous alerts are being investigated. This can be overwhelming for the analysts as they work hard to address all alerts. Microsoft Defender XDR has **automated investigation and response** (**AIR**) and **self-healing** capabilities that work across devices, email and identities and can help security teams address threats more efficiently.

AIR is a virtual assistant that mimics the steps a security analyst would take to prioritize and investigate an incident. It works tirelessly 24x7, has unlimited capacity and takes on the load of investigations and threat remediation. This frees up the security analysts to focus on more important threats. It dramatically increases the security team's capacity to deal with security incidents. It also helps in reducing the cost of investigating and responding to security threats. It can help your security teams in determining if a threat requires action, taking or recommending remediation actions and conducting other investigations.

Prerequisites

AIR requires that the following pre-requites be met:

Requirement	Details
License	One of the following: • Microsoft 365 E5 • Microsoft 365 E3 + Microsoft 365 E5 Security • Office 365 E5 + EMS E5 + Windows E5
Network	• AIR requires that • Microsoft Defender for Identity is enabled • Microsoft Defender for Cloud Apps is configured • Microsoft Defender for Identity integration

Requirement	Details
Windows	Windows 11 or Windows 10 version 1709 or above with Microsoft Defender for Endpoint and Microsoft Defender Antivirus running.
Protection for email and files	Microsoft Defender for Office with AIR capabilities configured in Microsoft Defender for Endpoint.
Roles	• Global Administrator • Security Administrator

Table 6.1: AIR pre-requisites

Configure devices

To be able to run AIR and execute remediation actions automatically the devices must be configured with the appropriate settings. This is done using **Device groups** in the Microsoft Defender portal. A default group exists that includes all the devices. Additional device groups can be created if different remediation levels need to be configured for different groups of devices. For example, you might want to create a device group for devices of information workers with remediation level set to full and other for executives with remediation level set to semi.

Following figure shows an example of the **Device groups** page:

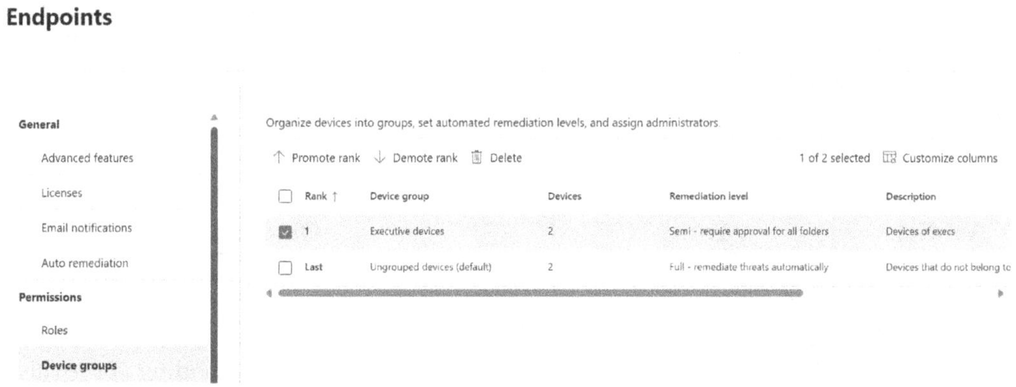

Endpoints

Figure 6.6: Device groups

Following are the steps to enable AIR to run automated remediation:

1. Login to **https://security.microsoft.com** and navigate to **Settings | Endpoints**. Under **Permissions,** click on **Device groups**.

2. In the right pane, select the appropriate device group and on the **General** page ensure that the **Remediation level** is set to **Full – remediate threats automatically**. Also, note the other remediation levels available as shown in the following figure:

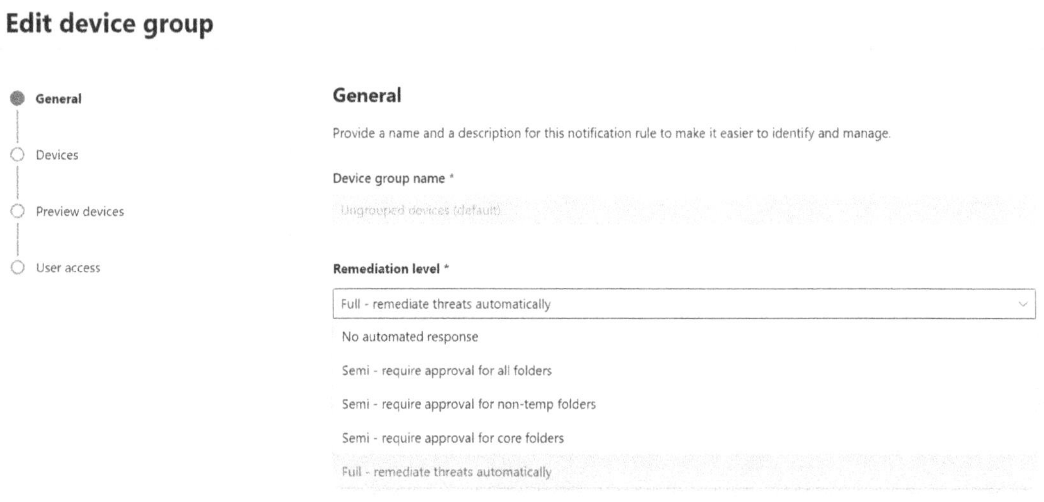
Edit device group
General
Devices
Preview devices
User access
General
Provide a name and a description for this notification rule to make it easier to identify and manage.
Device group name *
Ungrouped devices (default)
Remediation level *
Full - remediate threats automatically
No automated response
Semi - require approval for all folders
Semi - require approval for non-temp folders
Semi - require approval for core folders
Full - remediate threats automatically

Figure 6.7: *Configure remediation level*

Understand AIR

Once AIR is kicked off for an incident, it provides a verdict that will determine how the incident will be dealt with. It can also take remediation actions that could include quarantining a malicious file, stopping a process, isolating a device, blocking a URL, or disabling a user account. For a complete list of supported actions, refer to the Microsoft online documentation. Remediation actions might require approval or can be executed automatically, depending on the remediation level.

The following table summarizes the verdict and the outcomes:

Verdict	Entity	Outcome
Malicious	Devices	Remediation actions are taken automatically
Compromised	Users	Remediation actions are taken automatically
Malicious	Email (URLs or attachments)	Recommended actions are pending approval
Suspicious	Devices or email	Recommended actions are pending approval
No threats found	Devices or email	No remediation actions are needed

Table 6.2: *AIR verdicts and outcomes*

In addition to the automated remediation actions that follow automated investigations, security teams can also take manual actions like file quarantine, isolating device, soft-deleting email messages, resetting user passwords and so on.

All investigations performed by AIR for the incident show up in the **Investigations** tab of that incident. Analysts can explore each investigation and view its status and the time it took to complete the investigation. The details also show an **Investigation graph** that starts with alert received, entities investigated, evidence collected and remediation result. You might notice that the tabs are same as the ones on the incident page. The tabs on the investigation page however are in context of this particular investigation. All actions that were taken during the investigation are logged in the **Log** tab.

Refer to the following figure:

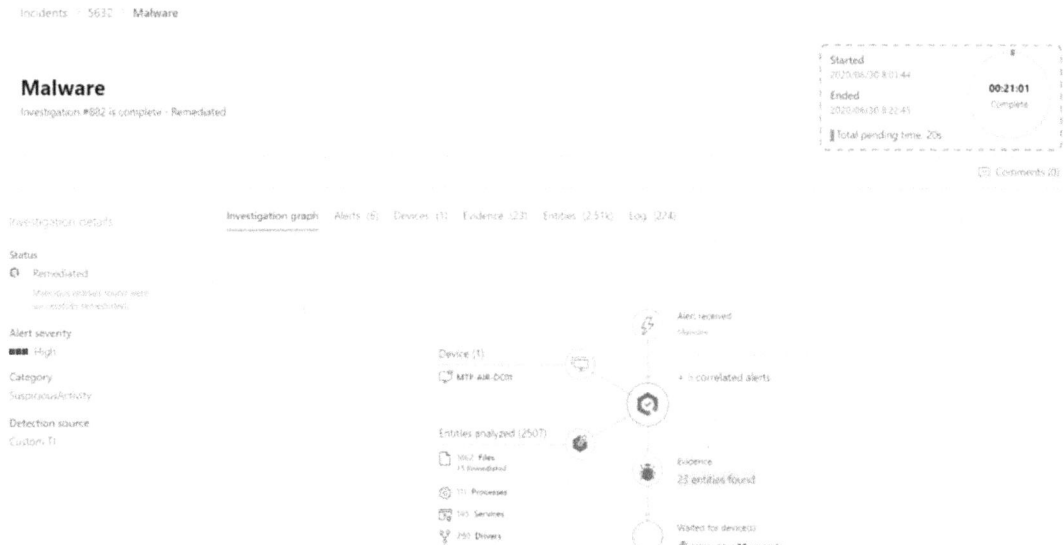

Figure 6.8: Incident investigation page

All recent actions are also listed in the **Action Center** on the Microsoft Defender portal. If an action requires approval, it will show up on the Pending tab, and the administrator will have the option to approve or reject it. Automatically approved actions show up in the **History** tab, which serves as an audit log for the remediation actions taken by AIR. If an administrator determines that the investigation action taken was not necessary because the device or file is not a threat, it can be undone on the **History** tab.

Following figure shows a snippet of the **Action Center**:

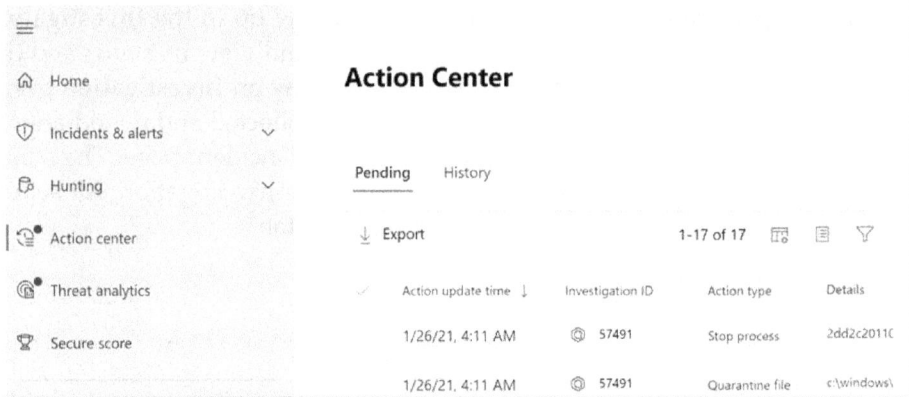

Figure 6.9: Action Center

While an incident is being investigated by AIR, any new related alerts are automatically added to the incident.

To view a list of ongoing investigations, go to the **Incidents** page, select an incident and click on the **Investigations** tab as shown in *Figure 6.5*.

If an administrator determines that the investigation action taken was not necessary because the device or file is not a threat, it can be undone on the **History** tab.

Automatic attack disruption

Microsoft Defender XDR has the capability to disrupt an attack that is in progress by automatically containing the assets that the attacker is using. This limits lateral movement and reduces the blast radius of the attack, thus saving costs and limiting loss of productivity. It considers the entire context of the millions of XDR signals across the entire stack of Microsoft Defender products to act at the incident level. It utilizes insights from the continuous investigation of thousands of incidents by Microsoft security research and advanced AI to disrupt complex attacks.

It uses Microsoft Defender XDR's response actions, as follows:

- **Contain device**: Using Microsoft Defender for Endpoint's capability, it can automatically contain a suspicious device by blocking any incoming or outgoing communication with the device.
- **Contain user**: Using Microsoft Defender for Identity's capability, it can automatically suspend compromised user accounts.
- **Disable user**: Using Microsoft Defender for Endpoint's capability, it can automatically contain suspicious user accounts to prevent lateral movement and remote encryption.

Prerequisites

To use automatic attack disruption the following pre-requisites must be met:

Requirement	Details
License	One of the following: • Microsoft 365 E5 • Microsoft 365 E3 + M365 E5 Security • M365 E3 + EMS E5 • Windows 10 E5 • Windows 11 E5 • EMS E5 • Office 365 E5 • Microsoft Defender for Identity • Microsoft Defender for Endpoint • Microsoft Defender for Cloud Apps • Defender for Office 365 (Plan 2) • Microsoft Defender for Business
Roles	• Global Administrator • Security Administrator
Deployment	Relevant Defender products should be deployed in the environment.
MDE	• The minimum sense agent required for contain user to work is v10.8470. • Device discovery should be set to standard discovery. • Automation level for devices should be configured as full – remediate threats automatically.
MDI	• Auditing should be enabled for AD Domain Controllers • Configure action accounts
MDCA	• Connect the Microsoft Office 365 app using connectors • Turn on App Governance
MDO	• Mailboxes should be hosted on Exchange Online • Enable mailbox audit logging • The Safelinks policy should be present

Table 6.3: Automatic attack disruption pre-requisites

Note: Some of the above concepts are discussed in subsequent chapters in this section.

Exclude users from automated response

If you would like to exclude certain users or user groups from containment you can exclude them by following the steps:

1. Login to **https://security.microsoft.com** and navigate to **Settings | Microsoft Defender XDR**. Under **Automation** select **Identity automated response**.

2. In the right pane, click on **Add user exclusion** and select the users to exclude as shown in the following figure:

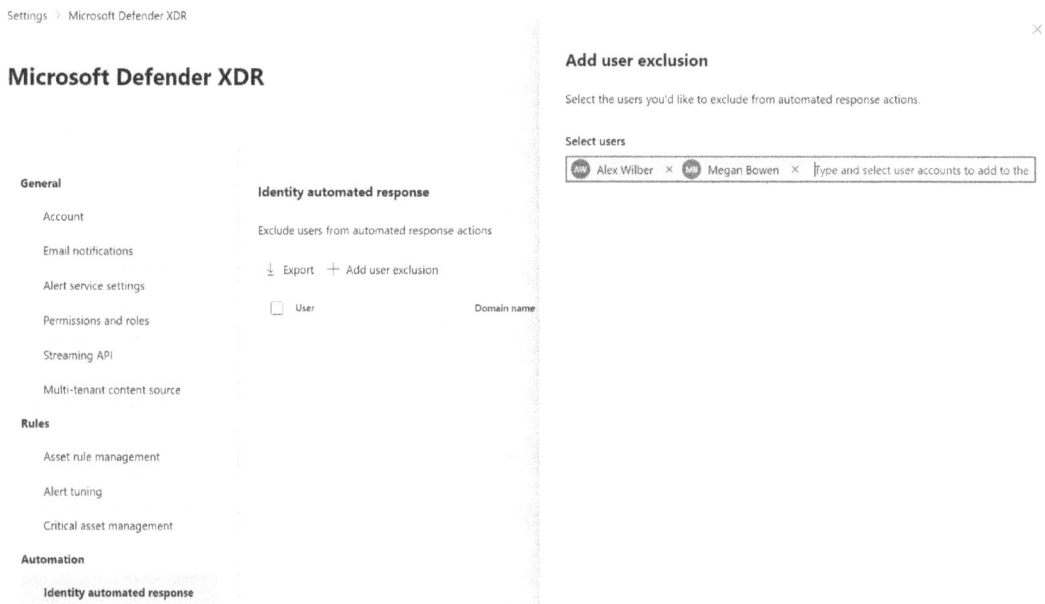

Figure 6.10: *Exclude users from automated response actions*

Understand automatic attack disruption

Once attack disruption kicks off for an incident, there are several visual cues available to the security analyst to show that attack disruption is in progress, as follows:

- The incident now has a tag **Attack Disruption** appearing next to it in the incident queue.

- The tab **Attack Disruption** also appears on the incident page as shown in *Figure 6.11*.

- A yellow banner appears at the top that highlights the automatic action taken as shown in *Figure 6.11*.

- If an action is done on an asset, the current status of the asset is shown in the incident graph.

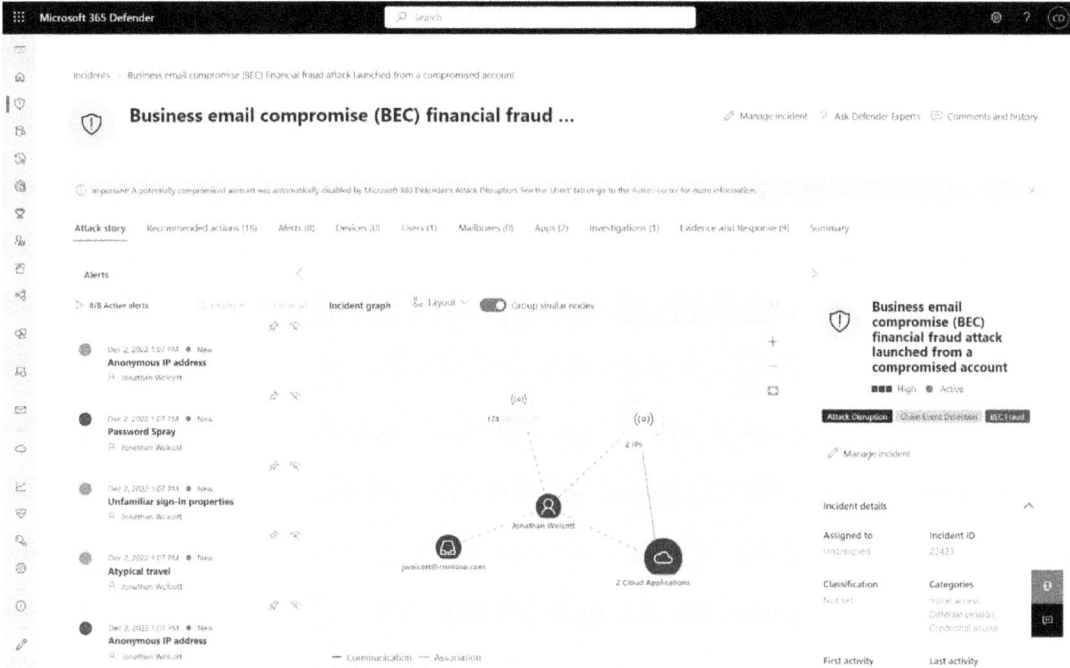

Figure 6.11: *Automatic attack disruption in progress*

Deception capability

Deception technology is a security technique that provides immediate alerts of a potential attack to security teams which enables them to respond to threats in real-time. It creates fake assets like devices and users that appear to belong to an organization. If an attacker interacts with these fake assets, it tips off the deception technology and the security analysts are warned of a potential attack. This allows the security teams to observe an attacker's methods and strategies and take appropriate protective actions.

Microsoft Defender XDR has built-in deception capability to detect human-operated lateral movement attacks with high confidence. It uses rules defined in the Microsoft Defender portal and machine learning to create **decoys** and **lures** that are specific to the organization, as follows:

- **Decoys** are fake devices that appear to belong to an organization.
- **Lures** are fake content like documents, cached credentials that are planted on the decoys and are used to attract attackers.

Prerequisites

Table 6.4 summarizes the requirements to use deception technology in Microsoft Defender XDR:

Requirement	Detail
License	One of the following: • Microsoft 365 E5 • Microsoft security E5 • Microsoft Defender for Endpoint Plan 2
Deployment	• MDE should be the primary EDR solution • AIR capabilities in MDE should be configured • Devices should be joined or hybrid joined to Microsoft Entra • PowerShell should be enabled on the devices • Windows 10 RS5 or later
Roles	• Global Administrator • Security Administrator

Table 6.4: Deception capability pre-requisites

Turning on deception capability

By default, deception capability is turned off. To use the deception capability in Microsoft Defender XDR, it needs to be turned on in the portal. The following are the steps:

1. Login to **https://security.microsoft.com** and navigate to **Settings | Endpoints | Advanced Features**.

2. In the right pane, turn switch the toggle next to **Deception** to **On**.

A default rule will be created automatically and turned on. This rule automatically generates decoy accounts and devices and plants them to all target devices. Administrators can modify this default deception rule and create their own rules if required. This is done from the **Endpoints** page by going to **Rules | Deception rules**.

Once **Deception** is turned on, if an attacker interacts with decoys or lures, high confidence alerts are generated. These alerts are correlated into incidents and appear in the **Incidents** queue on the Microsoft Defender portal. These alerts have deceptive in the title. The alert will contain the Deception tag, the decoy device or user account where the alert originated and the type of the alert.

Advanced hunting

Advanced hunting in Microsoft Defender XDR enables threat hunters to proactively hunt for threats in raw data using queries written in KQL. These queries can be manually written, or advanced query builder can be used. Copilot for security can also be used to generate KQL queries from natural language. Using advanced hunting queries administrators can explore up to 30 days of raw data. Data in Microsoft Defender XDR is stored in the form of tables. These tables are a part of the schema that provide structured data for building queries. This data can be categorized as follows:

- **Event or activity data**: This includes information about alerts, security events, system events and routine investigations. This data is received by advanced hunting immediately after the sensors that collect it can transmit to the corresponding cloud service.

- **Entity data**: This includes information about users and devices. To provide fresh data, tables are updated with any new information every 15 minutes. This might add rows that are not complete. Every 24 hours data is consolidated to insert a new row that contains the most comprehensive and updated data.

Advanced hunting uses **Universal Time Coordinated (UTC)** time zone and queries should be written in UTC.

Advanced hunting supports two modes discussed in this section.

Guided mode

The query builder allows guided mode allows analysts to craft hunting queries without knowledge of KQL or the data schema. Analysts can use the query builder to query data of the last 30 days to look for threats, investigate incidents and perform data analysis.

Following are the steps to build queries in guided mode:

1. In the Microsoft Defender portal, navigate to **Investigation and response** | **Hunting** | **Advanced hunting**.

2. Click on the plus (+) sign and click on **Query in builder** as shown in the following figure:

Advanced hunting

Figure 6.12: Guided query builder

3. This launches the guided query builder, and you can construct the query by selecting options from the dropdown menus.

Advanced mode

Use advanced mode if you are comfortable with KQL and prefer to build queries from scratch. To launch the advanced mode, click on **Query in editor** as shown in *Figure 6.12*. This will launch the query editor and you can start writing your queries.

Security Copilot in advanced hunting

Security analysts who are not familiar with KQL can also use Security Copilot and ask questions in natural language. Security Copilot converts the question into a KQL query and provides a response. This feature reduces the time taken to build or write a query so that threat hunters can focus on hunting threats. To use Security Copilot, go to the **Advanced hunting** page and click on the **Copilot** option. This opens the Copilot pane. You can type your question in natural language and review the query that Copilot generated. You can view the logic Copilot used to generate the query. Click on **Run query** to see the results.

Figure 6.13: Use copilot to generate KQL query

Microsoft also offers advanced hunting services called **Microsoft Defender Experts for Hunting**. It has been designed for organizations that have a SOC but want Microsoft to help them proactively hunt threats.

> **Note: Microsoft Defender Experts for Hunting is sold separately from other Microsoft Defender XDR products.**

Threat analytics

Threat analytics is a threat intelligence solution that is built into Microsoft Defender XDR. It is designed to help security teams to be efficient while dealing with emerging threats like active threat actors, new attack techniques, critical vulnerabilities, prevalent malware etc.

It can be accessed from the left navigation menu on the Microsoft Defender XDR portal by clicking on **Threat intelligence | Threat analytics**. *Figure 6.14* is a snippet of the threat analytics dashboard. It highlights the list of most recently published threats (**latest threats**), the threats that have the highest impact on the organization (**high-impact threats**) and the threats to which the organization has the highest exposure (**highest exposure threats**).

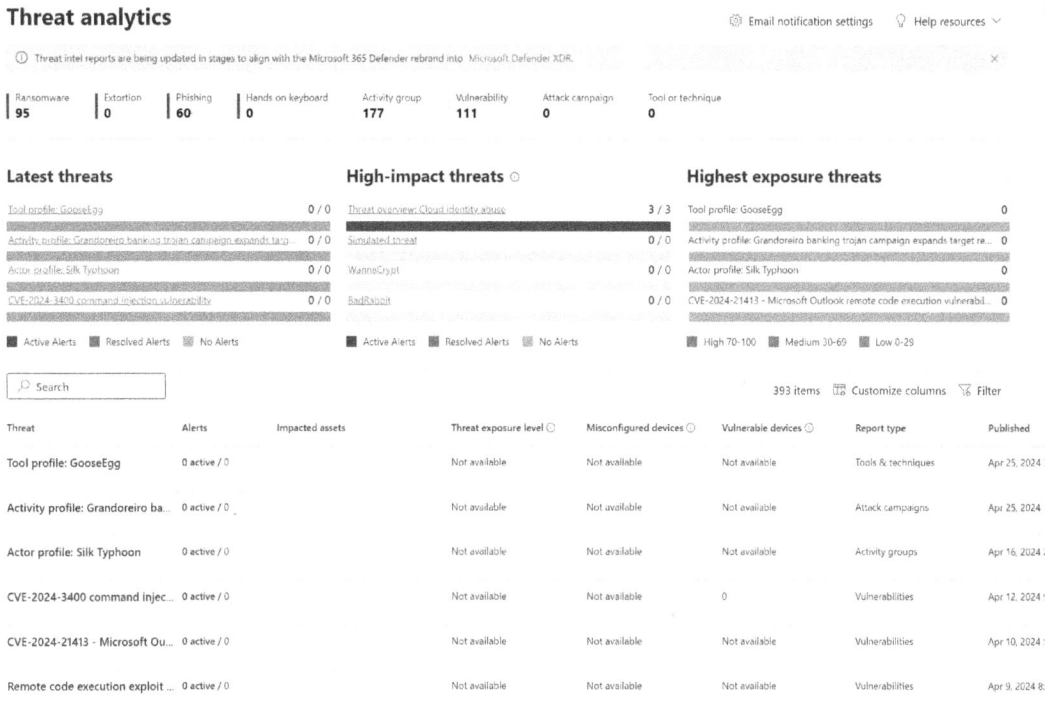

Threat analytics

⚙ Email notification settings   💡 Help resources ⌄

ⓘ Threat intel reports are being updated in stages to align with the Microsoft 365 Defender rebrand into Microsoft Defender XDR.   ✕

Ransomware	Extortion	Phishing	Hands on keyboard	Activity group	Vulnerability	Attack campaign	Tool or technique
95	0	60	0	177	111	0	0

Latest threats

Tool profile: GooseEgg	0 / 0
Activity profile: Grandoreiro banking trojan campaign expands targ...	0 / 0
Actor profile: Silk Typhoon	0 / 0
CVE-2024-3400 command injection vulnerability	0 / 0

■ Active Alerts   ■ Resolved Alerts   ▨ No Alerts

High-impact threats ⓘ

Threat overview: Cloud identity abuse	3 / 3
Simulated threat	0 / 0
WannaCrypt	0 / 0
BadRabbit	0 / 0

■ Active Alerts   ■ Resolved Alerts   ▨ No Alerts

Highest exposure threats

Tool profile: GooseEgg	0
Activity profile: Grandoreiro banking trojan campaign expands target re...	0
Actor profile: Silk Typhoon	0
CVE-2024-21413 - Microsoft Outlook remote code execution vulnerabili...	0

■ High 70-100   ■ Medium 30-69   ▨ Low 0-29

🔍 Search

393 items ▦ Customize columns ▽ Filter

Threat	Alerts	Impacted assets	Threat exposure level ⓘ	Misconfigured devices ⓘ	Vulnerable devices ⓘ	Report type	Published
Tool profile: GooseEgg	0 active / 0		Not available	Not available	Not available	Tools & techniques	Apr 25, 2024
Activity profile: Grandoreiro ba...	0 active / 0		Not available	Not available	Not available	Attack campaigns	Apr 25, 2024
Actor profile: Silk Typhoon	0 active / 0		Not available	Not available	Not available	Activity groups	Apr 16, 2024 :
CVE-2024-3400 command injec...	0 active / 0		Not available	Not available	0	Vulnerabilities	Apr 12, 2024 :
CVE-2024-21413 - Microsoft Ou...	0 active / 0		Not available	Not available	Not available	Vulnerabilities	Apr 10, 2024 :
Remote code execution exploit ...	0 active / 0		Not available	Not available	Not available	Vulnerabilities	Apr 9, 2024 8:

Figure 6.14: Threat analytics dashboard

Microsoft Defender Experts

Microsoft Defender Experts is a managed XDR service that augments your SOC by combining automation and Microsoft's security analyst expertise. Once you enable this service Microsoft security analysts manage your Microsoft Defender XDR incident queue and triage and investigate incidents on your behalf. They partner with your SOC team to respond to incidents. They also help with proactive threat hunting and conduct periodic check-ins with your service delivery teams to improve your security posture.

Microsoft Secure Score

All organizations today are under constant threat of cyber-attacks. They need to ensure that they have sufficient safeguards in place to protect themselves. They would like to know their current security posture and what steps they need to take to further strengthen it. **Microsoft Secure Score** provides a measurement of an organization's current security posture. It also provides recommendations to further strengthen it.

Following recommendations provided by Secure Score can help protect the organization against threats:

Secure Score helps organizations report on their current state, improve security by providing actionable guidance and compare benchmarks. It shows robust metrics and trends, integration with other Microsoft products, score comparison with other similar organizations and much more.

Secure Score is a measure of an organization's security posture with .a higher number indicating more actions have been taken. A higher number does not indicate that an organization is less likely to be breached. It represents the extent to which security measures have been adopted by the organization.

Microsoft Secure Score utilizes Microsoft Defender XDRs unified RBAC however, it still honors the Microsoft Entra global roles.

Secure Score is accessible in the Microsoft Defender portal from the home page. Secure Score includes recommendations for Microsoft and non-Microsoft products that include but are not limited to Microsoft Entra ID, Microsoft Defender for Identity, Microsoft Defender for Endpoint, Microsoft Defender for Office, Microsoft Information Protection, Citrix ShareFile, Okta, Zoom, Salesforce and ServiceNow. Figure shows the overall score of the organization, recommended actions and comparison with other similar organizations.

The following figure shows an example:

Overview   Recommended actions   History   Metrics & trends

Microsoft Secure Score is a representation of your organization's security posture, and your opportunity to improve it.

Applied filters: ▽ Filter

Your secure score	Include ⌄
Secure Score: 36.79%	
146.06/397 points achieved	

100%

50%

0%
07/31 02/07 02/14 02/18 02/15 02/13 02/20 04/03 04/10 04/17 04/24 04/29

Breakdown points by: Category ⌄

Identity	14.89%
Data	88.89%
Apps	39.44%

■ Points achieved   ▨ Opportunity

Actions to review

Regressed ⓘ	To address ⓘ	Planned ⓘ	Risk accepted ⓘ	Recently added ⓘ
1	65	0	0	0

Recently updated ⓘ
0

Top recommended actions

Recommended action	Score impact	Status	Category
Ensure multifactor authentication is enabled for all users i...	+2.52%	◯ To address	Identity
Ensure multifactor authentication is enabled for all users	+2.27%	◯ To address	Identity
Enable Conditional Access policies to block legacy authen...	+2.02%	◯ To address	Identity
Ensure that intelligence for impersonation protection is e...	+2.02%	◯ To address	Apps
Move messages that are detected as impersonated users ...	+2.02%	◯ To address	Apps
Enable impersonated domain protection	+2.02%	◯ To address	Apps
Set the phishing email level threshold at 2 or higher	+2.02%	◯ To address	Apps
Enable impersonated user protection	+2.02%	◯ To address	Apps

View all

Comparison

Your score	36.79 / 100
Organizations of a similar size	48.27 / 100

History

Date/Time	Activity
Apr 22, 2024 10:00 AM	▲ +6.00 points score change because Ensure internal phishing protection for Fo...
Apr 22, 2024 10:00 AM	+0.00 points score change because Block OneDrive for Business sync from unma...
Apr 22, 2024 10:00 AM	+0.00 points score change because Ensure SharePoint external sharing is manag...

Resources

Read about Secure Score capabilities
Learn about the recommended actions and how to improve your score.

Partner experience updates
Learn about temporary incompatibility with Identity Secure Score.

Messages from Microsoft

Get the inside scoop from Microsoft Security.

See recent blogs

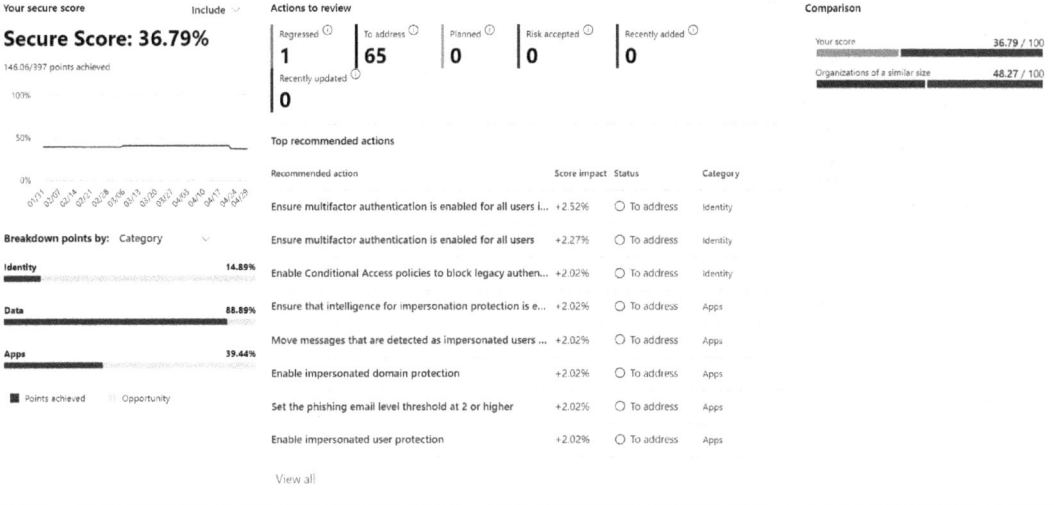

Figure 6.15: *Microsoft Secure Score*

Clicking on each recommended action will show detailed instructions on how to implement it. The status of each action can be updated by clicking on the **Edit status & action plan**.

Refer to the following figure:

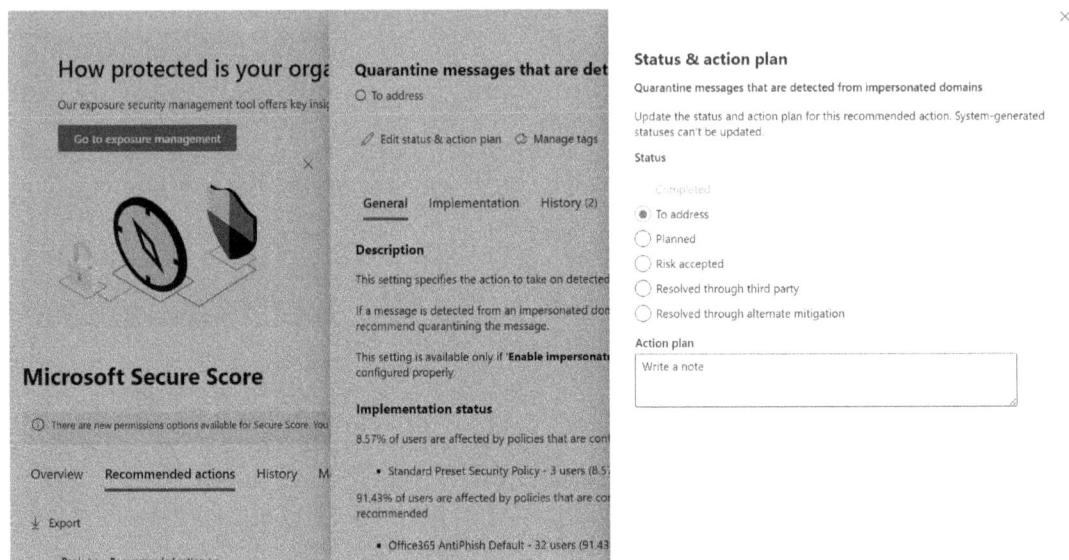

Figure 6.16: Updating recommended actions status

An organization is given points for configuring recommended security features using a Microsoft or non-Microsoft product. While some actions only give points if they are fully implemented, other actions give partial points if they are implemented for a subset of users or devices.

The customer data collected by Secure Score is stored in Azure data centers in the *European Union, United Kingdom* and *United States*.

Conclusion

This chapter introduced the incident response capabilities of the Microsoft security stack. It explored Microsoft Defender XDR as an extended detection and response solution that brings together signals from the other Microsoft Defender products to create a single pane of glass for the SOC analysts. It also explained how Microsoft Defender XDR uses AI capabilities like copilot to ease the work of the SOC analyst.

This chapter explained the incident investigation and response process in Microsoft Defender XDR including automated investigation and response. It also introduced the new concepts of automatic attack disruption and detection capability. It taught how analysts can use advanced hunting and threat analytics capabilities to proactively hunt for potential threats in their environment. The reader is encouraged to refer to Microsoft documentation to learn more about hunting threats using KQL and threat intelligence.

Finally, the chapter ended with explaining how organizations can assess and improve their security posture using Microsoft Secure Score.

Multiple choice questions

1. **Which of the Microsoft services do NOT send alerts to the Microsoft Defender XDR portal?**

   a. Microsoft Defender for Identity

   b. Microsoft Purview Data Loss Prevention

   c. Microsoft Purview eDiscovery

   d. Microsoft Defender for Office 365

2. **Which tab on the incident page shows the incident graph?**

   a. Attack story

   b. Evidence

   c. Assets

   d. Networks

3. **Which Microsoft Defender XDR capability would you use to proactive hunt for threats?**

   a. Threat analytics

   b. Advanced hunting

   c. Microsoft Defender Experts

   d. Detection capability

Answer key

1. c
2. a
3. b

Join our book's Discord space

Join the book's Discord Workspace for Latest updates, Offers, Tech happenings around the world, New Release and Sessions with the Authors:

https://discord.bpbonline.com

CHAPTER 7
Protecting Identities

Introduction

In the first part of this book, we discussed how to secure cloud identities using Microsoft Entra ID Governance capabilities, but organizations still have identities in their on-premises Active Directory that can be compromised by attackers. Organizations need to have tools to identify attacks against these identities and protect them from being stolen or abused. In this chapter we will explore how **Microsoft Defender for Identity (MDI)** helps organizations avoid breaches by spotting threats, investigating and responding to incidents. We will also discover how MDI proactively evaluates your identity posture and gives suggestions to improve it.

Structure

The chapter covers the following topics:

- Microsoft Defender for Identity
- System requirements
- Network requirements
- Installing MDI sensor
- Post-installation steps
- MDI domain controllers

- Investigate and respond
- Remediation
- Identity secure posture

Objectives

By the end of this chapter, readers will have an overview of MDI and its role in defending the identities throughout the cyberattack kill-chain. It shows you how to install and configure MDI on different servers in your environment. It also explains how to use the Microsoft Defender portal to examine and respond to identity related incidents. You will learn how to resolve security incidents and proactively check your identity posture and improve it. Finally, you will also learn about the reports and dashboards that MDI offers. By the end of this chapter, you should have a good understanding of protecting identities across on-premises and cloud environments.

Microsoft Defender for Identity

MDI, previously known as **Azure Advanced Threat Protection (Azure ATP)**, is a cloud-based security solution that protects identities across the organization. It works with Microsoft Defender XDR and uses signals from both on-premises AD and Microsoft Entra ID to find, discover and examine advanced identity threats. It enables the SecOps team to provide a complex and advanced **Identity Threat Detection and Response (ITDR)** solution by stopping breaches, finding threats, investigating unusual activities and responding to attacks.

MDI provides a view of the current identity posture helping understand, identify and resolve security issues before attackers get a chance to exploit them.

MDI can combine data from on-premises AD and Microsoft Entra ID to paint a complete picture of the identity environment. It monitors domain controllers. If required, it can also monitor **Active Directory Federation Services (AD FS)** and **AD Certificate Services (AD CS)** servers.

Attackers often target low-privileged users who have weaker and less visible identities. They use these users' credentials to access high-privileged users' accounts by moving sideways. MDI detects the threats along the cyberattack kill-chain and raises alerts providing you with a prioritized list of relevant security alerts.

Following table shows the threats and MDI's action at that stage:

Threat	Attacker	MDI
Reconnaissance	At this stage, the attackers run various tools to gather information about the users, group membership, IP address, and more.	Identifies the attackers attempt to gain this information.
Compromised credentials	Once an attacker has identified an account, they try to compromise it using various methods to move laterally.	Identifies the attackers attempt to compromise credentials by detecting brute force attacks, failed login attempts, group membership changes and more.
Lateral movements	Attackers try to move from one system to another trying to get more control of the network.	Identifies strategies such as Pass the Ticket, Pass the Hash, Overpass the Hash and more.
Domain dominance	If attackers could reach **domain controllers** (**DC**), they might try to run malicious code or try to duplicate the DC.	Identifies techniques such as DC shadow, malicious DC replications etc.

Table 7.1: *MDI protects across the cyberattack kill-chain*

Note: Discussing the cyberattack kill-chain in detail is beyond the scope of this book. The reader is expected to know the concepts.

MDI uses machine learning and advanced analytics to combine multiple low fidelity signals into fewer high-fidelity signals and prioritizes relevant and important security alerts thereby reducing noise. It seamlessly integrates with Microsoft Defender XDR, thus providing an additional layer of insight by correlating data from other systems.

MDI monitors the domain controllers by capturing events and network traffic.

Figure 7.1 shows how MDI works along with other Microsoft and third-party services to monitor traffic:

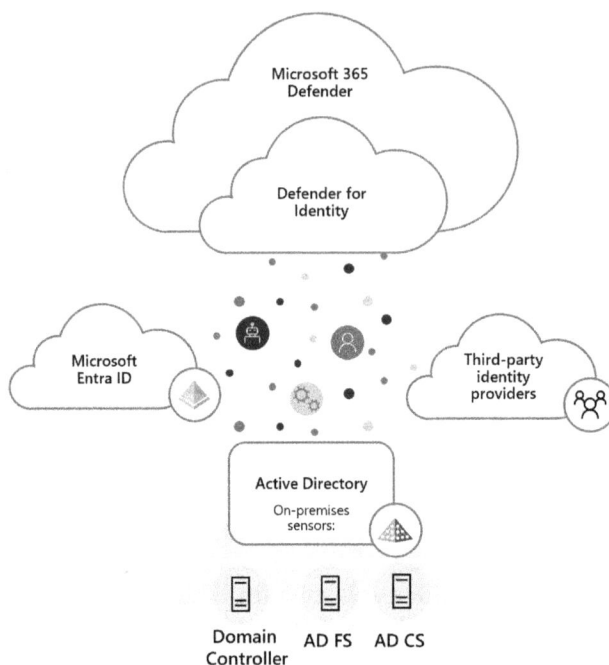

Figure 7.1: MDI architecture

MDI consists of three components, as follows:

- **Microsoft defender portal**: This is where the MDI workspace is created. It receives the data sent by the MDI sensors and displays the alerts. You can monitor, manage and investigate threats in this portal.

- **MDI sensors**: These are the sensors that are installed on the DC, AD FS and AD CS servers to monitor authentication requests, network traffic etc. These sensors send data directly to the Microsoft Defender portal.

- **MDI cloud service**: MDI cloud service currently runs in Azure data centers in UK, US, Europe, Australia, Switzerland, India and Asia. It is connected to Microsoft's intelligent security graph.

License requirements

MDI is included in one of the following licenses:

- Enterprise Mobility + Security E5
- Microsoft 365 E5
- Microsoft 365 E5 Security
- Microsoft 365 F5 Security + Compliance
- It can also be bought separately as a standalone MDI license

Roles in MDI

Table 7.2 summarizes the roles required to perform various tasks in MDI:

Activity	Role
Create MDI workspace	Global Administrator Security Administrator
Configure MDI settings	Global Administrator Security Administrator
View MDI settings	Global Reader Security Reader
Manage MDI security alerts and activities	Global Administrator Security Administrator Security Operator
View MDI security assessment	Managed by Microsoft Defender XDR RBAC
View the Assets I Identities page	Global Administrator Security Administrator Cloud App Security Administrator Compliance Administrator Compliance Data Administrator Security Operator Security Reader Global Reader
Perform MDI response actions	Global Administrator Security Administrator Security Operator Custom role with Response (manage) permissions

Table 7.2: MDI roles

System requirements

The MDI sensor is installed on domain controllers and can also be installed on AD FS and AD CS servers.

These servers should have the following minimum requirements:

- 2 cores
- 6 GB RAM
- 6 GB hard disk space

- Windows Server 2016, Window Server 2019 with KB4487044 and Windows Server 2022.
- .NET framework 4.7 later. If it is not installed, it will be installed during sensor installation and might require a system reboot.
- Npcap OEM version 1.0. If it is not installed, it will be installed during sensor installation.
- There should be trusted root certificates on the machine.
- Servers with desktop experience and server cores are supported. Nano servers are not supported.
- The servers should be able to reach the MDI cloud service. Ensure that you can access **https://<your_workspace_name>sensorapi.atp.azure.com/tri/sensor/api/ping.** To find the name of your workspace login to the Microsoft Defender portal and navigate to **Settings | Identities | About.** An **Ok** message with status code 200 should be displayed.
- If installing the MDI sensor on AD FS server ensure the following:
  o Verbose logging is enabled
  o The Directory Service Account has the db_datareader permissions on the AD FS database
- If installing the MDI sensor on AD CS server, ensure that the AD CS server has the Certification Authority Role Service.

Network requirements

Before you deploy the MDI sensor ensure that the following ports are opened:

Protocol	Transport	Port	From	To
Internet ports				
SSL (*.atp.azure.com)	TCP	443	MDI sensor	MDI cloud service
Internal ports				
DNS	TCP and UDP	53	MDI sensor	DNS servers
Netlogon (SMB, CIFS, SAM-R)	TCP/UDP	445	MDI sensor	All network devices
RADIUS	UDP	1813	RADIUS	MDI sensor
Localhost ports				
SSL	TCP	444	Sensor service	Sensor updater service

Protocol	Transport	Port	From	To
Network Name Resolution (NNR) ports				
NTLM over RPC	TCP	135	MDI sensor	All network devices
NetBIOS	UDP	137	MDI sensor	All network devices
RDP	TCP	3389	MDI sensor	All network devices

Table 7.3: MDI port requirements

Installing MDI sensor

To install the MDI sensor, you will first need to download it from the Microsoft Defender portal. Following are the steps:

1. Login to **https://security.microsoft.com** and navigate to **Settings | Identities | Sensors** and click on **Add sensor**. Click on **Download installer** and copy the **Access key**. This is a one-time passcode used during the installation. After this communication between the sensor and the MDI service uses certificates for authentication and TLS encryption, as shown in the following figure:

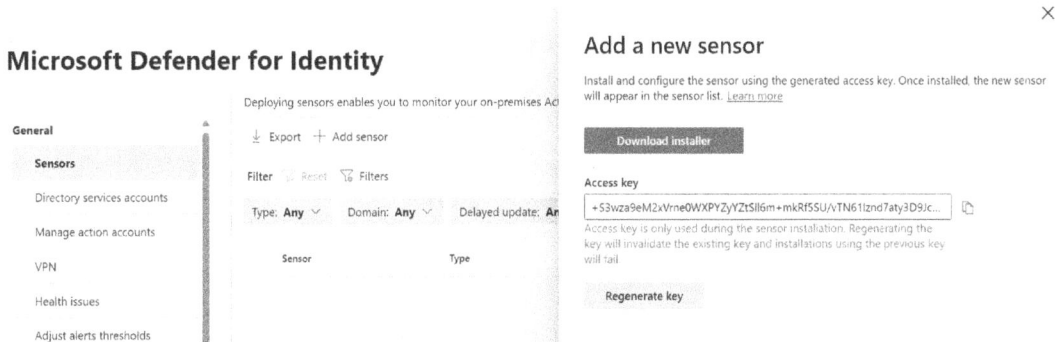

Figure 7.2: Download the MDI installer

2. Copy the installer package on the server of choice and extract the files from the `.zip` file. Right-click on **Azure ATP sensor setup.exe** and click on **Run as administrator**. On the **Welcome** page, select language and click **Next**.

3. On the **Configure the Sensor** page, select the **Installation path** and paste **Access key** copied in *step 1* and click on **Install**, as shown in the following figure:

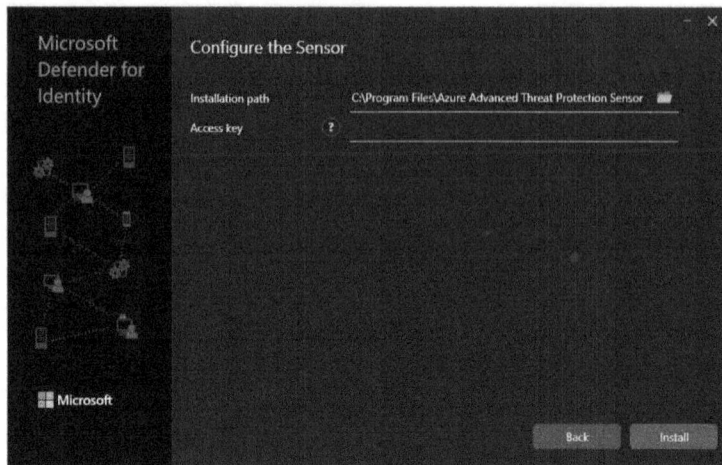

Figure 7.3: Configure the MDI sensor

4. Now, back in the Microsoft Defender portal navigate to **System | Settings | Identities | Sensors**. This page will display all the sensors installed on the servers in your environment as shown in the following figure:

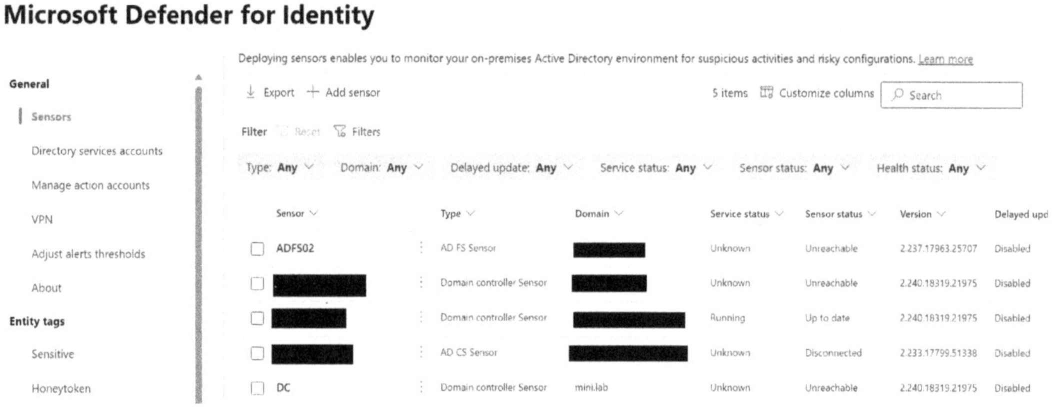

Microsoft Defender for Identity

Figure 7.4: Sensor view in the Defender portal

5. Click on a sensor to see more information about it and its health status. Scroll down on the fly out pane and click on **Manage sensor**. The following settings are available:

   a. An optional **Description**.

   b. The DC FQDN is required. All domain controllers whose traffic needs to be monitored via port mirroring must be listed here. If a DC is not listed suspicious activities from those DC will not be detected. At least one domain controller listed here should be a global catalog to enable the MDI to resolve computer and user objects in other domains in the forest.

c. Network adapters are required. All network adapters used for communication with other servers should be listed here.

6. To ensure that MDI sensor has been deployed successfully, go to the server and check that the status of the **Microsoft Advanced Threat Protection sensor** service is **Running**.

Post installation steps

Now that the sensor has been installed certain configuration needs to be done to ensure the relevant events are collected and reported. This section describes the post deployment configuration required for the MDI sensor.

Collect events

The MDI sensor is configured to automatically collect syslog events. For Windows events, it parses specific event logs from DC. For correct events to be audited and included in the Windows event logs accurate policies should be configured on the servers. These policies enable the sensor to collect information on users who perform actions like **NT LAN Manager** (**NTLM**) logons and security group modifications.

Review current configuration

It is recommended to review the current configuration settings before creating new event and audit policies. Following are the steps:

1. Download the MDI PowerShell module from the PowerShell gallery.
2. Run the following command to generate a report of the current domain configuration:

```
New-MDIConfigurationReport [-Path] <String> [-Mode] <String> [-Open-HtmlReport]
```

3. **Path** specifies the location where the report will be saved.
4. **Mode** specifies the Domain or LocalMachine mode. In Domain mode, the settings are extracted from Group Policy objects and in LocalMachine mode, the settings are extracted from the local machine.
5. **OpenHTMLReport** opens the report on the screen after it is generated.

Configure auditing on domain controllers

This section describes the policies that need to be updated to collect logs from domain controllers. Making these settings will begin capturing the below event ids in the Windows Event logs. These are required for all MDI sensors, as follows:

• **4662**: An operation was performed on an object

- **4726**: User Account Deleted
- **4728**: Member Added to Global Security Group
- **4729**: Member Removed from Global Security Group
- **4730**: Global Security Group Deleted
- **4732**: Member Added to Local Security Group
- **4733**: Member Removed from Local Security Group
- **4741**: Computer Account Added
- **4743**: Computer Account Deleted
- **4753**: Global Distribution Group Deleted
- **4756**: Member Added to Universal Security Group
- **4757**: Member Removed from Universal Security Group
- **4758**: Universal Security Group Deleted
- **4763**: Universal Distribution Group Deleted
- **4776**: Domain Controller Attempted to Validate Credentials for an Account (NTLM)
- **5136**: A directory service object was modified
- **7045**: New Service Installed
- **8004**: NTLM Authentication

Advanced Audit Policy

To update the Advanced Audit Policy, following are the steps:

1. Login to the DC as Domain Administrator.
2. Go to **Server Manager** | **Tools** | **Group Policy Management**.
3. Navigate to the **Domain Controllers** OU, right click on **Default Domain Controllers Policy** and click on **Edit**.
4. From the new window go to **Computer Configuration** | **Policies** | **Windows Settings** | **Security Settings** | **Advanced Audit Policy Configuration** | **Audit Policies**.
5. Under **Audit Policies** edit each of the following policies and select **Configure the following audit events** for both **Success** and **Failure** events.
   a. Account Logon | Audit Credential Validation
   b. Account Management | Audit Computer Account Management
   c. Account Management | Audit Distribution Group Management
   d. Account Management | Audit Security Group Management
   e. Account Management | Audit User Account Management

f. DS Access | Audit Directory Service Changes

g. System | Audit Security System Extension

h. DS Access | Audit Directory Service Access

6. From an elevated command prompt run the **gpupdate** command.

7. After this the new events will be visible in the **Event Viewer** under **Windows Logs | Security**.

Configure NTLM auditing

To configure NTLM auditing, following are the steps:

1. Open **Group Policy Management** and go to **Default Domain Controllers Policy | Local Policies | Security Options**.

2. Configure the following policies:

    a. **Network security**: Restrict NTLM: Outgoing NTLM traffic to remote servers to Audit all.

    b. **Network security**: Restrict NTLM: Audit NTLM authentication in this domain to Enable all.

    c. **Network security**: Restrict NTLM: Audit incoming NTLM traffic to Enable auditing for all accounts.

Domain object filtering

Following are the steps to collect events for object changes:

1. Open the **Active Directory Users and Computers** console and select the domain to audit. Click on **View** and select **Advanced Features**.

2. Right-click the domain and select **Properties**. Click on the **Security** tab and click on **Advanced**.

3. In the **Advanced Security Settings,** click on **Auditing** and click on **Add**.

4. Click on **Select a principal**. Under **Enter the object name to select** enter **Everyone** and click on **Check Names**. Click on **OK**.

5. In the **Auditing Entry** page, make the following changes:

    a. In the **Type** dropdown, select **Success**.

    b. In the **Applies to** dropdown, select **Descendant User objects**.

    c. In the **Permissions** sections click on **Clear all** and select the **Full control** check box. All permissions will be selected. Now clear the check boxes for **List contents, Read all properties** and **Read permissions** and click on **OK**.

6. Repeat the above steps, selecting the following in the **Applies to** dropdown one by one:

- Descendant Group Objects
- Descendant Computer Objects
- Descendant msDS-GroupManagedServiceAccount Objects
- Descendant msDS-ManagedServiceAccount Objects

Configure auditing on AD FS

If you are using MDI sensors to collect events from AD FS servers, make the settings described in this section. These will capture the event ids as follows:

- **1202**: The Federation Service validated a new credential.
- **1203**: The Federation Service failed to validate a new credential.
- **4624**: An account was successfully logged on.
- **4625**: An account failed to log on.

Following are the steps to configure auditing.

1. Open **Active Directory Users and Computers** and select the domain you want to enable the logs for.
2. Navigate to **Program Data** | **Microsoft** | **ADFS**.
3. Right-click on **ADFS** and click on **Properties**.
4. Click on the **Security** tab and go to **Advanced** | **Advanced Security Settings** | **Auditing**. Click on **Add** | **Select a principal**.
5. Under **Enter the object name to select,** enter **Everyone**. Click on **Check Names** and click on **OK**.
6. Back in the **Auditing Entry** page, make the following settings:

    In the **Type** dropdown, select **All**.

    In the **Applies to** dropdown, select **This object and all descendant objects**.

    Under **Permissions,** click on **Clear all** and then select **Read all properties** and **Write all properties**.
7. Click **OK**.

Configure auditing on AD CS

If you have a dedicated AD CS server and want to capture audit events from that server follow the steps in this section.

Once configured, the following event ids are collected and recorded in the Windows Event Viewer:

- **4870**: Certificate Services revoked a certificate
- **4882**: The security permissions for Certificate Services changed

- **4885**: The audit filter for Certificate Services changed
- **4887**: Certificate Services approved a certificate request and issued a certificate
- **4888**: Certificate Services denied a certificate request
- **4890**: The certificate manager settings for Certificate Services changed.
- **4896**: One or more rows have been deleted from the certificate database

Following are the steps to configure auditing:

1. Create a group policy to apply to the AD CS server. Go to `Computer Configuration\Policies\Windows Settings\Security Settings\Advanced Audit Policy Configuration\Audit Policies\Object Access\Audit Certification Services` and edit it to capture Success and Failure events.

2. To configure CA auditing, click on **Start | Certification Authority**, right-click on the CA name and click on **Properties**.

3. Click on the **Auditing** tab and select all the events on the page. Click on **OK**.

Configure auditing on configuration container

The last step is to configure auditing on the configuration container. This is done using the tool `ASDIEdit`.

Following are the steps:

1. Go to **Start | Run**. Type `ADSIEdit.msc` and click on **OK**.

2. On the **Action** menu click on **Connect to**.

3. Expand the **Configuration** container. Right-click on the **Configuration** node, beginning with **CN=Configuration,DC=....**, and click on **Properties**.

4. Click on the **Security** tab and click on **Advanced**.

5. In the **Advanced Security Settings,** click on the **Auditing** tab and click on **Add**.

6. Click on **Select a principal** and under **Enter the object name to select** enter **Everyone**. Click on **Check Names** and click on **OK**.

7. Back in the **Auditing Entry** page, make the following settings:

    a. In the **Type** dropdown, select **All**.

    b. In the **Applies to** dropdown, select **This object and all descendant objects**.

    c. Under **Permissions,** click on **Clear all** and then select **Write all properties**.

8. Click **OK**.

Directory Services Account

A **Directory Services Account** (**DSA**) is a special user account created to run specific services or applications. For MDI, a DSA is optional, however, it is required in the following scenarios:

- If you have a sensor installed on an AD FS or AD CS server.
- To request membership of local administrator group of devices on the network.
- To access the DeletedObjects container.
- When querying another domain using LDAP.

DSA must have read permissions to all the domains in the forest including the DeletedObjects container. In cases of disconnected forests, a DSA is required in each forest.

A DSA can use either a regular user account or a **Group Managed Service Account** (**gMSA**). A gMSA is the preferred option for a DSA because it offers better security and password management. The gMSA password is created and changed by AD, and no administrator or user ever knows it. To use a gMSA, the sensor has to get the password from AD. This requires the sensor to have the right permissions. The permissions can be given to each sensor individually, or a group can be used to give permissions to many sensors at once. If the sensor is not installed on AD FS or AD CA servers, the default DC security group can be used. If the sensor is installed on AD FS and AD CA servers, make a universal group and add the AD FS, AD CS and DC to the universal group.

Following are the steps to prepare a gMSA to be used as DSA:

1. Create a gMSA account.
2. Grant required DSA permissions.
3. Verify that the gMSA account has the required permissions.

> **Note: The detailed steps to create gMSA are beyond the scope of this book. Refer to the Microsoft documentation for details.**

Once this is done, you will need to configure a DSA in the Microsoft Defender portal.

Following are the steps:

1. Login to **https://security.microsoft.com** and navigate to **Settings | Identities**. In the left pane, click on **Directory services accounts** and click on **Add credentials**.
2. Enter the **Account name** of the gMSA account created earlier and check the box **Group managed service account**. Type in the **Domain** and click **Save** as shown in *Figure 7.5*. Notice that the **Password** option is deactivated. This is because AD manages the password of the gMSA account.

Microsoft Defender for Identity

Manage credentials used to connect sensors with your on-prem

General

Sensors

Directory services accounts

Manage action accounts

VPN

Health issues

Adjust alerts thresholds

About

⤓ Export   ＋ Add credentials

Filter   Reset ⛃ Filters

Domain: **Any** ∨   Group managed service account: **Any**

Account   Doma

Add credentials

Provide read-only Active Directory credentials to connect your on-premises Active Directory domains.

Account name *

mygMSA

☑ Group managed service account   ⟳

Domain *

contoso.com

☐ Single label domain

Password

Type password

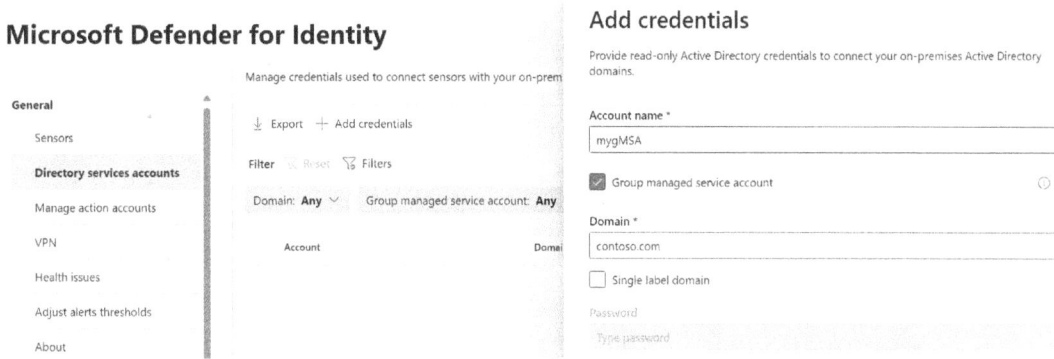

Figure 7.5: Configure gMSA as a DSA

The same procedure can be used to configure a standard user account as a DSA. Ensure that you generate a strong password each time the password is changed for the user account and remember to update the password here.

To identify lateral movements, MDI relies on queries that identify local administrator accounts on machines. This is done using the **Security Account Manager-Remote (SAM-R)** protocol. Windows clients and servers should allow the MDI DSA to perform SAM-R queries. This is done by modifying the Group Policy. Go to **Computer configuration | Windows settings | Security settings | Local policies | Security options**. In the right pane click on **Network access | Restrict clients allowed to make remote calls to SAM** and add the DSA to the list of approved accounts.

Action accounts

MDI can take remediation action on on-premises AD accounts in case of identity compromise. By default, it uses the LocalSystem account for this purpose. If required, this can be changed so that MDI uses a dedicated gMSA. This is optional and it is recommended that the default settings be used. If organizations would like to change this, it is crucial to ensure that the gMSA is granted the right permissions on the DC and that it has access to the required user or machine objects.

Following are the steps:

1. Create a new gMSA and grant it the **Log on as a service** permission on each domain controller running the MDI sensor.

2. Grant the gMSA the required permissions by going to **Active Directory Users and Computers**. Following are the steps. These settings are shown in *Figure 7.6*.

    a. Right click on the relevant domain or OU and click on **Properties**.

    b. Select the **Security** tab and click on **Advanced**.

c. Click on **Select a principal** and check the box next to **Service Accounts**. In the **Enter the object name to select** box, enter the name of the gMSA account and click on **OK**.

d. In the **Applies to** field, select **Descendant User objects**. In the **Permissions** and **Properties** section, make the selections as shown in *Figure 7.6* and click **OK**:

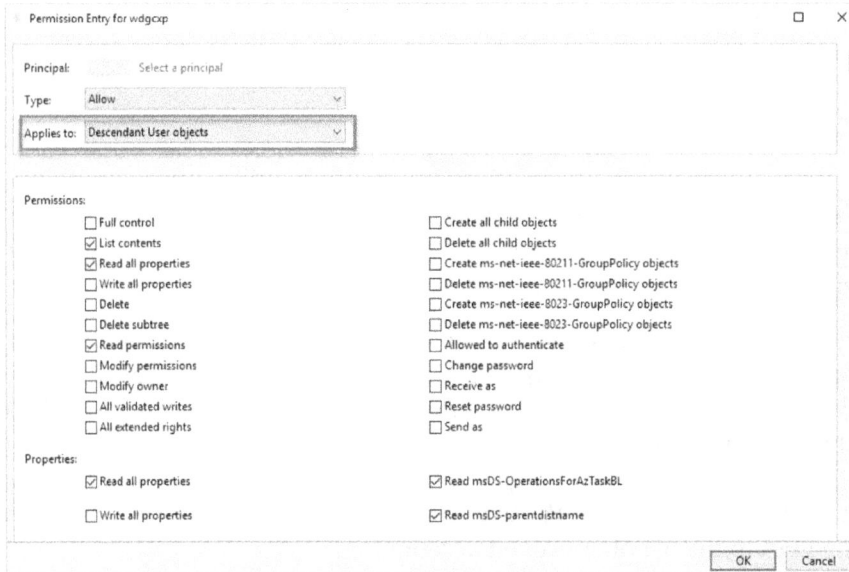

Figure 7.6: gMSA account permissions for action accounts

3. Login to **https://security.microsoft.com** and navigate to **Settings | Identities | Manage action account**. In the right pane click select the option **Manually configure your management account**. In the fly out pane, type the name of the gMSA account and the domain and click on **Save** as shown in the following figure:

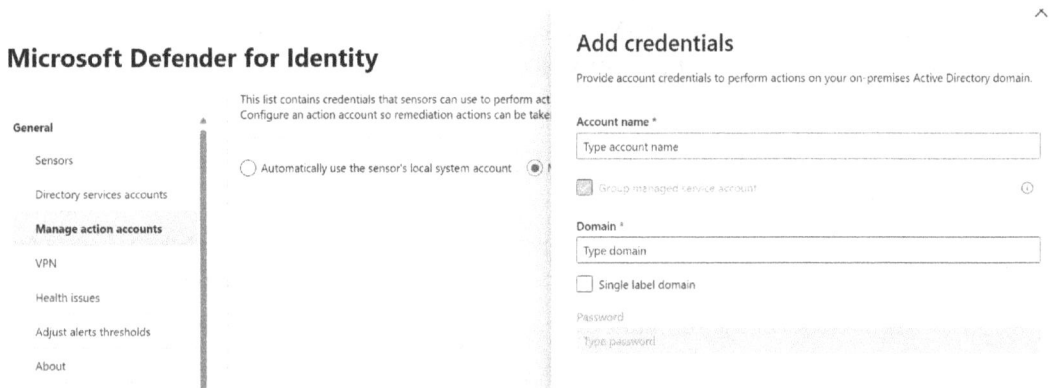

Figure 7.7: Add gMSA as action account

MDI domain controllers

If an organization has already onboarded DC to Microsoft Defender for Endpoint, they can activate MDI capabilities without installing the MDI sensor on the DC.

To use MDI capabilities without the MDI sensor, ensure that the following prerequisites are met:

- MDI sensor should not be installed on the DC.
- Ensure that the DC is Windows Server 2019 or Windows Server 2022 with the March 2024 cumulative update installed.
- The DC should be onboarded to MDE. This will be explained in *Chapter 8, Protecting Endpoints*.
- An account with the **Security Administrator** role.
- Network connectivity as required by MDE. This will be explained in *Chapter 8, Protecting Endpoints*.
- Configure Windows audit log collection policies as explained in the section *Configure auditing on domain controllers* earlier in this chapter.

To activate the MDI capabilities, following are the steps:

1. Login to **https://security.microsoft.com** and navigate to **Settings I Identities I Activation**. All eligible domain controllers will be listed on this page.
2. Click on the DC where you want to activate MDI capabilities and click on **Activate**. When prompted confirm your selection.
3. Once the activation is complete, a green banner is displayed. Click on **Click here to see the onboarded servers**. It will take you to the **Settings I Identities I Sensors** page.

> Note: At the time of this writing, this feature was in Public Preview.

Investigate and respond

MDI reports into the Microsoft Defender portal if any users or computers have performed suspicious activities or are suspected of being compromised. Security analysts can then investigate users and take remedial actions on compromised user accounts.

Investigate users

To investigate suspicious users, go to the **Assets** tab in the incident and then click on **Users** as shown in the following figure:

Figure 7.8: Investigating assets

Clicking on the user will open the details page for the user, where you can investigate further. Following figure shows the user page:

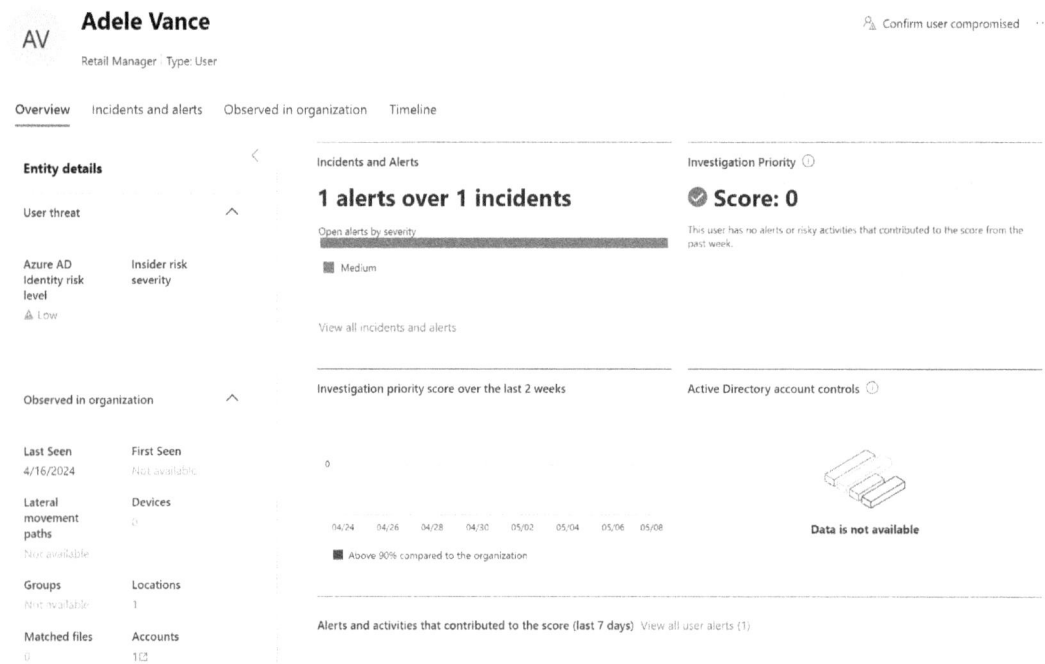

Figure 7.9: User page

- **Overview**: Shows general identity data such as the risk level, the number of devices assigned to the user etc.

- **Incidents and alerts**: Shows all the incidents and alerts involving the user from the last 180 days.

- **Observed in organization**: Shows the devices to which the user has signed on in the last 180 days, the locations where the identity was observed in the last 30 days, the on-premises groups for the identity and if any lateral movement path has been detected from the on-premises environment.

- **Identity timeline**: Shows all observed user activities across MDI, MDE and MDCA.

From this screen, you can **Confirm user compromise** by clicking on the option on the top right. More options are available by clicking on the ellipses as shown in the following figure:

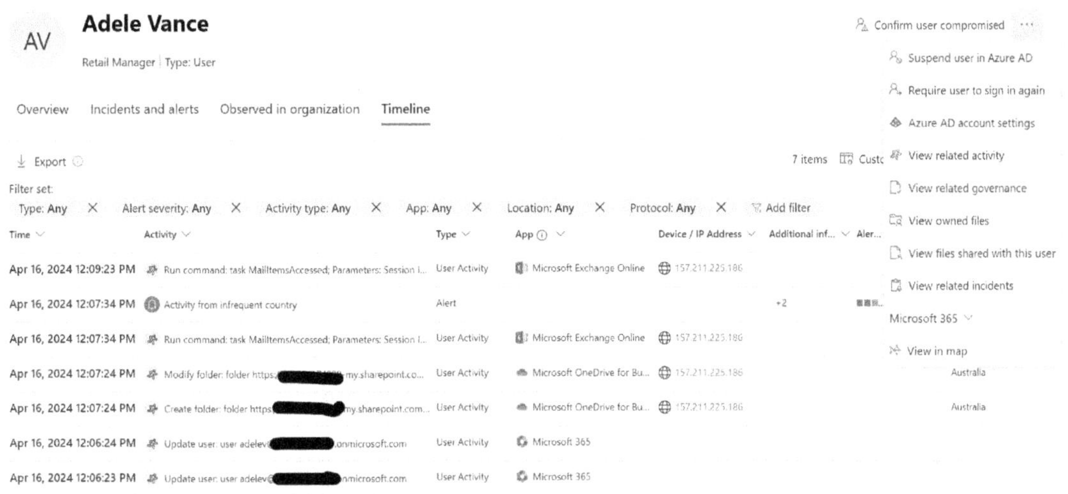

Figure 7.10: *User timeline page*

Investigating lateral movement

One of the main strategies that attackers use in attacks based on identity is moving sideways within the network. This is called **lateral movement**. They use an account with low permissions to get into an account with high permissions. They do this by finding machines that have saved credentials on them. MDI gives you security information about how attackers move sideways, **lateral movement paths** (**LMPs**). These are visual aids that help analysts see and recognize how attackers go from one machine to another in the network. Attackers have different ways of moving sideways. The usual ones are stealing credentials and Pass the Ticket.

If an identity discovered by MDI is suspected to be in an LMP it is listed under the **Lateral movement** section on the **Observed in organization** tab on the user page.

For sensitive user, potential LMPs leading to the user are shown and for non-sensitive users potential LMPs the entity is related to are shown. This example is shown in *Figure 7.11*, LMP for the admin user and the entities involved in it.

MDI displays the most recent LMP discovered, and it is saved for 48 hours post discovery. Past LMPs can be seen by selecting a date. You can also select a different user who initiated the LMP by selecting the **Path initiator**.

Refer to *Figure 7.11*:

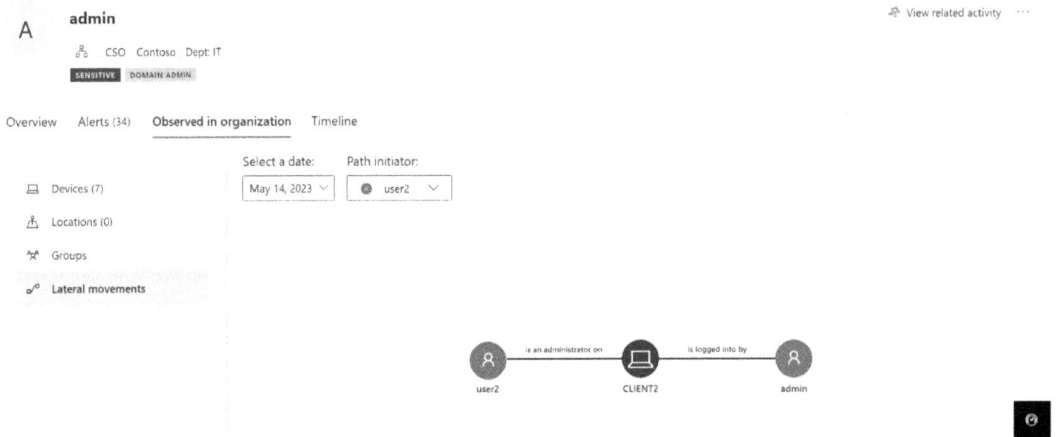

Figure 7.11: Investigating lateral movement

LMPs assist in investigation by providing evidence and entities involved in each potential lateral movement. Based on this evidence the security teams can determine the priority of the security alert and investigate the entities. It also makes it easier for the security teams to prevent the attacker from moving forward in the network.

MDI also highlights risky LMPs. LMPs are considered risky if they have three or more non-sensitive accounts that have the potential to expose sensitive credentials to bad actors. To view risky LMPs review LMP security assessment by going to **Microsoft Secure Score** on the Microsoft Defender portal and clicking on **Recommended actions**. Look for an entry called **Reduce lateral movement path risk to sensitive entities** as shown in *Figure 7.12*. It also suggests recommended actions that could be removing the entity from the group or removing its administrative privileges.

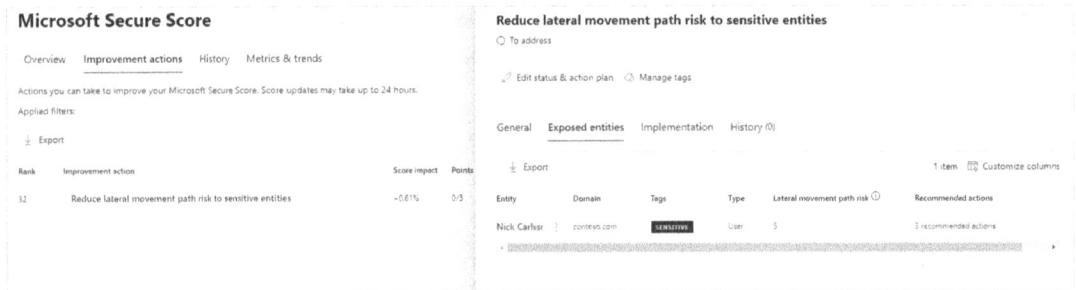

Figure 7.12: Risky LMP

Working with security alerts

As discussed in the previous chapter, MDI logs alerts in the Microsoft Defender portal. Since Microsoft Defender XDR is aligned to the MITRE ATT&CK framework, the MDI alerts are categorized into the following as per the phases seen in a cyber-attack kill-chain:

- **Reconnaissance alerts** which include activities like account enumeration, user and group membership enumeration, AD attribute reconnaissance.

- **Persistence and privilege escalation alerts** like golden ticket usage, suspicious additions to sensitive groups, modifications to domain trust relationships.

- **Credential access alerts** like brute force attacks, honeytoken authentication, password spray attacks.

- **Lateral movement alerts** like remote code execution on DNS, Pass The Hash, Pass The Ticket.

- **Other alerts** like DCShadow attack, suspicious VPN connection, group policy tampering.

In addition to the above, MDI also monitors Active Directory, network and event activities for suspicious activities. These include user account attribute changes, login operations, AD security principal operations and more.

> **Note: For detailed information on these categories and the alerts under each, refer to the Microsoft online documentation.**

MDI explains the alerts in plain language, uses graphics and colors to make them easy to understand. To review the alerts related to MDI in the Microsoft Defender XDR portal, go to **Incidents alerts | Alerts** and add a filter for **Service/detection sources** and filter by **Microsoft Defender for Identity** as shown in the following figure:

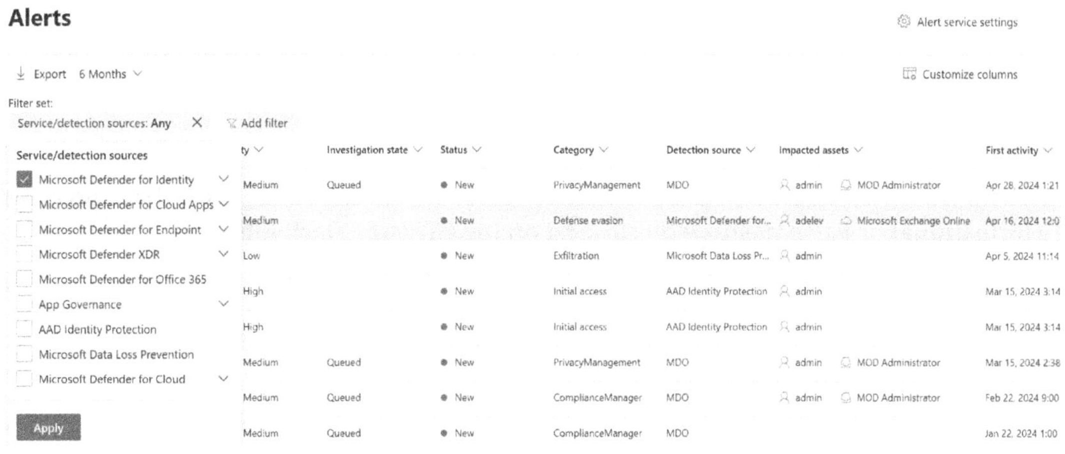

Figure 7.13: Viewing MDI alerts in Microsoft Defender XDR portal

Click on an alert to view the alerts details. The following figure shows an example of a MDI alert. Review the information provided on the page. Note that you can click on the **Manage alert** option to update the alert status, assignment and classification. It can also be exported as a detailed Excel report by clicking on the **Export** option. You can also link the alert to an incident.

Refer to the following figure:

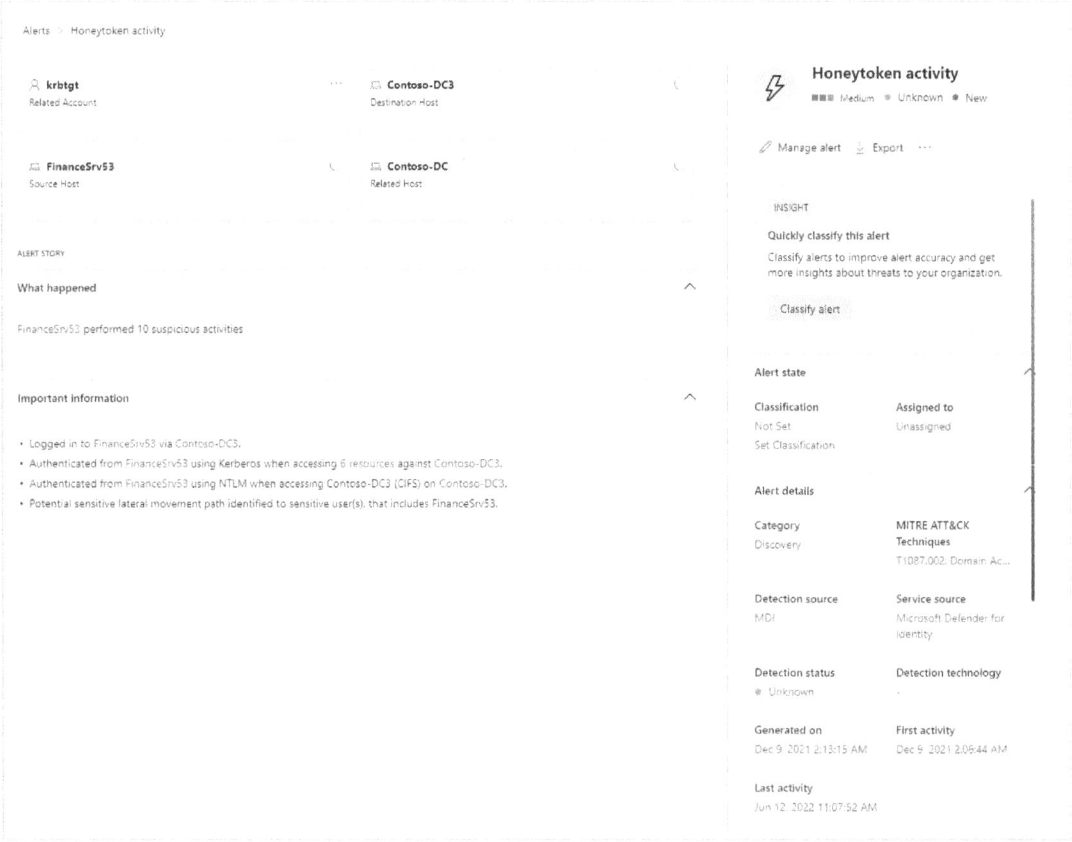

Figure 7.14: MDI alert

Based on the investigations carried out the alert can be classified as a **True positive**, **Informational** or **False positive** by clicking on the **Classify alert** button.

Remediation

MDI allows security analysts to take remediation actions of disabling user accounts or resetting their passwords. These actions are sent to AD via the MDI gateway and are logged in the **action center**. The next time AD synchronizes with Entra ID, the action is reflected in Entra ID as well. To ensure that hybrid remediation works you need to ensure that you have configured an **action account**. This is explained in the *Action accounts* section earlier in this chapter.

The actions taken on user accounts can be viewed from the user page, in the action center or using advanced hunting.

Identity security posture

Organizations today like to be proactive in understanding and strengthening their security posture. In the previous chapter, we learnt how to use Microsoft Secure Score. Microsoft Secure Score also offers assessments for MDI security posture and provides contextual data on known exploitable components and misconfigurations. It actively monitors the on-premises identities and identity infrastructure for weal spots. It provides accurate assessment reports or the organization's identity security posture. To access the security assessments for MDI, go to the **Microsoft Secure Score** page in the Microsoft Defender XDR portal and click on **Recommendations**. Filter by the **Category** and choose **Identity** to view all identity related recommendations. You will see all recommendations related to MDI and Microsoft Entra ID in one place. Select each recommendation to view detailed description and implementation steps.

Dashboards and reports

MDI offers various dashboards and reports that can be used to understand the threat landscape, proactively understand health issues and report to relevant stakeholders.

ITDR dashboard

The **MDI Dashboard** page shows data that helps understand the security posture, identify vulnerabilities and complete recommended actions. On this page you can view critical insights and real-time data about identity threats and response. The minimum role required to view the ITDR dashboard is **Security Administrator**. The **ITDR Dashboard** is accessible from the Microsoft Defender portal under **Identities | Dashboard**.

Following figure shows an example of the **ITDR Dashboard**:

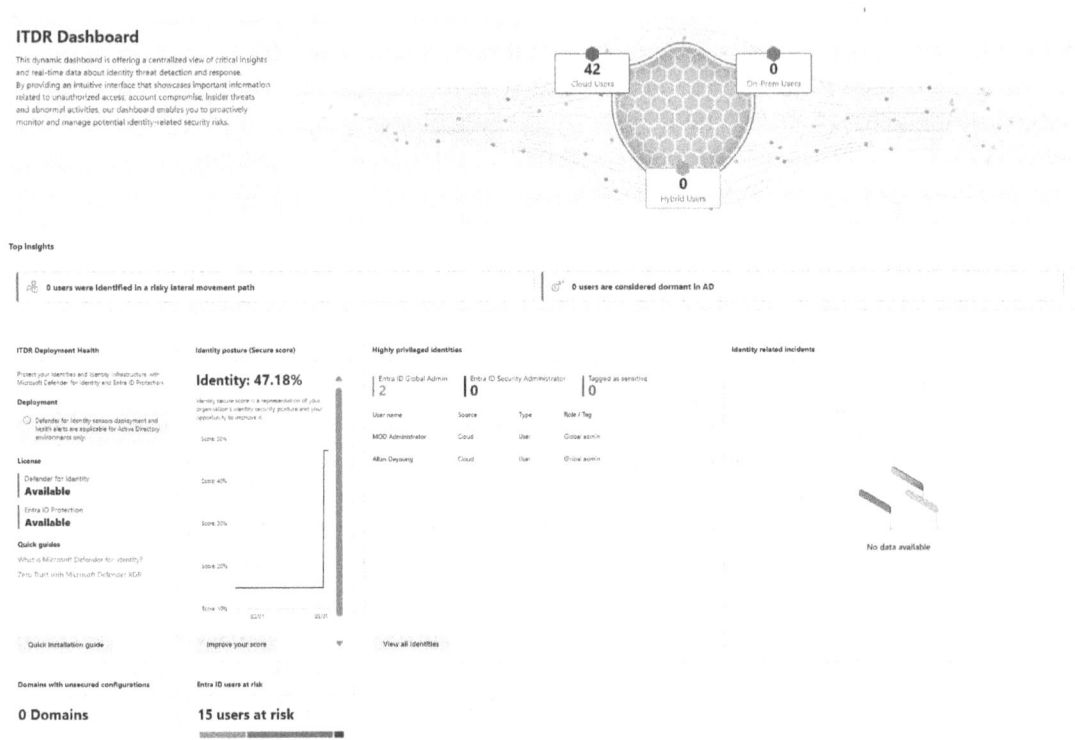

Figure 7.15: ITDR Dashboard

Viewing health issues

The **Health Issues** page under **Identities** on the Microsoft Defender page shows any health issues in your MDI sensors or the general MDI environment.

They are segregated under two tabs as follows:

- Domain related health issues are under the **Global health issues** tab. These could include issues like incorrect directory services user credentials, advanced auditing not enabled etc.

- MDI Sensor related issues are under the **Sensor health issues** tab. These could include issues like outdated sensor version, domain controller not reachable, sensor reaching a resource limit, service failed to start etc.

You can click on any of the issues to see more details or to close or suppress the issue as shown in the following figure:

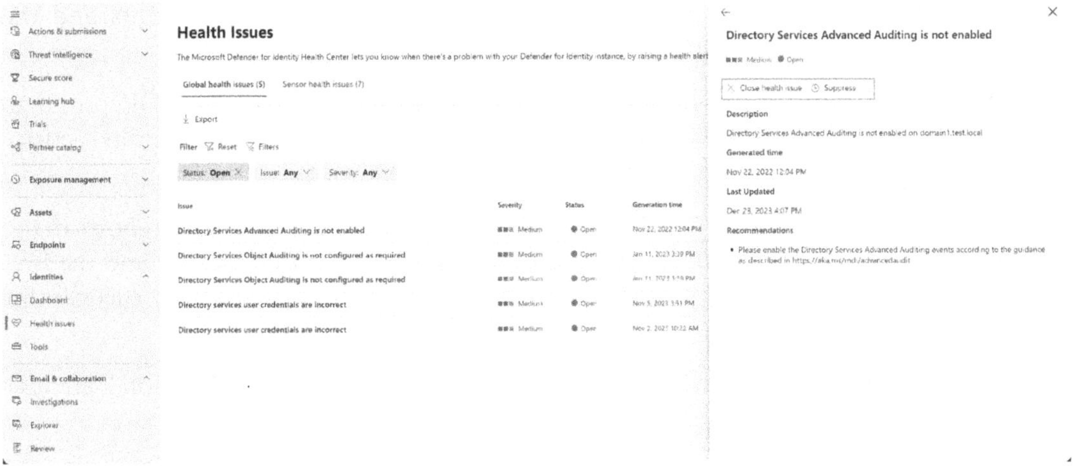

Figure 7.16: Health Issues

Microsoft Defender for Identity reports

Microsoft Defender now offers MDI reports which are accessible from the Microsoft Defender portal by going to the **Reports** section and clicking on **Reports Management** under **Identities** in the right pane. There are four types of reports available as shown in the following figure:

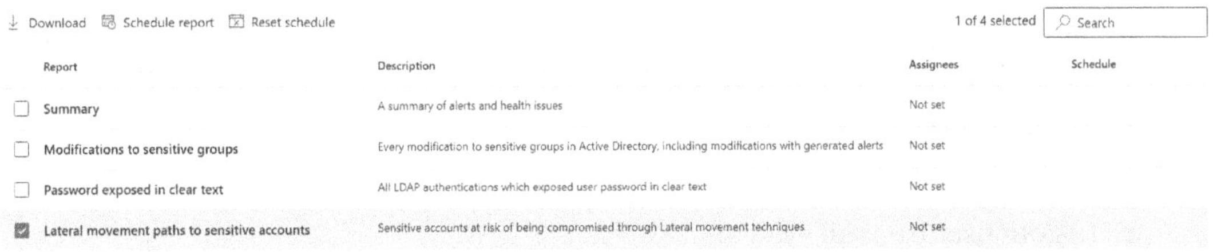

Figure 7.17: MDI reports

Reports can be scheduled to be sent to designated individuals by clicking on the check box next to the report and selecting **Schedule report**. Refer to *Figure 7.17*.

Reports can also be downloaded on demand by clicking on the name of the report. In the fly out pane, select the **Start date** and **End date** and click on **Download Report**.

Conclusion

This chapter taught you about MDI and its role in securing on-premises AD accounts. You should have learned about the different features of MDI and how it can help you identify, investigate and respond to attacks that target identities. You should be able to deploy the MDI sensor on servers in your environment and set policies to collect events.

This chapter also explained Directory Services accounts and action accounts and the scenarios in which they are required.

One of the skills you should have been using the Microsoft Defender XDR portal to examine users and lateral movement paths. You should also be able to handle security alerts and perform remediation actions on affected user accounts.

This chapter concluded with an explanation of the different dashboards and reports in the Microsoft Defender portal. With the information you learned in this chapter and the first part of the book, you can now design and implement a strategy for identity security for your organization.

In the next chapter, we will learn how to protect endpoint devices using Microsoft Defender for Endpoint.

Multiple choice questions

1. **On which server can the MDI sensor be installed? Select all that apply.**
   a. Domain Controller
   b. AD FS server
   c. Any member server
   d. AD CS server

2. **You are investigating a security incident, and you find a suspicious user account? What are the actions available to you to contain the spread of the attack?**
   a. Reset the user's password
   b. Delete the user account
   c. Logout user from all systems
   d. Force MFA for the user

3. **In the Microsoft Defender XDR portal where can you investigate LMPs?**
   a. On the incident page
   b. On the Assets tab in the alert
   c. On the Observed in organization tab on the user page
   d. In the Reports section

Answer key

1. a, b, d
2. a
3. c

CHAPTER 8
Protecting Endpoints

Introduction

In today's hybrid working environment, users use a multitude of devices from a multitude of locations. The days when users worked solely from their offices behind corporate firewalls are gone. This exposes user endpoints to threats like never before. At the same time, attackers are becoming increasingly sophisticated. Organizations need modern and intelligent tools to protect their users' devices from bad actors. **Microsoft Defender for Endpoint** (**MDE**) is an enterprise endpoint security platform designed to help enterprise networks prevent, detect, investigate, and respond to advanced threats. Coupled with Microsoft Defender Vulnerability Management, it offers proactive protection and visibility into the vulnerabilities in the environment and provides recommendations to strengthen the security posture. Organizations today also use **operational technology** (**OT**) and **Internet of Things** (**IoT**) devices. It is important for an organization to gain visibility into these devices and the threats surrounding them. Microsoft Defender for IoT provides device discovery and threat protection services for OT and IoT networks across cloud, on-premises and air-gapped infrastructure.

Structure

Following is the structure of the chapter:

- Microsoft Defender for Endpoint
- Configure MDE settings
- Microsoft Defender Vulnerability Management
- Microsoft Defender for IoT

Objectives

By the end of this chapter, readers will learn about the licensing options and features of MDE and how it is used to detect, investigate and protect endpoints from cyber threats. This chapter will also introduce you to Microsoft Defender Vulnerability Management to proactivity identify, assess and remediate vulnerabilities in the endpoints in your network. You will learn about the various licensing options and the features of MDE. You will also learn how MDE integrates with Microsoft Defender XDR to provide a complete picture of the threats in your environment. Lastly, this chapter will introduce Microsoft Defender for IoT and how it is used to protect connected devices that use OT and IoT networks.

Microsoft Defender for Endpoint

MDE is a cloud-based, agentless, enterprise level **endpoint protection (EPP)** and **endpoint detection and response (EDR)** solution. It helps organizations protect, identify, investigate and respond to cyber threats on end user devices like laptops, servers, tablets, PCs, routers and firewalls.

MDE uses built-in sensors in the Windows operating system, which means there is no need to install agents or anti-virus software on the endpoints. These sensors gather and process signals from the endpoints and send them to the MDE cloud service. It uses big data, machine learning and millions of signals received by Microsoft from all the enterprise (such as Microsoft 365) and consumer systems (such as Xbox) running worldwide. These signals are used to do behavioral analytics for early detection of threats. It uses threat intelligence generated by Microsoft researchers and security teams in addition to the intelligence provided by partners to identify tools, techniques and procedures used by attackers and matches them to the data received by the sensors to generate alerts.

Figure 8.1 shows the various capabilities of MDE:

Figure 8.1: MDE capabilities

These capabilities are explained as follows:

- **Core defender vulnerability management** uses a modern risk-based approach to discover, assess, prioritize and remediate vulnerabilities and misconfigurations on the endpoint.

- **Attack surface reduction** provides the first line of defense by ensuring that proper configuration settings and exploit mitigation strategies are applied. This includes network and web protection.

- **Next-generation protection** catches and blocks all types of emerging threats. Modern malware mutates continuously (polymorphic) to evade detection. MDE uses local and cloud-based machine learning models, behavior analysis and heuristics to bock malware.

- **Endpoint detection and response** capabilities are used to detect, investigate and respond to advanced threats that may have escaped the first two pillars.

- **Automated investigation and remediation** offer automatic remediation of threats that help reduce the volume of alerts to be triaged and investigated by a human.

- **Microsoft threat experts** is a managed threat hunting service provided by Microsoft that helps augment and further empower the customer security teams.

- **Centralized configuration and administration**, APIs enabled MDE to easily integrate with the existing workflows. It offers native integration with other Microsoft products like Microsoft Defender for Cloud, Microsoft Sentinel, Intune, Microsoft Defender for Cloud Apps, Microsoft Defender for Identity and Microsoft Defender for Office.

Data storage and privacy

MDE collects data from onboarded devices and stores it in customer dedicated segregated tenants. The data collected includes file data such as file names, sizes and hashes, process data such as running process and hashes, registry data, network connection data such as host IPs and ports, and device details such as device names and operating system version. This data is stored securely in Microsoft Azure data centers across UK, US, Europe and

Australia. This data is encrypted using 256-bit AES encryption at rest and in flight with key management within Azure Key Vault.

MDE shares this data among other products like Microsoft Sentinel, Microsoft Tunnel for Mobile Application Management, Microsoft Defender for Cloud, Microsoft Defender for Identity and Microsoft security Exposure Management.

Customer data is always isolated from other customers' data through authentication and logical segregation.

Data in MDE is retained for 180 days during which is visible across the portal. If the organization requires to retain the data for longer than that, consider exporting the data to an external system like log analytics.

If a customer decides to end the MDE service, the data is available to the customer till the license is under the grace period. At the end of this period the data is deleted from Microsoft's system within 180 days from contract termination date.

MDE has obtained several industry certifications like ISO, SOC, FedRAMP High and continues to achieve additional industry and regional certifications. For a complete list of certifications held by MDE visit the Microsoft Service Trust Portal at **https://aka.ms/stp**.

Licensing

MDE is available in two plans, as follows:

- **Microsoft Defender for Endpoint Plan 1**: It delivers the core protection capabilities like next-generation anti-malware, attack surface reduction rules, device control, endpoint firewall and network protection. It is available as a standalone user license subscription and as part of Microsoft 365 E3.

- **Microsoft Defender for Endpoint Plan 2**: It delivers additional endpoint protection that includes all capabilities of MDE Plan 1 plus EDR, **automated investigation and response (AIR)**, **Threat and Vulnerability Management (TVM)**, Threat Intelligence and Microsoft Threat Experts. It is available as a standalone user subscription and as a part of the following subscriptions:

  o Windows 10/11 Enterprise E5

  o Microsoft 365 E5

  o Microsoft 365 E5 Security

  o Microsoft 365 F5 Security & Compliance

  To onboard Windows Servers to the standalone versions of MDE, server licenses are required. The following are the available options:

  o Microsoft Defender for Endpoint for Servers Plan 1 or Plan 2 (as part of Defender for Cloud)

  o Microsoft Defender for Endpoint for Servers

Deploy MDE

Deploying MDE in your environment requires careful planning, stakeholder involvement and change management. Before you begin, you should understand your environment in terms of the number of endpoints and servers, the management engine, **security operations center (SOC)** processes and security incident monitoring tools in use. Conduct a comprehensive security product evaluation and start with a small subset of endpoints and servers and then slowly expand to all devices.

Prerequisites

Before you begin deploying MDE in your environment ensure the following prerequisites:

- **Roles**: To onboard the tenant to the MDE service you must be a Global Administrator or Security Administrator. MDE leverages Microsoft Defender XDR unified RBAC model. Once you turn on unified RBAC in Microsoft Defender XDR a role called **Microsoft Defender for Endpoint administrator** is created and available in the Microsoft Defender portal under **Settings** | **Endpoints** | **Roles**. This role has full permissions to the MDE service, and it cannot be modified. *Figure 8.2* shows the permission for this role. This role can be assigned to Microsoft Entra ID users and groups.

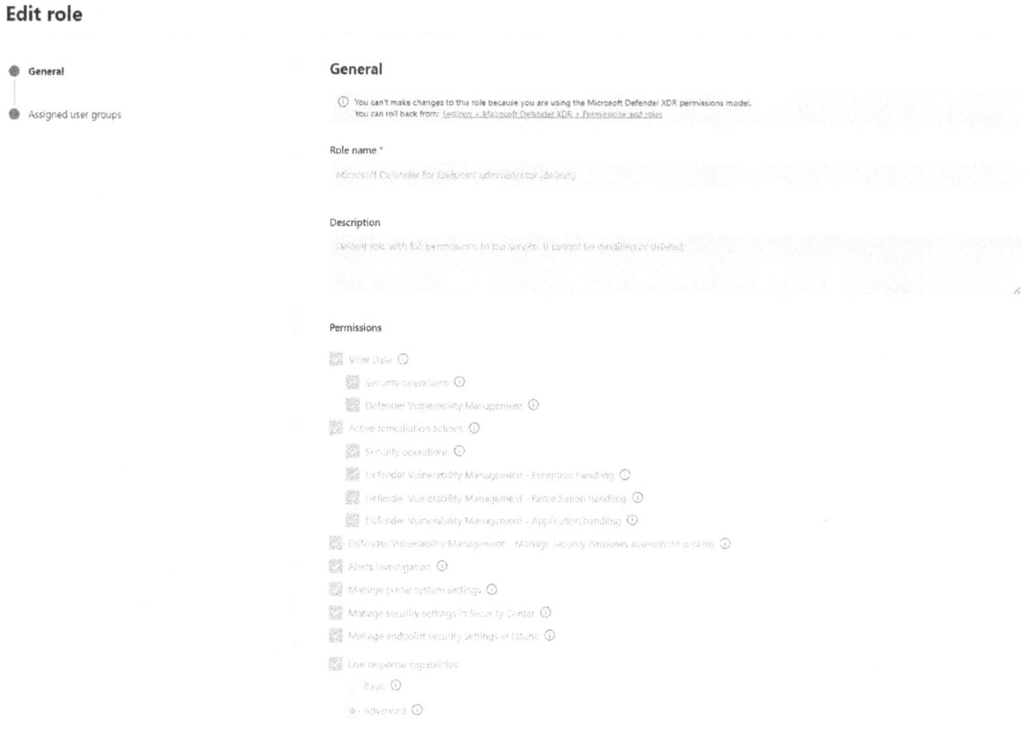

Edit role

● General

● Assigned user groups

General

ⓘ You can't make changes to this role because you are using the Microsoft Defender XDR permissions model.
You can roll back from: Settings > Microsoft Defender XDR > Permissions and roles

Role name *

Microsoft Defender for Endpoint administrator (default)

Description

Default role with full permissions to this service. It cannot be modified or deleted.

Permissions

☑ View Data ⓘ
  ☑ Security operations ⓘ
  ☑ Defender Vulnerability Management ⓘ
☑ Active remediation actions ⓘ
  ☑ Security operations ⓘ
  ☑ Defender Vulnerability Management - Exception handling ⓘ
  ☑ Defender Vulnerability Management - Remediation handling ⓘ
  ☑ Defender Vulnerability Management - Application handling ⓘ
☑ Defender Vulnerability Management - Manage security baselines assessment profiles ⓘ
☑ Alerts investigation ⓘ
☑ Manage portal system settings ⓘ
☑ Manage security settings in Security Center ⓘ
☑ Manage endpoint security settings in Intune ⓘ
☑ Live response capabilities ⓘ
  ○ Basic ⓘ
  ● Advanced ⓘ

Figure 8.2: Microsoft Defender for Endpoint administrator permissions

Custom roles can be created by going to **Permissions** and selecting **Roles** under **Microsoft Defender XDR**.

- **Hardware requirements**: Since MDE is a part of the Windows operating system there is no specific hardware requirement for MDE. Ensure that the devices meet the minimum hardware requirements for the operating system they are running. MacOS devices should be running x64 and ARM64 processors with 1GB of disk space available. Linux x64 (AMD64/EM64T) and x86_64 versions are supported.

- **Operating system requirements**: MDE supports a long list of Windows 10/11 and Windows Server versions. It also supports Azure Virtual Desktop and Windows 365. MacOS 14 (Sonoma), 13 (Ventura), 12 (Monterey) are supported. In addition, it supports a range of Red Hat Enterprise Linux, Cent OS, Ubuntu and many more operating systems. For a complete list of supported operating systems refer to the Microsoft documentation.

- **Supported browsers**: Since MDE is administered through a web browser ensure that you use Microsoft Edge or Google Chrome to access the console. Other browsers may work but they are not supported by Microsoft.

- **Network requirements**: Ensure that IPv4 is enabled on all onboarded devices to allow communication with the MDE service. The onboarded devices must be able to connect to the internet directly or through a proxy.

- **Configure Microsoft Defender Antivirus**: For endpoint protection capabilities like file scanning MDE depends on Microsoft Defender Antivirus. This is built into the Windows operating system, and updates are managed by the cloud service. Many organizations also use non-Microsoft anti-malware clients. If Microsoft Defender Antivirus detects the presence of a non-Microsoft anti-malware client, it goes into passive mode. It continues to receive updates and the `msmpeng.exe` service shows as running in the task manager. However, it does not run any scans on the system or replace the non-Microsoft anti-malware client. The user interface is disabled, and the users are not able to use Microsoft Defender Antivirus to run system scans or configure other options like Attack Surface Reduction, Network Protection, Controlled Folder Access etc.

Security intelligence updates should be configured regardless of whether Microsoft Defender Antivirus is the active anti-malware solution. Since the MDE service depends on Microsoft Defender Antivirus, it should not be turned off by Group Policy or any other methods.

If Microsoft Defender Antivirus is not your primary anti-malware solution and you are using Mobile Device Management solutions or Microsoft Configuration Manager make sure that Microsoft Defender Antivirus **Early Launch Antimalware** (**EALM**) driver is enabled.

Define deployment architecture

Each organization is unique and MDE can provide for an environment's requirements. There are various deployment options available depending on the current infrastructure setup.

Table 8.1 summarizes the different architectures available along with their use cases:

Architecture	Description
Cloud-native	Ideal for organizations that do not have an on-premises configuration management solution or are looking to reduce their on-premises footprint. It is recommended to use Microsoft Intune to onboard the endpoint devices to MDE.
Co-management	Ideal for organizations that use cloud capabilities but also have significant on-premises footprint. It is recommended to use Microsoft's Configuration Manager and Intune.
On-premises	Ideal for organization's that are largely on-premises but want to use the cloud capabilities provided by MDE. It is recommended to use their existing Configuration Manager and AD setup.
Evaluation	It is recommended that organizations test MDE in a small environment before rolling it out. For this Microsoft provides local scripts to onboard a small number of devices without the need of management software.

Table 8.1: MDE architecture

Selecting deployment tool

To take advantage of the MDE capabilities, endpoints need to be onboarded to the MDE cloud service. This can be done by using various tools.

Table 8.2 summarizes the tools available depending on the operating system on the endpoint:

Endpoint	Onboarding tool
Windows devices	Local script (up to 10 devices) Group Policy Microsoft Intune/Mobile Device management Microsoft Configuration Manager VDI scripts
Windows Servers	Integration with Microsoft Defender for Cloud

Endpoint	Onboarding tool
MacOS	Local script Microsoft Intune JAMF Pro Mobile Device Management
Linux devices	Local script Puppet Ansible Chef Saltstack
Android	Microsoft Intune
iOS	Microsoft Intune Mobile Application Manager

Table 8.2: MDE deployment tools

Onboard devices

As we have learnt, the devices must be able to reach the MDE service to be onboarded and managed by MDE. In many organizations this requires the use of proxy configurations. Earlier, administrators needed to allow a large list of MDE URLs in their proxy servers as static IP ranges were not supported. A simplified method called Streamlined connectivity is now available using which devices can be onboarded using lesser URLs or static IP ranges. For a list of these URLs and IP ranges, refer to Microsoft online documentation.

To onboard endpoints to the MDE service, following are the steps:

1. Login to **https://security.microsoft.com** and click on **Settings**. In the right pane click on **Endpoints**.

2. Under **Device management** click on **Onboarding**. In the right pane select the **operating system, Connectivity type** and **Deployment method** and click on **Download onboarding package** as shown in the following figure:

Endpoints

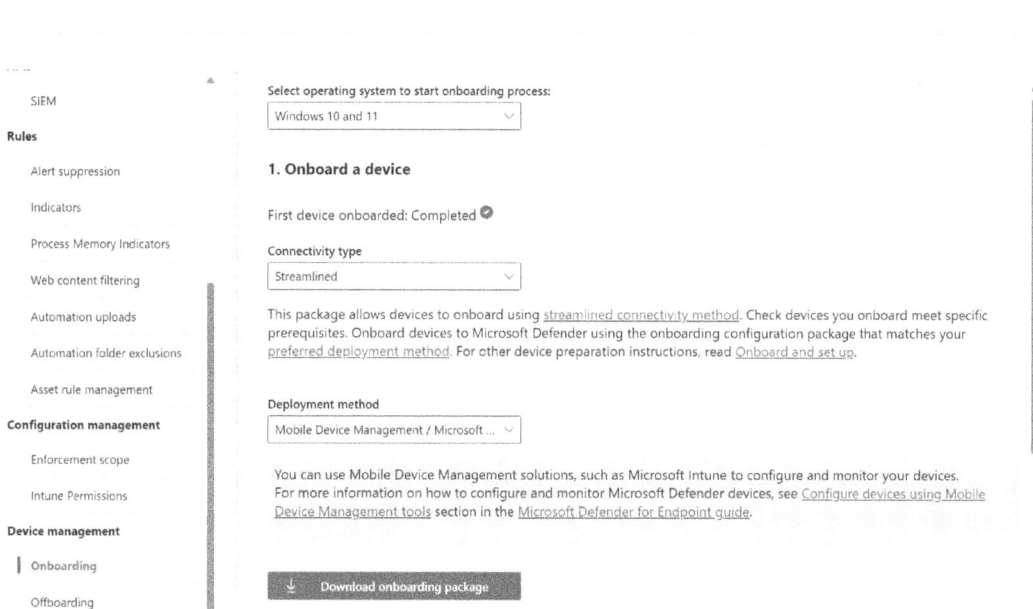

Figure 8.3: Onboarding devices to MDE

Note: The detailed onboarding steps for each operating system and deployment method is beyond the scope of this book. Refer to Microsoft online documentation for detailed steps.

Configure MDE settings

This section will discuss the various settings available for MDE in the Microsoft Defender portal. To access these settings, go to **https://security.microsoft.com** and click on **Settings**. In the right pane, click on **Endpoints**.

General

Under the General settings, you can configure advanced features, assign licenses, email notifications, and auto remediation settings. This section discusses the details:

Advanced features

Following settings are available:

- **Restrict correlation to within scoped device groups**: MDE correlates similar alerts into incidents to reduce the number of alerts that SOC analysts need to look at. By default, this considers alerts generated by all devices in the network. If this setting is turned on, incident correlation will only happen within device groups. Similar alerts across device groups will be treated as separate incidents. For example, if an organization has two device groups, device group A and device group B and if the same malware was seen on devices in both device groups, two alerts will be generated instead of one. This is useful in distributed SOC scenarios where local SOC teams would only like to see incident related to the devices they manage.

- **Enable EDR in block mode**: When turned on this feature proactively blocks malicious behaviors detected on the device even if Microsoft Defender Antivirus is running in passive mode. This feature is off by default.

- **Automatically resolve alerts**: This capability resolve alerts automatically if no threat was found or if the threats have been remediated. This works on MDE tenants created after Windows 10, version 1809 and is on by default. For MDE tenants created before this version it will have to be manually turned on.

- **Allow or block file**: This feature blocks malicious files on the network which prevents it from being read, written or executed on devices on the network. For this feature to work Windows Defender Antivirus must be running in active mode and cloud-based protection must be turned on.

- **Hide potential duplicate device records**: Enabling this feature ensures that the most accurate information about the devices is displayed as it hides the potential duplicate device records. Device records could be duplicated if **Device discovery** scans the network and discovers an already onboarded device or one that has been recently offboarded. Duplicate devices are identified based on their hostname and last seen time. This feature is on by default. Device discovery is covered later in this section.

- **Custom network indicators**: This feature lets you create indicators for IP addresses, domains or URLs that determine if they will be allowed or blocked on devices. The devices must be running Windows 10, version 1709 or later or Windows 11. They must have network protection configured in block mode and antimalware version 4.18.1906.3 or later. This feature is off by default.

- **Tamper protection**: This setting prevents bad actors from turning off the security features like antivirus, threat protection, cloud-delivered protection etc. This feature is on by default.

- **Show user details**: This feature shows the user details like name, title, department which are stored in Microsoft Entra ID in the **Alerts** and **Devices** view. This feature is on by default.

- **Skype for business integration**: This allows security analysts to communicate with end users using Skype for business, phone or email to work with end users to mitigate risks on their devices.

- **Microsoft Defender for Cloud Apps**: MDE can be integrated with Microsoft Defender for Cloud Apps and assist in Shadow IT discovery and sanctioning and blocking apps on devices onboarded to MDE. This feature is available with EMS

E5 license on devices running specific builds of Windows 10 version 1709, 1803, 1809 or later. This setting is off by default.

- **Web content filtering**: Using this setting access to unwanted sites like adult content, site requiring high bandwidth or child abuse sites, drugs, illegal software sites etc. can be blocked. For this a policy needs to be created. This will be explained later in the **Rules** section. This setting is off by default.

- **Unified audit log**: When this setting is turned on all auditable activities performed by a user or administrator is recorded in the Office 365 audit log. This setting is off by default.

- **Device discovery**: When this setting is turned on MDE proactively discovers all the unmanaged devices on the network. These devices include workstations, servers, mobile devices that are not onboarded to MDE, network devices like routers and switches and IoT devices like printers and cameras. This setting is on by default.

- **Download quarantined files**: This feature allows backing up quarantined files in a secure location so that they can be downloaded using the **Download file** option available on the file page. This feature is turned on by default.

- **Default to streamlined connectivity when onboarding devices in Defender portal**: Turned on by default this feature onboards devices to MDE using the streamlined connectivity method. Streamed connectivity has been explained earlier in this chapter.

- **Apply streamlined connectivity settings to devices managed by Intune and Defender for Cloud**: Turned on by default this feature enables devices managed by Intune and Defender for Cloud to connect to the MDE service using the streamlined connectivity method.

- **Live response**: This feature enables administrators with appropriate permissions to start a live response session on devices. This feature is off by default.

- **Live response on servers**: This feature enables administrators with appropriate permissions to start a live response session on Windows and Linux servers to which they have access. This feature is off by default.

- **Live response unsigned script execution**: This feature enables the use of unsigned scripts during a live response session. This feature is off by default.

- **Share endpoint alerts with Microsoft Compliance center**: Turning this feature on sends endpoint security alerts to the Microsoft Compliance Center thereby enhancing Insider Risk Management policies. **Security policy violation indicators** will have to be configured in insider risk management. This will be covered in the next section of this book. This feature is off by default.

- **Microsoft Intune connection**: Using this feature allows MDE to share device telemetry with Microsoft Intune to enable **device risk-based conditional access policies**. For example, if MDE detects that a device has been comprised and is at high risk, this signal can be shared with Microsoft Intune. A conditional access policy can then prevent high risk devices from connecting to internal resources. This feature is turned off by default and must be turned on in both MDE and Microsoft Intune. It is only available in tenants that have EMS E3 + Windows E5 or M365 Enterprise E5 and Intune-managed Windows devices that are **Microsoft Entra joined**. When this feature is turned on, a Conditional Access policy is created that is used to send status reports to Intune. This policy should not be deleted.

- **Authenticated telemetry**: Turned off by default, this feature prevents spoofing telemetry into the dashboard.

- **Preview features**: Turned off by default, this setting enables the preview features in your tenant. This includes **Endpoint Attack Notifications** that is a managed proactive hunting service from Microsoft. Once you sign up for this you start getting attack notifications for human operated ransomware, hands-on keyboard attacks or cyber espionage that can be viewed in the **Alerts** queue in the Microsoft Defender XDR portal.

Licenses

This page can be used to track and manage the availability and usage of MDE licenses in your organization. It shows the MDE plan your organization subscribes to and how many of those licenses are active.

Email notifications

Email notifications to stakeholders can be configured when alerts are generated, or vulnerabilities are identified. You can configure the severity threshold of the alerts and vulnerabilities that trigger the notification.

Figure 8.4 shows an example of a configured alert notification:

Endpoints

Figure 8.4: *Email notifications*

Permissions

Under this section, you can configure **Roles** and **Device groups**. Creating device groups and setting remediation levels has been covered in *Chapter 6, Microsoft Defender XDR.*

If you have unified RBAC turned on (recommended), the **Roles** page will be read-only, and you will be able to see the default role group **Microsoft Defender for Endpoint administrator**. This role has been explained in the previous section.

Rules

Under this section, you can create policies and rules for indicators of compromise, web content filtering and more. Let us explore each section here.

Indicators

Under this section, you can create indicators of compromise for File hashes, IP addresses, URLs/Domains, and **Certificates**. You can create up to 15000 indicators across these categories. Indicators can be added manually or be bulk imported in the form of a .csv file. *Figure 8.5* shows an example of a blocked URL:

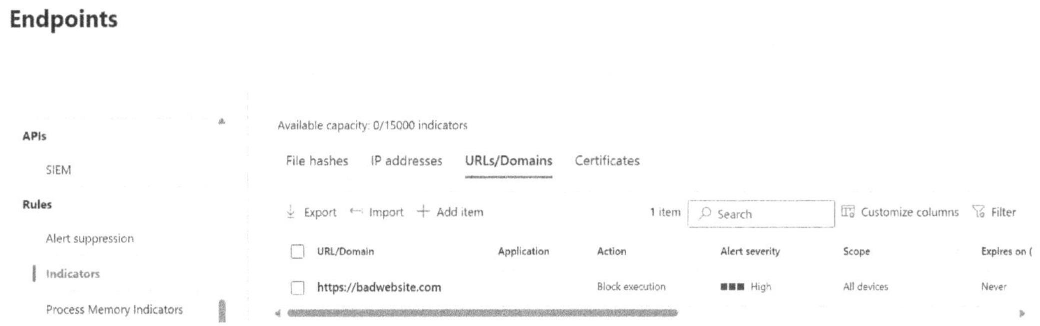

Figure 8.5: Indicators of compromise

Web content filtering

If you have web content filtering turned on in **Advanced features,** you can create a policy here to block specific web content. In the right pane click on **Add policy** to create the policy.

Figure 8.6 shows the list of categories that you can choose from. The policy can be scoped to all devices or specific device groups:

Figure 8.6: Web content filtering

Automation uploads

On this page, you can choose to submit suspicious files and memory content to MDE for automated investigation.

Figure 8.7 shows the settings on this page:

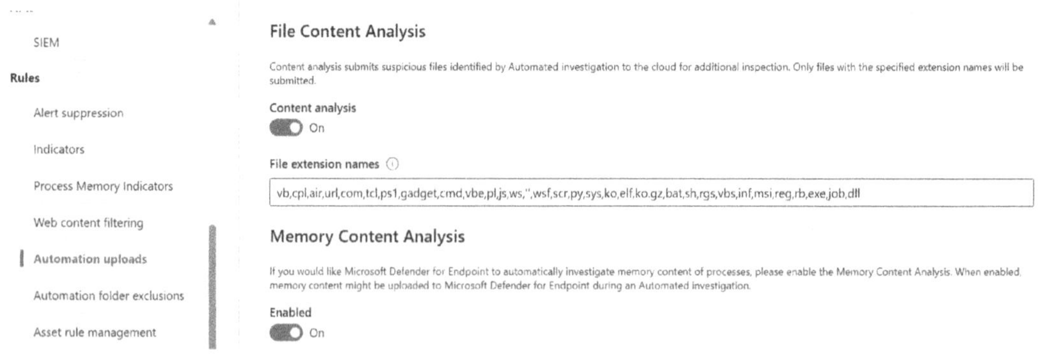

Figure 8.7: Automation uploads

Automation folder executions

On this page, you can list the folders, file extensions and file names that you want automated investigations to skip. Once these settings are configured, the folders, file extensions and file names listed here will not be scanned during automated investigations.

Configuration management

Microsoft Intune can be used to deploy endpoint security policies to manage the Defender security settings on devices that have been onboarded to MDE but not enrolled in Intune. This is called **Defender for Endpoint security settings management**. This enables extending the MDE policies to devices that are not capable of being enrolled in Intune. Devices that are enrolled in Intune continue to receive policies from Intune.

This integration needs to be enabled in both the Intune admin center as well as MDE. To turn this setting on in the Intune admin center login to **https://intune.microsoft.com**. In the left pane click on **Endpoint security**. Under **Setup** click on **Microsoft Defender for Endpoint**. Switch the toggle **Allow Microsoft Defender for Endpoint to enforce Endpoint Security Configurations** to **On** and click on **Save**.

Enforcement scope

To turn on security setting management in MDE switch the **Use MDE to enforce security configuration settings from Intune** to **On** and select the device platforms that you want to apply the settings to as shown in the following figure:

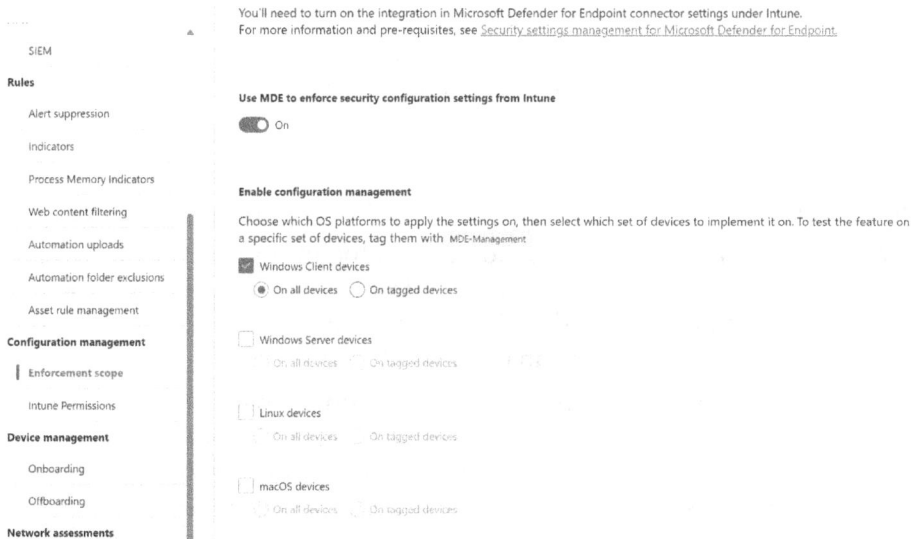

Figure 8.8: Defender for Endpoint security settings management

When devices are managed using security settings management you can use either Microsoft Intune admin center or the Microsoft 365 Defender portal to configure policies for MDE and assign the policies to Microsoft Entra ID groups. If using the Microsoft Defender portal navigate to **Endpoints | Configuration management | Endpoint security policies**.

On this page, you can create endpoint security policies for Windows, MacOS and Linux as shown in the following figure:

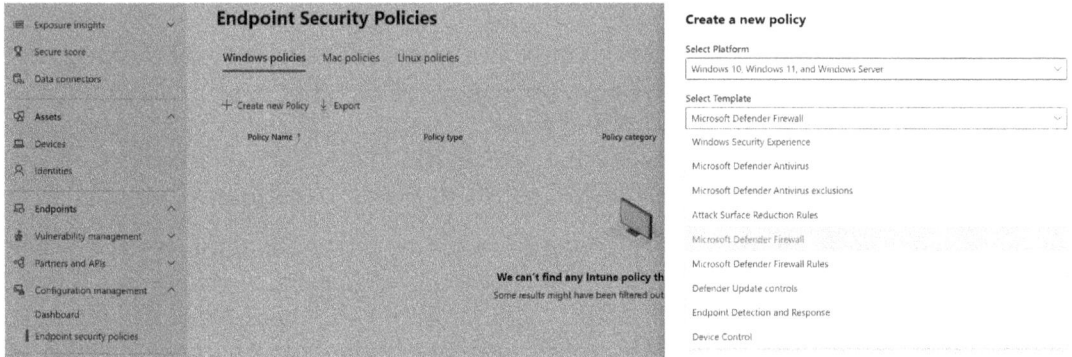

Figure 8.9: Endpoint security policies in the defender portal

Device discovery

To completely manage and protect your environment it is essential to take inventory of all devices on the network. This can be an arduous and time consuming task. MDE provides device discovery capabilities that help you discover unmanaged devices and equipment connected to the corporate network. This includes endpoints like workstations, servers and mobile devices that are not yet onboarded to MDE, IoT devices like printers, scanners and cameras and network devices like routers and switches. Once these devices have been discovered they can be onboarded to MDE, and policies can be configured to reduce the attack surface by patching vulnerabilities and closing configuration gaps.

There are two modes in which device discovery can be configured, as follows:

- **Basic discovery**: In this mode, onboarded endpoints passively collect events in the network and extract device information from them using the `SenseNDR.exe` and no network traffic is initiated. This results in limited visibility as it relies only on the network traffic as seen by an onboarded device.

- **Standard discovery (default)**: In this mode, onboarded endpoints actively seek devices in the network using common discovery protocols that use multicast queries. In this mode a negligible amount of network activity is generated by the discovery sensor. This mode helps in building a completer and more reliable device inventory.

Device discovery can be set up by going to the Microsoft Defender portal and going to **Settings** | **Device discovery** as shown in the following figure:

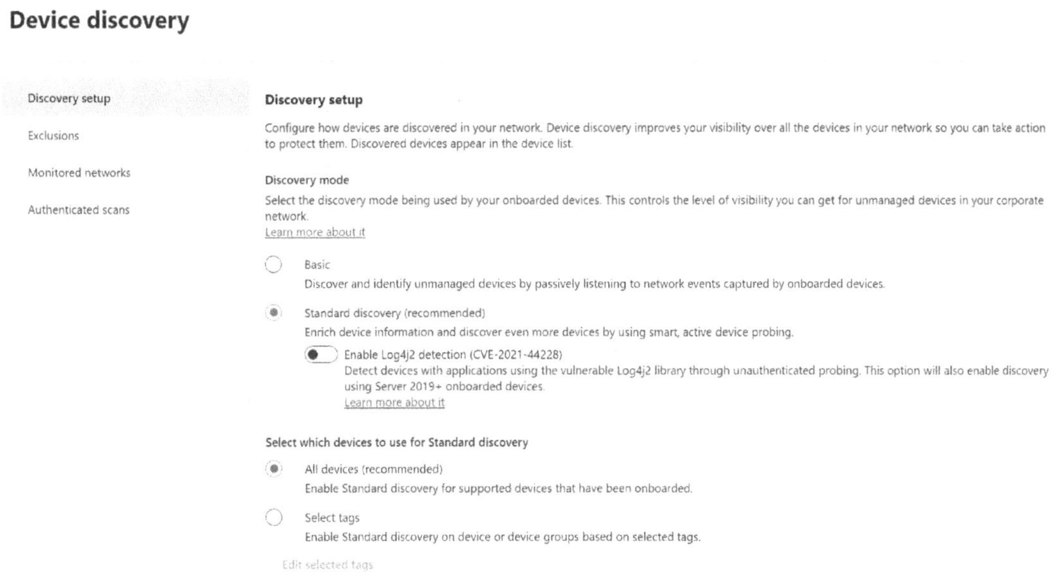

Device discovery

Figure 8.10: Device discovery setup

From *Figure 8.10*, you can configure the following additional settings:

- **Exclusions**: If there are devices that should not be actively probed you can add them to the exclusion list. These could be devices that are set up as decoys.

- **Monitored networks**: MDE monitors a network and determines if it is a corporate or non-corporate network. This is done by correlating network identifiers like default gateway and **Dynamic Host Configuration Protocol (DHCP)** server addresses. If majority of discovered devices have the same default gateway and DHCP server, it is considered to be a corporate network. A list of all discovered networks is available in the monitored networks page. Corporate networks are always scanned. You can configure non-corporate networks to be scanned for device discovery by clicking on the ellipses next to the network name and choosing if you want to monitor or ignore.

- **Authenticated scans**: In addition to managed Windows devices there are unmanaged Windows and other devices on a corporate network that cannot be managed by MDE as they do not have a MDE sensor built into them. To scan and discover these types of devices a designated MDE device is used to perform authenticated scans on preconfigured network devices. To configure authenticated scans, you will need a scanning device. A scanning device is a device that is already onboarded to MDE and will be used to scan the network. This can be a Windows 10, version 1903 or Windows Server, version 1903 or later machine. To install the scanner on this machine, click on the **Authenticated scans** option on the above screen and in the right pane click on **Download scanner**. Install the scanner on the designated machine and then configure the scan by clicking on **Add new scan** and following the instructions to configure a **Network device authenticated scan** or **Windows authenticated scan**.

The devices that are discovered in the last 30 days are listed under **Assets | Devices** page on the Microsoft Defender portal. On this page, you can see the discovered **Computers & Mobile**, **Network devices**, **IoT devices** and other **Uncategorised devices**.

These devices can have one of the following statuses:

- **Onboarded**: The device is onboarded to MDE.
- **Can be onboarded**: The device is supported and can be onboarded to MDE.
- **Unsupported**: The device is discovered but does not meet the minimum requirements to be onboarded to MDE.
- **Insufficient info**: There was not sufficient information to assess the supportability of the device. Turning on standard discovery can aid in enriching this information so that a decision can be made.

Detect and protect

Now that we have learned how to get started with MDE, onboard devices, and configure the MDE settings, let us explore how to use MDE capabilities to detect threats and protect endpoints.

Tamper resiliency

Attackers aim to launch a ransomware attack on the entire network. To evade detection, they try to impair the effectiveness of MDE by tampering with it. Anti-tampering capabilities built into MDE make it difficult to be tampered with. To provide effective defense against tampering, the devices must be as follows:

- Onboarded to MDE.
- Security intelligence and antivirus updates should be installed.
- Device must be managed centrally using a management solution like Microsoft Intune or Configuration manager.

MDE offers several controls to protect devices from being tampered with.

Table 8.3 summarizes the controls:

Control	OS	Technique
Tamper protection	Windows	• Terminating or suspending processes • Stopping or pausing or suspending services • Modifying registry settings including exclusions • Manipulating or hijacking DLLs • Manipulating or modification of the file system • Agent integrity
Tamper protection	MacOS	• Terminating or suspending processes • Manipulating or modification of the file system • Agent integrity
Attack surface reduction	Windows	Kernel drivers
Windows Defender Application Control	Windows	Kernel drivers

Table 8.3: Tamper techniques

Note: Windows Defender Application Control is a Windows feature and beyond the scope of this book. Refer to the Microsoft online documentation for understanding and configuring.

Tamper protection on Windows

Tamper protection is the capability in MDE that prevents security settings like virus and threat protection from being disabled or changed. Tamper protection is on by default on Windows 10 and 11, Windows Server 2022/2019/2016/2012 R2 and Windows Server, version 1803 or later.

Table 8.4 lists methods to turn tamper protection on or off:

Method	Capabilities
Microsoft Defender portal	Tamper protection can be turned on or off tenant wide. This is on by default.
Microsoft Intune or Configuration Manager	Tamper protection can be turned on or off tenant wide or scoped to a subset of users or devices.
Configuration management with tenant attach	Tamper protection can be turned on or off tenant wide or scoped to a subset of users or devices.
Windows Security app	Tamper protection can be turned on or off at an individual unmanaged device level.

Table 8.4: Tamper protection methods

Once tamper protection is turned on the following settings cannot be modified:

- Virus and threat protection remains enabled.
- Real-time protection remains turned on.
- Behavior monitoring remains turned on.
- Antivirus protection, including **IOfficeAntivirus (IOAV)** remains enabled.
- Cloud protection remains enabled.
- Security intelligence updates occur.
- Automatic actions are taken on detected threats.
- Notifications are visible in the Windows Security app on Windows devices.
- Archived files are scanned.
- Exclusions cannot be modified or added

Tamper protection on MacOS

Tamper protection on MacOS prevents bad actors from removing the MDE agent on MacOS. It also protects security files, processes and configuration settings from being tampered with. On MacOS tamper protection can be set to **disabled**, **audit** or **block**.

Tamper protection can be enabled on MacOS Big Sur (11) or later with MDE version 101.70.19. It is recommended that System Integrity Protection be enabled and that a MDM tool is used to configure MDE. Also ensure that MDE has **Full Disk Access** authorization.

Once tamper protection is turned on, the following activities are either audited or blocked, depending on the configuration:

- Action to uninstall MDE agent
- Editing or modification of MDE files
- Creation of new filed under MDE location
- Deletion of MDE files
- Renaming of MDE files

Attack surface reduction

Attack surface refers to all the places where an attacker could launch an attack to compromise an organisation's security. Reducing the attack surface means protecting these areas thereby leaving attackers with fewer avenues to launch an attack. Examples of attack surface reduction could include, using passwordless sign-ins, closing vulnerable network ports or encrypting sensitive data. MDE offers attack surface reduction capabilities that can contain software-based risky behaviours.

To apply **Attack Surface Reduction** (ASR) rules the following prerequisites must be met:

- Windows 11/10 version 1709 or later.
- Windows Server, version 1709 or later and Windows Server 2012 R2/2016/2019/2022.

- Microsoft Defender Antivirus must be running in active mode.
- Cloud-delivery protection must be on.
- Windows 10 E3 or E5 license.

Each ASR rule can be **Not configured, Off, Block, Audit, Warn**. ASR rules can be configured using Microsoft Intune, Microsoft Configuration Manager, Group policy or PowerShell.

To configure ASR rules in Intune, following are the steps:

1. Login to **https://intune.microsoft.com** and navigate to **Endpoint security | Attack surface reduction**.

2. In the right pane, click on **Create policy**. Under **Platform** select **Windows, 10, Windows 11, and Windows Server** and under **Profile** select **Attack Surface Reduction Rules** and click on **Create**.

3. Type in a **Name** and **Description** for the profile and click on **Next**.

4. On the **Configuration settings** page make the appropriate selections and click on **Next**.

   Figure 8.11 shows the options available:

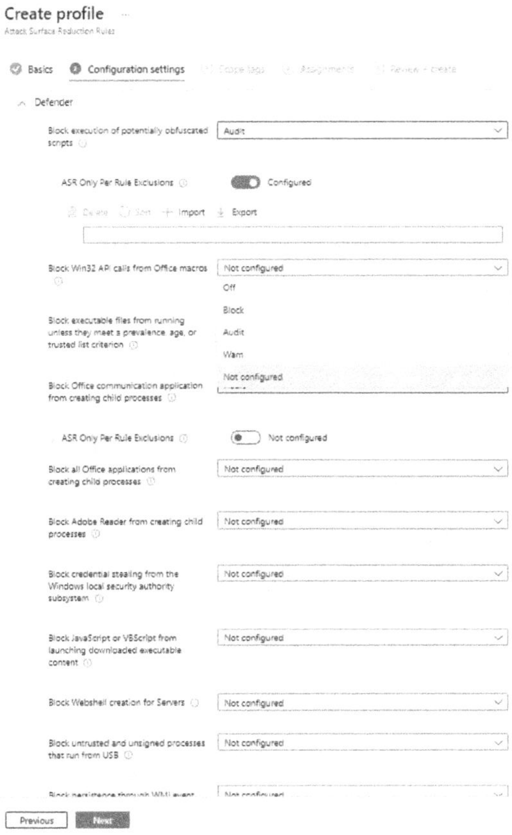

Figure 8.11: *ASR rules in Intune*

5. Click **Next** on the **Scope tags** page.

6. On the **Assignments** page, you can choose to include or exclude users or groups. Click on **Next** as shown in the following figure:

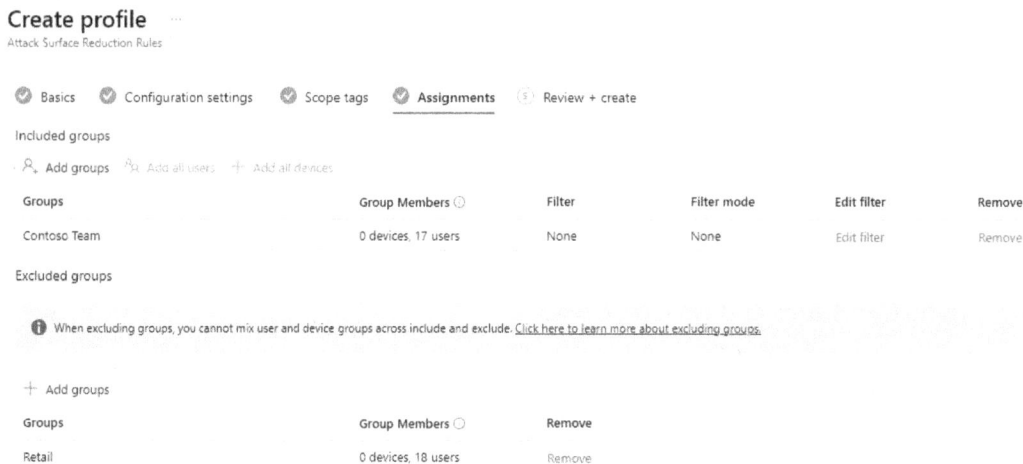

Create profile ⋯
Attack Surface Reduction Rules

✓ Basics	✓ Configuration settings	✓ Scope tags	✓ Assignments	(5) Review + create

Included groups

⊕ Add groups   ⊕ Add all users   + Add all devices

Groups	Group Members ⓘ	Filter	Filter mode	Edit filter	Remove
Contoso Team	0 devices, 17 users	None	None	Edit filter	Remove

Excluded groups

ⓘ When excluding groups, you cannot mix user and device groups across include and exclude. Click here to learn more about excluding groups.

+ Add groups

Groups	Group Members ⓘ	Remove
Retail	0 devices, 18 users	Remove

Figure 8.12: Assign the ASR policy

7. On the **Review + create** page, review your settings and click on **Create**.

Next generation protection

MDE delivers next-generation protection to catch and block all types of emerging threats. Modern malware is polymorphic meaning it constantly mutates to evade detection. This constantly mutating nature of malware requires defenders to create more creative and agile security solutions. MDE offers next-generation protection using Microsoft Defender Antivirus. It uses predictive techniques, ML and AI to block potential malware at the first sign of abnormal behavior. It uses behavior-based, heuristic, and real-time antivirus protection, also known as **real-time protection**, to detect and block unsafe apps. **Cloud-delivered protection** provides near real-time detection and blocking of new threats.

Microsoft Defender Antivirus is prebuilt into Windows 10 and 11 and in certain versions of Windows Server. It provides **anomaly detection** which adds a layer of protection for new malware that does not fit any predefined pattern. It has moved away from using static signature-based updates. Instead, it uses predictive techniques like ML, applied sciences and AI that are imperative in keeping organizations safe from the constantly evolving malware. Due to these modern techniques, Microsoft Defender Antivirus can block new malware within milliseconds of detection.

Microsoft Defender Antivirus uses advanced technologies that work under the hood to detect and stop a wide range of threats at multiple points. These are depicted in the following figure:

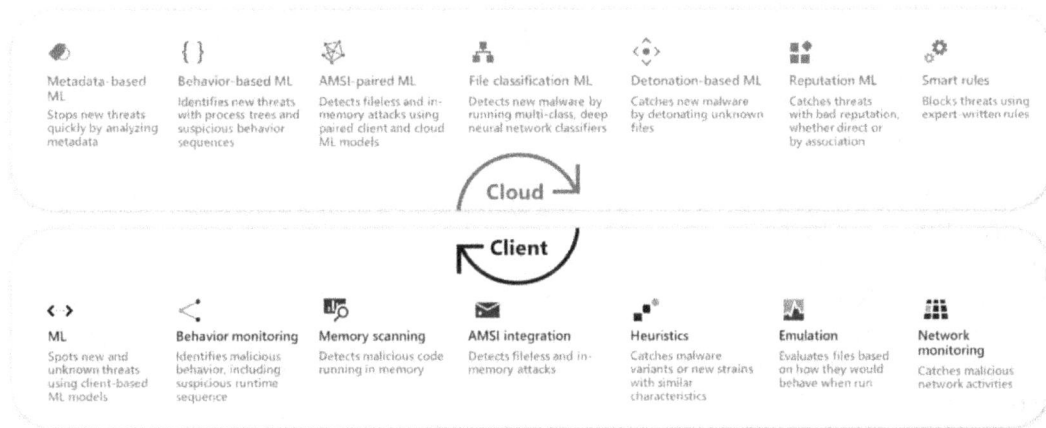

Figure 8.13: Advanced technologies behind Microsoft Defender Antivirus

Microsoft Defender Antivirus performs hybrid detection and response. The detection and protection first occur on the client device. It works with the cloud for newly developing threats for more effective and faster detection and protection. When the client encounters unknown threats it sends the metadata to the cloud for advanced analysis before it lets the endpoint interact with the file.

As explained earlier, Microsoft Defender Antivirus can coexist with other antivirus solutions running on the system. Depending on the configuration, it can run in any of the following modes:

- **Active mode**: In this mode it is the primary antivirus solution on the device. Files are scanned, risks are mitigated, and threats are reported to the Windows Security app.

- **Passive mode**: In this mode, it is not used as the primary antivirus solution. Files are scanned and threats are reported but remediation is not carried out. Microsoft Defender Antivirus runs in passive mode only on devices onboarded to MDE.

- **Disabled or uninstalled (not recommended)**: In this case, it is not used at all. Files are not scanned or remediated, and threats are not reported. It is important to note that if MDE is in use, features like EDR will continue to work.

To check the status of the Microsoft Defender Antivirus on your system click on **Start** and type **Security**. Open the Windows Security app. Click on **Virus & threat protection**. Under **Who's protecting me?** click on **Manage Providers**. The name of the antimalware solution will be listed there.

Like any other antimalware solution, Microsoft Defender Antivirus needs to be kept updated to ensure that the devices have access to the latest technology and features to protect against new malware and techniques. It receives monthly updates known as **platform updates**. These updates contain performance improvements, serviceability improvements and integration improvements. In addition to the monthly updates Microsoft Defender Antivirus also uses cloud-delivered protection to download dynamic **security intelligence updates**. Security intelligence updates occur on a scheduled cadence that can be configured via policy. They include engine updates that are released on a monthly cadence.

Endpoints can download updates from Microsoft update service, **Windows Server Update Service (WSUS)**, Microsoft Endpoint Configuration Manager and network file share. Depending upon your organization's network and how much control you would like on the devices receiving the update you can choose to use a combination of these services. The order in which the update sources are used can be managed using Group Policy, Microsoft Endpoint Configuration Manager, PowerShell and **Windows Management Instrumentation (WMI)**.

Cloud delivered protection

Microsoft Defender Antivirus provides near real-time protection against new and emerging threats. It works seamlessly with **cloud-delivered protection**. These cloud protection services are also called **Microsoft Advanced Protection Service (MAPS)**. To identify new threats, they use the millions of signals received by the Microsoft Intelligent Security Graph to deliver accurate and intelligent protection in real-time, sometimes even before a single endpoint is affected.

Following figure shows the capabilities of cloud protection:

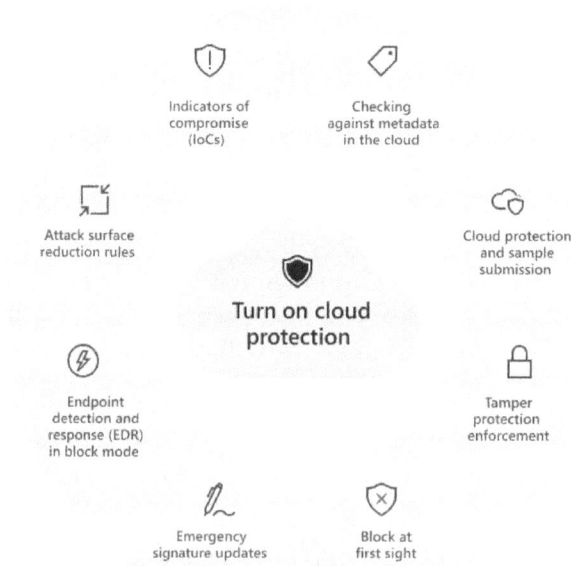

Figure 8.14: Cloud-delivered protection capabilities

These capabilities are explained as follows:

- **Checking against metadata in the cloud**: Microsoft Defender Antivirus cloud service uses ML models that include metadata. So, when a suspicious file is detected, its metadata is checked.

- **Cloud protection and sample submission**: Suspicious files can be sent to the Microsoft Defender Antivirus cloud service for detonation and analysis.

- **Tamper protection**: This protects against unauthorized changes to the security settings.

- **Block at first sight**: If a new suspicious file is detected, this capability queries the cloud backend and applies heuristics, ML and automated analysis to determine if the file is a threat.

- **Emergency signature updates**: When a new threat is detected, emergency fixes and updates are deployed within minutes rather than waiting for the next update cycle.

- **EDR in block mode**: This feature provides an extra layer of security by blocking suspicious behavior and files on the endpoint.

- **Attack surface reduction**: ASR rules can be configured to fix vulnerabilities that attackers could use to spread malware.

- **Indicators of compromise (IOCs)**: IOCs can be configured to define the detection and prevention of entities.

Cloud protection is turned on by default in your tenant. This enables fixes for malware issues to be delivered from the cloud within minutes instead of waiting for the next update to come in.

Real time protection

Microsoft Defender Antivirus uses behavioral, heuristic and real-time protection to block **Potentially Unwanted Applications (PUA)** like adware, browser modifiers and toolbars or fake antivirus applications. These applications are not considered malware but are deemed unsafe as they might cause endpoints to run slow, display ads or install other software that may be unsafe or unwanted. These applications increase the risk of your network being affected by actual malware and can make malware difficult to detect. MDE subscribers can use Microsoft Defender Antivirus to block PUA on devices using Microsoft Intune, Configuration Manager, Group Policy or PowerShell.

Cloud delivered protection, PUA restrictions and other settings in Microsoft Defender Antivirus can be configured using Microsoft Intune, Endpoint Security policies, Configuration Manager, Group Policy or PowerShell.

To configure these settings using Microsoft Intune following are the steps:

1. Login to **https://intune.microsoft.com** and navigate to **Endpoint security** | **Antivirus**.

2. On the **Summary** page, under **AV Policies,** click on **Create Policy.**

3. Select the **Platform** as **Windows 10, Windows 11, and Windows Server**.

4. Under **Profile,** select **Microsoft Defender Antivirus** and click on **Create**.

5. On the **Basics** page, provide a **Name** and **Description** for the policy and click **Next**.

6. On the **Configuration settings,** select the desired settings and click **Next**.

7. Click **Next** on the **Scope tags** page.

8. On the **Assignments** page select the groups that you want to apply the policy to and click **Next**. If no group is selected, the policy will be applied tenant-wide.

9. On the **Review + create** page, review the settings and click **Save**.

Investigate and respond

Now that we have understood how MDE can help detect and protect the infrastructure from threats, let us see what it has to offer in case a malware is detected and needs to be investigated. When a threat is detected, alerts are created for an analyst to investigate. Alerts with similar attack techniques or by the same attacker or including similar assets are grouped together as incidents. MDE continuously collects telemetry like process information, network activities, user login activities, registry changes etc. This information is stored for six months and aids in advanced hunting.

MDE alerts and incidents are available in the respective alerts and incidents queue on the Microsoft Defender XDR portal. Managing and investigating incidents has been explained in *Chapter 6, Microsoft Defender XDR*.

Now let us see what remediation actions are available for files and devices.

Remediation action on devices

Security analysts can investigate the details of an alert on a device to identify other behavior or events that may be related. Affected devices can be identified in several areas of the Microsoft Defender XDR portal like the devices list, alerts queue, any individual alert, any individual file details view and any IP address view. When you investigate a device, you can see several details. Review the various tabs available on the device screen in the following figure:

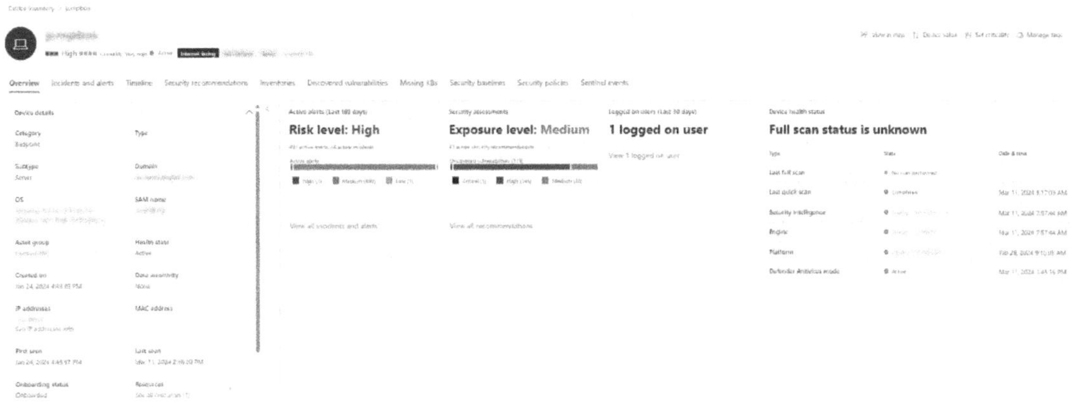

Figure 8.15: Investigating devices

Following options are available on devices:

- **Manage tags**: Tags aid in creating logical group affiliation.

- **Initiate automated investigation**: Automated investigations can be run on devices. This has been covered in detail in *Chapter 6, Microsoft Defender XDR*.

- **Initiate live response session**: This capability gives you instant access to the device via a remote shell using which investigators can collect forensic evidence, run scripts, send suspicious file for investigation and remediate threats.

- **Collect investigation package**: Using this, you can collect an investigation package from the device in a zip file. This helps in investigating the device's current state and understanding the tools and techniques used by the attacker.

- **Run antivirus scan**: Remotely execute an antivirus scan on the device using Microsoft Defender Antivirus.

- **Restrict app execution**: If the organization is using Microsoft Defender Antivirus you can contain an attack by stopping malicious processes from running.

- **Isolate device**: In certain cases, you might want to disconnect the device from the network to prevent the attack from spreading.

- **Contain device**: Containing a device will block any incoming and outgoing communications from the device. The device remains connected to the network to enable security teams to run investigation and collect investigation packages.

- **Consult a threat expert**: If the organization subscribes to Microsoft Defender Experts you can work with them to aid your investigation using this option. Microsoft Defender Experts is a paid service and is covered in *Chapter 6, Microsoft Defender XDR*.

Remediation action on files

Files associated with specific incidents and alerts can be investigated to determine if the file is malicious. It also helps understand the potential scope of the breach and identify the motivation behind the attack. You can reach the file page from several places in the Microsoft Defender XDR portal like using the search feature or click a link from the **Alert process tree**, **Incident graph** pages. The file details page shows file details like name and metadata and which incidents and alerts the file is associated with. Review the options as shown in the following figure:

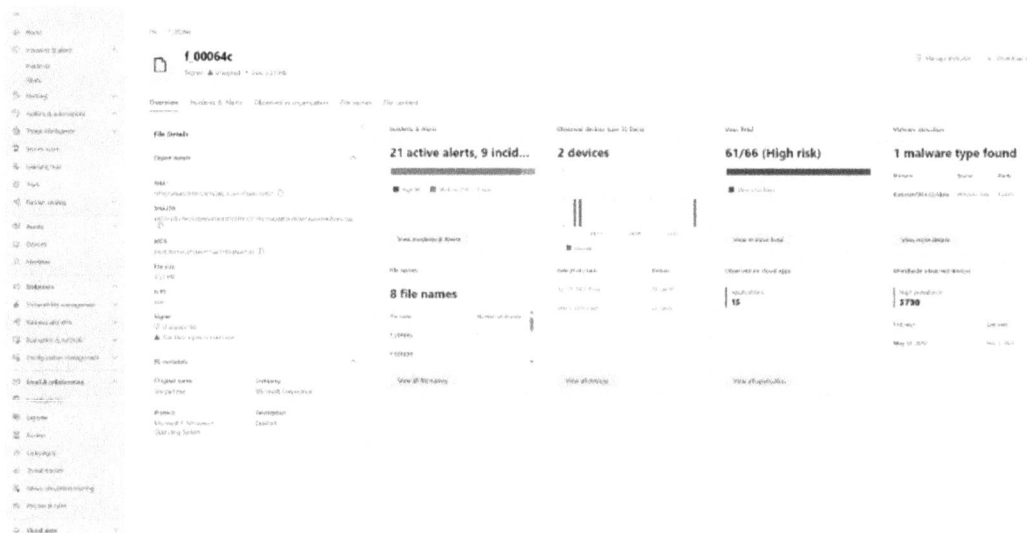

Figure 8.16: Investigate files

Following actions can be taken on the file:

- **Stop and quarantine**: Stop the file and any associated processed from running and quarantine the file.

- **Manage indicator**: Using this option you can add an IoC to prevent similar files from being read, written or executed.

- **Download file**: This option enabled you to download the file in a password protected archive file that you can use for investigation.

- **Ask Defender experts**: If the organization subscribes to Microsoft Defender Experts you can work with them to aid your investigation using this option.

- **Manual actions**: For MDE Plan 1 customers some manual actions are available like adding an Indicator of Compromise to block or allow a file.

- **Go hunt**: This feature provides pre-built queries that can aid in advanced hunting related to the file. For example, you might want to search for all devices in your network where this file has been detected.

- **Deep analysis**: This feature executes the file in a secure cloud environment. It shows the result of running the file like registry changes, new processes added, communication with external IP Addresses etc. This can take several minutes.

Microsoft Defender Vulnerability Management

Microsoft Defender Vulnerability Management provides security analysts real-time EDR insights correlated with endpoint vulnerabilities and automated remediation capabilities using Microsoft Intune or Microsoft Endpoint Configuration Manager.

It extends the capabilities of MDE by providing asset visibility, intelligent assessment and built-in remediation tools for Windows, Linux, MacOS and network devices. Using Microsoft Defender Vulnerability Management security teams can prioritize and address the most critical vulnerabilities and misconfigurations across the network.

Figure 8.17 shows the key capabilities of Microsoft Defender Vulnerability Management:

Microsoft Defender Vulnerability Management
Reduce cyber risk with continuous vulnerability discovery, risk-based prioritization, and remediation.

Continuous discovery & monitoring

Risk-based intelligent prioritization

Remediation & tracking

Figure 8.17: Microsoft Defender Vulnerability Management

Following is an explanation for each of the capabilities:

- **Continuous discovery and monitoring**: Microsoft Defender Vulnerability Management has built-in agents and scanners that continuously scan the environment for vulnerabilities even when devices are not connected to the network. It provides inventories using which you can view the software application, certificates, hardware and firmware and browser extensions running in your environment in real time.

- **Risk-based intelligent prioritization**: Microsoft Defender Vulnerability Management uses Microsoft's threat intelligence to predict likelihood of breaches, the business context and device assessments to provide a prioritized list of vulnerabilities in the environment. It focuses on emerging threats, pinpoints active breaches and helps protect high-value assets by giving a single view of prioritized recommendations that have been curated using multiple security feeds, known **Common Vulnerabilities and Exposures (CVEs)** and many more.

- **Remediation and tracking**: Microsoft Defender Vulnerability Management provides inbuilt remediation workflows that enable defenders to quickly block vulnerable applications, review mitigation alternatives and monitor the status of remediations and real-time.

Microsoft Defender Vulnerability Management stores data in the same location as your MDE instance and the same data security and privacy principles apply. It honors the Microsoft Defender XDR unified-RBAC permissions.

Licensing

MDE P2 includes some Vulnerability Management capabilities like device discovery, vulnerability assessment, and risk-based prioritization.

Following are the additional Microsoft Defender Vulnerability Management subscriptions available:

- **Defender Vulnerability Management add-on**: MDE Plan 2 customers can enhance their vulnerability management capabilities using the new advanced tools like blocking vulnerable applications, browser extension and digital certificate assessment, network share analysis etc. available in this plan.

- **Defender Vulnerability Management standalone**: Customers who do not have MDE Plan 2 can complement their existing EDR solution to meet their vulnerability management needs. This plan includes all vulnerability management capabilities that are a part of MDE Plan 2 and Defender Vulnerability Management add-on plan.

- **Defender Vulnerability Management add-on to Microsoft Defender Endpoint for servers**: Provides premium vulnerability management capabilities for customers who have Microsoft Defender for Endpoint for Servers Plan 1 and Plan 2. The vulnerability management capabilities are natively integrated with Defender for Cloud; however, client devices will need the Defender Vulnerability Management add-on license to access the premium features.

Operating system requirements

Microsoft Defender Vulnerability Management supports a range of Windows and non-Windows operating systems. All devices should be onboarded to MDE.

Note: Not all Vulnerability Management features are available on all operating systems. For details of feature availability by operating system refer to Microsoft documentation.

Inventories

In the previous section, we learnt how to discover devices and view the device inventory in the Microsoft Defender portal. This section will explain how to view and explore software inventories. Software inventory is a list of known software running on devices in your environment. Defender Vulnerability Management also collects vulnerability information from devices and from other security feeds. Software inventories can be viewed in the Microsoft Defender portal by navigating to **Endpoints** and clicking on **Inventories** under **Vulnerability Management**. On this page, you can see all discovered software, vulnerable components, browser extensions, certificates and hardware and firmware.

Working with Vulnerability Management

On the Microsoft Defender Vulnerability Management dashboard, you can view valuable insights that and take remediation action on discovered vulnerabilities.

Following figure shows an example of the dashboard. Explore the available information and actions available:

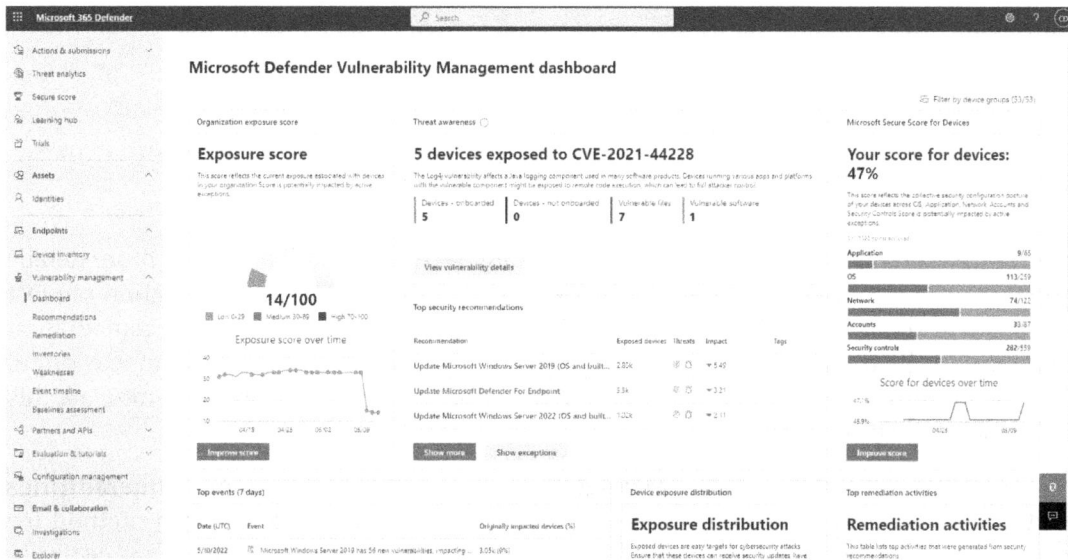

Figure 8.18: Microsoft Defender Vulnerability Management dashboard

The dashboard displays the **Exposure score** that reflects how vulnerable the devices in the organization are to cyber threats. It also displays the trend over time in the form of a graph. The exposure score is broken down in levels where a score of 0-29 denotes low exposure, 30-69 denotes medium exposure and 70-100 denotes high exposure. Microsoft Defender Vulnerability Management suggests remediation actions to improve your exposure score. Clicking on the **Improve score** button on the above screen will take you to the **Recommendations** page where you can view a list of security recommendations prioritized by impact. This page will also show you other security recommendations and exposed network shares.

Following is an example of the recommendations page in the Microsoft Defender XDR portal:

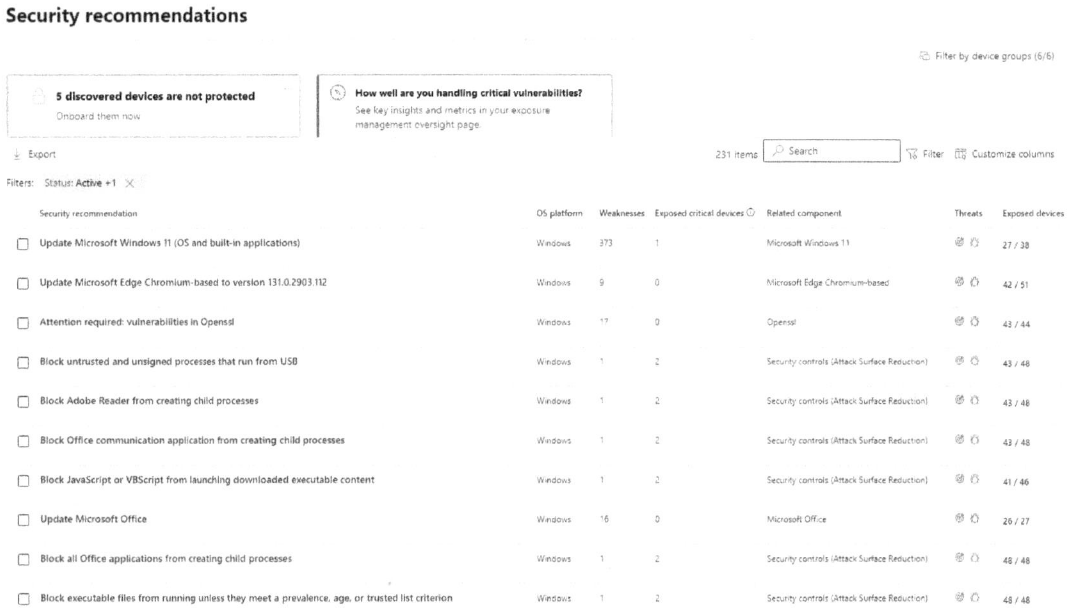

Security recommendations

Figure 8.19: Security recommendations page

Review the information on this page. Click on any recommendation to view more details about the recommendation. From the fly out pane you can submit a remediation request to open a ticked in Microsoft Intune for an IT administrator to work on. The remediation progress can be tracked from the **Remediation** page. You can also submit an exception, provide a justification and set the exception duration, if you are not able to remediate this vulnerability at this time.

Microsoft Defender Vulnerability Management also shows the **Common Vulnerabilities and Exposures** (**CVEs**) on the **Weaknesses** page. CVEs provide a standard method for organizations to view and track vulnerabilities in their environment. They are centrally tracked in the public register **https://www.cve.org**. Microsoft Defender Vulnerability Management not only shows all the CVEs on the **Weaknesses** page it also proactively scans your environment to detect these vulnerabilities in your network.

Following is an example of the **Weaknesses** page:

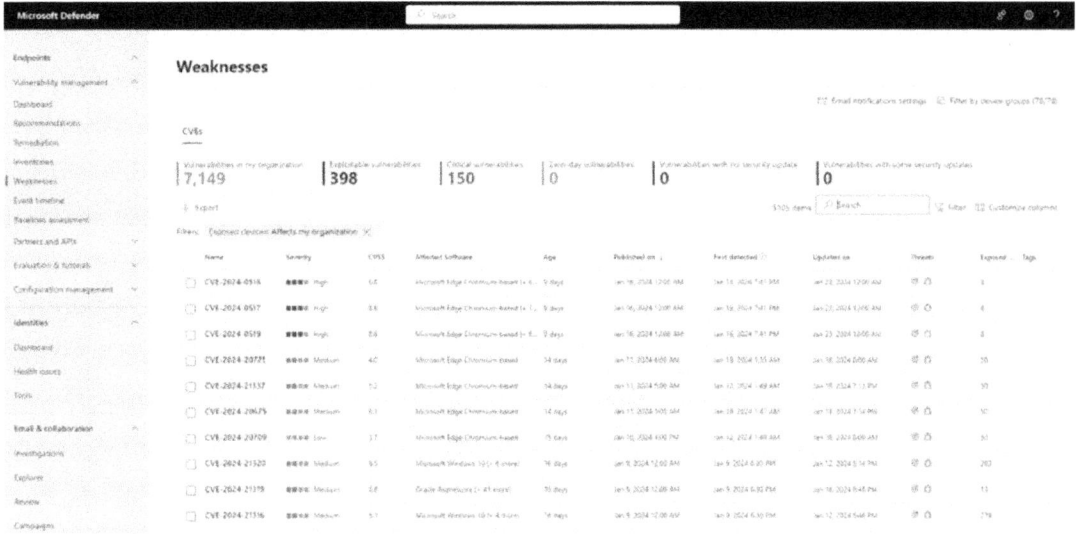

Figure 8.20: *Common Vulnerabilities and Exposures*

Notice that it shows you how many vulnerabilities are found in your organization. Clicking on any vulnerability will provide more information about it. You can also view the exposed devices and software in your environment. There is also an option to **Go to related security recommendation** which is usually a recommendation to fix the vulnerability by applying a security update.

Microsoft Defender for IoT

Business today use thousands of connected devices that use both OT and IoT. These devices use specialized protocol that can pose security challenges. Microsoft Defender for IoT uses agentless, network layer monitoring to discover and identify threats and vulnerabilities related to OT and IoT devices that do not have a built-in security agent. With integration with Microsoft Sentinel and other SIEM services it can also help remediate the discovered vulnerabilities.

Defender for IoT can connect to both cloud and on-premises components. It uses OT or enterprise IoT sensors deployed on virtual or physical machines to discover devices. The sensors can be cloud-connected or fully managed on-premises. These sensors are specifically built for OT/IoT networks and connect to the SPAN port or network TAP. They provide visibility into the risks within minutes of being connected. They use OT/IoT aware analytics and Layer 6 Deep Packet Inspection to detect threats. Data is collected, processed and analyzed on the sensor which makes it ideal for low bandwidth connectivity. Only telemetry and insights are transferred to the management portal. Azure portal is used for cloud managed environments and an on-premises management portal is available for air-gapped environments.

Following figure shows how data streams into Defender for IoT from the network sensors and third-party sources:

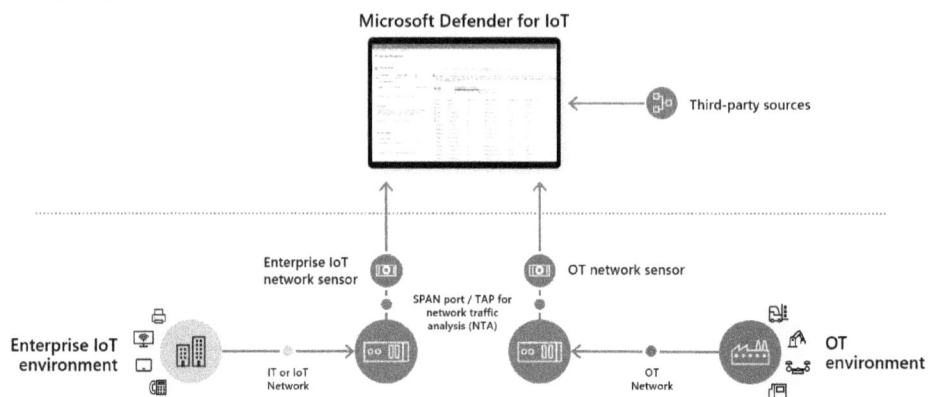

Figure 8.21: Defender for IoT

The sensors analyze traffic using built-in analytics engines and trigger alerts based on live and pre-recorded data. Analytics engines provide machine learning and profile analytics, risk analysis, a device database and set of insights, threat intelligence, and behavioral analytics. Defender for IoT includes the following analytics engines:

- **Protocol violation detection engine**: It identifies the use of packets that do not conform with the **Industrial Control Systems** (**ICS**) protocol specifications.

- **Policy violation**: It identifies any behavior which deviates from the defined or learnt baseline.

- **Industrial malware detection engine**: Identifies behavior that detects the presence of known malware like WannaCry, NotPetya etc.

- **Anomaly detection engine**: Detects unusual machine-to-machine communication.

- **Operation incident detection**: Detects issues like intermittent connectivity that can indicate early signs of equipment malfunction.

Currently, all traffic from European regions is routed through the Western Europe data center while all traffic from the rest of the world is routed through the East US data center.

Licensing

Microsoft Defender for IoT is included with M365 E5 subscription. With each user license organizations can protect up to five IoT devices. If you have more devices to monitor and you own Microsoft Defender for Endpoint Plan 2, purchase a per device add-on for **Microsoft Defender for IoT—Enterprise IoT security**.

For OT monitoring it is recommended that you estimate how many devices you want to monitor to estimate the number of sites that need to be licensed. Each site to be monitored needs a license and the fee differs based on the site size.

Permissions

In the Azure Portal, the permissions are managed by Microsoft Entra and Azure RBAC. The built-in Azure roles of **Security Reader, Security Admin, Contributor** and **Owner** have permissions to interact with Defender for IoT.

When working with OT network sensors, Defender for IoT services and data is also available from on-premises OT sensors and management console. The OT sensors are each installed with a default admin user that has access to advanced troubleshooting and setup tools. To set up the sensor, sign-in with the default admin user and create a user with Admin role. This user can then be used to create more users and assign permissions. The on-premises management console is installed with two privileged users called support and cyberx. To set up the management console, sign in with the support user and create a user with the Admin role. Use this user to create additional users and assign roles.

Table 8.5 summarizes these roles and the permissions assigned to them:

Role	Connects to	Permissions
admin	The OT sensor's configuration shell	• Has access to CLI commands • Can manage log files • Can start and stop services • Does not have filesystem access
support	The on-premises management console's configuration shell	• Has access to CLI commands • Can manage log files • Can start and stop services • Does not have filesystem access
cyberx	The on-premises management console's terminal (root)	• Is the root user and has unlimited privileges on the appliance. • It is used for • Changing default passwords • Troubleshooting • Filesystem access

Table 8.5: Default users and permissions

When using one of the above default built-in users to create new users, one of the following roles can be assigned:

- **Admin**: This user has access to all tools to configure the system, create and manage users and more.
- **Security analyst**: This user can perform actions on devices, acknowledge alerts and use investigation tools.

- **Read-only**: They can view alerts and devices on the device map.

Getting started

To get started with Microsoft Defender IoT ensure that you have valid licenses and then turn on enterprise IoT monitoring by logging into the Microsoft Defender portal and going to **Settings | Device discovery | Enterprise IoT** and switching the toggle to **On**. Once the IoT devices are discovered they will be available on the **Devices** page under the **IoT Devices** tab based on the IP and MAC address coupling. It identifies devices as following:

- **Individual devices**: These include IT, OT or IoT devices with one or more NICs like switches or routers. Devices with modules or backplane components like racks or slots are counted as individual devices.

- **Non-individual devices**: These are items like public internet IP addresses, multicast groups, broadcast groups and inactive devices. These items do not count against the licenses. OT devices are marked as inactive when there is no network activity detected for more than 60 days. Enterprise IoT devices are marked as inactive when there is no network activity detected for more than 30 days.

Note: The detailed steps for planning and deploying sensors in the OT environment is beyond the scope of this book. The reader is advised to refer to Microsoft documentation.

Device inventory

Using Defender for IoT you can identify details like manufacturer, type, serial number etc. for each discovered device. Defender for IoT supports device classes like manufacturing, building, health care, transportation, energy, endpoints, enterprise and retail. Some devices are classified as transient, which means that the device was visible only for a short duration. These devices should be investigated to understand their impact on the network. If devices are in the *unclassified* type, it means that there is no out-of-the box category defined for them. Following figure shows the **Device inventory** page on the Defender for IoT portal:

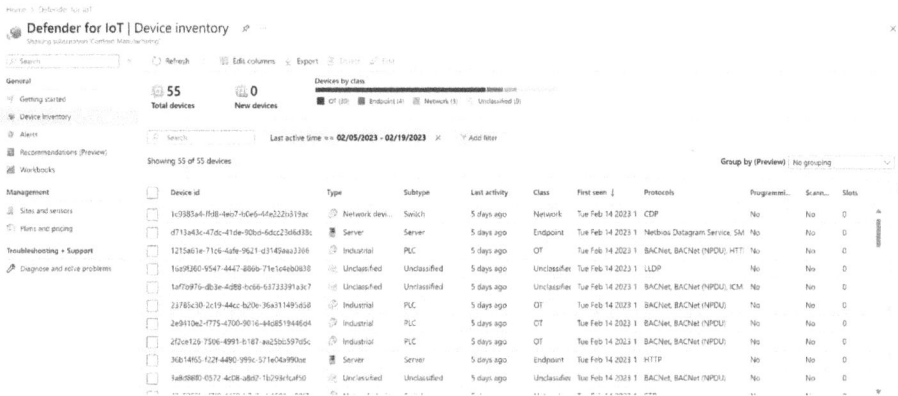

Figure 8.22: *Device inventory page in Defender for IoT portal*

When Defender for IoT is deployed at scale, it is possible that multiple sensors detect the same device. To avoid duplicate devices in the console Defender for IoT consolidates devices based on the zone where the device was found and some common characteristics. When Defender for IoT first discovers the devices, all are listed as authorized. Over time it learns and then any new devices are considered unauthorized and new. The new status is changed as soon as any of the device details are edited, or the device is moved to an OT sensor map. The unauthorized label needs to be manually changed to authorized. Some OT devices can also be marked as important to include them in extra tracking. Devices marked as unauthorized and important are included in the **attack vector** and **risk assessment reports**.

Alerts

Microsoft Defender for IoT generates alerts when the sensors detect changes or suspicious activity in the network traffic.

Following figure shows an example of the **Alerts** page on the Defender for IoT portal:

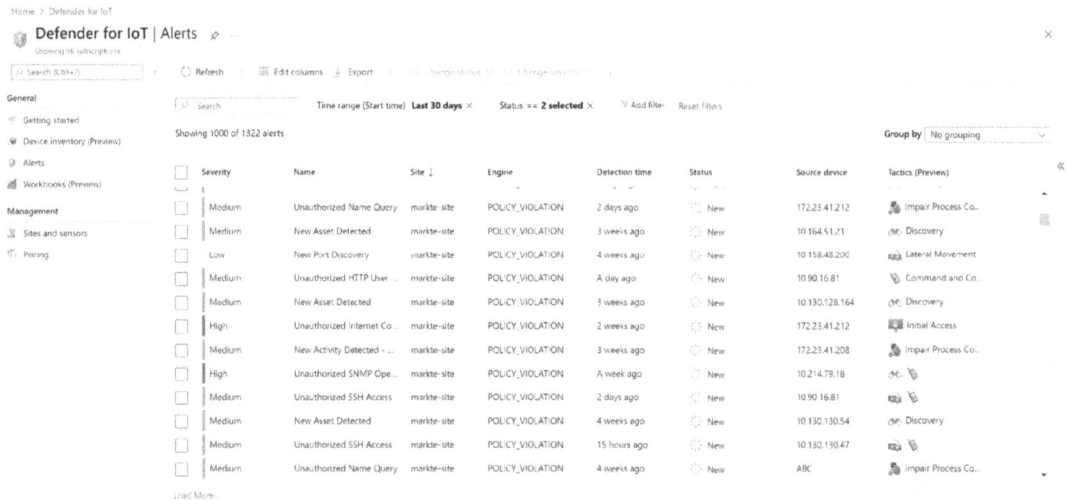

Figure 8.23: *Alerts on Defender for IoT portal*

Organizations receive numerous alerts related to both OT and IT traffic. Some of these alerts are irrelevant and cause alert fatigue. Defender for IoT focusses on alerts which can have business impact on an OT network. It reduces low value IT related alerts. All engines except the Malware engine generate alerts only if a related OT subnet or protocol is detected. The Malware engine generates alerts regardless of whether they are related to IT or OT devices.

In hybrid environments, security teams may be monitoring alerts in the Azure portal and the on-premises management console. Alerts status is fully synchronized between the Azure portal, OT sensor and the on-premises management console. Regardless of where the alert is managed, its status is updated everywhere else. New alerts are automatically closed if no identical traffic is detected within 90 days. If identical traffic is detected, then the 90-day count is reset. To help the SOC teams to triage and manage the alerts better, an **Admin** can create custom alert rules, add comments to alerts, create exclusion rules or forward the alerts to a SIEM. Alerts can have the following statues:

- **New**: These are alerts that have not yet been investigated or triaged.

- **Active**: When investigation starts the alert status can be set to active.

- **Closed**: Alert is fully investigated. Use this status if you want to be alerted for the same traffic again.

- **Learn**: Use this status if you want to add the traffic to the allowed traffic and don't want to be alerted for the same traffic again.

- **Mute**: Use this status if you do not want to be alerted for the same traffic again and do not want to add this traffic to allowed traffic.

Conclusion

In this chapter, we learned how Microsoft Defender for Endpoint helps protect, detect and respond to threats on endpoints on the network. We learnt about the operating systems supported by MDE and the different tools that can be used to onboard devices to MDE. We learnt in detail about collecting device inventory and how MDE integrates with other Microsoft solutions. This chapter covered the important topics of tamper protection, attack surface reduction and automated response and remediation. We learnt how to use Microsoft Intune to configure these settings on Windows and non-Window devices. This chapter also explained the remediation actions available to be taken on suspicious devices and files.

Further this chapter explained how Microsoft Defender Vulnerability Management can complement the existing vulnerability management capabilities available with MDE P2.

Lastly, we explored Microsoft Defender for IoT and how it can help protect OT and IoT networks from bad actors.

In the next chapter, you will learn how to protect Microsoft 365 applications using the capabilities of Microsoft Defender for Office 365.

Multiple choice questions

1. **You are planning to deploy MDE in your environment. You plan to start with a small subset of Windows machine to evaluate the solution. What method should you use to onboard devices to MDE.**

   a. Onboarding script

   b. Microsoft Intune

   c. Group Policy

   d. JAMF Pro

2. **Your organization uses cloud services but still have a significant footprint on-premises. You plan to deploy MDE to manage devices on the network. Which deployment architecture suits you the best?**

   a. Cloud-native

   b. On-premises

   c. Co-management

   d. Evaluation

3. **Your organization uses a non-Microsoft EDR solution but have devices onboarded to MDE. You want to take advantage of the attack surface reduction rules available in MDE. What should you do?**

   a. Configure attack surface reduction rules in Microsoft Intune

   b. Turn off Microsoft Defender Antivirus

   c. Offboard endpoints from MDE

   d. Ensure Microsoft Defender Antivirus is running in active mode

Answer key

1. a
2. c
3. d

Join our book's Discord space

Join the book's Discord Workspace for Latest updates, Offers, Tech happenings around the world, New Release and Sessions with the Authors:

https://discord.bpbonline.com

CHAPTER 9

Protecting M365 Apps

Introduction

Microsoft is the global leader in cloud-based collaboration services and is the preferred partner for organizations that want to move to cloud. Consequently, organization store a lot of their data in the M365 cloud, Exchange Online, SharePoint Online, OneDrive for Business and Teams. Attackers try to breach these applications using various techniques like malware, phishing and spoofing attacks. This chapter describes how organizations can use Exchange Online Protection and Microsoft Defender for Office 365 to defend, detect, investigate and respond to attacks targeting their M365 environment.

Structure

The chapter covers the following topics:

- Exchange Online Protection
- Microsoft Defender for Office 365
- Threat protection policies
- Deploy email protection
- Detect threats
- Investigate and respond

- Remediate

Objectives

By the end of this chapter, readers will learn how **Exchange Online Protection (EOP)** and **Microsoft Defender for Office 365 (MDO)** work together to secure M365 applications. You will be able to distinguish between EOP and MDO and explain how they complement each other to provide a comprehensive security strategy for your M365 environment. This chapter will guide you through the detailed steps of setting up email protection. It will show you how to create threat policies to defend your organization from malware, phishing and spoofing attacks. By the end of this chapter, you will be able to use the advanced features in MDO to run phishing simulations, investigate post-breach incidents and automate response actions.

Exchange Online Protection

An email gateway is a tool that all organizations use to send and receive email and protect against spam, phishing and spoofing attacks. These can be either on-premises or a cloud service. EOP is a cloud-based email gateway that comes with every subscription to Exchange Online and filters email messages and blocks common, large-scale email threats. This is the first layer of protection for organizations that have mailboxes on Exchange Online.

For any email gateway to receive email for an organization, it needs to be listed as the authority in the public DNS. This is done by publishing a **Mail Exchange (MX)** record with the domain registrar. If using EOP (standalone or the cloud version), MX record should point to EOP.

Following figure shows the mail flow from the internet to the recipient mailbox in Exchange Online via EOP:

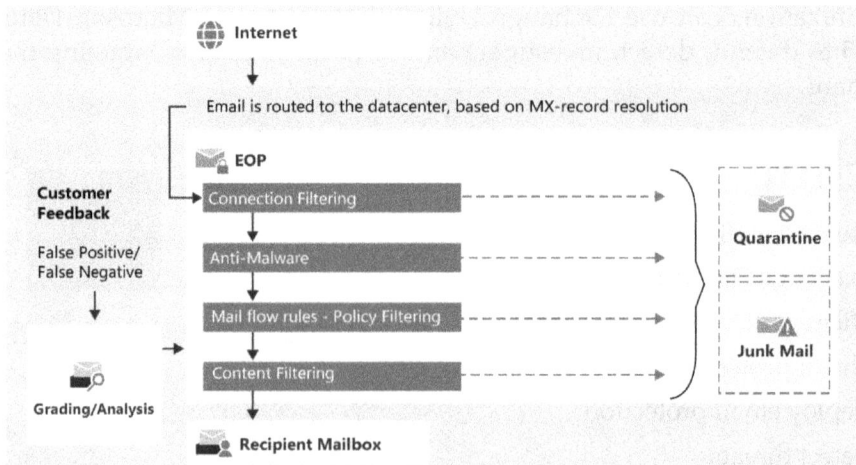

Figure 9.1: EOP in Exchange Online

It is important to understand the capabilities of EOP because MDO builds on these capabilities.

Table 9.1 summarizes the capabilities of EOP:

Prevent or detect	Investigate	Respond
Anti-malware protection Anti-spam protection Bulk email protection Anti-phishing protection Outbound spam filtering Connection filtering Quarantine False positive and false negative report Ability to allow and block domains, URLs, files.	Audit log search Message trace Email security reports	Zero-hour auto purge

Table 9.1: EOP capabilities

Protection policies in EOP

EOP is on by default and basic protection policies are available to all EOP subscribers. There are pre-created **Anti-malware**, **Anti-spam** and **Anti-phishing** policies that apply to all recipients. These policies are available in the Microsoft Defender portal under to **Email & collaboration** | **Policies & rules** | **Threat policies** as shown in the following figure:

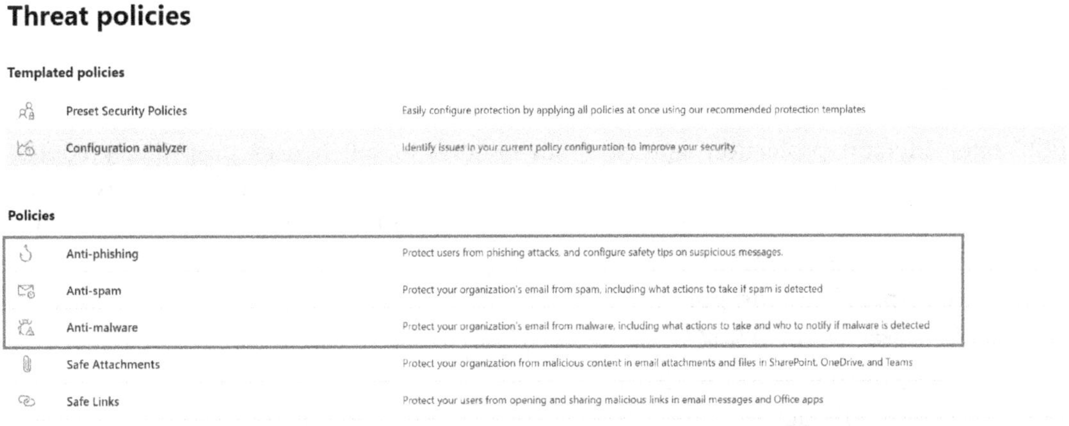

Figure 9.2: Default policies in EOP

Anti-malware

It is common for email messages to be infected with malware like viruses, spyware and ransomware. EOP provides a multi-layered defense that catches all known malware in Windows, Mac and Linux. EOP has an in-built Anti-malware policy that is on by default and applied to all recipients. This policy cannot be turned off. Administrators can change the security settings in this policy by going to the Microsoft Defender clicking on **Anti-malware** in the screen above and then clicking on **Default (Default)**. This will open the policy settings in a fly out pane, as shown in *Figure 9.3*. Review the various settings. To edit the settings, click on **Edit protection settings**.

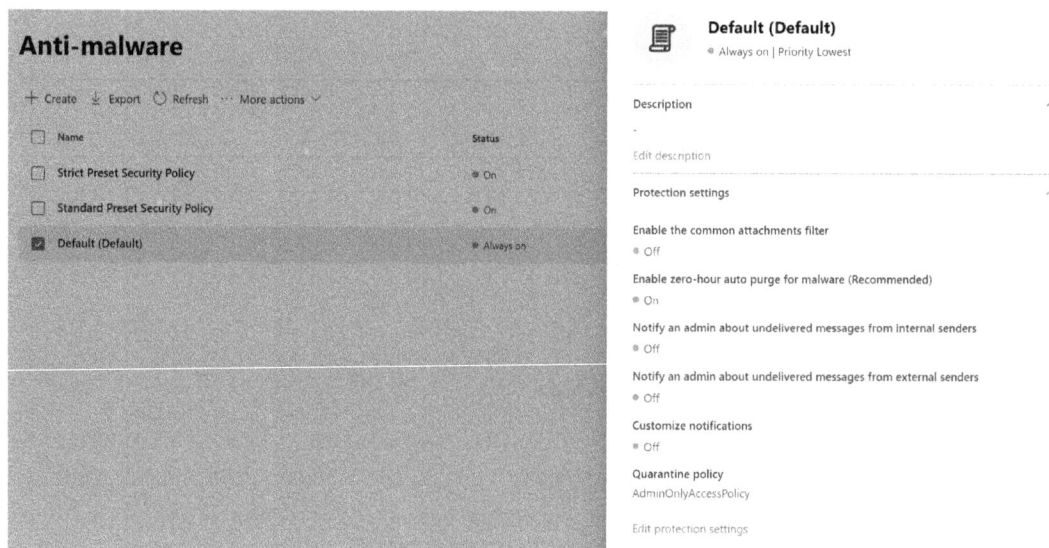

Figure 9.3: Default anti-malware policy

Anti-spam

EOP offers default protection against spam or junk email. It uses proprietary content filtering technologies to identify junk email. It continuously learns from known spam threats and user feedback to improve junk email detection. There are three default Anti-spam policies available, as follows:

- **Anti-spam inbound policy**: This policy scans all incoming email to identify spam. EOP uses the following criteria to identify messages as spam:
  - **Spam**: If the message has a *spam confidence level (SCL)* of 5 or 6 it is classified as spam. By default, these messages are moved to the `junk email` folder.
  - **High confidence spam**: If a message has SCL of 7, 8 or 9 it is classified as high confidence spam. By default, these messages are moved to the `junk email` folder.

○ **Phishing**: By default, these messages are moved to the `junk email` folder.

○ **High confidence phishing**: These messages are always quarantined and can only be released by an administrator.

○ **Bulk senders insight**: If the message source met or exceeded the configured *bulk compliant level (BCL)* the message is classified as bulk. By default, these messages are moved to the `junk email` folder.

Spam thresholds and actions are configurable, and administrators can change them in the policy settings. To do this, click on **Anti-spam** as shown in *Figure 9.2* and then click on **Anti-spam inbound policy (Default)**. The settings will open in a fly-out pane, as you will be able to edit the settings as shown in the following figure:

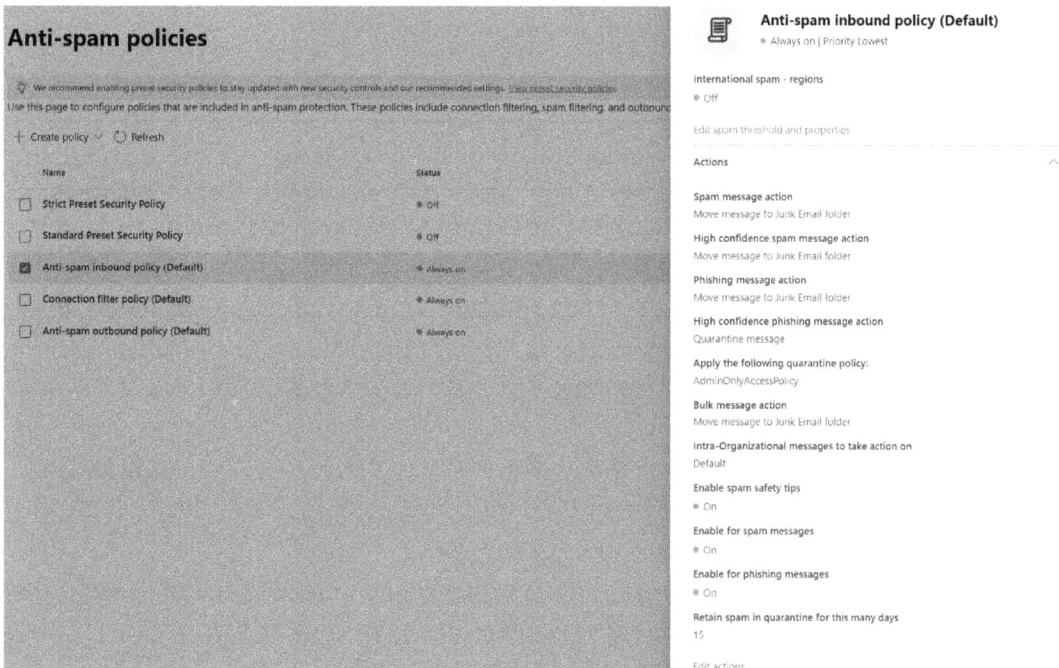

Figure 9.4: *Default anti-spam inbound policy*

- **Connection filter policy**: The connection filter policy identifies good or bad email servers based on the source IP Address. It uses the **IP Allow list**, **IP block list** and **Safe list** to make these decisions. To configure these, click on **Anti-spam** as shown in *Figure 9.2* and then click on **Connection filter policy (Default)**. The policy settings will open in a fly out pane and you will be able to add the allowed and block IP list. You can add a single IP, an IP range or CIDR IP. Safe list is a list of good senders that skip spam filtering. This list is managed by Microsoft and does not require any configuration. You can choose to turn it on or off as shown in the following figure:

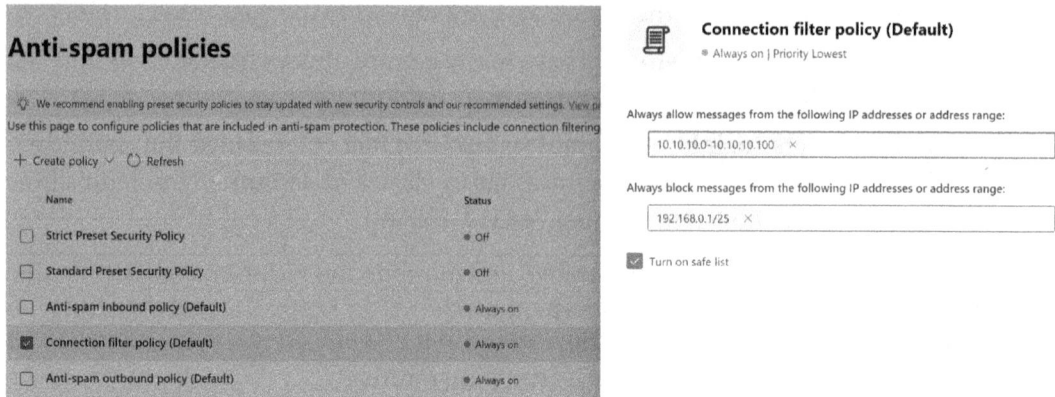

Figure 9.5: Default connection filter policy

- **Anti-spam outbound policy**: Just as organizations need to monitor incoming email for spam, they also need to ensure that spam is not being sent from within their organization. If the organization's email domain is seen as a source of spam, their reputation can be degraded, and the domain can be blacklisted leading to all email generated from within the organization to be rejected by recipient domains. EOP has sending limits to prevent spam and mass-mailing.

  EOP imposes the following sending limits at the service level to all mailboxes in the tenant:

  o **Recipient rate limits**: This limit is designed to discourage sending unsolicited bulk mail. EOP sets this at 10,000 recipients per sender per day.

  o **Recipient limits**: This is the maximum number of recipients allowed in the To, CC and Bcc boxes for an individual message. EOP sets this limit to 1000 recipients per message.

  o **Recipients proxy address limit**: This is the maximum number of email aliases that a single recipient mailbox can have. EOP sets this at 300.

  o **Message rate limit**: This limit specifies the maximum number of messages a user can send from their account within a specified period. EOP sets this at 30 messages per minute.

Some settings can be configured in the policy as well. To do this click on **Anti-spam** in *Figure 9.2* and then click on **Anti-spam outbound policy (Default)**. The settings will open in a fly out pane as shown in the following figure:

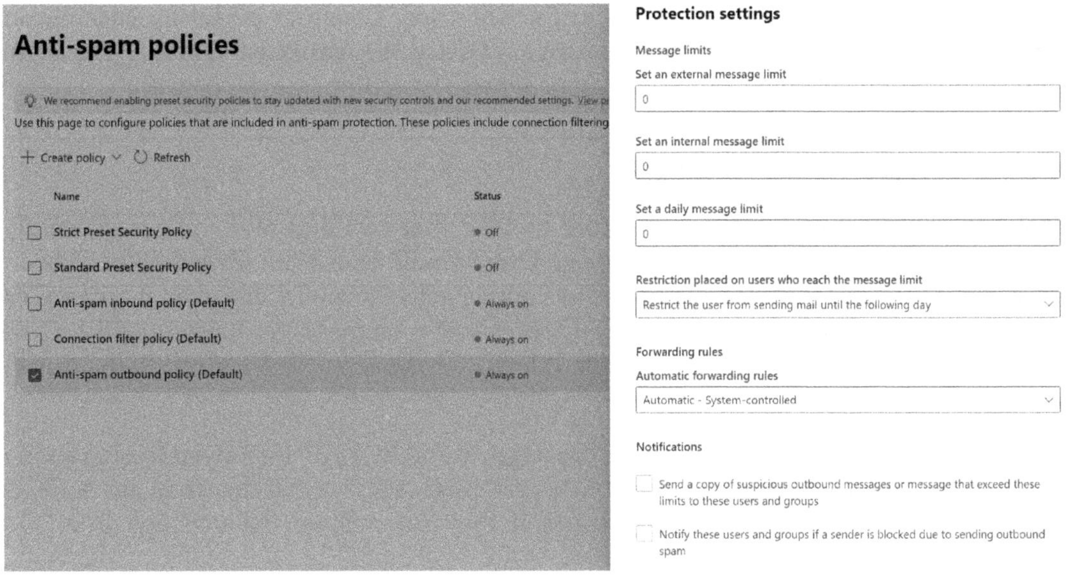

Figure 9.6: *Default anti-spam outbound policy*

For each of the limits above a value between 0-10000 can be specified. The default value is 0 which means that the service default is being used. You can also decide the action to be taken on users who exceed the limits.

Anti-phishing

Phishing is a type of email attack that attempts to steal sensitive information by luring the users to click on malicious links in email messages. For example, an email might appear to be from a bank asking the user to click on a malicious link and then prompting them to enter their login credentials in an attempt to steal them. These email messages look legitimate enough for users to trust. Phishing attacks are of several types as follows:

- **Spear phishing**: Attackers cast a wide net for using regular phishing messages. Spear phishing is focused attack tailored to targeted recipients. It is usually launched after the attacker has completed reconnaissance in the environment.

- **Whaling**: This is directed towards executives and other high value targets.

- **Business Email Compromise (BEC)**: This uses forged trusted senders like financial officers, partners to trick recipients into approving payments, transferring funds or revealing customer data.

- **Ransomware**: Most ransomware attacks that encrypt data and demand payment start with phishing messages. Anti-phishing protection cannot help decrypting the data, but it can help detect the initial message that is associated with the ransomware campaign.

EOP Anti-phishing policy is available in the Microsoft Defender portal by clicking on **Anti-phishing** in *Figure 9.2* and then clicking on **Office 365 AntiPhish Default (Default)**. The policy setting will open in a fly out pane where the settings can be edited.

Zero-hour auto purge

Zero-hour auto purge (**ZAP**) is a feature in EOP that can find and remove phishing, spam or malware messages from Exchange Online mailboxes even after they have been delivered. This helps when the message was not detected as malicious when it arrived, or it became harmful later. ZAP automatically takes action on messages in user mailboxes. It is on by default and users do not notice it. It looks for messages that arrived in the last 48 hours.

Malware and high confidence phishing messages found by ZAP are moved to quarantine which only administrators can view. Policies can be created so that the users are notified that a message has been quarantined and if they can release the message from the quarantine or permanently delete it.

Phishing, spam or high confidence spam messages are subject to the settings defined in the corresponding policy. ZAP either moves the message to the junk mail folder or quarantines the message. By default, users can view messages that were classified as spam or high confidence spam where they are the recipient. Administrators can create policies to define what the users can do with the messages in the quarantine or if they receive notifications.

Microsoft Defender for Office 365

Microsoft Defender for Office 365 is a cloud-based service that augments the capabilities of EOP to protect not just Exchange Online but also other M365 services like SharePoint Online, OneDrive for Business and Microsoft Teams. It helps safeguard the organization against advanced threats like phishing, business email compromise and malware attacks.

Microsoft Defender for Office 365 is available in two plans, as follows:

- **Microsoft Defender for Office 365 Plan 1 (MDO P1)**: MDO P1 has all capabilities of EOP, and some additional capabilities as summarized in *Table 9.2*. It protects the M365 services from zero-day malware, phishing and business email compromise. MDO P1 builds on the prevention and detection capabilities of EOP.

Prevent or detect	Investigate	Respond
Additional capabilities in anti-phishing capabilities User and domain impersonation protection Mailbox intelligence impersonation protection Advanced phishing thresholds Safe attachments Safe links SIEM integration for alerts	Real-time detections SIEM integration for incidents URL trace Reports	Same as EOP

Table 9.2: *MDO P1 capabilities*

- **Microsoft Defender for Office 365 Plan 2 (MDO P2)**: In addition to all capabilities that come with EOP and MDO P1, MDO P2 adds phishing simulations, post-breach investigations, advanced hunting, response and automation. MDO P2 expands the investigation and response capabilities of EOP and MDO P1.

The following table summarizes the additional features available with MDO P2:

Prevent or detect	Investigate	Respond
Attack simulation training	Threat Explorer instead of real-time detections Threat Trackers Campaigns	AIR SIEM integration for Automated Investigations

Table 9.3: *MDO P2 capabilities*

As is evident, each of these plans builds on the capability of the previous one, providing layers of security with each layer having a different security emphasis.

Before we move on, let us discuss some of the MDO protection features.

Safe Attachments in email

Safe Attachments in MDO provides an additional layer of protection for messages that have been scanned by the anti-malware policy in EOP. It uses a virtual environment to check attachments before they are delivered to the recipient using a process called **detonation**. This is particularly useful in cases of unknown or zero-day malware. For MDO P1 subscribers, Safe Attachments is enabled by default by the **Built-in protection** in the **Preset security policies** discussed in the next section. In addition, administrators can create **custom policies** that are specific to their requirements.

The following figure shows the available settings for a Safe Attachments policy:

Safe Attachments unknown malware response

Select the action for unknown malware in attachments. Learn more

Warning

- **Monitor** and **Block** actions might cause a significant delay in message delivery. Learn more
- **Dynamic Delivery** is only available for recipients with hosted mailboxes.
- For **Block** or **Dynamic Delivery**, messages with detected attachments are quarantined and can be released only by an admin.

◉ Off - Attachments will not be scanned by Safe Attachments.

◯ Monitor - Deliver the message if malware is detected and track scanning results.

◯ Block - Block current and future messages and attachments with detected malware.

◯ Dynamic Delivery (Preview messages) - Immediately deliver the message without attachments. Reattach files after scanning is complete.

Quarantine policy

AdminOnlyAccessPolicy	⌄

NotificationEnabledPolicy

DefaultFullAccessPolicy

AdminOnlyAccessPolicy

DefaultFullAccessWithNotificationPolicy

☐ Enable redirect ⓘ

Send messages that contain monitored attachments to the specified email address.

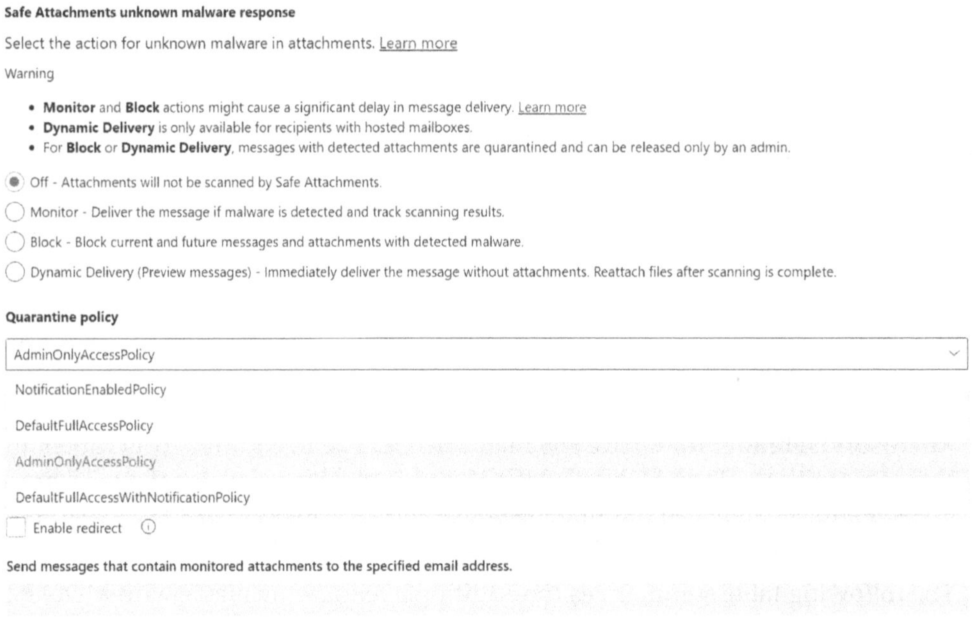

Figure 9.7: Safe Attachments policy settings

Safe Attachments in SharePoint, OneDrive and Teams

M365 uses a common virus detection engine for files that are uploaded to SharePoint Online, OneDrive and Teams. Safe Attachments for SharePoint, OneDrive for Business and Teams provides an additional layer of security for these files once they have been scanned by the common virus detection engine. It also uses the same detonation process to open the attachment in a virtual environment to see what happens. Safe Attachments for SharePoint, OneDrive for Business and Teams is turned on by default and this setting can be viewed from the Microsoft Defender portal by navigating to **Email & collaboration** | **Policies & rules** | **Threat policies** | **Safe Attachments**. Click on **Global settings** and in the fly out pane, ensure that the toggle for **Turn on Defender for Office 365 for SharePoint, OneDrive and Microsoft Teams** is **On**.

Following points should be considered while using this feature:

- MDO does not scan every single file in SharePoint Online, OneDrive for Business and Teams. Files are scanned asynchronously.
- SharePoint sites should be configured to use the Modern experience.

Safe Links for emails

Like Safe Attachments, Safe Links add an additional layer of protection for messages that are already scanned by anti-spam and anti-malware protection in EOP. Safe Links scans incoming email messages for URLs. All scanned URLs are wrapped using the Microsoft URL **https://nam01.safelinks.protection.com**. Post this they are scanned for malicious content. If the URL is found to be malicious, the action configured in the policy is taken which could be to reject the mail or quarantine it. If it is found to be safe it is forwarded on to the user mailbox with the rewritten URL.

Once Safe Links rewrites the URL, it is rewritten when the message is manually forwarded or replied to. Wrapping is done per messages recipient for both internal and external recipients. Links that are added to the replied or forwarded message are also rewritten.

If messages are automatically forwarded based on Inbox or SMTP forwarding rules, the URL is not rewritten unless the recipient is also protected by Safe Links or the URL was already rewritten in a previous communication.

If Safe Links protection is turned on URLs are scanned prior to message delivery regardless of whether the URLs are rewritten or not. In supported versions on Outlook on Windows, Mac and Web unwrapped URLs are checked by a client-side API call to Safe Links at the time of click. Administrators can choose to use only API calls for Safe Links scanning by selecting the option **Do not rewrite URLs, do checks vis Safe Links API only** in the Safe Links policy as shown in *Figure 9.8*.

Safe Links provides on-click protection of URLs in email messages. Since it is common for attackers to first send a non-malicious link in an email and then arm it with a malicious URL post-delivery, this feature ensures that each time a user clicks on the URL it is first checked by Safe Links to confirm that it is safe before users are directed to the website.

For MDO P1 subscribers, Safe Links is enabled by default by the **Built-in protection** in the **Preset security policies** discussed in the next section. Administrators can choose to create **Custom policies**.

Following figure shows the available settings for the Safe Links policy for email messages while creating a custom policy:

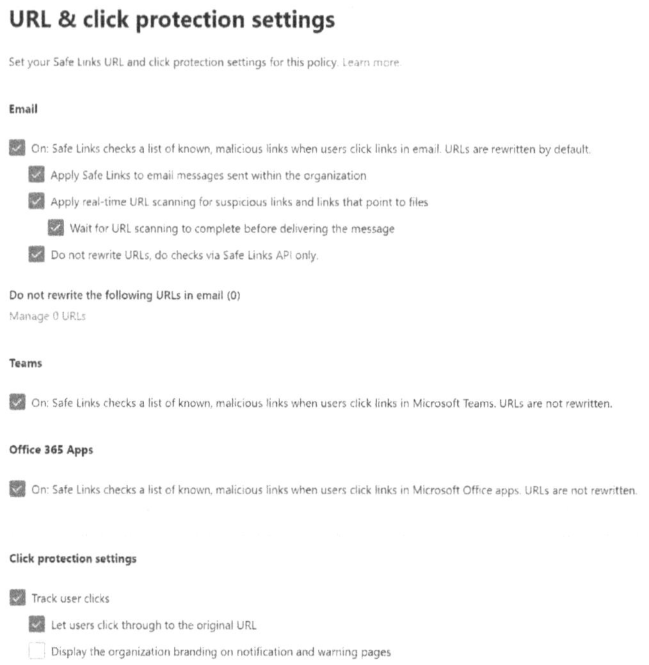

URL & click protection settings

Set your Safe Links URL and click protection settings for this policy. Learn more.

Email

☑ On: Safe Links checks a list of known, malicious links when users click links in email. URLs are rewritten by default.

   ☑ Apply Safe Links to email messages sent within the organization

   ☑ Apply real-time URL scanning for suspicious links and links that point to files

      ☑ Wait for URL scanning to complete before delivering the message

   ☑ Do not rewrite URLs, do checks via Safe Links API only.

Do not rewrite the following URLs in email (0)
Manage 0 URLs

Teams

☑ On: Safe Links checks a list of known, malicious links when users click links in Microsoft Teams. URLs are not rewritten.

Office 365 Apps

☑ On: Safe Links checks a list of known, malicious links when users click links in Microsoft Office apps. URLs are not rewritten.

Click protection settings

☑ Track user clicks

   ☑ Let users click through to the original URL

   ☐ Display the organization branding on notification and warning pages

Figure 9.8: Custom Safe Links Policy

Following are the steps on how Safe Links works in email messages:

1. Email goes through EOP and MDO where it is scanned for spam, malware and phish. URLs are rewritten to provide on-click protection before being delivered to the user's inbox.

2. User opens the message and clicks on the link in it.

3. Safe Links checks the URL before opening the site. It can take one of the following actions:

   a. If the URL points to a malicious site, the user is directed to a malicious site warning page.

   b. If the URL points to a site that downloads a file and the **Apply real-time URL scanning for suspicious links and links that point to files** is turned on, the downloadable file is inspected before being opened.

   c. If the URL is safe, the user is directed to the website.

Safe Links for Teams

URLs shared in Teams chat and channel messages are scanned for known malicious links when the user clicks on the link. MDO provides on-click protection, however, the URLs in Team messages are not rewritten. Safe Links for Teams can be turned on or off in the custom Safe Links policy as shown in *Figure 9.8*.

If the link is found to be malicious, the user can have one of the following experiences:

1. If the link was clicked in a Teams conversation, group chat or from a channel, a warning page shown opens in the user's default browser.

2. If the link was clicked for a pinned tab the warning page opens within the Teams interface.

3. If the **Let users click through to the original URL** setting as shown in *Figure 9.3* is enabled, then the user can open the original URL by clicking on the **Continue anyway (not recommended)** option as shown in *Figure 9.9*. It is recommended to not allow the users to continue to the original URL.

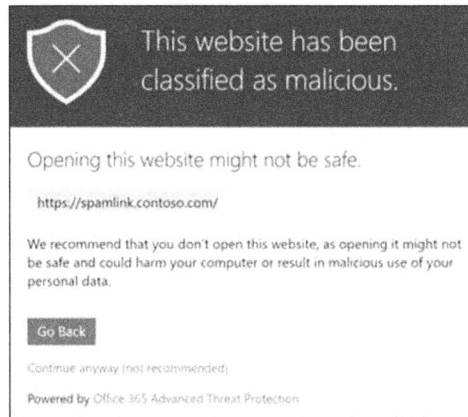

Figure 9.9: Teams Safe Links warning page

Safe Links for Office apps

Safe Links checks for links in Office documents that were attached in an email message. If a user receives an email with a Word file with links, once the user opens the attachment and clicks on a link, Safe Links for Office apps checks if the link is safe. This policy setting is shown in *Figure 9.8*.

Safe Links for Office apps require that the following prerequisites are met:

- Subscription version of Office should be used. This includes Microsoft 365 Apps or Microsoft 365 Business Premium. The following versions are supported:

  o Current versions of Word, Excel and PowerPoint on Windows or Mac

  o Web versions of Word, Excel, PowerPoint and OneNote

  o Office Apps for iOS and Android

  o Visio on Windows

  o Outlook for Windows when opening links from emails messages saved as EML or MSG files.

- Office apps and M365 services should be using modern authentication.
- Users signed into Office apps using the Work or School accounts.

Safe Links in Office Apps works the same way, Safe Links in email messages work. If Safe Links in unable to complete the scanning, the protection is not triggered. The user is warned to exercise caution while proceeding to the website.

Threat protection policies

Threat protection policies overlap between EOP and MDO. Some base settings are available with EOP while others are available with MDO P1 and P2. This section discusses all the policies and settings.

Preset security policies

These are predefined profiles that contain most of the available protection settings in EOP and MDO. The profiles are tailored to specific levels of protection like **Strict**, **Standard** and **Built-in protection**. In these profiles the security settings are locked and cannot be changed. As new security capabilities are added these profiles are automatically updated. Administrators can only change the users to which these policies apply.

These policies are available in Microsoft Defender portal by navigating to **Email & collaboration** | **Policies & rules** under **Threat policies** as shown in *Figure 9.2*. Click on the **Preset security policies** to view the three profiles available as shown in the following figure:

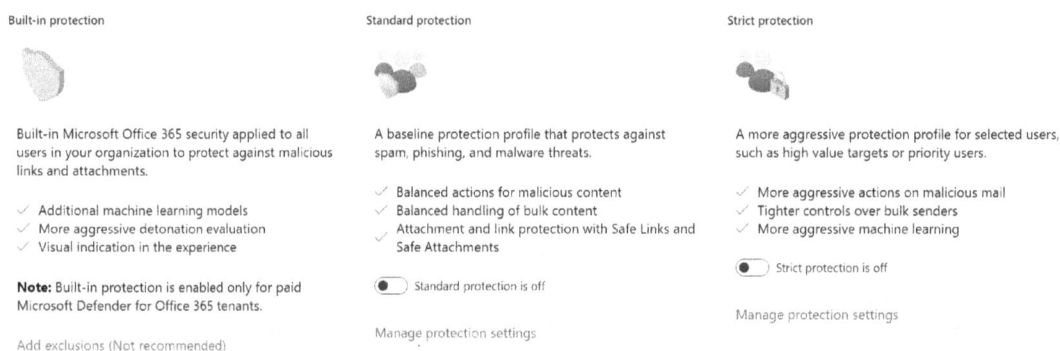

Built-in protection

Built-in Microsoft Office 365 security applied to all users in your organization to protect against malicious links and attachments.

✓ Additional machine learning models
✓ More aggressive detonation evaluation
✓ Visual indication in the experience

Note: Built-in protection is enabled only for paid Microsoft Defender for Office 365 tenants.

Add exclusions (Not recommended)

Standard protection

A baseline protection profile that protects against spam, phishing, and malware threats.

✓ Balanced actions for malicious content
✓ Balanced handling of bulk content
✓ Attachment and link protection with Safe Links and Safe Attachments

(●) Standard protection is off

Manage protection settings

Strict protection

A more aggressive protection profile for selected users, such as high value targets or priority users.

✓ More aggressive actions on malicious mail
✓ Tighter controls over bulk senders
✓ More aggressive machine learning

(●) Strict protection is off

Manage protection settings

Figure 9.10: Preset security policies

Built-in protection

Built-in protection is only available for paid MDO subscribers and is not available with EOP. For paid subscribers of MDO P1 or MDO P2 built-in protection is turned on by default and it adds the **Safe Links** and **Safe Attachment** policies. Administrators cannot change the security settings in these policies, but they can add users, groups and domains to be excluded from the policy by clicking on **Add exclusions (Not recommended)** in the above screen. The Safe Links and Safe Attachments policies can be accessed from the Microsoft Defender portal by navigating to **Email & collaboration | Policies & rules | Threat policies** as shown in *Figure 9.2*. These policies have been explained in detail in the previous section.

Strict and standard

The **strict** and **standard** profiles are available with EOP with some additional protection if the organization has MDO P1 or MDO P2 licenses. They are turned off by default. When turning on, you can specify the users, groups and domains who the profiles apply to by clicking on **Manage protection settings**. Once these are on, corresponding policies are created in Anti-spam, Anti-phishing, Anti-malware, Safe Attachment and Safe Links policies. These policies are explained in detail in the previous sections.

Following figure is an example of the Safe Attachments policy with all the preset profiles turned on:

Figure 9.11: Safe attachment policy with all profiles

Custom policies

If the default and preset security policies do not fulfil the needs of an organization, custom policies can be created for all Threat Protection policies as discussed above. These policies are fully customizable, and administrators can create any number of custom policies. To create a custom policy, navigate to the relevant policy on the **Threat Policies** page and click on **Create** at the top. Follow the instructions in the wizard to create the policy.

Following table summarizes the different policies and the protection feature it applies to:

Protection feature	Default policy	Preset security policies	Custom policies
Anti-malware	Yes	Yes (Standard and Strict)	Yes
Anti-spam	Yes	Yes (Standard and Strict)	Yes
Anti-phishing	Yes	Yes (Standard and Strict)	Yes

Protection feature	Default policy	Preset security policies	Custom policies
Safe Attachments	No	Yes (All)	Yes
Safe Links	No	Yes (All)	Yes

Table 9.4: Policies and protection features

Policy order

Now the question arises how these policies are evaluated and what happens if all policies are turned on for a specific protection feature.

Following considerations are applied while determining the policy order:

- Protection features like malware, spoofing and phishing have an unconfigurable order of processing. This means that Microsoft has already determined the order in which messages will be evaluated for these policies and this order cannot be changed or customized. For example, a message is always evaluated for malware before it is evaluated for phishing.

- If you are using all or some of the preset and custom policies, they are applied in the following order of precedence:

    1. Strict preset profile.
    2. Standard preset profile.
    3. Custom policies based on priority order.
    4. Built-in preset profile for Safe Links and Safe Attachments and default policies for anti-malware, ant-spam and anti-phishing.

This means that strict preset policy overrides the settings in the standard preset policy which overrides the settings in the custom policies and so on.

If a user is included in multiple policies for a specific protection feature, the first policy for the feature where the user is defined will determine what happens to the message.

Once a protection policy is applied to a message, policy processing stops, and the message is not evaluated against other policies.

Deploy email protection

All organizations with Exchange Online licenses benefit from the default level of protection provided by EOP. Administrators can take some additional action to configure EOP and MDO in a way that enables them to unleash the full potential of these products. This section will help you configure email protection offered by EOP and MDO in a way that will best protect your organization and show management that you are maximizing the benefits provided by MDO.

Configuring email authentication

Email authentication, also called email validation are standards that verify that email messages are legitimate and unaltered and come from sources expected from the sender's email domain. This section assumes that you have configured custom domains in your M365 tenant as described in *Chapter 1, Introduction to Microsoft Entra*. To configure email authentication, you need to create the register the below DNS records with your domain registrar for all custom domains configured in your tenant. This includes subdomains as follows:

- **Sender Policy Framework (SPF)**: This is a TXT record that helps prevent spoofing by validating that the source of the email is from senders in the domain.

- **DomainKeys Identified Mail (DKIM)**: Signs outbound messages and stores the signature in the message header.

- **Domain-based Message Authentication, Reporting, and Conformance (DMARC)**: Using this the recipient email servers can decide what to do with messages that fail the SPF or DKIM checks.

- **Authentication Received Chain (ARC)**: Some customers use services that modify the email headers of inbound emails before they are delivered. To prevent these messages from failing the SPF or DKIM checks you can add these services as trusted ARC sealers.

To ensure that the organization is sufficiently secure, MDO provides a **Configuration analyzer** that is a central location to find and fix security policy settings where the settings are less secure than the settings in the Standard and Strict protection profiles. It analyses all the policies listed in *Table 6.4* above and checks if SPF or DKIM records are detected in DNS and if native outlook external sender identifiers are enabled. Configuration analyzer can be accessed from the Microsoft Defender portal by navigating to **Email & collaboration** | **Policies & rules** | **Threat policies** | **Configuration analyzer** as shown in *Figure 9.5*.

The first tab shown is **Standard recommendation**. The first section on this page shows the type of policy and the number of settings in the policy that are lower than the recommended settings in the **Standard** policy. For example, in *Figure 9.12* there are eight settings in Anti-spam policy and 33 settings in the Anti-phishing policy that need improvement. If a policy type and number is not shown it means that it meets the standard and does not need improvement. You can switch to the **Strict Recommendations** tab to view the improvement actions for the Strict profile.

Figure 9.12: Configuration analyzer

Click on any recommendation to view details. The details pane is shown in *Figure 9.13*. To apply the recommendation, simply check on the box next to the recommendation and click on **Apply recommendation**.

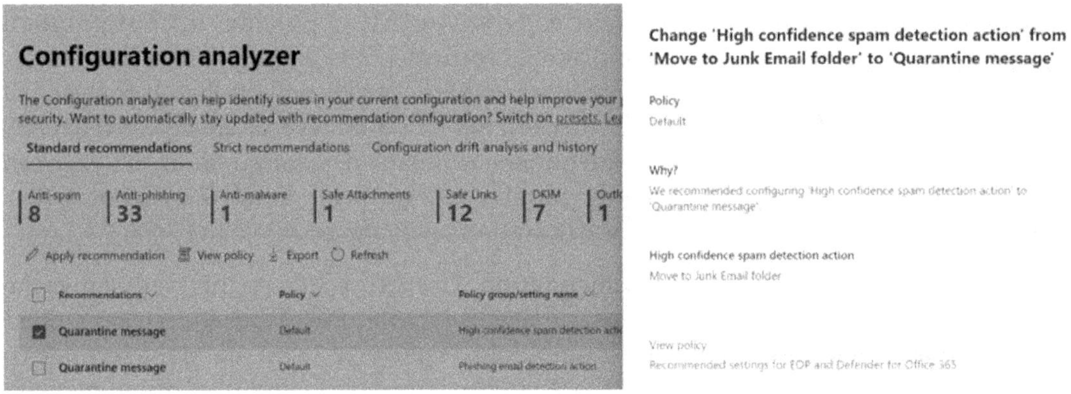

Figure 9.13: Apply recommendation

Using the **Configuration drift analysis and history** tab, administrators can track changes to the security policies and how these changes compare to the standard and strict profiles.

Configure protection policies

The next step would be to configure the Anti-spam, Anti-malware, Anti-phishing, Safe Attachments and Safe Links policies. Depending on the licenses you own and your organization's security requirements, you can choose to use the Default or Preset policies or create custom policies as discussed in the previous section.

Assign permissions to admins

To configure EOP and MDO one of the following permissions is required:

- Global Administrator or Security Administrator in Microsoft Entra
- Organization Management or Security Administrator in MDO
- Exchange Online Organization Management in Exchange Online

It is recommended to use the principle of least privilege to assign permissions to admins.

Setup priority accounts

Not all users in an organization have access to the same information. Some users may have access to more sensitive information than others, like customer financial data or product code. If attackers can compromise these accounts, they might gain access to this highly sensitive information which could pose a serious threat for the organization. These accounts are called **priority accounts**. These could be accounts of senior executives, admin accounts or accounts belonging to product developers. Attackers cast a wide net for regular user accounts using phishing attacks. Other attacks like spear phishing or whaling are used to target these priority accounts. Hence, these priority accounts require more protection than regular user accounts.

MDO improves security features for priority accounts by requiring MFA and disabling the use of legacy authentication protocols. They also require more stringent protection actions which can be implemented using preset security policies.

MDO allows administrators to tag user accounts as priority accounts for easier identification in alerts and reports. This is done by adding the user accounts to the **Priority Account** tag. This tag is built-in the Microsoft Defender portal. To add user accounts to the **Priority Account** tag, following are the steps:

a. Login to **https://security.microsoft.com** and navigate to **Settings | Email & collaboration**. Click on **User tags**.

b. In the right pane, you will see a tab for **Priority account** as shown in the following figure:

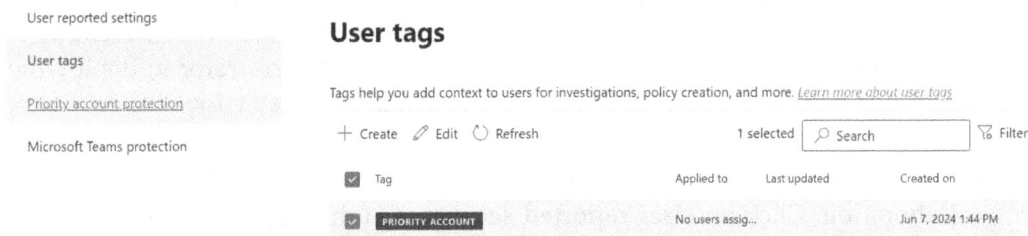

Figure 9.14: Priority account tag

c. Select the tag and click on **Edit**. Click on **Add members** and type the name of users would like to add to the tag. Click on **Add**.

Additional tags can be created from this page to suit your business requirements. For example, you might want to create a tag to identify account of executive admins or IT administrators.

Accounts tagged as **priority accounts** receive **Priority account protection** which offers additional tailored heuristics that apply to executives. Priority account protection is turned on by default in MDO. To view this setting, login to **https://security.microsoft.com** and navigate to **Settings | Email & collaboration**. Click on **Priority account protection** and ensure that the toggle next to **Priority account protection** is **On**. As accounts are added to the priority account tag, they start receiving additional protection as outlined in the following figure:

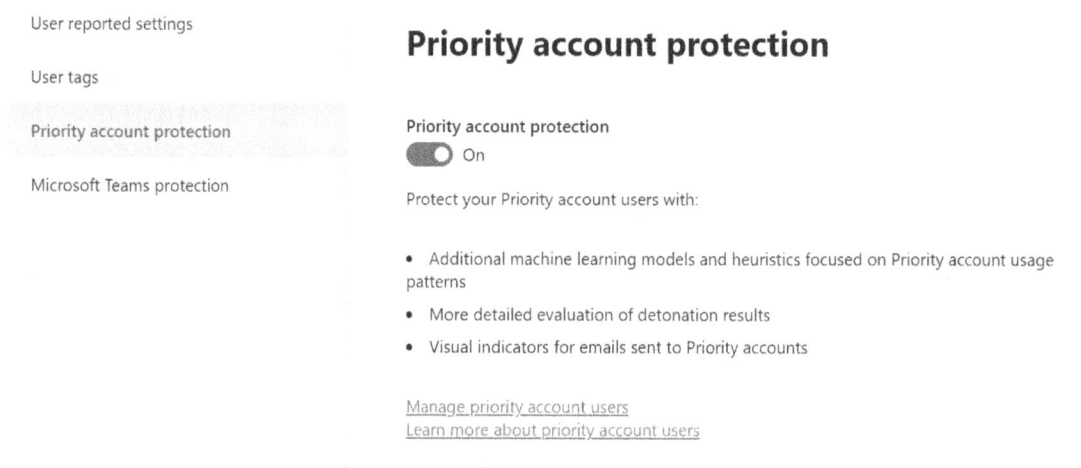

User reported settings

User tags

Priority account protection

Microsoft Teams protection

Priority account protection

Priority account protection
⬤ On

Protect your Priority account users with:

- Additional machine learning models and heuristics focused on Priority account usage patterns
- More detailed evaluation of detonation results
- Visual indicators for emails sent to Priority accounts

Manage priority account users
Learn more about priority account users

Figure 9.15: Priority account protection

Enable user reported messages

It is common practice to enable users to report suspected phishing or junk messages. Users can do this by clicking on a button in Microsoft Outlook and these messages are available for administrators to review in the Microsoft Defender portal under **Actions & submissions | Submissions | User reported**. MDO allows administrator to deploy the report message or report phishing add-in or a supported third-party tool. To configure these options, following are the steps:

1. Login to **https://security.microsoft.com** and navigate to **Settings | Email & collaboration**. Click on **User reported settings**. On this page you can customize how users report messages in Outlook. Review the available options as shown in *Figure 9.16.*

2. Check the box **Monitor reported messages in Outlook** and select **Use the built-in Report button in outlook** to enable the **Report** button in Outlook.

    a. When the **Ask the user to confirm before reporting** box is checked a pre-reporting pop-up is shown to the user asking them to confirm if the message is phishing, junk or not junk.

    b. Checking the **Show a success message after the message is reported** will display a success message to the user once they report phishing or junk message. This message can be customized by clicking on the **Customize messages** option as shown in the following figure:

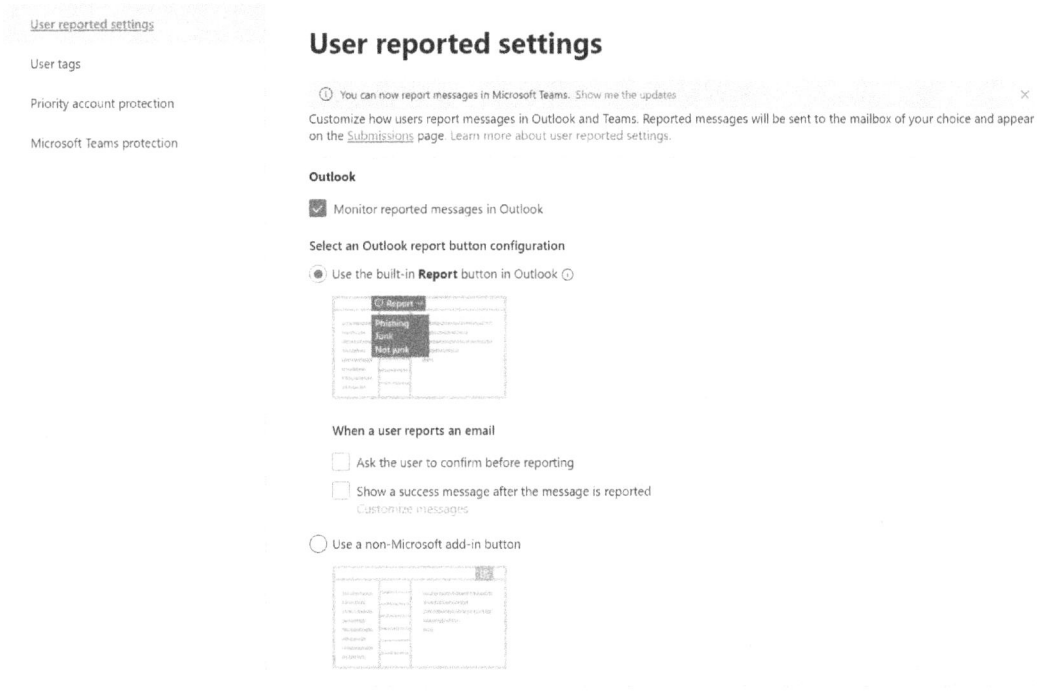

Figure 9.16: User reported settings

3. You can also choose to let the user know the result of the investigation by using the options as shown in *Figure 9.17*.

    a. Click on **Customize results email** to customize the text of the email message.

    b. Selecting the box **Automatically email users the results of the investigation** allow you to choose if you want to notify the user for phishing or malware, spam or no threats or all.

    c. Check the box **Specify a Microsoft 365 mailbox to use as the from address of email notifications** if you want to use a customized mailbox to send the result message. If not selected the messages are sent from **submissions@microsoft. com.**

   d. The last option allows you to customize the email by adding your company branding instead of the Microsoft logo.

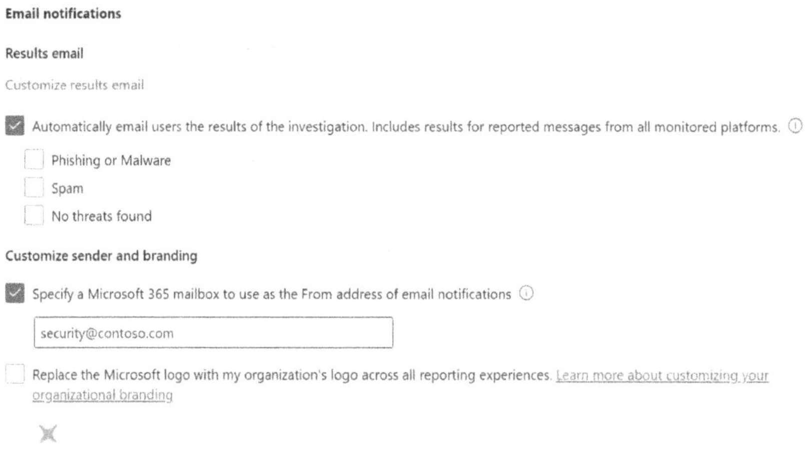

Email notifications

Results email

Customize results email

☑ Automatically email users the results of the investigation. Includes results for reported messages from all monitored platforms. ①

  ☐ Phishing or Malware

  ☐ Spam

  ☐ No threats found

Customize sender and branding

☑ Specify a Microsoft 365 mailbox to use as the From address of email notifications ①

  ┌───┐
  │ security@contoso.com   │
  └───┘

☐ Replace the Microsoft logo with my organization's logo across all reporting experiences. Learn more about customizing your organizational branding

✕

Figure 9.17: Result email settings

Block and allow entries

In certain scenarios, you might need to block or allow message senders, files and URLs. This is done by adding entries to the **Tenant Allow/Block List** available in the Microsoft Defender portal by navigating to **Email & collaboration** | **Policies & rules** | **Threat policies** | **Tenant Allow/Block List**. The following figure shows an example of the Tenant Allow/Block List page:

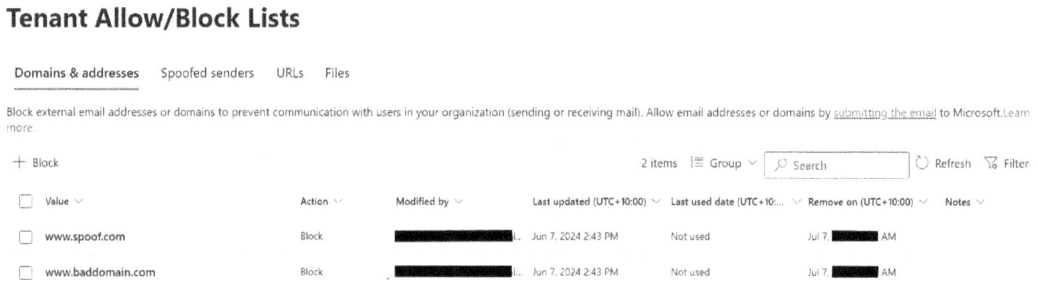

Tenant Allow/Block Lists

Domains & addresses   Spoofed senders   URLs   Files

Block external email addresses or domains to prevent communication with users in your organization (sending or receiving mail). Allow email addresses or domains by submitting the email to Microsoft.Learn more.

+ Block   2 items   ≡ Group ∨   🔍 Search   ↻ Refresh   ⊽ Filter

☐	Value ∨	Action ∨	Modified by ∨	Last updated (UTC+10:00) ∨	Last used date (UTC+10:... ∨	Remove on (UTC+10:00) ∨	Notes ∨
☐	www.spoof.com	Block	████████████L.	Jun 7, 2024 2:43 PM	Not used	Jul 7, ████ AM	
☐	www.baddomain.com	Block	████████████L.	Jun 7, 2024 2:43 PM	Not used	Jul 7, ████ AM	

Figure 9.18: Tenant Allow/Block List

Following are the guidelines for blocking and allowing entries:

   • **Block**: Using this setting you can prevent email addresses or domains from sending and receiving emails from users in your organization, specify spoofed senders that are always blocked and specify URLs, Files and IP addresses that the users cannot access. Items can be added to the block list in one of the following ways:

  o   Manually add domains and URLs in the **Tenant Allow/Block List**.

  o   Submit items to Microsoft for analysis from the **Submissions** page. This creates corresponding block entries in the Tenant Allow/Block List.

  o   Messages blocked by spoof intelligence are shown on the **Spoof intelligence** page. If manual changes are made to these entries, it becomes a manual block, and the entry is displayed on the **Spoofed senders** page in the Tenant Allow/Block List. Senders can also manually be added to the **Spoofed senders** page.

- **Allow**: This option allows email addresses and domains to communicate with users in your organization. Allow entries for domains and URLs cannot be created manually in the Tenant Allow/Block List. You can do so by submitting the message to Microsoft. While reporting the item you can choose to allow the item which creates an allow entry in the Tenant Allow/Block List.

  Messages allowed by spoof intelligence are shown on the **Spoof intelligence** page. If manual changes are made to these entries, it becomes a manual allow, and the entry is displayed on the **Spoofed senders** page in the Tenant Allow/Block List. Senders can also manually be added to the **Spoofed senders** page.

Train end users

MDO P2 offers attack simulation training for end users that enables administrators to run realistic campaigns that help end users identify the characteristics of a suspicious message so that they are better prepared to deal with such messages. It also helps organizations identify vulnerable users and provide them additional training before a real attack can impact the organization.

This training is an overall campaign. It sends a realistic but harmless message to the users. Administrators would decide the following:

- The target users who get the simulated message and how frequently they get it.
- The training that users receive is based on the action they take.
- The payload that is delivered with the message. This could be a URL or an attachment.
- The social engineering technique used.

MDO offers the following **social engineering techniques** in the attack simulation training. Most of these are curated from the MITRE ATT&CK framework. Different payloads are available for each technique, as follows:

- **Credential harvest**: This technique is used to steal user credential by asking them to click on a link that presents a well-known website that has been compromised or is a clone of the actual website, like a banking website. The user is prompted to enter their credentials.

- **Malware attachment**: This technique is used to infect a user's computer with malware by sending them an infected attachment. When the user opens the attachment an arbitrary code or a macro is run that helps the attacker to inject additional code to compromise the device.

- **Link in attachment**: This is a hybrid of the first two methods. In this case the malicious URL is embedded in an attachment in the email.

- **Link to malware**: In this case the user receives a link to an attachment on a well-known file sharing platform like SharePoint or Dropbox. When the user clicks on the link to open the attachment, code is run on the user's device that enables the attacker to inject additional code to compromise the device.

- **Drive by URL**: In this case the user receives an email with a URL. When the user clicks on the URL, they are redirected to a well-known website that has been compromised or is a clone of the actual website. This website runs code on the device to gather information about the recipient.

- **OAuth consent grant**: The attacker uses a malicious Azure Application that is used to gain access to data. The user is asked to provide consent so that the application can read their name, profile, inbox etc.

- **How to guide**: This is a training guide that teaches the users to do certain things like reporting suspicious messages.

To create simulations, following are the steps:

1. Login to **https://security.microsoft.com** and navigate to **Email & collaboration | Attack simulation training**. The **Overview** page will show you details about recent simulations launched, simulation coverage and repeat offenders.

2. Click on the **Simulations** page and click on **Launch a simulation**. On the **Select technique** pick one of the techniques listed above and click **Next**.

3. On the **Name simulation** page, give your simulation a meaningful name and description and click **Next**.

4. Next, you will select the payload. Different payloads are available for each type of simulation. Clicking on the name of the payload will show more details about the payload including the subject and body of the email message that will be sent, the sender email address and name. You will also be able to see the name and type of the attachment. Select one and click **Next**. You can also choose to **Send a test**.

5. On the **Target users** page, you can choose to launch this simulation to all users in the organization or select specific users. You can filter by user location, department and title to launch specific campaigns. You can also import a list of users. Make the appropriate selections and click **Next**.

6. On the next page, you can exclude some users if you like. Click **Next** to continue.

7. On the **Assign training** page select if you would like to deliver a training to the end users. You can choose to let Microsoft recommend the training or manually pick the training from the Microsoft catalogue. You can also choose your own custom trainings by redirecting users to a custom URL.

On the next page, select a landing page that provides a learning moment to the user after getting phished. This is the page that will open if they click on the malicious link or attachment sent in the simulation. There are **Global landing pages** available to choose from or you can also choose to create your own custom landing pages.

Following figure shows an example of a global landing page. Select a landing page and click **Next**:

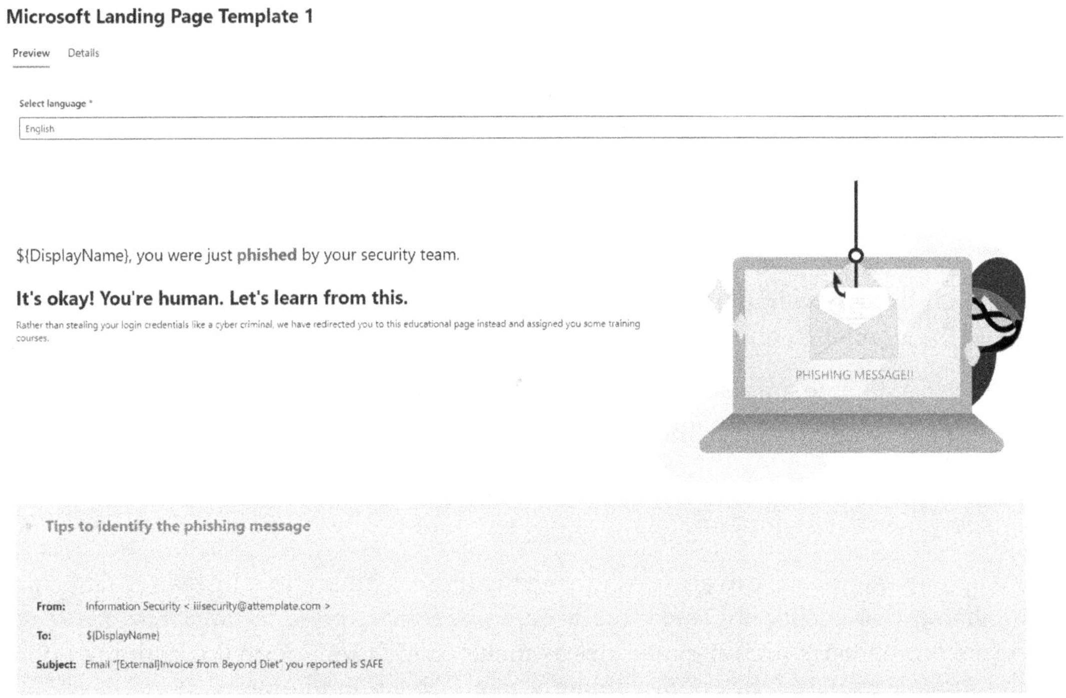

Figure 9.19: Phishing landing page example

8. On the **end user notification** page, you can choose to use the Microsoft default notification or use your customized ones.

9. On the **Launch details** page, select when the simulation should be launched and end.

On the next page, review the details and click on **Submit**.

The simulation will now show in progress on the **Simulations** page and users will receive emails. The details of the simulation will be visible on the **Reports** page as shown in the following figure:

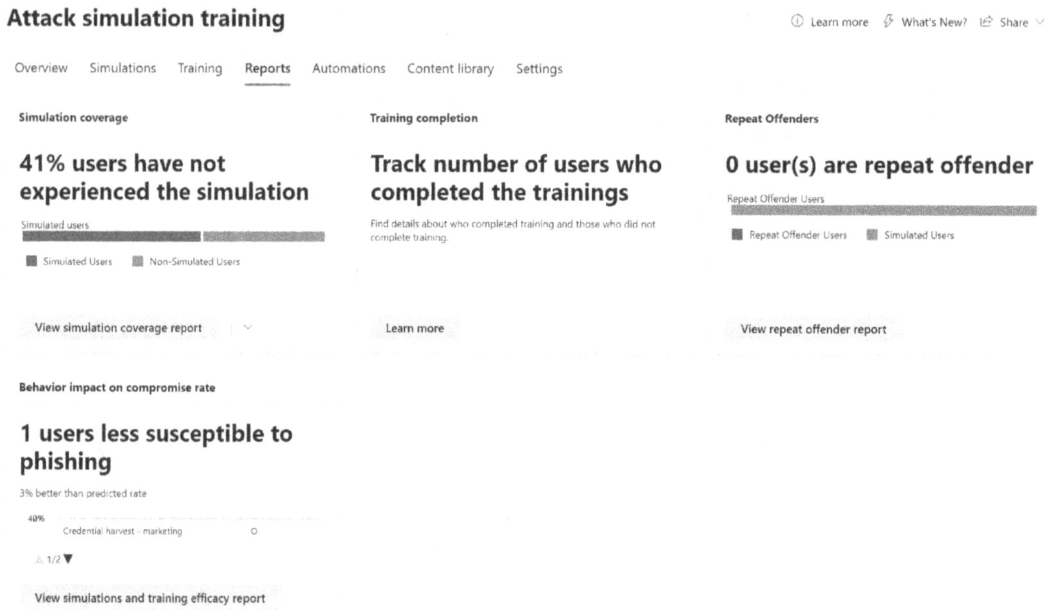

Attack simulation training

Overview   Simulations   Training   **Reports**   Automations   Content library   Settings

Simulation coverage	Training completion	Repeat Offenders
41% users have not experienced the simulation	**Track number of users who completed the trainings**	**0 user(s) are repeat offender**
Simulated users	Find details about who completed training and those who did not complete training.	Repeat Offender Users
▨ Simulated Users ▨ Non-Simulated Users		▨ Repeat Offender Users ▨ Simulated Users
View simulation coverage report ⌄	Learn more	View repeat offender report

Behavior impact on compromise rate

1 users less susceptible to phishing

3% better than predicted rate

40%

Credential harvest - marketing   0

⊿ 1/2 ▼

View simulations and training efficacy report

Figure 9.20: Attack simulation report

Clicking on the **View simulation coverage report** button will show the list of users who received the simulation and the results.

You can also automate simulations by using the **Automations** option as shown in *Figure 9.20* Simulation automations can contain multiple social engineering techniques and payloads and can start on an automated schedule. Creating an automated simulation is similar to creating an individual simulation except for the ability to select multiple techniques and payloads.

Training only campaigns can also be launched without a simulation. Instead of launching a simulation that eventually leads to a training you can choose to only train the users. There are more than 90 training modules available in MDO. Click on the **Training** option on the above screen and click on **Create new** to launch a training campaign.

With the initial setup now complete, you can use MDO to monitor and investigate threats in the organization.

Detect threats

EOP and MDO offer several tools to detect threat in the M365 organization. This section will cover some of those tools.

Alert policies

When users violate the conditions defined in the policies as discussed above, alert policies generate alerts in the **Alerts** dashboard in Microsoft Defender portal. There are several default alert policies that help administrators monitor unusual activities like privilege escalation in Exchange Online, malware attacks, phishing campaigns and so on.

In addition, administrators can configure custom Alert policies by following these steps:

1. Login to the Microsoft Defender portal and navigate to **Email & collaboration** | **Policies & rules** | **Alert policy**. In the right-pane click on **New Alert policy**.

2. On the first page, give your policy a **Name** and **Description**. Select a **Severity** for the alert. The available options are **Low**, **Medium** and **High**. Lastly select a **Category** and click **Next**, as shown in the following figure:

New Alert Policy

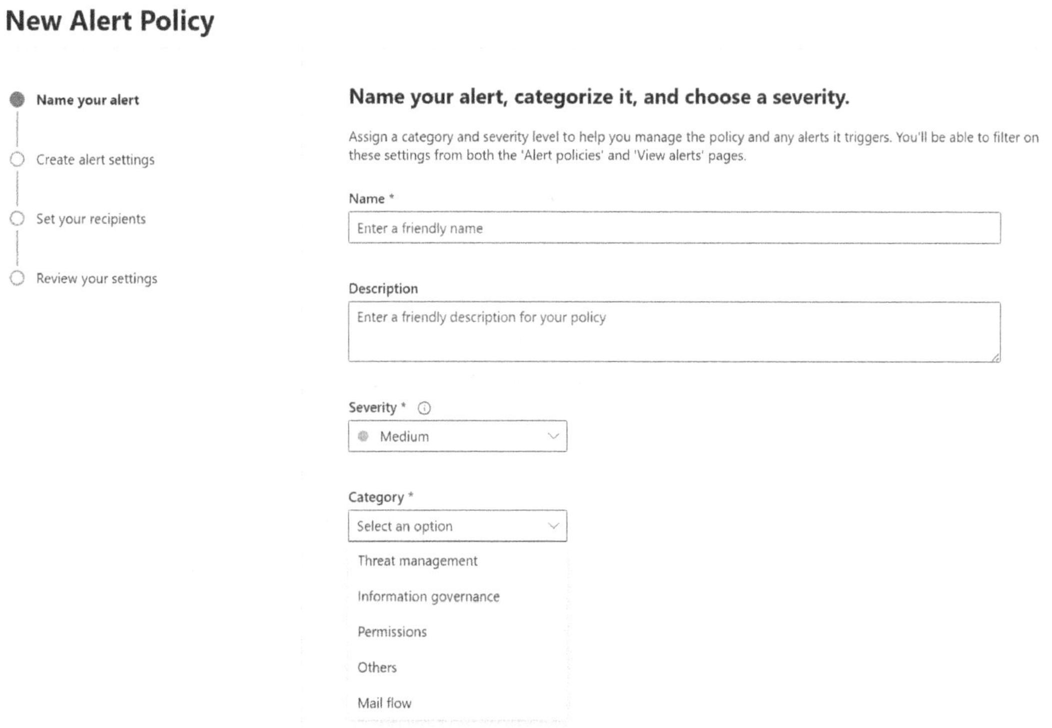

Figure 9.21: Alert policy

3. On the next page, you can choose the activity for which you want to trigger the alert. There is a wide range of user and admin activities to choose from. Additional conditions can be added depending on the activity selected. Lastly, you can choose if you want an alert each time an activity matches the rule or when the matched activities reach a threshold. Once done, click **Next** as shown in the following figure:

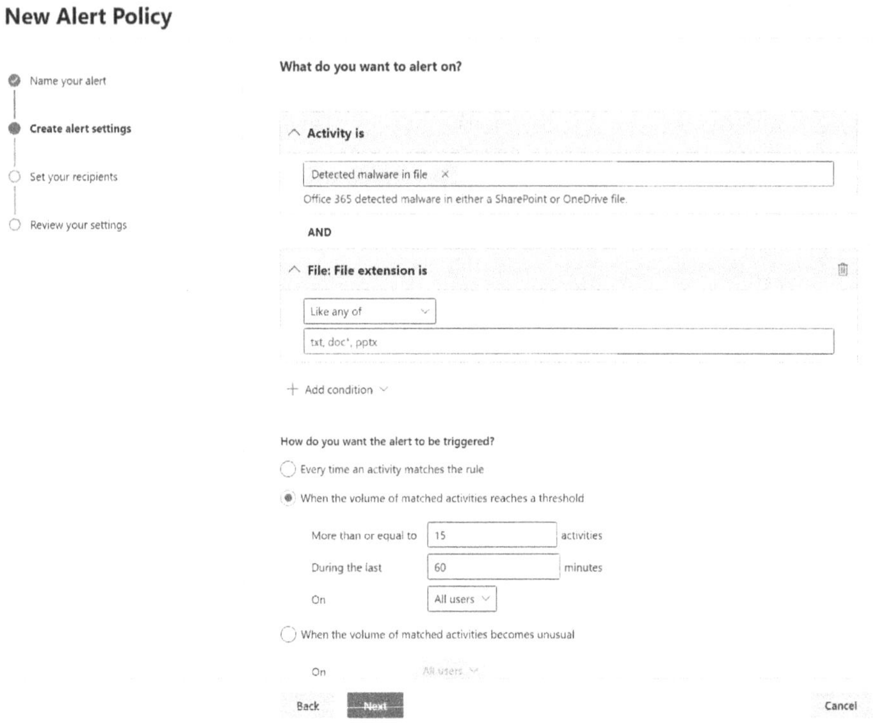

New Alert Policy

Name your alert

Create alert settings

Set your recipients

Review your settings

What do you want to alert on?

∧ **Activity is**

Detected malware in file ✕

Office 365 detected malware in either a SharePoint or OneDrive file.

AND

∧ **File: File extension is** 🗑

Like any of ∨

txt, doc*, pptx

+ Add condition ∨

How do you want the alert to be triggered?

○ Every time an activity matches the rule

◉ When the volume of matched activities reaches a threshold

More than or equal to   15   activities

During the last   60   minutes

On   All users ∨

○ When the volume of matched activities becomes unusual

On   All users ∨

Back   **Next**   Cancel

Figure 9.22: Configure activity and conditions

4. On the next page, you can select if you want to send email notifications when the alert is triggered. You can set a daily notification limit. Once done, click on **Next** as shown in the following figure:

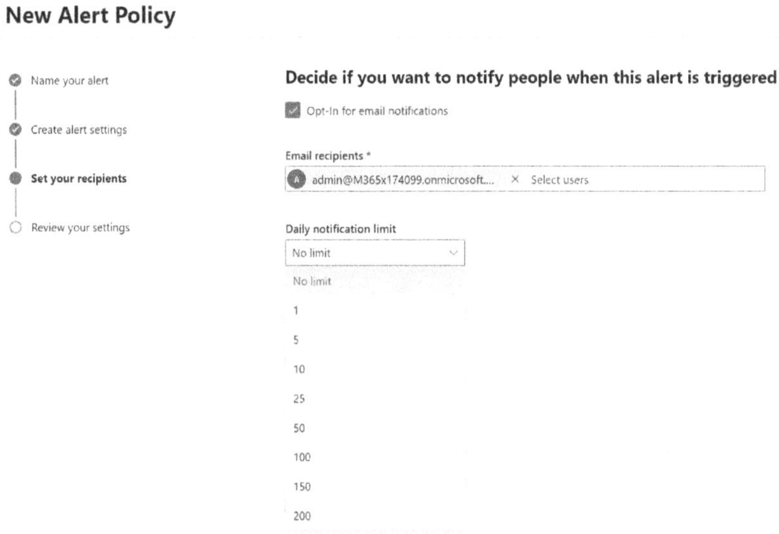

New Alert Policy

Name your alert

Create alert settings

Set your recipients

Review your settings

Decide if you want to notify people when this alert is triggered

☑ Opt-In for email notifications

Email recipients *

Ⓐ admin@M365x174099.onmicrosoft.... ✕ Select users

Daily notification limit

No limit ∨

No limit

1

5

10

25

50

100

150

200

Figure: 9.23: Email notifications

5. On the last page, you can review your settings and decide if you want to turn on the policy right away or later. Once done, click on **Submit**.

It can take up to 24 hours after creating or updating the policy for alerts to be generated.

Message trace

Message trace allows administrators to follow email messages as they travel through the organization. It helps determine if the message was received by the recipient, deferred, rejected or quarantined. It also shows what actions were taken on the message before it reached its final status. This information can be used to answer end user questions about missing messages, troubleshooting mail flow issues and validating policy changes.

To start a message trace in the Microsoft Defender portal, go to **Email & collaboration | Exchange message trace**. You will be redirected to the Exchange Online admin center. Click on **Start a trace** and fill out the details to trace the message as shown in the following figure:

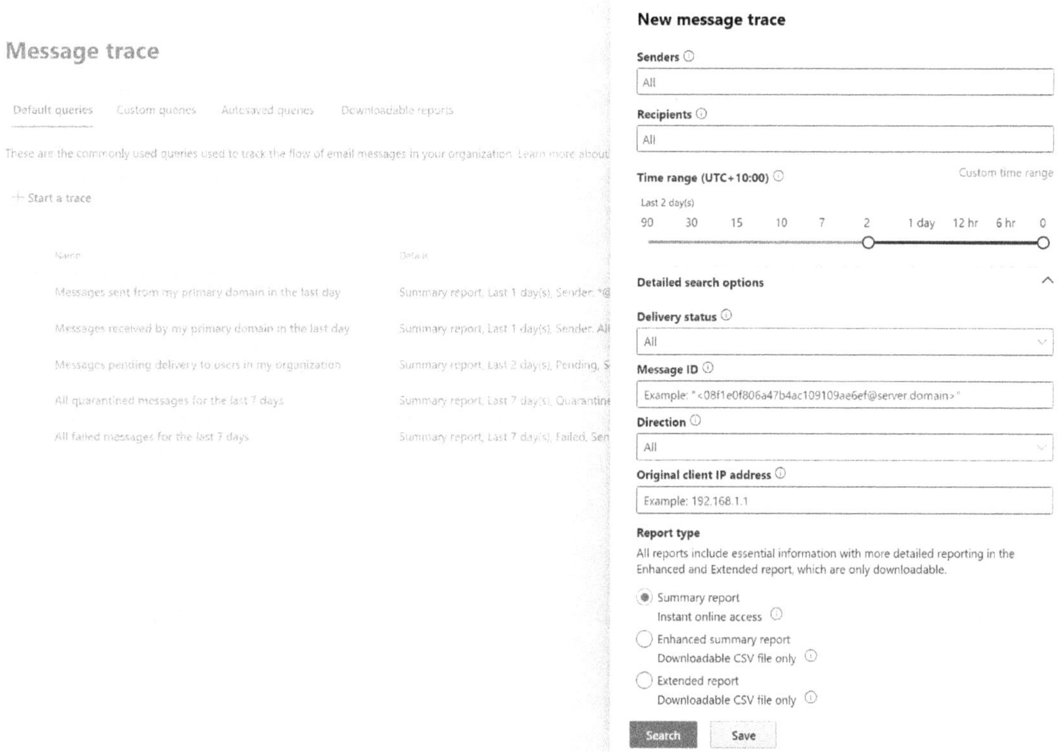

Figure 9.24: *Message trace*

Note that you can save the query to be used later. There are also some default queries available for use.

Quarantine

As we saw earlier, one of the actions that protection policies can take on potentially malicious email messages and files is to quarantine them. Admins can view, release, and delete all types of messages for the users. They can also manage files that were quarantined by Safe Attachments for SharePoint, OneDrive and Teams and messages that were quarantined by ZAP. They can also review and act on user reported Teams messages. Admin Quarantine is accessible in the Microsoft Defender portal by going to **Email & collaboration** | **Review** and clicking on **Quarantine** in the right pane.

Quarantine policies

Admins can use quarantine policies to define how users interact with the quarantined messages and if they receive notifications about the quarantine messages. Quarantine policies can be accessed from the Microsoft Defender portal by navigating to **Email & collaboration** | **Policies & rules** | **Threat policies**. Click on **Quarantine policies** under **Rules**. There are four default policies available as shown in the following figure:

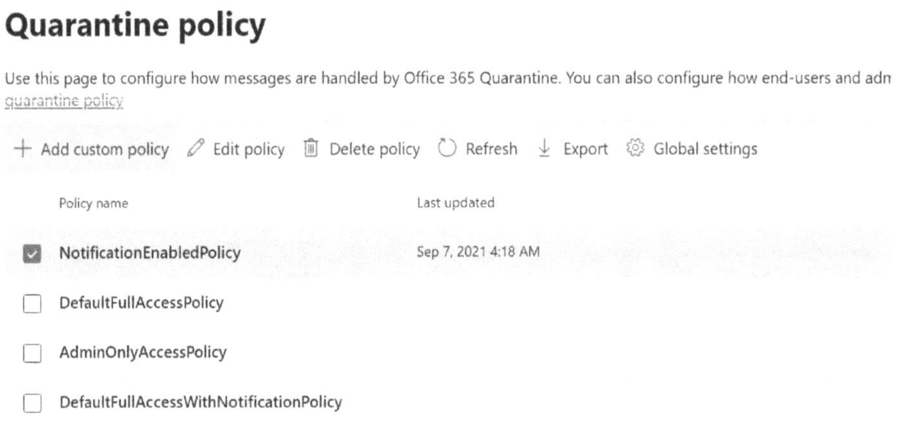

Quarantine policy

Use this page to configure how messages are handled by Office 365 Quarantine. You can also configure how end-users and adn
quarantine policy

+ Add custom policy   ✎ Edit policy   🗑 Delete policy   ↻ Refresh   ↓ Export   ⚙ Global settings

Policy name	Last updated
☑ NotificationEnabledPolicy	Sep 7, 2021 4:18 AM
☐ DefaultFullAccessPolicy	
☐ AdminOnlyAccessPolicy	
☐ DefaultFullAccessWithNotificationPolicy	

Figure 9.25: Default quarantine policies

These policies contain predefined permissions that are combined into preset permission groups. The preset permission groups are No access, Limited access and Full access.

Following table summarize the relationship between the permissions, permission groups and the default policies:

Permission	No access	Limited access	Full access
Permission to view header	Yes	Yes	Yes
Allow sender (sender will be added to the Allow senders list in their mailbox)	No	Yes	Yes
Block sender (sender will be added to the Blocked senders list in their mailbox)	No	No	No
Delete message from quarantine	No	Yes	Yes
Preview	No	Yes	Yes
Release from quarantine	No	No	Yes
Request release from quarantine	No	Yes	No

Table 9.5: Permissions mapping with permission groups

Following table summarize the relationship between the permission groups and the notifications enabled:

Policy	Permission group	Notifications enabled
AdminOnlyAccessPolicy	No access	No
DefaultFullAccessPolicy	Full access	No
DefaultFullAccessWithNotificationPolicy	Full access	Yes
NotificationEnabledPolicy	Full access	Yes

Table 9.6: Permissions group mapping with policy

Administrators can only edit and customize the NotificationEnabledPolicy by selecting the policy and clicking on **Edit policy** as shown in *Figure 9.25*. The other default policies cannot be customized.

Following are the steps to customize the **NotificationEnabledPolicy** policy:

1. In the **Edit policy** fly out pane, click on **Next**. Notice the policy name cannot be changed.

2. Edit the policy to the required setting. Refer to the following figure for the available settings. Once done, click on **Next**:

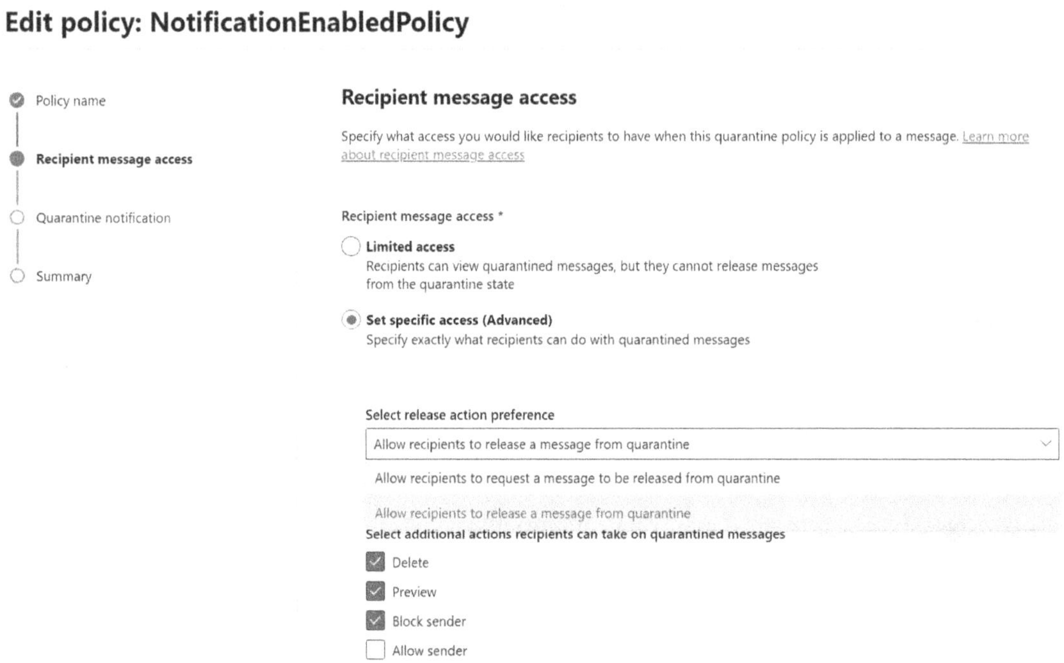

Edit policy: NotificationEnabledPolicy

- ✓ Policy name
- ● Recipient message access
- ○ Quarantine notification
- ○ Summary

Recipient message access

Specify what access you would like recipients to have when this quarantine policy is applied to a message. Learn more about recipient message access

Recipient message access *

○ **Limited access**
Recipients can view quarantined messages, but they cannot release messages from the quarantine state

◉ **Set specific access (Advanced)**
Specify exactly what recipients can do with quarantined messages

Select release action preference

Allow recipients to release a message from quarantine	⌄

Allow recipients to request a message to be released from quarantine

Allow recipients to release a message from quarantine

Select additional actions recipients can take on quarantined messages
- ☑ Delete
- ☑ Preview
- ☑ Block sender
- ☐ Allow sender

Figure 9.26: Edit policy

3. On the next page, select the settings for the **Quarantine notification**. Click **Next** to continue as shown in the following figure:

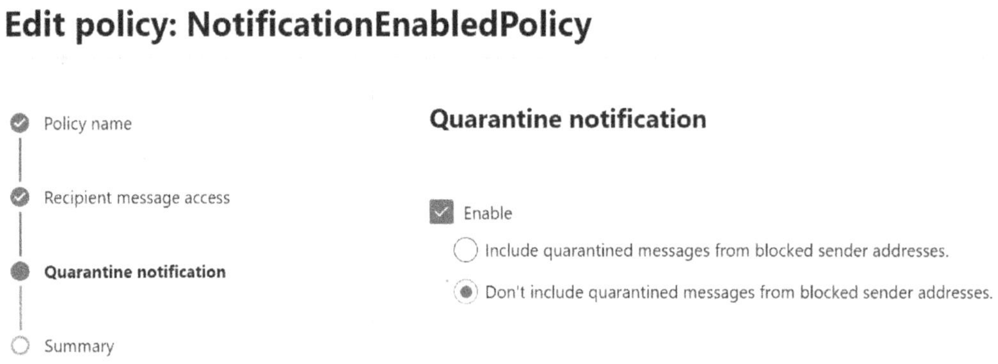

Edit policy: NotificationEnabledPolicy

- ✓ Policy name
- ✓ Recipient message access
- ● **Quarantine notification**
- ○ Summary

Quarantine notification

☑ Enable

○ Include quarantined messages from blocked sender addresses.

◉ Don't include quarantined messages from blocked sender addresses.

Figure 9.27: Quarantine notification settings

4. On the next screen, review your settings and click on **Submit**.

In addition to the default policies, administrators can also create custom policies from scratch by clicking on **Add custom policy** as shown in *Figure 9.25*.

Quarantine notifications

Administrators can use the **Global settings** option, as shown in *Figure 9.25* in quarantine policies to customize the format of the quarantine notifications that the users receive. A sender display name and sender address can be configured. Translations in up to three languages can be added and the company logo can be used to replace the Microsoft logo. Administrators can also define the frequency at which the end-users receive quarantine notifications. The options are **Within 4 hours**, **Daily** or **Weekly**.

When users receive quarantine notifications, the **Sender**, **Subject** and **Date** is shown for each quarantined message. Certain actions are available to be taken from within the message depending on the settings configured in the policy.

Following figure shows an example of a quarantine notification sent to the user:

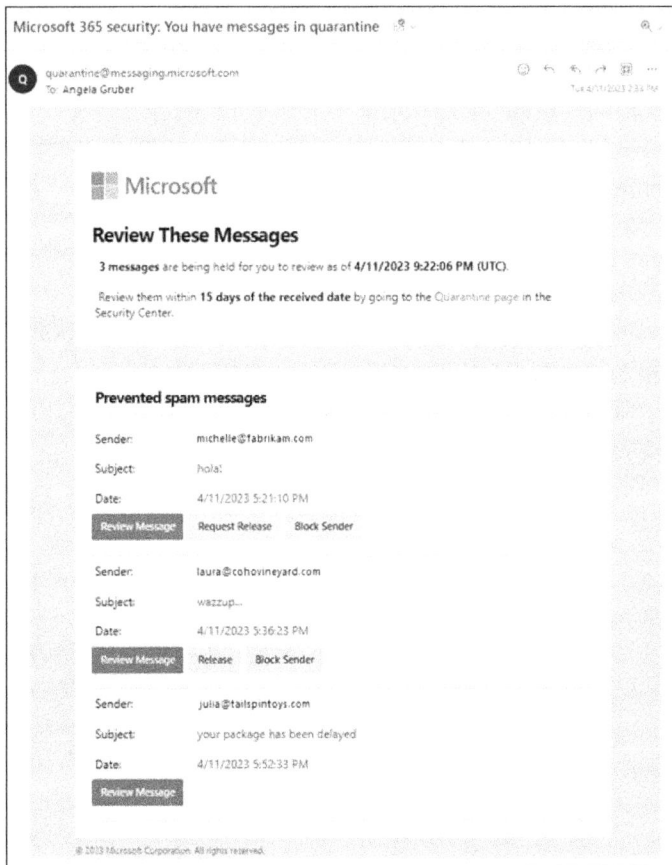

Figure 9.28: Quarantine notification

When users click on **Quarantine page** in the notification, they are taken to the Microsoft Defender portal where they are shown a view of quarantined messages only meant for them. From there the end users can take relevant action on the messages.

Advanced delivery

By default, EOP does not allow messages that are identified as malware or high confidence spam to bypass filtering but if organizations use third-party phishing simulations, receiving these emails is required. Security operation teams might also want to receive such email for advanced analysis and investigation. To enable these scenarios the advanced delivery policy can be used to prevent messages from being filtered. When advanced delivery is enabled as in the following:

- Filters in EOP and MDO do not take any action on these messages and malware filtering is bypassed only for SecOps mailboxes.
- ZAP for spam and phishing does not take action on malware messages in the SecOps mailbox.
- Safe Links does not block or detonate URLs. URLs are wrapped but not blocked.
- Safe Attachments does not detonate attachments.
- Alerts are not triggered for these scenarios.
- AIR ignores these messages.

Following is what happens when third-party phishing simulation tools are used:

- Admin submission generates a response highlighting that the message is a part of phishing simulation and not a real threat. Alerts and AIR are not triggered.
- When users report phishing messages, alerts are not generated. Links and files are not detonated but the message appears on the **User reported** tab of the **Submissions** page.

Since these messages are not security threats, they are marked as **Phishing simulation** or **SecOps mailbox** system overrides. Admins can view and analyze these messages in **Explorer** (MDO Plan 2) or **Real-time detection** (MDO Plan 1) in the Microsoft Defender portal by filtering on **Override source** as shown in the following figure:

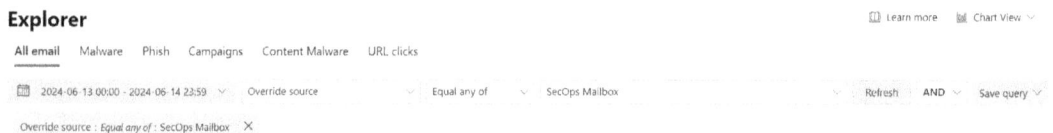

Figure 9.29: System override

SecOps mailbox and third-party phishing simulation can be configured from the Microsoft Defender portal by navigating to **Email & collaboration** | **Policies & rules** | **Threat policies** | **Advanced delivery**.

Audit logs

All administrative and user activities are logged in the unified M365 audit logs. Auditing is turned on by default for M365 enterprise organizations and retains audit logs for 180 days. The unified audit log is available in the Microsoft Defender portal. Login to the portal with the required permissions and add the appropriate search criteria to perform the search. Audit will be covered in more detail in the next section of this book on Microsoft Purview.

Email and collaboration reports

Subscribers of Microsoft Defender for Office 365 Plan 1 and Plan 2 can access a variety of security related reports in the Microsoft Defender portal. To access these reports in the Microsoft Defender portal, navigate to **Reports** | **Email & collaboration** | **Email & collaboration reports**. The following reports are available:

- Mailflow status summary
- Threat protection status summary
- Post-delivery activities
- URL protection report
- Top malware
- Spoof detections
- Compromised users
- Mail latency reports
- User reported messages
- Submissions
- Top senders and recipients
- Bulk senser insights

Following figure shows all the reports available. To view a report, click on **View details** on the relevant tile:

Email & collaboration reports

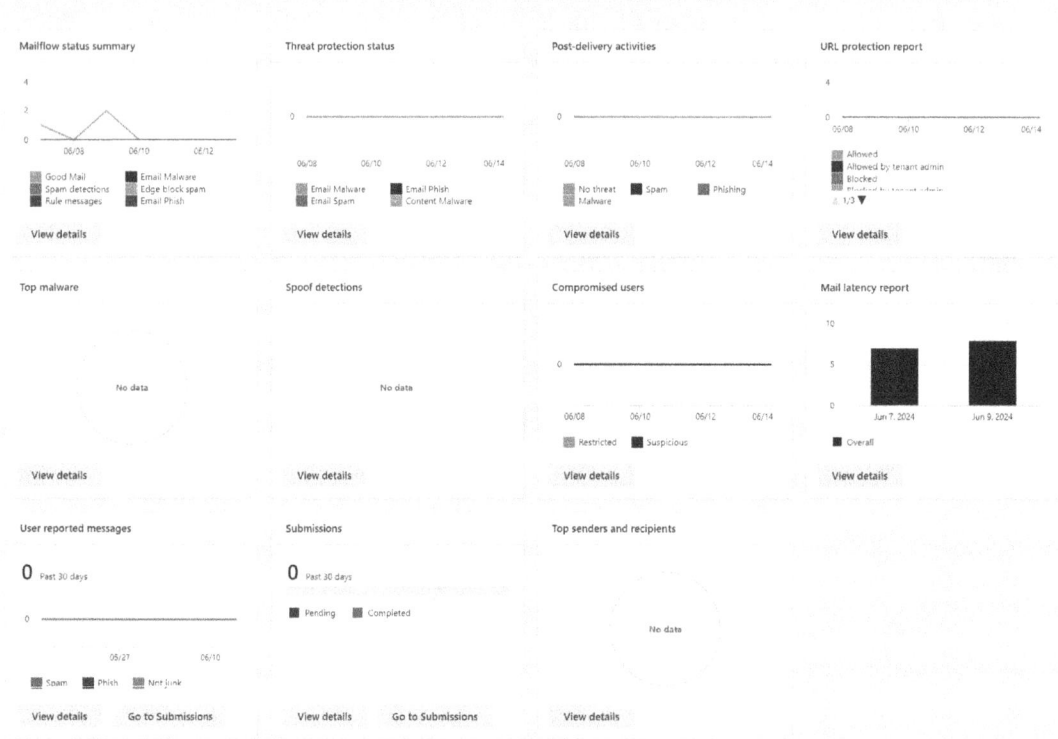

Figure 9.30: Email & collaboration reports

Investigate and respond

All incidents generated by EOP and MDO are logged in the incident queue in the Microsoft Defender XDR portal. Incident investigation and response is covered in detail in *Chapter 6, Microsoft Defender XDR*. In this chapter, we will explore the investigation and response capabilities specific to EOP and MDO.

Explorer

For MDO P2 customers, the **Explorer** view in MDO is the starting point for any security investigation. If using MDO P1 you will see **Real-time detections** instead of Explorer. These views are used to analyze threats, see volume of attacks and analyze threats by families, attacker infrastructure and more. They are available in the Microsoft Defender portal under **Email & collaboration**. The Explorer view is organized in tabs as follows:

- **All email**: This is the default tab in the Explorer view and has information about all incoming email to your organization or email exchanged by recipients within the organization.

- **Malware**: This is the default tab in the real-time detections view and contains information about all email that contains malware.
- **Phish**: Information about all emails classified as phishing messages.
- **Campaigns**: Information about emails that were identified as being part of a phishing or malware campaign.
- **Content malware**: Information about files containing malware that have been detected in SharePoint, OneDrive or Teams by Safe Attachments.
- **URL clicks**: Information about user clicks on URLs in emails, Teams and Office files in SharePoint or OneDrive.

Each of these views can be filtered by date ranges, message or file properties. You can also save commonly used queries for use in future investigations.

Campaigns

In MDO P2, the **Campaigns** view identifies coordinated phishing and malware attacks. Microsoft categorizes them into discrete campaigns to help organizations efficiently investigate and respond to email attacks and understand the scope of the attack. A *campaign* is a coordinated email attack against one or more organizations. To identify these targeted campaigns Microsoft applies anti-spam, anti-malware and anti-phishing intelligence gathered from the entire M365 service. It provides information like the attack source, message properties, recipients and the attack payload. The Campaigns page is available in the Microsoft Defender portal under **Email & collaboration**.

The following figure shows a view of the **Campaigns** page:

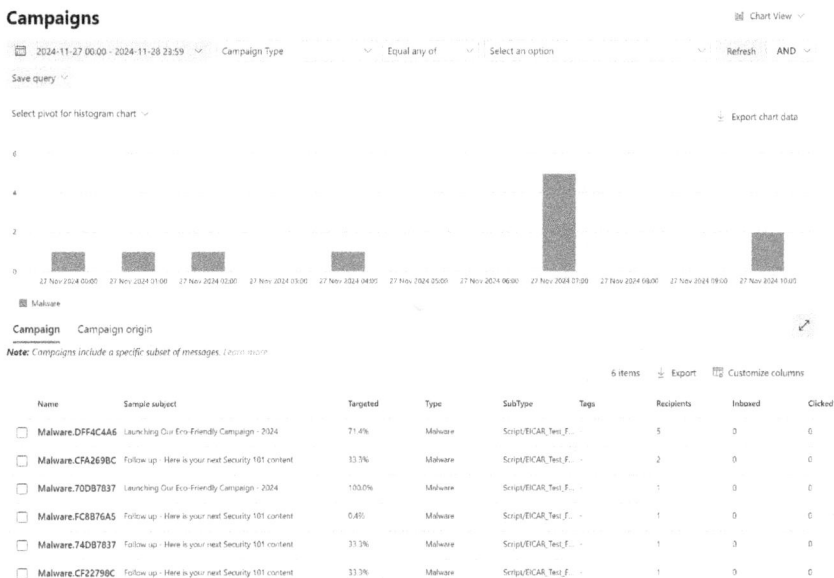

Figure 9.31: Campaigns

The **Campaigns** page is divided into three sections. At the top you can apply filters to search for specific Malware or Phishing campaigns. Additional filters can be applied by clicking on the **Campaign Type** drop down and selecting campaign name, subtype, sender domain etc. This will update the chart and details view. Review the information provided in the details area.

Investigate user reported messages

As was described in an earlier section, users can be enabled to report suspicious messages for investigation. These messages are available for review in the Microsoft Defender portal under **Investigation & response** | **Actions & submissions** | **Submissions** | **User reported**. From this page, administrators can trigger an investigation which will trigger an automated investigation using the AIR capability. The message can also be submitted to Microsoft for analysis, or the administrator can mark the message as safe or confirm Phishing or Spam as shown in the following figure:

Figure 9.32: User reported messages

Admin submissions

In addition to submitting user reported messages to Microsoft for analysis, administrators can also submit email messages, email attachments, URLs and Files to Microsoft for analysis manually by clicking on the relevant tab in the above screen and clicking on **Submit to Microsoft for analysis**.

Spoof intelligence insights

EOP offers **spoof intelligence** to protect against spoofing. Spoofing is a technique used by senders so that the email appears to be coming from within the organization or from an organization that commonly sends emails to you. EOP uses spoof intelligence insights to detect spoofed senders in messages from external and internal domains and automatically protects you against spoofing. Spoof intelligence insights are available in the Microsoft Defender portal to identify senders who are sending unauthenticated messages.

Spoof intelligence should be enabled in the Anti-phishing policy.

Following are the steps:

1. In the Microsoft Defender portal, navigate to **Email & collaboration** ⏐ **Policies & rules** ⏐ **Threat policies** ⏐ **Anti-phishing**.

2. Click on the policy you would like to edit and click on **Edit protection settings** under the section **Phishing threshold & protection**.

3. Check the box next to **Enable spoof intelligence** and click on **Save** as shown in the following figure:

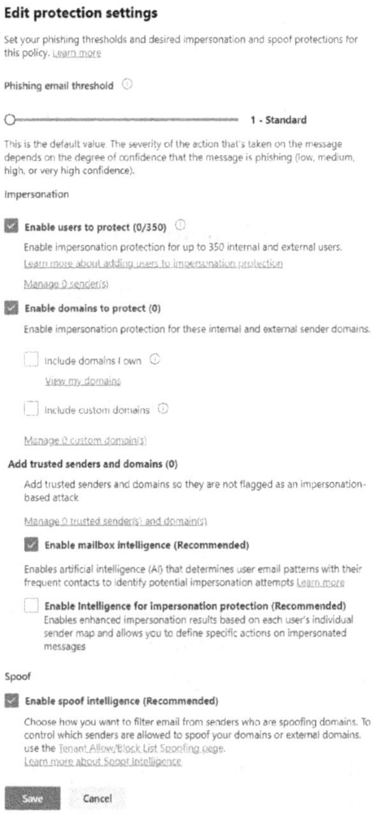

Figure 9.33: Enable spoof intelligence

To view the spoof intelligence insights, login to the Microsoft Defender portal and navigate to **Email & collaboration** ⏐ **Policies & rules** ⏐ **Threat policies** ⏐ **Tenant Allow/Block Lists** ⏐ **Spoofed senders**. On the page the spoof intelligence insights look as follows:

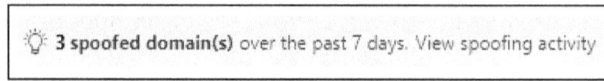

Figure 9.34: Spoof intelligence

Click on **View spoofing activity** to go to the **Spoof intelligence insights** page. On this page, you can override the verdict by choosing the sender to **Allow to spoof** or **Block from spoofing**.

Impersonation insights

Impersonation is when a sender of a message looks similar to a real or expected sender or domain. Attackers often use this technique to gain the trust of the recipient.

There are two types of impersonation, as follows:

- **Domain impersonation**: In this case, there are minute differences in the domain name. For example, contoso.com might be impersonated as c0nst0so.com. This is different from domain spoofing as the impersonated domain is a real registered domain that can pass the SPF, DKIM and DMARC checks.

- **User impersonation**: In this case the domain name remains the same but there might be minute differences in the email alias. For example, **lilly@contoso.com** might be impersonated as **1illy@contoso.com**.

Impersonation protection is a part of the Anti-phishing policies offered by MDO P1 and is not available with EOP. It can be enabled in the Anti-phishing policy through following steps:

1. In the Microsoft Defender portal, navigate to **Email & collaboration** | **Policies & rules** | **Threat policies** | **Anti-phishing**.

2. Click on the policy you would like to edit and click on **Edit protection settings** under the section **Phishing threshold & protection**.

3. Following are the available options:

    a. To protect users, check the box next **Enable users to protect**. Click on **Manage 0 sender(s)** to add users from your directory whose email accounts you would like to protect from impersonation.

    b. To protect domains, check the box next to **Enable domains to protect**. You can include your own domains and add custom domains by checking the relevant boxes as shown in *Figure 9.33*.

4. To view a list of impersonated domains and users in the Microsoft Defender portal navigate to **Email & collaboration** | **Policies & rules** | **Threat policies** |, **Anti-phishing**. On this page the impersonation insights appear as shown in the following figure:

> 💡 **5 impersonated domain(s) and user(s)** over the past 7 days. View impersonations

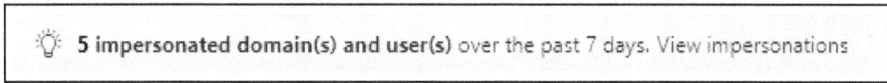

Figure 9.35: Impersonation insights

Click on the **View impersonations** link to go to the **Impersonation Insight** page. If impersonation protection is enabled in Anti-phishing policies, this page will show you the impersonated domains and users. If not, this page will show you the number of messages that would have been detected if impersonation protection was enabled.

You can see the impersonating sender domain or user, the number of messages received from these domains or senders in the last seven days, the policy that detected these messages and user account whose email account was protected by the impersonation policy.

Clicking on any entry shows insights into why the message was caught and recommended actions.

Mailbox intelligence

This feature uses AI to determine communication patterns among users who communicate regularly. For example, there is an internal user called **johndoe@contoso.com** that is protected from impersonation in an anti-phishing policy. There is an external user called **johndoe@tailspintoys.com** that some of the recipients in the policy communicate with frequently. In this case, because there is a communication history between the internal users and **johndoe@tailspintoys.com**, mailbox intelligence does not detect **johndoe@tailspintoys.com** as an impersonation of **johndoe@contoso.com**. To turn on mailbox intelligence, check the relevant boxes in the Anti-phishing policy as shown in *Figure 9.33*.

Threat tracker

MDO P2 subscribers have an additional feature called Threat trackers which are queries that can be built and saved in **Explorer**. These queries can be used to discover threats in the environment either manually or automatically. To access Threat trackers, go to the Microsoft Defender portal and navigate to **Email & collaboration | Threat tracker**.

There are three tabs on this page, as follows:

- **Saved queries**: These are all the queries that have been saved in Explorer.
- **Tracked queries**: Contains all queries saved in Explorer where Track query was selected. These queries automatically run periodically, and results are shown on this tab.
- **Trending campaigns**: This information is added by Microsoft to highlight new threats in your organization.

Remediate

In this last section, we will learn some techniques to respond to various threats like business email compromise or illicit consent grants.

Business email compromise

When an attacker steals a user's credentials, they can access the user's mailbox, SharePoint Online folder, and file on OneDrive. They can also use the mailbox to send bogus emails to other employees of the organization or external vendor, supplies or partners. They can also use the email account to exfiltrate data. Users may notice suspicious activity in their email accounts that might indicate that their account has been compromised, such as suspicious mailbox rules, missing email, profile changes, unusual email signature etc. To investigate these issues, administrators can use the audit logs or review the Entra ID sign-in logs. Microsoft offers Self Help tools to assist in the investigation. This is accessible by going to **https://admin.microsoft.com** and clicking on the question mark (**?**) on the top right. This will open a pane where you can type in the issue you are facing, and the system will prompt you for details and guide you through troubleshooting. It will also recommend some steps to take if the account is compromised as shown in the following figure:

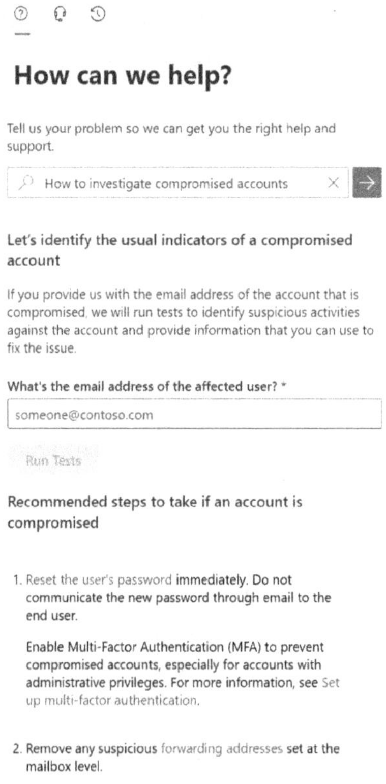

Figure 9.36: Investigate business email compromise

Illicit consent grants

Sometimes attackers use Azure-registered applications to access users' data. They first create an application and then use a phishing attack to trick users into granting access to that application or by injecting illicit code into the website. Once the application has been granted access, it has account-level access to user's data without needing their credentials or an account in the organization. Normal protection mechanisms like MFA do not protect against these types of attacks.

Administrators should search audit logs to find signs of such an attack and regularly inventory all the applications and their permissions.

Malicious email messages

Some malicious email messages might breach the organizations' defenses and find their way to user mailboxes. They need to be cleaned up. This can be done by ZAP as explained earlier in this chapter or by security teams manually or using AIR capabilities available with MDO P2.

Manual cleanup can be done by hunting for email messages categorized as Malware or Phish in **Explorer**. Once a set of messages has been identified administrators can take bulk actions of moving the message to deleted items or permanently deleting the items. Security operation teams can also trigger AIR from the Explorer view.

These actions are available for review under **Actions & submissions** | **Action center**.

The AIR process is explained in detail in *Chapter 6, Microsoft Defender XDR*.

Custom form injections

Once an attacker gains access to an organization they try to establish a method using which they can get back in if they are discovered. Custom form injections is one way of doing this. In this method an attacker steals the user credentials and uses them to sign in to their mailbox. They then insert a custom mail form template into the mailbox. This form is triggered when the user receives a specific message. The attacker then sends that message to the user mailbox which makes the mailbox load the form. This form launches an application on a remote server. This application can then be used to install malware on the user's machine using which the attacker can steal user credentials or other important data. Typical indicators of custom forms compromise include custom forms saved as their own message class, message class that contains executable code or a form names `IPM.Note.[custom name]`.

Since this will require examining each mailbox individually, administrators can use PowerShell scripts to dump all custom forms for all users in the organization and then troubleshoot with individual users.

Office rules

Another method for an attacker to get back into an organization if they are discovered is to use Outlook rules. In this method, once an attacker steals a user's credentials, they login to the user's mailbox and create an inbox forwarding rule that is triggered when a specific message is received. The attacker sends this message to the user mailbox that triggers the rule to launch an application on a remote server. This application can then be used to install malware on the user's machine or do other malicious activities. Typical indicators of compromise are if the rule starts an action or launches an EXE, ZIP or URL.

Since this requires examining each mailbox individually, administrators can use PowerShell scripts to dump all rules for all mailboxes in the organization and then troubleshoot with individual users.

Conclusion

In this chapter, we learned how administrators can protect their Microsoft 365 applications from compromise using the capabilities available in EOP and MDO. EOP and MDO work hand-in-hand to provide protection against spam, malware and phishing attacks. While EOP provides the base layer of security, MDO P1 brings in advanced protection like Safe Link and Safe Attachments while MDO P2 adds the threat intelligence component on top of the capabilities provided by EOP and MDO P1. You should now be comfortable with navigating the Microsoft Defender portal to access the various capabilities. You should be able to understand the default protection policies and configure custom threat protection policies. You should be able to detect threats using alert policies, message traces and quarantine. You should also be able to use the threat response features like Explorer, Campaigns and Threat tracker. Lastly, you should be able to understand the various forms of compromise and the methods to remediate them.

In the next chapter, you will learn how you can protect and govern non-Microsoft applications using Microsoft Defender for Cloud Apps.

Multiple choice questions

1. **Your organization has mailboxes hosted on Exchange Online. Which of the following provides default spam, malware and phishing protection to all users?**

   a. Exchange Online Protection

   b. Microsoft Defender for Office 365 P1

   c. Third-party email filtering

   d. Anti-spam policy

2. **You are an IT administrator for your organization. You have been asked to deploy email protection for all mailboxes. What should you do first?**

   a. Configure protection policies

   b. Setup priority accounts

   c. Train end users

   d. Configure email protection

3. **Your organization is using EOP and MDO P1 configure to block spam, malware and phishing messages from reaching end user mailboxes. As a SecOps administrator you want to receive unfiltered messages so that you can investigate spam, malware and phishing campaigns. What should you do?**

   a. Search the Audit logs

   b. Look in the quarantine

   c. Configure Advanced delivery

   d. Run a message trace

Answer key

1. a

2. d

3. c

Join our book's Discord space

Join the book's Discord Workspace for Latest updates, Offers, Tech happenings around the world, New Release and Sessions with the Authors:

https://discord.bpbonline.com

CHAPTER 10

Protecting Non-Microsoft Cloud Apps

Introduction

Today, end users have access to and use a wide variety of **software as a service (SaaS)** applications that help them work more efficiently. However, this poses a major challenge for Security Administrators as they might not have visibility of which applications are in use, their security posture and how they are being used. These applications introduce new threat vectors for an organization in terms of cyber-attacks and more avenues for data exfiltration. This chapter explores **Microsoft Defender for Cloud Apps (MDCA)** and how it can help you identify the use of unapproved applications, approve and disapprove applications and ultimately track the usage of those applications to protect your organization's data and assets.

Structure

The chapter covers the following topics:

- Microsoft Defender for Cloud Apps
- Network requirements
- Set up MDCA
- Cloud discovery
- Connect apps

- Working with policies
- Conditional Access app control
- Microsoft Purview Information Protection
- Microsoft Sentinel
- Additional Integrations
- Investigate and respond
- App governance

Objectives

By the end of this chapter, readers will be able to understand the threats unmonitored applications introduce in the environment and how a cloud access security broker can help you discover and monitor the use of these applications. You will be able to implement and configure MDCA to discover Shadow IT and sanction or block applications. You will be able to configure policies to protect the data in these applications from cyber-attacks and exfiltration. You will learn how MDCA integrates with other Microsoft products to help secure data in applications. Lastly, you will learn how you can use app governance to get insights into all non-Microsoft registered applications, protect users from malicious applications, be alerted if any anomalies are detected and automatically remediate anomalous app activity.

Microsoft Defender for Cloud Apps

Cloud applications are becoming more popular these days. They are easier for the organization to use because they are run by a provider in the cloud who handles the maintenance and management. However, they also create new risks as employees access resources outside the traditional corporate boundaries. To address these new risks, security teams need new tools that protect their data within the cloud apps. **Cloud Access Security Brokers** (**CASBs**) are security policy enforcers that sit between the users and the cloud applications and provide visibility and data control to detect and prevent threats.

MDCA is a CASB solution from Microsoft that provides protection for cloud applications by monitoring and protecting data.

It has the following main features:

- **Shadow IT discovery**: The term *Shadow IT* is used to refer to applications used by users that are not approved by IT. For example, in the absence of an approved file sharing platform, users might resort to using cloud-based file sharing services to collaborate. This poses threats as IT teams have no visibility on the applications being used, the data that is being uploaded to them and if it is being shared with unauthorized individuals. The Shadow IT discovery capability in MDCA provides complete visibility into the cloud applications being used, their risk score, their reputation and much more. MDCA evaluates each application for more than 90 risk indicators and assigns a risk score and identifies the users using that application. Based on this information the administrator can choose to block the use of the application or monitor the application for unusual behavior.

- **SaaS security posture management (SSPM)**: Using cloud applications, also called SaaS applications may introduce risks in your cloud environment. SSPM helps organizations assess the security posture of the cloud applications being used by users. MDCA reduces the burden of assessing each application individually by assessing the SaaS applications for risky configuration and providing recommendations in Microsoft Secure Score. It identifies misconfigurations and recommends actions to close security gaps for each connected application. These recommendations are based on **Center for Internet Security (CIS)** benchmarks and the best practices specified by the app developer. To turn on secure score recommendations for SaaS applications, in the Microsoft Defender portal, navigate to **Settings** ∣ **Cloud Apps** ∣ **App Connectors**. In the right pane, click on the ellipses next to the app and select **Turn on Secure Score recommendations**.

- **Advanced threat protection**: SaaS applications also introduce a new attack vector for bad actors to move laterally from email to connected applications to gain access to business-critical data. For example, an adversary might steal the user credentials using an email phishing campaign and then move laterally into a connected Salesforce application to steal the organization's customer data. MDCA has built-in adaptive access control and provides user entity behavior analytics to help mitigate malware. It also integrates with Microsoft Defender XDR, correlating signals from the Microsoft Defender suite giving SOC teams the complete picture of the attack kill chain.

- **Information protection**: SaaS applications are commonly used to exfiltrate data outside the organization. For example, a malicious employee might try to steal the company secrets by copying sensitive content from their work laptop to their personal OneDrive or DropBox account. MDCA integrates with Microsoft Purview to extend information protection and data loss prevention capabilities to SaaS applications. Using these capabilities organizations can apply controls such as encrypting sensitive content in SaaS applications, preventing uploading of sensitive content in SaaS applications or blocking download of sensitive files on unmanaged machines.

- **App-to-app protection**: Some OAuth applications require user consent and access to their profile information. These applications often fly under the radar, but they might have access to sensitive content in other apps on behalf of the user. MDCA helps protect inter-app data exchange. It identifies unused apps and monitors current and expired credentials to help maintain app hygiene.

MDCA collects network data, OAuth app configuration and usage, file metadata, system settings, users and group configurations and more. It stores data in Microsoft Azure data centers depending on the geographical region where the customer's M365 tenant is provisioned.

The data collected by MDCA is retained for up to 180 days. MDCA shares data with the following Microsoft products:

- Microsoft Defender XDR
- Microsoft Defender for Cloud
- Microsoft Sentinel
- Microsoft Defender for Endpoint
- Microsoft Purview
- Microsoft Entra ID Protection

Licensing

The complete feature set of MDCA is available as a part of either one of the following licenses:

- Microsoft 365 E5
- Enterprise Mobility + Security E5

Roles

Like all other Microsoft Defender products MDCA supports role-based access control.

The following Microsoft Entra ID roles have access to MDCA:

Role	Permissions
Global Administrator	Full access
Security Administrator	Full access
Cloud App Security Administrator	Full access
Compliance Administrator	• Read-only • Manage alerts
Compliance Data Administrator	• Read-only • Create and modify file policy • Allow file governance actions • View discovery reports
Security operator	• Read-only • Manage alerts

Role	Permissions
Security reader	• Read-only • Create API access tokens
Global reader	Full read-only access

Table 10.1: Entra ID roles and permissions in MDCA

In addition to the Microsoft Entra ID roles, MDCA specific roles can also be configured in the Microsoft Defender portal by navigating to **Permissions** and clicking on **Roles** under **Cloud apps**.

The following roles are available:

- **Global Administrator**: Full access only to MDCA.
- **Compliance Administrator**: Same permissions as Entra ID Compliance Administrator role but the scope is limited to MDCA.
- **Security reader**: Same permissions as Entra ID Security reader role but the scope is limited to MDCA.
- **Security operator**: Same permissions as Entra ID Security operator role but the scope is limited to MDCA.
- **App instance admin**: Full or read-only access to all data in a specific MDCA instance or app. For example, access can be given to a Salesforce US instance. In this case, the user will have access only to the data in the Salesforce US instance.
- **User group admin**: Full or read-only access to all data in MDCA that deals with a specified group of users. For example, if access is given to a user to the group Marketing, the admin will be able to view and edit information in MDCA for only the Marketing group.
- **Cloud discovery global admin**: Permissions to view and edit all Cloud Discovery settings and data.
- **Cloud discovery report admin**: Permissions to view all Cloud Discovery settings and data.

Network requirements

Depending on which data center your MDCA instance is hosted, you will need to allow some Microsoft IP Address and Ports in your firewall. To view your MDCA data center location, in the Microsoft Defender portal go to **Settings** | **Cloud Apps** | **Region**.

> **Note: The complete list of IP addresses and ports is subject to change and hence is not listed here. Refer to the Microsoft documentation for the latest list.**

Set up MDCA

In this section, you will learn the basic steps to get started with MDCA. It starts with setting up a MDCA environment.

Following are the steps:

1. Login to the Microsoft Defender portal and navigate to **Settings** | **Cloud Apps**.
2. Click on **Organization details** under **System**.

   a. Provide an organization display name. This name will be displayed on emails and web pages.

   b. Provide an environment name. This is important if you manage more than one tenant.

   c. An organization logo can be uploaded to be displayed in email notifications and web pages.

   d. Add a list of managed domains. These are used to identify internal users. Alerts from managed domains are considered internal for alerts, reports and file sharing access level.

   e. Click on **Mail settings**. Using these settings, you can customize the notifications sent to end users in case of breaches. The email sender display name and email address are default and cannot be modified. You can upload a custom email template in the form of an HTML file. The HTML file should include the company logo, a placeholder for the email title which is decided by the policy and a place for the content. Once uploaded you can test by sending a test email.

User groups

When apps are connected to MDCA using API connectors, you can import user groups from applications like Microsoft 365 and Microsoft Entra ID.

There are two types of groups, as follows:

- **Automatic groups**: These groups are created by default by MDCA. The are two automatic groups in MDCA as follows:

   o **Application user group**: This group enables you to see all activities performed by M365 and Microsoft Entra applications.

   o **External users' group**: This group includes users who are not members of any domains you configured in managed domains.

   Additionally, MDCA has the following automatic groups. If these applications are connected via APIs to MDCA, you will see the corresponding group listed in the

Microsoft Defender portal under **Settings** | **Cloud apps** | **User groups**. Refer to *Figure 10.1*.

- o   Dropbox administrator
- o   Microsoft 365 administrator
- o   Google Workspace administrator
- o   Box administrator
- o   All Salesforce standard and custom profiles

- **Imported groups**: In addition to the automatic groups, administrators can import groups from connected applications like Microsoft 365. You might want to do this to investigate specific scenarios like investigating suspicious activities in the executive group.

Following are steps to import user groups into MDCA:

1. In the Microsoft Defender portal, navigate to **Settings** | **Cloud apps** | **User groups**.

2. In the right pane, click on **Import user group**. In the pop-up screen, select the app from which you would like to import the users and then select the group to import. You can choose to be notified by email when the import is complete. Once done click on **Import** as shown in the following figure:

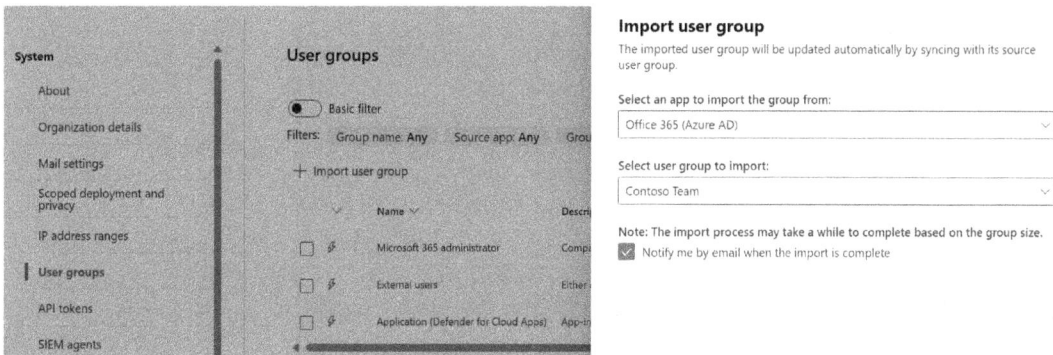

Figure 10.1: Import users to MDCA

Scoped deployment

In some scenarios, administrators might not want to deploy MDCA for all users. This might be due to license limitations or to run a pilot before mass rollout. MDCA allows you to scope the deployment to user groups. These user groups can be included or excluded from monitoring. An include rule will automatically exclude all users that are not members of the included group. An exclude rule will override included user groups. For example, if you include the user group AU-employees and exclude Legal, Legal users from AU will not be monitored even if they are members of the AU-employees group. Following are the steps to configure scoped deployment:

1. Login to the **https://security.microsoft.com** and navigate to **Settings** | **Cloud Apps** | **Scoped deployment and privacy**.

2. To monitor specific groups, click on **Add rule** under **Include**, in the right pane.

3. Give the rule a name and select the name of the group you want to include. Refer to picture below.

4. Next, choose which applications you want to scope this deployment for and click on **Create**. Refer *Figure 10.2*:

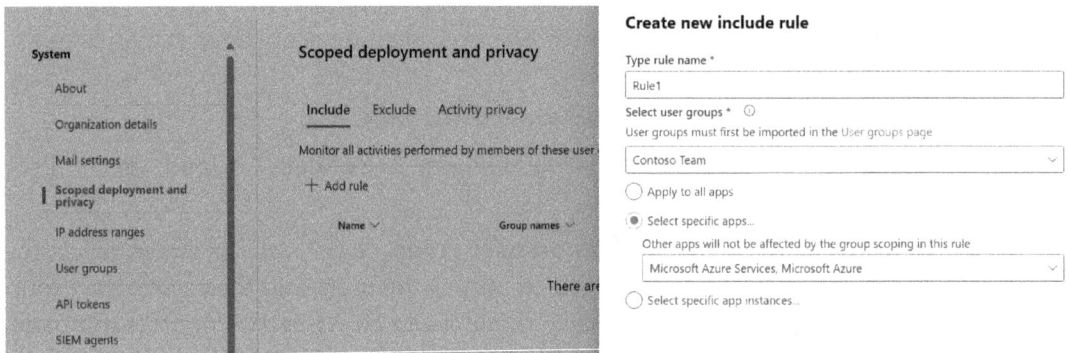

Figure 10.2: Scoped deployment

5. To create an exclude rule, go to the **Exclude** tab and follow the same steps.

Cloud discovery

Cloud discovery helps in discovering Shadow IT by analyzing network traffic logs against MDCA's app catalogue of more than 31,000 applications. These applications are scored against 90 risk parameters to assign a risk score which makes it easy for the administrators to decide if they want to block the app or let the end users use it.

The cloud discovery process consists of the following steps:

1. **Upload**: Network traffic logs are uploaded to the MDCA portal.

2. **Parse**: MDCA parses and analyses the traffic data using a dedicated parser for each data source.

3. **Analyze**: The traffic data is analyzed against the MDCA app catalogue of over 31,000 applications and the risk score is assessed. Users actively using the apps, and the machine IP addresses are also identified.

4. **Report**: A risk assessment report is generated and is available in the portal.

Network logs can be uploaded to MDCA in multiple ways as follows:

- **Snapshot report**: In this method, administrators manually upload a set of traffic logs from the firewall or proxy.

- **Cloud discovery API**: MDCA cloud discovery API can be used to automate traffic log upload and generate the cloud discovery report. The API can also be used to generate scripts to block unsanctioned applications.

- **Continuous reports**: MDCA can provide continuous monitoring of network traffic logs it receives. This is more efficient than a snapshot report as administrators do not have to manually upload logs and applications can be discovered immediately instead of waiting for logs to be uploaded manually. To generate these reports, MDCA offers seamless integration with **Microsoft Defender for Endpoint (MDE)** and **Secure Web Gateways (SWGs)** like Zscaler, iboss, Corrata, Menlo and Open Systems. You can also use a log collector to continuously upload the logs to MDCA.

The following sections explain the methods of generating continuous reports.

MDE integration

MDCA works seamlessly with MDE to help find and stop unauthorized applications. This integration let MDCA use the logs that the MDE agent creates as it tracks network connections. This enhances MDCA's protection capabilities outside the corporate network as it can now analyze network logs that are not just captured from the firewall. This integration does not require any extra configuration or log forwarding to work.

For MDCA and MDE integration to work seamlessly the following perquisites should be met:

- Microsoft Defender for Cloud Apps license
- Microsoft Defender for Endpoint Plan 2 license
- One of the following operating systems:
  - Windows 10 version 1709 (OS Build 16299.1085 with KB4493441)
  - Windows 10 version 1803 (OS Build 17134.704 with KB4493464)
  - Windows 10 version 1809 (OS Build 17763.379 with KB4489899), or later Windows 10 and Windows 11 versions
  - macOS, on devices with Defender for Endpoint version 20.123072.25.0 or higher
- If supporting integrations for macOS, network protection capabilities in MDE must be turned on. Network protection only audits TCP connection events hence, UDP protocols are not covered for macOS.
- It is recommended that real-time protection, cloud-delivered protection and network protection in block more be turned on in Microsoft Defender Antivirus.

To enable this integration, following are the steps:

1. Login to **https://security.microsoft.com** and navigate to **Settings | Endpoints | Advanced features**.

2. Toggle the **Microsoft Defender for Cloud Apps** to **On** and click on **Save preferences**.

The severity of alerts can be configured using the following steps:

1. Login to **https://security.microsoft.com** and navigate to **Settings | Cloud Apps | Microsoft Defender for Endpoint**.

2. Under **Alerts** choose the severity from **Informational, Low, Medium, High** and click on **Save**.

Secure Web Gateway integration

If your organization uses any of the supported SWGs you can take advantage of their integration with MDCA for seamless cloud discovery and automatic blocking of unsanctioned applications. You will need to have a valid license for SWG in addition to the MDCA license. Integration will also have to be configured on the SWG portal. The steps to configure MDCA integration with the SWG will be available on their website. To complete the integration on the MDCA side, the following are the steps:

1. Login to **https://security.microsoft.com** and navigate to **Settings | Cloud Apps | Automatic log upload**.

   In the right pane, on the **Data sources** tab, click on **Add data source**. Enter the **Name** and pick the **Source** and **Receiver type** from the dropdown lists and click on **Add.**

   Refer to the following figure:

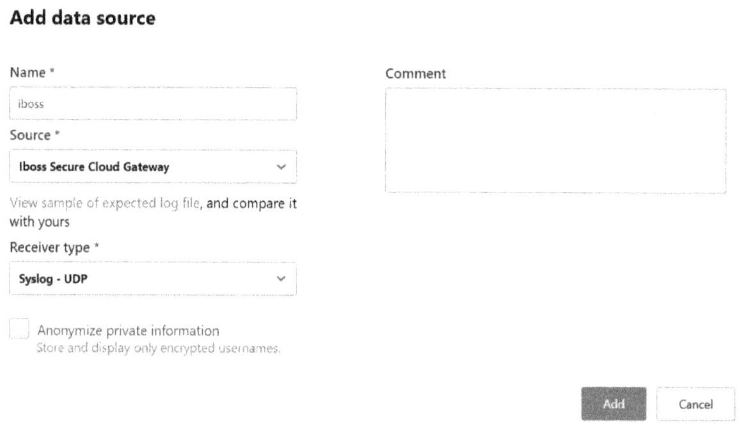

Figure 10.3: Configure SWG

Configure log collector

Using log collectors, you can easily automate the process of uploading logs from your network. The log collector can run on your network and receive logs over Syslog or FTP. Each log is processed and transmitted to the MDCA portal. FTP logs are uploaded to MDCA once the FTP transfer to the log collector is complete. For Syslog, the log collector writes the received logs to disk and uploads to the MDCA portal once the file size reaches 40GB. Once the log is uploaded to MDCA it is moved to a backup folder. The backup folder stores the last 20 logs. As new logs arrive, old ones are deleted. If the log collector disk runs out of space, new logs will be dropped till space is created. You will receive a warning in the Microsoft Defender portal under **Settings** | **Cloud Apps** | **Automatic log upload** | **Log collectors**.

The log collector supports the **Container** deployment mode and can be configured to run, as follows:

- In a Docker container in an on-premises Windows or Linux machine
- In a Docker or Podman container on Linux in Azure
- In a Docker container in Azure
- In a Docker container in Azure Kubernetes Services

View discovered apps

Once MDCA receives the logs in one of the ways mentioned above, it parses and analyzes the logs to generate the cloud discovery report. This is available in the **Cloud Discovery** dashboard in the Microsoft Defender portal.

Following figure shows an example of the **Cloud Discovery** dashboard:

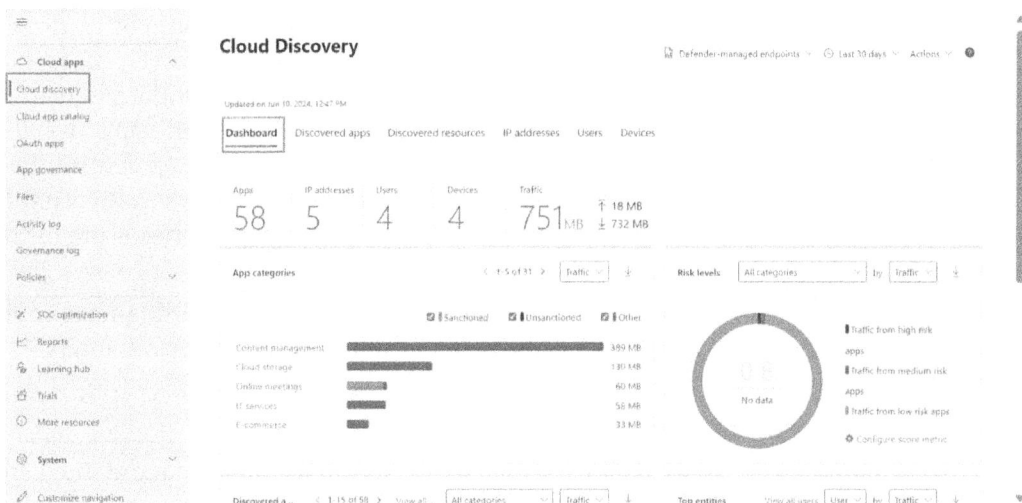

Figure 10.4: Cloud Discovery dashboard

Note that the main screen shows the number of discovered apps. It also shows the app categories, the amount of traffic from apps based on their risk level and the top users using the apps. You can dive deeper by going to the **Discovered apps** section. This page gives details about the applications, their risk score, the amount of data uploaded into the app, the number of users, devices and IP addresses that have interacted with the app. You can also sanction or block the apps from this page. There are filters available to help you see a filtered list of the discovered apps.

The **IP addresses** page shows the discovered IP addresses and how much traffic they generate with each SaaS application. You can dive deeper into each IP address to view the number of transactions, total traffic, uploads and downloads for each app.

The **Users** tab shows the transactions, total traffic, uploads and downloads for each user. By default, the username displayed is the username selected by the user in the SaaS application. This makes it difficult for administrators to understand which Entra ID user is interacting with the application. It is possible to populate the cloud discovery data with Microsoft Entra ID usernames. When this setting is enabled the application username that was received in the Microsoft Entra traffic logs is matched and replaced with the Microsoft Entra usernames. This helps relate a discovered app to a Microsoft Entra user for further investigation and reporting, like creating department specific reports. This setting is enabled in the Microsoft Defender portal by navigating to **Settings | Cloud Apps | User enrichment** and checking the box **Enrich discovered user identifiers with Azure Active Directory usernames**.

Lastly, the **Devices** tab shows the transactions, total traffic, uploads and downloads by device.

Identify risky apps

Once the cloud apps are discovered, the next step for an administrator would be to identify risky apps. The discovered applications are scored based on more than 90 risk factors. MDCA rates the risks based on regulatory certifications, industry standards and best practices. The risk score provided represents MDCA's assessment of the app's usability for enterprises. MDCA gives a score between 0-10 across the following categories. Each of these categories have more properties and each property receives a score between 0-10. The score of each of these properties is aggregated to provide an overall risk score for the category, as follows:

- **General**: This includes basic facts about the app developer including its domain, founding year and popularity. This is meant to show the company's stability.
- **Security**: This rates the apps on parameters such as MFA, encryption, data classification and data ownership.
- **Compliance**: This identifies if the app adheres to the compliance regulations like HIPAA, PCI-DSS etc.

- **Legal**: Accounts for policies to account for data protection, retention and privacy of users.

These scores are kept updated using data extracted from the app, data extracted using MDCA's algorithms, continuous analysis done by Microsoft security researchers and customer requests.

The following figure shows the risk analysis of an application discovered by MDCA:

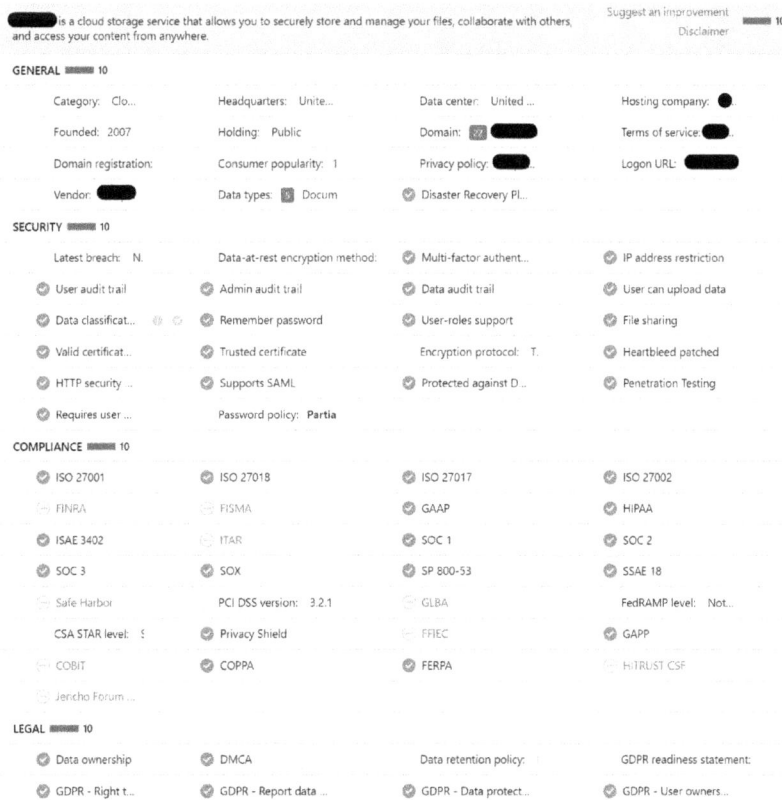

Figure 10.5: Risky application

All the parameters are given equal weightage by MDCA. If some parameters are more important for your organization, you can change them in the Microsoft Defender portal as follows:

1. Login to **https://security.microsoft.com** and navigate to **Settings | Cloud Apps | Cloud discovery | Score metrics**.

2. Adjust the **Importance** slider for each risk category to change the weightage. The available options are **Ignored, Low, Medium, High** or **Very high**.

3. Use the **N/A values** checkbox to determine if N/A value will be included in the score calculation or not. N/A values have a negative impact on the score.

The following figure shows the **Score metrics** screen:

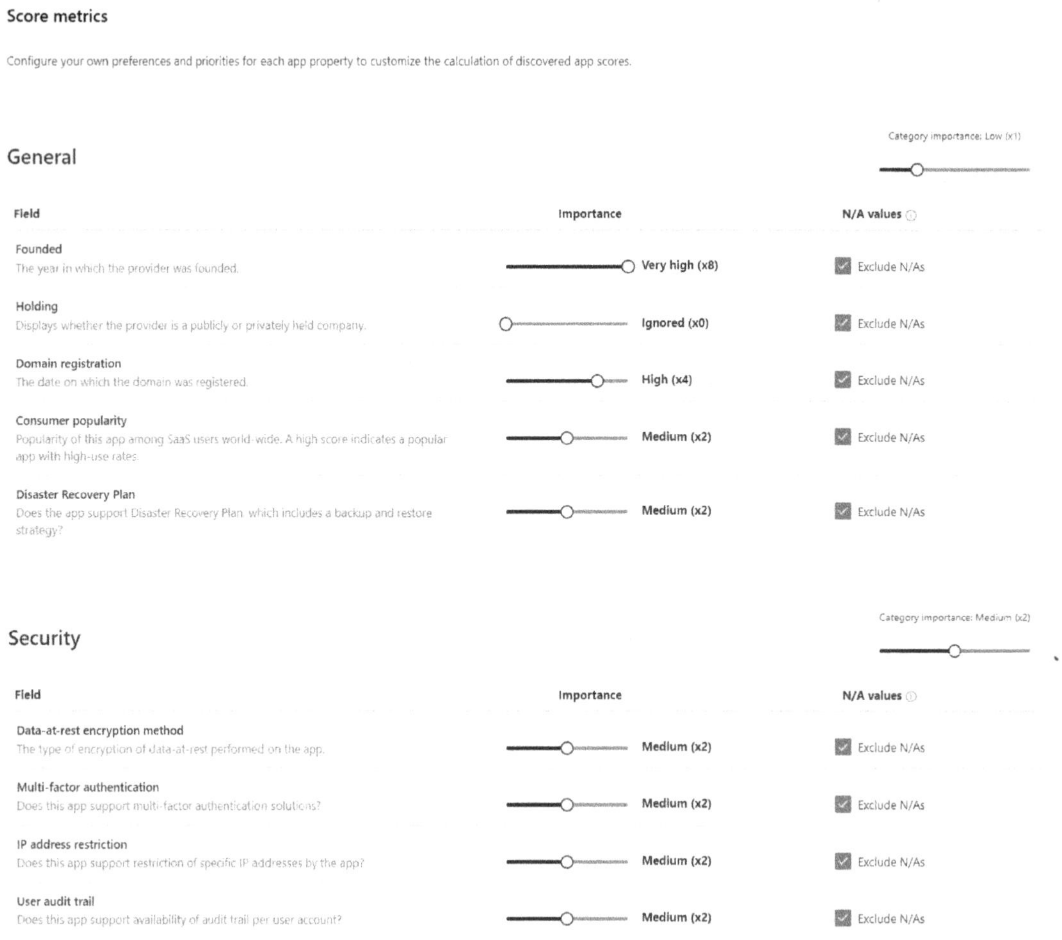

Score metrics

Configure your own preferences and priorities for each app property to customize the calculation of discovered app scores.

Category importance: Low (x1)

General

Field	Importance	N/A values
Founded The year in which the provider was founded.	Very high (x8)	✓ Exclude N/As
Holding Displays whether the provider is a publicly or privately held company.	Ignored (x0)	✓ Exclude N/As
Domain registration The date on which the domain was registered.	High (x4)	✓ Exclude N/As
Consumer popularity Popularity of this app among SaaS users world-wide. A high score indicates a popular app with high-use rates.	Medium (x2)	✓ Exclude N/As
Disaster Recovery Plan Does the app support Disaster Recovery Plan, which includes a backup and restore strategy?	Medium (x2)	✓ Exclude N/As

Category importance: Medium (x2)

Security

Field	Importance	N/A values
Data-at-rest encryption method The type of encryption of data-at-rest performed on the app.	Medium (x2)	✓ Exclude N/As
Multi-factor authentication Does this app support multi-factor authentication solutions?	Medium (x2)	✓ Exclude N/As
IP address restriction Does this app support restriction of specific IP addresses by the app?	Medium (x2)	✓ Exclude N/As
User audit trail Does this app support availability of audit trail per user account?	Medium (x2)	✓ Exclude N/As

Figure 10.6: Adjust score metrics

You can override the risk score of an application that has a low risk score but is approved for use by your organization. You can also request a score update for an application. This can be done by locating the application in the **Discovered apps** page and clicking on ellipsis next to it and selecting the appropriate option as shown in the following figure:

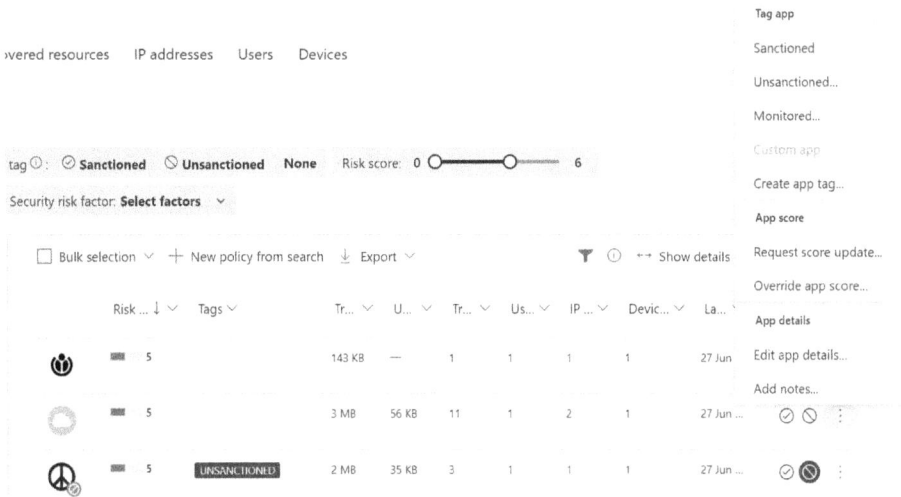

Figure 10.7: *App options*

Block risky apps

After you have identified the risky applications, you might want to block users in your organization from using them. This can be done by clicking on **Unsanctioned** as shown in *Figure 10.7*. Unsanctioned apps are denoted with a red icon as shown in *Figure 10.7*.

If your organization uses MDE, then once an application is unsanctioned it is automatically blocked. Ensure that you have the **Enforce app access** setting turned on in the Microsoft Defender portal by navigating to **Settings | Cloud Apps | Microsoft Defender for Endpoint**. The users will not be able to use the unsanctioned applications in their MDE onboarded devices. This blocking can be scoped to MDE device groups. Following are the steps to do this in the Microsoft Defender portal:

1. Navigate to **Settings | Cloud Apps | App tags | Scoped profiles**.

2. Click on **Add profile**. Give the profile a name and description. You can decide if the profile should be an **Include** or **Exclude** profile. If you choose **Include**, then the devices groups in the profile will be included in the block and not be able to access the unsanctioned application. If you choose to **Exclude**, then the device groups in the profile will be excluded from the block and will be able to access the unsanctioned application.

    In the following figure, the devices in the device group `Executive devices` will not be able to access the unsanctioned application:

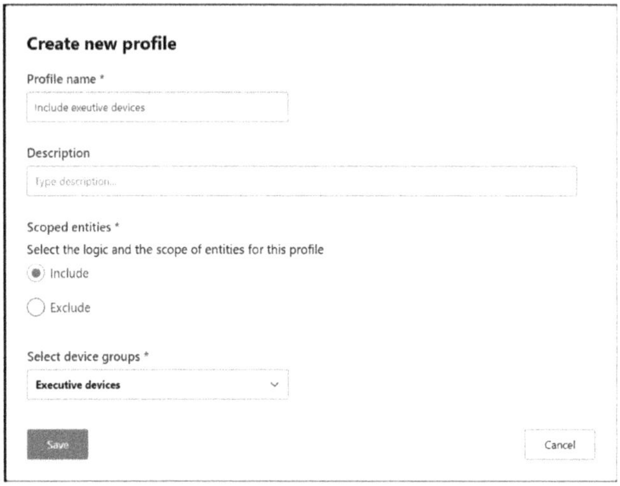

Figure 10.8: Scoping block to devices

3. Click **Save**.

4. Now, when you click on **Unsanctioned** in *Figure 10.7* you will be asked to select the profile as shown in the picture below. Select the profile and click on **Save**.

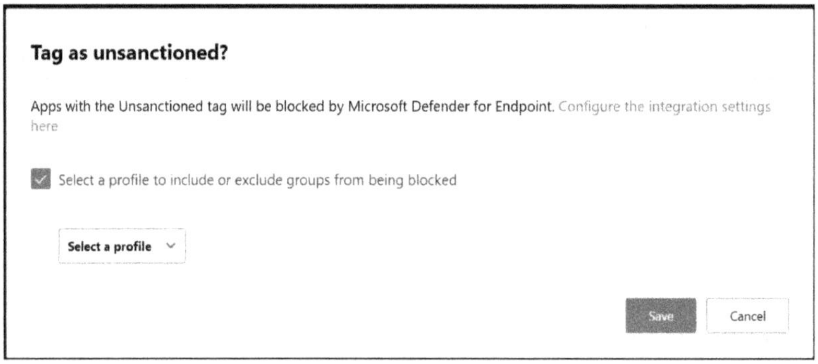

Figure 10.9: Block an application

If your organization uses any of the supported SWGs listed in the previous section, an unsanctioned application will be seamlessly blocked however, you will not be able to scope it by device groups.

If your organization uses any other appliance or SWG, MDCA can generate a block script for all the unsanctioned applications. To generate a block script, following are the steps:

1. In the **Cloud discovery** dashboard, click on **Actions** on the top right, and in the drop-down box click on **Generate block script**.

2. In the window that pops up, select the appropriate appliance and click on **Generate script**. The script will be saved on your local machine which can then be imported into your appliance.

Connect apps

To gain visibility and control over SaaS applications used by the organization, MDCA provides app connectors which leverage the APIs provided by the app provider to connect the application to MDCA. Communication between MDCA and the application is encrypted using HTTPS. Every application has its own architecture and limitations such as throttling and API limits among others. MDCA works with these services to optimize the use of APIs to provide the best performance. Some operations like scanning all files are resource intensive, hence the policies can sometimes run for hours or even days.

MDCA supports multiple instances of the same application. For example, if the organization uses two instances of Salesforce (one for sales and one for marketing) both instances can be connected to MDCA. They can be managed from the same console and be governed by different policies for granular control. Multi-instance support is available only for API connected apps and not for cloud discovered or proxy connected apps. It is not available for M365 and Azure.

The App Connector works, as follows:

- MDCA scans and saves authentication permissions.
- MDCA requests the list of users, activities and files. The scan might take longer the first time.
- Post the first scan, MDCA periodically scans users, groups and activities.

Depending on which app is connected the following items that may be available:

- **Account information**: Information about users, accounts, profile information, groups and permissions.
- **Audit trail**: Visibility into user and admin activities.
- **Account governance**: Ability to suspend and revoke user accounts.
- **App permissions**: Visibility into tokens and permissions.
- **App permission governance**: Ability to revoke tokens.
- **Data scan**: Scanning of unstructured data.
- **Data governance**: Ability to quarantine and overwrite files.

> **Note: For details on which features are available for which application, refer to Microsoft online documentation.**

To connect an app to MDCA you must have the required licenses and admin privileges in that application. Login to the Microsoft Defender portal and navigate to **Settings** | **Cloud Apps** | **App connectors**. In the right pane, click on **Connect an app** and select the app you would like to connect. From there follow the instructions for the selected app.

Working with policies

MDCA offers several policies using which you can control how users interact with the cloud applications. This enables you to detect risky behavior, policy violations and suspicious activities. Remediation workflows can be integrated to mitigate the risks.

The following table summarizes the various policies available in MDCA:

Policy type	Category	Description
Activity policy	Threat detection	This policy enables administrators to monitor specific user activity within SaaS applications.
Anomaly detection policy	Threat detection	This policy enables administrators to identify unusual user activity in cloud apps.
OAuth app policy	Threat detection	These policies are inbuilt in MDCA and cannot be created by administrators. These enable administrators to investigate, approve or revoke the permissions requested by OAuth applications.
Malware detection policy	Threat detection	These policies are in-built and cannot be created. They help identify malicious files in the SaaS applications and automatically approve or revoke them.
File policy	Information protection	These policies enable you to scan files stored in cloud apps for sensitive information and apply governance actions on the file.
Access policy	Conditional Access	These policies provide real-time monitoring and control over user logins to cloud apps.
Session policy	Conditional Access	These policies provide real-time monitoring and control over user activity in cloud apps.
App discovery policy	Shadow IT	These policies notify when new apps are discovered.
Cloud Discover anomaly detection policy	Shadow IT	These policies look at the logs used for cloud discovery and highlight unusual occurrences like more than usual transactions in an application.

Table 10.2: MDCA policies

MDCA helps mitigate risks in the cloud applications. Any of the above policies can be associated with the following risk categories:

- **Access control**: Identify which users access which files from which location. You can continuously monitor user behavior and detect anomalous activities like high-risk insider and external attacks and apply policies to alert or block actions within an app.

- **Compliance**: Ensure that you are meeting your compliance regulatory requirements.
- **Configuration control**: Monitor if there are unauthorized changes to the configuration.
- **Cloud discovery**: Identify if new apps are being used in the environment.
- **DLP**: Identify if sensitive information is being shared externally.
- **Privileged accounts**: Real-time activity monitoring of admin accounts.
- **Sharing control**: Inspect the content of files stored in the cloud and enforce internal and external sharing controls.
- **Threat detection**: Discover suspicious activities that threaten the cloud environment.

To control risk, you must create and fine tune a policy to generate the right kind of alerts. Then automated actions can be added to respond to and remediate risks.

Let us explore this in detail.

Following are the steps to create a policy:

1. Login to **https://security.microsoft.com** and navigate to **Cloud Apps | Policies | Policy templates**. You can filter the page by policy type and category. Click on the plus sign (+) next to the policy template you want to base the policy on as shown in the following figure:

Policy templates

Filters:

Advanced filters

| Type: **Select type** ⌃ | Severity: ▪▪▪ ▪▪▪ ▪▪▪ | Name: | Template name | Category: **Select risk category** ⌄ |

⚡ Activity policy			
☁ Cloud Discovery anomaly detection policy		No Templates found ▽ Hide filters ▤ Table settings ⌄	
▯ File policy			
☣ Malware detection policy		Severity ↓ ⌄	Linked policies ⌄	Published ⌄
☁ Anomaly detection policy	main (such as your competitor).	▪▪▪ High	2	Jan 22, 2024 12:30 AM	+
⌕ App discovery policy	wnloads within 1 minute.	▪▪▪ High	0	Jan 22, 2024 12:30 AM	+
🌐 Access policy				
🌐 Session policy	pp	▪▪▪ High	0	Jan 22, 2024 12:30 AM	+
⧉ OAuth app policy	gle, and fails more than 10 times within 5 ...	▪▪▪ High	0	Jan 22, 2024 12:30 AM	+

	by more than 500 users.			
⌕	New high volume app Alert when new apps are discovered that have total daily traffic of more than 500 MB.	▪▪▪ High	0	Jan 22, 2024 12:30 AM	+
⌕	New high upload volume app Alert when new apps are discovered whose total daily upload traffic is more than 500 MB.	▪▪▪ High	0	Jan 22, 2024 12:30 AM	+
⌕	New risky app Alert when new apps are discovered with risk score lower than 6 and that are used by more than 5...	▪▪▪ High	0	Jan 22, 2024 12:30 AM	+
⌕	Cloud storage app compliance check Alert when new cloud storage apps are discovered that are not compliant with SOC2, SSAE 16, ISA .	▪▪▪ High	0	Jan 22, 2024 12:30 AM	+
⌕	Collaboration app compliance check	▪▪▪ High	0	Jan 22, 2024 12:30 AM	+

Figure 10.10: MDCA policy templates

2. Give the policy a meaningful name and make the required selections. The available selections will depend on the policy type selected.

The following figure shows an example of a file policy created for detecting files shared with an unauthorized domain:

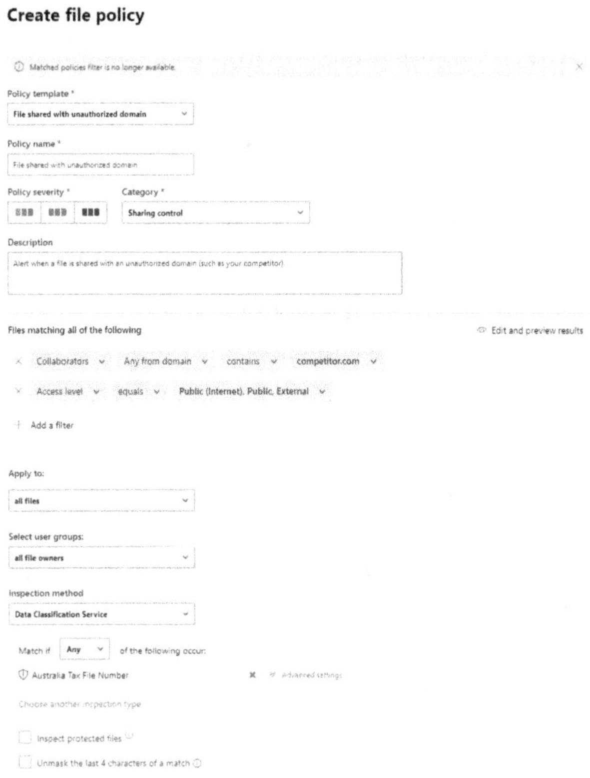

Figure 10.11: File policy example

3. Scroll down to configure alerts. The alerts will be sent to the incident queue in the Microsoft Defender portal. You can also configure alerts to be sent as email to a specific email address. For automatic remediation, a Power Automate flow can be triggered as shown in the following figure:

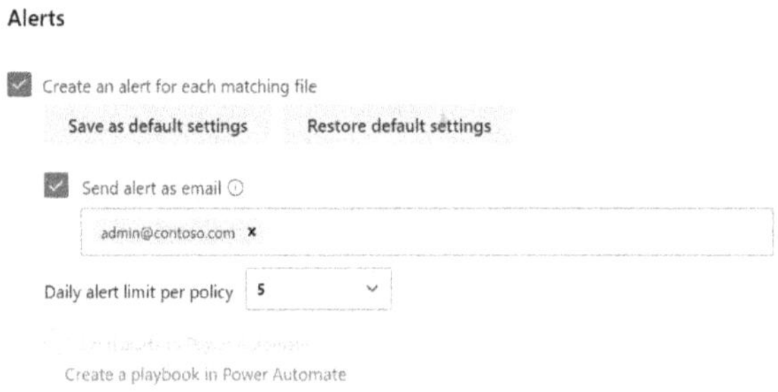

Figure 10.12: Configure alerts

4. Scroll down to configure the actions to be taken once a policy match occurs. Governance actions are available for the API connected apps and differ based on the application.

5. Once complete, click on **Create**. The created policy will now be visible as a linked policy with the policy template that was used to create it, as shown in *Figure 10.10*. Clicking on the number under the column **Linked policies** will show you all policies linked with the template.

Policies can be edited, enabled or disabled by clicking on the ellipses next to the policy by navigating to the **Policy management** page. You can also see if any policies triggered a match or an incident by looking at the **Count** column as shown in the following figure:

	Policy ∨	Count ∨	Se... ↓ ∨	Category ∨	Action ∨	Modified ∨		
🗐	Malicious OAuth app consent This policy uses Microsoft Threat Intelligence to scan OAuth apps conn...	0 active incidents	■■■ High	✪ Threat detection	⌂	Apr 22, 2024	⚙ ≣ ⋮	
							Edit policy	
🗐	Suspicious inbox forwarding This policy profiles your environment and triggers alerts when suspicio...	0 active incidents	■■■ High	✪ Threat detection	⌂	Apr 22, 2024	View all matches	
🗐	Suspicious inbox manipulation rule This policy profiles your environment and triggers alerts when suspicio...	0 active incidents	■■■ High	✪ Threat detection	⌂	Apr 22, 2024	View all incidents	
🗐	Ransomware activity This policy profiles your environment and triggers alerts when an activit...	0 active incidents	■■■ High	✪ Threat detection	⌂	Apr 22, 2024	Disable ⚙ ≣ ⋮	
🗐	Activity performed by terminated user This policy profiles your environment and alerts when a terminated use...	0 active incidents	■■■ High	✪ Threat detection	⌂	Apr 22, 2024	⚙ ≣ ⋮	
👤	Logon from a risky IP address Alert when a user logs on to your sanctioned apps from a risky IP addr...	0 active incidents	■■■ High	✪ Threat detection	⌂	Aug 7, 2020	⚙ ≣ ⋮	
👤	Mass download by a single user Alert when a single user performs more than 10 downloads within 5 mi...	0 active incidents	■■■ High	✪ Threat detection	⌂	Aug 7, 2020	⚙ ≣ ⋮	
🗋	File shared with◆unauthorized domain Alert when a file is shared with◆an unauthorized◆domain (such as yo...	0 matches	■■■ High	⛉ Sharing control	⌂	Oct 26, 2021	⚙ ≣ ⋮	
🗃	Risky OAuth apps	0 active incidents	■■■ High	✪ Threat detection	⌂	Aug 7, 2020	⚙ ≣ ⋮	
🗋	Publicly shared confidential files	1 matches	■■■ High	🔒 Compliance	⌂	Oct 26, 2021	⚙ ≣ ⋮	
🗋	File shared with unauthorized domain [Disabled - configur. Alert when a file is shared with an unauthorized domain (such as y...	0 matches	■■■ High	⛉ Sharing control	⌂	Apr 28, 2022	⚙ ≣ ⋮	
🗃	Malware detection [Disabled] This detection scans files in your cloud apps and runs suspicious files th...	0 matches	■■ Medi...	✪ Threat detection	⌂	Aug 4, 2020	⚙ ≣ ⋮	

Figure 10.13: View policy details

MDCA integrates with other Microsoft products to offer additional control capabilities. Let us explore some of these integrations.

Conditional Access app control

In today's cyber landscape, it is not enough to know what happened in the environment in the past. It is imperative that we stop breaches and data leaks from happening by ensuring that employees don't accidentally or unintentionally put the organization and data at risk. Organizations want the users to be able to use cloud apps and be productive anytime and anywhere, so they need the tools to ensure that data is protected. MDCA integrates with

Microsoft Entra ID Conditional Access to deliver this protection via *Access* and *Session* policies using a capability called Conditional Access app control.

Microsoft Entra ID Conditional Access assesses the user risk and then passes on to MDCA to apply app restrictions based on user risk. Users of Microsoft Edge will see a lock in their address bar indicating that the session is protected by MDCA. Users of other app browsers will see the suffix `*. mcas.ms` appended to the application URL.

This is a two-step process as defined in the following:

1. **Create a Conditional Access policy**: Following are the steps to create a Conditional Access policy:

    a. Login to **https://entra.microsoft.com** and navigate to **Protection | Conditional Access**.

    b. In the right pane, click on **Create new policy**.

    c. Select the users, applications, target resources and other conditions as per requirements.

    d. Under **Access controls** click on **Session** and check the box next to **Use Conditional Access App Control** and select the option **Use custom policy**.

    e. Switch the **Enable policy** toggle to **On** and click on **Create** to create the policy.

    f. Now, login to the application configured in the policy. You will see the application listed in the Microsoft Defender portal under **Settings | Cloud Apps | Conditional Access App Control apps**. Notice that under **Azure AD conditional access** is listed under the **Available controls** column. The application is now ready as shown in the following figure:

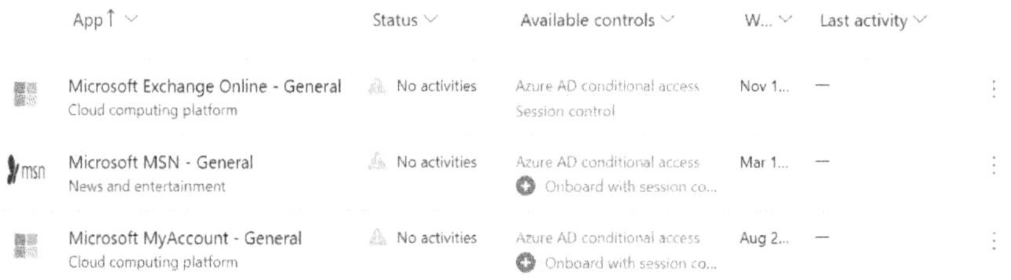

Figure 10.14: Conditional Access app control apps

2. Create a Session or Access policy: The next step is to create MDCA *Session* or *Access* policy. The policy you create depends on the control you want to apply on the application. Login to **https://security.microsoft.com** and navigate to **Policy Management | Conditional access** and click on **Create policy**. Select **Session policy** or **Access policy**. Next, select the requisite filters to apply.

Access policy

Access policies allow you to completely block access to applications depending on certain conditions. For example, you can use access policies to block access to sensitive applications from unmanaged devices or native clients. These conditions are configured using filters summarized in the following table:

Filter	Description
App	Use this to specify the app to be included in the policy. If you do not use this filter, then the policy will apply to all apps listed under **Settings** | **Cloud Apps** | **Conditional Access app control** apps as shown in *Figure 10.14*.
Client app	Specifies the client apps to apply the policy too. For example, browser or mobile or desktop apps.
Device	Filter for device by tag or type (mobile, PC, tablet).
IP address	Filter for IP address.
Location	Filter by geographic location.
Registered ISP	Filter for activities coming from a specific ISP.
User	Filter activities for a user or group of users.
User agent string	Filter by user agent string.
User agent tag	Filter by user agent tag like outdated browsers or operating systems.

Table 10.3: Filters in an access policy

In the **Actions** areas, select either **Audit** or **Block**. Configure the appropriate **Alerts** settings. The following figure shows an example of an access policy configured to block access to SharePoint Online from mobile, browser or desktop applications if the user is located outside Australia:

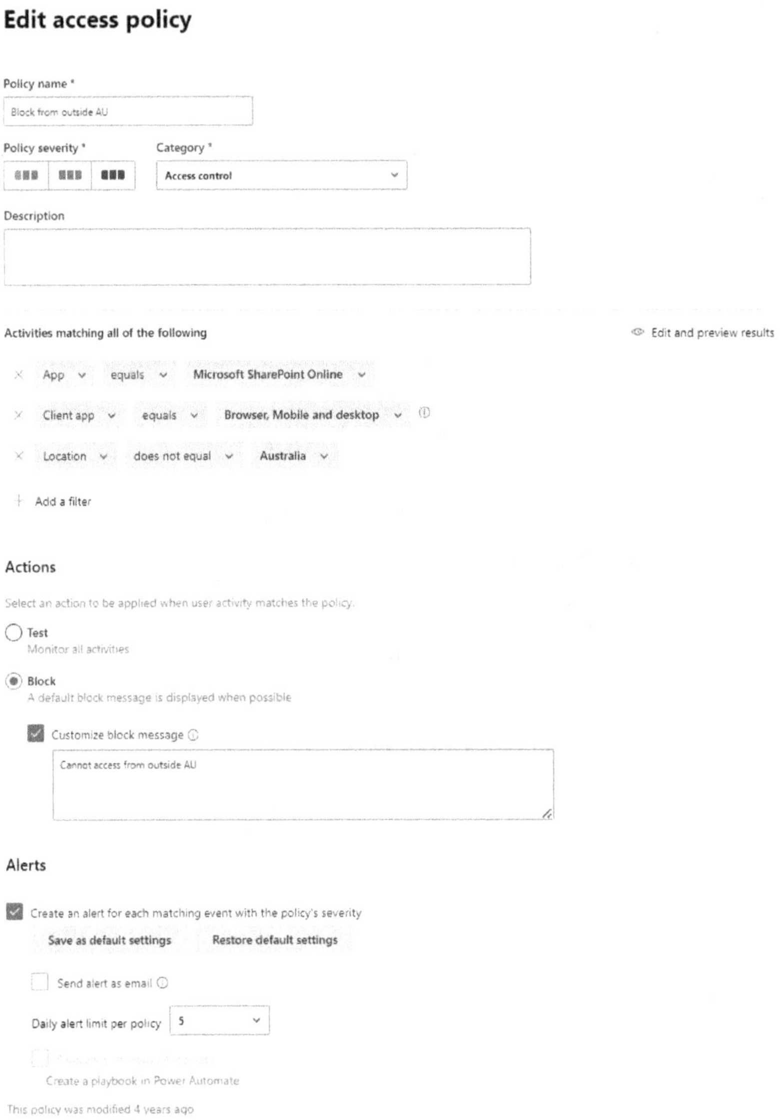

Edit access policy

Policy name *

```
Block from outside AU
```

Policy severity *   Category *

▮▮▮ ▮▮▮ ▮▮▮   Access control   ⌄

Description

```
[                                                  ]
```

Activities matching all of the following   👁 Edit and preview results

×   App ⌄   equals ⌄   Microsoft SharePoint Online ⌄

×   Client app ⌄   equals ⌄   Browser, Mobile and desktop ⌄   ⓘ

×   Location ⌄   does not equal ⌄   Australia ⌄

+   Add a filter

Actions

Select an action to be applied when user activity matches the policy.

◯ Test
    Monitor all activities

◉ Block
    A default block message is displayed when possible

    ☑ Customize block message ⓘ

```
Cannot access from outside AU
```

Alerts

☑ Create an alert for each matching event with the policy's severity

Save as default settings   **Restore default settings**

☐ Send alert as email ⓘ

Daily alert limit per policy   `5`   ⌄

☐ ~~...........~~
    Create a playbook in Power Automate

This policy was modified 4 years ago

Figure 10.15: Create access policy

Session policy

While Access policies completely block access, Session policies allow you to be more granular with the controls applied to users. For example, you might want to allow users to access apps from an unmanaged device but might want to block download of sensitive content on the unmanaged device. In a session policy, you need to select a **Session control type** which is the control you want to enable in the policy.

The following options are available:

- **Monitor only**: Use this to only monitor user activity on the selected apps.
- **Block activities**: Blocks the activities specified in the **Activity type** filter.
- **Control file download (with inspection)**: Use this to monitor file downloads. This can be combined with actions like blocking or protecting the downloaded file.
- **Control file upload (with inspection)**: Use this to file being uploaded. This can be combined with actions like blocking or protecting the file being uploaded.

Session policies have the same set of filters available as Access policies. There is one additional filter available for the **Block activities** session control type. This **Activity type** are actions like printing, copying, pasting or sharing of items.

In the actions area, in addition to **Audit** and **Block**, an additional action of **Protect** is also available if the **Control file download (with inspection)** session control type is chosen. This option protects files on download by applying an Information Protection Sensitivity label.

The following figure shows an example of a Session policy that applies an Information Protection Sensitivity label to files downloaded from SharePoint or OneDrive:

Figure 10.16: Create session policy

Microsoft Purview Information Protection

MDCA integrates with Microsoft Purview Information Protection, to encrypt and protect sensitive information in SaaS applications. This integration enables you to use the full potential of both services to secure files in SaaS applications. You can use the following:

- Apply sensitivity label as a governance action.
- View all classified files in a central location.
- Investigate according to classification.
- Create policies to ensure classified files are being handled correctly.

Prerequisites

Following are the prerequisites for integrating MDCA with Microsoft Purview Information Protection:

- A license that includes Microsoft Purview Information Protection.
- Connect M365 to MDCA using the app connectors.

Considerations

Keep the following considerations in mind:

- MDCA supports applying sensitivity labels for Office and PDF files only.
- MDCA supports scanning documents stored in Box, Google Workspace, SharePoint Online and OneDrive for Business.

Enable integration

To enable this integration, following are the steps:

1. Login to **https://security.microsoft.com** and navigate to **Settings | Cloud Apps | Microsoft Information Protection**.
2. In the right pane, check the box **Automatically scan new files for Microsoft Information Protection sensitivity labels and content inspection warnings**.
3. By default, MDCA scans labels defined by your tenant and those defined by other tenants. If you want to ignore the labels defined by other tenants check the box next to **Only scan files for Microsoft Information Protection sensitivity labels and content inspection warnings from this tenant** as shown in the following figure:

Microsoft Information Protection

Microsoft Information Protection settings

☑ Automatically scan new files for Microsoft Information Protection sensitivity labels and content inspection warnings
When enabled, the App connector will scan new files, searching for sensitivity labels embedded by Microsoft Information Protection.

☐ Only scan files for Microsoft Information Protection sensitivity labels and content inspection warnings from this tenant
When enabled, all Microsoft Information Protection sensitivity labels that were set by external tenants will be disregarded.

Get more info in the Microsoft Information Protection integration guide.

Save   We secure your data as described in our privacy statement and online service terms .

Inspect protected files

File policies can inspect content and/or read labels in Microsoft Information Protection protected files.
To inspect protected files, read labels from protected files, grant Defender for Cloud Apps permission in Azure AD.

✓ **Active**
Protected files can be inspected by file policies. Learn more

Figure 10.17: Configure MIP integration

Manually apply labels

Now, you can apply labels to files directly from the MDCA portal. Following are the steps:

1. Login to **https://security.microsoft.com** and click on **Files** under **Cloud apps**.

2. Locate the file to which you want to apply the label and click on the ellipses on the far right. In the menu that pops up, click on **Apply sensitivity label** and select the label from the drop-down menu and click on **Apply**.

Automatically apply labels

Labels can also be applied automatically using the **Governance actions** in file policy. Create a file policy with the requisite settings and under **Governance actions** choose the cloud app and check the box next to **Apply sensitivity label** and select the label from the drop-down list as shown in the following figure:

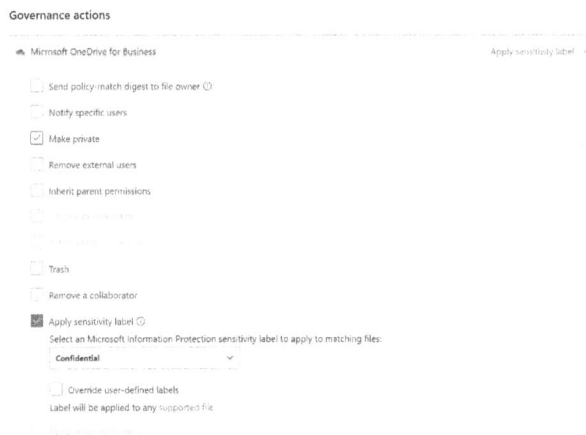

Governance actions

☁ Microsoft OneDrive for Business   Apply sensitivity label ∧

☐ Send policy-match digest to file owner ⓘ

☐ Notify specific users

☑ Make private

☐ Remove external users

☐ Inherit parent permissions

☐ Trash

☐ Remove a collaborator

☑ Apply sensitivity label ⓘ
   Select an Microsoft Information Protection sensitivity label to apply to matching files:
   Confidential   ⌄

   ☐ Override user-defined labels
   Label will be applied to any supported file

Figure 10.18: Governance actions

Microsoft Sentinel

Microsoft Sentinel is Microsoft's **Security Incident Event Monitoring** (**SIEM**) and **Security Orchestration and Response** (**SOAR**) solution. MDCA integrates with Microsoft Sentinel to help you better protect cloud applications and maintain the security workflow, automate security procedures, and correlate cloud and on-premises events.

To enable integration between MDCA and Microsoft Sentinel ensure that you have the following:

- An active Microsoft Sentinel environment.
- Global Administrator or Security Administrator role.

Following are the steps to enable this integration:

1. Login to **https://security.microsoft.com** and navigate to **Settings** | **Cloud Apps**. Under **System** click on **SIEM agents**.

2. In the right pane, click on **Add SIEM agent** and select **Azure Sentinel** from the drop-down list as shown in the following figure:

Figure 10.19: Select the SIEM

3. In the wizard, select the data types you want forwarded to Microsoft Sentinel. **Alerts** are automatically forwarded once the integration is enabled. In addition, **Discovery logs** can be forwarded. By default, all discovery logs are sent. You can choose to filter which discovery logs you want to send as shown in the following figure:

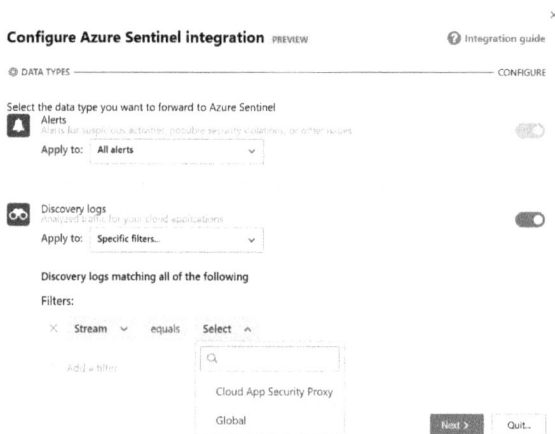

Figure 10.20: Integrate with Microsoft Sentinel

4. Once done, click on **Next**. You will be shown a success screen, and the alerts and discovery logs will start flowing into Microsoft Sentinel.

You can also integrate with other SIEM solutions by selecting **Generic SIEM** as shown in *Figure 10.19*.

Additional integrations

MDCA can be integrated with other security solutions to enable organizations to take advantage of their investments and enhance their security posture.

The following are a few solutions MDCA you can work with:

- **Threat Intelligence (TI) feeds**: MDCA allows organizations to bring their own TI feeds which can work with MDCA IP address range APIs and add new risky address ranges. These ranges can help you tag, categorize and customize how logs and alerts are displayed and investigated.

- **Mobile Device Management (MDM)/Mobile Threat Defence (MTD) solutions**: MDCA provides out of the box integration with Microsoft Intune, which is Microsoft's MDM solution to get device status which can be used to apply policy controls. However, if organizations use third-party MDM solutions, they can be integrated with MDCA through analysis of client certificates. MDCA can then receive signals from these MDM and MTD solutions and apply controls based on device status.

- **User Entity Behavior Analysis (UEBA) solutions**: Organizations use different UEBA solutions to identify suspicious and risky user behavior. These solutions can be integrated to MDCA to provide user risk signals, based on which MDCA can apply security controls like forcing password reset, requiring MFA or requiring that the user device be registered with the company MDM solution.

Investigate and respond

Once MDCA is configured and running in your environment you will need to learn the tools to gain deeper insights into what is happening. This section will explain some of the tools available to you to investigate apps, users and files.

Investigate Cloud Apps

To investigate apps in the Microsoft Defender portal, navigate to **Settings** | **Cloud Apps** | **App Connector** and click on the specific app. The **Dashboard** will show the user activities over time as shown in *Figure 10.21*. Notice the other tabs available at the top where you can get more information about the application's risk score as calculated by MDCA, user accounts accessing the app and any alerts generated by the app.

Figure 10.21: App dashboard

The **Activity log** tab gives detailed information about the users who are accessing the application, the IP addresses they are coming from, the admin activities, the locations from which the administrators are connecting, outdated devices in the environment and any failed login attempts. This view is also available by clicking on **Activity log** under the **Cloud Apps** menu.

Investigate files

To investigate files in the Microsoft Defender portal, navigate to **Cloud Apps** | **Files**. Here you can gain visibility into how many files are shared publicly, with which partners are files being shared, are there any files with sensitive names and if files are being shared from someone's personal accounts.

The following figure shows the files section. Notice that you can filter by application, file owner, access level, file type and more:

Files ❓

Queries: Select a query ∨ 💾 Save as   ⬤ Advanced filters

App: **Select apps** ∨   Owner: **Select users** ∨   Access level: **Select access level** ∨   File type: **Select type** ∨   Matched policy: **Select policy** ∨

☐ Bulk selection ∨ ➕ New policy from search ⬇ Export   1 - 20 of 489 files ↔ Show details ▽ Hide filters ⊞ Table settings ∨

	File name ∨	Owner ∨	App ∨	Collaborators ∨	Policies ∨	Last modified ↓ ∨	
🗐	CAS	▬▬▬▬▬	🔷 Microsoft SharePoint Online	🗐 22 collaborators	—	Apr 13, 2024	🔍 ⋮
🗐	_siteicon_.jpg	System Account	🔷 Microsoft SharePoint Online	🗐 3 collaborators	—	Apr 4, 2024	⋮
🗐	_siteicon_.jpg	System Account	🔷 Microsoft SharePoint Online	🗐 3 collaborators	—	Apr 4, 2024	⋮
🗐	_siteicon_.jpg	System Account	🔷 Microsoft SharePoint Online	🗐 3 collaborators	—	Apr 4, 2024	⋮
🗐	_siteicon_.jpg	System Account	🔷 Microsoft SharePoint Online	🗐 3 collaborators	—	Apr 4, 2024	⋮
🗐	_siteicon_.jpg	System Account	🔷 Microsoft SharePoint Online	🗐 3 collaborators	—	Apr 4, 2024	⋮
🗐	_siteicon_.jpg	System Account	🔷 Microsoft SharePoint Online	🗐 3 collaborators	—	Apr 4, 2024	⋮
🗐	_siteicon_.jpg	System Account	🔷 Microsoft SharePoint Online	🗐 3 collaborators	—	Apr 4, 2024	⋮
🗐	Payslip	▬▬▬▬	🔷 Microsoft SharePoint Online	🗐 3 collaborators	—	Mar 27, 2024	🔍 ⋮
📄	paystub_40.pdf	▬▬▬▬	🔷 Microsoft SharePoint Online	🗐 3 collaborators	—	Mar 27, 2024	⋮
📄	paystub_37.pdf	▬▬▬▬	🔷 Microsoft SharePoint Online	🗐 3 collaborators	—	Mar 27, 2024	⋮
📄	paystub_38.pdf	▬▬▬▬	🔷 Microsoft SharePoint Online	🗐 3 collaborators	—	Mar 27, 2024	⋮
📄	paystub_39.pdf	▬▬▬▬	🔷 Microsoft SharePoint Online	🗐 3 collaborators	—	Mar 27, 2024	⋮
📄	payslip_20.pdf	▬▬▬▬	🔷 Microsoft SharePoint Online	🗐 3 collaborators	—	Mar 27, 2024	⋮
📄	payslip_19.pdf	▬▬▬▬	🔷 Microsoft SharePoint Online	🗐 3 collaborators	—	Mar 27, 2024	⋮
📄	payslip_21.pdf	▬▬▬▬	🔷 Microsoft SharePoint Online	🗐 3 collaborators	—	Mar 27, 2024	⋮

Figure 10.22: Investigate files

Investigate users

To investigate users in the Microsoft Defender portal, click on **Identities** under **Assets**. Here, you can investigate if any accounts have been inactive for a long time, which users have a specific role, if terminated users still have access. You can revoke a user's permission for an app or force MFA. You can further investigate a user by clicking on the ellipses on the far right as shown in the below picture. Clicking on **View user page** will take you to the user's page from where you can confirm that the user is compromised, suspend the user account in Entra ID, require user to sign in again, view files owned by or shared with the user and view related activities or incidents.

Refer to the following figure:

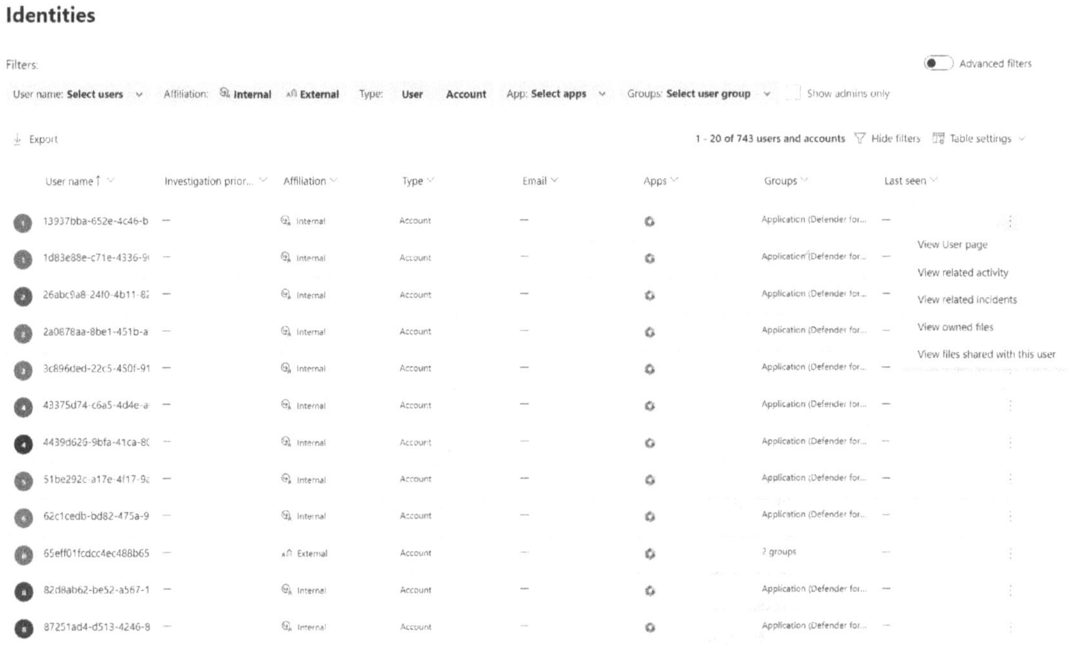

Identities

Figure 10.23: Investigate users

Behaviors

MDCA can assist in finding and examining unusual user actions. This may not mean a breach, but it alerts the security team to users who act differently from normal patterns. For this MDCA uses a specific data type, called **behaviors**.

Behaviors are linked to MITRE attack categories and techniques and offer a more detailed view of an event. Behaviors may be associated with security scenarios, but they do not always imply malicious activity. They are low-fidelity detections that provide contextual information about what happened at the time of the security incident.

Currently the following detections are supported:

- Activity from infrequent country
- Impossible travel
- Mass delete
- Mass download
- Mass share
- Multiple VMs deleted
- Multiple failed login attempts

- Suspicious administrative activities
- Suspicious impersonated activities
- Suspicious OAuth file download activities
- Suspicious Power BI report sharing
- Unusual addition of credentials to an OAuth application

Behaviors are accessible in the Microsoft Defender portal on the **Advanced hunting** page. There are two behavior tables available that can be queried for behavior data as follows:

- **BehaviorInfo**: This table contains the behavior metadata including behavior title, MITRE Attack category and technique.

- **BehaviorEntities**: This table contains the entities that were a part of the behavior.

Use KQL to query the information in these tables to investigate behavior tables.

Manage OAuth apps

Many applications used by business users request permissions to access user information and data. They sign in on behalf of the user in other cloud apps like M365, Google Workspace and Salesforce. When users access these apps, they often click accept without much thought or reviewing the permissions the app is requesting. The IT team may not have enough insight to balance the security risk against the productivity benefit provided by the app. Accepting third party app permissions is risky as attackers can use malicious apps to gain access to your organization. It is important for security teams to monitor the permissions these applications have.

MDCA enables you to see which user-installed OAuth applications have access to M365, Google Workspace and Salesforce. It tells you the permissions the application has and the users that granted that permission. Using this information, you can decide which apps you want to allow the users to access and which ones you would like to ban.

For this make sure you have one of the supported platforms (M365, Google Workspace or Salesforce) connected to MDCA. To access the OAuth apps, in the Microsoft Defender portal navigate to **Cloud apps** | **OAuth apps** as shown in the following figure:

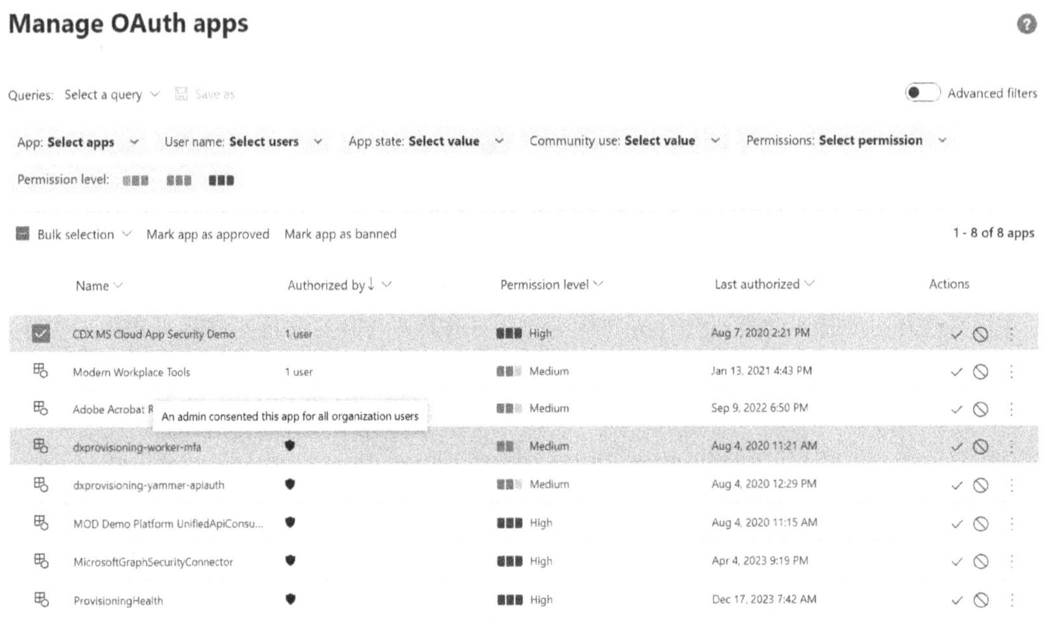

Manage OAuth apps

Figure 10.24: OAuth apps

This page shows you if the app was authorized by a user or an admin, the date when it was authorized and the permission level of the app. You can allow or ban the app by clicking on the check box and selecting the appropriate option or by selecting the icon under the **Actions** column. Clicking on the name of the app will open the app details page where you can see further details.

App governance

Apps deployed in organizations are increasingly vulnerable to cyber-attacks, as hackers use them to infiltrate, gain privileges, move across systems and steal data. To prevent and mitigate the threats posed by apps, organizations need to know what apps are running and how secure and compliant they are. App governance in MDCA is a solution that manages security and policies for OAuth-enabled apps registered with Microsoft Entra ID, Google and Salesforce. It helps you monitor, fix and control how users interact with these apps. With app governance, you can find out which OAuth apps installed by users can access data in M365, Google and Salesforce. You can also find out what permissions the users have granted to these apps.

App governance allows you to monitor all non-Microsoft registered applications, you can set up policies to prevent users from harmful applications, be notified if any unusual activities are detected and automatically fix any anomalous app behavior.

Licensing

App governance is available with the following licensing options:

- Microsoft 365 E5
- Microsoft 365 E5 Security
- Microsoft 365 E5 Compliance
- Enterprise Mobility + Security E5

Roles

One of the following roles is required to turn on and use app governance:

- Global Administrator
- Company Administrator
- Security Administrator
- Compliance Administrator
- Compliance Data Administrator
- Cloud App Security Administrator

Get started

To get started turn on app governance by going to the Microsoft Defender portal and navigating to **Settings | Cloud apps** and click on **Service status** under **App governance**. In the right pane, click on **Turn on app governance**.

> Note: Once app governance has been turned on, you might have to wait up to ten hours to start using it.

To access app governance in the Microsoft Defender portal, click **App governance** under **Cloud apps**. In the right pane, you will see the App governance **Overview** page. On this page, you can view the compliance posture of your apps and the latest incidents in your tenant. Review the information as shown in the following figure:

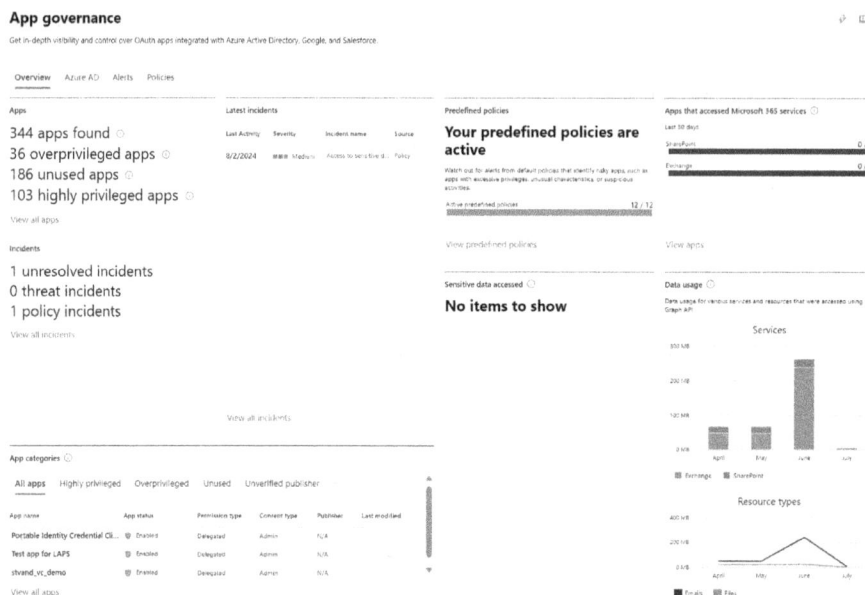

Figure 10.25: *App governance overview*

Investigate apps

You can view a list of all apps by clicking on **View all apps** links in the above screen. The **Azure AD** page lists all the applications that are integrated with Entra ID. If your organization has applications integrated with Google or Salesforce, these will show up as additional tabs and you could investigate each. Clicking on an app will open a fly out pane where you can see more details about the app like its data usage, the users who consented to and are using the app, the Graph API and legacy permissions the app has been granted and if they are in use and if the app has accessed any items which have a sensitivity label applied. You can also disable the app from this fly out pane.

App policies

App governance uses ML to detect anomalous app behavior and generate alerts. Policies are a way to generate alerts and perform automatic remediation for the specific apps in your organization. Policies can be used to manage OAuth apps in Microsoft Entra ID, Google and Salesforce. App governance has predefined policies that are tailored to your tenant. These allow you to start monitoring the apps without needing to set up your own policies. In addition, you can create your own policies.

The list of policies is available by clicking on the **Policies** tab in the above screen. On this page, you can see the predefined policies, their status, severity and if the policy has generated any alerts. You can disable the policy or edit the **Scope** and **Policy action** in the fly out pane that appears when you click on a policy as shown in the following figure:

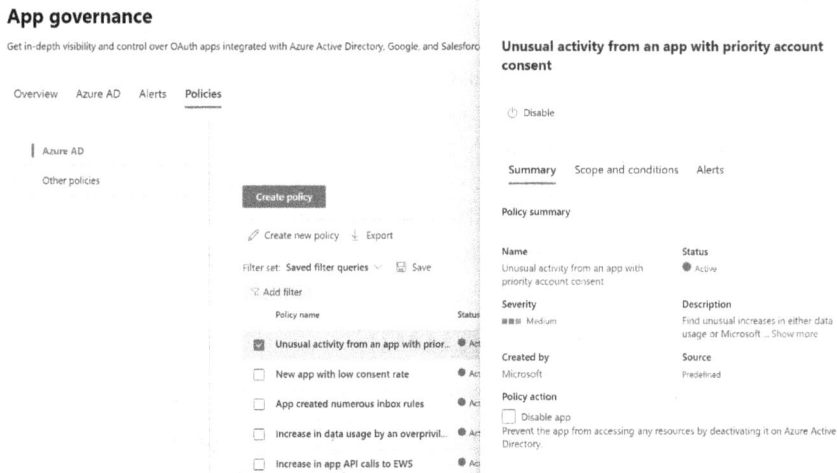

Figure 10.26: App governance policies

To create a new policy, click on the **Create policy** button on the above screen and follow the steps in the policy creation wizard.

Investigate alerts

App governance generates alerts when a predefined policy is violated. Predefined policies are nondeterministic, so alerts are only triggered when a behavior deviates from the norm. App governance alerts can be classified as follows:

- **True positive (TP)**: This is a confirmed malicious activity.
- **Benign true positive (B-TP)**: This is a suspicious activity but not necessarily malicious.
- **False positive (FP)**: This is an alert generated on a non-malicious activity.

To investigate alerts and gain a clear understanding of threats you can use the following guidelines. This will help in assigning the correct classification to the alert:

- Review the app severity level and compare with the other apps in the tenant. This helps in identifying which apps pose a greater risk.
- In case of a true positive, review all app activities to completely understand the impact.

All alerts generated by App governance and logged in the Microsoft Defender portal under **Incidents & alerts | Incidents**. Filter the **Service/detection source** by app governance.

Conclusion

This chapter introduced you to MDCA and how it helps discover, manage and govern SaaS applications. You should now be able to set up MDCA in your organization and integrate it with MDE and other SWGs to discover cloud apps being used by users in your organization. You also learnt how you can connect Microsoft and non-Microsoft applications to MDCA using APIs and how to control those applications using policies. This chapter explains how MDCA integrates with other Microsoft products and features like Conditional Access App Control, Microsoft Purview Information Protection and Microsoft Sentinel. It further goes on to explain how you can investigate and respond to threats using MDCA. Lastly, you learnt the app governance features of MDCA and how you can use the app policies to govern how users interact with applications.

Multiple choice questions

1. You are an IT administrator in your organization. You have been tasked with discovering the cloud applications are being used by users. All your users' endpoints are managed by Microsoft Defender for Endpoint. What should you do discover the applications?

   a. Set up a log collector

   b. Set up integration with MDE

   c. Set up integration with a SWG

   d. Import firewall logs into MDCA

2. You are the administrator for MDCA in your organization. You want to be alerted when files containing sensitive information are shared with personal email addresses. Which policy should you configure?

   a. Session policy

   b. Activity policy

   c. File policy

   d. Anomaly detection policy

3. Your organization is using app governance. You want to be alerted when an API connected app accesses sensitive data. What do you need to do?

   a. Create a custom policy in app governance

   b. Investigate the cloud app in the Cloud App Dashboard

   c. Explore user reported incidents

   d. Investigate the Incidents generated by the predefined policies in app governance

Answer key

1. b
2. c
3. d

CHAPTER 11
Security Management Using Microsoft Sentinel

Introduction

This chapter introduces you to the concepts of SIEM and SOAR. It then goes on to introduce Microsoft Sentinel as Microsoft's cloud-native SIEM and SOAR solution. It explains how Microsoft Sentinel helps SOC analysts manage hundreds of alerts daily, preventing critical security incidents. The chapter covers the setup of Microsoft Sentinel, connecting data sources, handling incidents, creating playbooks, and automating responses. It also highlights the integration with Microsoft solutions and non-Microsoft clouds, the use of Threat Intelligence, and the creation of visual reports. Additionally, it discusses the importance of understanding Azure architecture, data storage, and processing locations to meet data sovereignty requirements.

Structure

The chapter covers the following topics:

- Understanding SIEM and SOAR
- Microsoft Sentinel
- Understanding solutions and content
- Repositories
- Plan for Microsoft Sentinel

- Deploy Microsoft Sentinel
- Visualize data
- Hunt threats
- Create and investigate incidents

Objectives

By the end of this chapter, readers will learn the concepts of SIEM and SOAR and the difference between them. You will also learn the architecture of Microsoft Sentinel. This chapter explains how you can design and implement Microsoft Sentinel as the SIEM and SOAR solution for your organization. You will learn how to configure Microsoft and non-Microsoft data sources to ingest logs into Microsoft Sentinel. You will be able to connect threat intelligence and set up analytics rules to identify and report security incidents. You will also be able to set up automation rules and playbooks to automate responses to security incidents. This chapter also shows how you can use the Microsoft Sentinel dashboard, Workbooks and Power BI to visualize data and hunt threat proactively using Notebooks and Livestreams. Finally, you will learn how you can create and investigate incidents.

> **Note: Microsoft Sentinel is now available in the Microsoft Defender portal. This chapter will focus on the Microsoft Sentinel experience in the Microsoft Defender portal and not the Azure portal.**

Understanding SIEM and SOAR

The frequency and complexity of cyberattacks have escalated in recent times. This has resulted in more data breaches and an unprecedented volume of security alerts. As discussed earlier, all implemented security measures generate notifications. Analyzing and addressing these incidents manually is inefficient, time-intensive, and prone to mistakes. SOC teams need to survey different systems and correlate the information from the various alerts to determine the extent and impact of a cyber-attack comprehensively. SIEM and SOAR are essential tools in current cybersecurity strategies that support SOC teams in gathering, correlating, analyzing, and tackling cybersecurity events efficiently.

SIEM combines **Security Information Management** (**SIM**) and **Security Event Management** (**SEM**) into a single system. It collects, correlates, and analyses security data from various sources like applications, devices, servers and users to detect and respond to security events in real-time. SIEM provides valuable insights into potential threats, helping organizations monitor data loss, detect intrusions, and ensure compliance. It uses predetermined rules to define threats and generate alerts.

SIEMs vary in their capabilities but most of them serve the following use cases:

- **Log management**: As we have learnt so far, all the different IT systems generate large amounts of logs and events. SIEM systems help collate all these logs in one place, organize and correlate them to show signs of an attack or breach.

- **Event correlation**: SIEM systems use built-in logic, Threat Intelligence and Artificial Intelligence to identify relationship patterns in the logs to detect and respond to threats.

- **Event monitoring and response**: SIEM monitors security incidents across the network and generates alerts and audits of all events related to an incident.

SIEM can help mitigate cyber risks by detecting suspicious user activity and monitoring user behavior. It offers many advantages like providing a single pane of glass for all potential threats related to users, applications and devices. It also helps maintain regulatory compliance auditing and reporting.

In today's world, SIEM is an important part of an organization's cybersecurity ecosystem. It provides a central place to collect, aggregate and analyze large volumes of data. It provides operational capabilities like incident monitoring and compliance reporting.

SOAR is a set of technologies that focuses on automated prevention and response to cyberattacks. It reduces the workload on security teams by handling repetitive tasks and enabling rapid response to security incidents. It is a combination of two components as follows:

- **Security orchestration**: SOAR connects with other tools to consolidate data and respond to incidents as a group even when they are spread across the environment.

- **Automation**: SOAR can program tasks that can be automatically executed based on a trigger. This way the SOC teams can focus on tasks that matter rather than sorting through repetitive signals.

SOAR integrates with various security tools, allowing for seamless communication and coordination, ultimately improving the efficiency and effectiveness of incident response. SOAR systems offer greater productivity, faster responses and a centralized view of activities.

Together, SIEM and SOAR enhance an organization's ability to detect, analyze, and respond to security threats, creating a robust and proactive cybersecurity posture. In this chapter, we will learn about Microsoft Sentinel which is Microsoft's cloud-native SIEM and SOAR solution.

Microsoft Sentinel

Microsoft Sentinel is a scalable, cloud-native SIEM and SOAR solution that sits within Microsoft Azure. Sentinel delivers intelligent security analytics and threat intelligence across the enterprise, providing a single solution for alert detection, threat visibility, proactive hunting, and threat response. It collects data at cloud scale across all users, devices, applications, and infrastructure, both on-premises and in multiple clouds. Sentinel helps detect previously undetected threats and minimizes false positives using Microsoft's analytics and unparalleled threat intelligence. Sentinel integrates seamlessly with other Microsoft services, such as Microsoft Defender, to provide a unified security operations platform. This integration helps security teams find and resolve threats faster by bringing together previously discrete security tools into a unified experience powered by threat intelligence and generative AI.

Before we move on, let us spend some time to understand Microsoft Azure and its architecture and how Sentinel sits within it. This will help in understanding the concepts in this chapter better.

Microsoft Azure is a comprehensive cloud computing platform that provides a wide range of services, including computing, analytics, storage, and networking. At a high level, Azure's architecture is designed to be flexible, scalable, and secure, enabling organizations to build, deploy, and manage applications efficiently.

In Azure, **management groups** are used to organize and govern your Azure subscriptions. They provide a way to apply policies and access controls across multiple subscriptions, making it easier to manage large environments. Management groups can be nested, allowing for a hierarchical structure that mirrors your organization's needs.

Subscriptions are the next level in the hierarchy. Each subscription is a logical container for resources and services in Azure. Subscriptions help manage and control access, billing, and resource allocation. They provide a way to separate different environments, such as development, testing, and production, or to allocate resources to different departments or projects.

Within each subscription, **resource groups** are used to organize and manage related resources. A resource group is a container that holds related resources for an Azure solution. These resources can include virtual machines, storage accounts, virtual networks, and databases. Resource groups provide a way to manage and deploy resources as a single unit, making it easier to monitor, update, and scale your applications.

This hierarchical structure of management groups, subscriptions, and resource groups allows for efficient organization, governance, and management of resources in Azure, ensuring that your cloud environment is secure, scalable, and aligned with your business needs.

The following figure shows an example of an Azure environment:

Note: Explaining the detailed Azure architecture is beyond the scope of this book. The reader is advised to refer to Azure documentation.

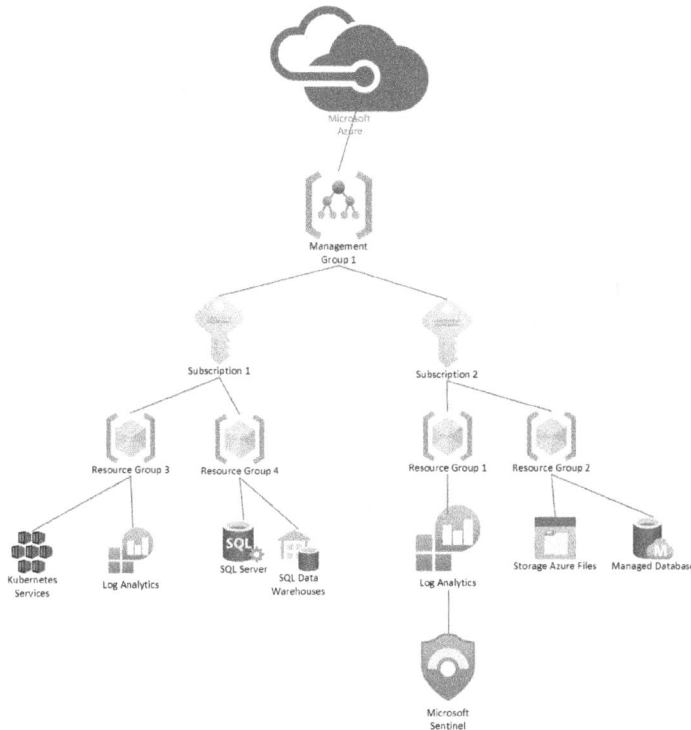

Figure 11.1: *Microsoft Sentinel architecture*

Microsoft Sentinel enables you to ingest data at scale from multiple data sources across users, devices, applications and infrastructure both on-premises and in multiple clouds. It offers data connectors across Microsoft solutions like Microsoft Entra and Microsoft 365 and non-Microsoft clouds like AWS and Google. Using these connectors Microsoft Sentinel can receive logs from these services at scale. It helps you reduce noise and minimize the number of alerts you must review by detecting threats out-of-the-box. It is aligned with MITRE ATT&CK tactics and techniques to better help visualize the nature and coverage of an attack. It integrates with Microsoft's own TI to detect malicious activity and provides security context to SOC teams to make informed decisions. It helps create visual reports using built-in workbook templates that allow you to quickly gain insights into your data. It offers deep investigation tools that can help you understand the complete impact and find the root cause of a security threat. Microsoft Sentinel helps in responding to incidents rapidly by simplifying orchestration using playbooks which are Azure Logic Apps based workflows.

Microsoft Sentinel is a non-regional service which means that it does not have dependency on a specific Azure region and does not let customers specify a deployment region. It operates globally to deliver functionality to customers. Customers must understand where the data is stored and processed as this will be critical in meeting their data sovereignty requirements and be a key factor in designing their Microsoft Sentinel architecture. It is built on top of Azure Monitor Logs which is a regional service, therefore, it stores data in the same region as the Log Analytics workspace associated with Microsoft Sentinel. Data is processed in two locations. If the Log Analytics workspace is in Europe, customer data is processed in Europe. For all other locations, customer data is processed in the US.

> **Note: For a complete list of regions that can run Microsoft Sentinel, refer to Microsoft Online documentation.**

Understanding solutions and content

Microsoft Sentinel content is SIEM components that help ingest data, monitor, alert, hunt, investigate, respond and connect with different products, platforms and services. Content in Microsoft Sentinel are of the following types:

- **Data connectors**: These provide connectivity with data sources for Microsoft Sentinel to receive events and logs.
- **Parsers**: These provide log formatting and transformation.
- **Workbooks**: Provide rich reporting capabilities to highlight meaningful insights.
- **Analytics rules**: Generate alerts to help SOC teams take actions on incidents.
- **Hunting queries**: SOC teams use them to proactively hunt for threats.
- **Notebooks**: SOC teams can use them to access advanced hunting features in Jupyter and Azure Notebooks.
- **Watchlists**: Support ingestion of specific data for enhanced threat detection.
- **Playbooks and Azure Logic Apps connectors**: Help in automating investigation, remediation and incident response.

These content types are available as solutions or standalone items. Solutions are packages of content that fulfil an end-to-end solution. These might be focused on a specific product, domain or industry verticals. Both solutions and standalone items are available in the **Content hub**. Administrators can either customize out of the box content or create their own.

To discover out of the box content, in the Microsoft Defender portal navigate to **Microsoft Sentinel | Content management | Content hub**.

The following figure shows the content hub. Notice that you can filter it by categories, content type and more. There is also a text search available for you to search using keywords:

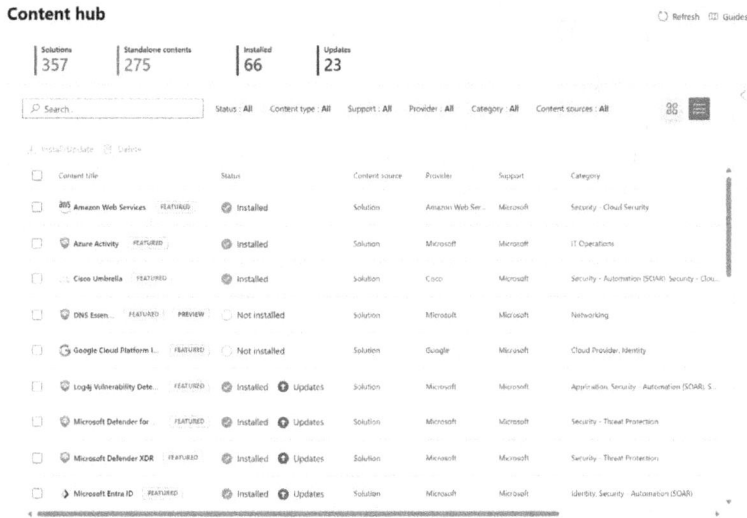

Figure 11.2: *Content hub*

Repositories

Microsoft Sentinel can be deployed as code using Repositories. They allow connections to external source control for **continuous integration/continuous delivery (CI/CD)**. This removes the overhead of manually updating and deploying custom content.

Currently connections to GitHub and Azure DevOps are supported. The Microsoft Sentinel application must have **Contributor** access with Actions enabled for GitHub and Pipelines enabled for Azure DevOps. Repositories require the **Owner** role in the resource group that contains the Microsoft Sentinel workspace so that a connection can be created between the Microsoft Sentinel workspace and the source control repository.

The following Microsoft Sentinel content types can be deployed using a repository:

- Analytics rules
- Automation rules
- Hunting queries
- Parsers
- Playbooks
- Workbooks

To connect a repository to the Microsoft Sentinel workspace login to **https://security. microsoft.com** and navigate to **Microsoft Sentinel** | **Content management** | **Repositories**. In the right pane, click on **Add new** and follow the steps in the wizard.

Note: At the time of this writing, this feature is in Public Preview.

Plan for Microsoft Sentinel

Adequate preparation is key to a successful implementation. To effectively deploy and operate Microsoft Sentinel, it is critical to recognize the necessary prerequisites and the planned architecture. **Role-based access control** (**RBAC**) is a vital aspect in Microsoft solutions and is significant in Microsoft Sentinel. It is important to comprehend the different roles within Microsoft Sentinel, Log Analytics, and Azure to establish suitable permissions. Ascertain the data sources that need to be incorporated into Microsoft Sentinel and plan for the necessary rules, automation, and reporting.

Prerequisites

Microsoft Sentinel requires the following components to be in place:

- A Microsoft Entra ID license and tenant.
- An Azure subscription for creating resources and billing.
- A dedicated Azure Resource Group for Microsoft Sentinel is recommended.
- A dedicated Log Analytics workspace where logs will be ingested. You can use an existing Log Analytics workspace; however, it is recommended that you create a new one only for Microsoft Sentinel. The Log Analytics workspace should also meet the below requirements.
  - It must not have a resource lock applied.
  - It must be a pay-as-you-go pricing tier or a commitment tier.
- Assign appropriate permissions to the subscription.

Roles and permissions

Microsoft Sentinel uses **Azure role-based access control** (**Azure RBAC**) to provide permissions to users, groups and services in Azure. There are some Microsoft Sentinel specific roles in Azure that give permissions only on data in the Microsoft Sentinel workspace. In addition, there are some Azure roles and Log Analytics roles that give access to more than just the Microsoft Sentinel workspace. These roles are summarized in this section.

Microsoft Sentinel roles

These roles grant access only to the Microsoft Sentinel workspace. These roles and their permissions are summarized, as follows:

- **Microsoft Sentinel reader**: These users can view data, incidents, workbooks and other Microsoft Sentinel resources. Paired with the Workbook Contributor Azure Monitor role they can also create and delete workbooks.

- **Microsoft Sentinel responder**: In addition to permissions assigned by the reader role, these users can assign, dismiss and change incidents. Paired with the Workbook Contributor Azure Monitor role they can also create and delete workbooks.

- **Microsoft Sentinel contributor**: In addition to the permissions assigned by the reader and responder role, these users can install and update solutions from content hub and create and edit Microsoft Sentinel resources like workbooks and analytics rules.

- **Microsoft Sentinel playbook operator**: These users can list, view and manually run playbooks. Paired with the Logic App Contributor role, these users can also create and edit playbooks.

- **Microsoft Sentinel automation contributor**: This role is not meant for users. It allows Microsoft Sentinel to add playbooks to automation rules.

It is recommended that these roles be assigned at the Azure resource group level that contains the Microsoft Sentinel workspace. This way all resources under the resource group will inherit the permissions.

There might be scenarios where users need access to specific data for the resources they own and not the entire Microsoft Sentinel environment. In these cases, permission should be granted on the specific resources and not the entire Microsoft Sentinel workspace. This is called **resource-context RBAC**. When resource-context RBAC is configured, users access Microsoft Sentinel data via the resource itself or via Azure Monitor.

In addition to the above roles, users might need to be granted additional roles depending on the tasks they are trying to accomplish. Following is the explanation:

- **Connect data sources**: To add data connectors, the users must have the **Write** permissions to the Microsoft Sentinel workspace. The specific permissions required to configure each data connector is listed on the **Data connectors** page in the Microsoft Defender portal.

- **Allow guests to assign incidents**: If your organization uses an external provider to triage first level incidents, you might require guest users to assign incidents. In this case, they will need the Microsoft Entra **Directory Reader** role in addition to the **Microsoft Sentinel Responder** role.

Azure roles

These roles grant access to all Azure resources including Log Analytics workspace and Microsoft Sentinel. These roles are **Owner**, **Contributor** and **Reader**. In addition to these built-in roles, custom Azure roles can also be used to assign permissions to Microsoft Sentinel.

Log Analytics roles

These roles grant access only to the Log Analytics workspace. These are **Log Analytics Contributor** and **Log Analytics Reader**.

These roles work together to determine the exact permissions that a user or group will have on a resource. For example, if a user has the **Microsoft Sentinel Reader** role and the **Azure Contributor** role, they will be able to edit items in the Microsoft Sentinel workspace. It is therefore important to take stock of all permissions a user has across the above roles to determine the level of access they will have on a resource.

Costs

As organizations plan for Microsoft Sentinel deployment, they want to understand how much it will cost them to implement and run. They want to understand the pricing and billing to optimize their costs. Microsoft Sentinel stores data in Azure Monitor Log Analytics workspace. Billing is based on the amount of data **analyzed** in Microsoft Sentinel and **stored** in the Log Analytics workspace.

As you begin, you can start using Microsoft Sentinel for free by enabling the **Free trial** for 31 days. In these 31 days, the first 10 GB per day is free. Up to 20 workspaces can be created in the free trial.

To estimate the cost of running Microsoft Sentinel, it is recommended that you use the **Microsoft Sentinel pricing calculator**. For this, you would need to have an initial understanding of the data sources, you will connect to your Microsoft Sentinel workspace. The following data sources are free:

- Azure Activity Logs
- Microsoft Sentinel Health
- Office 365 Audit logs
- Security alerts from Microsoft Defender XDR, Microsoft Defender for Cloud, Microsoft Defender for Office 365, Microsoft Defender for Identity, Microsoft Defender for Endpoint and Microsoft Defender for Cloud Apps.
- Alerts from Microsoft Defender for Cloud and Microsoft Defender for Cloud Apps.

There are two billing methods, as follows:

- **Pay-as-you-go**: This is the default billing method. In this method, the customer pays for the actual amount of data stored in Log Analytics.
- **Commitment tier**: Log Analytics and Microsoft Sentinel have commitment tiers which is the combined cost of data stored in Log Analytics and processed in Microsoft Sentinel. The pricing starts at 100 GB per day. If an organization expects to ingest more than 100 GB data in a day, the commitment tiers might offer

significant cost savings over pay-as-you-go model. Organizations can increase their commitment tier anytime as the data grows.

The Log Analytics workspace enabled for Microsoft Sentinel store logs for free for the first 90 days. If organizations want to retain logs beyond 90 days, they are subject to **Log Analytics retention pricing**. Alternatively, they can move the logs to other low-cost storage.

Deploy Microsoft Sentinel

Now that we understand the features, prerequisites, roles and cost associated with Microsoft Sentinel, let us discuss how we deploy it in our environment. Before you begin, ensure that all the prerequisites have been met. Deploying Microsoft Sentinel in your tenant involves adding Microsoft Sentinel to a Log Analytics workspace and configuring data connectors These are described as following:

Add Microsoft Sentinel

Following are the steps to add Microsoft Sentinel to your Log Analytics workspace:

a. Login to **https://portal.azure.com**.

b. In the search box search and select **Microsoft Sentinel**.

c. Click on **Create Microsoft Sentinel**.

d. Select the Log Analytics workspace you want to use or create a new one.

Ingest data

Once Microsoft Sentinel has been added, it needs to receive logs from data sources. This can be done in the ways listed, as follows:

Out-of-the-box data connectors

Microsoft Sentinel has several out of the box connectors for a variety of data sources ranging from Akamai, Palo Alto, Azure, AWS, GCP and many more. To connect data sources to Microsoft Sentinel, following are the steps:

a. Login to **https://security.microsoft.com** and navigate to **Microsoft Sentinel | Content Management | Content hub**. This is a centralized location to discover and manage all out-of-the-box content. Find the solution you would like to add and click on **Install/Update**.

The following figure shows some of the available solutions:

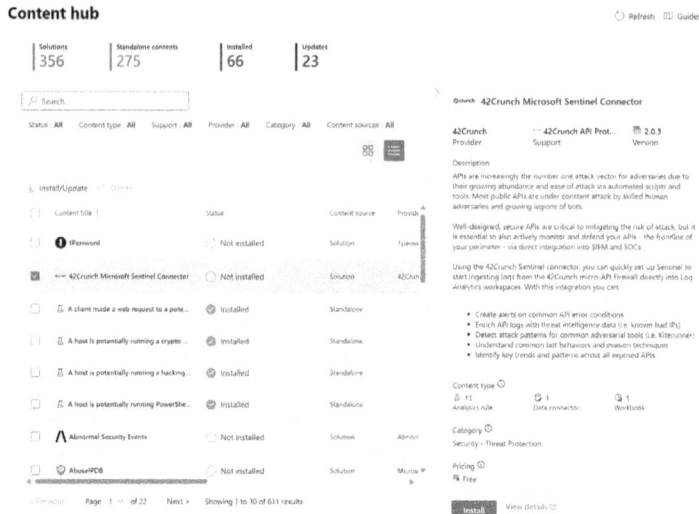

Figure 11.3: Install a connector

b. Click on **Data connectors** under **Configuration**. This page lists all the data sources that can be connected to Microsoft Sentinel so that it can receive logs from these data sources. Select the connector you want to configure and click on **Open connector page** as shown in the following figure:

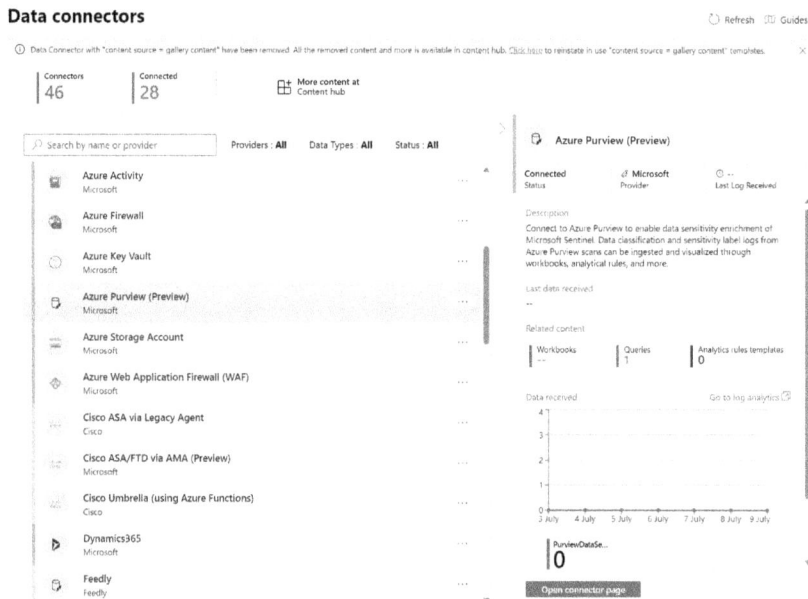

Figure 11.4: Data connectors in Microsoft Sentinel

c. This page shows the prerequisites and instructions to set up this connector. The following figure shows the details of the **Azure Purview** data connector:

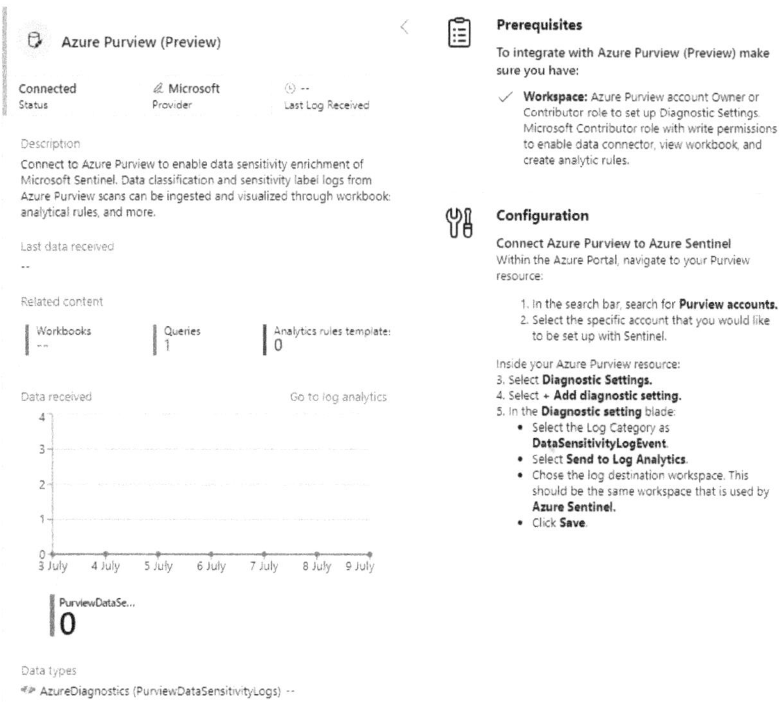

Figure 11.5: Data connector page

d. Click on **Launch Azure Policy Assignment Wizard**. On the **Basics** tab, select the **Subscription** and **Resource group**. This will be the subscription on which Microsoft Sentinel is configured.

e. Click on **Parameters**. Set the **Primary Log Analytics workspace**. This should be the workspace where you installed the Microsoft Sentinel solution in *Step 1*.

f. Select **Review + create** and click on **Create**.

Custom connectors

In addition to out of the box data connectors, Microsoft Sentinel allows you to create custom connectors using one of the methods listed. You can use a custom connector if you are unable to connect your data source using the built-in connectors, as follows:

- **Codeless Connector Platform (CCP)**: This method does not require deep technical expertise and can be used to create SaaS connectors using a configuration file. It supports all capabilities available with the code.

- **Log Analytics agent**: This method is used to collect files from on-premises and IaaS sources.

- **Logstash**: This method is used to collect data from on-premises and IaaS sources for which a plugin is available.

- **Logic Apps**: This method is best for low-volume cloud data sources. It is codeless, expensive and provides limited flexibility.
- **PowerShell**: This method is best for prototyping and file collection.
- **Log Analytics API**: This method caters for unique collection requirements and is suitable for ISVs to implement integration. It supports all capabilities available with the code.
- **Azure Functions**: This method is best for high-volume cloud data sources. It caters for unique collection requirements and supports all capabilities available with the code.

In SIEM solutions, the most common form of CTI are **indicators of compromise (IoC)** and **indicators of attack (IoA)**. These threat indicators associate IP addresses, file hashes, domains etc. with known threat activity like phishing or malware.

Microsoft Sentinel offers the following connectors to import threat intelligence feeds:

- Microsoft Defender Threat Intelligence data connector
- Threat Intelligence **Trusted Automated eXchange of Intelligence Infromation (TAXII)**
- Threat Intelligence upload indicators API

Organizations can use any or all these connectors to import threat intelligence feeds.

Set up analytics rules

Once Microsoft Sentinel has been set up to collect data from the configured data sources, you need to keep investigating the data to detect security threats. For this, Microsoft Sentinel offers analytics rules that run regularly to query and analyze the data to discover threats. There are three types of rules available discussed in this section.

Scheduled analytics rules

These are the most common type of rules and are based on **Kusto queries**. They are configured to run periodically, and they query raw data from a specified period. If the number of results captured exceeds the configured threshold an alert is generated. There are several rule templates available in Microsoft Sentinel. While it is possible to create a scheduled rule from scratch, it is highly recommended to use the out of the box rules templates to create your rules as the queries are written by security and data science experts from Microsoft or from the vendor that provides the solution. To view the analytics rule templates, following are the steps:

a. Login to **https://security.microsoft.com** and navigate to **Microsoft Sentinel** | **Configuration** | **Analytics**. In the right pane, click on **Rule templates**.

b. Click on a rule name to see its configuration as shown in *Figure 11.6*. You can click on the **Create rule** button to start the rule creation wizard. Review the settings and create the rule.

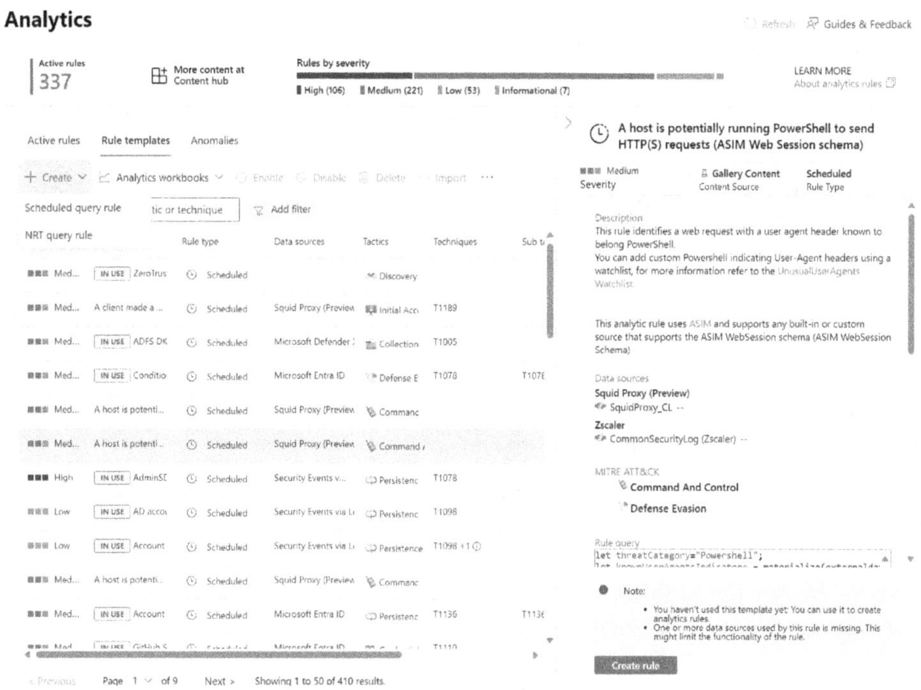

Figure 11.6: *Analytics rules*

c. Once the rule is turned on, it will appear on the **Active rules** tab in the above screen.

To create a rule from scratch, click on **Create | Scheduled query rule** in the screen above and follow the steps in the wizard.

There are additional capabilities available to enhance the quality of detections as follows:

- **Entity mapping**: Enriches the incidents and alerts generated by the rule with information that helps investigation and remediation. These **entities** are recognized by Microsoft Sentinel. Up to ten entities recognized by Microsoft Sentinel can be mapped in a rule. Some examples of entities are Account, Host, IP, URL. Attributes can be used as **identifiers** for each entity type. For example, Name, UPNSuffix, AadUserId are identifiers that can be used as attributes with the Account entity. Up to three identifiers can be mapped to an entity.

- **Custom event details in alerts**: Analytics rules analyze *events* from data sources connected to Microsoft Sentinel and generate alerts. These alerts are further analyzed and grouped into **incidents** which require investigation by a SOC team. However, when SOC team receives the incident, they do not see the information in the events. Getting this information requires them to do some digging. Using the custom details feature, the information from the events can be included in the alerts so that it is immediately visible to the SOC team, thus increasing speed and efficiency.

- **Customize alert details**: The first step while creating a rule is to give it a name, severity and selecting the MITRE ATT&CK tactic. All alerts generated by the rule inherit these details regardless of the nature of the alert. Using the alert details feature, you can override these settings as follows:

  o Creating custom names and descriptions for the alert by selecting fields in the alert query output whose contents can be included in the name and description of each alert.

  o Customize the severity and tactics with values of relevant fields from the query output.

All the settings are configured while creating the analytics rule on the **Set rule logic** page as shown in the following figure:

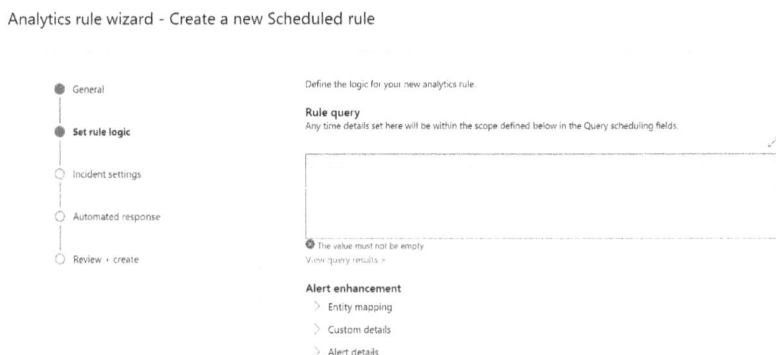

Figure 11.7: Customize analytics rules

Near-real-time analytics rules

Organizations today are faced with hundreds of threats every minute. It is therefore important that organizations respond to these threats quickly. Microsoft Sentinel's **near-real-time** (**NRT**) rules are a subset of the scheduled rules and are designed to run every minute to capture threats in events ingested in the preceding minute. These query the events ingestion time instead of the time they were generated at the source. To create NRT rule, click on **NRT query rule** in the above screen and follow the wizard to create the rule. All the customizations available with scheduled analytics rules like entity mapping, custom details and alert details are available with NRT rules.

Anomaly detection rules

These rules use machine learning to observe specific types of behavior over time to determine a baseline. Each rule has its own parameters and thresholds specific to the behavior being observed. Once the observation is complete, the baseline is set. Now, when the rule observes a behavior that deviates from the baseline, the behavior is flagged as anomalous. Anomalies do not necessarily indicate malicious behavior; hence these rules do not generate alerts, but they can be used to improve detections, investigations and threat hunting by providing additional signals and evidence during investigations. Threat hunters can use anomalies as a starting point for proactive threat hunting.

There are out of the box anomaly templates available with Microsoft Sentinel. These are activated by default and cannot be edited or deleted. To customize a rule, you must create a duplicate of the rule and then edit the duplicate.

The anomaly rules can be accessed by clicking on **Anomalies** tab as shown in the following figure:

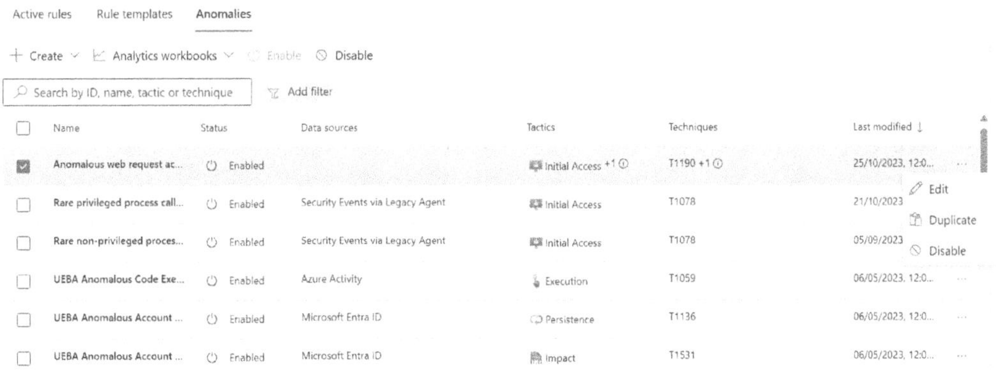

Figure 11.8: Anomalies

Set up automation rules

SOC teams are bombarded with hundreds of alerts every day. This can lead to the SOC teams being overwhelmed with the amount of information and they may end up ignoring or missing important alerts. Many alerts and incidents can be addressed with a standard set of responses and remediation actions. These actions can be automated that can take the load off the SOC team so that they can focus on more important and critical alerts.

Microsoft Sentinel offers automation rules that allow SOC analysts to automatically handle incidents from a central location. They can be used to manage and orchestrate threat responses to improve the effectiveness and efficiency of the SOC teams. Using automation rules, SOC analysts can automatically assign, tag or close an incident, automate responses for multiple rules with a single click, create lists of tasks that should be performed while triaging, investigating and remediating incidents and much more.

An automation rule has three components as follows:

- **Triggers** are events that cause an automation rule to be executed.

- **Conditions** determine the circumstances under which the rule will be run.

- **Actions** change the incident in some way like updating, closing or tagging or calling a playbook.

Designing an automation rule is a three-step process as follows:

a. **Determine the scope**: The first step in designing an automation rule is to determine which incident and alerts you want it to apply to. You might want to create tasks for SOC teams to follow in investigating incidents, suppress noisy incidents, or tag, escalate or resolve incidents.

b. **Determine the trigger**: Automation rules can be triggered when an incident is created or updated or when an alert is created.

c. **Create the rule**: The final step is to create the rule. Following are the steps to create the rule:

   i. Login to **https://security.microsoft.com** and navigate to **Microsoft Sentinel | Configuration | Automation**. In the right pane, click on **Create | Automation rule**.

   ii. In the fly out pane, give the rule a name, choose the trigger when you want to run the rule and the action you want it to take.

   The following figure is an example of an automation rule designed to assign an owner when a high severity incident is created:

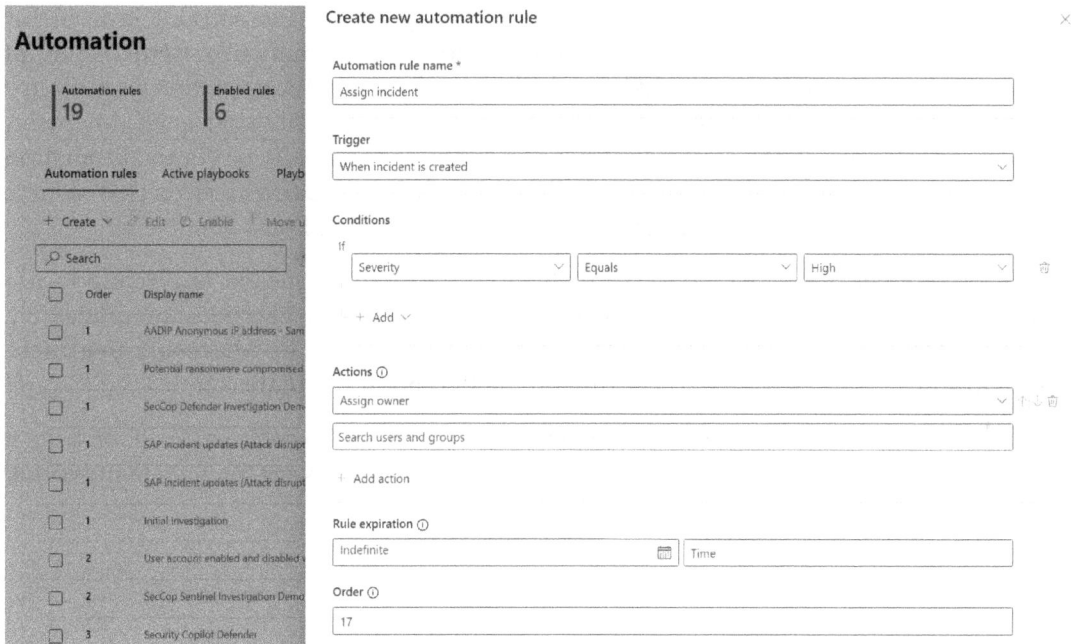

Figure 11.9: Create automation rule

Set up playbooks

Microsoft Sentinel offers playbooks that can run a preconfigured set of actions to automate and orchestrate the threat response. The playbooks can be run automatically in response to a specific alert. For example, if a user account is confirmed compromised, the playbook can block the user account in Entra ID.

Microsoft Sentinel playbooks run on Azure Logic Apps and can be used to enrich the data set, sync with other ticketing systems like ServiceNow, orchestrate and respond to security incidents with minimal human intervention.

One of the following roles is required to use Logic Apps to create and run playbooks in Microsoft Sentinel:

- **Owner**: Lets you grant access to playbooks in the resource group.
- **Logic App Contributor**: Manage logic apps and run playbooks but cannot grant access to the playbooks.
- **Logic App Operator**: Read, enable and disable logic apps but cannot edit or update.
- **Microsoft Sentinel Contributor**: Attach a playbook to an automation or analytics rule.
- **Microsoft Sentinel Responder**: Run a playbook from within an incident.
- **Microsoft Sentinel Playbook Operator**: Run the playbook manually.

Microsoft Sentinel uses a service account to run playbooks. This account is used for playbooks triggered by incidents or when a playbook is run manually from within an incident. This service account should have the Microsoft Sentinel Automation Contributor role on the resource group that contains playbooks. Once this role is granted, Microsoft Sentinel can run any playbook in the resource group either manually or via an automation rule. To grant this role to the service account, you must have the **Owner** role on the resource group in Azure or **User Access Administrator** role in Microsoft Entra ID.

Microsoft Sentinel offers playbook templates that are prebuilt, tested and ready-to-use workflows. Administrators can use them to create playbooks. Playbook templates are accessible from the Microsoft Defender portal by navigating to **Microsoft Sentinel | Configuration | Automation** and clicking on the **Playbook templates** tab.

The following figure shows the available playbook templates. To create a playbook from a template, click on the template name and in the right pane, click on the **Create playbook** button:

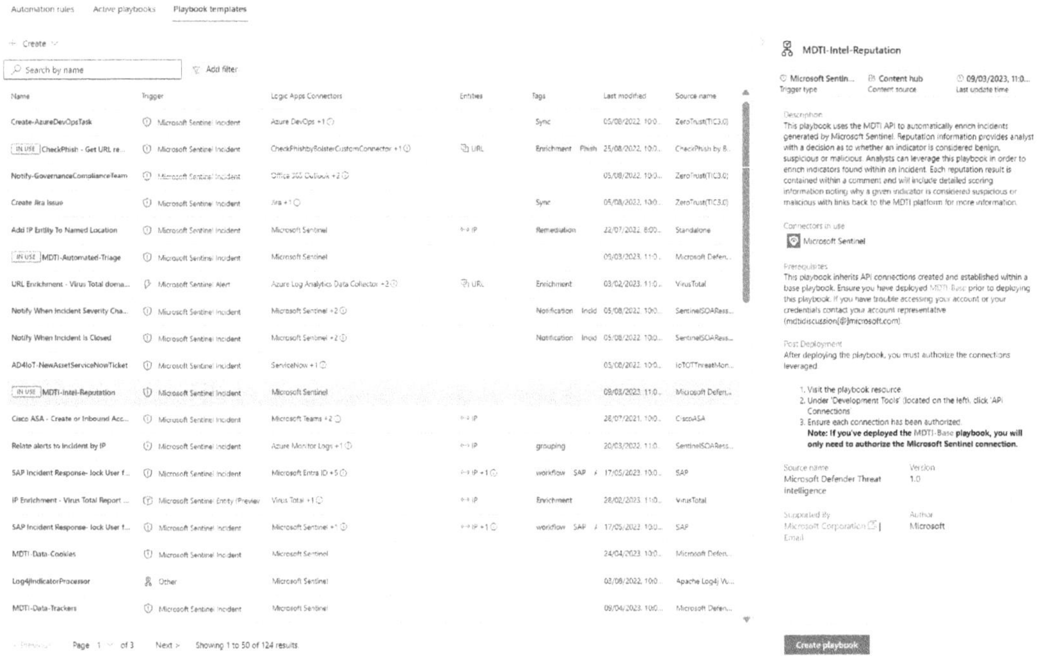

Figure 11.10: Playbook templates

The **Active playbooks** tab on this page displays all the playbooks currently active in the environment.

Set up watchlists

Administrators might want to watch some assets more closely than others. For example, high-value servers, accounts of terminated or executive employees or service accounts.

Watchlists offer a way to correlate data from these data sources to the events received in the Microsoft Sentinel environment. Watchlists can be used in searches, detection rules, threat hunting and playbooks. They are stored as name-value pairs in Microsoft Sentinel.

Following are a few scenarios where watchlists can help:

- Investigate threats and respond to incidents by importing IP addresses or file hashes. This imported data can be used to filter alerts rules.

- Import users with privileged access or terminated employees. Use this to create allow or block lists to allow or prevent these users from logging in.

- Allowlists can be used to suppress alerts from some users or IP addresses. This will prevent benign events from becoming incidents.

- Enrich event data with name-value combinations.

Watchlist can be uploaded to Microsoft Sentinel in the form of .csv files from a local folder or an Azure storage account.

Following are the steps to create a watchlist:

a. Login to **https://security.microsoft.com** and navigate to **Microsoft Sentinel | Configuration | Watchlist**.

b. Microsoft Sentinel offers Watchlist templates that you can use to create your watchlists. Click on **Templates (Preview)** to view a list of available templates. Select the name of the template you want and click on **Create from template** as shown in the following figure:

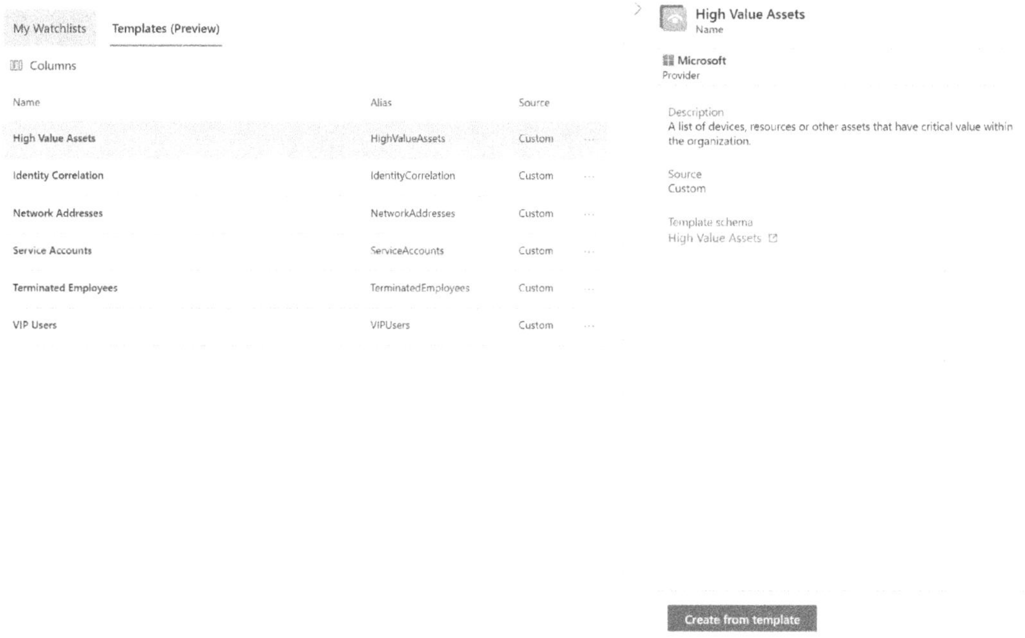

Figure 11.11: Create watchlist from template

c. Accept defaults on the **General** page and click on **Next: Source**.

d. On the **Source** page, click on **Download schema** to download a sample of the required `.csv` file. Make the necessary changes to the file and upload the file and click **Next: Review + Create** as shown in the following figure:

Download schema   View template schema

Upload file *   High Value Assets.csv

                                       Drag and drop the files or Browse for files

SearchKey *   Asset FQDN

Reset

File preview | First 50 rows and first 5 columns

Asset Type	Asset Id	Asset Name	Asset FQDN	IP Address	Tags
PC	12234	Computer1	Computer1.cont...	10.1.1.20	
Laptop	34567	Computer2	Computer2.cont...	10.1.1.50	

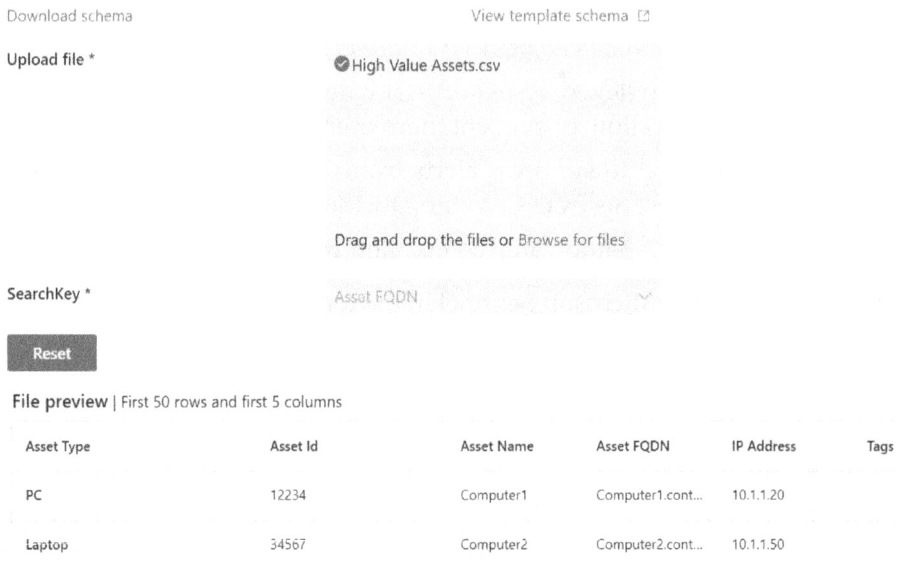

Figure 11.12: Watchlist source

e. In the **Review + create** screen, review the settings and click on **Create** to create the watchlist.

You can also create a watchlist from scratch without using the available templates. To do that, just click on **New** on the **My Watchlists** page to launch the watchlist creation wizard. You can also edit or delete watchlists from this page as shown in the following figure:

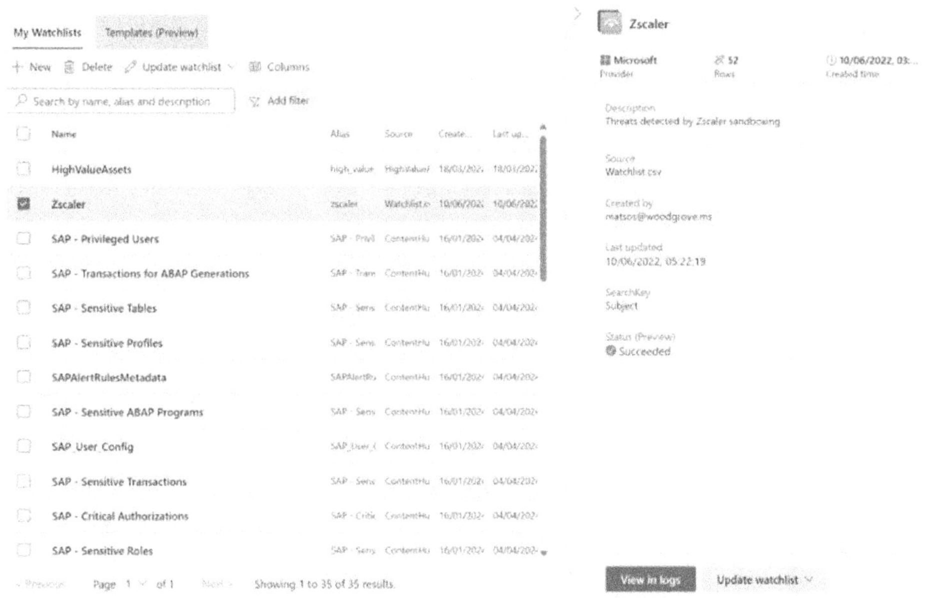

Figure 11.13: My Watchlists

To use a watchlist in a search query, you will have to use a Kusto query with the `_GetWatchlist(watchlist-name)` function and use the **SearchKey** as shown in *Figure 11.12*, for the join. To do so, select to the watchlist in the **My Watchlists** page and click **View in logs** in the right pane. This will take you to the **Advanced hunting** page. Write the query here and click on **Run query**.

Watchlists can also be used in analytics rules using the `_GetWatchlist(watchlist-name)` function in the **Rule query**.

Visualize data

Once the data sources have been connected and Microsoft Sentinel begins to receive data from the sources, you can use the **Overview** page to view, monitor and analyze activities.

The following figure shows a snapshot of the **Overview** page. Review the different widgets and the data displayed:

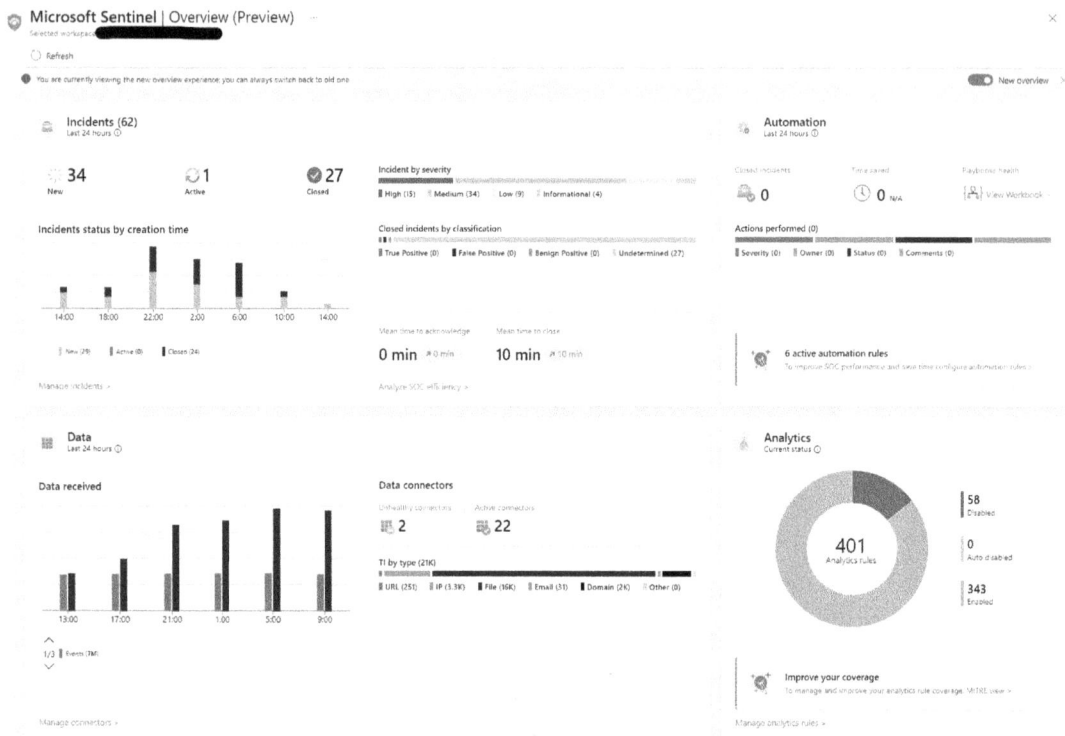

Figure 11.14: Visualize data

Workbooks

In addition to this **Overview** page, you can also create customized dashboards called **Workbooks**. Several workbook templates are available as a part of solutions or standalone content in the content hub. To use a workbook template, install the solution that contains the workbook or the standalone workbook from the content hub. You must have the **Workbook reader** or the **Workbook contributor** permission on the resource group that contains the Microsoft Sentinel workspace.

Microsoft Sentinel workbooks are based on Azure Monitor workbooks and like any other Azure resource permissions can be assigned to them to limit access.

Following are the steps to create a workbook using a workbook template:

1. Install the solution that contains the workbook or the standalone workbook from the content hub.

2. In the Microsoft Defender portal, navigate to **Microsoft Sentinel | Threat management | Workbooks**. In the right pane click on **Templates** to see the templates installed in the previous step.

3. Select the workbook name that you want to use and in the flyout pane, click on **Save**. Select the location where you want to save the workbook and click on **Yes** as shown in the following figure:

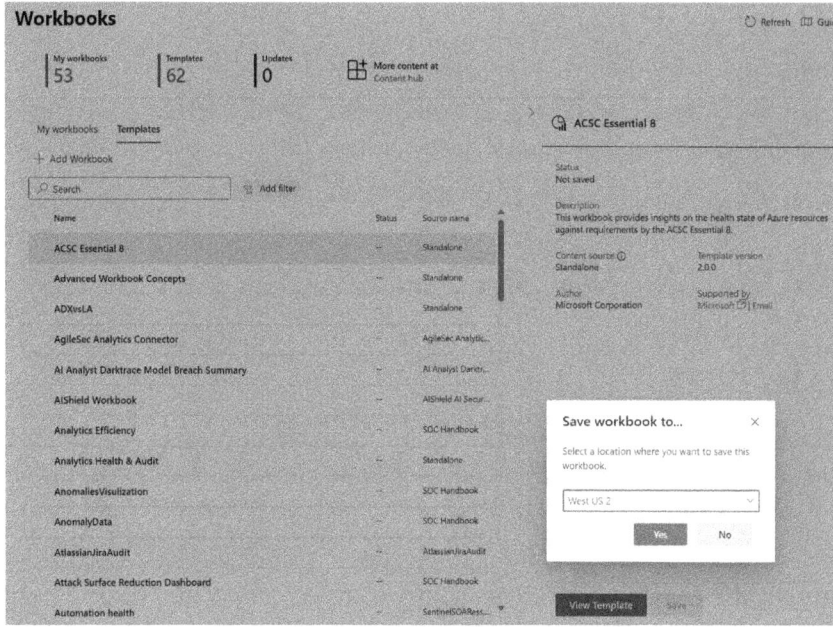

Figure 11.15: Save workbook template

4. Click on the **My workbooks** tab and select the workbook just saved. In the flyout pane, click on **View saved workbook**. The workbook will open in a new window. Click on **Edit** to customize the workbook as per your requirements. Once done, click on the save icon as shown in the following figure:

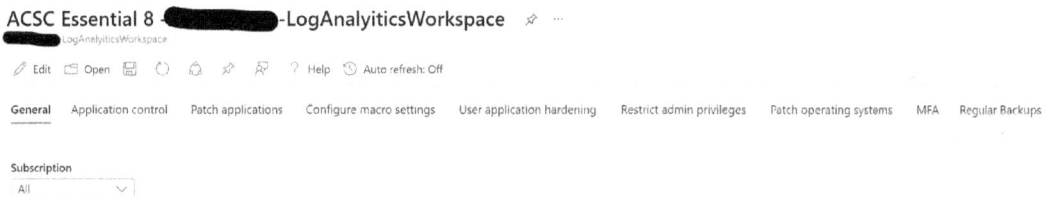

Figure 11.16: Edit a workbook

You can also create a workbook from scratch by clicking on **Add workbook** as shown in *Figure 11.15*.

Power BI

Another option to visualize Microsoft Sentinel data is to use Power BI which is a rich reporting and analysis tool that turns data into immersive and interactive visualizations. It can connect to various data sources and discover relationships. It is a perfect tool to make threat data available to management.

Following are the high-level steps to generate a Power BI report using Microsoft Sentinel as the source:

1. Create a query in Microsoft Sentinel using KQL.
2. Export the query from Microsoft Sentinel in the Power BI M query format.
3. Open Power BI desktop and run the exported query to get the data.
4. Now that you have the data in Power BI, you can create visualizations.
5. Create a Power BI workspace and share it with the stakeholders.
6. You can schedule data refresh from Microsoft Sentinel.

Hunt threats

Security analysts and researchers want to be proactive in looking for threats in the environment. However, the various security systems generate enormous amounts of data making it very difficult to translate them into meaningful information. Microsoft Sentinel offers powerful hunting and query tools to proactively look for anomalies in the data.

Using **Hunts** in Microsoft Sentinel, security researchers can look for undetected threats and malicious behavior by creating a hypothesis, searching data, validating the hypothesis and taking action when required.

Using hunts, you can perform the following activities:

- Proactively hunt for threats to gain early insights into events that might show a bad actor in the environment. It can also point to the potential vulnerabilities that need addressing.
- During a compromise, livestream can be used to actively monitor user events to confirm if a compromise is still taking place.
- After an incident to ensure that security coverage has been improved so that future incidents can be prevented.

Hunting queries can be accessed from the Microsoft Defender portal by navigating to **Microsoft Sentinel | Threat management | Hunting**. In the right pane, select the **Queries** tab. This page shows all queries that were installed with security solutions from the **Content hub** and the ones that were manually created. Each query provides a description of what it does and the MITRE ATT&CK tactics and techniques. A single or multiple queries can be run by selecting them and clicking on **Run selected queries** option as shown below. Click on **New query** to create a custom query. Refer to *Figure 11.17*:

Note: Hunting queries are written in KQL which is beyond the scope of this book.

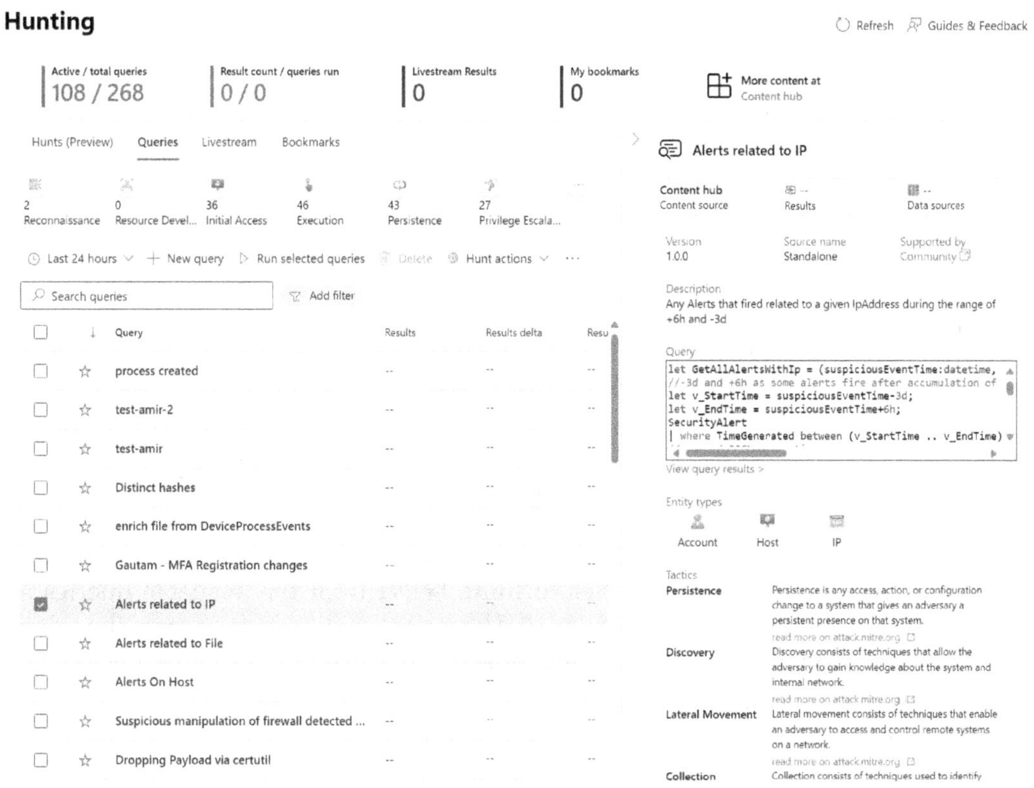

Hunting

Figure 11.17: Hunting queries

To perform an end-to-end hunt, following are the steps:

1. Define a hypothesis first. A hypothesis is open ended and flexible. Most used hypotheses are suspicious behavior, a new threat campaign or a detection gap.

2. Use a **Hunt** to prove or disprove the hypothesis. In *Figure 11.17*, click on **Hunts (Preview)**, and then on **New hunt**. Fill in the details and click on **Create** as shown in the following figure:

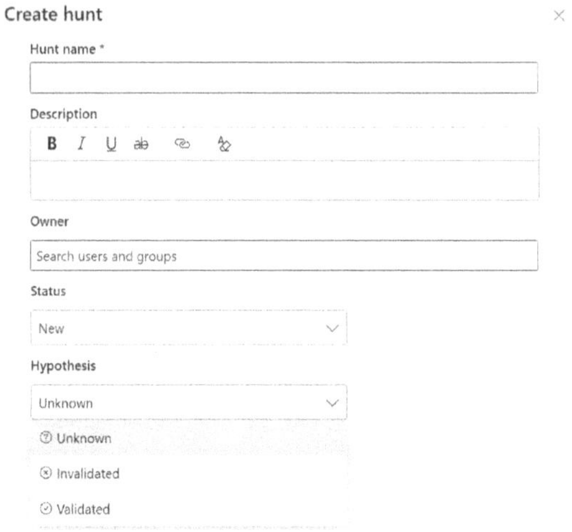

Figure 11.18: Create a new hunt

3. The next step is to add queries to the hunt. Click on the newly created hunt and click on **Actions | Add queries to hunt**. Select from the available queries and click on **Add** as shown in *Figure 11.19*. The queries will be cloned from the original location and will be specific to this hunt. You can modify or delete them without impacting the original query.

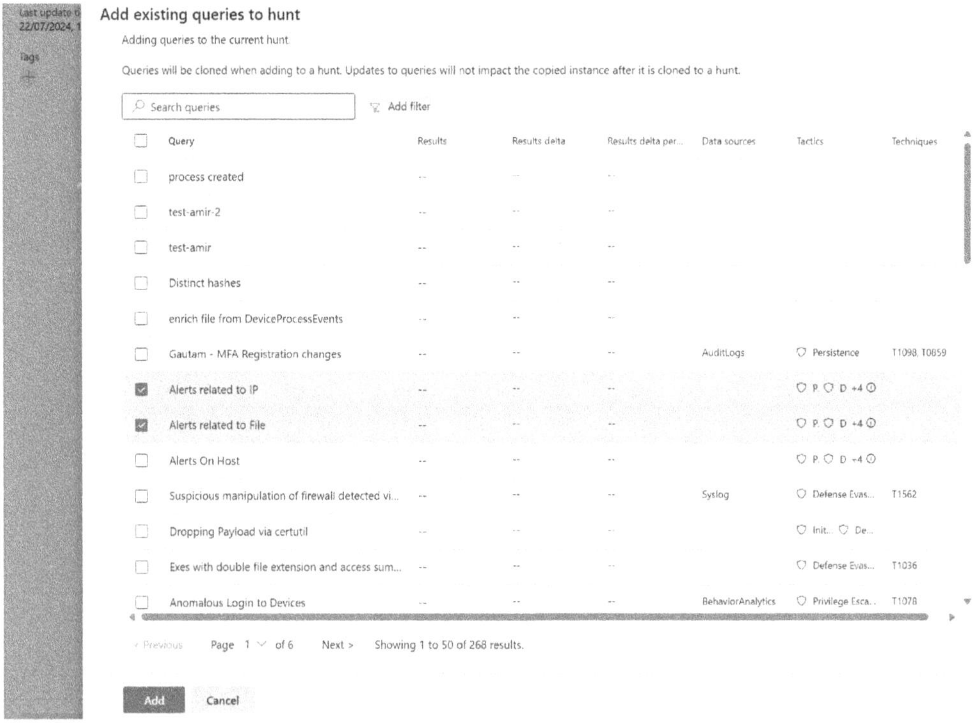

Figure 11.19: Add queries to hunt

4. Run the queries by selecting the query and clicking on **Run query**.

5. If you find results that are meaningful or interesting, you can bookmark them by selecting the desired rows and clicking on **Add a bookmark**. The bookmarks are available on the **Bookmark** tab, and they help preserve queries and results that are relevant for your investigation. Contextual observations can be recorded by adding notes and tags to bookmarks.

6. If you find evidence of suspicious activity that needs to be investigated, create an incident by selecting **Actions | Create incident** as shown in the following figure:

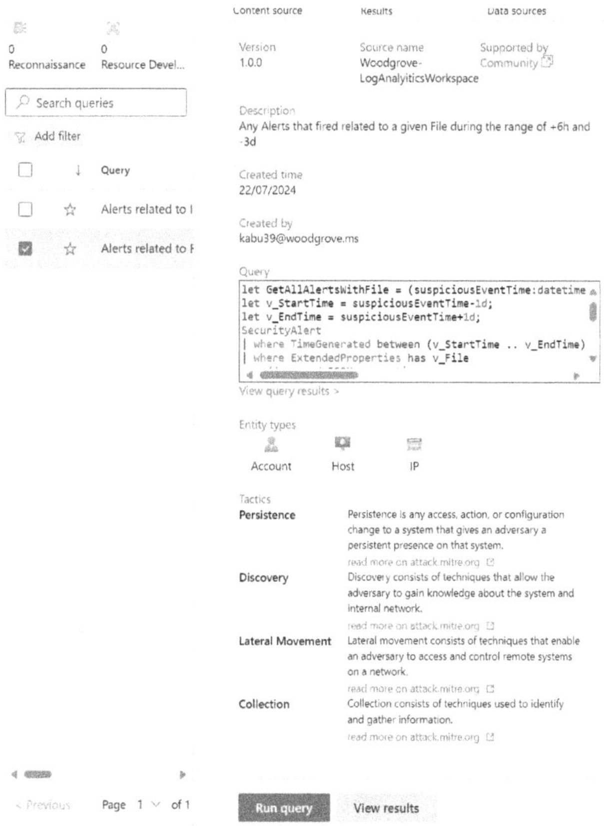

Figure 11.20: Run the query

7. In the right pane, click on **View results**.

8. All entities found by the queries in the hunt are listed on the **Entities** page in the hunt. Actions like running a playbook or adding to TI can be done from this page.

9. Once you have enough information to validate or invalidate your hypothesis, change the status and state of the hypothesis by opening the hypothesis and selecting the appropriate options.

Livestreams

Hunting livestream helps you create interactive sessions to test queries. You can get notifications and launch investigations as incidents occur and match the query created. Following are the steps to create a livestream session:

1. Login to **https://security.microsoft.com** and navigate to **Microsoft Sentinel | Threat management | Hunting**.

2. In the right pane, click on the **Queries** pane. Right click on the required query and select **Add to livestream**. The livestream will be visible on the **Livestream** tab.

Notebooks

Microsoft Sentinel offers Jupyter Notebooks as a tool for security investigation and hunting. Jupyter Notebooks are an open-source tool that supports interactive code execution, rich media integration and data visualization. Microsoft Sentinel relies on its data store that it accesses using an API. This same API is available for external tools like Jupyter Notebooks which extends the scope of what this data can be used for. For example, notebooks can be used to perform analytics and create visualizations that are not provided out-of-the-box by Microsoft or integrate with data sources that are outside of Microsoft Sentinel. The Jupyter experience is integrated with Microsoft Sentinel to simplify the creation and usage of notebooks for data analysis. The `Kqlmagic` library allows you to take KQL queries from Microsoft Sentinel and run them directly inside a notebook.

Notebooks are accessible from the Microsoft Defender portal by navigating to **Microsoft Sentinel | Notebooks**. There are several templates available to get started. Click on the **Create from template** button to customize the notebook for your environment as shown in the following figure:

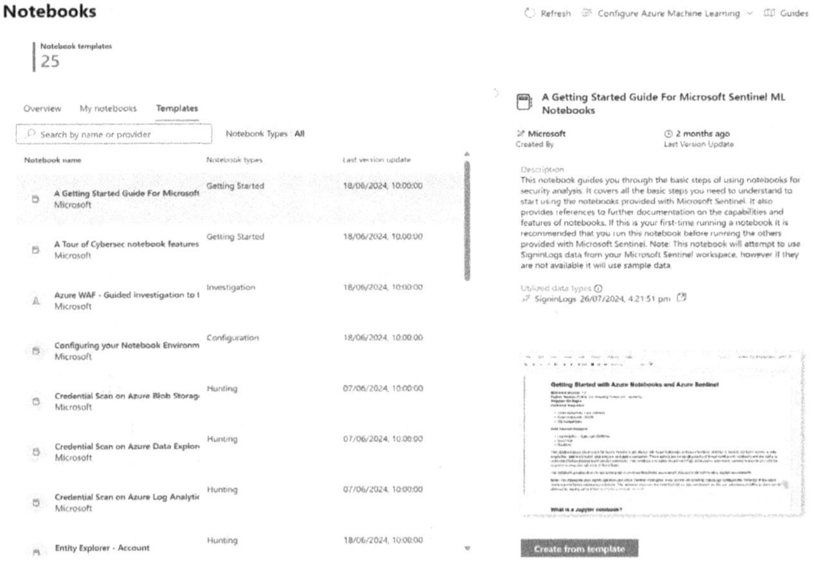

Figure 11.21: Notebooks

Create and investigate incidents

Alerts created in Microsoft Sentinel from connected data sources do not automatically generate incidents. When a Microsoft solution is connected to Microsoft Sentinel, any alerts generated by that incident are stored in the **SecurityAlert** table in the Microsoft Sentinel workspace.

The most common method of generating incidents for Microsoft security solutions is using the data connector. While configuring the data connector, simply click on **Enable** next to **Create incidents** and enable the default analytics rule to create incidents automatically. The rule can then be edited by going to **Active rules** under **Analytics** as shown in the following figure:

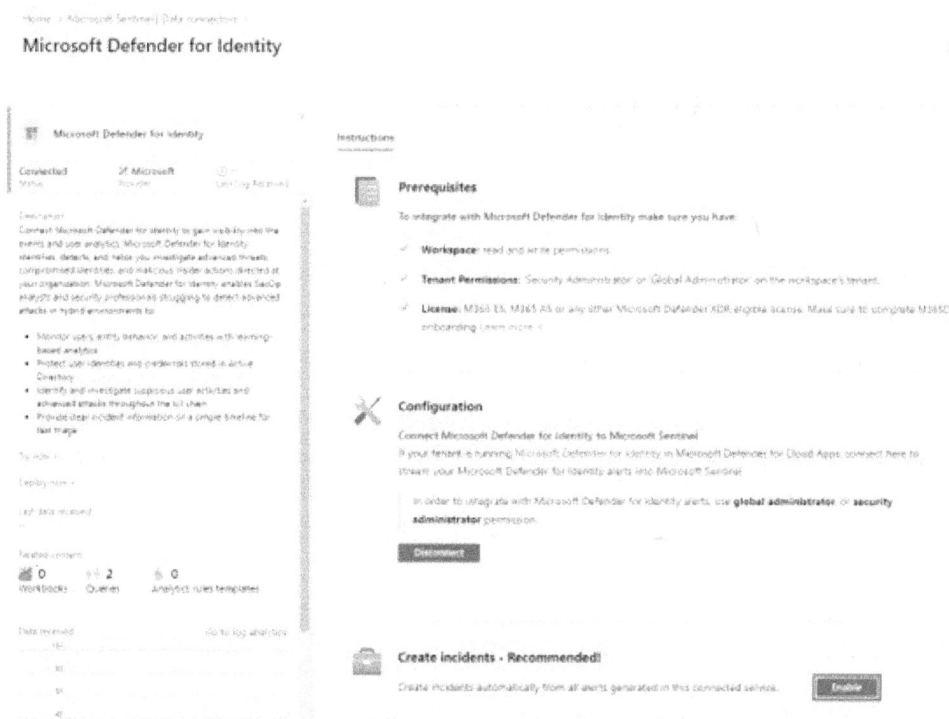

Figure 11.22: Create incidents for Microsoft security solutions

Incidents can also be created using analytics rules discussed in the previous section. Use the available rule templates to customize and create incidents as per your requirements.

Incidents in Microsoft Sentinel are used to refer to case files that contain the complete set of alerts, entities and insights related to a particular event. The incidents can be enriched by adding comments or tags. All actions taken by security teams to investigate and respond to the event are also added to the incident.

Microsoft Sentinel incidents can be investigated in the Microsoft Defender XDR portal by navigating to the **Incidents** page and filtering by **Microsoft Sentinel** as the product source.

Conclusion

This chapter introduced the concepts of SIEM and SOAR. You should now be able to understand and explain the difference between these two important security management concepts. You should now be able to plan, design and implement a Microsoft Sentinel environment for your organization's SOC teams. You should be able to articulate the difference between the different types of rules available in Microsoft Sentinel and when to use them. You should be able to use Workbooks and Power BI to create visualizations for different stakeholders. The chapter also explained how to automate incident response using automation rules and playbooks and hunt threats proactively using hunts and notebooks.

In the next chapter, we will discuss how you can protect and govern sensitive data using the capabilities in Microsoft Purview.

Multiple choice questions

1. **What is the primary function of Microsoft Sentinel?**
    a. To manage email communications
    b. To detect cyber threats, facilitate investigations, respond to incidents, and proactively hunt for dangers
    c. To create and edit documents
    d. To manage financial transactions

2. **Your organization decided to use Microsoft Sentinel for their SIEM and SOAR needs. You have been tasked with designing the solution. Your organization has an existing Azure subscription. What is the first thing you should do?**
    a. Create a new Azure subscription for Microsoft Sentinel
    b. Configure connectors in Microsoft Sentinel
    c. Create a new Log Analytics workspace for Microsoft Sentinel
    d. Add the Microsoft Sentinel solution to an existing Log Analytics workspace

3. **You organization wants to use the SOAR capabilities of Microsoft Sentinel to respond to incidents. What capabilities does Microsoft Sentinel offer in this space? Select all that apply.**
    a. Analytics rules
    b. Automation rules
    c. Workbooks
    d. Playbooks

Answer key

1. b   2. c   3. b, d

CHAPTER 12

Protect and Govern Sensitive Data

Introduction

Data stands as the most valuable asset for any organization. In the modern era, data is ubiquitous. Many organizations struggle with identifying sensitive data within their environment, determining its location, and understanding who has access to it. Additionally, there is a critical need to safeguard this data against unauthorized access and data breaches. Proper disposal of data after its business utility, while remaining compliant with industry standards, is another crucial responsibility. Given the vast amount of data, executing these tasks manually is infeasible. Organizations require robust tools to accomplish these tasks effectively and on a large scale. This chapter introduces Microsoft Purview and outlines how it helps organizations discover, protect, and manage their sensitive data at scale.

Structure

The chapter covers the following topics:

- Microsoft Purview
- Data security and governance
- Know your data
- Protect your data
- Prevent data loss

- Govern your data
- Gain visibility

Objectives

By the end of this chapter, readers will have an overview of Microsoft Purview product suite, followed by an in-depth examination of its data protection and governance features. We will explore how Microsoft Purview Information Protection aids organizations in detecting and safeguarding sensitive information both on-premises and within the Microsoft 365 cloud environment. The content further delves into how Microsoft Purview Data Loss Prevention assists in monitoring and averting accidental or unauthorized data leakage. Additionally, we will discuss Microsoft Data Lifecycle Management and records management and their significance in retaining and disposing of sensitive information to comply with regulatory and compliance standards. By the end, you should be equipped to design, configure, and implement a comprehensive data security and governance strategy for your organization.

Microsoft Purview

Microsoft Purview is a suite of solutions designed to help organizations govern, protect, and manage data, no matter where it resides or moves. It consolidates Microsoft tools for data security, risk, and compliance, formerly Microsoft 365 Compliance and data governance, previously Azure Purview, under the unified brand name **Microsoft Purview**, making data security and governance simpler for customers. These solutions enable organizations to gain insight into their data across the digital landscape, safeguard and manage sensitive data throughout its lifecycle, address risks associated with data and meet regulatory compliance standards.

Figure 12.1 shows the individual products that comprise Microsoft Purview:

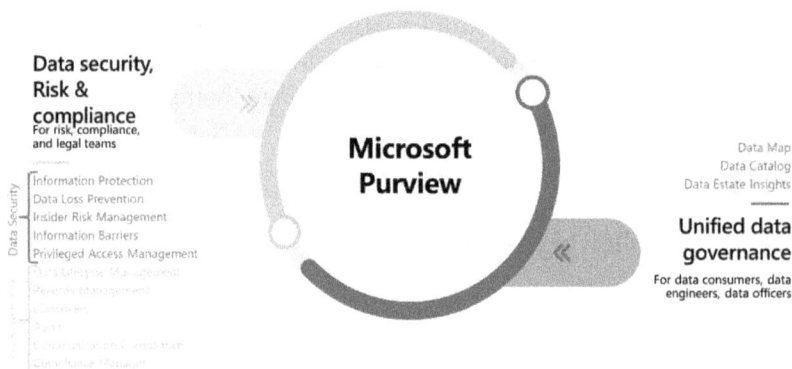

Figure 12.1: Microsoft Purview products

Microsoft Purview has its own portal from where all the above products can be configured and administered. This portal is available at **https://purview.microsoft.com**.

Before we explore the solutions, let us understand some concepts that are common to all and will be key in understanding the solutions.

Role-based access control

Microsoft Purview implements its own role-based access control that allows users detailed permissions within the Microsoft Purview solutions. In Microsoft Purview, permissions are organized into role groups. Each role group encompasses a set of related roles. Users are assigned to these role groups instead of individual roles. Once assigned to a role group, users inherit all roles included in that group. In certain scenarios, these role groups might grant more permissions than necessary. Administrators have the option to create custom role groups, incorporating only the required permissions, and subsequently assign users to these custom role groups.

> **Note: Describing each role and role group is beyond the scope of this book. The reader is advised to refer to the Microsoft documentation for details.**

These roles groups are available in the Microsoft Purview portal by clicking on **Settings** and navigating to **Roles and scopes** | **Role groups**.

The following figure shows some of the available roles in Microsoft Purview. To create a new role group, click on **Create role group**:

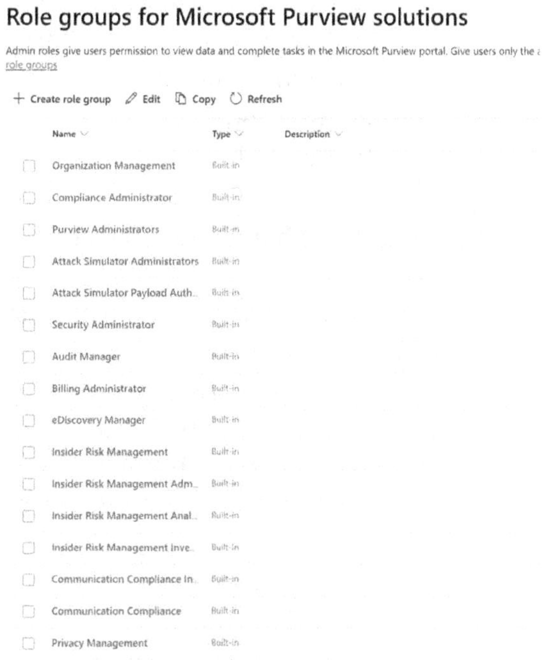

Figure 12.2: Role groups for Microsoft Purview solutions

Adaptive scopes

When creating a policy in Microsoft Purview, you will need to select a scope. This scope comprises groups or user accounts, mailboxes, or SharePoint sites that the policy will cover. Administrators must manually identify and define this list within the policy. Managing this can be complex as users transition between roles or geographies, necessitating frequent policy updates. For example, if you have a policy for all users in the legal department, you would include all members of the legal team in the policy scope. When a user transfers from the legal department to the finance department, they must be manually removed from the initial policy and added to another. This process becomes cumbersome when there are hundreds of user changes daily.

Adaptive scope makes this easy by automating these user changes. They use a query to determine the users, M365 groups or SharePoint sites that will be included in the scope. These queries run daily so that the scope remains current. For example, you can define an adaptive scope to include all users whose **Department** attribute in Entra ID is **Legal.** When the user moves from the Legal department to the Finance department and their **Department** attribute is updated, they are automatically removed from this scope. Consequently, any policy using this scope is also updated.

Currently, adaptive scopes are available to use with Data Lifecycle Management, records management and communication compliance solutions.

Following are the steps to create an adaptive scope:

1. Login to the Microsoft Purview portal by clicking on **Settings** and navigating to **Roles and scopes | Adaptive scopes.** Click on **Create scope.**

2. Give the scope a name and description and click **Next.**

3. Select the **Entra ID Administrative Unit** you would like to include in this scope and click **Next.** Administrative units have been discussed in *Chapter 3, Identity Management.*

4. Define the scope type as **Users, SharePoint sites** or **Microsoft 365 Groups** and click **Next.**

5. Depending on the selection you made in the previous step, you can define the attributes for the objects to be included in this scope.

   Figure 12.3 shows an example of a user scope that includes all users whose Entra ID **Department** attribute is **Legal.** You can build complex queries by adding more attributes or by using the **Advanced query builder.** Click **Next** once done.

Figure 12.3: Defining query in adaptive scope

6. Review the settings and click on **Submit** to create the scope.

Data security and governance

Before we begin, it is important to understand the data lifecycle. Every artifact created, be it an email or a file, has a lifecycle that starts from the time it is created and ends once it is safely disposed of.

Following figure shows the data lifecycle from creation till deletion:

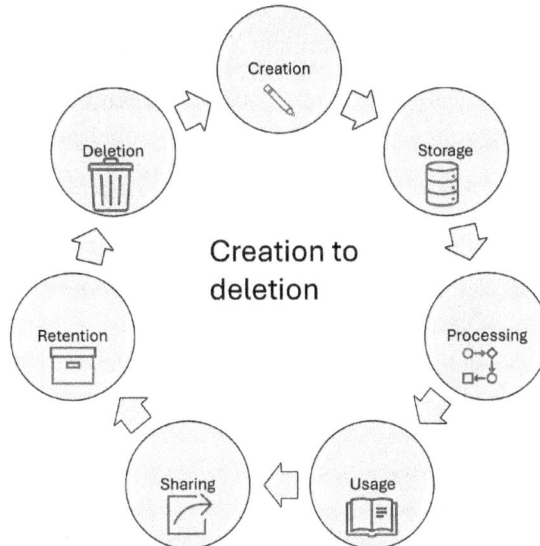

Figure 12.4: Data lifecycle

There are risks associated with each stage in the data lifecycle. Some of them are as follows:

- **Creation**: Data is created every day by users and stored in different locations. These could range from corporate OneDrive accounts to personal file sharing services like DropBox or from a network file share to a local hard drive on a computer. Most organizations lack visibility of the data that is being created by workers every day. They do not know where the data created is stored or if it has sensitive information.

- **Storage**: Since organizations do not have visibility of the data created and stored, they may be unable to apply security controls to adequately protect the content.

- **Processing**: Regulatory requirements state how and where the data is processed. For example, **European Union (EU) General Data Protection Regulation (GDPR)** specifies that the data of EU citizens be processed with the EU geographical boundaries.

- **Usage**: There are significant regulatory requirements around usage of data. Regulations demand that sensitive customer data be used in accordance with the data privacy requirements laid out by the country or industry that the organization operates in.

- **Sharing**: Organizations need visibility into how the data is being shared. They need to know if sensitive content is shared with unauthorized parties.

- **Retention**: Business requirements and regulatory requirements can require retaining certain content for a specified period. Organizations need to apply specific controls to be able to protect business critical content from accidental or intentional deletion.

- **Deletion**: Several regulations require safe disposal of sensitive content once it has served its business purpose. Organizations need tools to do this at scale.

Based on this, the challenges faced by organizations throughout the lifecycle of data can be summed up in four stages.

Figure 12.5 shows the four stages along with the tasks organizations must do to protect data and the Microsoft Purview solution that provides the tools to accomplish the tasks:

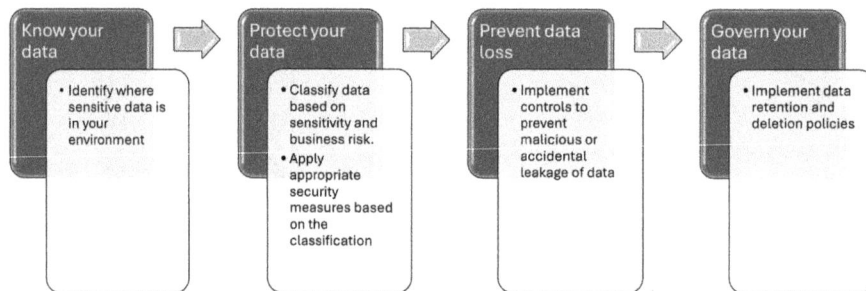

Figure 12.5: Stages of data security and governance

Before we can discover sensitive information, it is important to determine what is meant by sensitive information. This is different for different organizations. For a financial institution, customers financial records might be sensitive, for a hospital patient record might be sensitive and for an educational institution student records might be sensitive. To identify sensitive information Microsoft Purview uses **sensitive information types (SITs)** and **trainable classifiers (TCs)**.

Sensitive information types

SITs are pattern-based classifiers. They detect sensitive information like passport numbers, credit card numbers, driving license numbers or bank account numbers to help identify sensitive documents. Microsoft Purview has more than 300 SITs available by default.

SIT has four primary components, as follows:

- **Primary element**: This is the sensitive information you are looking for. It can be a regular expression with or without a checksum validation, a keyword list, a keyword dictionary or a function.

- **Supporting element**: This is a piece of information that serves as supporting evidence. For example, when looking for credit card information the words **credit card number**, **CC**, **CC No.** etc. when found in proximity of the primary element, could serve as supporting elements. This results in higher confidence that the 16-digit number detected is indeed a credit card number.

- **Confidence level**: There are three confidence levels with respect to detected matches, that is, high, medium and low. These reflect how much supporting evidence was found with the primary element.

- **Proximity**: This defines how close the supporting element should be to the primary element. This is defined in terms of the number of characters between them.

Built in SITs

These are SITs pre-created and configured by Microsoft and they show up in the Purview portal by default. These are based on regex patterns, keywords and keyword dictionaries cannot be modified. They can be used as templates to create new SITs by copying and then editing the copy. Some examples are driving license numbers, social security numbers, bank account numbers, credit card numbers etc.

Named entity SITs

These are also pre-created and configured by Microsoft and show up in the Purview portal by default. They use complex dictionaries and pattern-based classifiers to detect entities like names of people, physical addresses, medical terms etc. These cannot be copied or edited. Named entity SITs can be bundled or unbundled. **Unbundled** SITs have a narrower focus. For example, Australian physical addresses or US physical addresses. **Bundled** SITs, on the other hand, are a collection of related unbundled SITs. For example, all physical addresses that contain unbundled SITs like Australian physical addresses and US physical addresses. Named entity SITs are only available with one of the following licenses:

- Microsoft 365 E5
- Microsoft 365 E5 Compliance
- Microsoft 365 E5 Information Protection & Governance

SITs are available in the Purview portal by clicking on any of the **Information Protection, Data Loss Prevention, Data Lifecycle Management** or **records management** tiles. Navigate to **Classifiers | Sensitive info types**.

Custom SITs

Organizations have the flexibility to create their own SITs if the default ones do not work for them. For example, an organization might want to create SIT to detect employee numbers. To create a custom SIT, click on **Create sensitive info type** to launch the wizard. You will be taken through the steps to define patterns and rules to detect sensitive information.

Document fingerprinting

This feature converts a standard form into SIT making it easier to protect sensitive information in commonly used forms. For example, a bank might have an account opening form used by customers to open a bank account. The bank can create a document fingerprint based on a blank form. When a form is filled with information like names, addresses, phone numbers etc. it will be detected as containing the same pattern as the original form. Organizations can apply **data loss prevention (DLP)** policies to protect information in these forms. To create a document fingerprint, click on **Create Fingerprint based SIT**. You will have to upload a blank form and define the confidence thresholds to create SIT. Document fingerprinting is only available with one of the following licenses:

- Microsoft 365 E5
- Microsoft 365 E5 Compliance
- Microsoft 365 E5 Information Protection & Governance

Exact data match SIT

Exact data match (EDM) SITs are used to detect items that have exact values. For example, a bank might want to create EDM SIT to detect only the credit card numbers issued by them and not all credit card numbers that will be detected by using the built-in credit card number's SIT. To create an EDM SIT, you will have to upload a database containing the sensitive information into the Purview portal. This database can have 100 million rows of data and can be refreshed daily. EDMs are only available with one of the following licenses:

- Microsoft 365 E5
- Microsoft 365 E5 Compliance
- Microsoft 365 E5 Information Protection & Governance
- Office 365 E5

Trainable classifiers

This is a method of identifying sensitive information that cannot be easily identified using SITs. This method uses a classifier to identify an item based on what it is, rather than by the patterns it contains. These are **machine learning (ML)** algorithms that learn to identify content by looking at examples of the content to be detected. Microsoft Purview offers more than 100 pre-trained classifiers which cannot be edited or retrained. Built-in trainable classifiers are available in the Purview portal by clicking on any of the **Information Protection**, **Data Loss Prevention**, **Data Lifecycle Management** or **records management** tiles. Navigate to **Classifiers | Trainable classifiers**. Some commonly used classifiers are bank statements, business plans, employment agreements and financial audit reports. In addition to the built-in ones, organizations can create their own custom classifiers by providing between 50 and 500 positive and negative samples. Trainable classifiers are only available with one of the following licenses:

- Microsoft 365 E5
- Microsoft 365 E5 Compliance
- Microsoft 365 E5 Information Protection & Governance

Know your data

As is evident, the biggest challenge organizations face is knowing where sensitive information is stored. Microsoft Purview Information Protection helps discover sensitive content in unstructured data across the Microsoft 365 cloud and on-premises file shares and SharePoint servers. Formerly called **Microsoft Information Protection** (**MIP**), this capability enables organizations to discover, classify and protect sensitive information regardless of where it lives or travels.

Microsoft 365 cloud

Most organizations have the bulk of their content in the Microsoft 365 cloud in the form of emails, files on SharePoint online and OneDrive for Business and content in Microsoft Teams. Microsoft Purview Information Protection discovers the content in these locations by default without the need to configure any policies. The discovered content is displayed in the **Data Explorer** in the Microsoft Purview portal as shown in *Figure 12.6:*

Note: Both the built in and custom SITs and trainable classifiers are used to discover the sensitive content.

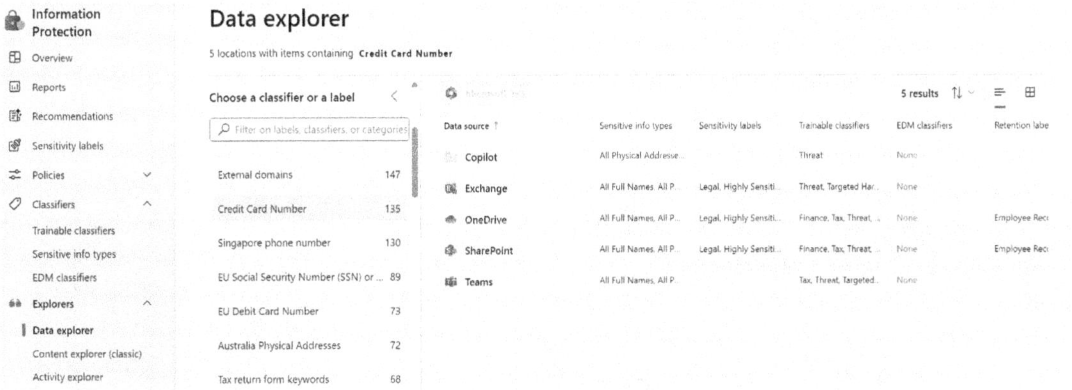

Figure 12.6: Data explorer

This feature requires one of the following licenses:

- M365 E5
- M365 E5 Compliance
- M365 E5 Information Protection & Governance

To be able to access the **Data explorer** tab, you must have one of the following Entra ID roles:

- Global Administrator
- Compliance Administrator
- Security Administrator
- Compliance Data Administrator

However, membership of these roles does not allow viewing the list of items or the content of items. This is highly restricted as the content is expected to contain sensitive information. To be able to view the list of items and content in items, following additional permissions are required:

- Content explorer list viewer
- Content explorer content viewer

On-premises

While the move to cloud is rapid, most organizations still have a large data footprint on-premises. These are mainly in the form of network file shares and SharePoint document libraries. Microsoft Purview Information Protection offers an on-premises scanner to discover, classify and protect files on network file shares that use the **Server Message Block** (**SMB**) protocol and SharePoint servers from SharePoint 2013 to SharePoint 2019. In this section, we will learn how we can use the on-premises scanner to discover files.

The information protection scanner runs as a service on a Windows Server and can inspect any file that Windows can index. It uses SITs to classify these files.

Following figure shows the scanner architecture at a high level:

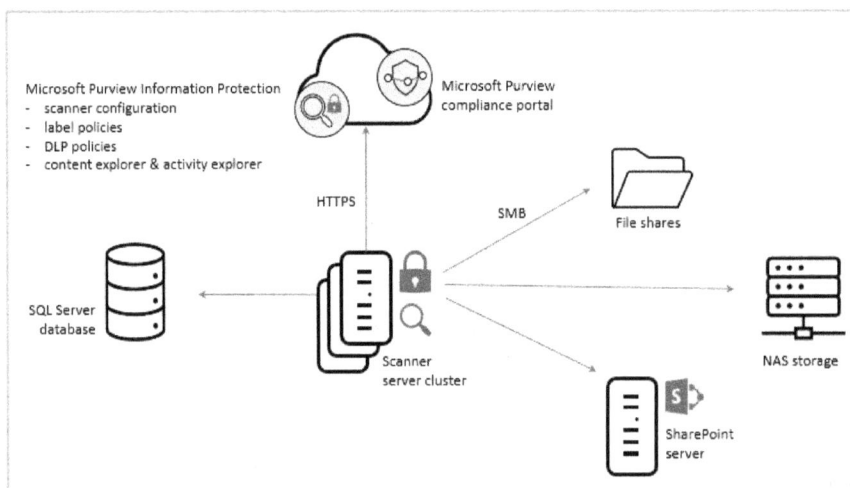

Figure 12.7: Information protection scanner architecture

The scanner can accomplish the following tasks:

- Run in discovery mode to create reports.
- Discover files that contain sensitive information.
- Run automatically to apply sensitivity labels.
- Include or exclude certain file types from scanning.

Pre-requisites

Before you can install and configure the scanner, ensure that the following pre-requisites are met:

- **Windows server requirements**: The scanner needs to be installed on a virtual or physical Windows Server computer that must meet the following minimum requirements:
  - 4 core processors
  - 8 GB RAM
  - 10 GB free space
  - 64-bit versions of Windows Server 2022/2019/2016/2012 R2
  - Install the Microsoft Office Filter to scan for sensitive information in `.zip` files
- **Network connectivity requirements**: The scanner computer must be able to connect to the following URLs over port 443:
  - `*.aadrm.com`
  - `*.azurerms.com`
  - `*.informationprotection.azure.com`
  - `informationprotection.hosting.portal.azure.net`
  - `*.aria.microsoft.com`
  - `*.protection.outlook.com`
- **Service account requirements**: The scanner uses a service account to authenticate to Microsoft Entra ID and download the scanner policy. This service account must be an Active Directory account synchronized to Microsoft Entra ID. This service account has the following requirements:
  - Log on locally user right assignment
  - Log on as a service user right assignment
  - Permissions on the data repositories to be scanned, as follows:
    - For file shares, **Read**, **Write** and **Modify** permissions should be granted.
    - For SharePoint, **Full Control** must be granted.
    - If scanner is running only in discovery mode, **Read** permission is enough.

- o Enable the super user feature in Azure information protection using the PowerShell cmdlet **Enable-AipServiceSuperUserFeature**. Add the service account as super user using the cmdlet **Add-AipServiceSuperUser**.

- o To scan and discover sites and subsites grant the **Site Collector Auditor** permission on the SharePoint farm level.

- o Assign an information protection license to the service account.

- **SQL server requirements**: SQL server local or remote instance is used to store the scanner configuration data. Following are the minimum requirements:

- o SQL Server Enterprise or Standard 2016.

- o An account with Sysadmin role to install the scanner.

- o Storage requirements differ depending on the number of files to be scanned and average length of the file name. Typically, the following formula is used:

  100 KB + <file count> *(1000 + 4* <average file name length>)

- **Minimum role requirements**: To configure the scanner settings, you should have one of the following roles assigned:

- o Compliance Administrator

- o Compliance Data Administrator

- o Security Administrator

- o Organizational Management

Configuring scanner settings

Before the scanner can be installed on the Windows Server, certain settings must be configured in the Purview portal. Following are the steps:

1. Sign in to **https://purview.microsoft.com** and in the left navigation bar click on **Settings | Information Protection | Information protection scanner**.

2. In the right pane, click on **Add** under **Clusters**. This cluster defines your scanner and is used to identify the scanner instance during installation and upgrades. Give a name and description to the cluster and click on **Save**. For example, you might name you client Europe to identify the geographical location of the repositories scanned by this scanner.

3. Next, click on **Content scan jobs** and click on **Add**. This is where you define the scanner configuration. Make the following settings:

   a. **Name**: Give the job a meaningful name.

   b. **Description**: Give the job a meaningful name.

   c. **Cluster**: Select the cluster created in the previous step.

   d. **Schedule**: Set the schedule to **Manual**.

e. **Info types to be discovered**: Select **All**.

Accept defaults for all other settings and click **Save**.

4. Back in the **Content scan jobs** page, open the job just created and click on the **Repositories** tab. This is where you define the repositories that will be scanned by this scanner. Click on **Add** and define the **Universal Naming Convention** (**UNC**) path for file shares and SharePoint server URLs that you want to scan. Accept the other defaults and click on **Save**. Repeat this step to create as many repositories as you would like to scan using this scanner.

Installing scanner

Once the scanner settings have been configured, you can now install the scanner software on the Windows Server. Following are the steps:

1. Login to the Windows Server computer that will serve as the scanner with an account that has local administrator permissions and permissions to write to the master SQL database.

2. Download and install the latest version of the **Microsoft Purview Information Protection client** from the Microsoft Download Center.

3. Open a Windows PowerShell session with the **Run as administrator** option.

4. Run the following PowerShell cmdlet specifying the SQL Server instance on which the database for the scanner will be created and the scanner cluster name defined. Enter the scanner service account credentials when prompted.

    ```
    Install-Scanner -SqlServerInstance <name> -Cluster <cluster name>
    ```

5. Verify that the service is installed by going to **Administrative Tools** | **Services**. Look for the service **Microsoft Purview Information Protection Scanner** and endure that it is configured to run using the service account.

The service account needs a token from Microsoft Entra to be able to authenticate to the Microsoft Purview Information Protection service enabling the scanner to run unattended. This is done by creating an app registration in Microsoft Entra using the following steps:

1. Login to **https://entra.microsoft.com** and navigate to **Applications** | **App registrations**.

2. In the right pane, click on **New registration**.

3. Enter the name as `InformationProtectionScanner`.

4. Leave the **Supported account types** as default.

5. Under **Redirect URI**, select **Web** in the dropdown box and enter **http://localhost** in the textbox and click on **Register**.

6. From the **Overview** page, note down the **Application (client) ID** and **Directory (tenant) ID**.

7. In the left pane, click on **Certificates & secrets**. In the right pane, click on **New client secret**. Enter a description for your secret and set expiry to 12 months and click on **Add**. You will now be able to see the secret value. Copy it. This is the only time the secret value is visible so ensure that you copy it now as it will be needed later.

8. In the left pane, click on API permissions and in the right pane, click on **Add a permission**. Select **Azure Rights Management Service** and then click on **Application permissions**. Select `Content.DelegatedReader` and `Content.DelegatedWriter` and click on **Add permissions**.

9. Click on Add a permission again, and this time click on **APIs my organization uses**. Search for **Microsoft Information Protection Sync Service** and select it. Select Application permissions and select `UnifiedPolicy.Tenant.Read.` Click on **Add permissions**.

10. Sign back in to the Windows Server with the scanner service account and start a Windows PowerShell session. Run the following PowerShell cmdlet specifying the values copied:

```
Set-Authentication -AppId <ID of the registered app> -AppSecret
<client secret sting> -TenantId <your tenant ID> -DelegatedUser
<Azure AD account>
```

The scanner now has a token that is valid for 12 months. At the end of 12 months, the procedure must be repeated.

Running scanner

The scanner is now ready to discover files. To start a scan, following are the steps:

1. Login to **https://purview.microsoft.com** and navigate to **Settings** | **Information protection** | **Information protection scanner**.

2. In the right pane, click on **Content scan jobs** and select the scan job created earlier. Click on **Scan now** to start the scan.

3. Once the scanner has crawled through all the files in the data store, the **Last scan results** and the **Last scan end time** columns in the scan job will be updated.

4. The report will be stored on the scanner computer under `%localappdata%\Microsoft\MSIP\Scanner\Reports`. Open the report in `.csv` format to view the results.

Protect your data

Now that you have learnt how to discover sensitive content in your environment, the next step is to protect that data to prevent it from being misused or accessed by unauthorized parties. Microsoft Purview Information Protection does this using sensitivity labels and label policies.

Sensitivity labels

Sensitivity labels let you classify and protect sensitive content while enabling productivity and collaboration. A sensitivity label is like a stamp that is applied to a document that specifies its business importance. A typical example of sensitivity labelling schema in an organization could be **Personal, General, Confidential, Highly Confidential** where the personal sensitivity label could be used to classify non-business content and highly confidential could be used to classify content of high business importance like board papers or intellectual property. Following are some of the key features of sensitivity labels:

- They are **customizable** as per an organization's requirements. IT admins can create categories depending on the business needs.
- They are stored in **clear text** in the metadata of files and emails so that they can be consumed by non-Microsoft applications and services.
- Since the sensitivity labels are written in the metadata of the file, they are **persistent**, which means that they travel with the file regardless of where the file lives or travels. This protects the file from unauthorized access even if it leaves your M365 tenant.

Organizations can use sensitivity labels for the following:

- Protect content in files by applying encryption settings and visual markings like watermark, header or footer.
- Protect content in Office applications across platforms and devices including Office on the web, desktop apps and mobile devices including macOS, iOS and Android.
- Protect content in non-Microsoft cloud applications using Microsoft Defender for Cloud Apps.
- Protect content in containers like Team, M365 groups and SharePoint site.
- Protect meetings and chat by labelling meeting invites.
- Protect Power BI.
- Extend sensitivity labels to assets in Microsoft Purview Data Map.
- Extend sensitivity labels to non-Microsoft apps using the Microsoft Information Protection SDK.
- Label the content without applying encryption.
- Protect over exposure of data when Microsoft copilot is used. Microsoft copilot understands and honors sensitivity labels.

Sensitivity labels can do the following:

- Be applied manually by users by picking the appropriate sensitivity label from the Office toolbar. They can also be recommended or automatically applied based on the content of the file in use.

- Be automatically applied to content at rest in SharePoint Online and OneDrive and on-premises file shares using the on-premises scanner discussed in the previous section.

- Be grouped using sublabels. This is the way to group labels under a parent label. For example, you might want to specify additional labels under the Confidential label. This will be as follows:

  Confidential | All Employees, Confidential | Partners only and **Confidential | Board members only**.

Following is an example of a sensitivity label hierarchy and how it appears in an Office application:

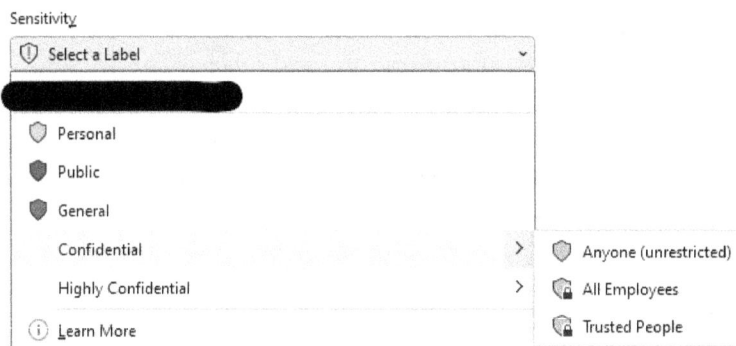

Figure 12.8: Sensitivity label hierarchy

Label settings

Several settings need to be configured while creating a sensitivity label. This section will explain the label settings available. The specific settings you choose will depend on the organization's data security policy and use cases.

Basic details

When you first create a label, you will have to provide the following basic details.

- **Name**: This is the name that the admins will see in the Purview portal. This name cannot be changed once the label is saved.

- **Display name**: This is the name that the users will see in the Office applications where the label is published.

- **Description for users**: This is the description users will see when they hover over the label name in their Office application.

- **Description for admins**: This is the description that is for admins who will manage this label.

- **Label color**: Label colors are used to visually differentiate between the labels. They appear next to the label in the Office app.

Scope

The label scope determines the applications and services that this label will be available for. Labels can be applied to individual items like files, emails and meetings or to containers like SharePoint sites, M365 Groups or Teams. They can also be extended to data assets in Microsoft Purview Data Map.

Protection settings

Using sensitivity labels you can control who can access the labelled items, apply content marking like watermark, header and footer and protect Teams meetings and chats if Teams was selected as a location in the label scope.

Access control settings

This is where you define the protection settings that will be enforced on the content when this label is defined. There are several settings, and it is important to understand them to ensure the correct settings are being enforced. The first step is to decide between defining permissions while creating a label or letting users choose the permissions when they apply the label.

Refer to the following:

- **Assign permissions now**: Also called **admin-defined permissions** this option lets administrators define the permissions users will get on the document when this label is applied. When this option is selected, the following settings are available:

  - **User access to content expires**: This setting allows administrators to determine if users should have indefinite access to content or it should expire on a specific date or after a specified number of days.

  - **Allow offline access**: This setting allows administrators to specify if the user should be able to access the content if they are not connected to the internet. The available options are **Always**, **Never** or **Only for a number of days**.

  - **Assign permissions to specific users and groups**: This is where the administrator can define the users or groups who will be able to consume the content protected by this label. You can choose the following:

    - All users and groups in the organization or specific users and groups.

    - Any authenticated user which includes any user that has an email address authenticated by Microsoft Entra ID or a federated social provider or Microsoft account or users that use a one-time email passcode.

- Specific email addresses or domains. For example, you might have a partner with which you need to collaborate on content protected by sensitivity labels.

o **Choose permissions**: This setting defines the permissions the users and groups selected earlier will have on the file. The available options are **Co-Owner**, **Co-Author**, **Reviewer**, **Viewer** and **Custom**.

o **Use dynamic watermarking**: When this option is enabled the email address of the user accessing the document is automatically inserted as a watermark on each page of the file. This watermark persists when the file is printed and cannot be removed by the user.

o **Use double key encryption**: Microsoft Purview Information Protection uses Microsoft managed keys to protect data. These keys are generated and managed by Microsoft and organizations have no control over this. However, in some scenarios organizations might require an extra layer of protection for some highly sensitive content or to maintain compliance with some regulatory requirements. In these scenarios, they can use **Double Key Encryption (DKE)**. When DKE is used, two keys are used to protect content, one key is in the organization's control and is stored securely in Microsoft Azure. The other key is controlled by Microsoft. Viewing the content protected by DKE requires access to both these keys.

- **Let users assign permissions when they apply the label**: It is also called **User-Defined Permissions (UDP)**, this option prompts the user to assign permissions when they apply the label to the file. The following options are available:

o **In Outlook**: Enforce one of the following restrictions. These settings define how an email will behave when it is encrypted using user-defined permissions.

- **Do not forward**: When this option is selected the recipient of the email will be able to read the message but will not be able to forward, print or copy it.

- **Encrypt-only**: When this option is selected the email is encrypted and the recipients must be authenticated. They have no restrictions except that they cannot remove the encryption from the message.

o **In Word, PowerPoint, and Excel, prompt users to specify permissions**: When users select this label while working on a file in Word, Excel or PowerPoint, a dialog box will appear asking them to choose one of the predefined permissions, specify the users or groups who those permissions apply to or set an expiry date for the file.

o **Use DKE**: Microsoft Purview Information Protection uses Microsoft managed keys to protect data. These keys are generated and managed by Microsoft and organizations have no control over this. However, in some scenarios organizations might require an extra layer of protection for some highly sensitive content or to maintain compliance with some regulatory requirements. In these scenarios, they can use **DKE**. When DKE is used, two keys are used to protect content, one key is in the organization's control and is stored securely in Microsoft Azure. The other key is controlled by Microsoft. Viewing the content protected by DKE requires access to both these keys.

Content marking

You can select to apply a watermark, header and footer to the content when this label is applied.

Microsoft Teams meetings and chats

If you chose to protect Microsoft Teams meetings and chats you can choose to apply controls like users who are allowed to bypass the lobby, who can present, record and transcribe. You can also prevent copying of the meeting chat. Some of the settings require a Teams Premium license and you would not be able to configure them if a Teams Premium license is not found in the tenant. For those settings you will see an information bar telling you that your organization does not have a license.

Auto-labelling for files and emails

It is also called **client-side auto labelling**. This feature allows administrators to either recommend or enforce a sensitivity label on a file stored in Microsoft 365 when it is in use. Administrators can define the conditions that should be present in the file to trigger auto-labelling. This is done using SITs and trainable classifiers. When this setting is enabled, Microsoft Purview Information Protection inspects the content of the file in use and if it matches the conditions defined in the label it can either recommend or enforce the label. For example, you can choose to enforce a label to a file that contains full names and addresses and Australian Bank Account numbers or Finance documents.

Figure 12.9 shows an example of a label automatically applied to a Microsoft Word document when certain keywords were detected. You can also see that the sensitivity label applied a header and watermark to the document.

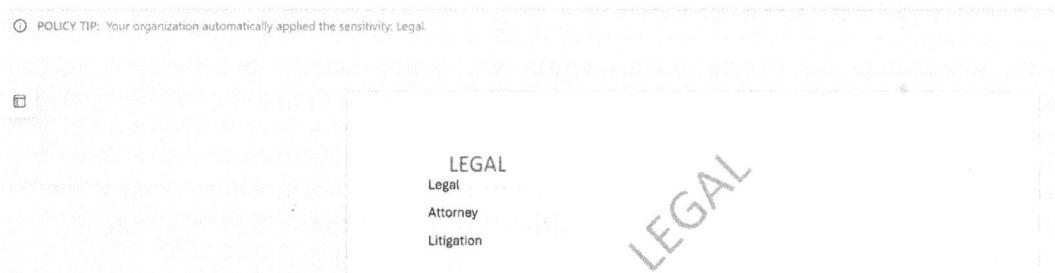

Figure 12.9: Client side auto-labelling in Microsoft Word

Groups and sites

The following settings are available to protect groups and sites:

- Control the level of access internal and external users will have to labelled Teams and M365 groups. The following options are available:

  o **Public**: Anyone in the organization can access this group or team and add members.

  o **Private**: Only team owners and members can access this group or team and add members.

  o **None**: Team and group members can decide the privacy settings themselves.

  You can also choose to let team owners add people to from outside your organization as guests.

- Control the external sharing and configure Conditional Access settings to protect labelled SharePoint sites. The following options are available:

  o You can configure that the content in the labelled SharePoint site be shared with anyone, new and existing guests, existing guests or only people in your organization.

  o Microsoft Entra Conditional Access policies can be used to control the level of access users have from unmanaged devices (devices not managed by Microsoft Intune). This could be full access, limited access which allows them to only view content with no ability to download or completely block access.

  o Use Conditional Access Authentication context to secure data in SharePoint site protected by this label.

- Decide whether private Teams will be discoverable in searches. By default, private Teams are not discoverable, but this option enables users to search for private teams that have this label applied. The users must be added to a Teams policy that has **Private Teams discovery** turned on.

- Control the types of teams that can be invited to shared channels. You can choose from **Internal only**, **Same label only** and **Private teams only**.

Schematized data assets

Using this option, you can automatically apply sensitivity labels to assets governed by Microsoft Purview Data Map like database columns in SQL, Azure SQL, Azure Synapse, AWS RDS etc.

To create a sensitivity label login to **https://purview.microsoft.com** and click on the Information Protection tile. Click on **Sensitivity label** and then click on **Create a label**. This will launch the label creation wizard. Choose from the above options to create labels based on your organization's requirements.

Label order

When labels are created in the Microsoft Purview portal they appear in a list on the labels page. The order of the label is important because it sets their priority. The label that appears on the top of the list has the lowest priority and the label that appears on the bottom of the list has the highest priority. Typically, lower priority labels will be less restrictive than higher priority labels. Label priority is used in the following scenarios:

- Asking users to provide a justification to lower the sensitivity of a file. The label priority is used to determine which label is lower.

- When auto-labelling content, the file can match multiple labels, but since only one label can be applied to a file the highest priority label is selected.

A new label is created with the highest priority by default. The priority can be adjusted by clicking on the ellipses next to the label name and moving it up or down as shown in the following figure:

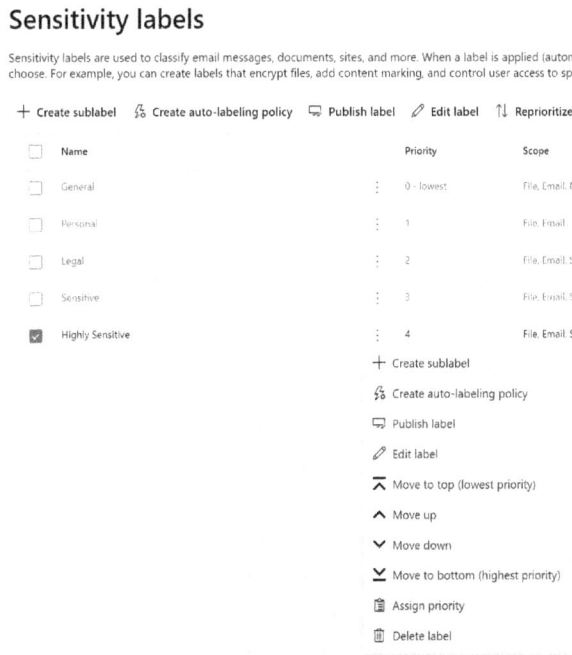

Figure 12.10: Label priority

Publish labels

Once labels are created, they need to be made available in Office applications for the users to use them. This is called **publishing labels** and is done using **publishing policies**. Multiple labels can be published in a single policy. Policies can be scoped to groups of users to make different sets of labels available for them. For example, you might want the **General**,

Personal and **Confidential** labels to be available for everyone in your organization but have specific labels for users in the Legal or Finance teams.

Following table is an example of how multiple policies can be used to publish different labels to different groups of users:

Publishing policy	Labels	User groups
Org wide	Personal General Confidential	All company
Legal policy	Legal\Internal only Legal\Business partners	Legal department
Finance	Payslips Financial reports	Finance department

Table 12.1: Publishing policies

To publish a label, click on **Publish label** as shown in *Figure 12.10* and then following are the steps:

1. Choose the sensitivity labels to be published using the policy and click **Next**.
2. Choose the **Admin Units** to include in the scope of this policy and click **Next**.
3. Select the users or groups to which these labels will be available and click **Next**.
4. Configure the policy settings. The following options are available. Select the appropriate options and click **Next**.

   a. Users must provide a business justification to remove a label or lower its classification.

   b. Require users to apply a label to their emails and documents. When this option is selected, users must select a label before sending an email or saving a file. This is also called **mandatory labelling**.

   c. Require users to apply a label to their Fabric and Power BI content.

   d. Provide users with a link to a custom help page. You will be able to provide a link to a site where users can learn more about sensitivity labels in use in your environment.

5. In the next set of screens, you will be asked to provide a default label to documents, emails, meetings, sites and groups and Fabric and Power BI. This is called **default labelling** and is used to provide a default label when files are created or modified.

This label is applied if the user does not choose a label manually. However, the user can always choose a better label for their file. Make the appropriate setting and click **Next**.

6. Lastly, name your policy and click on **Submit**.

Note: **When you apply a default label to an email and the email has an attachment you can configure that the email is assigned the same label as the attachment. If multiple attachments are added to the email and each document has a different label, then the email gets the highest priority label. This is called label inheritance.**

Auto labelling content

So far, we have learnt how we can label newly created files or files that are in use. However, most organizations have petabytes of historical data in on-premises shared folders, SharePoint servers or in SharePoint Online and OneDrive for business. Most of this content is not accessed or used actively. Manually classifying and protecting this content is an arduous task. To simplify and automate this, Microsoft Purview Information Protection offers the ability to auto label content at rest both on-premises and in the Microsoft 365 cloud.

Auto labelling content on-premises is accomplished using the Microsoft Purview Information Protection scanner tool by toggling the **Enforce sensitivity labelling policy** to **On** and selecting the appropriate sensitivity label.

To label content in Microsoft 365 cloud Microsoft Purview Information Protection offers auto-labelling policies. Using these policies, you can apply sensitivity labels to data at rest in SharePoint Online and OneDrive and data in transit in Exchange Online. This is called **service-side labelling**.

Following are the steps to create an auto-labelling policy:

1. Login to **https://purview.microsoft.com** and click on the **Information Protection** tile.

2. Click on **Policies | Auto-labeling policies**. In the right pane click on **Create auto-labeling policy**.

3. In the first screen of the policy, you will be asked to select the type of content you would like to label using this policy. You can choose from templates or start from scratch by selecting the **Custom** option. The following figure shows the available templates. Make the appropriate selections and click **Next**.

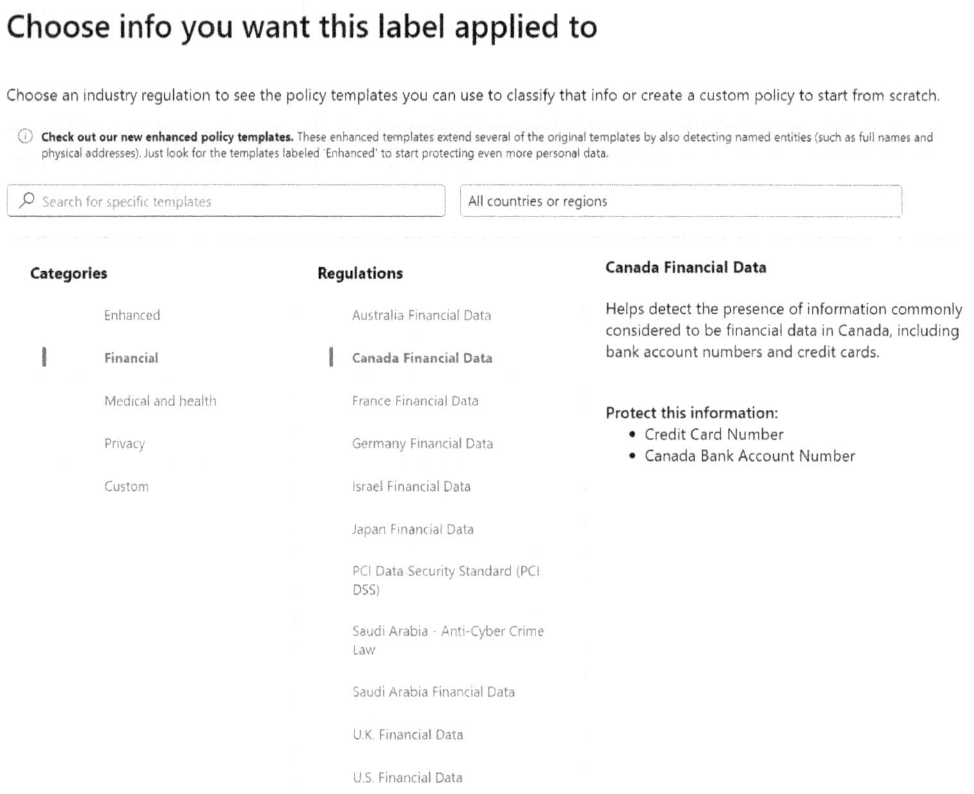

Choose info you want this label applied to

Choose an industry regulation to see the policy templates you can use to classify that info or create a custom policy to start from scratch.

ⓘ **Check out our new enhanced policy templates.** These enhanced templates extend several of the original templates by also detecting named entities (such as full names and physical addresses). Just look for the templates labeled 'Enhanced' to start protecting even more personal data.

○ Search for specific templates	All countries or regions

Categories	**Regulations**	**Canada Financial Data**
Enhanced	Australia Financial Data	Helps detect the presence of information commonly considered to be financial data in Canada, including bank account numbers and credit cards.
▎ Financial	▎ Canada Financial Data	
Medical and health	France Financial Data	**Protect this information:**
Privacy	Germany Financial Data	• Credit Card Number
Custom	Israel Financial Data	• Canada Bank Account Number
	Japan Financial Data	
	PCI Data Security Standard (PCI DSS)	
	Saudi Arabia - Anti-Cyber Crime Law	
	Saudi Arabia Financial Data	
	U.K. Financial Data	
	U.S. Financial Data	

Figure 12.11: Select content to label

4. In the next screen, provide a name and description for the policy and click **Next**.

5. Select the locations you would like to include in the policy and click **Next**. You can select all Exchange mailboxes, SharePoint sites, and OneDrive accounts, or scope the policy to specific locations. You can also include or exclude specific mailboxes, SharePoint sites or OneDrive accounts.

6. In the next screen, define the policy rules. If you chose a template in *Step 3*, the relevant SITs will already be picked for you. If you would like to apply the same rules for all locations selected in *Step 5*, leave the default selected and click on **Next**. If you choose a custom policy or you would like to define different rules for each location, select **Advanced rules** and click **Next**.

   Following figure shows a rule that is looking for files that contain names, **Canada Physical Addresses** and **Credit Card Number** or **Canada Bank Account Number**. Notice that you can create complex conditions to suit your requirements. Click **Save**.

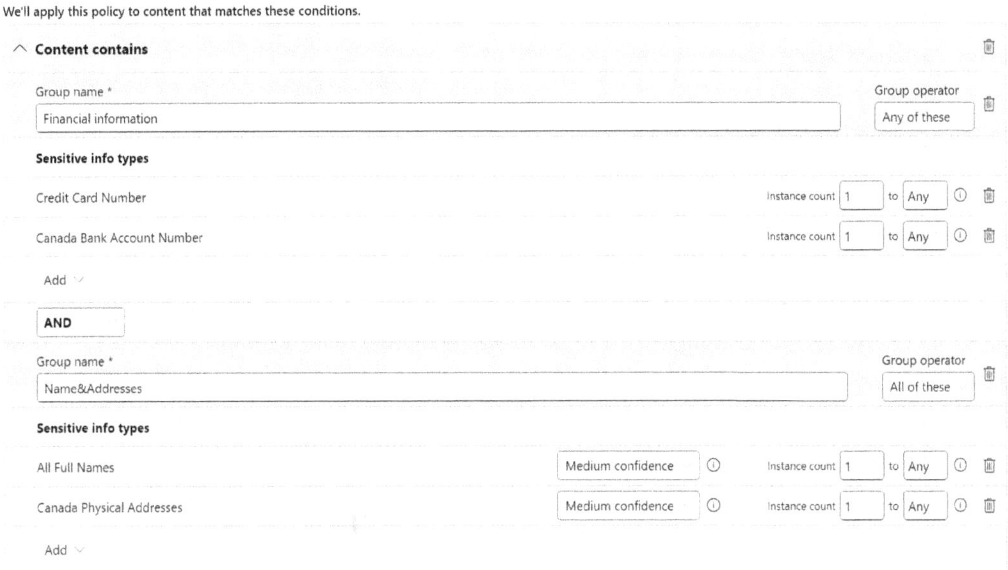

We'll apply this policy to content that matches these conditions.

∧ **Content contains**   🗑

Group name *   Group operator
| Financial information | | Any of these | 🗑

Sensitive info types

Credit Card Number   Instance count [1] to [Any] ⓘ 🗑

Canada Bank Account Number   Instance count [1] to [Any] ⓘ 🗑

Add ∨

| **AND** |

Group name *   Group operator
| Name&Addresses | | All of these | 🗑

Sensitive info types

All Full Names | Medium confidence | ⓘ   Instance count [1] to [Any] ⓘ 🗑

Canada Physical Addresses | Medium confidence | ⓘ   Instance count [1] to [Any] ⓘ 🗑

Add ∨

Figure 12.12: Choose content to discover

7. Now, select the label that you would like to apply to the discovered content and click **Next**.

8. You can also choose to relabel already labelled files if the existing label has a lower priority than the one defined by this policy. Click **Next**.

9. In the last step, you can choose to run the policy in simulation mode. This will gather the items that will be labelled but will not apply the label. You can review the items and then edit or turn on the policy depending on the results. This is highly recommended because if the files are encrypted with the wrong label, it is very difficult to reverse the process. Click on **Finish** to create the policy.

Once the labels are applied, they are visible under the **Sensitivity** column in the SharePoint document library. If you hover over the label name, you can see that the label was automatically applied as shown in the following figure:

	Name ∨		Modified ∨	Modified By ∨	Sensitivity ∨	+
📄	Document.docx		October 20, 2022	▬▬▬	Legal	
📝	file with legal label.docx		October 21, 2022	▬▬▬	Legal	
📝	important.docx	⊖ 🔗 ⋯	December 7, 2023	▬▬▬▬	Financial	
📄	Important.pdf	⊖	August 16, 2022	▬▬▬ This file has been automatically labelled	

Figure 12.13: Service side auto-labelling in SharePoint

Auto-labelling content in M365 locations requires one of the following licenses:

- M365 E5

- M365 E5 Compliance
- M365 E5 Information Protection & Governance

Prevent data loss

Most organizations have sensitive content like financial data, medical records, intellectual property and more. They need a way to prevent their users from accidentally or maliciously sharing this content with unauthorized parties. This is called Data Loss Prevention (DLP). **Microsoft Purview Data Loss Prevention** uses SITs and trainable classifier to detect sensitivity content using deep content analysis. For example, you can have a DLP policy that looks for **All Full name**, **All Physical Addresses** and **Credit Card Number** in email messages and applies controls. If your organization uses Microsoft Information Protection sensitivity labels, you can use them to apply DLP policy. For example, you could have a DLP policy that prevents users from sharing files with the **Confidential** label to external recipients.

Implementing a data loss prevention program for an organization needs proper planning and testing to ensure that the correct policies are being implemented to prevent loss of productivity for users. It is not expected that the IT department will be aware of what data is sensitive and the controls that should be implemented to protect it. Therefore, it is important to include stakeholders from all the business units that create, manage and own data to identify the data that is critical for them, the controls they would like to implement and the regulatory requirements that they need to adhere to. These stakeholders could be data protection officers, risk and compliance officers, legal officers and business owners.

Defining DLP strategy will typically include the following steps.

- Prioritize data
- Categorize and label data
- Define and develop policies

Once you have worked with these stakeholders and defined a DLP strategy you can proceed with creating the DLP policies. DLP policy can be applied to the following locations:

- Exchange Online
- SharePoint Online & OneDrive accounts
- Teams chat and channel messages (Teams DLP)
- Windows 10/11 and macOS (Endpoint DLP)
- Non-Windows cloud applications using Microsoft Defender for Cloud Apps
- On-premises files shares and SharePoint servers
- Fabric and Power BI

Microsoft Purview DLP allows you to create a single policy for all locations. This is called **unified DLP**. The only exception is Power BI for which a separate policy must be created.

DLP policy comprises of one of more rules. Each rule has conditions and actions. Depending on the conditions, the rule takes certain actions including but not limited to notifying the user and generating alerts. The available conditions and actions differ based on the locations selected.

DLP for Exchange

The most common method of data exfiltration is emails. Users can accidentally or maliciously send sensitive content to unauthorized parties over email. Microsoft Purview DLP offers several controls that can warn or prevent users from oversharing content. DLP for Exchange is included in M365 E3 licenses.

Administrators can define several conditions to detect data exfiltration. These include using SITs, trainable classifiers and sensitivity labels to detect sensitive content. Other commonly used conditions are sender, recipient, sender domain, recipient domain, document property, words or patterns in subject and body, attachment type and size.

Based on these conditions, actions like preventing sending email to external recipients, prepending text in the email subject, forwarding the message for approval, copying the sender's manager or starting a Power Automate workflow can be taken.

Email DLP allows sending notifications to the user to let them know that they are violating a DLP policy. This can be done by way of emails or policy tips. In addition, users can be provided with the option of overriding the policy and asked to provide a business justification for doing so. When the user clicks on **Override**, they will be prompted to enter a business justification and then they will be able to send the email as shown in the following figure:

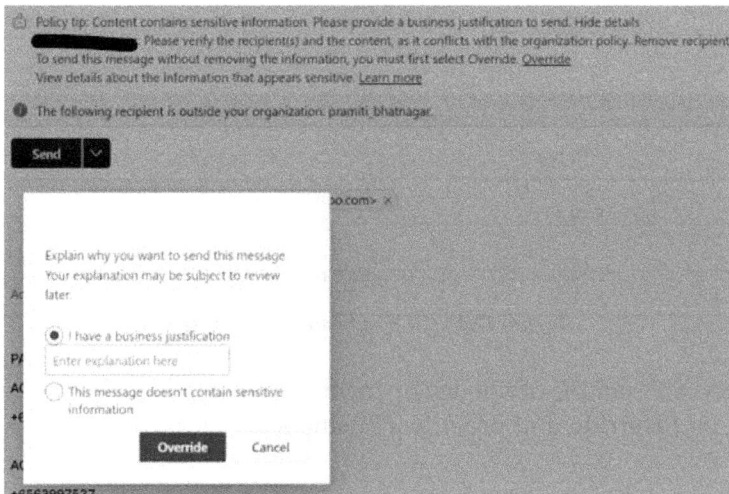

Figure 12.14: DLP in Exchange

DLP for SharePoint and OneDrive

Nowadays, it is common to share files as links from SharePoint and OneDrive as it helps in better collaboration by enabling co-authoring and co-editing content. Users can accidentally or maliciously overshare files with unintended recipients. Microsoft Purview DLP offers capabilities that detect and prevent users from sharing sensitive content with unintended recipients. DLP for SharePoint and OneDrive is included with M365 E3 licensing. This also includes files that are shared through Teams because Team uses SharePoint and OneDrive to share files.

Just like with Exchange DLP, administrators can define conditions to detect sensitive content in documents using SITs, trainable classifiers and sensitivity labels. In addition, other predicates like document property, file extensions, document author can be used. Based on these conditions the following actions can be taken:

- Block everyone which will block all internal and external users from accessing the document. Only the document owner, last modifier and stie admin will have access.
- Block people outside the organization.
- Block people who were given access using **Anyone with the link** option.

Administrators can configure user notifications to alert users that they are violating DLP Policy. This can be done by way of emails or policy tips. In addition, users can be provided with the option of overriding the policy and asked to provide a business justification for doing so. Users can click on **Override** and provide a business justification if they would like to share the file. Files that are protected by a DLP policy are denoted by a red icon as shown in the following figure:

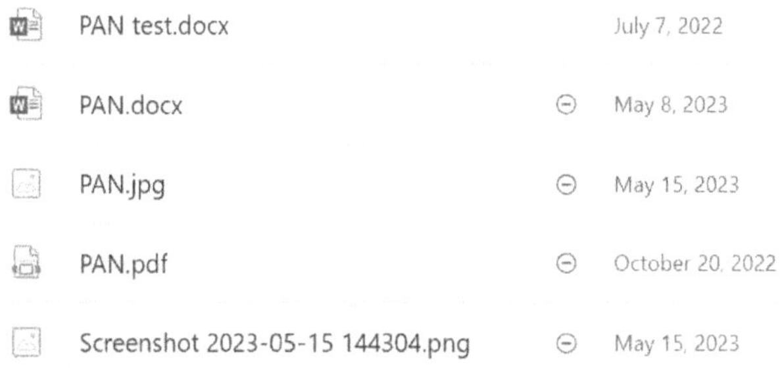

PAN test.docx		July 7, 2022
PAN.docx	⊖	May 8, 2023
PAN.jpg	⊖	May 15, 2023
PAN.pdf	⊖	October 20, 2022
Screenshot 2023-05-15 144304.png	⊖	May 15, 2023

Figure 12.15: DLP in SharePoint Online

Figure 12.16 shows an example of a policy tip in SharePoint Online with the override option. Users can click on **Override** and provide a business justification to continue sharing the file.

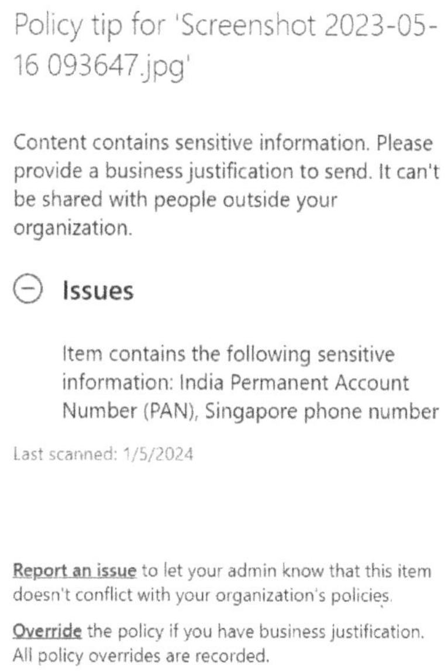

Policy tip for 'Screenshot 2023-05-
16 093647.jpg'

Content contains sensitive information. Please
provide a business justification to send. It can't
be shared with people outside your
organization.

⊖ **Issues**

Item contains the following sensitive
information: India Permanent Account
Number (PAN), Singapore phone number

Last scanned: 1/5/2024

Report an issue to let your admin know that this item
doesn't conflict with your organization's policies.

Override the policy if you have business justification.
All policy overrides are recorded.

Figure 12.16: DLP policy tip in SharePoint Online

Teams DLP

Microsoft Teams is being increasingly used by users to collaborate and share files both internally and externally. Users can inadvertently share sensitive information in chat and channel messages or share sensitive files on Teams. Microsoft Purview provides DLP capabilities to detect and block such sharing. Teams DLP requires one of the following licenses:

- Microsoft 365 E5
- Microsoft 365 E5 Compliance
- Microsoft 365 E5 Information Protection & Governance

Administrators can define various conditions ranging from content detected by SITs and trainable classifiers to recipient, recipient domain, sender and sender domain. Based on these conditions the following actions can be taken:

- **Block everyone**: No recipient will receive the sensitive information.
- **Block people outside the organization**: Recipients outside the organization will not receive the sensitive information.

User notifications can be sent by way of policy tips, and the users can be given the override option to override the policy and continue sending the message. *Figure 12.17* shows an example of a Teams message blocked by a Teams DLP policy. When the user clicks on **What can I do?** they are given more details about why this message was blocked along with the override option.

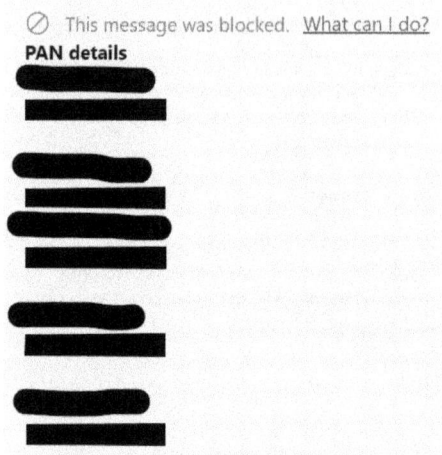

Figure 12.17: Teams DLP sender view

Following figure shows the view from the recipient side when they receive a message blocked by a Teams DLP policy:

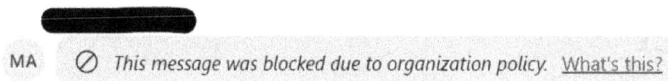

Figure 12.18: Teams DLP recipient view

Endpoint DLP

Microsoft Purview DLP extends the monitoring and protection capabilities of DLP to sensitive items stored on Windows 10/11 and macOS devices. For DLP policies to be applied to devices, the devices must be onboarded to Microsoft Purview. This is like onboarding devices to Microsoft Defender for Endpoint which has been explained in *Chapter 8, Protecting Endpoints*. If your organization is already using MDE, no further step is necessary. If not, follow the steps in *Chapter 8, Protecting Endpoints* to onboard devices

Endpoint DLP requires one of the following licenses:

- Microsoft 365 E5
- Microsoft 365 E5 Compliance
- Microsoft 365 E5 Information Protection & Governance

The endpoint DLP rule can detect sensitive content based on SITs, trainable classifiers and sensitivity labels. Additionally, conditions like file type, extension, document name and size can be used.

Using endpoint DLP, the following activities on endpoints can be audited, blocked or blocked with the option to override:

- Unloading sensitive content to a restricted cloud service domain or unallowed browser.
- Pasting sensitive content to supported browsers.
- Copying sensitive content to clipboard.
- Copying sensitive content to USB.
- Copying sensitive content to file shares.
- Printing sensitive content.
- Copying or moving sensitive content to unallowed Bluetooth applications.
- Copying or moving sensitive content using RDP.
- Restricted applications accessing sensitive content.

Users can be notified that they are violating DLP policy using policy tips that show up as toast notifications on their desktop as shown in *Figure 12.19*. Users can click on **Allow** to enter a business justification and continue the operation.

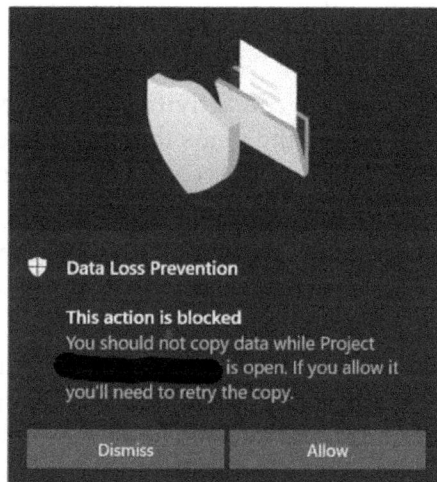

Figure 12.19: *Endpoint DLP policy tip*

Endpoint DLP settings

Much of the behavior of Endpoint DLP is controlled centrally by settings that are applied to DLP policies for devices. These settings are used to control behaviors like data egress to cloud locations, browser and domain restrictions, file path exclusions and more.

These settings are accessed from the Purview portal by clicking on **Settings** and then selecting **Data Loss Prevention | Endpoint DLP settings**. The following settings are available:

- **Advanced classification scanning and protection**: With this setting turned on Microsoft Purview can use advanced classification techniques like EDM SITs, trainable classifiers, credential classifiers and named entities to scan items stored on the device, classify them and return the results to the local machine. Since, content is sent from the local device to the cloud service for scanning and classification bandwidth is utilized. If that is a concern, administrators can set a per-device limit on the maximum bandwidth that can be used in 24 hours. Once that bandwidth limit is reached, data is not sent to the cloud and scanning continues on the local device. At this point, advanced classification techniques listed above cannot be used. When the cumulative bandwidth usage drops below the limit in a rolling 24-hour window, communication with the cloud resumes. This feature is supported on the following operating systems:

  o Windows 11

  o Windows 10 versions 20H1/20H2 or higher

  o Windows 10 RS5

- **File path exclusions for Windows**: Use this option to add locations on Windows devices that should not be monitored by DLP policies.

- **File path exclusions for Mac**: Use this option to add locations on Mac devices that should not be monitored by DLP policies.

- **Setup evidence collection for file activities on devices**: This option is used if administrators want to collect the items that match the DLP policy as evidence. When an item matches a policy, it is copied to an Azure storage account. This option is useful for auditing and troubleshooting.

- **Network share coverage and exclusions**: This setting extends the DLP protection to new and edited files on network shares. Use this option to exclude certain network shares from DLP protection.

- **Restricted apps and app groups**: This option specifies the actions that DLP takes when a sensitive file is accessed by an application. For example, you can prevent certain file sharing applications from accessing sensitive files. Application groups are used to create a collection of applications that can be used in DLP policies.

- **Unallowed Bluetooth apps**: Use this setting to define a list of Bluetooth apps where users are not allowed to copy sensitive content.

- **Browser and domain restrictions to sensitive data**: This setting is used to specify browsers that are not allowed to access sensitive content. When users use these unallowed browsers to access sensitive content, they are prompted to use Microsoft Edge. You can also specify a **Block** or **Allow** list of service domains that are not allowed to access sensitive content.

- **Additional settings for endpoint DLP**: This setting allows you to customize the text of the policy tips that appear on the user's desktop when a DLP policy is matched. You can show the default options and a custom text box or only the default options or only a custom text box.

- **Endpoint DLP support for onboarded servers**: By default, when Windows Servers are onboarded to Microsoft Purview, endpoint DLP is not enabled for them. To enable endpoint DLP for onboarded Windows Servers, switch this option to **On**.

- **Always audit file activity for devices**: With this option turned on, all file activities on onboarded Window devices for Office files, PDF and CSV are automatically audited and reported in the **Activity Explorer**. This option is on by default.

- **Printer groups**: This option is used to apply different restrictions to different sets of printers. For example, you might want to prevent users from printing sensitive content on any printer other than the ones on the corporate network.

- **Removeable USB device groups**: This option is used to apply different restrictions to different sets of USB devices. For example, you might want to prevent users from copying sensitive content to any USB device other than the ones issued by the organization.

- **Network share groups**: This option is used to apply different restrictions to different groups of network shares. For example, you might want to prevent users from copying sensitive content to any network share other than the ones on the corporate network.

- **VPN settings**: You can choose to apply different DLP restrictions when users are connected to the corporate network using the VPN addresses listed in this setting.

Just-in-time protection

Endpoint DLP does not scan content at rest on endpoints. It can only apply the DLP protection to new or in-use files. Users may have historical files stored on their devices which will not be evaluated for DLP unless they are manually accessed. This can expose these files to risk. With just-in-time protection enabled, files are evaluated for DLP at the time of egress. For example, if a user tries to copy a file that has not been scanned by the DLP engine to a USB drive, the DLP engine can block access to the files unless DLP scanning is complete. This setting is available in the Purview portal by going to **Settings | Data Loss Prevention | Just-in-time protection**. You can add the locations to monitor and choose the outcome if the DLP scanning fails. There are additional settings available for customizing the notification and adding app, file path and file extension exclusions.

DLP for non-Microsoft applications

Microsoft Purview can extend DLP protection to non-Microsoft applications that are connected to Microsoft Defender for Cloud Apps. Currently, support for Box, Dropbox, Google Workspace, Salesforce and Cisco Webex is available. SITs, trainable classifiers and sensitivity labels can be used as conditions.

DLP for on-premises repositories

Microsoft Purview DLP offers protection to on-premises repositories. The Microsoft Purview Information Protection scanner implements DLP policies. SITs, sensitivity labels, file extension and document property can be used as conditions. When a file matches these conditions, access can be blocked, permissions can be inherited from the parent folder, or the file can be moved to a quarantine location.

Creating DLP policy

Following are the steps to create a DLP policy:

1. Login to **https://purview.microsoft.com** and click on the **Data Loss Prevention** tile.

2. Click on **Policies** and then click on **Create policy**.

3. In the first screen, you will be asked to select the sensitive content. Select the appropriate option and click **Next**.

4. In the next screen, give your policy a name and description and click **Next**.

5. Select the **Admin units** you would like to apply the policy to and click **Next**.

6. Next, you will be asked to select the locations that this policy will be applied to. Choose the locations and click **Next**.

7. In the next screen, you will be asked to create the DLP rules. The rules you create will depend on the locations you want to cover in the DLP policy. Use the above information to define the rule as per your requirements and click **Next**.

8. Select the policy mode. The following options are available:

    a. **Run the policy in simulation mode**: In this case the policy is created but stays off. There will be no user impact. You can choose to show user notifications while the policy is in simulation mode, however, the users will not be blocked from taking any action. You can review the impact of the policy.

    b. **Turn the policy on immediately**: The policy will turn on however, it can take up to an hour for the changes to be enforced.

    c. **Leave the policy off**: You can choose to use this option if you would like to leave the policy to be turned on later.

9. Choose the appropriate option and click **Submit** to create the policy.

DLP alerts

As discussed in this section, DLP policies can be configured to generate alerts. These alerts are available in the Microsoft Purview portal by clicking on the **Data Loss Prevention** tile and selecting the **Alerts** option. Alerts can be generated each time a DLP rule is matched. This can be noisy as the number of alerts can be very high. Administrators can choose to generate aggregated alerts based on the number of matches or the volume of items over time.

Following figure shows the alerts configuration option available in a DLP rule:

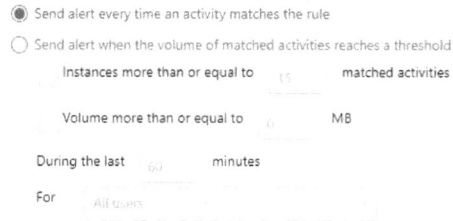

Figure 12.20: DLP alerts configuration

Single event alerts are available for all tenants that have an E1 license. To configure aggregated alerts one of the following licenses must be available:

- M365 E5
- M365 E1 + Office 365 Advanced Threat Protection Plan 2
- M365 E1 + M365 E5 Compliance
- M365 E1 + M365 eDiscovery and Audit

Govern your data

So far, we have gone through the know your data, protect your data and prevent data loss aspects of the data journey. Now let us focus on govern your data. This refers to managing the retention and safe disposal of data. Microsoft Purview offers two solutions when it comes to governing data, Microsoft Purview Data Lifecycle Management and Microsoft Purview Records Management. While these two solutions seem to be doing the same thing, there are significant differences between them.

Following is an explanation:

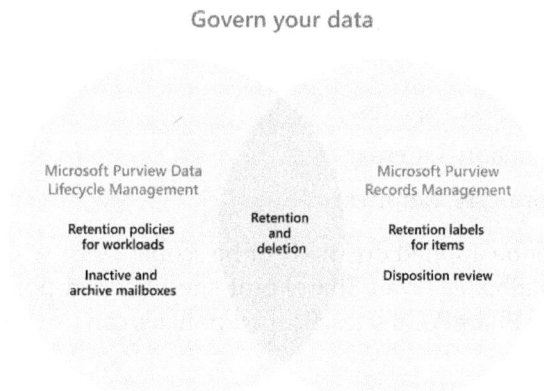

Figure 12.21: Govern your data

Both solutions support the retention and deletion of documents, however, there are differences in the way they are applied and managed as follows:

- **With Data Lifecycle Management**:
  o Create overarching retention policies that apply to entire locations like Exchange mailboxes, SharePoint sites and OneDrive accounts.
  o Create retention labels that can be applied at the document level.
  o Retain mailboxes of users who leave the organization once their Entra ID account is deleted.
  o Provide archive mailboxes to end users that provide additional storage space.
  o Bulk-import `.pst` files to Exchange Online.

- **With records management**:
  o Create retention labels, called **file plan**, which support additional information that help you track business or regulatory requirements.
  o Declare items as **Records**.
  o Trigger disposition review of content before it is permanently deleted.
  o Export information about all disposed items.

Retention policy

For most organizations managing the volume of data created can be a daunting task. It is important to effectively manage and govern this information to comply with regulatory and industry requirements and reduce risk in events of data breach. Microsoft Purview Data Lifecycle Management offers retention policies that help organizations manage and govern data at scale. A retention policy is an overarching policy that applies to an entire location.

The locations covered by a retention policy are as follows:

- SharePoint sites and OneDrive accounts
- Mailboxes
- M365 Group mailboxes & sites
- Teams chat and channel messages
- Viva Engage (formerly Yammer)

These policies can either be applied org-wide or be scoped. Org-wide policies apply to the entire tenant like all mailboxes or all SharePoint sites. Scoped policies apply to a subset like some mailboxes and SharePoint sites. Scoped policies can use static scopes or adaptive scopes.

Using retention policies organizations can do the following:

- **Retain content**: For specific periods of time. This will prevent accidental or intentional deletion of data that is required to be retained for legal or regulatory purposes.
- **Delete content**: Permanently delete content that has served its business purpose.

With both these actions, retention settings can be configured to achieve one of the following outcomes:

- **Retain-only**: Retain content forever or for a specified period.
- **Delete-only**: Permanently delete content after a specified period.
- **Retain and then delete**: Retain content for a specified period and then permanently delete.

Following are the steps to create a retention policy:

1. Login in **https://purview.microsoft.com** and click on **Data Lifecycle Management** tile.
2. Navigate to **Policies | Retention policies** and click on **New retention policy**.
3. Give the policy a name and description and click **Next**.
4. Choose the **Admin Units** you would like to apply the policy to and click **Next**.
5. Choose the scope as **Adaptive** or **Static** and click on **Next**.
6. If you chose adaptive scope, then select the adaptive scope you want to use. If you chose static scope, then manually select the locations you would like to include in the policy and click on **Next**.
7. In the next page, you will be asked to choose the retention settings. Choose the appropriate settings depending on your conditions and click **Next**.
8. On the last page, review the settings and click **Submit**.

When content has retention settings applied, it remains in the original location. Nothing changes for users, and they can continue to work with their documents normally. But if they edit or delete content that is included in the scope of a retention policy, a copy of that item is retained in a separate location and held there till the item reaches its retention period after which the actions specified in the retention policy is applied. For example, a retention policy specifies that all files in a SharePoint document library should be retained for seven years after creation and then deleted. A user deletes a file from the document library after two years of creation, the document is moved to a separate location and remains there for the next five years after which it is deleted. These locations are not visible to end users and most of the time, they are not even aware that they exist.

The location where the item is moved depends on the location it was deleted from, as follows:

- Files deleted from SharePoint and OneDrive are moved to a folder called **Preservation hold library**.

- Emails deleted from an Exchange mailbox are moved to the **Recoverable items** folder.

- Messages deleted from Teams and Viva Engage are moved to a hidden folder called **SubstrateHolds** which is a subfolder in the Exchange **Recoverable items** folder.

Retention labels

Retention policies apply blanket retention and deletion settings to entire locations. However, there can be situations where the specific items under these locations might have separate retention and deletion requirements. In such cases, retention labels and label policies in Microsoft Purview Data Lifecycle Management can be used. A retention label is a visual label that specifies the retention settings for a file. Retention labels can be used in combination with retention policies. For example, you might need to have all content in a SharePoint site to be retained for seven years and then deleted, but certain files might need to be retained for longer. In such cases you can specify a retention policy at the SharePoint site level and apply retention labels to the individual items that have longer retention requirements.

A retention label can retain items for a specific period from when items were created, modified or label applied. Event-based retention like retention to start at the end of the financial year or upon contract termination can also be applied. You can also just label the items without applying any retention or deletion settings.

Following actions can be taken once the retention period expires:

- **Delete the items automatically**: This will permanently delete the item.

- **Start a disposition review**: Some highly sensitive documents might need to be approved for disposal before they can be deleted. Using a disposition review, administrators can define up to five levels of reviewers to approve before the item is deleted.

- **Change the label**: A new label can be applied at the end of the retention period.

- **Run a Power Automate flow**: Customized flows can be run to meet specific business needs not met by the in-built options.

- **Deactivate retention settings**: All retention settings will be deactivated at the end of the retention period and the item will not be deleted.

To create a retention label, login in **https://purview.microsoft.com** and click on **Data Lifecycle Management** tile. Select on **Retention labels** and then click on **Create a label** to launch the label creation wizard.

File plan

Although retention labels can be created in Data Lifecycle Management, file plan in Records Management offer additional capabilities like marking items as records, bulk-creating retention labels by importing from a spreadsheet, exporting existing labels for analysis and offline collaboration and adding optional file plan descriptors that provide more information about the label.

Marking items as records

The key difference between a retention label and a file plan is that using a file plan you can mark an item as a record or a regulatory record.

Refer to the following:

> **Note: This is an additional capability, and you can always use a file plan even if you are not marking items as a record or a regulatory record.**

- **Record**: When an item is marked as a record, certain restrictions are placed on the item in terms of what actions are allowed or blocked, additional activities about the item are logged and a proof of disposition is maintained when the item is deleted at the end of its retention period. Placing these restrictions may be required by some industry or compliance regulations. Organizations also might want to protect some highly sensitive content from intentional or accidental changes by marking them as records. For example, legal contracts might need to be protected from change after final signatures. It is possible to start with an unlocked record while it is in draft mode and lock it once it is complete. An unlocked record can be edited; however, it cannot be moved to other locations.

- **Regulatory record**: Marking an item as a regulatory record places additional restrictions on the file. Due to this, the option to mark an item as a regulatory record is not available by default and must be enabled using the PowerShell cmdlet `Set-RegulatoryComplianceUI-Enabled $true`. Once this is done the option to mark items as regulatory records appears in the file plan creation wizard. Refer to *Figure 12.24*.

Labels that mark items as regulatory records have the following restrictions enforced:

- No one can remove the label. This includes the global administrator.
- The retention period can only be extended. It cannot be made shorter.
- The label must be applied using a label policy. It cannot be automatically applied.
- The label cannot be applied to items that are checked out in SharePoint.

Items marked as records are denoted with lock icon in SharePoint Online as shown in the following figure:

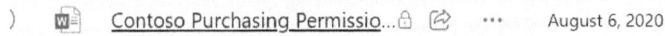

) 　 🗎　 Contoso Purchasing Permissio...🔒 ↪ 　···　　August 6, 2020

Figure 12.22: Items marked as records in SharePoint

Following are the steps to create a file plan:

1. Login to **https://purview.microsoft.com** and click on the **Records Management** tile.

2. Click on **File plan** and in the right pane click on **Create a label**.

3. Give the label a name and description and click **Next**.

4. In the next page, you will be asked to specify the file plan descriptors and click **Next**. Refer to the following figure for an example:

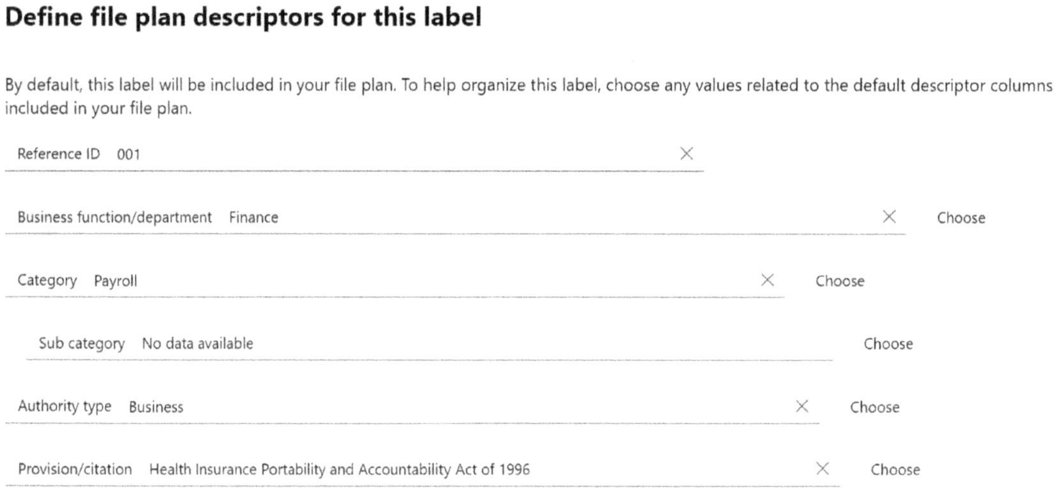

Define file plan descriptors for this label

By default, this label will be included in your file plan. To help organize this label, choose any values related to the default descriptor columns included in your file plan.

Reference ID　001　　　　　　　　　　　　　　　　　　　　　　✕

Business function/department　Finance　　　　　　　　　　　　　　✕　　Choose

Category　Payroll　　　　　　　　　　　　　　　　　　　　✕　　Choose

Sub category　No data available　　　　　　　　　　　　　　　　　　　Choose

Authority type　Business　　　　　　　　　　　　　　　　　✕　　Choose

Provision/citation　Health Insurance Portability and Accountability Act of 1996　　✕　　Choose

Figure 12.23: File plan descriptors

5. In the next screen, define the label settings and click **Next**.

6. Specify the time for which items should be retained and click **Next**.

7. You can now choose to mark the item as a record or a regulatory record. Refer to the following figure:

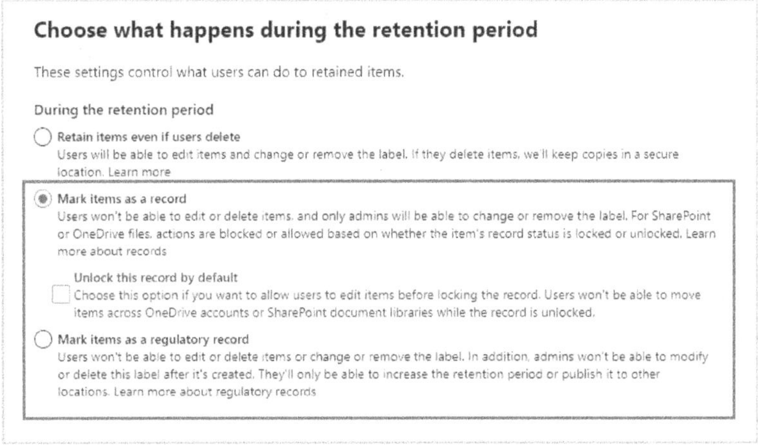

Figure 12.24: Declaring items as records

8. Now choose what happens once the item reaches its retention period and click **Next**. The options available are the same as creating a retention label.

9. Review the settings and click on **Create label**.

Following are the points to be kept in mind while deciding if an item should be marked as a record:

- Editing properties of a locked record is allowed by default but can be changed by going to the Purview portal and clicking on the **Settings** tile. Navigate to **Records Management** | **Retention labels**. Switch the **Allow users to edit record properties** to **Off**.

- When labelled items are deleted from SharePoint and OneDrive locations, they appear deleted to the user, but they are moved to the **Preservation hold library** where they live out their retention time. Deleting labelled items can be blocked in the Purview portal by clicking on the **Settings** tile and navigating to **Records Management** | **Retention labels**. Switch the settings **Allow users to delete items on OneDrive** and **Allow users to delete items on SharePoint sites** to **Off**.

Label policies

Once the label is created it will have to be published to make it available for applications and users. Just like sensitivity labels, retention labels can be applied manually by users or automatically based on conditions like SITs, keywords and trainable classifiers. Labels can also be applied to cloud attachments that are shared as links in Exchange, Teams, Viva Engage and M365 copilot. Publishing a label is called creating a label policy.

Like retention policies, label policies can either be applied org-wide or be scoped. Org-wide policies apply to the entire tenant like all mailboxes or all SharePoint sites. Scoped policies apply to a subset like some mailboxes and SharePoint sites. Scoped policies can use static scopes or adaptive scopes.

Following are the steps to create a label policy:

1. Login in **https://purview.microsoft.com** and click on the **Data Lifecycle Management** or **Records management** tile.
2. Navigate to **Policies** | **Label policies** and in the right pane click on **Publish labels**.
3. In the first step, choose the labels to publish using this policy and click **Next**.
4. Choose the **Admin Units** to which this policy will apply and click **Next**.
5. Choose the scope as **Adaptive** or **Static** and click **Next**.
6. If you chose adaptive scope, then select the adaptive scope you want to use. If you chose static scope, then manually select the locations you would like to include in the policy and click **Next**.
7. Name your policy and click **Next**.
8. Review the settings and click on **Submit**.

To auto-apply a label, following are the steps:

1. Login in **https://purview.microsoft.com** and click on **Data Lifecycle Management**.
2. Navigate to **Policies** | **Label policies** and in the right pane click on **Auto-apply a label**.
3. In the first screen, enter a name and description for the policy and click **Next**.
4. In the next screen, choose the information you would like to label and click **Next**.
5. Choose the **Admin Units** that you would like to include in the scope of the policy and click **Next**.
6. Choose the scope as **Adaptive** or **Static** and click on **Next**.
7. If you chose adaptive scope, then select the adaptive scope you want to use. If you chose static scope, then manually select the locations you would like to include in the policy and click on **Next**.
8. Choose the label you would like to apply and click **Next**.
9. Lastly, choose to turn the policy on immediately or run the policy in simulation mode and click on **Next**. In simulation mode, no content will be labelled but you will be able to monitor the content picked by the policy and make changes if required.
10. Review the settings and click **Submit**.

As is clear from the steps, retention labels, retention policies and file plans have many overlaps, but each serves specific purposes.

Use the following table to understand the differences and help you choose which option to use in which scenario:

Capability	Retention policy	Retention label	File plan
Delete, retain-only, delete-only	Yes	Yes	Yes
Workloads	• Exchange • SharePoint • OneDrive • M365 Groups • Teams • Viva Engage	• Exchange • SharePoint • OneDrive • M365 Groups	• Exchange • SharePoint • OneDrive • M365 Groups
Applied to	Locations	Items	Items
Automatically applied	Yes	Yes	Yes
Manually applied	No	Yes	Yes
Retention applied based on conditions	No	Yes	Yes
Retention persists when item is moved	No	Yes, within the tenant	Yes, within the tenant
Disposition review	No	Yes	Yes
File plan descriptors	No	No	Yes
Declare item as record	No	No	Yes

Table 12.2: Difference between retention policy, retention label and file plan

Licensing

The following table summarizes the minimum licensing requirements for using the various capabilities in Data Lifecycle Management and Records Management:

Capability	Minimum license required
Retention policies	Office 365 E3
Retention labels	Office 365 E1
If retention labels have the below settings Event based retention Disposition review Mark items as records At the end of retention period change the retention label	M365 E5 Information Protection & Governance
Retention label policies	Office 365 E1

Capability	Minimum license required
If retention label policies have the below settings Auto apply a retention label using SIT or keywords Apply default retention label to a SharePoint site, document library or folder Adaptive scopes	Office 365 E5
If retention label policies have the below setting Auto apply a retention label using a trainable classifier	M365 E5 Information Protection & Governance
File plan	Office 365 E5

Table 12.3: Minimum license requirement

Principles of retention

Since a single item can be in scope of multiple retention policies and have a retention label applied, the question arises that what happens in case of a conflict.

Following principles of retention apply to resolve a conflict:

- Retention always wins over deletion.
- If conflicts remain, the longest retention period wins.
- If conflicts remain, explicit deletions win over implicit deletions.
    - A retention label provides explicit retention in comparison to retention policies. For example, a retention policy applied on a SharePoint site deletes content after 7 years but some documents in the site have a retention label applied that deletes content after five years. The file will be deleted after five years.
    - Scoped policies win over org-wide policies for deletion. For example, an org-wide retention policy deletes all mails after ten years and a scoped retention policy deletes mails after five years. Mails in mailboxes subject to both policies will be deleted after five years.
- If conflicts remain and retention is applied using multiple scoped retention policies, then the shortest deletion wins. For example, a mailbox is subject to two scoped policies where one deletes content after ten years and the other after five years, the content will be deleted after five years.

Managing data disposition

Many industry regulations require organizations to not just dispose of data safely, but they also have requirements that organizations be able to provide a proof of disposal in cases of audit or litigation. As we have learnt, data can be automatically deleted by policy or be subject to a disposition review. Disposition reviews are configured while creating a file plan. Each item can be sent to five levels of review before a decision is made. Administrators can also configure a number of days ranging from 7-365 for auto-approval.

Refer to the following figure for disposition review configuration while creating a file plan:

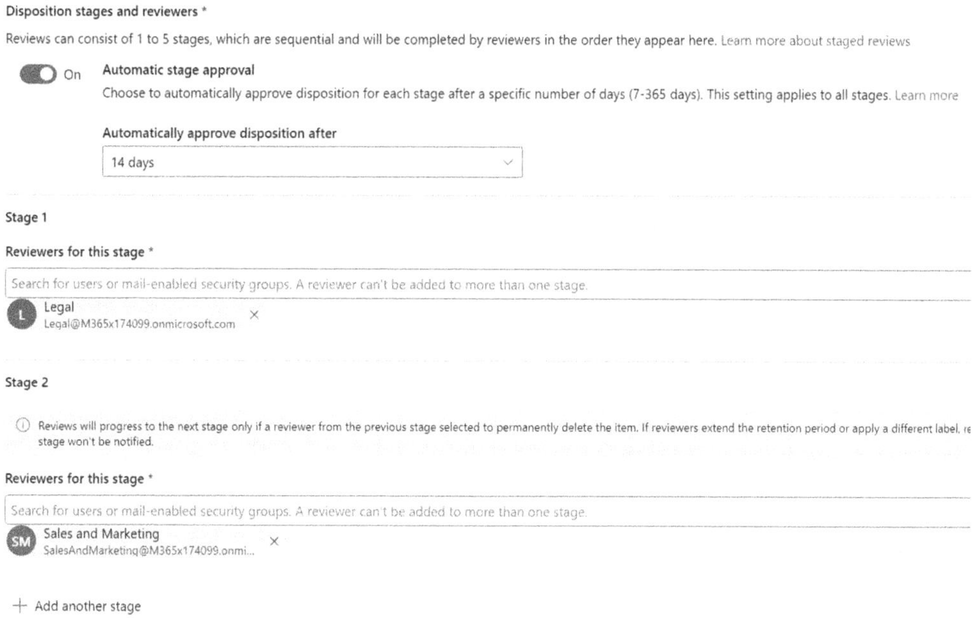

Disposition stages and reviewers *

Reviews can consist of 1 to 5 stages, which are sequential and will be completed by reviewers in the order they appear here. Learn more about staged reviews

⬤ On   **Automatic stage approval**

Choose to automatically approve disposition for each stage after a specific number of days (7-365 days). This setting applies to all stages. Learn more

Automatically approve disposition after

14 days	⌄

Stage 1

Reviewers for this stage *

Search for users or mail-enabled security groups. A reviewer can't be added to more than one stage.

Ⓛ   Legal
Legal@M365x174099.onmicrosoft.com   ✕

Stage 2

ⓘ Reviews will progress to the next stage only if a reviewer from the previous stage selected to permanently delete the item. If reviewers extend the retention period or apply a different label, re stage won't be notified.

Reviewers for this stage *

Search for users or mail-enabled security groups. A reviewer can't be added to more than one stage.

Ⓢⓜ   Sales and Marketing
SalesAndMarketing@M365x174099.onmi...   ✕

＋ Add another stage

Figure 12.25: Disposition review configuration

When items are up for disposition, the reviewers receive an email asking them to approve or deny the disposition. They will be directed to the **Disposition** page in **Records Management** tile in the Purview portal. From here they will be able to approve disposal, relabel the file, extend the retentions period or add additional reviewers.

Since data disposal is a critical task, the reviewers must be members of the **Disposition Management** role group. This role is included in the **Records Management** role group which has other privileges as well. If you would like the reviewers to only be able to dispose of items and not perform other activities like viewing or configuring other records management features, create a custom role group and add only the **Disposition Management** role to it.

> **Note: By default, Global Administrator does not have the Disposition Management role.**

Each person that accesses the **Disposition** page can only see items that are assigned to them for review. For a records management administrator to be able to see all items assigned to all reviewers, additional configuration needs to be made as described in the following steps:

1. Create a mail-enabled security group in Exchange Online and add the records managers to it.

2. Login to **https://purview.microsoft.com** and click on **Settings** | **Records Management** | **Disposition**.

3. In the right-pane, add the mail-enabled security group under **Mail-enabled security group for disposition** and click **Save**. Once this group is added, it can only be removed using PowerShell.

Now all members of the above mail-enabled security group will be able to see all items assigned to all reviewers on the **Disposition** page. The proof of disposition on this page is maintained for seven years and can be used for internal investigation or litigation purposes. *Figure 12.26* shows an example of items disposed of by a retention label. You can use the **Export** option to export this information in a **.csv** format.

Figure 12.26: Items disposed of by a retention label

Gain visibility

Microsoft Purview provides **Activity explorer** to monitor what is being done with data in your environment. It provides a historical view of activities performed on the content. This information is collected from the M365 audit logs and is available in the activity explorer for 30 days. Activity explorer is accessible in the Purview portal from any of the solutions discussed in this chapter and click on **Explorers** | **Activity explorer**.

The following figure shows a view of the activity explorer:

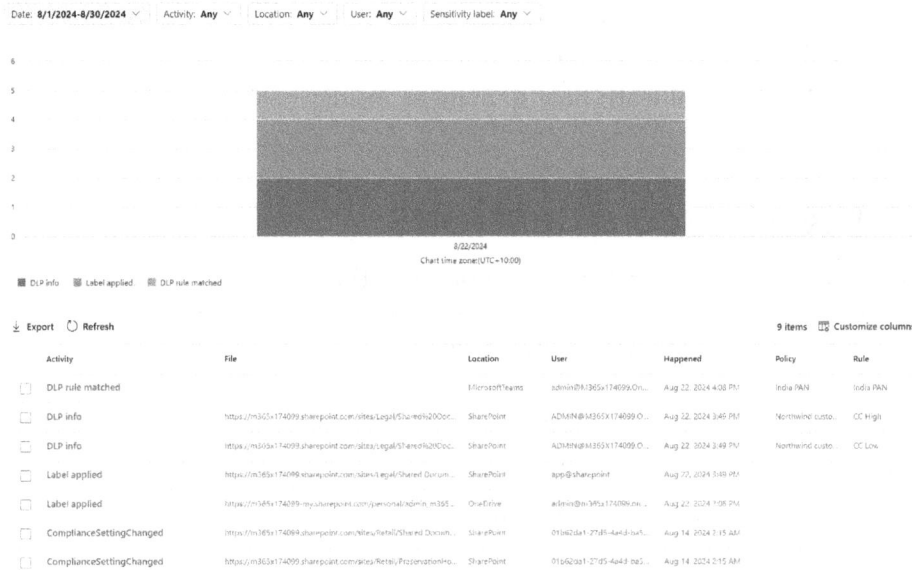

Figure 12.27: Activity explorer

Activity explorer requires one of the following licenses:

- Microsoft 365 E5
- Office 365 E5
- Advanced Compliance E5 add-on
- Advanced Threat Intelligence E5 add-on
- M365 E5 Information Protection & Governance
- M365 E5 Compliance

Conclusion

In this chapter, we have learned about the significance of data security and governance, and how Microsoft Purview solutions facilitate organizations in achieving this efficiently and at scale. The chapter detailed data classifiers such as SITs and TCs, and their use in identifying and protecting sensitive information. We explored how to find content in the M365 cloud and employ the Microsoft Information Protection on-premises scanner to detect and safeguard sensitive information in on-premises repositories. Additionally, we covered the use of sensitivity labels and label policies to secure data both in use and at rest. Furthermore, the chapter provided an in-depth explanation of how to prevent intentional or accidental data exfiltration using the DLP capabilities of Microsoft Purview across Exchange, SharePoint, OneDrive, Teams, non-Microsoft cloud applications, and endpoints. Lastly, we discussed retaining and disposing of content through Microsoft Purview Data Lifecycle Management and Records Management. You should now be well-prepared to design, plan, and implement a comprehensive data security and governance solution for your organization.

In the next chapter, we will learn how to manage insider risks using Microsoft Purview solutions.

Multiple choice questions

1. **You are the IT administrator of your organization. You have been asked to create a list of all files in SharePoint Online that contain credit card numbers. You need to use Data Explorer to discover this content. What are the two perquisites to use Data Explorer.**

   a. M365 E5 Information Protection & Governance license

   b. Install the Microsoft Purview Information Protection Scanner

   c. Onboard devices to Microsoft Purview

   d. Context explorer list viewer permissions

2. **Your organization was working on a top-secret project for a new car design. Before you could announce the design, the exact same design was announced by your competitor. Upon investigation, you discovered that an employee emailed the car designs to their friend working for the competitor. What can you do to prevent these incidents in the future? Select the most appropriate answer.**

   a. Use sensitivity labels to encrypt the files.

   b. Implement DLP policies to prevent users from emailing sensitive content to external recipients.

   c. Design and implement a comprehensive data loss prevention strategy for the organization.

   d. Block all employees from sending any external email.

3. **Your organization is subject to an industry regulation that requires them to retain all content for 7 years. Which of the below should you use to accomplish this? The solution should require the least amount of administrative effort.**

   a. Retention labels

   b. Retention policies

   c. File plans

   d. Mark all items as records

Answer key

1. a, d
2. c
3. b

CHAPTER 13
Managing Insider Risks

Introduction

Data does not move itself; people move data. Many data breaches occur due to insiders, whether they are acting maliciously or simply being careless. Therefore, it is crucial to understand how data flows within or outside the organization, as well as the user's intentions behind moving the data. With this knowledge, administrators can make informed decisions in the event of a data breach and prevent insider threats by identifying patterns in user behavior that may lead to data exfiltration. Microsoft Purview provides solutions to help organizations detect these early warning signs and take measures to protect their data.

Structure

The chapter covers the following topics:

- Microsoft Purview Insider Risk Management
- Microsoft Purview Communication Compliance
- Microsoft Purview Information Barriers

Objectives

By the end of this chapter, readers will have an understanding of the various tools provided by Microsoft Purview that help organizations understand risky user behavior and prevent data exfiltration. It begins with *Microsoft Purview Insider Risk Management* and demonstrates how it can be used to monitor user activities and detect early signs of potential data breaches. The chapter goes on to describe how adaptive protection within insider risk management can dynamically assign risky users to more restrictive DLP policies. Additionally, it covers how *Microsoft Purview Communication Compliance* can be utilized to detect violations of conduct policies. Finally, it explains how *Microsoft Purview Information Barriers* can create segments within an organization to prevent communication between different parts.

Microsoft Purview Insider Risk Management

In today's environment, employees can more readily create, manage, and share data across various platforms and services. This enhanced access introduces threats such as data breaches, **intellectual property** (IP) theft, insider trading, fraud, and policy violations. Organizations often face resource constraints in identifying and addressing these risks. Microsoft Purview Insider Risk Management leverages signals from both the M365 cloud and non-Microsoft services to correlate data that aids administrators in detecting, prioritizing, and responding to malicious or negligent user activities. Adhering to the privacy by design principle, it pseudonymizes usernames. It also employs role-based access control to safeguard audit logs, ensuring user privacy.

Microsoft Purview Insider Risk Management requires one of the following licenses:

- M365 E5 Insider Risk Management
- M365 E5 Compliance
- M365 E5

Prior to deploying Insider Risk Management in your organization, collaborating with stakeholders to devise a strategy is crucial. This strategy should encompass the identification of risky activities and specify the actions to be taken once risky users are detected. Additionally, it is vital to comprehend the regional and industry-specific regulatory and compliance standards that your organization must follow. Ensure involvement from IT, security, compliance, privacy, HR, and legal departments, among others.

Getting started

Microsoft Purview Insider Risk Management offers a quick onboarding guide that enables you to get started quickly. It guides the user through the following steps:

Get permissions

To view Insider Risk Management as a menu item in the Microsoft Purview portal, you must be assigned to one of the following role groups:

- Microsoft Entra Global Administrator
- Microsoft Entra Compliance Administrator
- Microsoft Purview Organizational Management
- Microsoft Purview Compliance Administrator
- Insider Risk Management
- Insider Risk Management Admins

There are further role groups available that offer granular permissions over the tasks available in Insider Risk Management. They are as follows:

- Insider Risk Management Analysts
- Insider Risk Management Investigators
- Insider Risk Management Auditors
- Insider Risk Management Approvers
- Insider Risk Management Session Approvers

Depending on the tasks you want to assign to individuals, you can assign them to these role groups in the Purview portal by clicking on **Settings | Roles and scopes | Role groups**. If these role groups do not suffice, custom roles can be created from this page.

Enable auditing

Microsoft Purview Insider Risk Management uses the M365 Audit logs for user insights and risky activities. Auditing is enabled by default in M365 tenants. Some organizations may have disabled it. Insider Risk Management requires that auditing is enabled.

Enable analytics

By turning on Insider Risk Management analytics you can conduct an evaluation of potential insider risks without making any changes or creating policies. This can help you identify areas of user risk and can aid in deciding what type of policies need to be configured. It also provides real-time recommendations on the policy thresholds that help in fine-tuning the policies and reducing noise.

Following are the steps to enable Insider Risk Management thresholds:

a. Login to **https://purview.microsoft.com** and click on **Settings**.

b. Click on **Insider Risk Management | Analytics**. In the right-pane, switch the toggle to **On** and click on **Save**.

c. Wait for about 48 hours for the analytics results to start showing up.

Configure connectors

Microsoft Purview Insider Risk Management integrates with several non-Microsoft systems to receive signals that enrich the risk detection and enhance visibility into risky activities performed by the users. This is done by configuring data connectors. To configure data connectors, in the Microsoft Purview portal navigate to **Settings** | **Data connectors** | **All connectors**.

Following connectors are available:

- **Microsoft 365 HR connector**: This connector enables you to import signals like termination dates, last employment dates, performance review plan notifications and job level changes from non-Microsoft human resource platforms.

- **Physical badging connector**: Using this connector you can connect Insider Risk Management to employee access and badging system and can help enrich the user risk data with insights like accessing office buildings after working hours or accessing restricted areas.

- **Healthcare specific data connectors**: These connectors enable Insider Risk Management to receive signals from a non-Microsoft electronic medical record system. This provides visibility for patient data misuse.

- **Insider Risk Indicator**: This connector helps extend insider risk management by importing detections from non-Microsoft workloads like Salesforce and Dropbox.

Configure Insider Risk Management settings

There are several settings available in Insider Risk Management for you to get the most out of your implementation. Accurately configuring these settings will help in ensuring that you get the most accurate insights and are able to uncover insider risks before any damage is done. This section discusses the settings are available in the Microsoft Purview portal under **Settings** | **Insider Risk Management**.

Data sharing

Using this setting you can choose the following:

- Export Insider Risk Management alerts to SIEM of your choice. When you turn on this setting, you can use Office 365 Management Activity APIs to export the alert details to other applications that can be used to manage or aggregate insider risk data.

- Share insider risk management user risk levels with Microsoft Defender and Microsoft Purview DLP alerts bringing unique user context to these solutions. Adding this data enhances the data available with these solutions enabling analysts to prioritize alerts.

Policy indicators

Microsoft Purview Insider Risk Management offers policy templates that define the type of risk activities that will be detected. Each policy looks for specific indicators that corresponds to triggers and risk activities. There is a list of global indicators that are disabled by default, for them to be available in a policy, they should be enabled.

Microsoft Purview Insider Risk Management offers the following built-in indicators:

- **Office indicators**: These include indicators from SharePoint sites, Teams and emails. Some examples are downloading sensitive content from SharePoint sites, deleting content from SharePoint, sending Teams messages that contain SITs.

- **Device indicators**: These include device specific activities like copying files to USB, printing files, creating hidden files on the device.

- **MDE indicators**: These are attempts to bypass security controls or using unapproved software.

- **Risky browsing indicators**: These indicators report on users' browsing habits like accessing malware, hacking, phishing or criminal activity websites.

- **Physical access indicators**: These indicators report is a user is accessing the office premises after they have been terminated or attempting to enter restricted areas. For this to work, priority physical assets must be configured, and the **Physical badging** data connector must be configured.

- **MDCA indicators**: These monitor user activity in applications connected to MDCA. The indicators include mass download or sharing of files from a connected app, failed logons, impossible travel or anonymous IP activity.

- **Health record indicators**: These indicators look for users accessing health records. A healthcare-specific data connector and the **human resource (HR)** data connector must be configured.

- **Cumulative exfiltration detection**: This indicator detects when the number of exfiltration activities performed exceeds the normal amount performed by users in the organization over the past 30 days.

- **Risk score boosters**: This setting increases the severity of an alert, if a user's activity is above their usual activity for a day or they have had a previous policy violation or they are a member of a priority user group or a high impact user.

- **Cloud storage indicators**: This includes indicators for Google Drive, Box and Dropbox that you can use to detect techniques used to exfiltrate data. These apps must first be connected in Microsoft Defender.

- **Cloud service indicators**: These include indicators for Amazon S3 and Azure to detect techniques used to avoid detection by disabling logs to steal sensitive data. These apps must first be connected in Microsoft Defender.

- **Generative AI apps**: This detects user entering risky prompts in copilot or receiving sensitive response from copilot.

- **Microsoft Fabric indicators**: These include activities like deleting Power BI reports or dashboards, downgrading the sensitivity labels of Power BI artifacts or downloading Power BI reports.

- **Communication Compliance indicators**: This set of indicators detect when users send inappropriate content or images in Microsoft Teams, email or Viva Engage. A Communication Compliance policy must exist to be able to use these indicators.

You can also create variants of these built-in indicators to tailor detection for different set of users. These are used along with **Detection groups**.

In addition to built-in indicators, custom indicators can be created using the **Insider Risk Indicators** connector to bring in signals from non-Microsoft data sources.

Detection groups

Detection groups are used in conjunction with policy indicators to create indicator variants which help policies ignore or detect user activity related to domains, file paths, file types, keywords, SITs, SharePoint sites and TC. This helps reduce false positives.

Following example explains how detection groups and policy indicators work together:

- You want to detect the deletion of SharePoint files that contain a **Credit Card Number**.
- You create detection groups containing the **Credit Card Number Sensitive Information Type (SIT)**.
- Then create a variant of the indicator **Deleting files from SharePoint**.
- Configure the variant to detect only the activity involving the detection group.

This new indicator can now be used in policies which will help reduce noise by reporting and deleting events of only the files that contain a credit card number instead of reporting all deleted files.

Global exclusions

This setting enables policies to exclude domains, email signature attachments, file paths, file types, keywords, SITs, SharePoint sites and TC to be evaluated by policies to help reduce noise. When using this setting, detection groups can be used to tailor detections for different sets of users.

Inline alert customization

When activities meet the threshold defined in policies, alerts are generated. To reduce the number of alerts generated by a policy, you can adjust the policy thresholds or remove the activity from the policy. This setting allows administrators to quickly tune a policy from the Alert dashboard while reviewing the alert. Members of the

Insider Risk Management Analysts and Insider Risk Management Investigator roles can customize alerts. If this setting is not enabled, only members of the Insider Risk Management Admins or Insider Risk Management Admins role groups can edit the policy conditions from the policy editor.

Intelligent detections

This setting can be used to accomplish the following tasks:

- **File activity detection**: Using this setting you can specify the number of daily events that should occur to boost the risk score for download activity. For example, if you specify this threshold as 20 and a user downloads 10 files every day for 30 days but one day they download 15 files, the risk score will not be boosted as their daily file download is less than 20. However, if 25 files were downloaded, the risk score will be boosted as this indicates unusual behavior and could be a data exfiltration attempt that requires further investigation

- **Alert volume**: Risky user activities detected are assigned a risk score that determines the alert severity of low, medium or high. By default, insider risk management generates a certain amount of low, medium and high alerts. This can be adjusted to suit requirements. You can choose from the following options:

  o **Fewer alerts**: You will see all high-severity alerts, fewer medium-severity alerts and no low-severity alerts. Some alerts could be missed if this setting is chosen.

  o **Default alerts**: You will see all high-severity alerts and a balanced number of medium and low-severity alerts.

  o **More alerts**: You will see all medium and high-severity alerts and most low-severity alerts. If this setting is chosen you could see more false positives.

- **Microsoft Defender for Endpoint alert statuses**: To get better visibility of security violations, you can import MDE alerts for activities used in insider risk management policies. These alerts are imported daily.

- **Domains**: Using this setting you can specify unallowed and third-party domains to boost detections. For example, you might want to detect all activities where content is shared with a gmail.com address or if your organization uses a non-Microsoft cloud storage for business purposes, you might want to detect risky sharing activities.

Microsoft Teams

Insider risk management integrates with Microsoft Teams for better collaboration between stakeholders while investigating alerts. Each time an insider risk management case is created and associated Team is created where all members who are assigned the Insider Risk Management, Insider Risk Management Analysts, Insider Risk Management

Investigators role groups are added.

Notifications

Using this setting you can choose to send emails to administrators when the first alert is generated for a new policy, a daily email when high-severity alerts are generated, a weekly email summarizing the policies that have unresolved warnings, a monthly email summarizing new analytics scan insights an email when analytics is turned off.

Policy timeframes

This setting allows you to define the past and future review periods triggered after a policy is matched.

Following settings are available:

- **Activation window:** This setting determines how long the policy will remain active for the user. It is activated when the user performs the first activity matching a policy. It can range from 1 to 30 days for any user assigned to a policy. If you have configured a policy and set the activation window to 30 days, once the triggering event occurs, the policy is active for that user for 30 days.

- **Past activity detection**: This setting determines the number of days the policy will look back to detect user activity. It is triggered when a user performs the first activity that matches a policy. It uses the M365 Audit logs to look back, and it can range from 0 to 90 days. If you have configured a policy and the past activity detection is set to 30 days, the policy will look back 30 days in the audit logs for matching activity once the user performs the first activity that matches the policy.

  For example, if you set the activation window to 15 days and past activity detection to 30 days. A user triggers a policy match on 1st July, the policy will retrieve user activity from 30 days ago (1st June) and will continue to record new activity for an additional 15 days (July 16th).

Power Automate flows

Power Automate is a workflow automation service from Microsoft. It enables you to create flows that automate actions across applications and services. These flows can be created from templates or manually.

Following Power Automate templates are available for Insider Risk Management:

- Notify users when they are added to an insider risk policy.
- Request information from HR or business about a user in an insider risk case.
- Notify manager when a user has an insider risk alert.
- Create record for insider risk case in ServiceNow.

Priority physical assets

There are physical assets in every organization that are more critical than others. These might be restricted company buildings, data centers or server rooms. These assets can be added to the priority physical assets list. This works with the **physical badging** data connector to integrate signals from physical control systems and user activities to detect users accessing these assets outside working hours or unauthorized access to secure areas.

Priority user groups

Not all users in an organization need to be monitored at the same level. Depending on their level of access to sensitive information, some might require closer monitoring than others. Use priority user groups to define users that need closer inspection and more sensitive risk scoring. Alerts, cases and reports related to users might also require to be reviewed only by certain reviewers instead of being open to review by all analysts. Members of the built-in Insider Risk Management, Insider Risk Management Analysts and Insider Risk Management Investigators role group can be assigned permissions to review these users.

Privacy

Use this setting to determine if you would like to show pseudonymized versions of usernames or actual usernames across insider risk management features like policies, alerts and cases.

Additional configuration

Depending on your organization and the business case you might want to make additional settings to receive signals from other systems.

Some of them are listed, as follows:

- Onboard devices to Microsoft Purview to receive risk signals from endpoints. This is the same process as onboarding devices to MDE or for endpoint DLP.
- Connect cloud applications in Microsoft Defender to receive signals from cloud storage and service applications.
- Configure DLP policies to help identify malicious or accidental sharing of sensitive information.
- Configure MDE to receive security violation incidents from endpoints.

Creating insider risk management policy

Once the above settings have been configured, you can proceed with creating insider risk management policies. Microsoft Purview Insider Risk Management offers policy templates based on which policies can be created. Following templates are available:

- Data theft by departing employees
- Data leaks
- Data leaks by risky users
- Risky AI usage
- Security policy violations
- Security policy violations by departing users
- Security policy violations by priority users
- Health record misuse
- Risky browser usage

To configure an Insider Risk Management policy, following are the steps:

1. Login to **https://purview.microsoft.com** and click on the **Insider Risk Management** tile.
2. Click on **Policies** and in the right pane click on **Create policy**.
3. Select a policy template and click **Next**.
4. Enter a **Name** and **Description** for the policy and click **Next**.
5. If you would like to assign this policy to an **Admin unit**, click on **Add or remove admin units**, select the admin unit and click **Next**.
6. In the next screen, select if you would like to apply the policy to the following:

   a. **All users, groups and adaptive scopes**: You will be asked to select users and groups to exclude from the policy. Make the appropriate selections and click **Next**. If you do not want to exclude any users, groups or adaptive scopes from this policy, just click **Next**.

   b. **Specific users, groups and adaptive scopes:** You will be asked to select the users, groups and adaptive scopes to be included in the policy. Make the appropriate selection and click **Next**.

7. On the next screen, select the content that this policy should look for.

   Following options are available:

   a. SharePoint sites

   b. Sensitivity labels

   c. Sensitive into types

   d. File extensions

   e. Trainable classifiers

   Make the appropriate selections and click **Next**. The next screens will walk you through selecting the specific SharePoint sites, sensitivity labels, SITs, file extensions and trainable classifiers depending on your selections.

8. On the next screen, choose the event that will trigger this policy. Depending on the policy template chosen, options on this screen can differ. Make the appropriate selections and click **Next**.

9. On the next screen, you can choose to apply the built-in thresholds for the policy or choose your own thresholds and click **Next**.

10. Next, select the policy indicators. These are the actions that will be used to generate alerts for this policy. Click **Next**.

11. On the next screen, you can select the detection options. These advanced detection options like sequence detections, cumulative exfiltration detection and risk score boosters provide additional insights into the activities. Click **Next**.

12. Finally, you can choose to apply the thresholds provided by Microsoft or customize your own thresholds and click **Next**.

13. Review the selections and click **Submit** to create the policy.

Investigate activities and manage alerts

Once you have configured insider risk settings and created the policies, you will start receiving insights into risky user activities. Depending on the policies, some of these activities might also generate alerts. Managing these risky user activities and alerts is an important step in minimizing insider risks in your organization. Microsoft Purview Insider Risk Management provides the below tools to investigate risky user activities and alerts.

User activity reports

As we have learnt, users will be assigned to an insider risk management policy that will generate alerts when users perform certain activities. In some scenarios, however, you may want to examine potential risky user activities for specific users for a defined time period without having to add them to an insider risk policy. These might be users you have received a tip about. Once you have configured the policy indicators in insider risk management settings, all potentially risky user activity associated with the selected indicators is detected regardless of whether an alert is generated or not. User activity reports are created for each user and can include all activities for a 90-day period.

The user activity data will be available for reporting approximately 48 hours after the activity occurs. For example, if a user performs an activity on 15th September, it will be reported by 17th September.

To create a user activity report, following are the steps:

1. Login to **https://purview.microsoft.com** and click on the **Insider Risk Management** tile.

2. On the **Overview** page click on **Manage reports** in the **User activity reports** card.

3. On the **User activity reports** page, click on **Create user activity report**.

4. In the fly out pane, select the **Start date**, **End date** and **Users**. Click on **Create report**.

5. The system will process the report, and, in a few seconds, you will see a **Close** button to close the fly out pane.

The report will be available on the **User activity reports** page with a status of **Not ready**. It takes about ten hours for the report to be ready for review. Wait for the status of the report to update to **Report ready** before starting investigation.

Figure 13.1 shows an example of the **User activity reports** page. Notice that the usernames are anonymized to protect user privacy.

Users must be a member of the Insider Risk Management Investigators role group to be able to view this page.

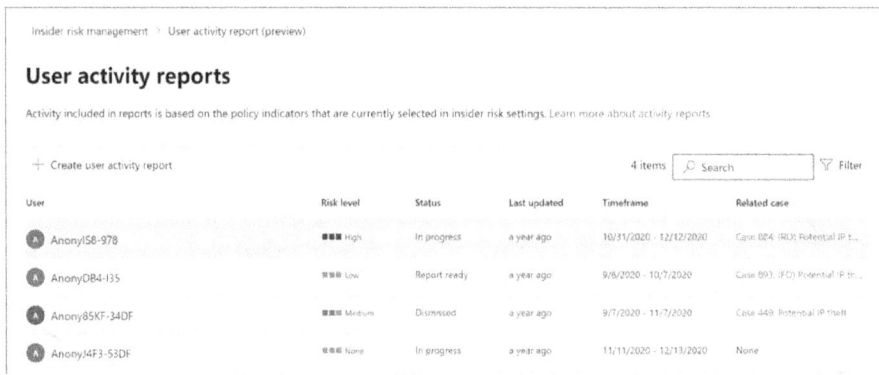

Figure 13.1: User activity reports

Click on any user to view their activity. *Figure 13.2* shows an example of user activity:

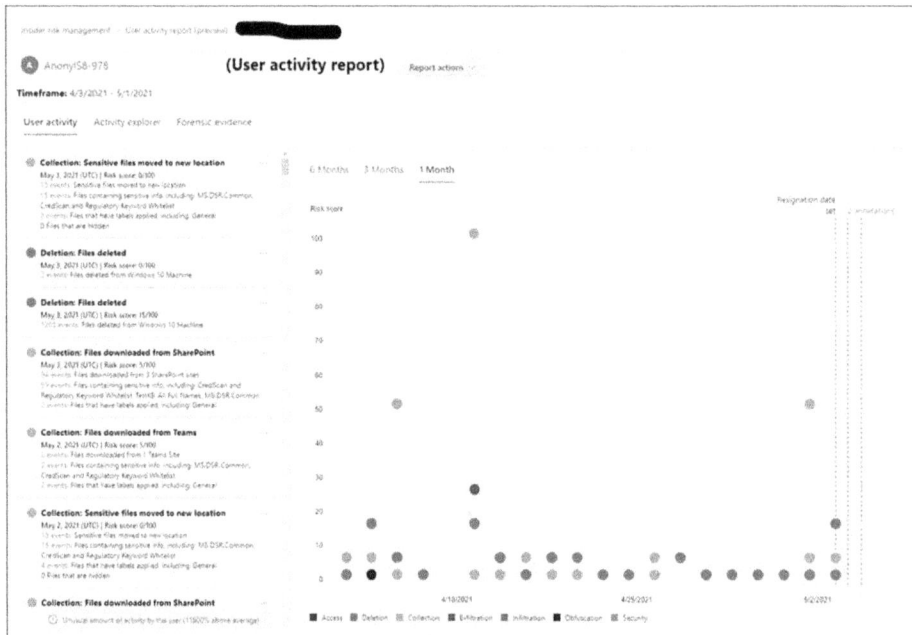

Figure 13.2: User activity details

Following information is available on the tabs in this page:

- **User activity**: This is a chart view to investigate risky activities and activities that occur in a sequence. For example, a user downloading sensitive files from a SharePoint site, downgrading the label and copying them to a USB. This tab enables you to quickly review the user and includes a historical timeline or all activities, the user's risk score and the sequence of events.

- **Activity explorer**: This is a comprehensive tool that provides detailed information about activities.

Alert dashboard

Insider risk management policies generate alerts when users perform activities that are configured in the policies. These alerts are available on the **Alerts** page under **Insider Risk Management**.

Following figure shows an example of the alerts generated by various insider risk management policies:

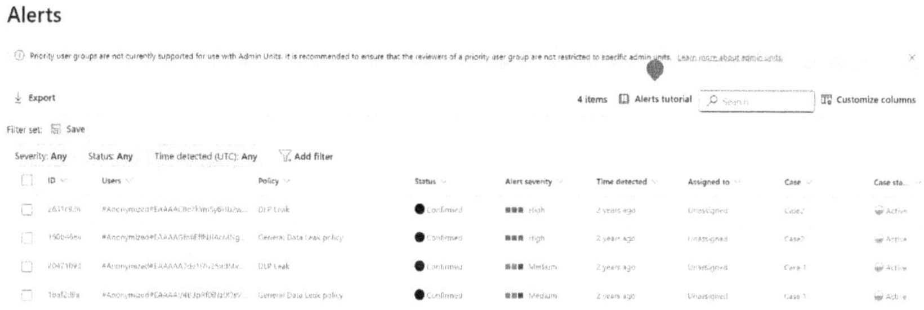

Figure 13.3: Insider risk alerts

Click on any alert to view more details about the alert. *Figure 13.4* shows an example of the alert details. You can use the information on this page to triage the alert and decide whether to dismiss it or confirm and create a case for further investigation.

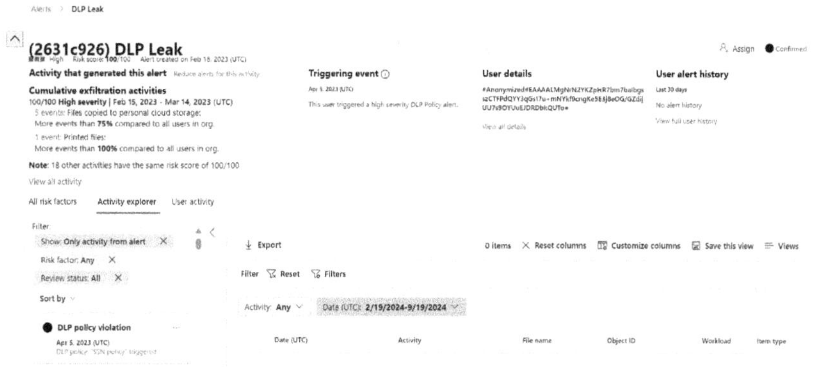

Figure 13.4: Alert details

If you choose to create a case, it will be available under the **Cases** page as shown in the following figure:

Figure 13.5: Cases in Insider Risk Management

Click on any case to view the details as shown in the following figure:

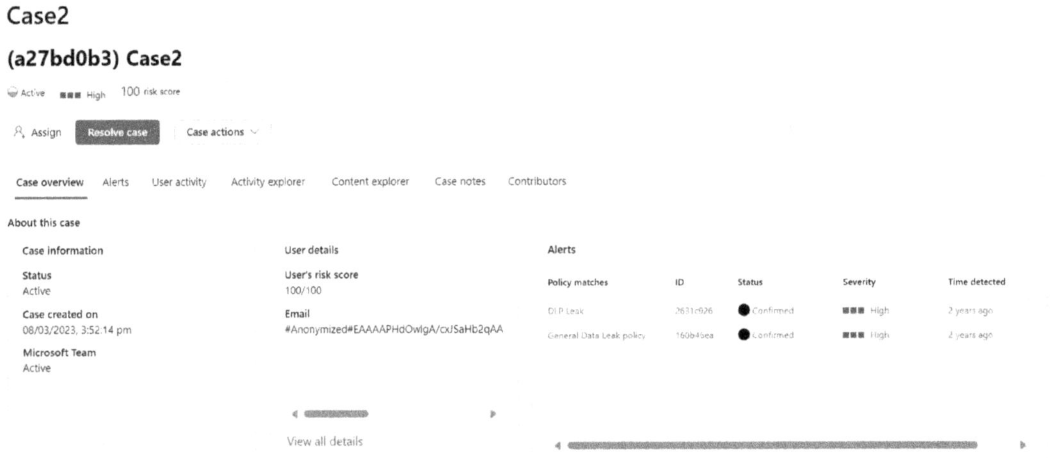

Figure 13.6: Case details

On this page, you can perform the following tasks:

- Assign the case to an investigator for further investigation and analysis.
- Resolve the case.
- Use the tabs to view details about the case and take appropriate action.
- Add more contributors to the case to aid in investigation and decision making.
- Use the **Case actions** button for the following:

o   Send an email notice to the user.

o   Escalate the case to eDiscovery for further investigation.

o   Run a Power Automate flow.

o   Use Microsoft Teams to collaborate with all contributors.

o   Turn off pseudonymization to be able to view actual usernames.

Note: Caution should be exercised while turning off pseudonymization as investigators will be able to see actual usernames. While this may be required in some cases for deeper investigation, it can lead to violation of user privacy and potential bias decision making.

Following figure summarizes the flow of information in Insider Risk Management:

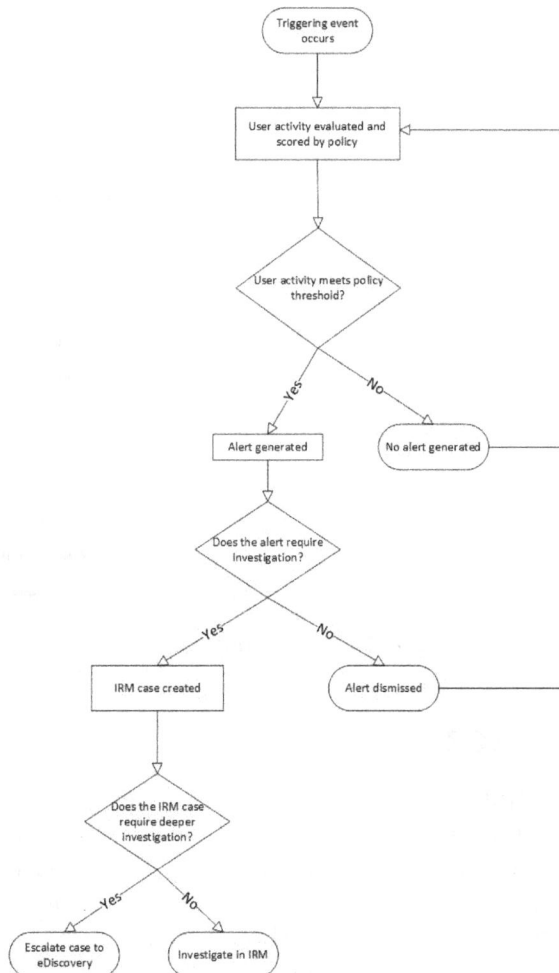

Figure 13.7: *Case management in Insider Risk Management*

Audit log

The insider risk audit log enables administrators to stay informed about the activities performed in Insider Risk Management. Actions taken by users who are assigned to any of the Insider Risk Management role groups are recorded here. This log is enabled by default and cannot be disabled. To view the audit log, select the **Audit log** option under **Insider Risk Management**.

Following figure shows an example of the insider risk audit log:

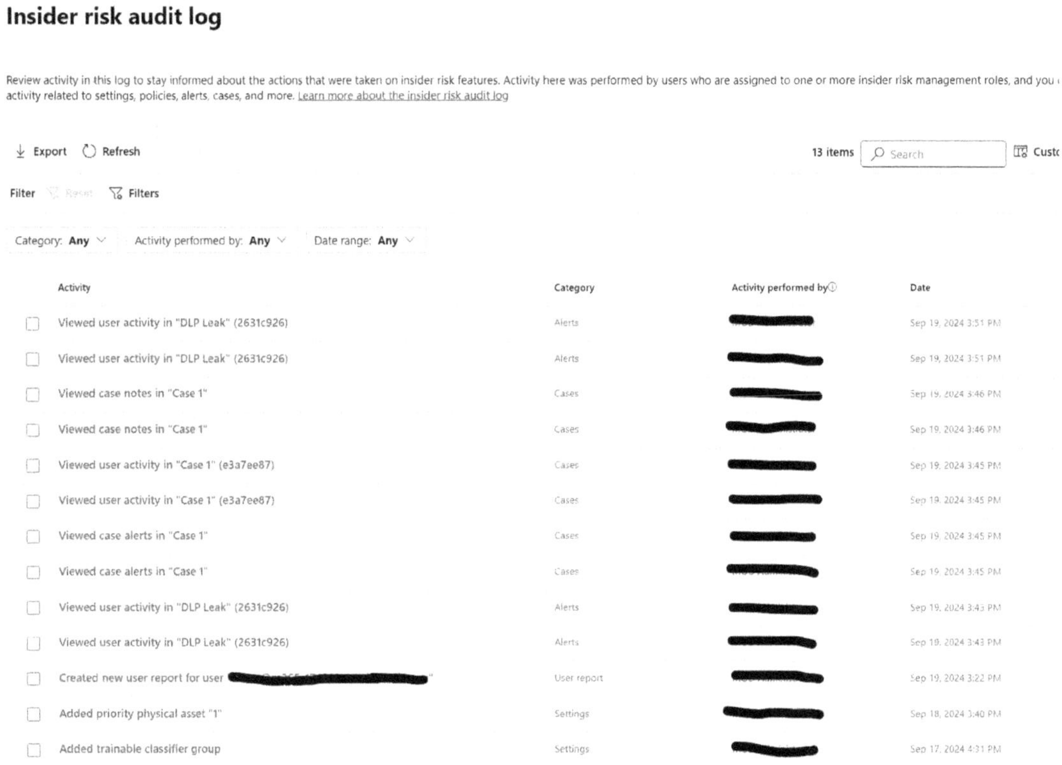

Figure 13.8: Insider risk audit log

Forensic evidence

Forensic evidence is an optional add-on feature in Insider Risk Management that gives security teams visual insights into potential insider data security incidents. Using forensic evidence security teams can capture screen activity across user devices to better understand and respond to data risks like data exfiltration. Security teams can decide the policies they want to create including what risky events should trigger screen capturing and if users should be notified when forensic capturing is activated. This feature is off by default.

Following are the key capabilities of this feature:

- **Visual capturing**: This enables organizations to record clips of security-related user activities. For example, screen recording can be triggered when the user mounts a USB to their device.

- **Protecting user privacy**: Multiple levels of approvals are required to activate screen capture for a user.

- **Continuous or event-based capturing**: Security teams can decide if they want to capture the screen whenever it is active or based on events like mounting a USB drive or downloading a sensitive file from SharePoint.

- **Strong RBAC**: The ability to start screen capture and to view the captures clips is tightly controlled and is only available to users with the right permissions.

Licensing and billing

Forensic evidence is an add-on feature and is not included with your M365 subscription. If you want to use this feature, you can opt-in to purchase the forensic evidence add-on for Insider Risk Management in units of 100GB per month which translates to about 1100 hours of recording captures at a video resolution of 1080p. This is used to store the clips captures by forensic evidence and is reset on the first of every month. Unused capacity does not carry over. The capture clips are retained for 120 days.

Microsoft offers a free trial of 20GB for organizations that want to evaluate forensic evidence before buying it. This 20GB is available till it runs out or till one year from activation. If you purchase forensic evidence before the trial runs out, you will be able to use the remaining capacity before the system starts billing the purchased capacity. To sign up for the trial, in the Purview portal, navigate to **Insider Risk Management** | **Forensic evidence** | **Capacity and billing** and click on **Claim 20GB of capacity**.

This section describes how security teams can configure and use this feature.

Configure your environment

Ensure that the following domains are allowed in your firewall and proxy server to allow forensic evidence to store clips:

- `compliancedrive.microsoft.com`
- `*.events.data.microsoft.com`
- `officeclient.microsoft.com`
- `odc.officeapps.live.com`
- `hrd.svc.cloud.microsoft`

Configure supported devices

Collecting forensic evidence is supported on Windows 10 and Windows 11 devices and virtual machines. In addition to being onboarded to the Insider Risk Management solution, the devices should also have the Forensic Evidence client installed. This client can be downloaded from the Purview portal by navigating to **Insider Risk Management | Forensic Evidence | Client installation**. Download the installer package and use your preferred software distribution method to distribute the software to the users' devices.

Configure settings

There are several settings in forensic evidence that provide flexibility for the types of security-related user activity captured, capturing parameters, bandwidth limits and offline capturing options. To configure setting for forensic evidence, in the Purview portal, navigate to **Insider Risk Management | Forensic evidence | Forensic evidence settings** and make the appropriate selections. Following figure shows the available settings:

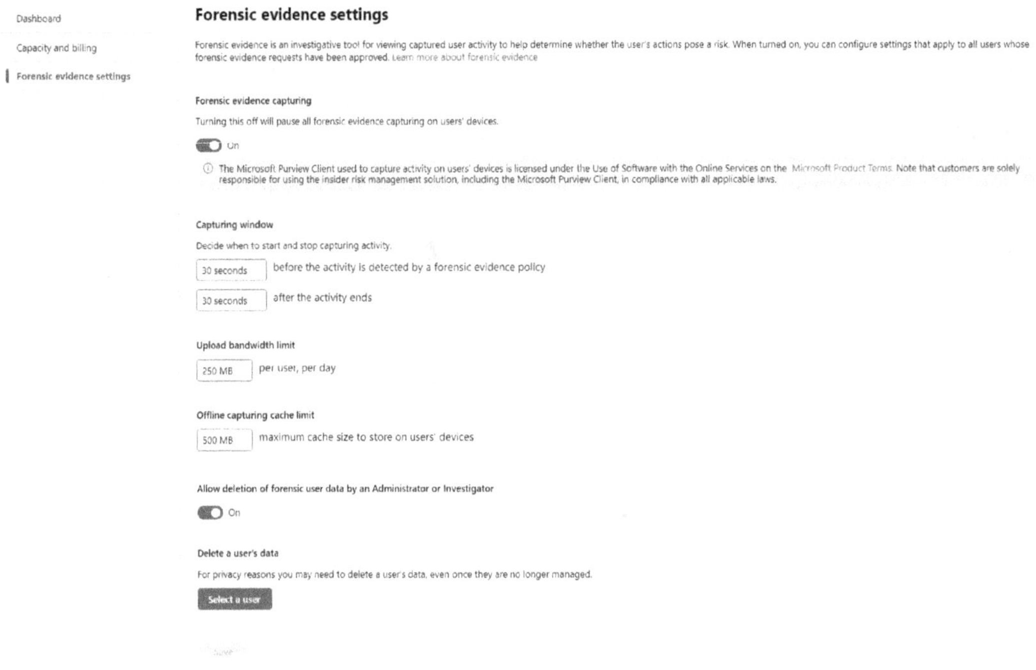

Figure 13.9: Forensic evidence settings

Create a policy

Policies in forensic evidence define the scope of security-related user activity to be captured. There are two types of policies, as follows:

- **All activities**: This policy captures user activity whenever the user is active on their device. This is usually used for a specific time, for example, when you suspect a user of being involved in potentially risky activities. To preserve capacity and user privacy, you can choose to exclude certain applications and/or websites from the capture.

- **Specific activities**: These policies are configured to trigger recording when a user performs certain activities like mounting a USB drive or printing a file. You can also choose to capture activity for specific applications and/or websites.

To create forensic evidence policy, following are the steps:

a. Login to the **https://purview.microsoft.com** and click on **Insider Risk Management**.

b. Navigate to **Forensic evidence** | **Forensic evidence policies** | **Create forensic evidence policy**.

c. Select **Specific activities** or **All activities** and follow the policy creation wizard to create the policy.

Define and approve users

Before screen capture can start, administrators must create an approval request for users to be added to the policy. This request must then be approved. Simply adding users to the policy does not make those users eligible for capturing.

Administrators in the Insider Risk Management or Insider Risk Management Admins role groups can submit approval requests and members of the Insider Risk Management Approvers role group can approve.

Following are the steps to create an approval request:

a. Login to the **https://purview.microsoft.com** and click on **Insider Risk Management**.

b. Navigate to **Forensic evidence** | **User management** | **Manage forensic evidence requests** | **Create request**.

c. On the **Users** page, click **Add users**. Search for the user and click on **Add** | **Next**.

d. On the **Forensic evidence policy** page, select the policy to which the user should be added and click **Next**.

e. On the next page, write a justification to let the reviewer know why the user is being added to the policy and click **Next**.

f. On the **Email notifications** page, you can optionally choose a template to notify the user that screen capture will be turned on for them. This email will be sent to the user only if the request is approved. Click **Next** and **Finish**.

Pending requests can be viewed by navigating to **Insider Risk Management** | **Forensic evidence** | **Pending requests**.

The approvers will receive an email for the approval request. To approve or decline the request, following are the steps:

a. Login to the **https://purview.microsoft.com** and click on **Insider Risk Management**.

b. Navigate to **Forensic evidence | Pending requests**.

c. Select a user to review and click on **Approve** or **Reject** as applicable and click **Close**.

Approved requests can be revoked if the need arises. Revoking approval does not delete any clips that have already been captured. To revoke a request, following are the steps:

a. Login to the **https://purview.microsoft.com** and click on **Insider Risk Management**.

b. Navigate to **Forensic evidence | User management | Approved users**.

c. Select the user and click **Remove**.

d. On the removal confirmation page, select **Remove** to revoke capturing.

Viewing captured clips

Captured clips can be viewed by selecting the Forensic evidence tab under Insider Risk Management. Members of the Insider Risk Management and Insider Risk Management Investigators role groups can view the capture clips.

Adaptive protection

Adaptive protection in Microsoft Purview uses machine learning to identify the most critical risks and dynamically apply protection from Microsoft Purview DLP, Microsoft Purview Data Lifecycle Management and Microsoft Entra Conditional Access. This integration helps organizations automate responses to insider risks and reduce the time required to identify and remediate threats. They can be proactive and prevent data exfiltration instead of being reactive and investigating a data exfiltration event.

To use Adaptive Protection, in the Purview portal go to **Insider Risk Management | Adaptive Protection | Adaptive Protection settings** and switch **Adaptive Protection toggle** to **On** and click on **Save**.

Adaptive protection uses context-aware detections, dynamic controls and automated mitigations to assign a risk score to the users based on the activities they perform. This risk score is then used to dynamically assign appropriate DLP, data lifecycle management and conditional access policies to users. For example, if a user has submitted their resignation and are downloading sensitive content from SharePoint, adaptive protection can raise the users risk level and dynamically assign them to a restrictive DLP policy that can prevent them for all external sharing, printing and copying data to USB thereby, preventing IP theft.

Administrators can configure risk factors or activities based on the organization's needs.

The risk levels are updated continuously and automatically based on user activity so when a user's risk increases or decreases their risk levels are adjusted accordingly. Adaptive protection assigns risk levels. These risk levels determine how risky a user's activity is based on the defined criteria. These risk levels have built-in definitions that can be customized as needed, as follows:

- **Elevated risk level**: This is the highest risk level. Users with at least three sequence insights that have a high severity alert for specific activities, or one or more confirmed high severity alerts are assigned this risk level.

- **Moderate risk level**: This includes users with medium severity alerts or users with at least two data exfiltration activities with high severity scores.

- **Minor risk level**: This is the lowest level for users with low severity levels or users with at least one data exfiltration activity with a high severity score.

These risk levels can be configured in the Purview portal by going to **Insider Risk Management** | **Adaptive Protection Insider risk levels**.

Figure 13.10 shows the available settings.

Notice that you can configure how far back Adaptive Protection looks to detect if a user meets the conditions defined in the risk levels and how long a user will remain in a risk level before it is reset. For example, if a user has been assigned elevated risk level, how long do they remain there before their risk level is lowered if they do not perform further risky activities and no longer meet the elevated risk level criteria.

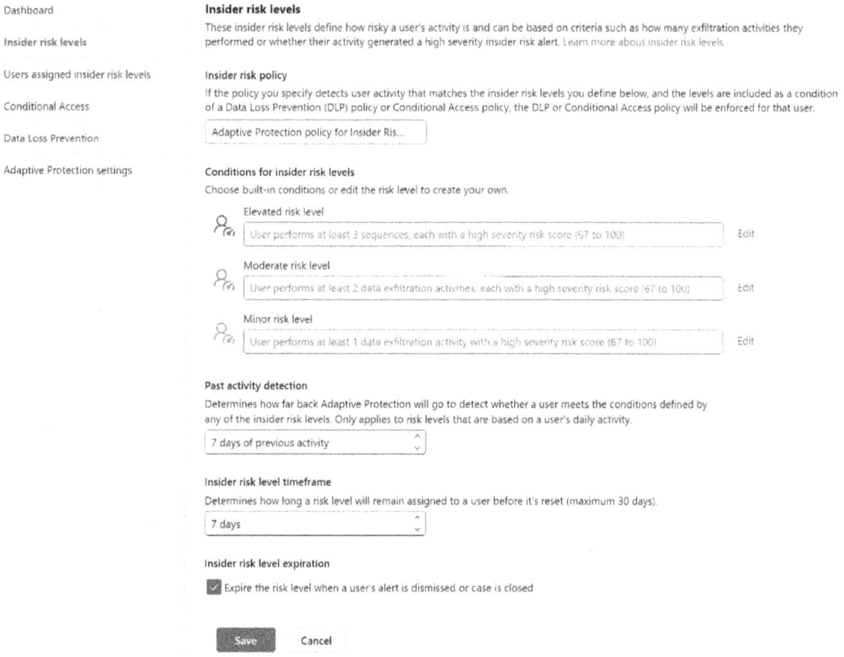

Figure 13.10: Insider risk levels

Users that meet the conditions for insider risk levels and are assigned a risk level are listed on the **Users assigned insider risk levels** page, as shown in *Figure 13.10*.

Now, let us explore how insider risk levels are used to apply controls. Consider the following examples:

- **Data loss prevention**
  - o Allow users with **Minor risk level** to receive policy tips on best practices of handling sensitive data.
  - o Users with **Moderate risk level** receive a block with override option. This way you can encourage them to think before they act.
  - o Users with **Elevated risk levels** are blocked from sharing sensitive data.
- **Data lifecycle management**
  - o If Insider Risk Management determines that a user is at an **elevated risk level**, data lifecycle could be used to ensure that any content deleted by the user is retained for 120 days.
- **Conditional Access policies**
  - o Users with **Minor risk levels** can be required to accept Terms of Use before accessing and application.
  - o Users with **Medium risk levels** can be prompted for MFA before they access certain applications.
  - o Users with **Elevated risk levels** can be blocked from accessing any applications.

Permissions

Since Adaptive Protection interacts with other solutions, administrators may need additional permissions as described in the following table:

Task	Permission
Configure Adaptive Protection	Insider Risk Management Insider Risk Management Admins
Create and manage DLP policies with Adaptive Protection condition	Compliance Administrator Compliance Data Administrator DLP Compliance Management Global Administrator
Create and manage Conditional Access policies with Adaptive Protection condition	Global Administrator Conditional Access Administrator Security Administrator

Task	Permission
View details on users' assigned insider risk levels	Insider Risk Management
	Insider Risk Management Analysts
	Insider Risk Management Investigators

Table 13.1: Roles required for Adaptive Protection

The above categories correspond to the tabs available on the Adaptive Protection page, as shown in *Figure 13.10*. If you are not assigned to the appropriate role group, you will not see the tab.

Configuring Adaptive Protection

To use Adaptive Protection with DLP, data lifecycle management and Conditional Access, certain steps need to be completed. You can choose between quick setup and custom setup depending on your organization. Quick setup is the fastest way to get started. You do not need any pre-existing insider risk management, DLP, data lifecycle management or Conditional Access policies and you do not need to pre-configure any settings or features.

Quick setup makes the following settings. If you choose custom setup, you will have to make these settings manually:

- Insider risk settings like policy indicators, risk boosters, admin notifications, depending on what is already configured in your environment.
- A new insider risk data leaks policy.
- Adaptive protection risk levels.
- Two DLP policies, that is, one for Team and Exchange and one for Endpoints. These policies include a **block** rule for users with Elevated risk level and an **audit** rule for users with high and low risk levels. These policies are configured in simulation mode which means that user actions are not blocked, and no alerts are generated. You can view the results of the simulation and adjust the settings to suit your requirements before turning the policies on.
- An org-wide auto-apply label policy that monitors users with Elevated risk level and preserves any content that they delete for 120 days.
- A Conditional Access policy in report-only mode that blocks access for users with **Elevated risk level**.

Once Adaptive Protection is enabled, additional conditions are added to the DLP and Conditional Access policies. Refer to *Figure 13.11*:

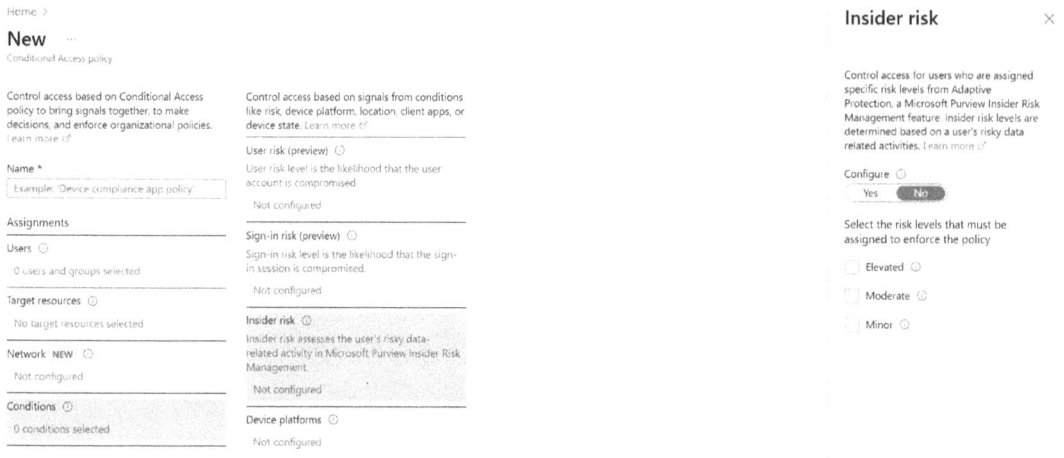

Figure 13.11: Insider risk levels in Conditional Access policy

Refer to *Figure 13.12* for more details:

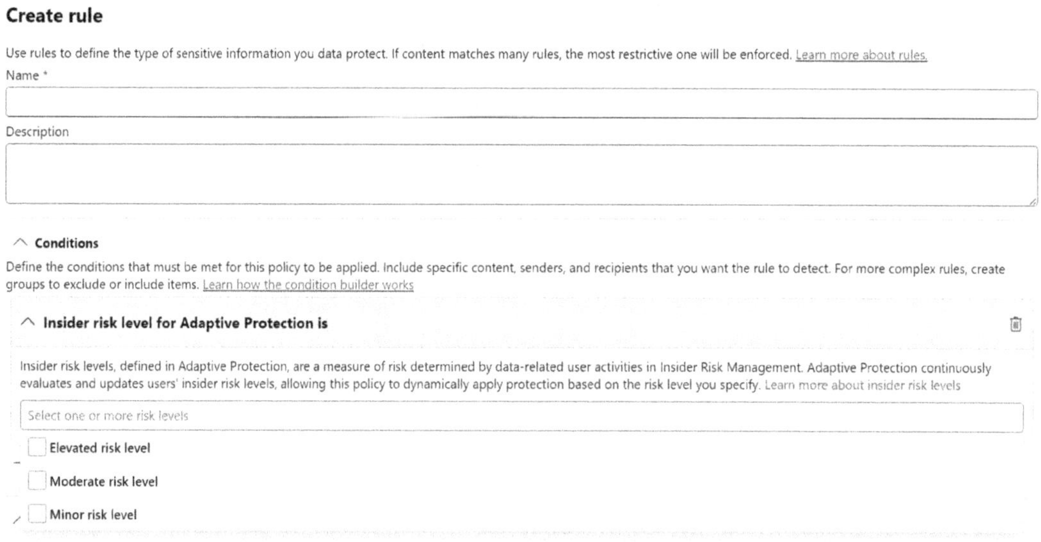

Figure 13.12: Insider risk levels in DLP policy

Microsoft Purview Communication Compliance

Most organizations have strict code of conduct guidelines that employees need to follow when communicating with fellow employees. These could include the use of explicit, discriminatory, offensive or threatening language. Organizations do not have the tools to monitor electronic communication for these violations and must rely on employee reports. Some employees might not report such behavior fearing backlash. Microsoft Purview Communication Compliance is a tool that helps organizations detect and act on code of conduct policy violations in email, Teams chat and channel messages, M365 and Microsoft Copilot, Viva Engage and non-Microsoft communication applications like Facebook, WhatsApp and more. Communication Compliance helps organizations in ensuring employees comply with corporate policies. It also helps managing insider risks as they can get early indications of possible insider trading, IP theft, disgruntled employees or conflict of interest. Lastly, it also helps in meeting regulatory compliance as certain industries require organizations to implement oversight over employee communication.

Microsoft Purview Communication Compliance offers customizable policy templates, flexible remediation workflows and actionable insights that help organization gain early visibility into possible insider threats. Workplace stress and dissatisfaction is often a factor that leads employees to malicious behavior. Communication Compliance can send signals concerning employee communication to Insider Risk Management so that those employees can be more closely monitored using insider risk policies.

Microsoft Purview Communication Compliance requires one of the following licenses:

- M365 E5 Insider Risk Management
- M365 E5 Compliance
- M365 E5

Before implementing Communication Compliance work with the stakeholders in your organization to identify the type of communications that are considered risky and the actions that should be taken on policy violations. The stakeholders can include people from IT, Compliance, Privacy, Risk, Security, HR and Legal departments.

Getting started

Microsoft Purview Communication Compliance offers an onboarding guide that helps you get started quickly. It guides you through the following steps:

Get permissions

Viewing Communication Compliance as a menu option in the Microsoft Purview portal requires one of the following role assignments:

- Microsoft Entra ID Global Administrator
- Microsoft Entra ID Compliance Administrator
- Microsoft Purview Organization Management
- Microsoft Purview Compliance Administrator
- Communication Compliance
- Communication Compliance Admins

There are further role groups available that offer granular permissions over the tasks available Communication Compliance. These are as follows:

- Communication Compliance Analysts
- Communication Compliance Investigators
- Communication Compliance Viewers

Enable auditing

Microsoft Purview Communication Compliance uses the M365 Audit logs for user insights and risky activities. Auditing is enabled by default in M365 tenants. Some organizations may have disabled it. Communication Compliance requires that auditing is enabled.

Configure Communication Compliance settings

There are several settings available in Communication Compliance for you to get the most out of your implementation. Accurately configuring these settings will help in ensuring that you get the most accurate insights and are able to uncover insider risks before any damage is done. This section discusses the settings that are available in the Microsoft Purview portal under **Settings** | **Communication Compliance.**

Privacy

Use this setting to determine if you would like to show pseudonymized versions of usernames or actual usernames across communication compliance features like policies, alerts and cases.

Notice templates

This option enables you to create email templates that can be sent to users. These are available to use any time you need to send an email notice to users about a communication compliance policy.

Sentiment analysis

Powered by the Azure Cognitive Service for Language, this option enables assigning labels like Positive, Negative, and **Neutral** to messages detected by a communication compliance policy. This helps reviewers in prioritizing which messages to investigate first.

Cross-policy resolution

If this setting is turned on and an investigator resolves a message in a policy, all instances of that message appearing in other policies are also resolved.

Teams

When collecting messages from Teams, communication compliance includes Teams meetings transcripts by default. Using this setting you can collect recordings as well. For this communication compliance needs access to your organization's SharePoint and OneDrive content. Click on the **Grant access** button to grant the access.

Convert Viva Engage to Native Mode

When Viva Engage is in Native Mode, all users are stored in Microsoft Entra ID, all groups are Office 365 Groups, and all files are stored in SharePoint Online. For communication compliance policies to detect content from your Viva Engage tenant, ensure that it is in Native Mode.

Configure connectors

The process of configuring connectors is explained in the previous section. The connectors for communication compliance include Bloomberg message, Signal, WhatsApp and more.

Create a communication compliance policy

Once all settings have been configured you can proceed with creating a communication compliance policy. Microsoft Purview offers the following policy templates based on which you can create policies:

- Detect Microsoft 365 Copilot interactions
- Detect inappropriate content
- Detect inappropriate text
- Detect inappropriate images
- Detect sensitive info types
- Detect financial regulatory compliance
- Detect conflict of interest

In addition to these you can also create a policy from scratch by choosing the **Custom policy** action.

Following are the steps to create a policy:

1. Login to **https://purview.microsoft.com** and click on the **Communication Compliance** tile.
2. Click on **Policies** and in the right pane click on **Create policy**.
3. Select a policy template or a Custom policy, and click **Next**.
4. Give your policy a **Name** and **Description** and click **Next**.

5. If you would like to assign this policy to an **Admin unit** click on **Add admin units**, select the admin unit and click **Next**.

6. On the **Choose users and reviewers** page, select if you would like to apply this policy to **All users**, **Select users** or **Select adaptive scopes**. You can also choose to exclude user and groups from the policy. Select the **Reviewers** for this policy and click **Next**.

   Refer to the following figure:

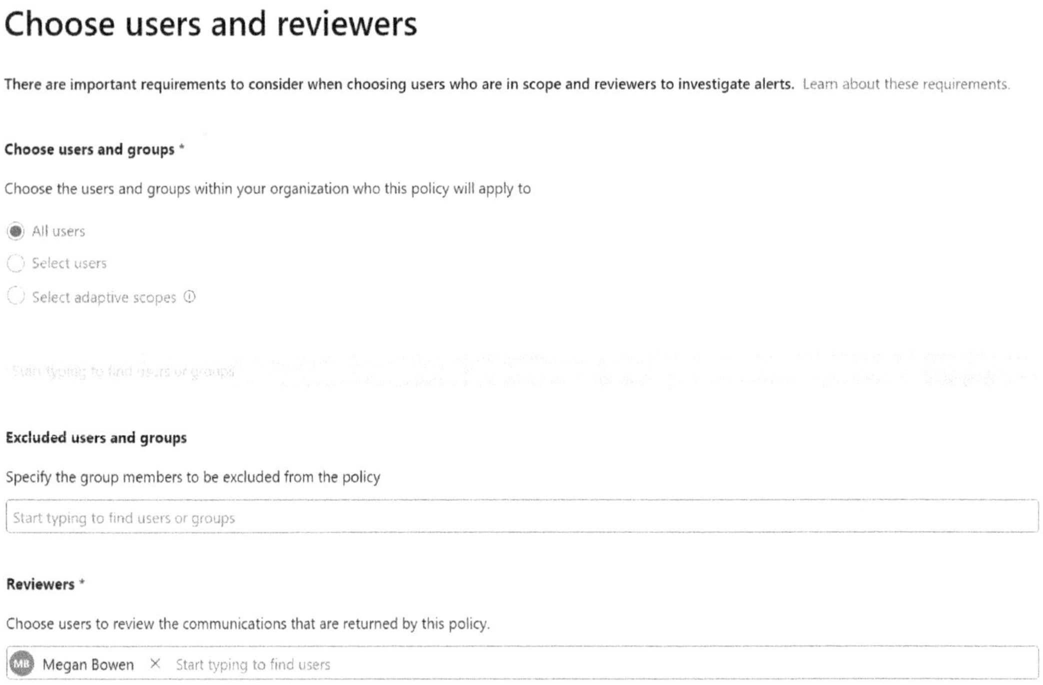

Choose users and reviewers

There are important requirements to consider when choosing users who are in scope and reviewers to investigate alerts. Learn about these requirements.

Choose users and groups *

Choose the users and groups within your organization who this policy will apply to

◉ All users

◯ Select users

◯ Select adaptive scopes ⓘ

Start typing to find users or groups

Excluded users and groups

Specify the group members to be excluded from the policy

Start typing to find users or groups

Reviewers *

Choose users to review the communications that are returned by this policy.

〔 MB 〕 Megan Bowen ✕ Start typing to find users

Figure 13.13: Users and reviewers

7. On the next page, choose the locations where this policy will apply. You can select from **Exchange**, **Teams**, **Viva Engage**, **Microsoft 365 Copilot** and any non-Microsoft apps that you have connected using connectors. Click **Next**.

8. On the next screen, you can make the following selections and click **Next**. Refer to *Figure 13.14*.

   a. Select the direction of the communication.

   b. Conditions like trainable classifiers, SITs, file extension, sender, recipient etc. If you chose to use custom policy, you would have to make all these selections manually. However, if you chose a template, certain conditions would already be selected for you. You can make changes as appropriate.

   c. Check the box next to **Use OCR to extract text from images** if you want to look for embedded text in pictures that matches the conditions content.

d. Review percentage.

e. Filter out messages from email blasting services.

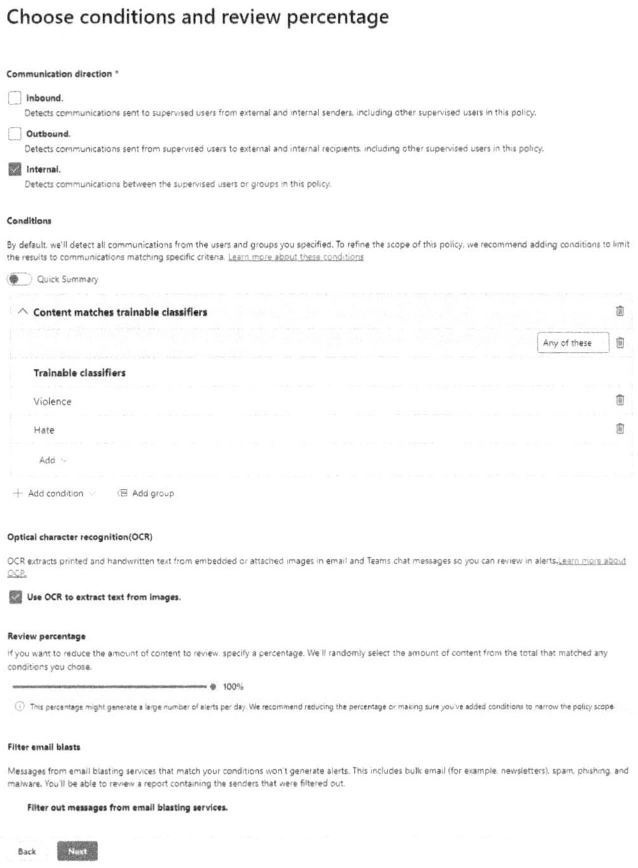

Figure 13.14: Communication compliance policy conditions

9. Review the settings and click **Create policy**.

Review policy matches

Members of the Communication Compliance Analysts, Communication Compliance Investigators or Communication Compliance role group or people assigned as Reviewers in the Communication Compliance policy will be able to review the items matched by the policy. Following are the steps to review the items:

1. Login to **https://purview.microsoft.com** and click on the **Communication Compliance** tile.

2. Click on **Policies** and in the right pane click on the policy to review.

3. The matched items will be shown as in *Figure 13.15*. Notice the information that you can review and the actions available.

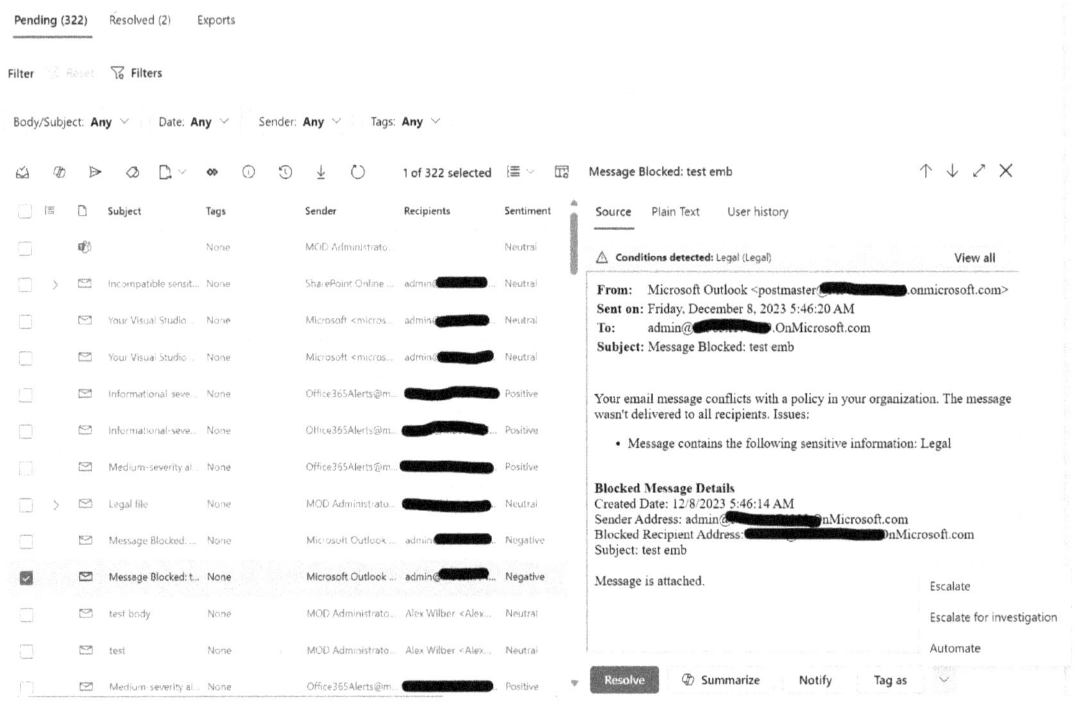

Figure 13.15: Policy matches in communication compliance

Manage alerts

Communication compliance policies generate alerts when messages matching conditions are detected. Members of Communication Compliance Analysts and Communication Compliance Investigators role groups and people assigned as Reviewers in the communication compliance policy can view and act on alerts. To view the alerts in the Purview portal, click on the **Communication Compliance** tile and then click on **Alerts**. Last 30 days of alerts are grouped by policy matches. An alert consists of multiple policy matches. After the required number of policy matches is met for a particular policy, an alert is created, and it appears on this page.

Reports

The **Reports** page under Communication Compliance is the central location to view all reports related to Communication Compliance. You must be a member of the Communication Compliance Viewers role group to view and manage reports.

Following figure shows a snippet of the reports page:

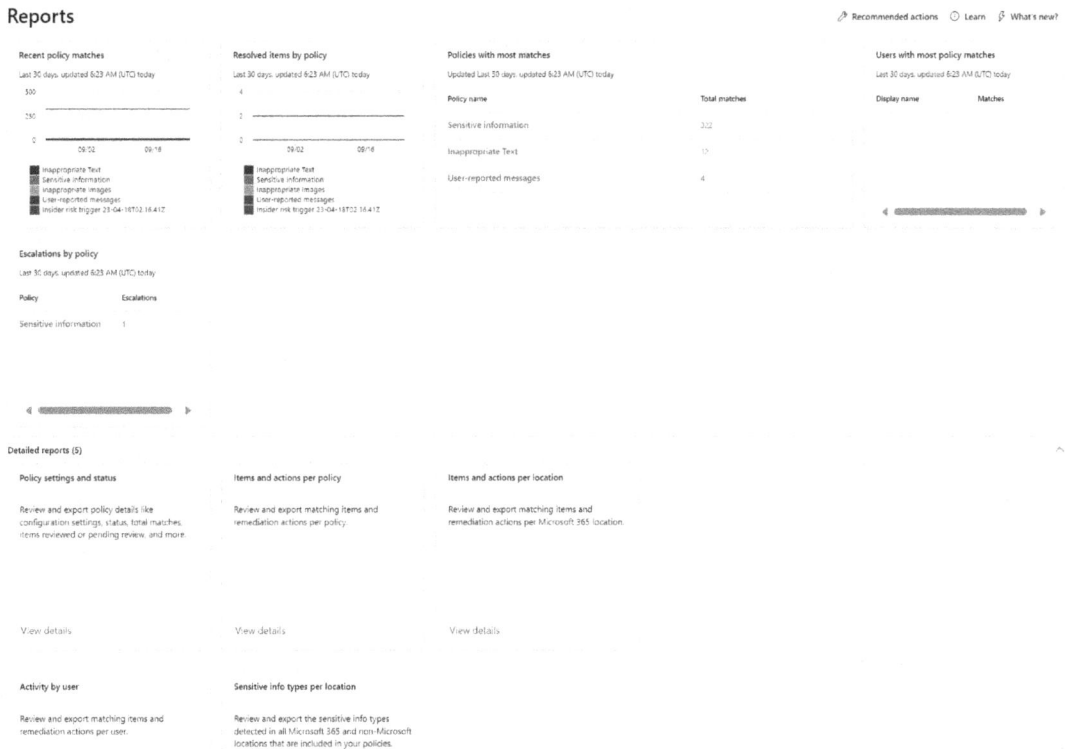

Figure 13.16: Reports in Communication Compliance

Microsoft Purview Information Barriers

Microsoft Purview Information Barriers allows organizations to restrict two-way communication between different groups thereby drawing virtual boundaries within the organization. This is often used in highly regulated industries to avoid conflicts of interest or safeguard the flow of information between users.

Information Barriers may be useful in the following scenarios:

- Teachers in one school should not be able to communicate with students at a different school.
- A research team working on a top-secret product design should only be able to communicate with a product development team.
- IT staff supporting a government defense department should not be able to communicate with the IT staff supporting other customers.

Information Barriers only supports two-way restriction. For example, a scenario where Marketing cannot communicate with Sales, by Sales can communicate with Marketing is not supported.

When Information Barriers is enabled between two groups of users the following restrictions are imposed in **Microsoft Teams**:

- Users will not be able to search for users that belong the other group.
- Not able to add members of the other group to a Team.
- Start a chat session with members of the other group.
- Starting a group chat with members of the other group included.
- Invite members of the other group to join a meeting.
- Share a screen with members of the other group.
- Call a member of the other group in Teams.
- Share a file with a member of the other group.
- Give access to a file through a file sharing link.

Following restrictions imposed in SharePoint and OneDrive. There are further restrictions that depend on the IB mode and are explained under the section *Configure IB modes* later in this chapter.

- Adding a member to a site.
- Accessing site or content by a user.
- Sharing site or content with another user.
- Searching a site.

Microsoft Purview Information Barriers requires one of the following subscriptions.

- Office 365 E5
- M365 E5 Compliance
- M365 E5

Getting started

Before you start with configuring Information Barrier policies in your environment, it is important to understand some terms and concepts.

- **User account attributes**: These are the account attributes defined in Microsoft Entra ID. They are used to assign users to segments.
- **Segments**: These consist of the set of users to whom the Information Barriers policies will apply. For example, if you want to restrict communication between the **Marketing** and **Research** group, then the **Marketing** team becomes one segment and the *Research* team becomes another segment. Defining these segments does not affect the users unless these segments are included in an Information Barriers policy. An organization can have a maximum of 5000 segments and a single user can be assigned to a maximum of 10 segments. Each segment can have only one

policy applied. It is not necessary that every user in the tenant is included in a segment. Some users can be **unsegmented**.

Consider the following points while defining segments:

o   If there are any internal, legal or industry regulations that require communication be restricted between groups of users.

o   Determine the Entra ID attribute that should be used in defining segments. You can use attributes like `Department`, `Company`, `MemberOf`. In addition, custom attributes can also be used.

- **Information Barrier policies**: These policies are used to determine if you want to allow or block communication between the segments. Consider the following scenarios:

  o   **Block communication between segments**: In this scenario, you will create two policies, as follows:

    ▪   Block policy preventing communication from Segment A to Segment B.

    ▪   Block policy preventing communication from Segment B to Segment A.

  o   Allow a segment to communicate with only one other segment. In this scenario, the following policies will be created:

    ▪   Allow policy allowing communication from Segment A to Segment B.

    ▪   Allow policy allowing communication from Segment B to Segment A.

This section describes how you can configure Information Barriers in your organization.

Get permissions

To create and manage Information Barriers policies, you must have one of the following roles:

- Microsoft 365 Global Administrator
- Office 365 Global Administrator
- Compliance Administrator
- Information Barrier Compliance Administrator

Enable auditing

Microsoft Purview Information Barriers uses the M365 Audit logs for user insights and risky activities. Auditing is enabled by default in M365 tenants. Some organizations may have disabled it. Information Barriers requires that auditing is enabled.

Enable IB for SharePoint and OneDrive

If you want to use Information Barriers for SharePoint and OneDrive, you will have to enable it on these services. This should also be done if you are using Information Barriers with Teams as when a Team is created an associated SharePoint site is also created. To enable Information Barriers for SharePoint and OneDrive, following are the steps:

1. Download and install the latest version of the SharePoint Online Management Shell.

2. Connect to SharePoint Online as a Global Administrator or SharePoint Administrator.

3. Run the following PowerShell cmdlet. Wait for about one hour for the changes to take effect:

```
Set-SPOTenant -InformationBarriersSuspension $false
```

Configure IB modes

IB modes strengthen access, sharing and membership of a M365 resource. They are supported on M365 groups, Teams, SharePoint and OneDrive and are automatically applied to new or existing configurations.

Open

No IB policies or segments are associated with the resource and files and folders. File can be shared based on the IB policy applied to the user. For a user to access a OneDrive file, the file must be shared with the user. If the file is on SharePoint the user must have access to the site.

Owner moderated

This mode is useful when you want to allow collaboration between incompatible segments. Only the resource owners can add users to the resource. To set a OneDrive or SharePoint to this mode use the following PowerShell cmdlet:

```
Set-SPOSite -Identity <siteurl> -InformationBarriersMode OwnerModerated
```

Following restrictions are applied on OneDrive and SharePoint:

- The option to share with **Anyone with the link** is disabled.
- The option to share with **Company-wide link** is disabled.
- The site and its content can be shared with existing members.
- The site and its content can only be shared by the owner as per the IB policy.

For a user to access a file from a OneDrive or SharePoint site in owner moderated mode the user must have access to the site.

Implicit

This is the default mode when a SharePoint site is provisioned by Microsoft Teams. A **Global Administrator** or **SharePoint Administrator** cannot manage segments with implicit mode configuration.

With this mode enabled the following restrictions are imposed on SharePoint sites:

- The option to share with **Anyone with the link** is disabled.
- The option to share with **Company-wide link** is disabled.
- The site and its content can be shared with existing members via a sharing link.
- New users cannot be added to the site. Team owners should add users to the Team's group using Microsoft Teams.

For a user to access SharePoint sites with implicit mode configurations

- The user must be a member of the M365 group connected to the site.
- The user who is not a member of the M365 group cannot access the site.

Explicit

SharePoint sites and OneDrive become explicit in the following scenarios:

- When a segmented user creates a new SharePoint site.
- When a SharePoint Administrator adds a segment to a site.
- When a segmented user provisions their OneDrive within 24 hours of enablement.

Following restrictions are imposed in this mode:

- The option to share with **Anyone with the link** is disabled.
- The option to share with **Company-wide link** is disabled.
- Files and folders can be shared only with users in the same segment.
- New users can be added to the SharePoint site if they are in the same segment.

For a user access content on SharePoint sites, the user must be in the same segment and have permissions to access the site. To access content in OneDrive they must be in the same segment and the file must be shared with the user.

Mixed

This is only available with OneDrive. In this mode the user is allowed to share with unsegmented users. This is an opt-in mode, and the SharePoint administrator can set it for the OneDrive of a segmented user.

Following restrictions are imposed in this mode:

- The option to share with **Anyone with the link** is disabled.

- The option to share with **Company-wide link** is disabled.
- Files and folders can be shared only with users in the same segment and with unsegmented users.

For a segmented user to access content from a OneDrive in mixed mode, the user must be in the same segment and the file must be shared with the user. Unsegmented users must have site access permissions.

Segment users

Following are the steps to segment users:

1. Login to **https://purview.microsoft.com** and click on the **Information Barriers** tile.
2. Click on **Segments** and in the right pane click on **New segment**.
3. Give your segment a **Name** and click **Next**.
4. In the **Add users** page select the attribute using which you want to define the segment and click **Next**.
5. Review the settings and click **Submit**.

Repeat the steps to create as many segments as required by your organization.

Create information barriers policies: Following are steps to create a policy:

1. Login to **https://purview.microsoft.com** and click on the **Information Barriers** tile.
2. Click on **Policies** and in the right pane click on **Create policy**.
3. Give your policy a **Name** and click **Next**.
4. On the **Assigned segment** page click on **Choose segment**. In the fly out pane pick a segment (marketing) from the list and click **Add**.
5. On the next page choose if communication and collaboration should be **Allowed** or **Blocked**. Pick the segment with which you want to allow or block the communication (research) and click **Next**.
6. On the next screen, you can choose to set your policy status to active or keep it off. Click **Next**.
7. Review your settings and click **Finish**.

Create a second policy where you will choose Research in *step 4* and marketing in *step 5*.

Apply the policies

Information Barriers policies do not take effect until they are set to active status and applied.

Following are the steps of policies to apply the policy:

1. Login to **https://purview.microsoft.com** and click on the **Information Barriers** tile.
2. Click on **Policy application** and in the right pane click on **Apply all policies**.
3. It can take up to 30 minutes for the policies to be applied. Policies are applied by user. The system processes about 5000 user accounts per hour.

You can use PowerShell to view the status of user accounts, segments, policies and policy applications. The following table summarizes the cmdlets:

Information	Cmdlet
User accounts and associated attributes and IB policies	`Get-InformationBarrierRecipientStatus -Identity <value>`
List all segments	`Get-OrganizationSegment`
List all IB policies	`Get-InformationBarrierPolicy`
Recent IB policy application	`Get-InformationBarrierPoliciesApplicationStatus`
All IB policy applications	`Get-InformationBarrierPoliciesApplicationStatus -All`

Table 13.2: PowerShell cmdlets for IB

Configure user discoverability

When IB policies block communication between segments, users in one segment cannot search for the users of the other segment in the people picker.

Following figure is an example of a user trying to look for a user in **Microsoft Teams** when IB policy is blocking communication:

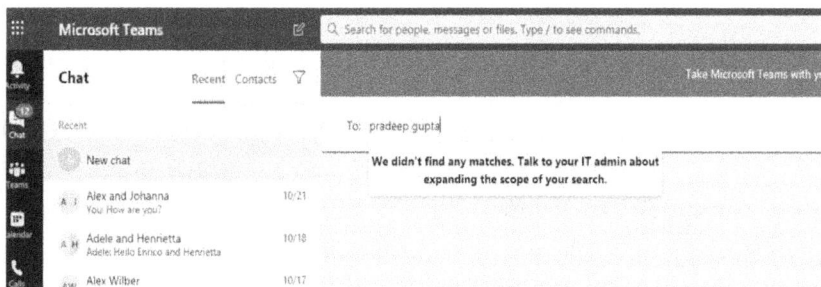

Figure 13.17: IB policy blocking user discoverability

Administrators can disable this restriction using the following PowerShell cmdlet:

```
Set-PolicyConfig -InformationBarrierPeopleSearchRestriction 'Disabled'
```

Conclusion

In this chapter, you learned how you can use Microsoft Purview Insider Risk Management to identify potentially risky user behavior to recognize early signs of a data breach. You also learnt how you can use the forensic evidence feature in Insider Risk Management to capture clips of risky user activity. This chapter also explained how Insider Risk Management integrates with Microsoft Purview DLP, and Microsoft Entra Conditional Access to dynamically act on risky users based on their risk levels. The chapter explained how you can use Microsoft Purview Communication Compliance to identify code of conduct policy violations, understand user sentiment, identify disgruntled employees that could potentially lead to a data breach. Lastly, you learnt how you can use Microsoft Purview Information Barriers to draw virtual boundaries within the organization to restrict communication between groups of users. You should now be well equipped to work with your stakeholders and chart out an insider risk strategy for your organization.

In the next chapter, we will discuss how to use Microsoft Purview eDiscovery to find and collect information that can be used as evidence in internal investigation or legal cases.

Multiple choice questions

1. **You are the IT administrator for your organization. You have been asked to monitor users who have submitted their resignation for possible data exfiltration activity. What should you do? Choose two.**

   a. Create a priority user list.

   b. Configure the HR connector.

   c. Create a Data theft by departing employee policy.

   d. Configure forensic evidence for users.

2. **You are the IT administrator for your organization. You want to ensure that users whose insider risk level is elevated should not be allowed to access critical applications. You are already using adaptive protection for DLP. What should you do?**

   a. Turn on Adaptive Protection

   b. Go to the Adaptive Protection dashboard and click on Quick setup next to Conditional Access.

   c. Create a Conditional Access policy in Microsoft Entra ID.

   d. Create a new DLP policy.

3. Your organization's HR team is receiving complaints about inappropriate communication between employees. You have been tasked with monitoring employee communications to identify threatening and discriminatory behavior. Which communication compliance policy should you create?

   a. Detect sensitive info types

   b. Detect financial regulatory compliance

   c. Detect inappropriate text

   d. Detect conflict of interest

Answer key

1. b, c
2. b
3. c

Join our book's Discord space

Join the book's Discord Workspace for Latest updates, Offers, Tech happenings around the world, New Release and Sessions with the Authors:

https://discord.bpbonline.com

Chapter 14
Managing eDiscovery Cases

Introduction

In an era where digital information proliferates at an unprecedented rate, the need for eDiscovery has never been more critical. Organizations are compelled to manage vast amounts of electronic data, which may be pivotal in legal proceedings. The ability to quickly and accurately identify, preserve, and retrieve relevant data not only helps in ensuring compliance with legal mandates but also significantly reduces the risk of hefty fines and legal repercussions. Moreover, effective eDiscovery practices can aid organizations in maintaining their reputation and operational integrity by demonstrating a commitment to transparency and accountability.

It is also important for organizations to be aware of user and admin activity happening in their environment to ensure accountability, transparency and security. Audit logs serve as a comprehensive record of system activities, user actions, and changes to data, which can be pivotal in investigating and resolving incidents of unauthorized access, data breaches, or other security violations. By systematically documenting these events, organizations can detect and respond to suspicious activities more effectively, thus mitigating potential risks. The meticulous maintenance of audit logs not only fortifies an organization's defense against cyber threats but also reinforces its commitment to ethical practices and governance.

Structure

The chapter covers the following topics:

- Microsoft Purview eDiscovery
- Microsoft Purview Audit

Objectives

By the end of this chapter, readers will know the intricacies of managing eDiscovery with Microsoft Purview. Microsoft Purview eDiscovery enables legal and compliance teams to efficiently handle large volumes of data, ensuring that relevant information is easily accessible for legal proceedings and investigations. You will learn the different eDiscovery tools available with Microsoft Purview and how you can use them to manage cases, put content on hold, collect, analyze and export data that can be legally defensible.

In addition to exploring the capabilities of Microsoft Purview eDiscovery, this chapter will also examine Microsoft Purview Audit. This robust auditing solution provides detailed insights into user activities and system changes, enhancing transparency and accountability within an organization. With powerful tracking and reporting features, Microsoft Purview Audit empowers teams to monitor compliance with internal policies and regulatory requirements, thus safeguarding the integrity of their operations.

Microsoft Purview eDiscovery

Electronic discovery or eDiscovery is the process of identifying, collecting, and producing **Electronically Stored Information** (**ESI**) in response to a legal request or investigation. Traditionally, eDiscovery tools presented significant challenges, particularly in the initial stages of data collection. Administrators often had to manually extract content from its original location before any meaningful search could be conducted. This process was not only labor-intensive but also fraught with the risk of data corruption, loss, and exfiltration as multiple copies of data were created. The extracted data then needed to be transferred to a separate environment where it could be indexed and searched. This multi-step process consumed valuable time and resources, delaying legal proceedings and increasing the likelihood of errors.

Using Microsoft Purview eDiscovery, administrators can perform in-place search on the data, review and analyze the data in place and then extract only the data relevant for the case. This saves time and money and keeps the data safe in its original location.

Microsoft Purview eDiscovery offers various tools that you can use to search for content in Exchange Online, SharePoint Online, One Drive for Business, Microsoft Teams, Microsoft 365 Groups and Viva Engage teams.

Following table covers the eDiscovery features and capabilities:

Capability	eDiscovery	Premium eDiscovery
Search for content	Yes	Yes
Keyword queries and search conditions	Yes	Yes
Search statistics	Yes	Yes
Export search results	Yes	Yes
Role-based permissions	Yes	Yes
Case management	Yes	Yes
Place content locations on hold	Yes	Yes
Advanced indexing	No	Yes
Review sets	No	Yes
Support for cloud attachments and SharePoint versions	No	Yes
Optical character recognition	No	Yes
Conversation threading	No	Yes
Search statistics and reports	No	Yes
Review set filtering	No	Yes
Tagging	No	Yes
Analytics	No	Yes
Computed document metadata	No	Yes
Transparency of long-running processes	No	Yes
Full reporting for all processes	No	Yes
Enhanced data source mapping	No	Yes

Table 14.1: Microsoft Purview eDiscovery solutions

Licensing

Before you get started it is important to understand the licensing requirements for each of the above options. If the organization wishes to use these features, they should have the licenses listed as follows:

- **eDiscovery (Standard)**: Office 365 E3/E5 or Microsoft 365 E3/E5.
- **eDiscovery (Premium)**: Office 365 E5 or Microsoft 365 E5 or Microsoft 365 E5 Compliance or Microsoft 365 E5 eDiscovery and Audit.

To remain compliant with Microsoft licensing guidelines and to get the best results, each person who benefits from the service should be assigned a license.

Use the following points as a guide:

- Any user whose mailbox or OneDrive account is put on hold or included in an eDiscovery search must be assigned a license.

- Owners and members of a Microsoft Team or SharePoint site that is put on hold or included in an eDiscovery search must be assigned a license.

Let us take a few examples:

- **Scenario one**: You want to search for email conversation between two users. In this scenario you will need to assign a license to both the users as both their mailboxes will be included in this search.

- **Scenario two**: You want to search for documents related to a particular project on a SharePoint site that has 30 members. You will need to assign a license to each of the 30 users.

Permissions

The main eDiscovery related role group is called the **eDiscovery Manager**. There are two subgroups in this role group, as follows:

- **eDiscovery Manager**: This role group can perform the following activities:
    o Search content locations.
    o Preview and export search results.
    o Create and manage eDiscovery cases.
    o Add members to eDiscovery cases they create.
    o Place content on hold.
    o Run searches are associated with an eDiscovery case created by them.
    o Access case data of eDiscovery cases created by them.

    An eDiscovery Manager can only access and manage the cases they create and not the cases created by other eDiscovery Managers.

- **eDiscovery Administrator**: As eDiscovery Administrator can view and access all eDiscovery cases. They can audit and oversee all cases and associated searches. This role is a member of the eDiscovery Manager role group and can perform all activities that an eDiscovery Manager can perform. In addition, it can perform the following activities:
    o Access all eDiscovery cases.
    o Configure eDiscovery solution settings.
    o Access process and hold reports.
    o Access case data for any eDiscovery case.
    o Add themselves as a member of any eDiscovery case and manage it.
    o Remove members from an eDiscovery case.

To add users to the eDiscovery Manager role group, in the Purview portal navigate to **Settings | Roles and scopes | Role groups**. In the right pane click on the eDiscovery Manager role and click on **Edit**. The wizard will guide you through the steps to add users as eDiscovery Manager and eDiscovery Administrator subgroups:

Consider the following points while adding users to the above subgroups:

- You can add a mail-enabled security group as a member of the eDiscovery Managers subgroup by using the following cmdlet in the Security and Compliance PowerShell:

  ```
  Add-RoleGroupMember "eDiscoveryManager" -Member <name of security group>
  ```

- Exchange distribution groups and Microsoft 365 are not supported.

- You cannot make a mail-enabled security group a member of the eDiscovery Administrators subgroup. Only individual users can be added to as eDiscovery Administrators.

- Mail-enabled users cannot be added as members of individual cases.

- An eDiscovery Administrator can access all cases created in eDiscovery which gives them the ability to access potentially sensitive content, the membership of this group should be limited.

eDiscovery workflow

Depending on the licenses that your organization owns, you will get access to specific eDiscovery or premium eDiscovery features in the Microsoft Purview portal.

Following figure describes a standard workflow to create and manage eDiscovery cases to quickly identify, investigate and act on the information stored in your organization:

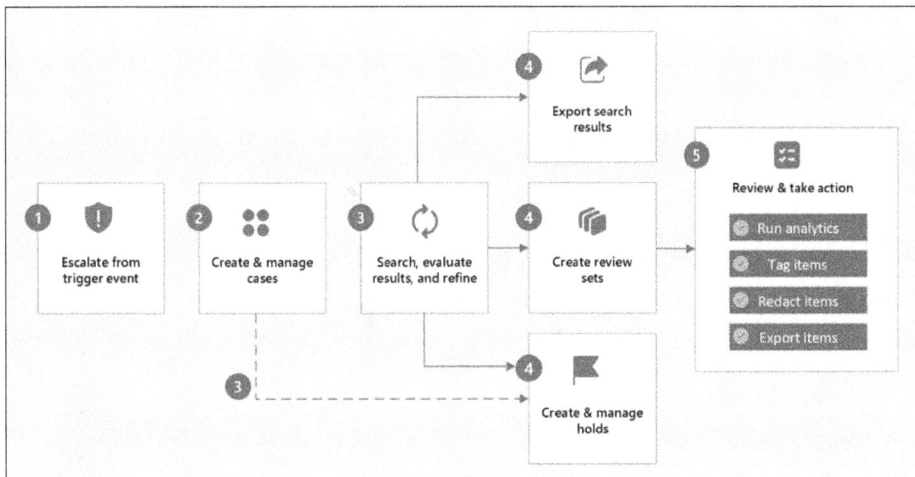

Figure 14.1: eDiscovery workflow

Cases in eDiscovery can be created manually or based on a trigger like a case escalation from Microsoft Purview Insider Risk Management. Once a case is created, you can assign members to the case to control who has access to the contents of the case. Use eDiscovery hold to prevent modification of content that may be important for the case. The in-built search tools can be used to build queries to search the locations using keywords, sensitive information types, file size, date time and much more. Once the query is complete, the search results can be exported directly to your local computer or added to a review set to search, filter, tag and analyze the content. Sensitive information can be redacted and annotations added. Once the review is complete the final content can be exported.

eDiscovery components

Before learning how to create and manage eDiscovery cases, it is important to understand the important components that make up an eDiscovery investigation.

Cases

A case is the primary component of the eDiscovery workflow. It contains data sources, people, holds, search queries and review sets related to an investigation. Members can be assigned to cases to control who can access and view a case.

Data sources

Data sources are locations where holds are applied, and searches are performed. They organize data locations in a hierarchical tree structure with two levels. For example, the user would be the top-level and the associated mailbox and OneDrive site would be the second level. Data sources are divided into three groups, as follows:

- **Users**: Users are people in the organization that include mailboxes or OneDrive accounts.
- **Groups**: These include group mailboxes, groups sites and shared and private Teams and SharePoint sites.
- **Organization-wide sources**: These are all users and groups and all public folders in the organization.

Hold and hold policies

Hold policies are used to create eDiscovery holds to preserve content that might be relevant to a case.

The following locations can be put on hold:

- Exchange mailboxes
- SharePoint sites

- OneDrive accounts
- Mailboxes and SharePoint sites that are associated with Microsoft Teams, M365 groups and Viva Engage groups.

When content is placed on hold, users cannot modify or delete it until the hold is released. It can take up to 24 hours for the hold to take effect.

The following options are available while placing content on hold:

- Create an infinite hold where all content in the specified locations is placed on hold. Alternatively, create a query-based hold where only content that matches a query is placed on hold.
- Specify a date range to preserve content that is sent, received or created within a date range. Alternatively, all content in a specified location can be placed on hold regardless of when it was sent, received or created.

Searches

A search is used to find content in Microsoft Exchange, SharePoint sites, OneDrive locations and Microsoft Teams. The search tool can be used to build queries to search for information based on keywords and other parameters. Multiple searches can be associated with a single eDiscovery case.

Search samples

A sample is a representative set of items returned from a search query. This helps you determine if the query is accurate, or it needs to be refined to produce the desired results.

Processes

eDiscovery includes a Process report that lists all activities performed in eDiscovery such as running searches, exporting content, creating review sets. eDiscovery Administrators and eDiscovery Managers can access this report.

Review sets

Review sets in Microsoft Purview eDiscovery are crucial for the effective management and analysis of collected information. Once search is complete, the results can be added to a review set which securely stores the content in a dedicated Microsoft Azure location. Review sets provide a static, unalterable collection of data that enables thorough examination and accurate tagging. This ensures that relevant content is preserved and easily accessible for legal and compliance purposes, facilitating efficient and reliable eDiscovery processes. You can choose to include or exclude content from the final export, tag relevant content and redact any sensitive information. This helps in reducing the size of the final package that can then be used for legal purposes.

Configure eDiscovery settings

Depending on the needs of the organization, you may need to review and configure the global eDiscovery settings that apply to all cases. These settings are accessible from the Microsoft Purview portal by clicking on the **Settings** tile and selecting **eDiscovery**.

Following settings are available:

- **Analytics**: Use this setting to turn on attorney-client privilege detection. This helps flag documents that are likely to be privileged. This flag is based on the content by comparing participants against a user-provided attorney list. This setting is **off** by default. If you turn it on you will need to provide a file containing a list of attorneys.

- **Guest users**: Using this setting you can determine if guest users are allowed to be invited to review eDiscovery cases. This is useful in scenarios where you might want to invite an external legal team to do an in-place review of content. This helps preserve privacy as the content does not leave your M365 tenant. This setting **off** by default.

- **Collections**: This setting lets you specify how items are searched, retrieved and processed. You can choose to include guest user mailboxes, shared Teams channels, include inactive mailboxes. You can also choose to retrieve content from Teams and Yammer conversations; include cloud attachments, all document versions from SharePoint and items that are partially indexed.

- **Tags templates**: Tags help organize content in a review set to complete various workflows. They can be reused across multiple review sets by using these templates. You can group tags by sections and allow single or multiple-choice tagging. For example, you could use tags like Financial, PII to tag items. These tags can be used to filter content and run other workflows.

- **Communication library**: Use this to create email templates that can be sent to users when their accounts are placed on hold or released from hold.

- **Issuing officer**: Using this setting you can define which user in the organization will be displayed as the officer that has placed content on hold. This can be included in the email communication sent to the users.

- **Historical versions**: This feature allows organizations to search for content not only in the most recent version of the file but across all previous versions stored on SharePoint Online. To use this feature, toggle the option to **On** and add the SharePoint sites that you want to enable historical versioning for.

Creating and managing cases in eDiscovery

The section discusses how to create and manage cases in eDiscovery. Depending on the licenses you have, some features may not be available for you. Refer to *Table 14.1* for a list of features available in content search, eDiscovery and premium eDiscovery.

Following are the steps to create a case in eDiscovery:

1. Login to **https://purview.microsoft.com** and click on the **eDiscovery** tile and then click on **Cases**. This page displays all cases created using eDiscovery and all searches performed using content search. Refer to the following figure:

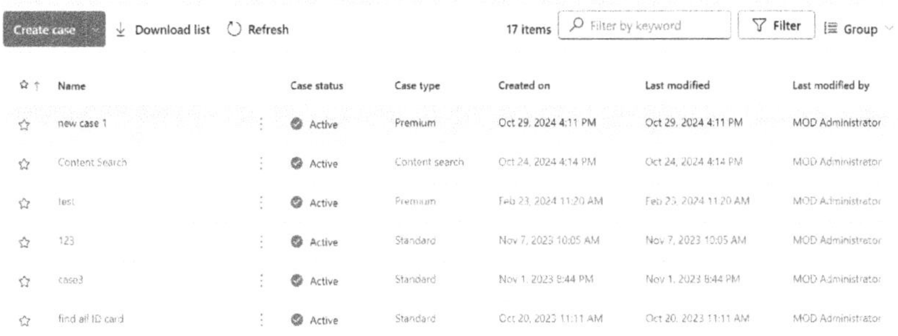

Figure 14.2: Case in eDiscovery

2. To create a case, click on **Create case** and give your case a name and description and click on **Create**.

3. On the case page, click on **Case settings** to specify settings for this case. Following settings are available:

   • **Case**: This tab displays the case id, case name, case number and case description. It also displays the current license. To use premium features for this case, toggle the **eDiscovery (Premium)** toggle to on. You can also close or delete the case by using the **Actions** button. Refer to the following figure:

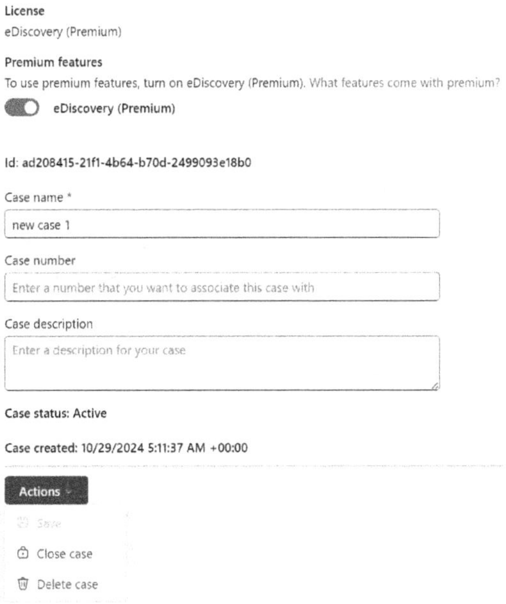

Figure 14.3: Case settings

4. **Access and permissions**: These settings allow you to add or remove users from the case. The person who created the case is automatically added as a user. You can add other users and role groups to the case. If guest users are enabled in eDiscovery, you can invite guest users to collaborate on this case.

Refer to the following figure:

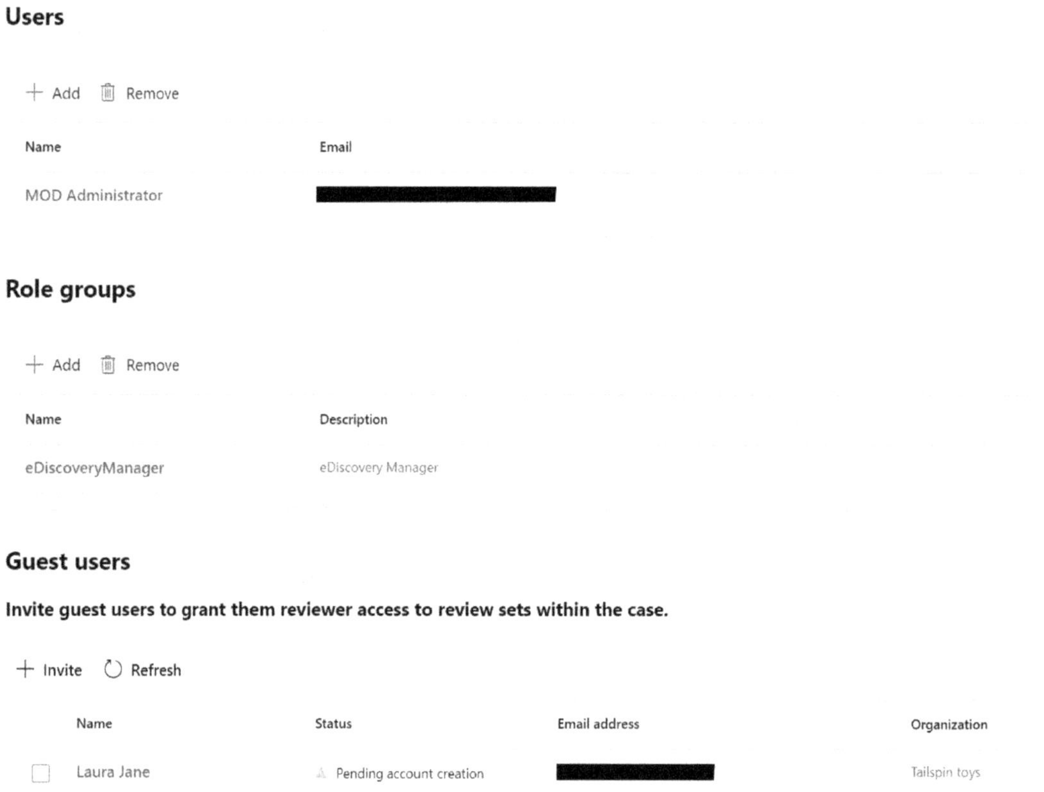

Users

+ Add   🗑 Remove

Name	Email
MOD Administrator	████████████████

Role groups

+ Add   🗑 Remove

Name	Description
eDiscoveryManager	eDiscovery Manager

Guest users

Invite guest users to grant them reviewer access to review sets within the case.

+ Invite   ↻ Refresh

Name	Status	Email address	Organization
☐ Laura Jane	⚠ Pending account creation	███████████	Tailspin toys

Figure 14.4: Adding users to a case

Once a guest user is invited, an eDiscovery manager must approve their access by going to **Settings** | **eDiscovery** | **Guest users**. Select the user's name and click on **Approve** in the fly-out pane as shown in *Figure 14.5*. Once approved, guest users will receive an email to accept the invitation and start collaborating on the case.

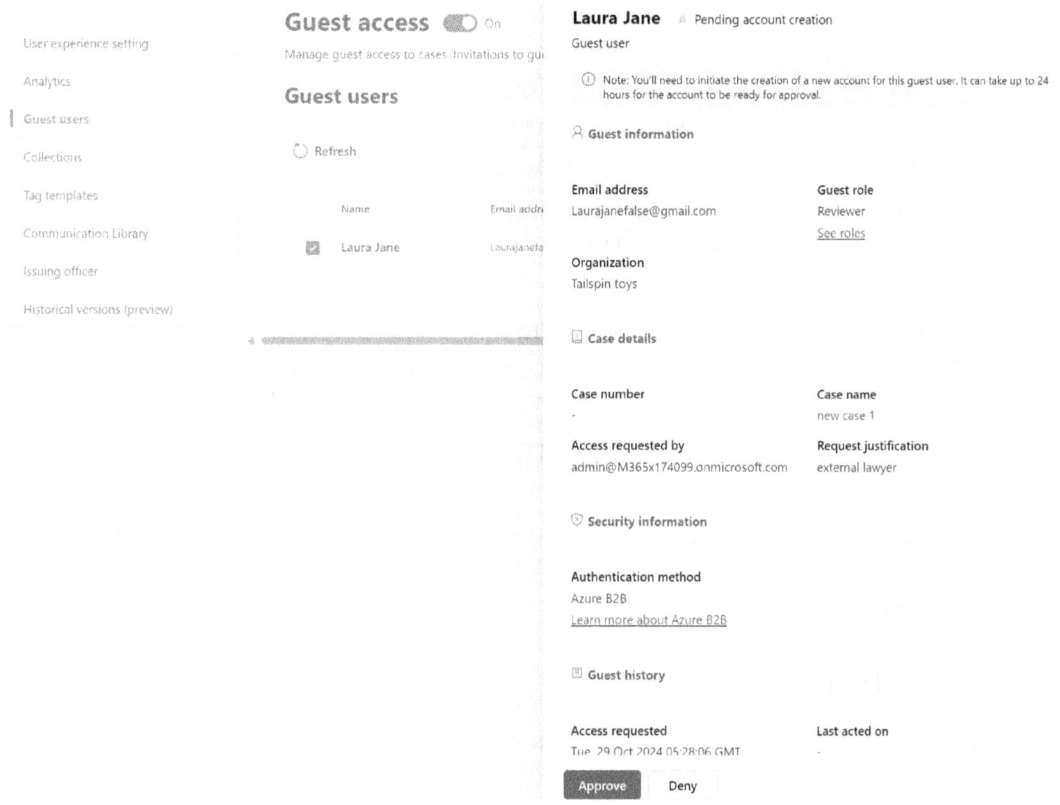

Figure 14.5: Approving guest users

5. **Data sources**: This setting allows you to specify the data sources that will be included in the searches. Choose one or more of the following and click on **Apply**:

   • All people and groups including unlicensed, on-premises and guest users.

   • All people and groups including share Teams channels.

   • All people and groups including departed users.

6. **Search and analytics**: Use this option to control the following functionality:

   • **Near duplicates and email threading**: If this setting is turned on, eDiscovery detects duplicate and near duplicate items. It also threads related emails into a conversation for better contextual understanding. You can specify the similarity threshold in terms of percentage. For example, if you set it at 70%, if the similarity level of two documents is above this threshold, they are considered duplicates and put in the same near duplicate sets.

   • **Themes**: This functionality analyzes documents in a review set to parse out common themes. eDiscovery labels each document with the themes that appear in it. Since one document can have many types of subject matter, eDiscovery often assigns multiple themes to a single document. This is called a **themes list**. The most prominent theme is designated as the **dominant theme**. You can specify the maximum number of themes that can be generated or let eDiscovery dynamically adjust the maximum number of themes. Using regular expressions is supported.

- **Autogenerated review set query**: Enabling this option automatically generates a query called for review. This query leaves out duplicate items from the review set.

- **Ignore text**: Use this option in situations where certain text dilutes the quality of the analytics, like disclaimers or terms of use. If you know that documents contain text that can be ignored you can specify the text string in this option.

- **Optical character recognition**: This setting enables eDiscovery to extract text from images and include it in searches.

7. **Review set settings**: Use this setting to control how data in a review set is grouped and displayed. When enabled, review set items are grouped by **Group ID** and **Thread ID**.

Create hold policies

Before you search for content, you might want to place some content on hold. This is done using **Hold policies**.

Following are the steps to create a policy:

1. In the eDiscovery case, click on the **Hold policies** tab and click on **Create policy**.

2. Give the policy a name and description and click on **Create**.

3. Add the data sources that you want to put on hold by clicking on **Add data sources**. Select the data sources from the fly-out pane and click on **Save and manage** as shown in *Figure 14.6*:

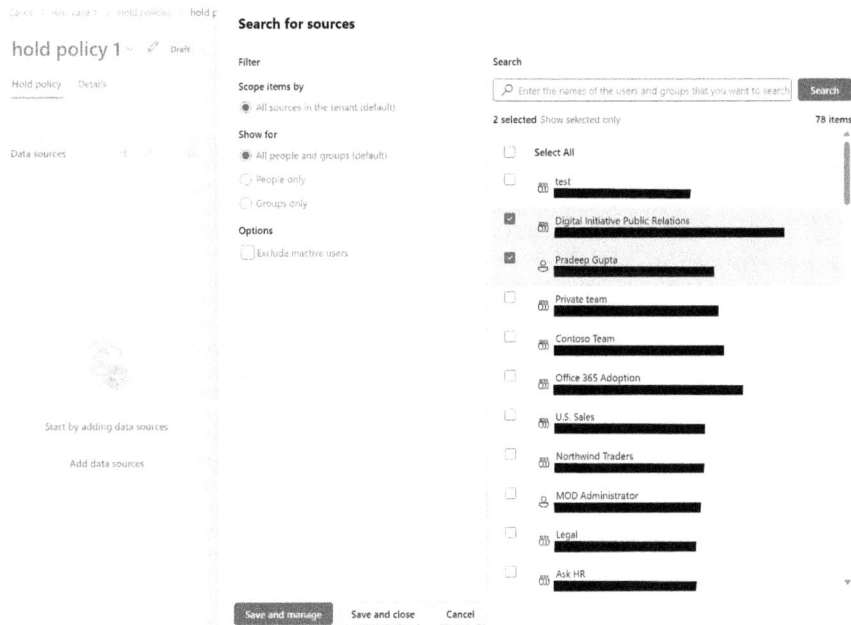

Figure 14.6: Selecting content to be placed on hold

4. The next page shows the content that will be included in this search. You can select all or omit some data sources.

   Following example shows a user mailbox and OneDrive account, and a Microsoft Teams location included in the search. If you want to search only the user mailbox and not the OneDrive location, you can uncheck the relevant box as shown in *Figure 14.7*. Once done, click on **Save**.

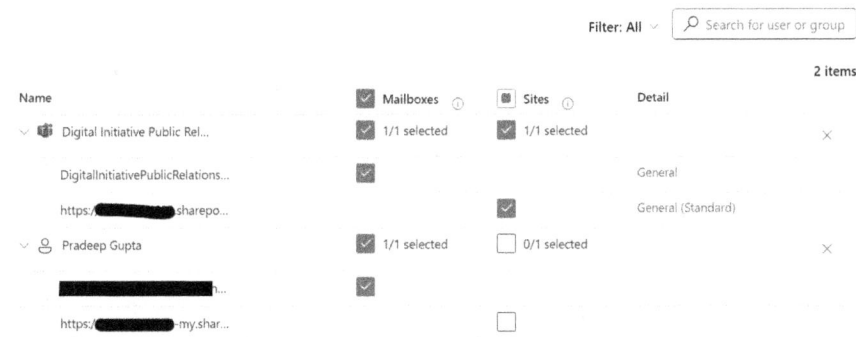

Figure 14.7: Select data sources

5. Click on **Apply hold**.

Search for content

Once you create a case and add locations on hold, you can begin to search for content. Following are the steps to create and run a content search:

1. Login to **https://purview.microsoft.com** with an account that has the eDiscovery Manager role assigned. Click on the **eDiscovery** tile.

2. In the left pane, click on **Content Search**.

3. In the right pane, click on **Create search** and enter a name and description for your search and click on **Create**.

4. In the next page, click on **Add data sources** and pick the data sources you would like to include in your search and click on **Save and manage** as shown in *Figure 14.8*. If you do not select any data sources here, the locations specified in the case settings will be searched.

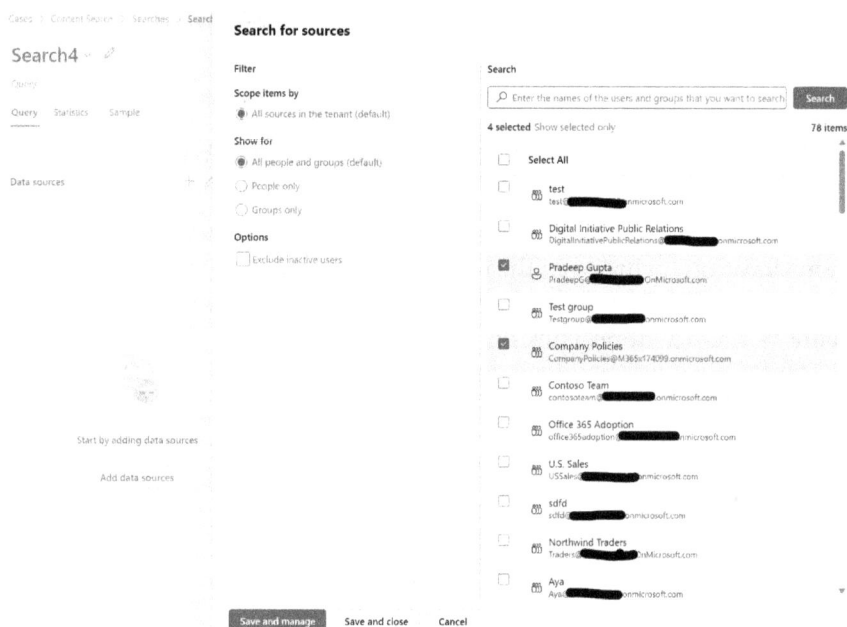

Figure 14.8: Select data sources

5. The next page shows the content that will be included in this search. You can select all or omit some data sources. The following example shows a SharePoint site, a user mailbox and OneDrive account and a Microsoft Teams location included in the search. If you want to search only the user mailbox and not the OneDrive location, you can uncheck the relevant box as shown in *Figure 14.9*. Once done, click on **Save**.

Manage sources

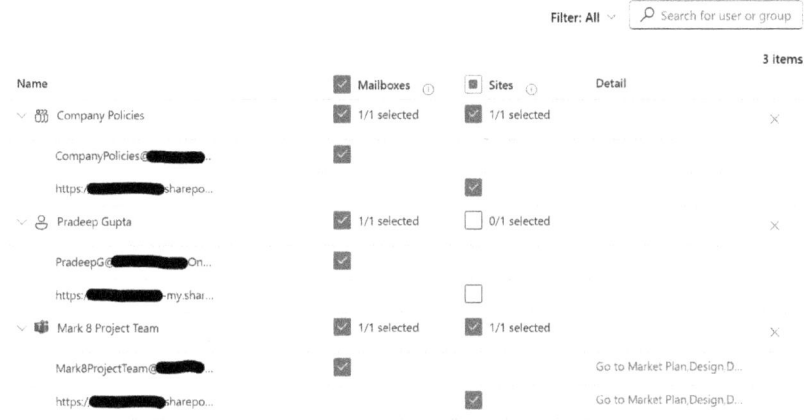

Figure 14.9: Select the locations

6. Back in the search page, you can now specify the search criteria using the **Condition builder**. The search query can include keywords, date, sender/author, file size, email subject, document title, retention or sensitivity label, sensitive information type and many more.

    Figure 14.10 shows a search query looking for credit card numbers in email messages and documents before a particular date. Once done click on **Run query**.

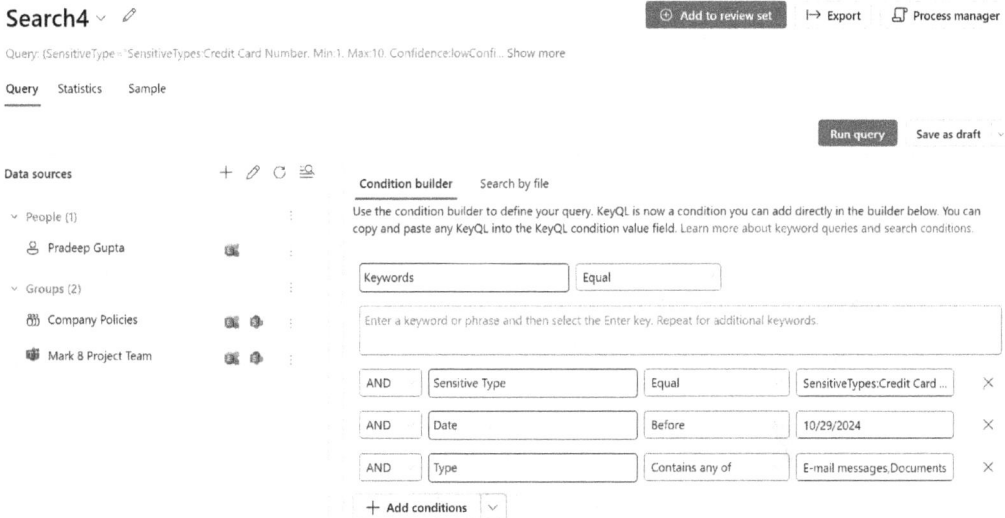

Figure 14.10: Specify search criteria

7. In the fly out pane, select the options to format your search results and click on **Run query**. Refer to the following figure:

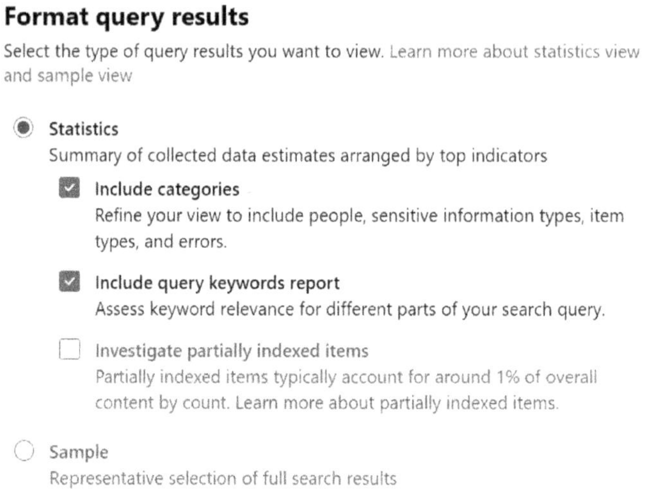

Format query results

Select the type of query results you want to view. Learn more about statistics view and sample view

- ◉ **Statistics**
  Summary of collected data estimates arranged by top indicators

  - ☑ **Include categories**
    Refine your view to include people, sensitive information types, item types, and errors.

  - ☑ **Include query keywords report**
    Assess keyword relevance for different parts of your search query.

  - ☐ **Investigate partially indexed items**
    Partially indexed items typically account for around 1% of overall content by count. Learn more about partially indexed items.

- ○ **Sample**
  Representative selection of full search results

Figure 14.11: Format query results

8. Once the search query is complete, you can view the statistics on the **Statistics** tab. Refer to *Figure 14.12*:

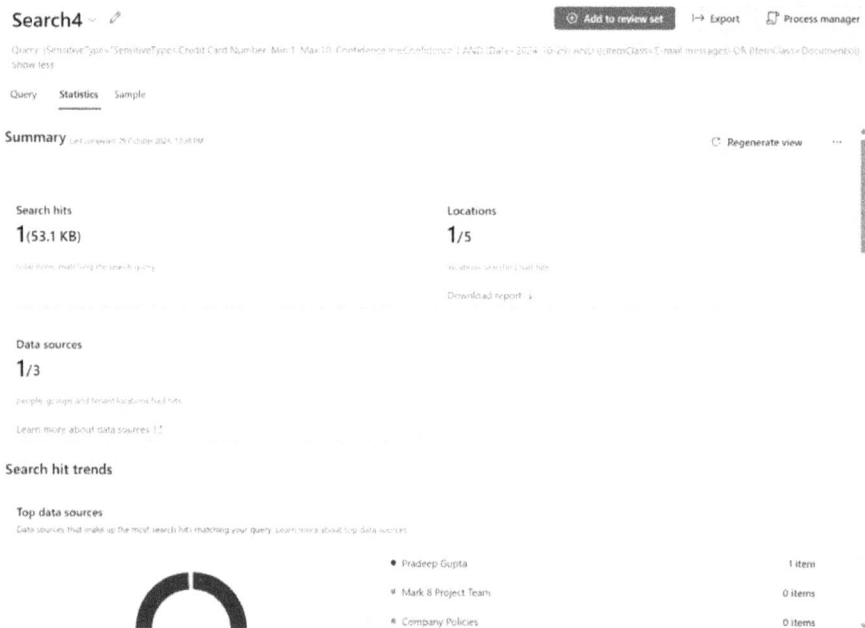

Figure 14.12: Content search statistics

9. If you would like to review a sample of the results, click on the **Sample** tab and then click on **Generate sample results**. In the fly out pane, select how many sample items per location and how many locations you would like to include in your sample and click on **Run query**. Refer to the following figure:

Cases > Content Search > Searches > Search4

Search4 ∨ ✎

Query: (SensitiveType="SensitiveTypes:Credit Card Number. Min:1. Max:10. Confidence:lowConfidence") AND (D
Show less

Query   Statistics   Sample

Generate sample view
Generate sample view settings. Learn more about sample view and relevant settings.

Samples per location
Specify how many sample items per location to generate

| 10 |

Sampled locations
Specify how many locations in specified data sources to sample from

| 1000 |

No results yet

Get sample results for your see
query to review items and ma
changes if needed.

Generate sample results

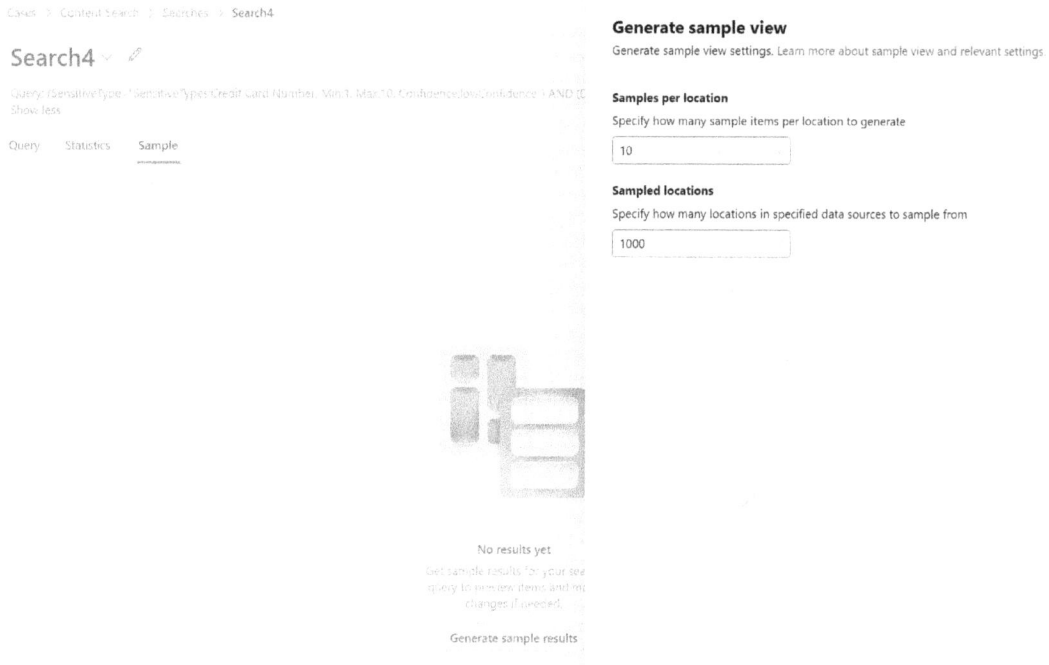

Figure 14.13: Generate sample

10. Wait for the query to complete and then review the sample as shown in the following figure:

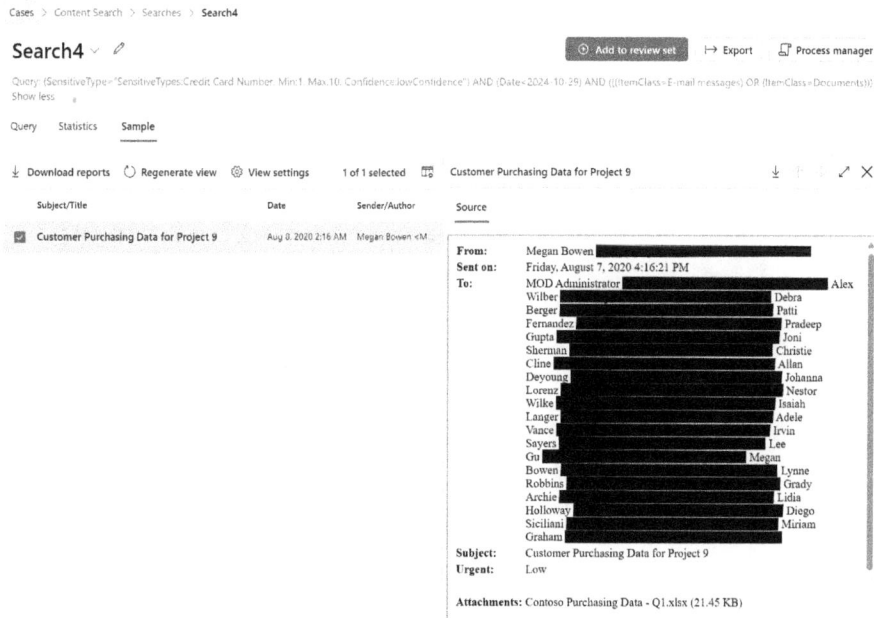

Cases > Content Search > Searches > **Search4**

Search4 ∨ ✎   ⊕ Add to review set   ↦ Export   ⬚ Process manager

Query: (SensitiveType="SensitiveTypes:Credit Card Number. Min:1. Max:10. Confidence:lowConfidence") AND (Date<2024-10-29) AND ((ItemClass=E-mail messages) OR (Item-Class=Documents))
Show less

Query   Statistics   **Sample**

↓ Download reports ↻ Regenerate view ⚙ View settings   1 of 1 selected   🗔   Customer Purchasing Data for Project 9   ↓ ↑ ↓ ↗ ✕

	Subject/Title	Date	Sender/Author		Source
☑	Customer Purchasing Data for Project 9	Aug 8. 2020 2:16 AM	Megan Bowen <M		

From: Megan Bowen
Sent on: Friday, August 7, 2020 4:16:21 PM
To: MOD Administrator   Alex
             Wilber   Debra
             Berger   Patti
             Fernandez   Pradeep
             Gupta   Joni
             Sherman   Christie
             Cline   Allan
             Deyoung   Johanna
             Lorenz   Nestor
             Wilke   Isaiah
             Langer   Adele
             Vance   Irvin
             Sayers   Lee
             Gu   Megan
             Bowen   Lynne
             Robbins   Grady
             Archie   Lidia
             Holloway   Diego
             Siciliani   Miriam
             Graham

Subject: Customer Purchasing Data for Project 9
Urgent: Low

Attachments: Contoso Purchasing Data - Q1.xlsx (21.45 KB)

Figure 14.14: Review sample data

11. If the sample data meets your expectations, you can now either add the results to a review set or export the results to your local computer by using the options in the above picture. If not, you can go back and edit the search query till you get the desired results. To export the results, click on **Export**. In the fly-out pane, give a name for your export. You can also select other options like exporting only the latest version of a SharePoint file, organize Teams conversations as HTML transcripts. Make the appropriate selection and click on **Export**.

Adding results to a review set

Once you have the result of your search, you can add them to a review set for further analysis and review. To do this, click on **Add to review set**. Give the review set a name and click on **Add to review set** as shown *Figure 14.5*:

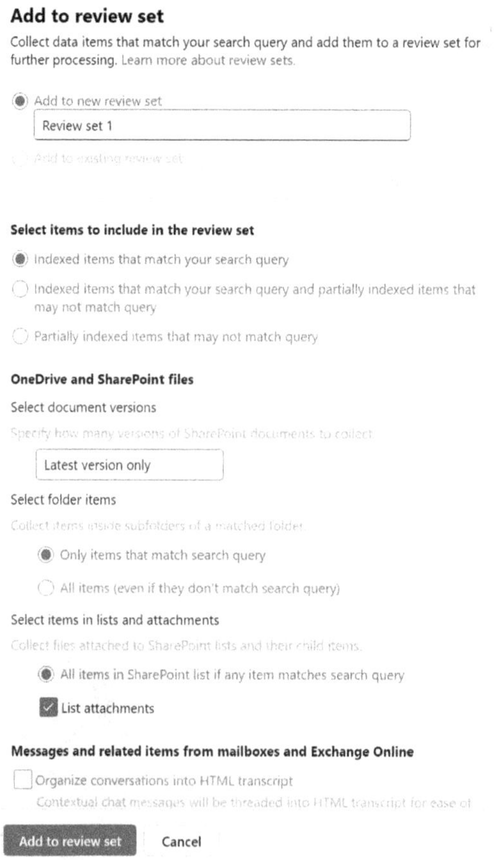

Add to review set

Collect data items that match your search query and add them to a review set for further processing. Learn more about review sets.

◉ Add to new review set

> Review set 1

◯ Add to existing review set

Select items to include in the review set

◉ Indexed items that match your search query

◯ Indexed items that match your search query and partially indexed items that may not match query

◯ Partially indexed items that may not match query

OneDrive and SharePoint files

Select document versions

Specify how many versions of SharePoint documents to collect.

> Latest version only

Select folder items

Collect items inside subfolders of a matched folder.

◉ Only items that match search query

◯ All items (even if they don't match search query)

Select items in lists and attachments

Collect files attached to SharePoint lists and their child items.

◉ All items in SharePoint list if any item matches search query

☑ List attachments

Messages and related items from mailboxes and Exchange Online

☐ Organize conversations into HTML transcript

Contextual chat messages will be threaded into HTML transcript for ease of

[Add to review set]   Cancel

Figure 14.15: Add to review set

The review set will be created, and you will be able to see all the items that matched your search criteria. From here you can perform further analysis like searching, tagging, annotating and redacting the content.

Following figure shows the review set screen and the various options available:

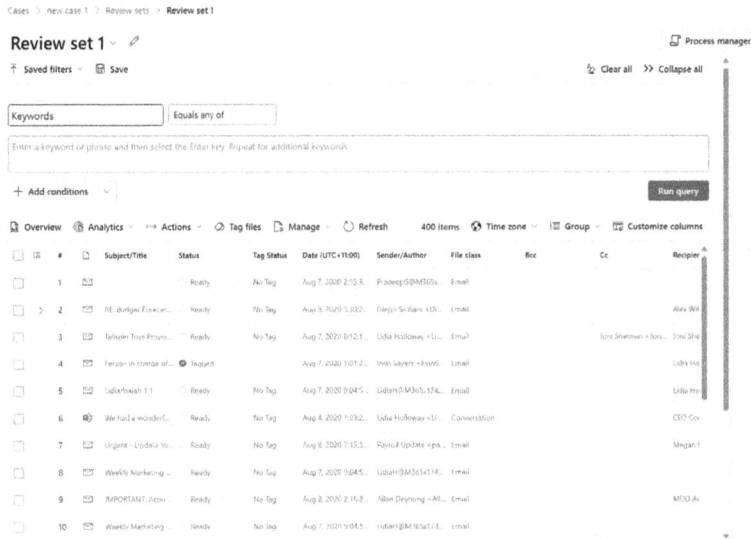

Figure 14.16: Review set

Export content

Once you have finished reviewing the content, you can export the review set and download it to your local computer by clicking on **Actions | Export** as shown in *Figure 14.16*, to track the progress of the export job, click on **Process manager**. Once the export is ready you can download it from this page as shown in *Figure 14.17*:

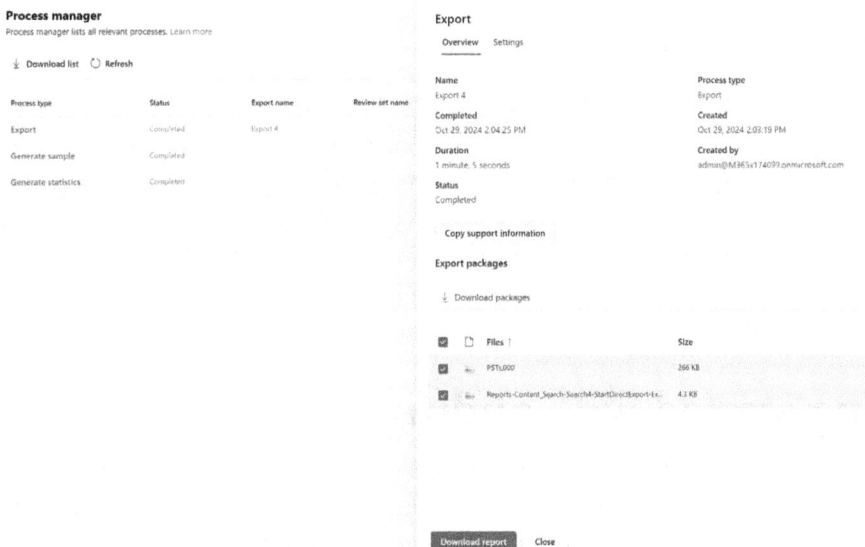

Figure 14.17: Download export

Microsoft Purview Audit

Microsoft Purview auditing solutions help organizations to respond to security incidents, forensic incidents, internal investigations and compliance obligations. All user and admin activities across Microsoft services are recorded and retained in the unified audit log.

Microsoft Purview offers two auditing solutions, as follows:

- **Audit (Standard)**: This is enabled by default for all organizations with the appropriate subscriptions. Users with the correct role can search the audit log from the Microsoft Purview portal, using Graph API or the `Search-UnifiedAuditLog` PowerShell cmdlet. Audit logs are retained for 180 days and can be exported to a CSV file.

- **Audit (Premium)**: Audit (Premium) builds on the capabilities of Audit (Standard) by providing audit log retention policies, longer retention of audit logs and higher bandwidth access to the Office 365 Management API. Audit logs are retained for one year. Organizations have the option to retain the audit logs for up to ten years by purchasing an add-on per-user license.

Licensing requirements

To ensure that the auditing events for users are captured, the users must be assigned one of the following licenses:

- **Audit (Standard)**: Office 365 E1/E3/E5, Microsoft 365 E3/E5

- **Audit (Premium)**: Office 365 E5, Microsoft 365 E5 eDiscovery & Audit, Microsoft 365 E5 Compliance, Microsoft 365 E5

Roles required

To search for and export the audit logs, members of the investigation team must be assigned to at least one of the following role groups in the Microsoft Purview portal:

- **Audit manager**: This role group has the **Audit Logs** and **View-Only Audit Logs** roles. Users assigned to this role group can search and export the audit log and can enable or disable auditing for the tenant.

- **Audit reader**: This role grants only the **View-Only Audit Logs** role and a user assigned to this role group can only search and export the audit logs.

Getting started with auditing

Once you have assigned the appropriate licenses to the users and assigned roles to members of the investigation team, you can begin with setting up Audit and searching the audit log. The following are the steps to get required to configure auditing:

1. **Enable SearchQueryInitiated events**: `SearchQueryInitiated` events logs events when users perform searches in Exchange and SharePoint online. These must be explicitly enabled in your tenant using the following PowerShell cmdlet:

   `Set-Mailbox <user> -AuditOwner @{Add="SearchQueryInitiated"}`

2. **Set up audit retention policies**: This step is required if you are using Audit (Premium). Organizations using Audit (Standard) can skip this step. The Audit (Premium) default policy retains audit logs for Microsoft Entra ID, Exchange, SharePoint and OneDrive for one year. This policy cannot be modified. Additional audit log retention policies can be created to meet the organization's security, IT and compliance requirements. Consider the following points before creating an audit log policy:

   - You must be assigned the **Organization Configuration** role in the Microsoft Purview Portal.

   - A maximum of 50 audit log retention policies can be created.

   - All custom audit log policies created take presence over the default audit log policy.

Following are the steps to create an audit log policy:

1. Login to **https://purview.microsoft.com** and click on the **Audit** tile.

2. Click on **Policies** and in the right pane click on **Create audit retention policy**.

3. In the fly out pane, enter the details as follows:

   - **Policy name and description**: Enter a meaningful name and description for the policy.

   - **Users**: You can select specific users for whom you want to enable the audit policy. If this field is left blank the policy will apply to all users who have the appropriate license assigned. If you leave this blank, you must select a record in the **Record type** box.

   - **Record type**: This specified the records that will be logged. If you leave this box blank, you must select a user in the **Users** box.

   - **Duration**: You can choose a duration of 7 days, 30 days, 90 days, 6 months, 9 months, 1 year, 3 years, 5 years, 7 years and 10 years. If you choose a duration of more than 1 year, users should have the 10-year advanced audit add-on license assigned.

   - **Priority**: This defines the priority of the policy in relation to the other policies. It is defined as a numeric value ranging from 1-10000 where 1 is the highest priority and 10000 is the lowest.

   Refer to *Figure 14.18* for example.

4. Click on **Save** to save the policy.

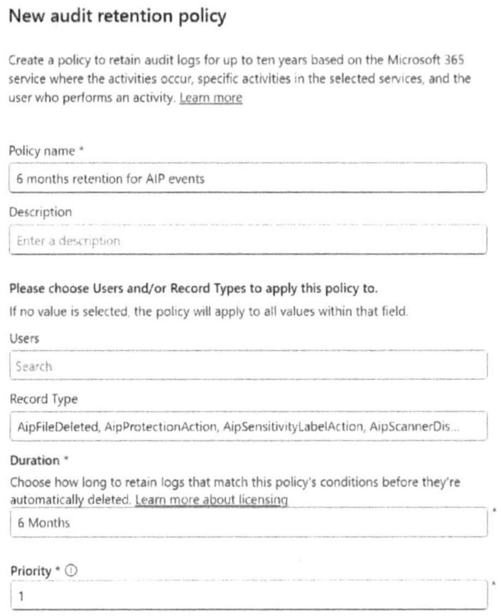

New audit retention policy

Create a policy to retain audit logs for up to ten years based on the Microsoft 365 service where the activities occur, specific activities in the selected services, and the user who performs an activity. Learn more

Policy name *

6 months retention for AIP events

Description

Enter a description

Please choose Users and/or Record Types to apply this policy to.
If no value is selected, the policy will apply to all values within that field.

Users

Search

Record Type

AipFileDeleted, AipProtectionAction, AipSensitivityLabelAction, AipScannerDis...

Duration *

Choose how long to retain logs that match this policy's conditions before they're automatically deleted. Learn more about licensing

6 Months

Priority * ⓘ

1

Figure 14.18: Audit log retention policy

5. **Search the audit log**: Now that all the settings are configured, you are ready to search the audit log. Consider the following points.

   - Completed search jobs are stored for 30 days which gives you historical reference to audit searches performed in the past.

   - Each admin Audit account can have a maximum of 10 concurrent search jobs in progress.

To search the audit log, following are the steps:

1. Login to **https://purview.microsoft.com** and click on the **Audit** tile.

2. Click on **Search**.

3. Make the necessary selections and click on **Search**. Refer to *Figure 14.19*:

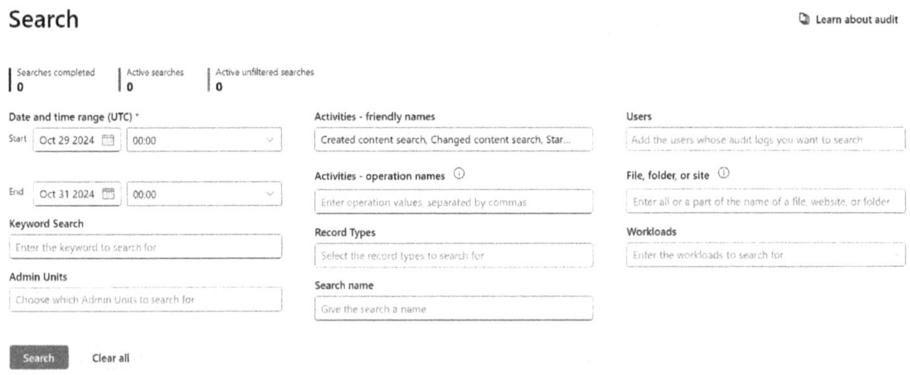

Search   Learn about audit

| Searches completed | Active searches | Active unfiltered searches |
| 0 | 0 | 0 |

Date and time range (UTC) *   Activities - friendly names   Users

Start Oct 29 2024   00:00   Created content search, Changed content search, Star...   Add the users whose audit logs you want to search

                                   Activities - operation names ⓘ   File, folder, or site ⓘ

End   Oct 31 2024   00:00   Enter operation values, separated by commas   Enter all or a part of the name of a file, website, or folder

Keyword Search   Record Types   Workloads

Enter the keyword to search for   Select the record types to search for   Enter the workloads to search for

Admin Units   Search name

Choose which Admin Units to search for   Give the search a name

[Search]   Clear all

Figure 14.19: Search the audit log

4. Once the search is completed, the search job is available in the search dashboard as shown in the following figure:

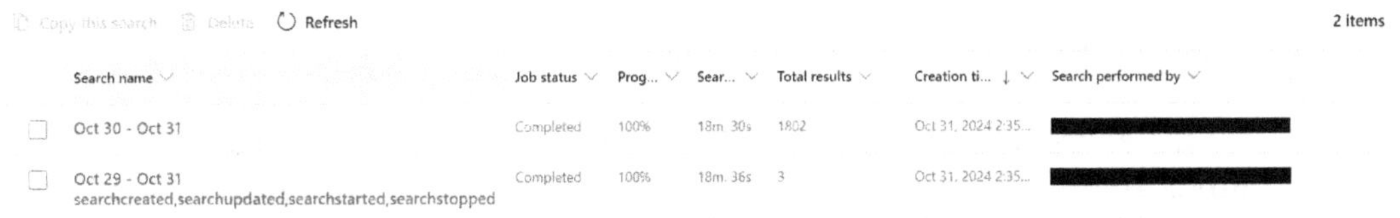

	Search name	Job status	Prog...	Sear...	Total results	Creation ti... ↓	Search performed by
	Oct 30 - Oct 31	Completed	100%	18m 30s	1802	Oct 31, 2024 2:35...	██████████████
	Oct 29 - Oct 31 searchcreated,searchupdated,searchstarted,searchstopped	Completed	100%	18m 36s	3	Oct 31, 2024 2:35...	██████████████

Copy this search   Delete   ◯ Refresh   2 items

Figure 14.20: Completed search jobs

5. Click on the search job to view the search results. The results can be exported by clicking on the **Export** option as shown in *Figure 14.21*:

Audit › **Audit search**

Search Query Information: Wed, 30 Oct 2024 00:00:00 GMT to Thu, 31 Oct 2024 00:00:00 GMT , ,

Total Result Count: 1802 items

⤓ Export   150 items ⫶ Filter

Date (UTC) ↓	IP Address	User	Record Type	Activity	Item	Admin Units	Details
Oct 30, 2024 9:13 PM		NT AUTHORITY\SYSTEM (...	ExchangeAdmin	Set-ConditionalAccessPolicy	████████		
Oct 30, 2024 9:13 PM		NT AUTHORITY\SYSTEM (...	ExchangeAdmin	Set-ConditionalAccessPolicy	████████		
Oct 30, 2024 7:09 PM		System	MDCRegulatoryComplianc...	MDCRegulatoryComplianc...			
Oct 30, 2024 7:09 PM		System	MDCRegulatoryComplianc...	MDCRegulatoryComplianc...			
Oct 30, 2024 7:09 PM		System	MDCRegulatoryComplianc...	MDCRegulatoryComplianc...			
Oct 30, 2024 7:09 PM		System	MDCRegulatoryComplianc...	MDCRegulatoryComplianc...			
Oct 30, 2024 7:09 PM		System	MDCRegulatoryComplianc...	MDCRegulatoryComplianc...			
Oct 30, 2024 7:09 PM		System	MDCRegulatoryComplianc...	MDCRegulatoryComplianc...			

Figure 14.21: Search results

Conclusion

In this chapter, we explored the critical aspects of managing eDiscovery cases using Microsoft Purview. We delved into the functionalities of Microsoft Purview eDiscovery and Microsoft Purview Audit, highlighting their importance in ensuring compliance, transparency, and accountability within an organization. By leveraging these tools, organizations can efficiently handle large volumes of data, maintain detailed audit logs, and safeguard their operations against potential legal and security risks. The effective implementation of eDiscovery and auditing practices not only fortifies an organization's defense against cyber threats but also reinforces its commitment to ethical practices and governance. As digital information continues to proliferate, the need for robust eDiscovery solutions will remain paramount in navigating the complexities of legal and regulatory landscapes.

In the next chapter, we will learn how you can use Microsoft Purview Compliance Manager to ensure your organization's compliance with regulatory and industry standards.

Multiple choice questions

1. You are the eDiscovery administrator for your organization. You have been asked to conduct an investigation to provide evidence for a legal case. You need to search for all documents related to Project Ninja on a SharePoint site. You need to ensure that the content in the SharePoint site is not modified while you are conducting your investigation. The content on SharePoint site includes Office file, pdf files and images. Which eDiscovery solution do you need to use?

   a. Content search

   b. eDiscovery

   c. Premium eDiscovery

   d. Any of them will work

2. You are the eDiscovery administrator for your organization. Your organization has 200 user mailboxes on Exchange Online. You have been asked to conduct an investigation to provide evidence for a legal case. You need to search for any email sent and received with the subject Project Ninja. How many eDiscovery licenses do you need?

   a. 1

   b. 200

   c. 2

   d. You need eDiscovery (Premium) licenses for this

3. You are responsible for conducting a forensic investigation for your environment. You need to retain audit logs for the finance department for three years. There are ten users in the finance department. Audit logs for the rest of the organization need to be maintained for one year. What and how many licenses do you need?

   a. Microsoft 365 E3 licenses for the entire organization

   b. Microsoft 365 E5 licenses for the entire organization

   c. Microsoft 365 E3 licenses for the entire organization plus ten 10-year Advanced Audit Add-on licenses assigned to the finance users.

   d. Microsoft 365 E5 licenses for the entire organization plus ten 10-year Advanced Audit Add-on licenses assigned to the finance users.

Answer key

1. c
2. b
3. d

CHAPTER 15
Managing Regulatory Compliance

Introduction

Regulatory compliance refers to the adherence of organizations to laws, regulations, guidelines, and specifications relevant to their business processes. Effective regulatory compliance ensures that companies operate within the bounds of legal and ethical standards, thereby protecting themselves from legal penalties, financial forfeitures, and reputational damage. The regulatory compliance landscape is constantly evolving, driven by changes in legislation, technological advancements, and shifting market dynamics. Organizations must therefore maintain a robust compliance framework that includes regular risk assessments, employee training, and the implementation of effective control measures. Compliance management also involves the meticulous documentation and reporting of compliance activities, as these records are often subject to regulatory scrutiny. The advent of compliance management tools, such as Microsoft Purview Compliance Manager, has significantly streamlined this process, allowing organizations to automate and monitor their compliance efforts efficiently. By integrating these tools into their compliance strategy, businesses can better navigate the complexities of regulatory requirements, ensuring they remain compliant while focusing on their core operations and strategic objectives.

Structure

The chapter covers the following topics:

- Microsoft Purview Compliance Manager
- Building and managing assessments

Objectives

By the end of this chapter, readers will have an understanding of Microsoft Purview Compliance Manager as an essential tool in the compliance journey. It details how organizations can utilize built-in regulatory compliance templates to create assessments and monitor their progress meeting regulatory requirements. The chapter also outlines the features of Compliance Manager, including risk assessments, control management, and continuous monitoring, which assist organizations in maintaining compliance with regulatory standards. It also explains multi-cloud support in Compliance Manager, allowing for compliance monitoring in the Microsoft 365 cloud and across Azure, AWS, and GCP. Furthermore, it describes how connectors can be used to monitor applications such as Salesforce and Zoom. Finally, the chapter discusses how to create alert policies to remain informed about any changes in the compliance landscape.

Microsoft Purview Compliance Manager

Maintaining regulatory compliance presents numerous challenges for organizations. The dynamic nature of regulations means that businesses must continuously stay informed about changes and updates, which can vary significantly across different jurisdictions and industries. Additionally, the complexity and volume of regulations can be overwhelming, requiring specialized knowledge and resources to interpret and implement effectively. Organizations must also address the potential for human error and the risk of non-compliance, which can arise from inadequate training, insufficient internal controls, or lack of employee awareness. Furthermore, the integration of compliance requirements with existing business processes and systems can be cumbersome and resource intensive. The need for ongoing monitoring, auditing, and reporting adds to the administrative burden, making it essential for organizations to invest in robust compliance management solutions and foster a culture of compliance throughout the organization. To effectively manage regulatory compliance, organizations utilize a variety of sophisticated tools and software solutions. These tools are designed to streamline the compliance process, mitigate risks, and ensure adherence to applicable laws and regulations.

One of the most widely used tools is Microsoft Purview Compliance Manager, which helps automatically assess and manage compliance across a multi-cloud environment. It assists organizations throughout the compliance journey from taking stock of the current risks to providing guidance to implementing controls and staying current with changing regulations. It offers a range of features, including risk assessments, control management, and continuous monitoring, all of which help organizations maintain compliance with regulatory requirements. By automating many of the compliance tasks, Microsoft Purview Compliance Manager reduces the administrative burden and allows businesses to focus on their core operations.

Microsoft Purview Compliance Manager offers the following important features that help organizations maintain compliance and reduce risk:

- Pre-built assessment templates for common industry and regional standards.
- Workflow capabilities to efficiently complete risk assessment using a single tool.
- Detailed step-by-step guidance on suggested improvement actions.
- A risk-based compliance score that helps organizations understand their compliance posture.

Compliance Manager is available in the Microsoft Purview portal. To access it login to **https://purview.microsoft.com** and click on the **Compliance Manager** tile. The **Dashboard** shows the organization's compliance score, key improvement actions and various other information. Refer to *Figure 15.1*:

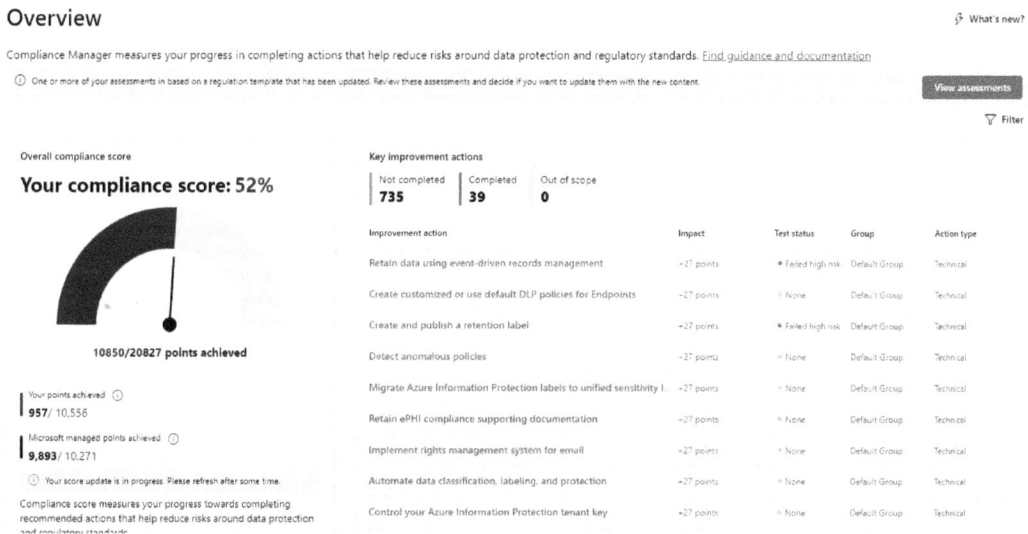

Figure 15.1: Compliance Manager dashboard

License requirements

The minimum license required to use Compliance Manager in the Microsoft Purview Portal is Microsoft 365 E1 or Office 365 E1. With these licenses, customers can use the **Data Protection Baseline** assessment template.

Organizations with Microsoft 365 E3 licenses get access to the **Compliance Score** feature in the Purview Portal in addition to the Data Protection Baseline assessment template.

Organizations with M365 E5 licenses get three premium templates for free in addition to the Data Protection Baseline template and Compliance Score. In addition, they are also able to create a new template, customize an existing template and add customized actions to a given template.

All organizations can purchase additional premium templates from the Purview Portal.

Permission requirements

Compliance Manager uses RBAC permission model. *Table 15.1* explains the actions available by role type:

Role	Action
Compliance Manager Reader	Read but not edit data
Compliance Manager Contributors	Edit data and create assessments
Compliance Manager Assessor	Edit data only
Compliance Manager Administrators	Manage assessments, regulatory templates and tenant data. Assign improvement actions

Table 15.1: Compliance Manager roles

Following are the steps to assign users to Compliance Manager roles:

1. Login to **https://purview.microsoft.com** and click on **Settings**.
2. Navigate to **Roles and scopes | Role groups**.
3. Search for the above groups and assign users as required.

Compliance score

When you first get started with Compliance Manager, the initial score is based on the Data Protection Baseline template that is available to all organizations regardless of the licensing type. Compliance Manager collects signals from your Microsoft 365 solutions to calculate your compliance score. You can see immediately your organization's performance relative to the key data protection regulations and take actions to improve your score.

Improvement actions have points, and they contribute to your compliance score. Once you complete an improvement action, the status is updated in the dashboard and the points are added to your compliance score within 24 hours.

Actions are assigned points depending on whether they are mandatory, discretionary, preventative, detective or corrective. These are explained as follows:

- **Mandatory actions** cannot be passed. For example, a password policy with complex requirements.

- **Discretionary actions** rely on users to understand and adhere to a policy. For example, locking a computer when leaving it unattended.

- **Preventative actions** address specific risks. For example, using encryption to protect sensitive data.

- **Detective actions** monitor systems to identify irregularities or risks. For example, auditing.

- **Corrective actions** try to minimize the effects of a security incident by taking some action. For example, isolating a rogue device.

Table 15.2 summarizes the points assigned to these actions:

Type	Score
Preventative mandatory	27
Preventative discretionary	9
Detective mandatory	3
Detective discretionary	1
Corrective mandatory	3
Corrective discretionary	1

Table 15.2: Improvement actions score

Multi-cloud support

Most large organizations have resources running in multiple clouds like Azure, AWS, GCP. Compliance Manager integrates with Microsoft Defender for Cloud, which allows organizations to build and manage assessments that align with specific regulations, regardless of the cloud service provider. This approach allows for seamless integration and consistent compliance management, ensuring that organizations can operate confidently across multiple cloud platforms while meeting all necessary regulatory requirements. The Compliance Manager can track configurations in your organization's Azure and Microsoft 365 environments and detect signals from other services like AWS and GCP so you can assess your progress in meeting controls for regulations you need to comply with.

With the integration with Microsoft Defender for Cloud, you can now select a supported assessment in Compliance Manager and select the service to assess. The Compliance Manager then provides automatic monitoring of configuration in your selected service and determines if controls are passing or failing. Using signals from Defender for Cloud, Compliance Manager automatically detects the test status of improvement actions that pertain to the supported services.

> **Note: Not all Compliance Manager templates are supported in Microsoft Defender for Cloud. For a list of supported assessments, refer to the Microsoft documentation. To take advantage of this integration, organizations must have an Azure subscription with Defender for Cloud enabled.**

In addition to the multi-cloud support, Compliance Manager also offers connectors to connect to non-Microsoft SaaS applications. These connectors provide a seamless integration into the non-Microsoft services used by your organization so that you can include them in your assessment and take advantage of the automatic monitoring and control testing. Connectors for corporate sustainability, Salesforce and Zoom are currently available. Only members of the Data Connector Administrator or Global Administrator role groups can set up a connector in Compliance Manager.

To create a connector in Compliance Manager, some settings need to be configured on each service to get the basic authentication information. The steps differ depending on the connector you are trying to set up. Refer to the Microsoft documentation for details on each. **https://learn.microsoft.com/en-us/purview/compliance-manager-connectors**

Once the service side settings are done, activate the connector in Compliance Manager using the following steps:

1. Login to **https://purview.microsoft.com** and navigate to **Settings** | **Compliance Manager** | **Connectors**.

2. In the right pane, select the appropriate connector and click on **Activate connector** as shown in the following figure:

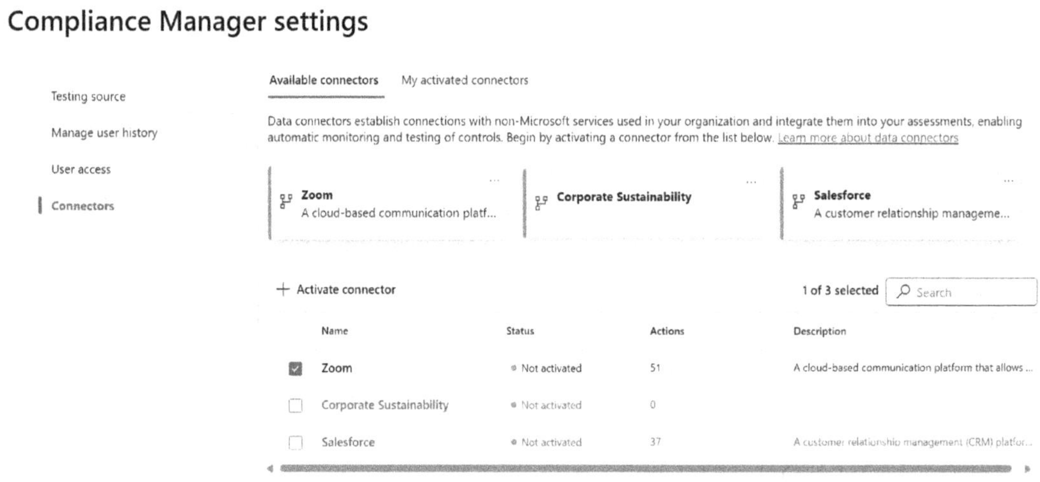

Compliance Manager settings

Figure 15.2: Activate connector

3. Click on **Accept** to accept the terms of use.

4. Enter a name for the connector and click **Next**.

5. On the **Authentication** page, enter the service side authentication information and click on **Validate connection** to ensure the connection works and click **Next**.

Following figure shows an example of the Salesforce connector:

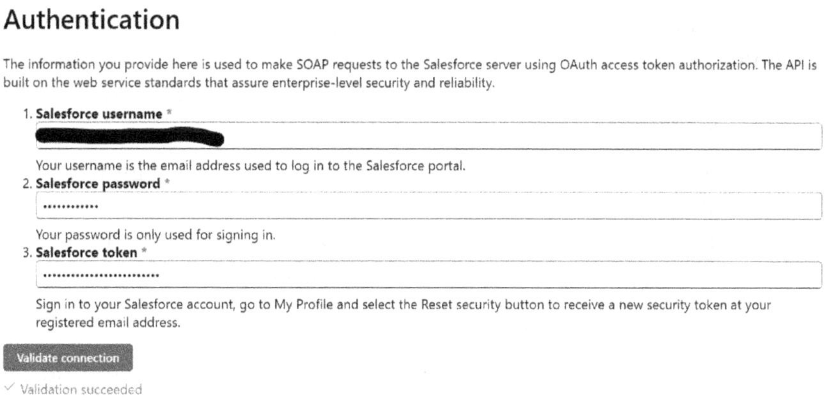

Authentication

The information you provide here is used to make SOAP requests to the Salesforce server using OAuth access token authorization. The API is built on the web service standards that assure enterprise-level security and reliability.

1. **Salesforce username** *

Your username is the email address used to log in to the Salesforce portal.

2. **Salesforce password** *

Your password is only used for signing in.

3. **Salesforce token** *

Sign in to your Salesforce account, go to My Profile and select the Reset security button to receive a new security token at your registered email address.

Validate connection

✓ Validation succeeded

Figure 15.3: Authenticate connector

6. Review the settings and click **Finish**. The connector will now appear in the **My activated connectors** tab. You will be able to add the configured service to assessments.

Understanding regulations

Compliance regulations are rules and standards that organizations must follow to ensure they operate ethically, safely, and within the law. These regulations can vary significantly across different industries and jurisdictions, and they are designed to protect consumers, employees, and the environment. Examples of compliance regulations include the **General Data Protection Regulation** (**GDPR**), which governs data protection and privacy in the European Union, and the **Health Insurance Portability and Accountability Act** (**HIPAA**), which sets standards for the protection of health information in the United States. Adhering to these regulations helps organizations avoid legal penalties, maintain their reputation, and build trust with stakeholders. Failure to comply with such regulations such can lead to substantial financial penalties, loss of customer trust, or legal ramifications. Therefore, maintaining compliance is not only a regulatory obligation but also a strategic business decision.

Compliance Manager provides more than 370 regulations as templates which organizations can use. The Data Protection Baseline regulatory template is the default available for all organizations. This assessment draws elements from important frameworks like NIST, ISO, FedRAMP and GDPR. This template aims to help all organizations evaluate their basic compliance posture. In addition, following categories of regulations are available:

- **Sub-service compliance readiness**: These templates provide a way for an organization to understand Microsoft's compliance posture before they deploy

Microsoft services in their environment. Using these templates, organizations can analyze how Azure services can contribute to their overall compliance posture with respect to ISO/IEC 27001:2013, NIST 800-53 rev.4, PCI DSS v4.0 and SOC 2. At the time of this writing, this feature is in Public Preview.

- **Premium AI templates**: Compliance Manager provides four templates to help organizations strengthen compliance with AI regulations. The included regulations are EU Artificial Intelligence Act, ISO/IEC 23894:2023, ISO/IEC 42001:2023, and NIST AI **Risk Management Framework (RMF)** 1.0.

- **Premium templates**: These include all other global, regional and industry regulations like ISO, FedRAMP, GDPR etc. For a complete list of regulations, refer to the Microsoft documentation: **https://learn.microsoft.com/en-us/purview/compliance-manager-regulations-list# premium-regulations**

Following are the steps to access these templates:

1. Login to **https://purview.microsoft.com** and click on the **Compliance Manager** tile.

2. Click on **Regulations**. *Figure 15.4* shows a sample of the available regulation templates.

3. Select any regulation template to view details about it and add it as an assessment.

4. You can also customize a template by clicking on the box next to it and selecting **Customize regulation**. This will create a copy of the template that you can modify as per your requirements.

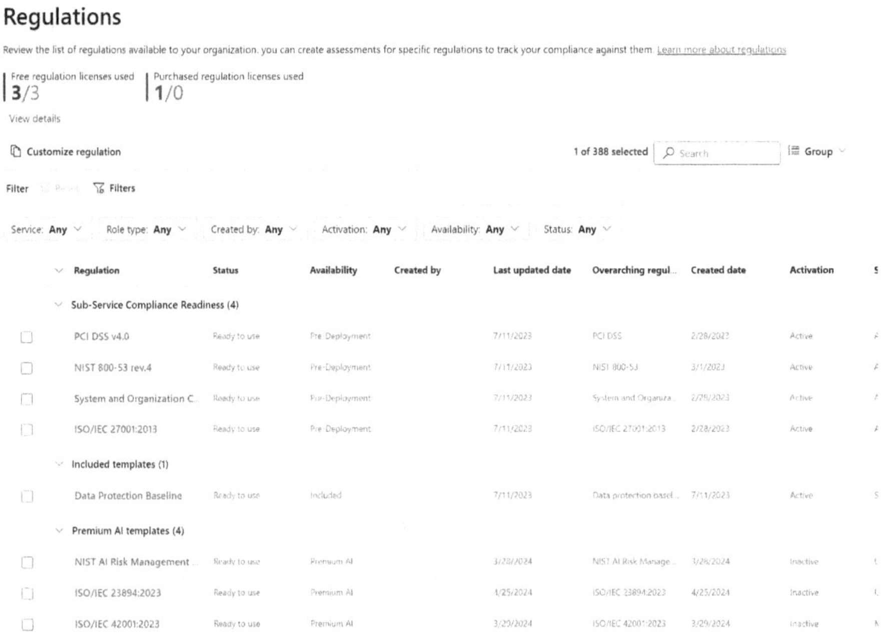

Figure 15.4: Compliance manager templates

Building and managing assessments

An assessment is a group of controls pertaining to a specific regulation. Completing the actions within an assessment is the way to meet the requirements of the regulation and be compliant with that regulation. You can select the required regulation and add it as an assessment in Compliance Manager.

Following are the steps to add a regulation as an assessment:

1. Login to **https://purview.microsoft.com** and click on the **Compliance Manager** tile.

2. Click on **Regulations** and select your template of choice.

3. The assessment page shows you an overview of the regulation, the controls, your actions and Microsoft actions. Click on the ellipses (…) in the top right corner and select **Create assessment** as shown in the following figure:

Figure 15.5: Create assessment

4. Give the connector a name and select a group or create a new group and click **Next**. A group is a collection of assessments that are logical for your organization. You could group assessments by year, geographical location or business units. For example, you could have a group created by year and add all assessments completed in that year to that group as shown in the following figure:

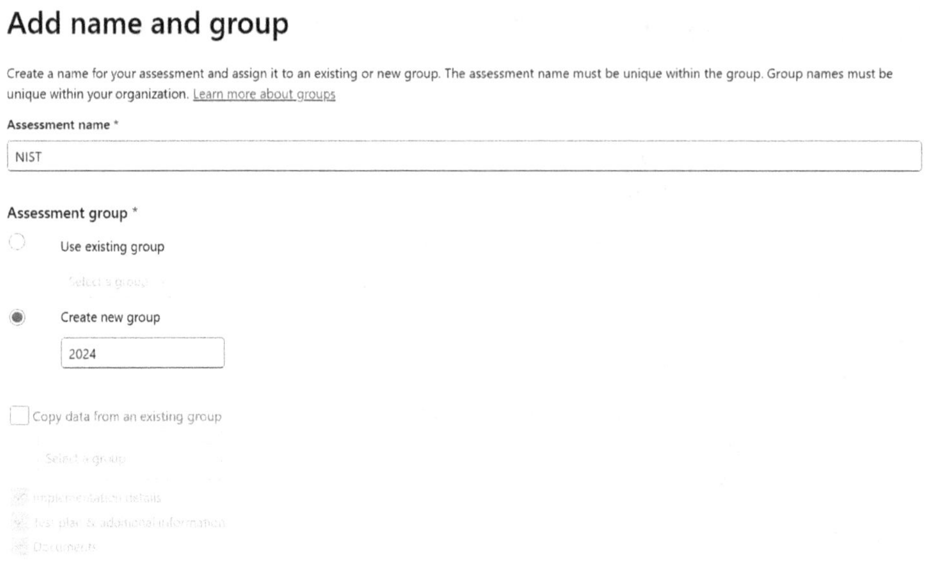

Add name and group

Create a name for your assessment and assign it to an existing or new group. The assessment name must be unique within the group. Group names must be unique within your organization. Learn more about groups

Assessment name *

NIST

Assessment group *

○ Use existing group

Select a group

● Create new group

2024

☐ Copy data from an existing group

Select a group

☑ Implementation details

☑ Test plan & additional information

☑ Documents

Figure 15.6: Add assessment

5. On the next page, you can select the services which the assessment applies to. Click on **Select services** and select the appropriate services and click **Update** as shown in *Figure 15.7*. Click **Next** to continue.

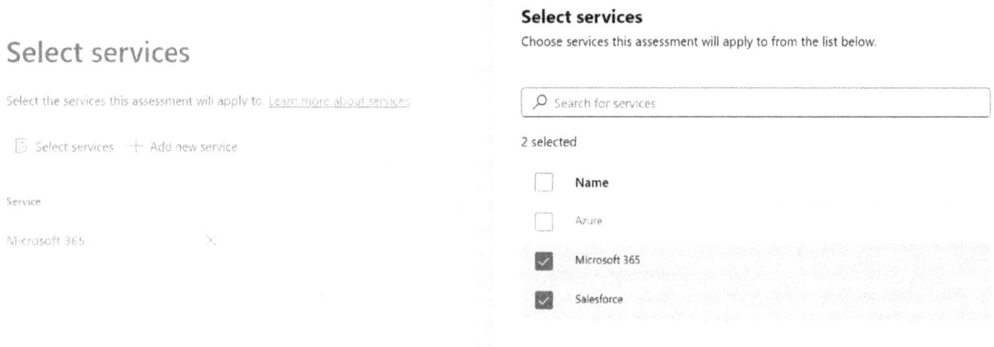

Select services

Select the services this assessment will apply to. Learn more about services

🗟 Select services   + Add new service

Service

Microsoft 365   ✕

Select services

Choose services this assessment will apply to from the list below.

🔍 Search for services

2 selected

☐ Name

☐ Azure

☑ Microsoft 365

☑ Salesforce

Figure 15.7: Select services

Note: Non-Microsoft services are available if multi-cloud support has been configured.

6. If non-Microsoft services have been selected, you will be prompted to select the service instance as shown in *Figure 15.8*. Click on **Manage service instance** and select the configured connector and click **Update**. Click **Next** to continue.

Figure 15.8: *Select service instance*

7. Review the settings and click on **Create assessment**. Once the assessment is created, click **Done**.

Each assessment has a details page that provides information about the progress and the actions taken in completing the assessment.

Figure 15.9 is an example of the assessment created in the previous steps. Note the details available to you. The **Overview** section provides the basic details like name and group of the assessment. The **Progress** section shows the percentage of progress toward assessment completion.

You can assign reader, assessor and contributor permissions to compliance managers by clicking on the **Manage user access** option on the top right.

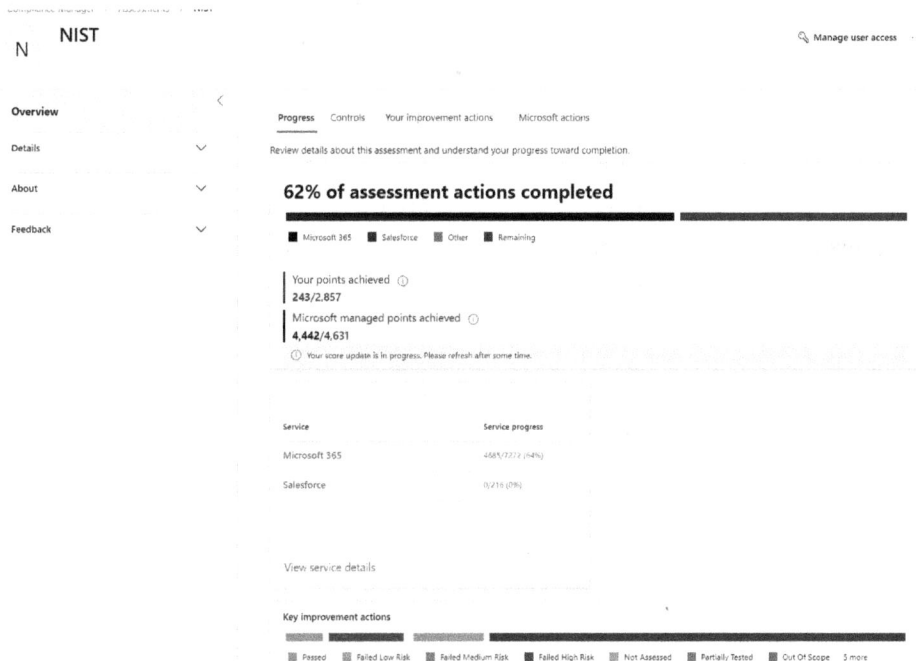

Figure 15.9: *Assessment overview*

Controls

Control is a requirement of a regulation. It defines how you assess and manage configuration, processes and people for meeting specific requirements. Assessments in Compliance Manager have the following categories of controls:

- **Microsoft managed controls**: These are controls pertaining to the Microsoft cloud services like Azure or Microsoft 365 that Microsoft must meet.

- **Customer managed controls**: These are controls that need to be implemented by the customer to meet the regulatory requirements.

- **Shared controls**: These are the controls that are the responsibility of both Microsoft and the customer. For example, to implement MFA, Microsoft is responsible for providing the tools and infrastructure necessary to implement MFA while, the customer is responsible for configuring and managing MFA policies and ensuring that users enroll for MFA.

Click on the **Controls** tab to view a list of all controls and their status. Refer to *Figure 15.10*. The page shows a graphical representation of the controls with their status. The detailed pane shows the **Control ID**, which is the control's unique identification number assigned by its regulation. It also shows the number of points that can be achieved if all improvement points in that control are completed.

Controls are grouped by categories and can have the following statuses:

- **Passed**: At least one improvement action related to the control have a test status of passed the rest are out of scope or all improvement actions have a test status of passed.

- **Failed**: At least on improvement, action has a test status of failed.

- **None**: All improvement actions have not been tested.

- **Out of scope**: All improvement actions are out of scope.

- **In progress**: Improvement actions have one of the following statuses like: in progress, partial credit or undetected.

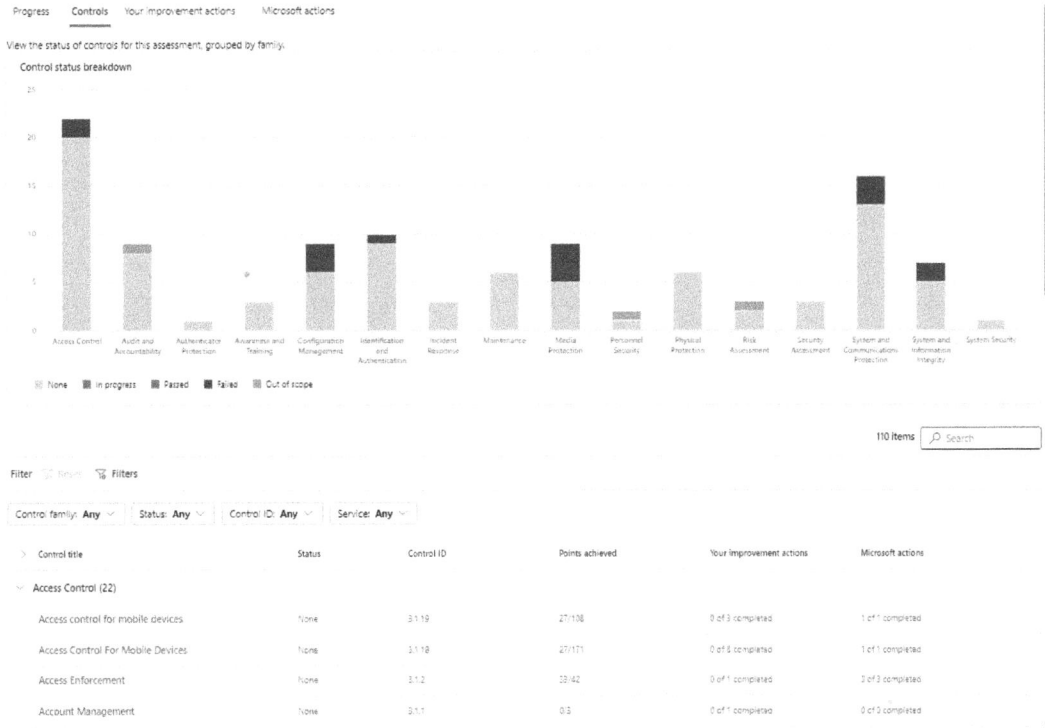

Figure 15.10: Controls

Improvement actions

Improvement actions are the specific activities that need to be performed to meet the control. A single control can have multiple improvement actions associated as shown in *Figure 15.11*. Click on any control to view its details page. A graph shows the status of the improvement actions associated with that control.

A   Access Control For Mobile Devices

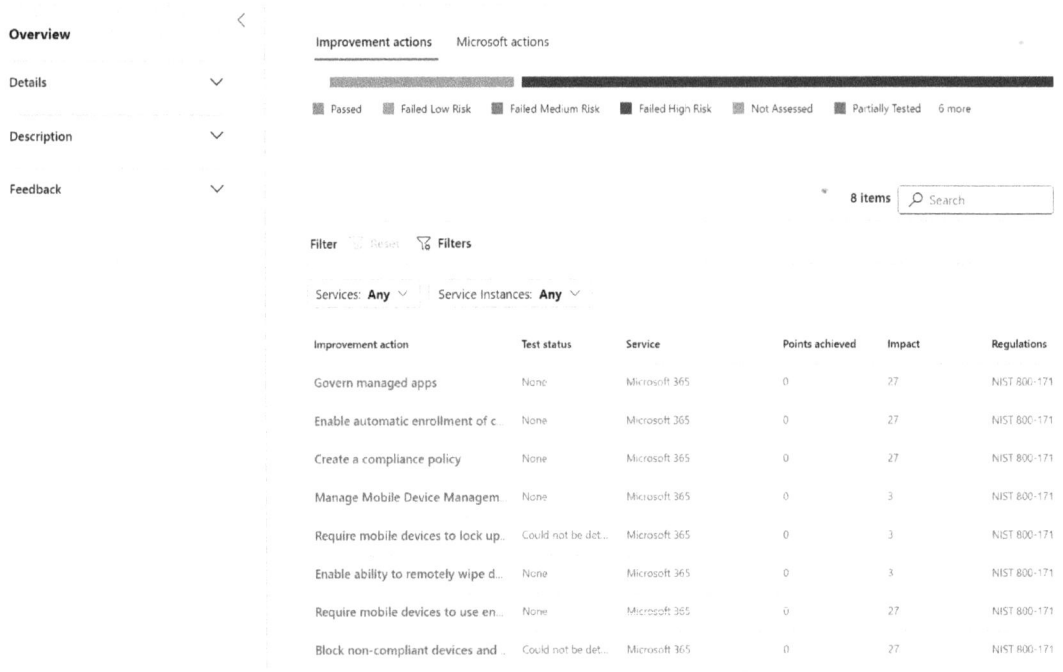

Figure 15.11: *Improvement actions*

Click on any improvement action to open its details page. Refer to *Figure 15.12*. On this page, you can get the status of the action from the top information bar. On the **Details** tab, you can see detailed instructions on how to implement the improvement action. You can upload evidence related to the implementation and testing work in the form of files or links by clicking on the **Evidence** tab. The **Related controls** tab shows all controls that include this improvement action. You would need to perform the action only once and it will satisfy all related controls.

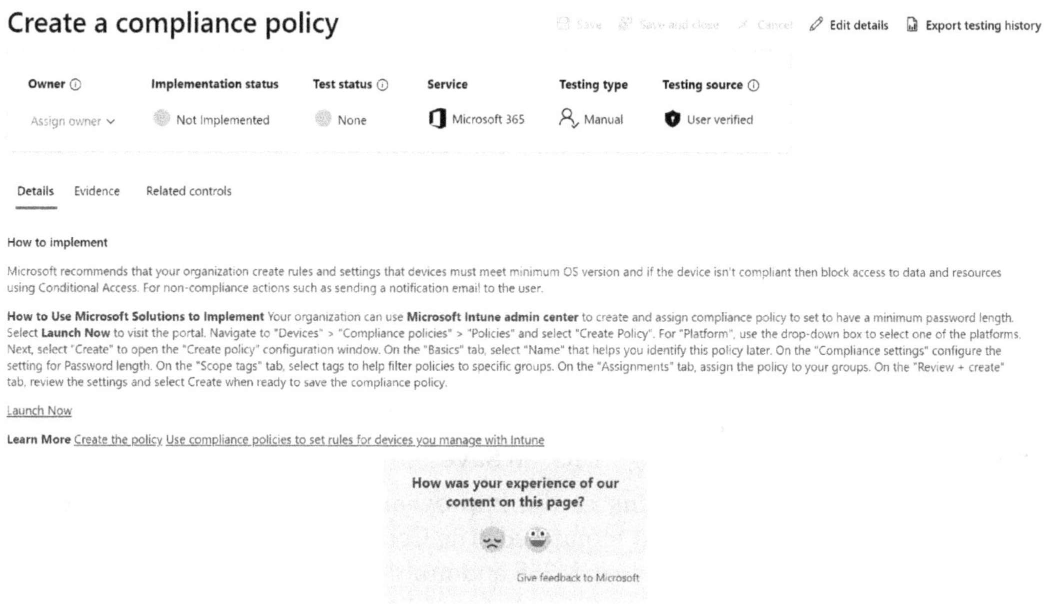

Create a compliance policy

▣ Save ▨ Save and close ✕ Cancel ✐ Edit details ▣ Export testing history

Owner ⓘ	Implementation status	Test status ⓘ	Service	Testing type	Testing source ⓘ
Assign owner ∨	◍ Not Implemented	◍ None	▣ Microsoft 365	ዱ Manual	🛡 User verified

Details   Evidence   Related controls

How to implement

Microsoft recommends that your organization create rules and settings that devices must meet minimum OS version and if the device isn't compliant then block access to data and resources using Conditional Access. For non-compliance actions such as sending a notification email to the user.

How to Use Microsoft Solutions to Implement Your organization can use **Microsoft Intune admin center** to create and assign compliance policy to set to have a minimum password length. Select **Launch Now** to visit the portal. Navigate to "Devices" > "Compliance policies" > "Policies" and select "Create Policy". For "Platform", use the drop-down box to select one of the platforms. Next, select "Create" to open the "Create policy" configuration window. On the "Basics" tab, select "Name" that helps you identify this policy later. On the "Compliance settings" configure the setting for Password length. On the "Scope tags" tab, select tags to help filter policies to specific groups. On the "Assignments" tab, assign the policy to your groups. On the "Review + create" tab, review the settings and select Create when ready to save the compliance policy.

Launch Now

Learn More Create the policy Use compliance policies to set rules for devices you manage with Intune

How was your experience of our content on this page?

😖 😃

Give feedback to Microsoft

Figure 15.12: Improvement action details

To begin implementation work, you can either assign the action to yourself or to another user using the **Assign owner** option as shown in *Figure 15.12*. After following the implementation guidance under **How to implement**, change the implementation status to one of the following by selecting **Edit details** and selecting the relevant option in the **Implementation** tab and click **Save** as shown in *Figure 15.13*:

- **Not implemented**: The improvement action has not been implemented.
- **Implemented**: The improvement action has been successfully implemented.
- **Alternative implementation**: Use this option if non-Microsoft tools are used to complete the improvement action.
- **Planned**: The improvement action is planned to be implemented later.
- **Out of scope**: Action is not relevant to the organization.

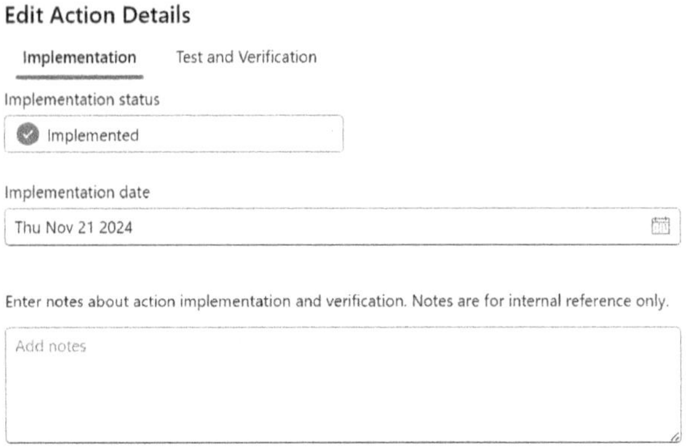

Edit Action Details

Implementation   Test and Verification

Implementation status

✓ Implemented

Implementation date

Thu Nov 21 2024   🗓

Enter notes about action implementation and verification. Notes are for internal reference only.

Add notes

Figure 15.13: Update implementation status

Back on the improvement action page, click on **Save**.

You can also update the **Test status** of the improvement action. Some improvement actions are automatically tested and monitored. The Compliance Manager automatically identifies configuration settings in your M365 and multi-cloud environments that satisfy the requirements and updates the test status. Automatic testing is turned on by default for all actions that can be automatically tested.

You can turn this option off by going to **Settings** | **Compliance Manager** | **Testing source** in the Microsoft Purview portal and selecting the option **Turn off automatic testing for all improvement actions**. You can also choose to **Turn on automatic testing for all improvement actions** or **Turn on automatic testing per improvement action** as shown in *Figure 15.14*:

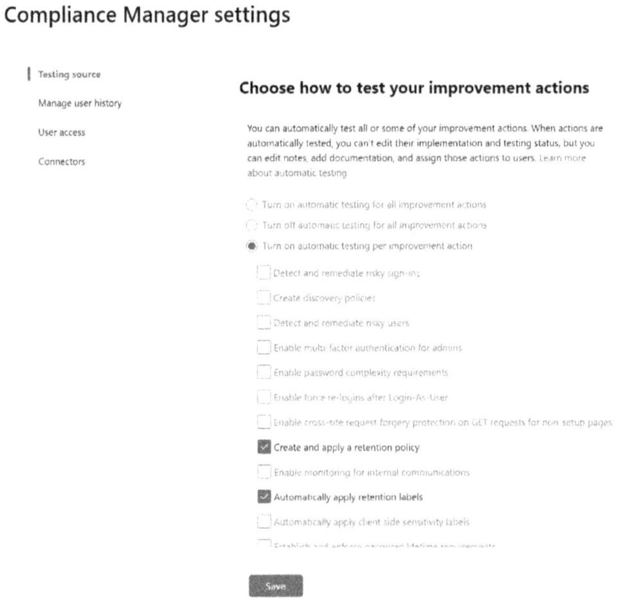

Compliance Manager settings

| Testing source

Manage user history

User access

Connectors

Choose how to test your improvement actions

You can automatically test all or some of your improvement actions. When actions are automatically tested, you can't edit their implementation and testing status, but you can edit notes, add documentation, and assign those actions to users. Learn more about automatic testing.

○ Turn on automatic testing for all improvement actions

○ Turn off automatic testing for all improvement actions

◉ Turn on automatic testing per improvement action

☐ Detect and remediate risky sign-ins

☐ Create discovery policies

☐ Detect and remediate risky users

☐ Enable multi-factor authentication for admins

☐ Enable password complexity requirements

☐ Enable force re-logins after Login-As-User

☐ Enable cross-site request forgery protection on GET requests for non-setup pages

☑ Create and apply a retention policy

☐ Enable monitoring for internal communications

☑ Automatically apply retention labels

☐ Automatically apply client side sensitivity labels

☐ Establish and enforce required lifetime requirements

Save

Figure 15.14: Testing source

There are four types of automation as follows:

- **Built-in automation**: Compliance Manager has built-in functionality to receive signals from other Microsoft and non-Microsoft services. It detects signals from other Microsoft Purview solutions like Data Lifecycle Management, Information Protection, Communication Compliance, Data Loss Prevention and Insider Risk Management. It also detects signals from Microsoft Priva.

- **Microsoft Secure Score automation**: Compliance Manager detects signals from improvement actions that are monitored by Microsoft Secure Score.

- **Microsoft Defender for Cloud automation**: Integration with Microsoft Defender from Cloud enables Compliance Manager to detect signals from connected cloud services like Azure, AWS and GCP.

- **Connectors**: Using connectors the Compliance Manager can detect signals from cloud services like Salesforce and Zoom.

When signals indicate that an improvement action has been successfully implemented you automatically receive the eligible points.

For actions that are not automatically tested, manual testing must be performed. The test status is displayed on the **Details** page. After an improvement action has been implemented, you can update the test status by clicking on **Edit details | Test and Verification** as shown in *Figure 15.15*.

Following are the available options:

- **None**: No work has been started on the action.
- **Not assessed**: The action has not been tested.
- **Passed**: The implementation has been verified by an assessor.
- **Failed low risk**: An assessor determines that the action does not meet the requirement but is of low risk.
- **Failed medium risk**: An assessor determines that the action does not meet the requirement and is of medium risk.
- **Failed high risk**: An assessor determines that the action does not meet the requirement and is at high risk.
- **Out of scope**: The action is out of scope and does not contribute to the score.
- **To be determined**: The test plan is yet to be determined.
- **Could not be determined**: The test plan could not be determined.
- **Partially tested**: The improvement action has been partially tested.
- **In progress**: The testing is in progress.
- **Remediated**: The testing is successful.

Select the relevant option and click on **Save**. Back on the improvement action page, click **Save**.

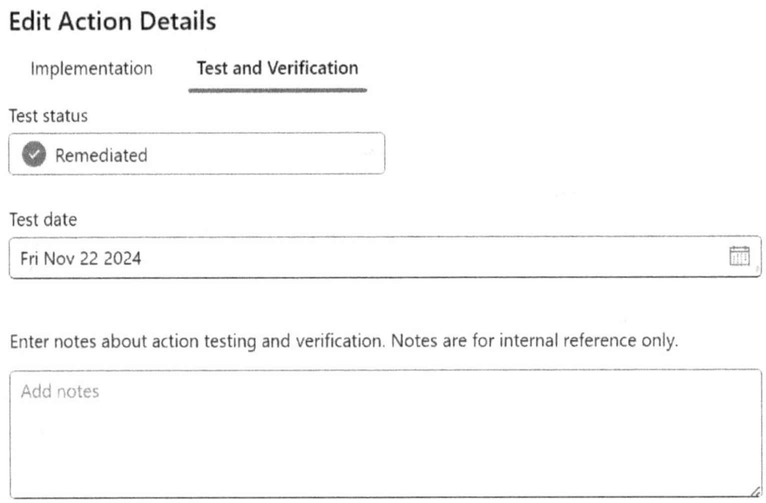

Edit Action Details

Implementation   **Test and Verification**

Test status

✅ Remediated

Test date

Fri Nov 22 2024   📅

Enter notes about action testing and verification. Notes are for internal reference only.

Add notes

Figure 15.15: Update test status

After you complete the work, conduct testing and upload evidence, assign the improvement action to an assessor for validation. The assessor will validate the work, examine evidence and update the test status to either **Pass** or **Fail**. If the action is set to pass, the action is complete, and the points will be added to your compliance score. If the action is set to fail, the assessor might assign the action back to the appropriate user for rework.

Alert policies

The Compliance Manager can alert you of changes like dropping compliance scores. This enables you to take quick actions and stay on track to meet your compliance goals. To generate alerts, alert policies must be created as described in the following steps:

1. Login to **https://purview.microsoft.com** and select the **Compliance Manager** tile.
2. Click on **Policies** and on the right pane, click on **Add**.
3. Give the policy a name and description and click **Next**.
4. Alerts can be generated for the following conditions. Click on **Add sub-condition** and select the relevant options and click **Add**. Click **Next** to continue. Refer to *Figure 15.16*.

   a. **Assignment change**: An improvement action has been assigned or reassigned.

   b. **Evidence changes**: Evidence has been uploaded or deleted.

   c. **Implementation status change**: The implementation status of an improvement action has been updated.

   d. **Score change**: Compliance score change due to implementation of improvement actions.

e. **Test status change**: The testing status of an improvement action has been updated.

Refer to the following figure:

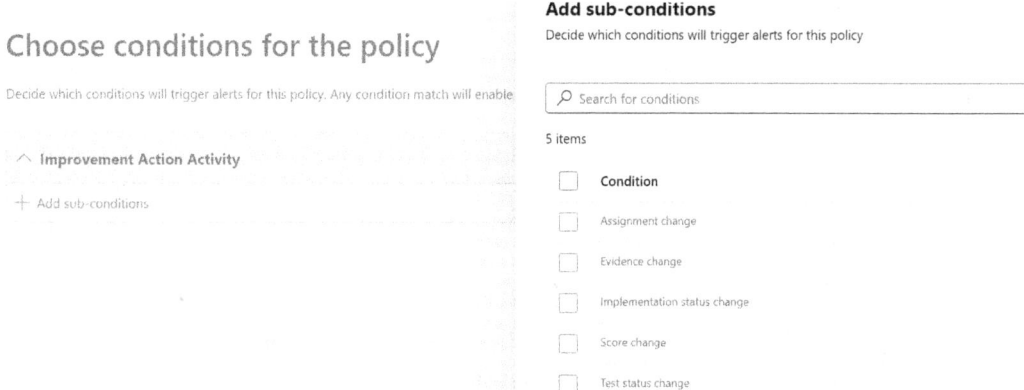

Choose conditions for the policy

Decide which conditions will trigger alerts for this policy. Any condition match will enable

∧ **Improvement Action Activity**

+ Add sub-conditions

Add sub-conditions

Decide which conditions will trigger alerts for this policy

🔍 Search for conditions

5 items

☐ **Condition**

☐ Assignment change

☐ Evidence change

☐ Implementation status change

☐ Score change

☐ Test status change

Figure 15.16: Add conditions for policy

5. On the outcomes page, select the severity of the alert and specify if you want to send email notifications for each match or after a specified threshold is reached as shown in *Figure 15.17*. Click **Next** to continue.

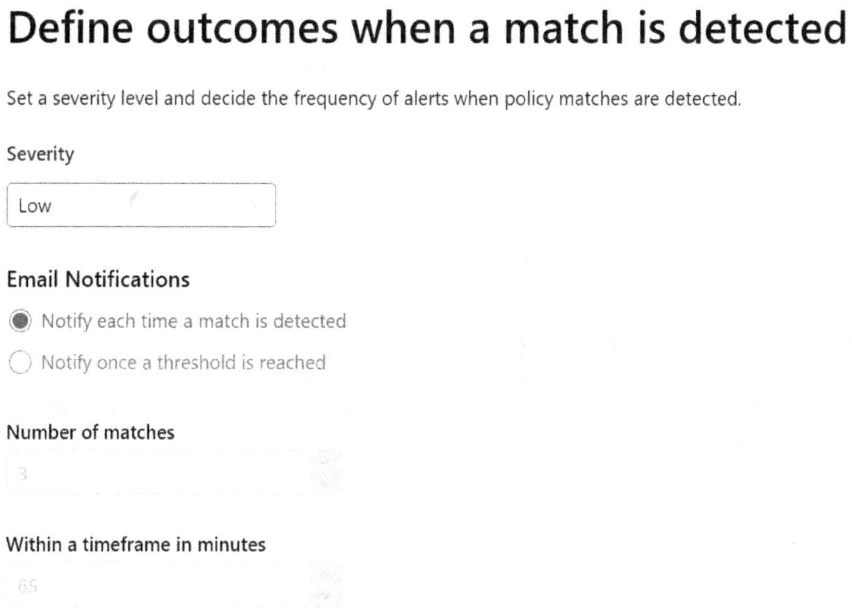

Define outcomes when a match is detected

Set a severity level and decide the frequency of alerts when policy matches are detected.

Severity

Low

Email Notifications

◉ Notify each time a match is detected

○ Notify once a threshold is reached

Number of matches

3

Within a timeframe in minutes

65

Figure 15.17: Select alert severity

6. On the next page, select the recipients who will receive the email notifications and click **Next**.

7. Review the settings and click **Create policy**.

Policies are activated as soon as they are created, and alerts are visible on the **Alerts** page. You can choose to disable a policy by selecting the policy and selecting the **Disable** option on the **Policies** page.

From the alerts page, the alerts can be assigned to someone for investigation. The status can be updated to **Active**, **Investigating**, **Resolved** or **Dismissed**.

All Compliance Manager role groups except the Compliance Manager Reader role, can create and edit compliance policies and work on alerts. In addition to Compliance Manager roles, users also need the following Microsoft Entra roles to work with alert policies and alerts.

- To view alerts and alert policies, the **Security reader** role is required.
- To create and update alert policies, the **Compliance administrator**, **Compliance data administrator**, **Security administrator** or **Security operator** role is required.

Conclusion

In this chapter, you learnt how you can manage regulatory compliance using Microsoft Purview Compliance Manager. You learnt how you can use the built-in assessment templates to build your own compliance and track your progress in meeting the requirements to be compliant with the regulations. You learnt how you can configure multi-cloud support in Compliance Manager so that you can manage compliance across your cloud landscape from a single source. You learnt how you can build and manage assessments and work on improvement actions. You should now be able to use Compliance Manager to meet your organization's regulatory compliance requirements.

In the next chapter, we will discuss how you can protect your customers' privacy and respond to subjects' rights requests using Microsoft Priva.

Multiple choice questions

1. **What is the minimum license required to access Compliance Manager?**

    a. Office 365 E1

    b. Microsoft 365 E3

    c. Microsoft 365 E5 Compliance

    d. Office 365 E3

2. **What is the default assessment template that is available to all organizations regardless of license type?**

    a. CIS Foundation Level 2

    b. Data Protection Baseline

    c. PCI-DSS

    d. NIST 800-171

3. **How does the Compliance Manager offer multi-cloud support? Choose all that apply.**

    a. It has assessment templates for non-Microsoft services

    b. Integration with Microsoft Defender for Cloud

    c. Compliance Manager does not offer multi-cloud support

    d. Using connectors

Answer key

1. a

2. b

3. a, b, d

Join our book's Discord space

Join the book's Discord Workspace for Latest updates, Offers, Tech happenings around the world, New Release and Sessions with the Authors:

https://discord.bpbonline.com

CHAPTER 16
Managing Privacy

Introduction

In today's digital age, securing personal information has become an imperative aspect of managing privacy. The rapid advancement of technology and the proliferation of online services have resulted in an unprecedented collection and exchange of personal data. This data, often containing sensitive information is vulnerable to various threats, including cyberattacks, identity theft, and unauthorized access. The consequences of such breaches can be severe, ranging from financial loss and reputational damage to emotional distress and legal repercussions. Therefore, implementing robust security measures to protect personal information is crucial. By prioritizing the security of personal data, organizations can foster trust with their users, comply with regulatory requirements, and ultimately safeguard the rights and freedoms of individuals. In essence, secure data management is not only a technical necessity but also a fundamental aspect of ethical responsibility in the modern world.

Structure

The chapter covers the following topics:

- Microsoft Priva
- Investigating and remediating alerts
- Creating and managing deleted request

Objectives

By the end of this chapter, readers will be introduced to Microsoft Priva, Microsoft's first privacy management solution and its various components. The chapter explains in detail how you can use Privacy Risk Management policies to identify privacy risks like overshared data, stale data and unauthorized data transfers. It shows how **Subject Rights Requests (SRRs)** can be used to service data subjects' requests for data export, access and deletion. It also briefly explains the preview capabilities of Tracker Scanning, Consent Management and Privacy Assessments.

Microsoft Priva

Data privacy has become a critical concern for organizations. The increasing scrutiny regarding the handling of personal information necessitates compliance with regulatory requirements. Personal information, which includes data such as name, date of birth, and passport number, can be used to identify an individual. To address these concerns effectively, organizations must adopt privacy **by default** approach. Implementing robust privacy solutions is essential not only for protecting personal information but also for ensuring adherence to regulations. Additionally, such measures contribute to building and maintaining trust with customers.

Microsoft Priva, Microsoft's first privacy management solution is a set of controls that supports privacy operations across an organization's data landscape. It helps an organization to consolidate privacy protection, adhere to regulatory compliance, manage privacy risks, foster customer trust and confidence and accelerate digital transformation. Priva utilizes the capabilities of Microsoft Purview like SITs to help identify personal information in Microsoft 365 services like Exchange Online, SharePoint Online, OneDrive for Business and Microsoft Teams.

Microsoft Priva includes the following solutions that help organizations manage, define and track privacy operations at scale and help ensure that personal data remains secure and compliant with regulations:
- Privacy assessments (Preview)
- Privacy risk management
- Tracker scanning (Preview)
- Consent management (Preview)
- Subject Rights Requests for Microsoft 365
- Subject Rights Requests for data beyond Microsoft 365 (Preview)

Privacy Risk Management

Microsoft Priva Privacy Risk Management enables you to identify and remediate privacy risks in your Microsoft 365 environment. Privacy risk management can detect overexposed personal information, spot and limit transfers of personal data across business units or regional borders and identify unused personal data. It offers built-in policy templates to help administrators easily create policies.

Getting started with Privacy Risk Management

Before getting started with Microsoft Priva Privacy Risk Management you must ensure that you have the required licenses, and roles assigned, as follows:

- **Microsoft Priva Privacy Risk Management** is a per user per month subscription and is available as an add-on to any of the following subscriptions:
  - Office 365 A1/E1/G1/E3/A5/E5
  - Microsoft 365 A3/E3/A5/E5/G5

Microsoft Priva uses RBAC permissions model. Users must be assigned an appropriate role to be able to access and administer Priva. The Global Administrator must assign these roles.

The following table summarizes the roles available to administer and use Privacy Risk Management:

Role	Description
Privacy Management	This role has all permissions for the Priva solutions. It is recommended to have at least one person in this role.
Privacy Management Administrators	This role has broad access to Priva solutions including permissions and settings and creating, modifying and deleting policies.
Privacy Management Analysts	Members can investigate policy matches, view file metadata and take remediation action but cannot view the content of the files.
Privacy Management Investigators	Members can investigate policy matches, view associated file content and take remediation actions. They can also view the content of the files.
Privacy Management Viewers	Members can view reports, insights and policy trends.

Table 16.1: Privacy Risk Management roles

Privacy Risk Management is available on the Microsoft Priva portal at **https://purview. microsoft.com/priva**. Click on the **Privacy Risk Management** tile to go to the **Overview** page as shown in *Figure 16.1*. Note that it shows the top SITs and the top locations with sensitivity labels detected.

Privacy Risk Management

Stay on track with data privacy requirements and protect against risks. Learn more about Privacy Risk Management

Looking for the classic compliance portal?
You're currently on the new Priva portal. Before the classic Microsoft Purview compliance portal retires, you can always switch back. Learn more

Setup tasks

1. Register and scan multicloud data sources
   Bring in data from platforms like Azure and AWS so we can start detecting sensitive data
   Highly recommended   30 minutes

2. Learn more about the new Microsoft Priva
   Familiarize yourself with default privacy features to detect privacy risks.
   Optional   2 minutes

Recommendations   View all recommendations →

Connect sources

Register and scan multicloud data sources

Bring in data from platforms like Azure and AWS so we can start detecting sensitive data

Reports   View all reports →

Instances of sensitive info types
Top sensitive info types across data sources

Legal   160
India Permanent Account Number (PAN)   160
Credit Card Number   155
Singapore phone number   120
Tax return form keywords   80

■ Microsoft 365

Top locations with sensitivity labels

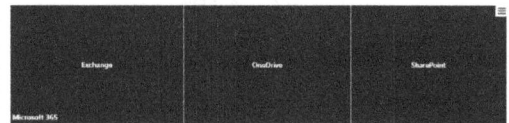

Exchange   OneDrive   SharePoint

Microsoft 365

Explore more sensitivity labels

Explore Reports

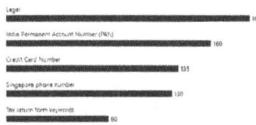

Figure 16.1: Privacy Risk Management dashboard

Click on **Explore Reports** to get more insights. This page contains a range of reports about the personal data found in the organization's data landscape including Microsoft 365, Microsoft Azure and AWS.

Some of the key insights shown are as follows:

- **Items with most personal data**: This lists content that has large amount of personal data and presents a higher risk of exposure. You might want to ensure that they are covered by a privacy risk management policy. It shows the number of unique personal data types and content owners detected.

- **Active alerts**: This card shows the active alerts generated by privacy risk management policies.

- **Privacy regulations**: This card shows insights from Microsoft Purview Compliance Manager. Improvement actions that require configuration in Microsoft Priva are listed here. This enables organizations to understand how they can improve their compliance posture by taking certain actions in Priva. The **Privacy score** indicates your rate of progress in strengthening your privacy posture. Refer to *Figure 16.2*:

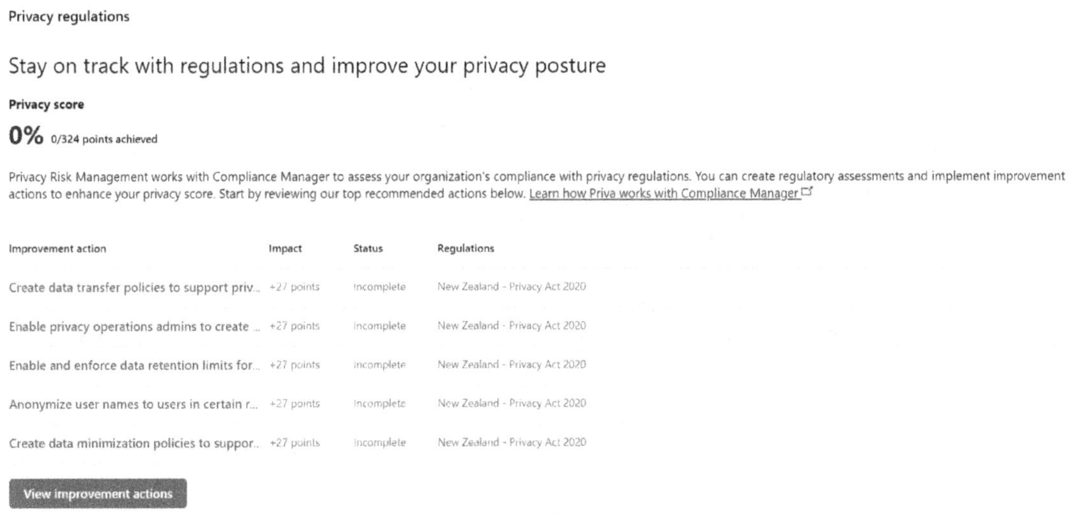

Privacy regulations

Stay on track with regulations and improve your privacy posture

Privacy score

0% 0/324 points achieved

Privacy Risk Management works with Compliance Manager to assess your organization's compliance with privacy regulations. You can create regulatory assessments and implement improvement actions to enhance your privacy score. Start by reviewing our top recommended actions below. Learn how Priva works with Compliance Manager ◻

Improvement action	Impact	Status	Regulations
Create data transfer policies to support priv...	+27 points	Incomplete	New Zealand – Privacy Act 2020
Enable privacy operations admins to create ...	+27 points	Incomplete	New Zealand – Privacy Act 2020
Enable and enforce data retention limits for...	+27 points	Incomplete	New Zealand – Privacy Act 2020
Anonymize user names to users in certain r...	+27 points	Incomplete	New Zealand – Privacy Act 2020
Create data minimization policies to suppor...	+27 points	Incomplete	New Zealand – Privacy Act 2020

View improvement actions

Figure 16.2: Privacy score

- **Personal data types by region**: For multi-geo M365 environments, this tile shows personal data types found in the content by region in a map format.

- **Personal data found in the organization**: This card shows how much personal data matching the policy settings has been found over time and in which data location.

- **Overexposed personal data**: This card shows personal data that has been overshared either within the organization or externally.

- **Data transfers detected**: This card shows personal data that has been transferred outside your organization or between departments or between regions in case of multi-geo M365 organizations. This is based on policy settings.

- **Unused personal data**: This card shows data in your Microsoft 365 environment that has not been accessed or modified in a configured time frame.

- **Top five sensitivity labels**: This shows the top five sensitivity labels in use in the organization.

- **Top five sensitive information types**: This card shows the top five SITs that occur most frequently in your data landscape.

- **Top locations with sensitivity labels**: This card shows the locations like SharePoint Online or OneDrive where the most sensitivity labels are applied.

Creating and managing policies

Microsoft Priva offers in-built policy templates that organizations can use to build their own policies. These templates address the risk scenarios that are important to most organizations. Following policy templates are available:

- **Data overexposure policy**: Data overexposure policy can help detect situations where items containing personal information are too widely shared. It detects scenarios like an internal SharePoint site containing payroll information that has been shared with everyone in the organization or a file containing sensitive customer information has been shared from a OneDrive account using an anonymous link. Data overexposure policies can detect and alert you about data overexposure, enabling you to take action to protect this data.

  Using this policy, you can detect overexposed data in SharePoint sites, OneDrive accounts, Azure Storage, Azure SQL and Amazon S3. To detect overexposed data in non-Microsoft 365 data sources, these data sources must be set up in the **Microsoft Purview Data Map**.

Note: Explaining Microsoft Purview Data Map is beyond the scope of this book. Refer to Microsoft online documentation for details: https://learn.microsoft.com/en-us/purview/purview-portal#get-started-with-data-governance-solutions.

  This policy detects data in Microsoft 365 locations with any of the following access levels:

  o **Public**: Anyone with a link has access.

  o **External**: Specific people outside the organization have access.

  o **Internal**: All users in the organization have access.

- **Data transfer policy**: Transferring data involves risk, especially when it is transferred outside the organization or sent between certain departments or across regions. It can detect scenarios like personal data related to **European Union (EU)** citizens transferred outside the EU borders or sensitive customer data shared from the marketing department to an external vendor. Using this policy, you can detect data transfers in Exchange email, OneDrive accounts, Teams chat and channel messages and SharePoint sites.

  Data transfers in the following scenarios can be detected:

  o **Transfers outside of your organization**: Detects when personal data is transferred to external users using email, files shared from OneDrive or SharePoint or in Microsoft Teams.

  o **Transfers across country boundaries or regions**: In multi-geo M365 scenarios this policy detects when data is transferred from one country to another. You will need to select the sender and recipient countries.

- o **Transfers between users**: Detects when data is transferred between employees with certain attributes like department, job titles etc. For example, personal data transferred from an employee in the Marketing department to an employee in the Sales department.

- o **Transfer between Microsoft 365 groups**: Detects data transferred from one Microsoft 365 group to another.

- o **Transfer between SharePoint sites**: Detects when personal data is copied or moved from one SharePoint site to another. You will have to specify the sender and recipient sites.

When the data transfer policy detects a match, you can choose to give users policy tips in Microsoft Teams about responsible use of personal data.

- **Data minimization policy**: Most people do not delete data, thus accumulating large amount of data. This data can contain personal data of employees or customers that is no longer required or has already served it business purpose. This type of data should be safely disposed of to limit privacy risks. Data minimization policies help detect unused data in Exchange email, OneDrive accounts, Teams chat and channel messages and SharePoint sites. You can choose the number of days from the last modification date for the data to be considered stale. The available options are 120, 90, 60 and 30 days.

These policy templates can be accessed in the Priva portal by clicking on **Policies** under the **Privacy Risk Management** tile. You can choose to create a policy using one of the templates or create a custom policy from scratch. If you choose a policy template some settings like data sources, data to monitor, users in scope and outcome are pre-defined for you. You can edit this as per your organization's requirements.

Following steps describe how you can create a policy from scratch:

1. Login to **https://purview.microsoft.com/priva** and click on the **Privacy Risk Management** tile.

2. In the left pane, click on **Policies**. This page will show you the default policies available. To create a new policy, click on **Create a policy**.

3. In the fly out pane, click on **Create** under **Custom** to create a policy from scratch.

4. Select the policy template and give your policy a name and description and click on **Next**. Refer to *Figure 16.3*:

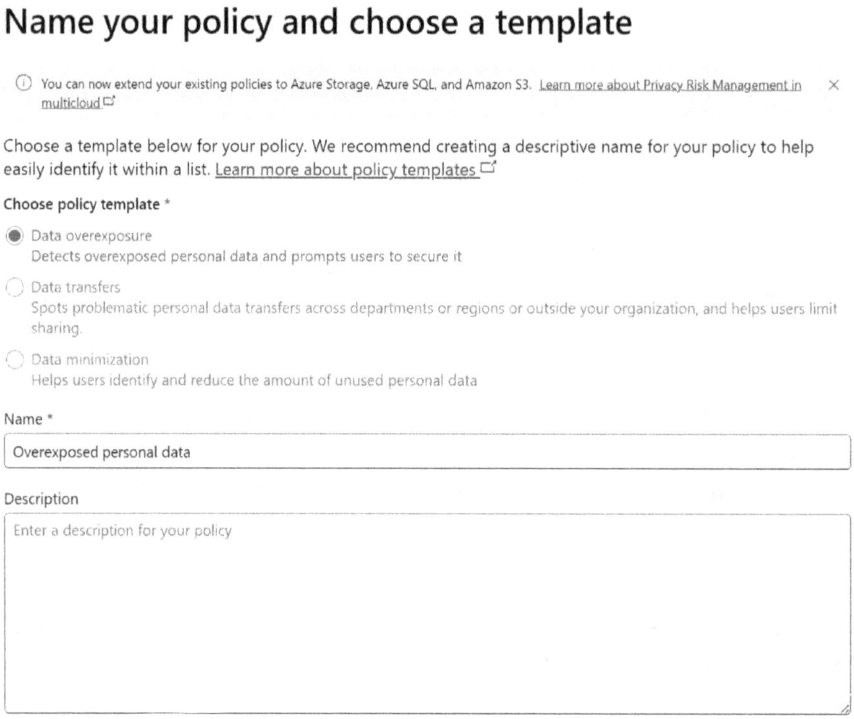

Name your policy and choose a template

ⓘ You can now extend your existing policies to Azure Storage, Azure SQL, and Amazon S3. <u>Learn more about Privacy Risk Management in multicloud</u> ⊏   ✕

Choose a template below for your policy. We recommend creating a descriptive name for your policy to help easily identify it within a list. <u>Learn more about policy templates</u> ⊏

Choose policy template *

⦿ Data overexposure
  Detects overexposed personal data and prompts users to secure it

◯ Data transfers
  Spots problematic personal data transfers across departments or regions or outside your organization, and helps users limit sharing.

◯ Data minimization
  Helps users identify and reduce the amount of unused personal data

Name *

Overexposed personal data

Description

Enter a description for your policy

Figure 16.3: Policy name and description

5. On the next page, select the data sources where you want this policy to apply and click **Next**.

6. On the data to monitor page, select the type of data this policy should monitor. The following options are available:

   a. **Classification groups**: These are a group of SITs that belong to a specific regulation. For example, there is a classification group for Australia Privacy Act that includes SITs like Australia driver's license number, Australia passport numbers, medical terms and conditions and Australian names and physical addresses.

   b. **Sensitive information types or trainable classifiers**: You can choose to define your own set of SITs and trainable classifiers if your requirements do not match any of the available classification groups.

Figure 16.4 shows the policy detecting content that contains full names and Australia bank account number or full names and Australia driving license numbers. Note that you can use groups to make complex policy conditions to detect the exact content you want. Make the appropriate selections and click **Next**.

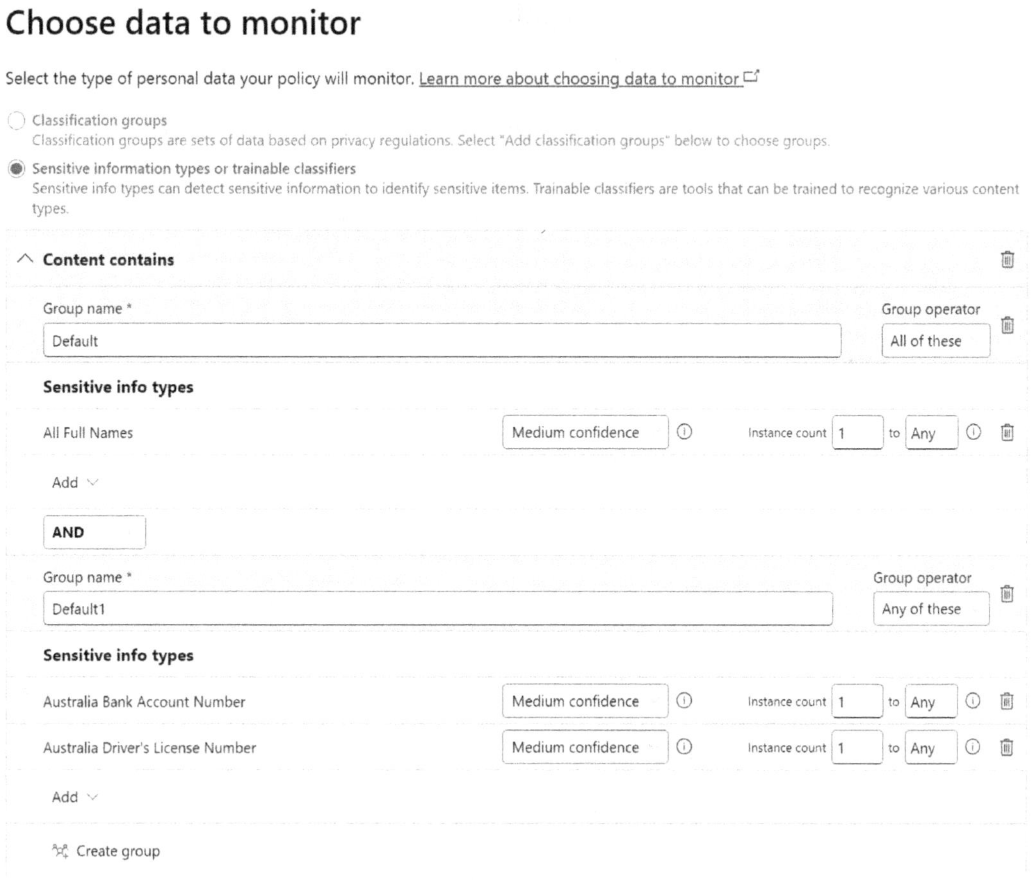

Choose data to monitor

Select the type of personal data your policy will monitor. Learn more about choosing data to monitor ⊑⁷

○ Classification groups
Classification groups are sets of data based on privacy regulations. Select "Add classification groups" below to choose groups.

◉ Sensitive information types or trainable classifiers
Sensitive info types can detect sensitive information to identify sensitive items. Trainable classifiers are tools that can be trained to recognize various content types.

∧ **Content contains**			🗑

Group name *		Group operator	🗑
Default		All of these	

Sensitive info types

All Full Names	Medium confidence ⓘ	Instance count 1 to Any ⓘ 🗑

Add ∨

AND

Group name *		Group operator	🗑
Default1		Any of these	

Sensitive info types

Australia Bank Account Number	Medium confidence ⓘ	Instance count 1 to Any ⓘ 🗑
Australia Driver's License Number	Medium confidence ⓘ	Instance count 1 to Any ⓘ 🗑

Add ∨

⚙ Create group

Figure 16.4: Content to monitor

7. On the next page, you can choose to apply this policy to all users or groups in the organization or select specific users or groups. Make the appropriate selections and click **Next**.

8. On the **Conditions** page, select the conditions as per the policy template selected in *Figure 16.3* and click **Next**.

9. On the next page, you choose what happens when a policy match occurs. You can choose to send an email notification to the users prompting them to take corrective action. This email can be sent daily, weekly or monthly. You must also include a link to privacy training. Once done, click **Next**. Refer to *Figure 16.5*:

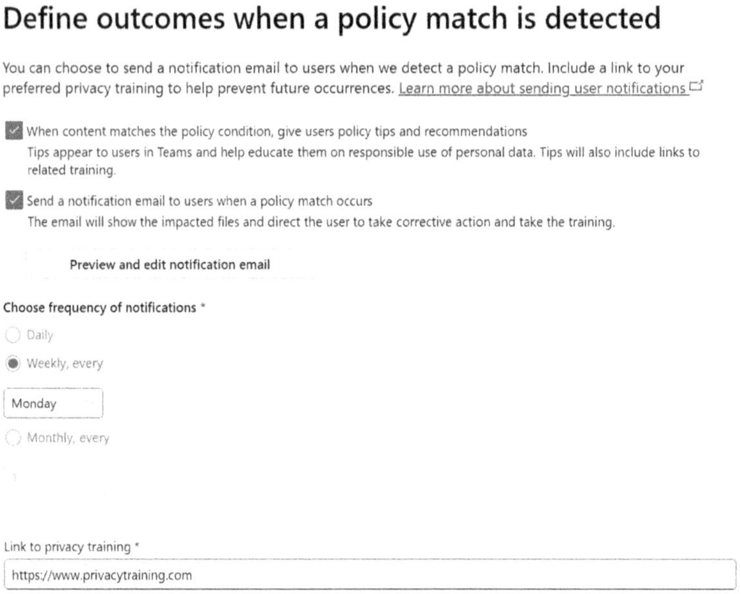

Define outcomes when a policy match is detected

You can choose to send a notification email to users when we detect a policy match. Include a link to your preferred privacy training to help prevent future occurrences. <u>Learn more about sending user notifications</u> ⊏⁺

☑ When content matches the policy condition, give users policy tips and recommendations
Tips appear to users in Teams and help educate them on responsible use of personal data. Tips will also include links to related training.

☑ Send a notification email to users when a policy match occurs
The email will show the impacted files and direct the user to take corrective action and take the training.

Preview and edit notification email

Choose frequency of notifications *

◯ Daily

◉ Weekly, every

Monday

◯ Monthly, every

Link to privacy training *

https://www.privacytraining.com

Figure 16.5: Define outcomes

10. Next, you can choose to generate alerts when a policy match occurs. Alerts can be generated each time a policy is matched, or they can be aggregated to reduce the number of alerts. You can also choose the severity of these alerts as shown in *Figure 16.6*. Make the appropriate selections and click **Next**.

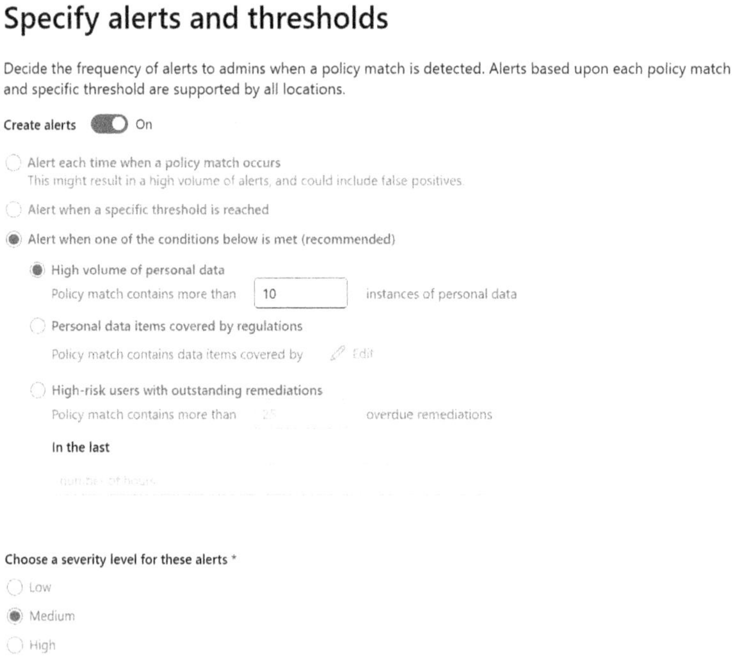

Specify alerts and thresholds

Decide the frequency of alerts to admins when a policy match is detected. Alerts based upon each policy match and specific threshold are supported by all locations.

Create alerts ⬤ On

◯ Alert each time when a policy match occurs
This might result in a high volume of alerts, and could include false positives.

◯ Alert when a specific threshold is reached

◉ Alert when one of the conditions below is met (recommended)

◉ High volume of personal data
Policy match contains more than [10] instances of personal data

◯ Personal data items covered by regulations
Policy match contains data items covered by ✐ Edit

◯ High-risk users with outstanding remediations
Policy match contains more than overdue remediations

In the last

Choose a severity level for these alerts *

◯ Low

◉ Medium

◯ High

Figure 16.6: Generate alerts

11. Lastly, you can choose to turn the policy on right away or test it out before turning it on. It is recommended to first test the policy as in test mode, you will be able to see the impact of the policy by reviewing alerts, but any restrictions configured will not be enforced and users will not receive notification emails.

12. On the last page, review your settings and click **Submit**.

Once a policy is created, it is available on the **Policies** page. Clicking on the policy will open the policy **Overview** that will show if the policy is **On** or in **Testing** mode.

If the policy is in testing mode, the number of days it has been in testing is displayed. It is looking for matches based on the conditions set. A recommendation is provided when it is a good time to turn the policy on. You can turn it on by clicking on **Turn on policy** on the top right. There are also options to edit or delete the policy.

When the policy is on metrics like the number and percentage of remediation actions taken by users and admins in displayed.

Further insights like matches by location, user and data type and the number of user notifications generated are also displayed.

The **Matched items** tab displays all the content that matched the conditions defined in the policy. You can select any item to view its preview.

Investigating and remediating alerts

Once the policies have been created and turned on, they start monitoring activity and when an activity matches the conditions in the policy, alerts are generated based on the settings defined in the policy. Admins can review alerts and identify cases that need attention. This is done by creating Issues, which provide a structured way to review content, assign severity and work collaboratively towards remediation. If the policies have been set to send email notification to content owners, then they can also help with remediating issues.

To view the alerts, the following are the steps:

1. Login to **https://purview.microsoft.com/priva** and click on **Privacy Risk Management**.

2. In the left-pane, click on **Alerts**.

3. The right-pane will show the alerts generated in the last one month.

4. Select an alert to view the details like the number of matching items and alert severity.

5. Click on the **Content** tab to view the files involved in this. This tab contains additional metadata about the files like their location and type of personal data in the file.

6. If the alert needs further investigation click on **Create issue**. You will be asked to give the issue a name and add any comments for context. If the alert does not require further investigation click on **Dismiss**.

Issues are created by admins for the alerts that require further investigation.

The following are the steps to work with issues:

1. Login to **https://purview.microsoft.com/priva** and click on **Privacy Risk Management**.
2. In the left pane, click on **Alerts**.
3. If any issues have been created, they will show up in a title on this page. Click on the tile to go to the **Issues** page.
4. Click on an issue to view details. The following details are available:
   - **Overview**: Essential information about the issue including status, severity and recommended actions. You can also view the associated policy.
   - **Alerts**: A list of alerts related to the issue.
   - **Content**: A list of all files associated with the issue. You can view the details about the file by selecting each file. This includes any remediation action taken. You can also take remediation action such as notifying owner, deleting the file, applying a sensitivity or retention label, revoking user access or marking as not a match.

> **Note: Here you can view any notes that have been added by other investigators. You can also add your own notes.**

   - **Collaborators**: Here you can view the users who are collaborating on this issue. You can also add more collaborators. Adding collaborators allows sharing the issue with additional people via a secure Teams channel, email or a link to the issue page in Priva. Click on the **Share** button to view these options.
5. Once all actions have been taken, you can close the issue by clicking on **Resolve**.

Subject Rights Requests

Subject Rights Requests (SRRs) are a critical aspect of modern privacy management that deals with granting individuals, also called **data subjects,** more control over their personal data held by organizations. These requests allow individuals to exercise their rights under various data protection regulations, such as the GDPR in the EU or the **California Consumer Privacy Act** (**CCPA**) in the United States.

The significance of SRRs lies in their ability to empower individuals to manage their personal information. Through SRRs, individuals can request access to their data, seek rectification of inaccuracies, request deletion of their data, and even restrict or object to the processing of their data. This level of control is essential for maintaining trust between individuals and organizations, as it demonstrates a commitment to transparency and respect for privacy.

From a regulatory perspective, the handling of SRRs is not just a best practice but a legal requirement. Organizations are required to respond to these requests within a specific timeframe. Failure to comply with these requirements can result in significant fines and penalties, highlighting the importance of having robust processes in place for managing SRRs. Companies usually store a large amount of data and finding the relevant information in a timely fashion is critical to meeting these timelines and avoiding fines.

Microsoft Priva Subject Rights Requests is designed to help organizations navigate the complexity and time involved in responding to these requests. It provides automation, insights and in-built workflows to help organizations respond to these requests confidently and efficiently.

Microsoft Priva Subject Rights Requests is a per request subscription and is available as an add-on to any of the following subscriptions:

- Office 365 A1/E1/G1/E3/A5/E5
- Microsoft 365 A3/E3/A5/E5/G5

The following table lists the roles required to use Subject Rights Requests in Microsoft Priva:

Role	Description
Subject Rights Request Administrators	This role has full rights to create and manage SRRs.
Subject Rights Requests Approvers	Members can approve SRRs where they are added as approvers.
Privacy Management Contributors	This role is automatically assigned when a user is added as a collaborator on a SRR case.

Table 16.2: Subject Rights Requests roles

To access SRRs login to **https://purivew.microsoft.com/priva** and click on the **Subject Rights Requests** tile. This opens the **Overview** page as shown in the following figure:

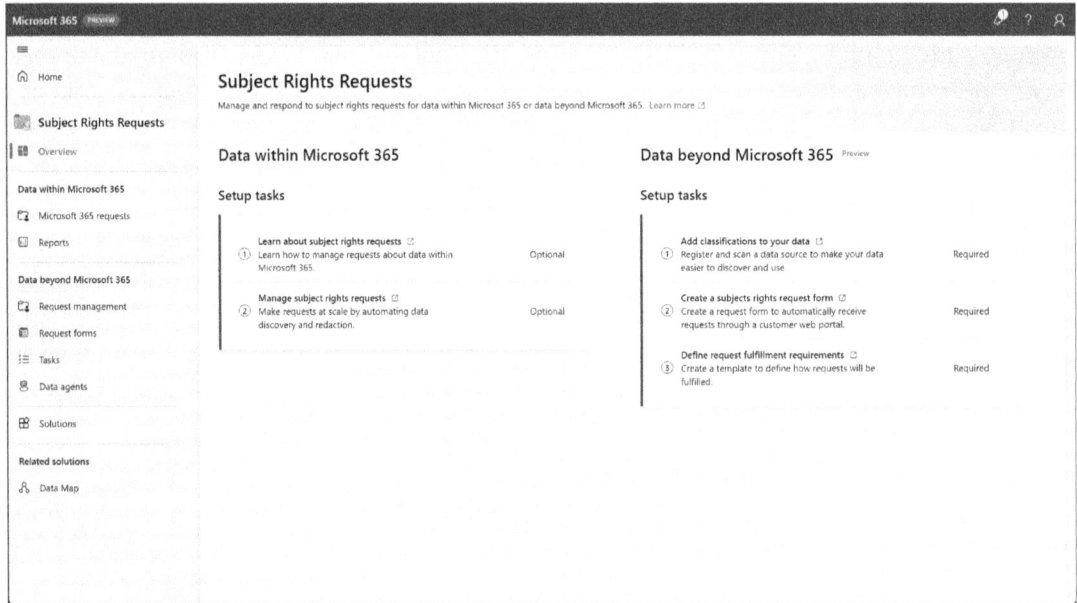

Figure 16.7: *SRR overview*

Using Priva, you can fulfil SRRs for both data in Microsoft 365 and data in non-Microsoft 365 locations. Let us explore each of these.

SRR for data in M365

Using this option, you can search for all data related to a data subject in Microsoft 365 locations like Exchange Online, SharePoint Online, OneDrive for Business and Teams.

Following are some of the key capabilities of SRR:

- **Prioritizing content to review**: SRR might result in large volumes of data collected for the data subject. To help the reviewer in prioritizing the content insights like files marked with sensitivity or retention labels or files containing information about multiple individuals are provided.

- **Teams' collaboration**: Once SRR is created, a dedicated Teams channel is created for this request. This helps with better collaboration between the stakeholders managing the request.

- **In-built tools**: Priva has built-in redaction tools which enable reviewers to redact sensitive information from the files before they are sent to the data subject. Tags can be defined and attached to files, if they require further investigation or review.

- **Reports**: Once you are done, reviewing the items reports like audit logs, the summary of tagged files is automatically generated.

- **Integration with Power Automate**: SRR integrates with Power Automate using which you can automate common tasks like creating calendar reminders or creating records in ServiceNow.

Each SRR goes through multiple stages. *Figure 16.8* shows different stages. Some stages progress automatically, while others must be advanced manually after completion of certain activities like reviewing files.

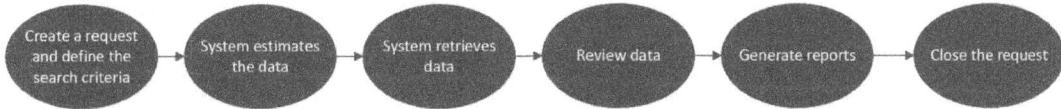

Figure 16.8: SRR workflow

Now, let us learn how to create and manage an SRR. Following are the steps:

1. Login to **https://purview.microsoft.com/priva** and click on **Subject Rights Requests** tile.

2. In the left pane, click on **Microsoft 365 requests**. The right pane shows the existing requests and their status as shown in the following figure:

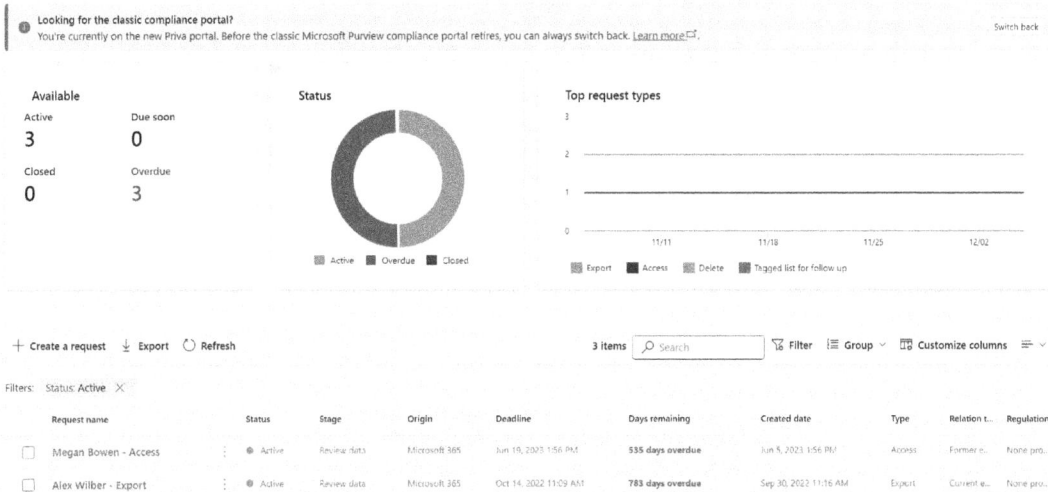

Figure 16.9: SRR overview

3. Click on **Create a request** to get started. Choose the type of request you would like to create and click on **Get started**. Following request types are available:

- **Data access**: This type of request provides a summary of the data subject's personal information held in your organization's M365 environment.

- **Data export**: Using this type of request you can export files containing the data subject's personal information.

- **Data tagged for further action**: This type of request generates a summary of files that were tagged during a data review of another request.

- **Data deletion**: This type of request enables you to delete all files containing the data subject's personal information. These requests are required by certain regulations that give data subjects the right to be forgotten. Creating and managing a delete request involves unique steps. They are described in the next section, *Creating and managing deleted request*.

4. You will be asked to choose the relationship of the data subject to the organization. The available options are **Current employee**, **Customer**, **Former employee**, **Prospective employee** or **Other**. Type a name of the data subject. You can specify their country of residence, the regulations under which this search is being conducted and the time frame as shown in the following figure:

Data export

template ⌕

How is this person related to your organization?

Relationship to organization

Current employee

What happens when you create this request

We'll run a default search for items in your organization's environment that avoid content created by this data subject, since current employees can usually access their emails and docs.

We've tailored locations and conditions to match the search criteria. Select **View settings** to see all configurations for this search. You can edit settings now or create your request with these defaults. Once you create this request, the data retrieval process will start automatically and your request will show up on the subject rights requests page.

View settings

Enter employee details

Search for a data subject *

AW Alex Wilber ✕

Can't find data subject? Enter their details manually.

Residency

Other / Not specified

Regulations

General Data Protection Regulation (GDPR)

Timeframe

Last 12 months

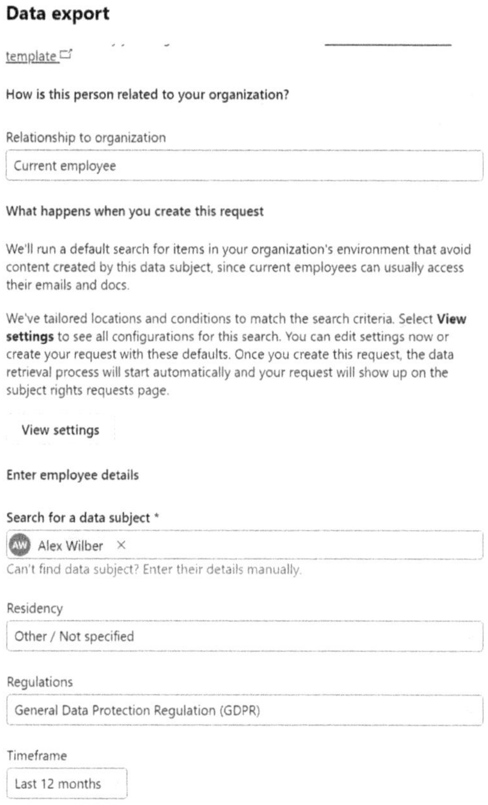

Figure 16.10: Create SRR

5. Based on the information provided, the system automatically runs a default search. You can view the details by clicking on **View settings**. You can either choose to continue with the default or click on **Edit settings** to edit the search criteria as shown in the following figure:

Data export

View settings

Here are the settings we've configured for you. Click **Edit settings** below to change them.

Edit settings

Residency
Other / Not specified

Locations

Exchange   None

SharePoint   SHAREPOINT_ALL

Conditions
(c:c)(date>=2023-12-05)

Request type
Export

Regulations
None

Deadline
Dec 19, 2024 3:52 PM

Search settings
Include authored content? No
Include all versions of items? No
Provide data estimate first? No

Figure 16.11: Edit search criteria

6. This will take you through a wizard where you can enter data subject identifiers like name, nickname, email addresses, physical addresses, phone number, date of birth and so on. You can also specify the locations to search in, like specific Exchange mailboxes and SharePoint sites. Once done, click on **Create**.

   Once the SRR is created, it appears on the SRR overview page. The **Stage** column displays **Data estimate**. Click on the request to view details.

   Refer to the following figure:

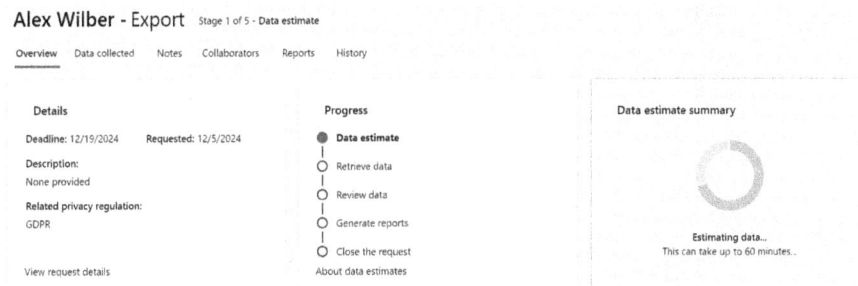

Figure 16.12: SRR data estimate stage

7. Once the data estimate is complete, the request automatically moves to the **Retrieve data** stage. This can take some time depending on the amount of data to be retrieved. Refer to *Figure 16.13* You can click on **View search query details** to view the search query and preview the results.

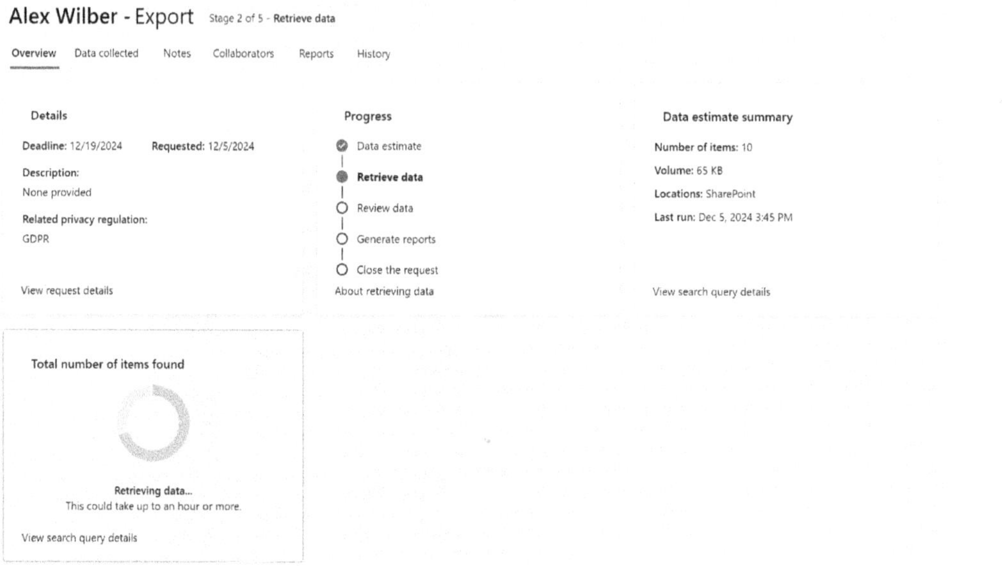

Figure 16.13: SRR retrieve data stage

8. Once the system has finished retrieving the data, you will see a summary on the **Overview** tab as shown in *Figure 16.14*:

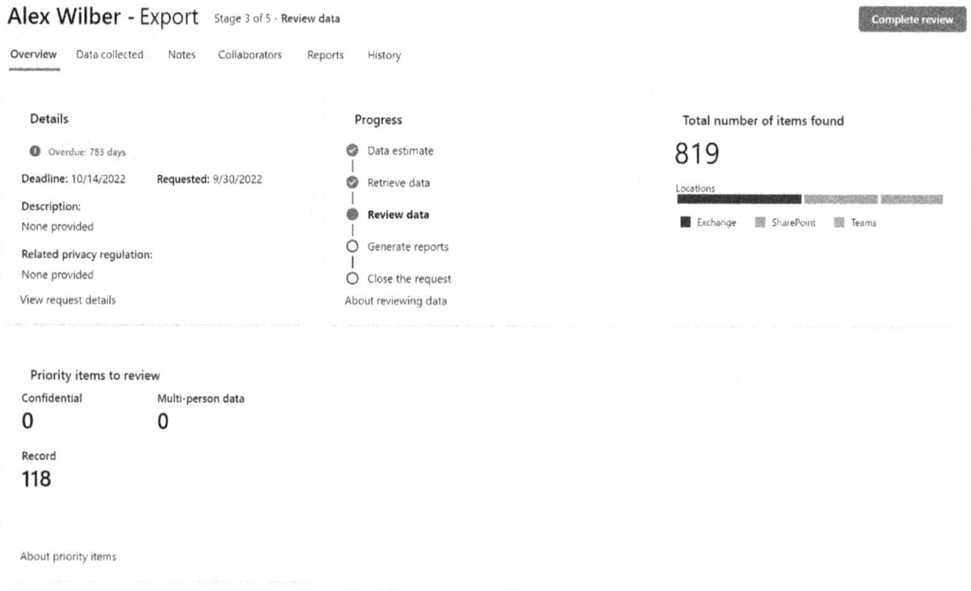

Figure 16.14: SRR review data stage

9. Click on the **Data collected** tab to view the content collected by the query. Use the available filters to view the content most relevant to your search. Click on any item in the list to see the content and details about the file as shown in *Figure 16.15*. From this screen you can take the following actions:

- Read the content of the file in plain text.
- Redact any sensitive or irrelevant content by clicking on the **Redact** tab.
- Choose to include or exclude the file from the result set.
- Apply tags or mark the file as not matching the search criteria.
- Add additional people to work on the request by clicking on the **Collaborators** tab.

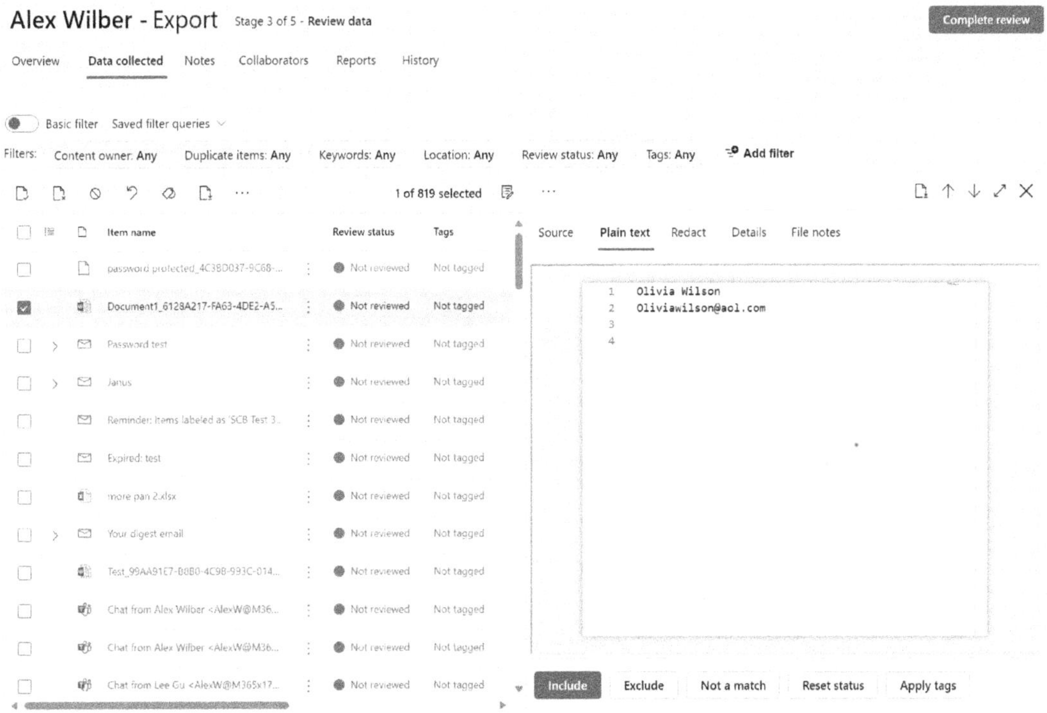

Figure 16.15: Review content

10. After you have finished reviewing the content you can click on **Complete review** to move to the next stage. When you complete the review, a final report is created and made available in the **Reports** tab for download. Reports are divided into the following sections:

- **Reports for the data subject**: These reports contain the files that were marked as **Included** during the data review stage.

- **Reports for internal use**: These reports are for internal use by your organization. They include an audit log and a list of files to which tags were applied.

Once the report status is **Ready to download**, you can select click on report and download it as shown in the following figure:

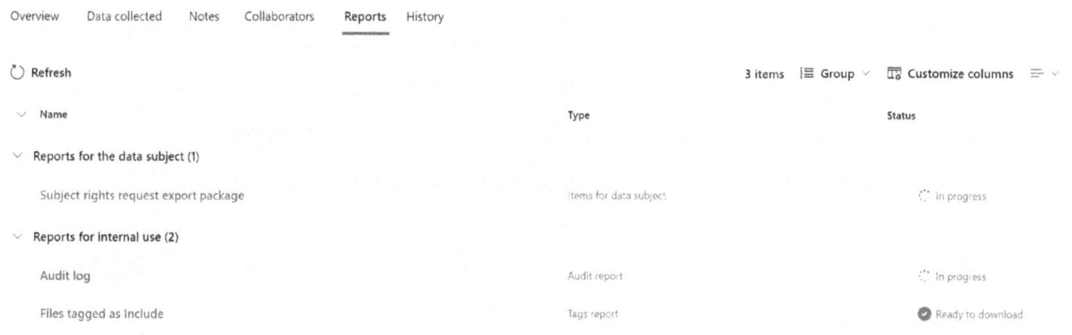

Name	Type	Status
⌄ Reports for the data subject (1)		
Subject rights request export package	Items for data subject	⟳ In progress
⌄ Reports for internal use (2)		
Audit log	Audit report	⟳ In progress
Files tagged as Include	Tags report	✓ Ready to download

Figure 16.16: Reports

11. When you have performed all the necessary actions related to the SRR you can close the request by clicking on **Close the request**. Closed requests cannot be reopened but you can view the details and notes.

Creating and managing delete request

A delete request allows you to mark items for deletion in your M365 environment. After items for deletion are identified, specified approve the request. All included items are then marked for deletion and are deleted within 30 days.

The following steps describe how delete requests are created and managed:

1. Login to **https://purview.microsoft.com/priva** and click on **Subject Rights Requests** tile.
2. In the left pane, click on **Microsoft 365 requests**.
3. In the right pane, click on **Create a request**.
4. In the fly out pane, click **Get started** under **Data deletion**.
5. In the fly out, enter the data subject name, select the relationship to the organization, residency, timeframe and regulations. Additionally, you must also specify one or more approvers. Once done click **Create**.
6. The request then follows the same steps of **Data estimate**, **Retrieve data** and **Review data**.
7. Collaborators review the data and mark the data to be deleted as **Include**. Once the review is complete, select **Complete review** and notify the approvers. The request status is now **Approval**. This is a substage of the **Review data** stage.

8. The approvers can find the data to be deleted on the **Data for approval** tab of the SRR. They review these items and click on **Complete approval**. In the fly out pane, the following options are available. Refer to *Figure 16.17*.

    - **Approve**: If the approvers are satisfied that all the data must be deleted, they can approve the request by selecting this option. If this option is selected, the **Data for approval** tab becomes read-only and no further changes can be made. The delete workflow begins automatically and the request moves to the **Generate reports** stage.

    - **Recommend changes**: If the approvers feel that the request cannot be approved as-is, they can recommend changes. They can use tags to mark the files for review and use the notes field to enter comments and recommendations. If this option is selected, the request remains in **Review data** stage and collaborators must review the data again and resend it for approval.

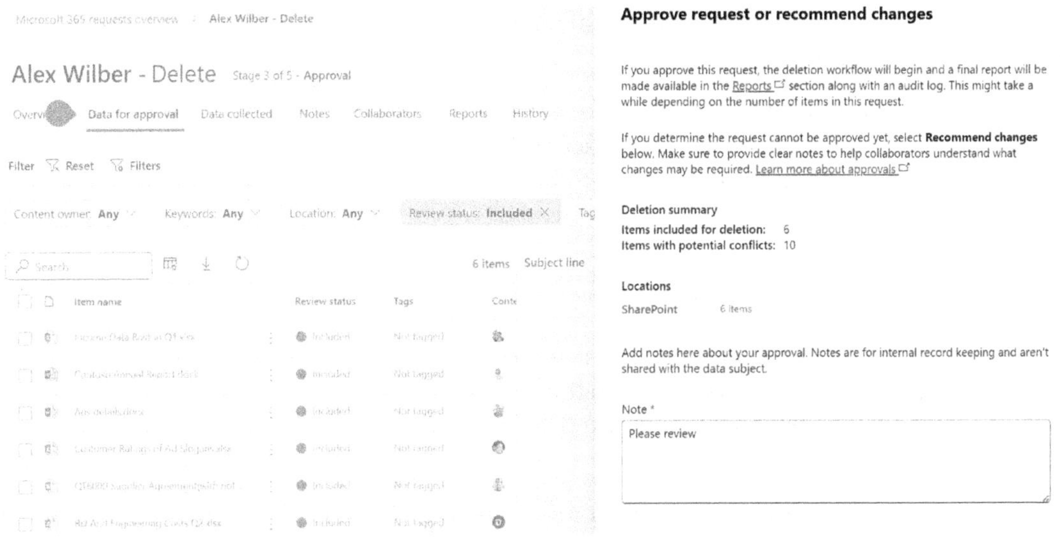

Figure 16.17: Approve delete requests

Delete workflow

When the first delete request is created, Priva creates a retention label called **PrivaDelete**, with an outcome of delete. Once the deletion request is approved, a workflow begins for each item to determine if there are any conflicts that can prevent the deletion of that item. If no conflict is found the **PrivaDelete** label is applied to that item.

This label might not be applied in the following scenarios:

- The items are in a location that is not supported by retention labels.
- The item is protected by a retention label. These items are highlighted for review in the **Priority items to review**.

Once the **PrivaDelete** label is applied to all items with no conflict and the reports are ready, the **Action summary** card shows the status as **Completed**. **Completed** does not mean that all items have been deleted. Deletion can take up to 30 days.

Priva and Microsoft Purview Data Lifecycle Management

If your organization uses Microsoft Purview Data Lifecycle Management capabilities such as retention labels to retain content for regulatory compliance purposes, the Priva delete workflow honors these labels. The **PrivaDelete** label will not apply to items that have a retention label applied.

When the **PrivaDelete** label is applied to an item, the system performs conflict resolution based on the principles of retention described in *Chapter 12, Protect and Govern Sensitive Data*. If a conflict is found the SRR admin has visibility of the conflict through the action execution log.

Action execution log

An action execution log is a report that is generated once the deleted request reaches the **Generate reports** stage. This is found on the **Reports** tab of the SRR. It can be downloaded as a CSV file. Each approved item marked as **Include** is represented as a row in the CSV file.

The following information is available for each item:

- **Approval UPN**: The user who approved the delete request.
- **Approval date**: The date of the deletion was approved.
- **Action**: Value is **ApplyRetetionLabel**.
- **Action status**: A value of **True** means that the **PrivaDelete** label was applied and a value of **False** means that it was not.
- **Action status details**: When the action status value is **False**, this column gives the reason the **PrivaDelete** label could not be applied.
- **Action date**: The date the action was applied.

The following figure shows a sample of the action execution log downloaded as a CSV file:

Id	Workload	Size	File class	File create	Immutable	Internet m	Path	Subject/Ti	Author/Se	Approval	Approval	Action	Action Status	Action Status Details	Action Date
0cc834adl	SharePoin	22458	Documen	8/6/2020	SharePoin		https://m:	Income D	debrab@r	admin@M	12/6/2024	ApplyRetentionLabel	True	None	12/6/2024 3:05:24 AM
10199bd9	SharePoin	21921	Documen	8/6/2020	SharePoin		https://m:	Contoso A	pattif@m:	admin@M	12/6/2024	ApplyRetentionLabel	True	None	12/6/2024 3:05:24 AM
16e0d4f28	SharePoin	19081	Documen	7/8/2022	SharePoin		https://m:	Aus detail	alexw@m:	admin@M	12/6/2024	ApplyRetentionLabel	False	LabelAlreadyExist	12/6/2024 3:05:24 AM
1a4c03abr	SharePoin	97856	Documen	8/6/2020	SharePoin		https://m:	Customer	christlec@	admin@M	12/6/2024	ApplyRetentionLabel	True	None	12/6/2024 3:05:24 AM
27e72341r	SharePoin	19443	Documen	8/6/2020	SharePoin		https://m:	QT6000 Si	irvins@m:	admin@M	12/6/2024	ApplyRetentionLabel	True	None	12/6/2024 3:05:24 AM
2812da4dr	SharePoin	18434	Documen	8/6/2020	SharePoin		https://m:	RD And En	diegos@n	admin@M	12/6/2024	ApplyRetentionLabel	True	None	12/6/2024 3:05:24 AM

Figure 16.18: Action execution log

SRR for data beyond M365

This capability enables admins to fulfil Subject Rights Requests for data that resides in non-Microsoft 365 data sources. It relies on **Microsoft Purview Data Map** and requires that data sources be registered in it.

The following steps describe the workflow:

1. Create a request intake form for people outside the organization to be able to submit a request. The form can be created in the Priva portal by going the **Subject Rights Requests** tile and selecting **Data beyond Microsoft 365** | **Request forms and templates**. This can be published on the web for a data subject to fill out.

2. Build a template that outlines the requirements for how to fulfil requests such as response deadline and associated intake forms. The template can be created in the Priva portal by going the **Subject Rights Requests** tile and selecting **Data beyond Microsoft 365** | **Request forms and templates**.

3. A request can be submitted either by a user internal to the organization or by a data subject using the request intake form. **Export** and **Delete** requests are supported.

4. A submitted request goes through the following stages.

   - **Not started**: All requests begin here.

   - **Identity validation**: The data subject's identity is validated.

   - **Analyzing data**: The system searches for the SITs selected in the request form within the assets in the Data Map. Once assets are identified tasks are created for data owners to review the access and find the data subject's personal information.

   - **Working on tasks**: Tasks assigned and are in progress.

   - **Approving tasks**: Tasks are complete and ready for approval.

   - **Ready to respond**: Tasks have been approved and ready to respond to the data subject.

5. Once the result of the request has been communicated to the data subject, the request can be closed.

To manage SRRs for data in non-Microsoft locations administrators require the following roles:

- **Data reader**: Required for accessing classification in the Data Map when creating new requests.
- **Privacy curator**: Create new requests and edit existing ones.
- **Privacy reader**: See details of existing requests.

Data agents

Data agents help automate exports and delete tasks. For non-Microsoft 365 data this is done through a Priva connector that integrates with Power Automate. For example, you can create a data agent to automate the creation of export packages or delete records.

The creation of a data agent follows the three basic steps, as follows:

1. Create a data agent and assign assets to it.
2. Create a Power Automate flow using the Priva Subject Rights Requests Power Automate connector.
3. Link the data agent to the Power Automate flow and publish the connector.

> **Note: At the time of this writing, SRR for data beyond M365 is in Public Preview.**

Tracker scanning

Tracker scanning is a vital tool for ensuring data privacy and regulatory compliance. By scanning and identifying trackers on websites and within applications, organizations can gain visibility into how user data is being collected and used. This process involves monitoring scripts and cookies that may be tracking user behavior, often without their explicit consent.

Effective tracker scanning helps organizations detect unauthorized data collection activities and take corrective actions to protect user privacy. It also ensures compliance with data protection regulations such as GDPR and CCPA, which mandate transparency and user consent for data collection.

Organizations can leverage **Microsoft Priva Tracker Scanning** to audit their digital properties regularly, ensuring that all tracking mechanisms are documented and aligned with user consent preferences. This not only helps in maintaining regulatory compliance but also builds user trust by demonstrating a commitment to safeguarding personal data. By integrating tracker scanning with broader data governance strategies, businesses can create a more secure and privacy-focused digital environment. Microsoft Priva Tracker Scanning enables organizations to automatically identify tracking technologies across multiple web categories, thereby driving efficient management of website privacy compliance.

Tracker scanning provides automatic scanning for trackers. Organizations can register web domains and set up scanning to identify tracking technologies on their websites. They can use scan configurations to identify missing compliance elements and streamline compliance reporting by scanning for areas of noncompliance and continuously monitoring compliance issues.

Tracker scanning also provides organizations with the following:

- A **common tracker database** where commonly used trackers are listed.
- A **tracker library** that can be curated for your organization's trackers. You can define which ones to use for new or updated websites.
- An advanced scanning capability to bypass authentication-based pages and website interactions for scenarios such as providing date of birth or some other interaction.
- An extension for Microsoft Edge.

Tracker scanning can identify the following types of tracker technologies:

- **Cookie**: Web cookies are small pieces of data stored on a user's device by a website to track and remember information about their visit and preferences.
- **Fingerprint**: Digital fingerprints use devices and browser data to uniquely identify devices.
- **Local storage object**: This is information stored on the user's device that is needed within the website, such as user preferences.
- **Web beacon**: A web beacon is a small, often invisible graphic image embedded in a web page or email that tracks user behavior and collects data on their interactions.

To be able to work with tracker scanning, users in the organizations require one of the following roles:

- **Data source administrator**: Can register a website and edit and update registered websites.
- **Privacy curator**: Can view and edit all privacy objects, create and categorize trackers, promote trackers and view associated tags.
- **Privacy reader**: Can review scan results, view the tracker library, view list of trackers identified by the scan. Cannot edit.

Microsoft Priva Tracker Scanning can be accessed from the Microsoft Priva portal by clicking on the **Tracker scanning** tile.

The following are the steps to set up and use tracker scanning:

1. Register websites
2. Create tracker categories
3. Run a scan
4. View scan results

Note: At the time of this writing this capability is in Public Preview.

Consent management

Consent management is a critical aspect of maintaining regulatory compliance in today's data-driven world. It ensures that organizations handle personal data transparently and with explicit permission from individuals, aligning with laws such as the GDPR and CCPA. Effective consent management involves obtaining, storing, and tracking user consents, allowing individuals to access, update, or withdraw their consent at any time. This not only safeguards user privacy but also builds trust and fosters customer confidence. Robust consent management practices mitigate the risk of legal penalties and reputational damage that can arise from non-compliance.

Microsoft Priva Consent Management is a solution for streamlining the management of consented personal data. It has customizable consent models and a centralized process for publishing them at scale to multiple regions. It ensures that the data collected is aligned to the right to use and used only according to the consent preferences.

Using Microsoft Priva Consent Management, you can create consent models that cater to the specific needs of your organization. Priva allows for the creation of detailed consent models that are adaptable to various regulatory requirements and business needs. The centralized management system ensures that these models can be easily deployed and maintained across different regions and jurisdictions, providing a seamless experience for both organizations and their customers.

One of the key features of Microsoft Priva Consent Management is its ability to store and track user consents comprehensively. This functionality not only facilitates compliance with regulations like GDPR and CCPA but also empowers individuals by allowing them to manage their consent preferences. Organizations can quickly respond to user requests to access, update, or withdraw consent, thereby enhancing transparency and trust.

Furthermore, Microsoft Priva Consent Management integrates with various data management systems, streamlining the process of ensuring that all data collected aligns with the given consents. This reduces the risk of non-compliance and helps maintain the integrity of personal data handling practices. By leveraging Priva, organizations can effectively mitigate legal risks and avoid potential reputational damage associated with data privacy violations.

There are two types of consent. Consent type controls what happens when someone visits the website, as follows:

- **Explicit**: Also referred to as opt-in consent, a visitor to the website must make an affirmative choice to accept trackers. Nonessential trackers are off by default unless the visitor gives consent.

- **Implicit**: Consent is implied through actions. Nonessential trackers are on by default. This type assumes that the visitor has given unless they say no. This is also called opt-out consent.

Following **consent models** are supported by Microsoft Priva Consent Management:

- **Tracker**: Used to turn cookies on and off.
- **Generic**: Type of consent not related to collecting cookie consent

To be able to work with consent management, users in the organizations require one of the following roles:

- **Privacy curator**: Can create consent models and layouts, generate packages, configure publishing profiles and read reports.
- **Privacy reader**: Can view consent models and layouts and read reports.

Microsoft Priva Consent Management can be accessed from the Microsoft Priva portal by clicking on the **Consent Management** tile.

Creating consent model

Consent models are created and managed on the **Models and layout** page. This page contains the following tabs:

- **Consent models' tab**: This tab contains cards representing each consent model and basic details like the type (tracker or generic), implicit or explicit, description and status (draft, in progress, complete, published).
- **Layouts tab**: This tab shows the default layouts available in consent management and any custom layouts created by your organization. A custom layout allows you to customize the look and feel of the consent experience that aligns with your website and brand.
- **Tracker categories tab**: This tab displays the tracker categories created by your organization.

The following are the basic steps to create a consent model:

1. **Create a custom layout (optional)**: This is not mandatory. Each consent model has out-of-box layouts that can be used. However, you can create customer layouts if you want to create unique experiences for your site visitors.
2. **Create a consent model**: Use the default or custom layout to create a consent model. This includes providing the consent model name, description, contact, consent type (implicit or explicit), target countries, default language and text.
3. **Add translations**: If you would like to make the consent available in multiple languages, you can add translations manually or import translations from a downloadable template. You can also choose to do auto translation which starts with a source language and allows you to multi-select other languages.

4. **Preview the consent model**: You can do a live preview to see how your model will look like once it is deployed on your website.

5. **Mark the consent model as complete**: Mark the consent model status as **Complete** so that it can be added to a consent model package and is available for deployment to a website.

Publishing consent model

A consent management package is used to generate the configuration file for consent models. This package is deployed on endpoints. Multiple consent models can be added to a package to enable group deployment.

Publishing a profile allows you to set up specific profiles for your websites. A profile can connect different websites that have multiple consent models so that multiple packages can be published to a group of websites at once.

The following types of profiles are supported:

*   **Content delivery network (CDN)/Storage**: The packages are published to a central location from where they can be connected to multiple websites.

*   **Offline**: This is for manual deployments. You can download the package and website configuration.

Both these options require some setup before a publishing profile can be created.

Refer to Microsoft online documentation for the detailed steps: **https://learn.microsoft. com/en-us/privacy/priva/consent-management-packages-profiles**

Use the **Packages and publishing** page in consent management to create consent model packages and manage publishing profiles. This page has the following tabs:

*   **Packages**: Lists of the consent packages including their status and number of consent models included in each package. Packages are based on consent model type and can only contain one type, either tracker or generic.

*   **Profiles**: Lists of the publishing profiles and the associated websites.

*   **Websites**: Lists of the websites registered in Tracker Scanning. You can also register more websites to be associated with profiles.

To publish the consent model, you will need to create a package and a publishing profile.

Note: At the time of this writing, this feature was in Public Preview.

Privacy assessments

Organizations must maintain documentation regarding the justified use of data across their data estates. The assessment of privacy data usage often involves manual processes that are time-consuming and cumbersome. Privacy impact assessments are usually performed retrospectively, and they fail to reflect the actual state of data usage.

Microsoft Priva Privacy Assessment seeks to automate the discovery, documentation and evaluation of personal data usage. It enables organizations to automate privacy assessments, monitor personal data use and evaluate privacy risks on a scale. It allows you to discover and automate instances of personal data usage to capture the type of data being used and the nature of usage.

Users need to be assigned proper permissions to be able to complete tasks in privacy assessments, as follows:

- **Data curator**: Can create a project in Data Catalog and curate relationships between the project and technical data assets.

- **Privacy curator**: Can review all registered projects, create and edit assessments, review and approve privacy assessment responses, export assessment responses and create privacy rules.

- **Privacy reader**: Can review projects and any associated assessments but is unable to create, edit or approve privacy objects.

Microsoft Priva Privacy Assessment is based on Microsoft Purview Data Map and you must ensure that your organization has access to it and that it has been set up for Privacy Management. This includes configuring a metamodel and registering an asset. Refer to the Microsoft online documentation for detailed guidance.

Microsoft Priva Privacy Assessments can be accessed from the Microsoft Priva portal by clicking on the **Privacy Assessments** tile. Once the relevant configurations have been completed in Data Map you can create privacy assessments.

Assessments are created and managed on the **Assessment management** page in privacy assessment. This page has the following tabs:

- **Assets**: This tab lists all the assets that were registered in the metamodel created in Data Map.

- **Assessments**: This tab lists all assessments with their status and versions.

- **Assessment responses**: Lists all responses to assessments including users who answered and the answer details.

Assessment workflow

To create a privacy assessment, you must first build a questionnaire that the respondents will answer. You can start with a template or a blank assessment. You can maintain and use multiple assessments for different use cases. A single assessment can be assigned to an unlimited number of projects or business assets.

The following is the basic workflow of a privacy assessment:

1. **Create the assessment**: It is created by using a template or start from scratch.

2. **Assign reviewers**: This is a list of users with the Privacy Curator role who can approve or reject an assessment that has been submitted for review.

3. **Build the questionnaire**: Add the required questions to the questionnaire. You can give respondents the ability to provide text answers or have multiple choice questions. A risk factor can be assigned to each question that specifies the level of risk revealed by the answer.

4. **Publish the assessment**: It is done to make it available to be assigned to a user.

5. **Assign assets**: The assets are assigned to the assessment; the asset owner gets an email to respond to the assessment. Once they complete the questionnaire the assessment is available for review.

6. **Approve or reject responses**: The designated approvers review the responses and either approve or decline the assessment. If the assessment is declined the project owner will be notified and they can resubmit the assessment with revised responses.

Privacy rules

Privacy rules can be created so that assessments are automatically assigned to assets when certain conditions are met. This can be based on SITs, data classifications or other metadata like attributes. The rule periodically scans the data map to determine if any assets satisfy the conditions of the rule. If conditions are satisfied the assessment is automatically assigned to the data asset.

Note: At the time of this writing Privacy Assessments is in Public Preview.

Conclusion

This chapter introduced you to Microsoft Priva and its various capabilities. You learnt how you can use Privacy Risk Management to detect and remediate privacy risks like overshared data, unused data and unauthorized data transfers. You also learnt how you can use Subject Rights Requests to respond to data subject's requests for information access, export and deletion timely and with confidence. Lastly, this chapter also introduced you to the preview capabilities of Tracker Scanning, Consent Management and Privacy

Assessments. You learnt how Microsoft Priva can be an end-to-end privacy management solution for your organization.

In the next chapter, you will learn some best practices for administering and managing Microsoft Entra, Microsoft Defender and Microsoft Purview solutions.

Multiple choice questions

1. **Microsoft Priva Privacy Risk Management serves the following use cases. Select all that apply.**

    a. Identify unused guest user accounts.

    b. Identify stale data in Microsoft 365 locations.

    c. Identify unauthorized data transfers.

    d. Block sending of sensitive content to external recipients.

2. **Which of the following is not a use cases for Microsoft Priva Subject Rights Requests?**

    a. Delete all data related to a data subject.

    b. Prevent access to external recipients to internal data.

    c. Export all data related to a data subject.

    d. Prevent departing employees from exfiltrating content.

3. **In a delete request, Subject Rights Request assigns the PrivaDelete retention label to files that can be deleted. In which scenario does the label not apply?**

    a. If the file is in a location that does not support retention labels.

    b. If there is no conflict found.

    c. If the file already has a retention label applied.

    d. The label always applies.

Answer key

1. b, c
2. a, c
3. a, c

Join our book's Discord space

Join the book's Discord Workspace for Latest updates, Offers, Tech happenings around the world, New Release and Sessions with the Authors:

https://discord.bpbonline.com

CHAPTER 17
Best Practices

Introduction

When it comes to implementing Microsoft security products, adhering to best practices is of utmost importance. These practices are designed to optimize security measures, making them more effective and efficient. Adhering to these standards ensures a structured environment where sensitive information is protected, operational efficiency is enhanced, and potential threats are mitigated. This disciplined approach not only secures the organization but also streamlines administrative processes, ensuring that the users are protected, and the organization adheres to regulatory requirements.

Structure

Following is the structure of the chapter:

- Identity best practices
- Security best practices
- Compliance best practices

Objectives

By the end of this chapter, readers will be provided with a comprehensive guide on the best practices for implementing Microsoft security products. It aims to enhance security measures, protect sensitive information, and improve operational efficiency within organizations. This chapter also strives to minimize potential threats by adhering to principles such as least privilege and JIT access, and to ensure compliance with regulatory requirements. Additionally, it offers structured guidelines on identity management, security, and compliance to help administrators secure their environment effectively.

Identity best practices

Following best practices while implementing Microsoft Entra is crucial to ensuring that security measures are both effective and efficient. By adhering to these guidelines, organizations can significantly reduce the risk of unauthorized access and potential data breaches. Best practices such as applying the principle of least privilege and using **Privileged Identity Management** (**PIM**) to grant JIT access help create a well-structured and secure environment. This not only protects sensitive information but also enhances operational efficiency by granting administrators the exact permissions they need, only when they need them, thus minimizing the attack surface and mitigating potential threats.

Microsoft Entra roles

As we have learnt Microsoft Entra follows RBAC, and roles are assigned to administrators to be able to perform their day-to-day tasks. This section discusses the guidelines that should be followed while assigning roles to keep your admins and environment safe from bad actors.

Apply the principle of least privilege

While planning an access control strategy, it is recommended to use the principle of least privilege. The principle of least privilege means that administrators are given exactly the permissions that are required to do their job. For example, if an administrator is only responsible for creating new user accounts in Microsoft Entra they can be applied the **User Administrator** role instead of a Global Administrator role.

Consider the following three aspects:

- The set of permissions required.
- The scope for which permissions are required.

- The duration for which permissions are required.

By limiting assigning broader permissions you limit the resources that are at risk if the admin account is compromised or if an admin goes rogue. Currently, Microsoft Entra supports over 65 built-in roles to choose from and custom roles can be created.

Use PIM to grant just-in-time access

Another aspect of the principle of the least privilege is granting access only when it is needed. Microsoft Entra PIM allows you to make admin users eligible for a role which they can activate when they need to perform a task that requires elevated permissions. For example, if an administrator's task is to create Conditional Access policies, they can be made eligible for the Conditional Access Administrator role. They can activate the role at the time that they need to create the policy. The role can be activated for a pre-defined duration. It can either be approved manually or be auto approved. The administrator can perform the task and when the duration expires their access is revoked.

Turn on MFA for all admin accounts

It is best practice to turn on multi-factor authentication for all administrative accounts. Studies show that an account is 99.9% less likely to be compromised if MFA is enabled.

Configure access reviews

Use Entitlement Management access reviews to periodically audit privileged role membership. This ensures that administrators' access is current and most suited for their job duties. This also prevents bad actors from compromising unused privileged accounts.

Limit the number of Global Administrators

Microsoft recommends that the number of administrators in the Global Administrator group should not exceed five. If you have more than five Global Administrators an alert card is displayed on the Microsoft Entra home page.

Microsoft also recommends that organizations should have two cloud-only emergency accounts that are permanently assigned to the Global Administrator role. These accounts are not assigned to individuals. These accounts are called **break glass** and are used in case of emergency when normal accounts are accidentally locked out.

Limit the number of privileged role assignments

Some roles include privileged permissions like the ability to reset passwords. Microsoft recommends that these roles should have less than ten members. If there are more than ten members in any of these privileged roles, a warning is displayed on the **Roles and administrators'** page.

Use groups for role assignments

Consider assigning roles to groups instead of individual users. Role-assignable groups can be managed using PIM to ensure that there are no standing members in these groups. Owners can be assigned who can then decide who is added or removed from the group. This way the owners become responsible for the role assignments.

Activate multiple roles as once

In many cases, a single user may be eligible to activate multiple privileged roles through PIM. They will need to activate each role individually leading to loss of productivity. You can use PIM for Groups in this case. A group can be given permanent access to all the resources that the user needs access to, and the user can become an eligible member of this group. Now when they need access to resources, they can just activate their group membership and gain access to all resources.

Use cloud-native accounts

Microsoft recommends using Microsoft Entra ID cloud-native accounts for privileged roles to avoid the complexity of syncing on-premises accounts to Microsoft Entra ID. Ensure that these accounts are protected by strong and non-phishable authentication methods like passkeys.

Risk policies

We have learnt that there are two kinds of risk policies in Microsoft Entra ID Conditional Access, that is, User risk policy and sign-in risk policy. These policies can be used to automate responses to risks by allowing users to self-remediate risks. Microsoft recommends the following best practices.

User risk policy

If user risk is detected as **High**, configure the policy to require a secure password change. A secure password change is the only way to self-remediate user risk.

Sign-in risk policy

When the sign-in risk is detected as **Medium** or **High**, configure the policy to require Microsoft Entra multifactor authentication. This is the only way to self-remediate the sign-in risk.

Conditional Access policies

Conditional Access policies are powerful tools that can be used to govern access to the organization's critical resources. It is recommended that the following accounts be excluded from the policies:

- **Emergency access or break-glass accounts**: There should be an emergency account, also called break-glass account, that can be used if all administrators are locked out of the tenant. This emergency administrative account should be able to log in to the tenant and take recovery steps.

- **Service account and service principles**: Service accounts are non-interactive accounts that do not belong to an individual. They are used by applications to access system resources. These accounts should be excluded from the Conditional Access policies so that they are not blocked while making calls to applications. You can use Conditional Access for workload identities to define policies for service principals.

Security best practices

When implementing Microsoft Defender and Sentinel, adhere to best practices to enhance your security posture. Ensure high-privileged users operate only from hardened computers and limit administrative permissions to essential users and resources. Regularly review and minimize unnecessary privileges. Utilize Microsoft Defender for Identity to monitor **lateral movement paths** (**LMPs**) and detect potential threats. In Microsoft Defender for Office 365, leverage default and standard preset security policies for comprehensive user protection. Exclude emergency and service accounts from Conditional Access policies to maintain access continuity. Following these guidelines helps prevent unauthorized access and mitigate risks effectively.

Microsoft Defender for Identity

Security insights help in predicting and preventing the next attack. Investigating LMPs offer insights into where the attacker gained privileges and the path they took to get into your network.

The following are some preventative best practices that prevent an attacker from elevating privileges:

- Make sure that the highly privileged users use their administrative credentials only on hardened computers.

- Ensure that users do not have unnecessary administrative permissions.

- Ensure that they have access only to necessary resources.

Microsoft Defender for Office 365

In *Chapter 9, Protecting M365 Apps,* we learnt how to use **Microsoft Defender for Office 365 (MDO)** to create protection policies to protect the users in your organization. It is imperative to decide how to use the EOP and MDO policies to ensure the best protection for your users.

Use the following guidelines to determine your protection strategy:

- Remember that default policies and built-in protection in Office 365 automatically protect all users in the organization. So even if you do nothing all users get the default protection.
- If you do not have a compelling business requirement, it is recommended to start with the standard preset security policy for all users.
- If you want to use the strict policy for some users and standard for other users, keep in mind the order of precedence.
- Use unambiguous groups in each preset security policy. For example, use different groups or lists of recipients for the standard and strict preset security policies.
- Configure exceptions at each level as required. For example, configure recipients who need custom policies as exceptions to the standard and strict preset security policies.
- Globally turn on **Safe Attachments** and **Safe Documents**. Any remaining recipients that aren't identified at the higher levels get the default policies or built-in protection in Defender for Office 365 (Safe Links and Safe Attachments).

Following protection features are unaffected by the preset security policies and can be used independently:

- Outbound spam policies (custom and default)
- The default connection filter policy (IP Allow List and IP Block List)

If you have the following business scenarios, you may decide to use custom policies instead of or in addition to the preset policies:

- Users require security settings that are different from the unmodifiable settings in the present policies.
- Users require settings that are not configured in preset policies.
- Users need a quarantine experience that is different from the unmodifiable setting in the preset policies.

If you choose to have multiple custom policies for a specific, keep the following guidelines in mind:

- Users in custom policies cannot be included in the Standard or Strict preset policies due to the order of precedence.

- Assign fewer users to higher priority policies and more to the lower priority policies.
- Configure higher priority policies to have stricter rules.

Responding to business email compromise

Business email compromise (**BEC**) is a type of cybercrime in which attackers gain access to a business email account and use it to deceive employees, customers, or partners into transferring funds or sensitive information to the attacker. Users might notice and report unusual activity in their mailboxes like missing email, receiving email without any corresponding email in Sent Items, suspicious Inbox rules or unusual profile changes and email signatures. You need to respond immediately to investigate these user reports.

The following tools are available for investigation:

- **Unified audit logs**: Filter and examine the audit logs using a date range that starts immediately before the reported suspicious activity till the present day.
- **Microsoft Entra sign-in logs**: Examine the Microsoft Entra sign-in logs and other risk reports for IP addresses, sign-in locations, sign-in times, sign-in success or failures.

To secure and restore the email function for a compromised Microsoft 365 mailbox the following steps are recommended:

1. Reset the user's password.
2. Block the user from signing-in till you feel it is safe to re-enable access.
3. Remove suspicious email forwarding addresses.
4. Disable suspicious Inbox rules.
5. Remove the account from administrative roles.

Microsoft Defender for Cloud Apps

As we have learnt, **Microsoft Defender for Cloud Apps** (**MDCA**) provides visibility and control over the applications and services used in your organization. It helps identify and mitigate risks by analyzing user behavior, detecting anomalies, and enforcing policies across cloud environments. To get the most value out of MDCA the following best practices are recommended:

- **Integrate MDE**: This gives you the ability to use cloud discovery beyond your corporate boundaries. With the combined user and device information you can identify risky users or devices for further investigation.
- **Enable Shadow IT Discovery using MDE**: MDCA utilizes the traffic logs collected by MDE to identify apps being used on the endpoints. It analyzes these apps against the cloud catalog and provides compliance and security information.

- **Configure App Discovery policies**: App Discovery policies make it easier to proactively identify risky, non-compliant and trending apps.

- **Manage OAuth apps**: Many users grant OAuth permissions to third-party apps without much thought. IT has no visibility to this making it difficult to assess security risk. MDCA makes it easy to monitor the app permissions the users have granted. You can use this information to investigate suspicious apps. You can also use OAuth app policies to notify you when an OAuth app meets a predefined threshold like an app with high permissions being accessed by many users.

- **Tag apps and export block scripts**: Once apps have been discovered, it is best practice to use the **Sanction** and **Unsanctioned** tag to allow or block the use of apps in your environment. You should also export a script to block unsanctioned apps on your on-premises security equipment.

- **Connect M365 and other apps**: Connect M365 and other non-Microsoft applications to MDCA to gain visibility into user activities like file sharing.

- **Remove sharing with personal accounts**: MDCA gives you the ability to create policies that block sharing sensitive connect with personal file sharing or email accounts.

- **Integrate with Microsoft Purview Information Protection**: Integration with Microsoft Purview Information Protection gives you the ability to automatically apply protection on sensitive files in non-Microsoft applications.

- **Create data exposure policies**: MDCA file policies help to detect information sharing and scan for confidential information in connected cloud apps.

  The following policies should be created to send alerts when data exposures are detected:

  o Files shared externally contain sensitive data.

  o Files shared externally and labeled as **Confidential**.

  o Files shared with unauthorized domains.

  o Protect sensitive files on SaaS apps.

- **Review reports on the Files page**: Once apps have been connected, MDCA scans files stored in these apps. Use the **Files** page to investigate files to ensure that the files are not at risk of exposure.

- **Integrated with Microsoft Purview Data Loss Prevention**: Use file policies to detect when users try to share sensitive files with someone external to the organization.

- **Block and protect data on unmanaged devices**: Session policies can be used to monitor high risk, low trust sessions. Using conditional access app control, you can create session policies that can block download of sensitive content on unmanaged devices. You can also apply sensitivity labels on files to download.

- **Monitor sessions with external users**: Use session policies to monitor sessions between internal and external users. This provides the ability to monitor the session and limit specific activities.

- **Tune anomaly detection policies**: Anomaly detection policies trigger alerts when there are unusual activities performed by users. These policies should be fine-tuned so that the settings fit your organization requirements.

- **Detect activity from unexpected locations**: Use activity policies to alert you when users sign-in from unexpected locations or countries. This alerts you if you have potentially compromised accounts in your environment.

- **Use audit trail for forensic investigation**: Alerts are triggered when users or admins do not comply with policies. Investigate these alerts to identify potential threats in your environment.

- **Connect cloud platforms**: Connect cloud platforms like Azure, AWS and GCP to improve your threat detection capabilities in multi-cloud environments.

- **Onboard custom apps**: Your line-of-business applications can be onboarded to MDCA to monitor usage.

Microsoft Sentinel

Microsoft recommends following the deployment guide for Microsoft Sentinel to get the best out of your Sentinel deployment. This section provides best practices for how to use Microsoft Sentinel features for incident management and response.

Refer to the following:

- **Incidents**: Incidents generated by Sentinel are displayed on the **Incidents** page on the Microsoft Defender page. On the incidents page, view the title, severity, related alerts and logs to triage the incident.

- **Investigation graph**: Investigation graph is an interactive tool using which you can deep dive into an alert to show the full scope of an attack. Use this to construct a timeline of events and estimate the extent of the threat chain. Entities like accounts, URLs, host names etc. help understand if the incident is a false positive or true positive. If the incident is a false positive it can be closed without further investigation. If it is a true positive, actions can be taken from the **Incidents** page to investigate logs, entities and the threat chain. Once the threat has been identified and a plan of action is created, use the other tools available in Microsoft Sentinel to investigate.

- **Information visualization**: Use the Microsoft Sentinel dashboard to get a sense of security posture.

- **Threat hunting**: The built-in threat hunting queries aid in investigating incidents and searching for root causes. Use **Livestream** to monitor in real time if there are any lingering malicious events.

- **Entity behavior**: Use **User Entity Behavior Analytics (UEBA)** to review actions and alerts for specific entities. This helps in understanding if an entity is performing actions that are not normal.

- **Watchlists**: Use a watchlist that combines data from internal and external sources. For example, you can create a watchlist for recently terminated employees. Use the watchlists in combination with playbooks to gather enrichment data like adding malicious IP addresses to watchlists and use them during threat hunting.

Roles and permissions recommendations

In *Chapter 11, Security Management Using Microsoft Sentinel,* we learnt the different roles available in Microsoft Sentinel. Let us look at some best practices in assigning these roles.

The following table explains the best role based on user profile:

User profile	Role	Resource group
Security analysts	Microsoft Sentinel Responder	Microsoft Sentinel's resource group.
	Microsoft Sentinel Playbook Operator	Microsoft Sentinel's resource group or the resource group with playbooks are stored.
Security engineers	Microsoft Sentinel Contributor	Microsoft Sentinel's resource group.
	Logic Apps Contributor	Microsoft Sentinel's resource group or the resource group with playbooks are stored.
Service principal	Microsoft Sentinel Contributor	Microsoft Sentinel's resource group.

Table 17.1: Microsoft Sentinel roles

Compliance best practices

The most common problem reported by SOC and IT teams is the number of alerts they must review after configuring policies. They either receive an overwhelming number of alerts or far too few alerts. Let us review some best practices to manage alert volumes in Insider Risk Management and Communication Compliance.

Insider risk management

Quickly acting on alerts is imperative to minimizing risk insiders might cause to your organization either inadvertently or maliciously. When you configure Insider Risk Management policies you may either receive too many alerts or too few. Let us learn what to do in both scenarios.

The following are the guidelines if you receive very few alerts:

- **Update settings**: Enable more policy indicators to include a larger list of activities to detect. You could also adjust the alert volume slider to see all medium and high severity alerts and most low severity alerts.

- **Modify the policy**: If you have scoped the policy to a subset of users try to include more users in the policy. You could also try to lower the policy to trigger threshold and add more indicators to the policy.

If you are receiving too many alerts or have many low severity alerts, you could try the following actions:

- **Enable analytics**: Analytics help identify risk areas. This can help determine the type and scope of the policies that should be configured.

- **Get real-time insights**: Threshold recommendations in analytics give real-time insights that help you to adjust indicators and thresholds that are more suited for your organization.

- **Enable inline alert customization**: This feature allows analysts and investigators to edit policies while reviewing alerts.

- **Bulk delete alerts**: Where possible, bulk dismiss alerts to save time.

Managing resource constraints

Shortage of IT and security skills are common in the modern workplace. The workers have a wide variety of responsibilities making a lot of demands on their time.

Consider the following actions to help address these resource constraints:

- Focus analyst and investigator efforts on the highest risk alerts first.

- Use Microsoft Copilot to summarize alerts without even opening it. This helps speed up the triage process.

- Assigning the right users to the right IRM roles is an important part of the alert review process.

- Use automated IRM features like sequence detection and cumulative exfiltration detection to discover risks that are otherwise harder to find.

- Fine-tune risk score boosters and use features exclusions, detections groups and variants.

- Fine tune minimum indicator threshold settings for policies.

Communication Compliance

As is the case with IRM, Communication Compliance policies might also generate a high volume of alerts. Use the following list of best practices to help create policies that generate actionable alerts and reduce the number of non-actionable alerts:

- **Understand keyword list volumes**: If you use keyword lists in your policies, it is important to understand the volume of matches for each keywork. Utilize the Sensitive information type per location report to analyze keywords that trigger most matches. You can also use message details reports to get data on keyword matches for a specific policy.

- **Use the data classification dashboard**: Use the **Content Explorer** in the data classification dashboard to understand the volume of data for each trainable classifier and sensitive information type.

- **Filter email blasts**: Filter out emails that are generic or intended for mass communications like spam, newsletters etc.

- **Filter our email signatures or disclaimers**: Exclude email signatures, footers and disclaimers from the scanning to reduce the number of false positives.

- **Use sentiment evaluation**: Sentiment evaluation categorizes messages as **Positive**, **Negative** or **Neutral**. This helps prioritize the messages you want to evaluate first.

- **Report messages as misclassified**: Reporting messages as misclassified helps Microsoft to improve the models that will help reduce the number of false positives.

- **Filter out specific senders**: If some senders consistently trigger detection, you can filter them out using the condition: `Message is not received from any of these domains.`

- **Use communication direction to target users**: Use communication direction (Inbound or Outbound) to detect the communication you want to scan.

- **Combine trainable classifiers**: For the best results consider combining two or more trainable classifiers.

- **Lower the percentage of reviewed communications**: Reduce the percentage of communications to review if you just want to sample a subset of the messages.

Conclusion

The strategies outlined in the chapter provided a comprehensive approach to managing and classifying data efficiently within your organization. By leveraging the capabilities of the data classification dashboard, filtering out irrelevant emails and signatures, utilizing sentiment evaluation, and reporting misclassifications, you are well-equipped to maintain the integrity and accuracy of your data. Filtering out specific senders and targeting users based on communication direction allows for a more focused and effective scanning process. Additionally, combining trainable classifiers can enhance the precision of your data classification efforts. Finally, adjusting the percentage of reviewed communications ensures that you can balance thoroughness with efficiency. By implementing these best practices, you can significantly reduce the occurrence of false positives and improve the overall quality of your data management system.

Multiple choice questions

1. **What is the maximum number of Global Administrators that Microsoft recommends a tenant should have?**

   a. 1

   b. 5

   c. 10

   d. 15

2. **As per Microsoft what should you do if a user risk is detected as High?**

   a. Configure a sign-in risk policy to enforce multi-factor authentication.

   b. Configure a Conditional Access policy to block user sign-in.

   c. Configure a user-risk policy to force a password reset.

   d. Investigate the sign-in logs.

3. **What actions can you take if you are receiving too many Insider Risk Management alerts? Select all that apply.**

   a. Enable more policy indicators.

   b. Turn on analytics.

   c. Include more users in the scope of the policy.

   d. Enable inline alert customization.

Answer key

1. b

2. c

3. b, d

Join our book's Discord space

Join the book's Discord Workspace for Latest updates, Offers, Tech happenings around the world, New Release and Sessions with the Authors:

https://discord.bpbonline.com

Index

D

E

www.ingramcontent.com/pod-product-compliance
Lightning Source LLC
Chambersburg PA
CBHW061737210326
41599CB00034B/6706